SOUTH AMERICA

EUROPE

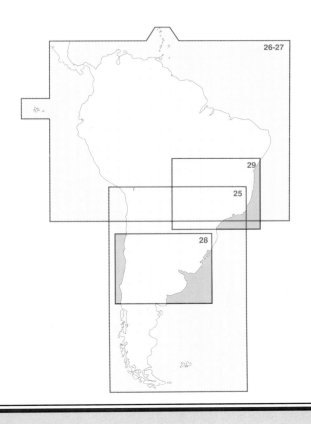

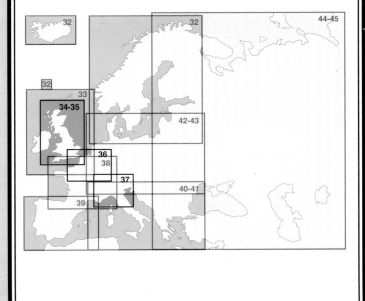

Bartholomew
A Division of HarperCollins Publishers
Duncan Street, Edinburgh EH9 1TA

First published by Bartholomew 1987
Revised edition 1994

© Bartholomew 1994

A CIP catalogue record for this book is available from the British Library

ISBN 0-7028-2616-2

Printed in Great Britain by Bartholomew, The Edinburgh Press Limited.

Details included in this atlas are subject to change without notice. Whilst every effort is made to keep
information up to date Bartholomew will not be responsible for any loss, damage or inconvenience caused
by inaccuracies in this atlas. The publishers are always pleased to acknowledge any corrections brought to
their notice, and record their appreciation of the valuable services rendered in the past by map users in
assisting to maintain the accuracy of their publications.

GH7492

Acknowledgements

The Publishers acknowledge the assistance of the following in the preparation of material used in this
publication: Dr Walter Stephen, Senior Adviser, Curriculum, Dean Education Centre, Edinburgh; Alister
Hendrie, Assistant Headteacher, Portobello High School, Edinburgh; Andrew Grant, Principal Teacher,
Geography, Wester Hailes Education Centre, Edinburgh; Stephen Hamilton, Principal Teacher, Geography,
Broughton High School, Edinburgh.

The Publishers are grateful to the following for providing the photographs used in this atlas:
(picture number(s) shown in italics)
Travel Photo International: pages xxii-xxiii, savanna, rain forest, prairie, northern forest; page xxii, *7;* page
xviii, *2;* page xv , *11;* page xvi , *4, 5, 13, 14;* page xx , *7;* page xxi , *2;* page vi , *3, 4;* page viii,*3,4.*
Photographers' Library: page xxii-xxiii, scrub *Chris Knaggs photograph,* desert *Oliver Martel photograph;*
page x , *8 Clive Sawyer photograph;* page xiv, *8 Ian Wright photograph;* page xvii, *9 Tom Hustler
photograph;* page xx , *4 Robyn Beeche photograph.* Biofotos: page x , *5 Heather Angel photograph;* page
xx , *6 Andrew Henley photograph;* page xxi , *3 Soames Summerhays photograph. The Photo Source:*
page xii,*10;* page xviii, *4;* page xiv, *7. Wade Cooper Associates,* Edinburgh: page xvi , *12;* page xvii, *10;*
page vi , *1. Pictor International:* page xiv, *6;* page vi , *2. B. and C. Alexander:* page xxii , tundra. *Bruce
Coleman Ltd:* page viii, *6 WWF/Eugen Schuhmacher. Mepha:* page xviii, *1 C. Osborne photograph. Michael
Scott:* page xxii , woodland and grass. *Yorkshire and Humberside Tourist Board:* page xi, *2. Spectrum
Colour Library:* page xiii, *12, 14.*

CONTENTS

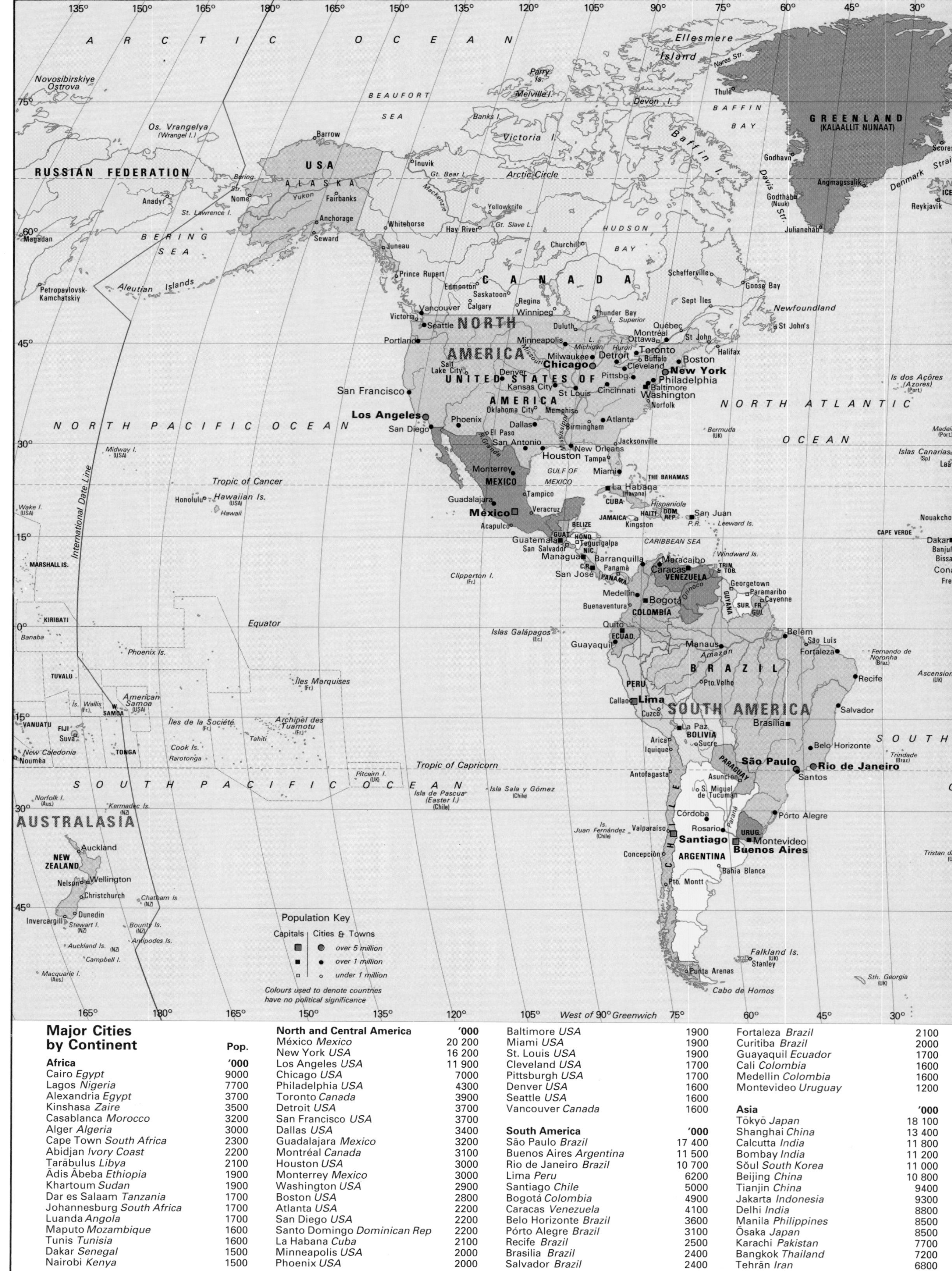

Major Cities by Continent

Africa	Pop. '000
Cairo *Egypt*	9000
Lagos *Nigeria*	7700
Alexandria *Egypt*	3700
Kinshasa *Zaire*	3500
Casablanca *Morocco*	3200
Alger *Algeria*	3000
Cape Town *South Africa*	2300
Abidjan *Ivory Coast*	2200
Tarābulus *Libya*	2100
Ādis Ābeba *Ethiopia*	1900
Khartoum *Sudan*	1900
Dar es Salaam *Tanzania*	1700
Johannesburg *South Africa*	1700
Luanda *Angola*	1700
Maputo *Mozambique*	1600
Tunis *Tunisia*	1600
Dakar *Senegal*	1500
Nairobi *Kenya*	1500

North and Central America	'000
México *Mexico*	20 200
New York *USA*	16 200
Los Angeles *USA*	11 900
Chicago *USA*	7000
Philadelphia *USA*	4300
Toronto *Canada*	3900
Detroit *USA*	3700
San Francisco *USA*	3700
Dallas *USA*	3400
Guadalajara *Mexico*	3200
Montréal *Canada*	3100
Houston *USA*	3000
Monterrey *Mexico*	3000
Washington *USA*	2900
Boston *USA*	2800
Atlanta *USA*	2200
San Diego *USA*	2200
Santo Domingo *Dominican Rep*	2200
La Habana *Cuba*	2100
Minneapolis *USA*	2000
Phoenix *USA*	2000

	'000
Baltimore *USA*	1900
Miami *USA*	1900
St. Louis *USA*	1900
Cleveland *USA*	1700
Pittsburgh *USA*	1700
Denver *USA*	1600
Seattle *USA*	1600
Vancouver *Canada*	1600

South America	'000
São Paulo *Brazil*	17 400
Buenos Aires *Argentina*	11 500
Rio de Janeiro *Brazil*	10 700
Lima *Peru*	6200
Santiago *Chile*	5000
Bogotá *Colombia*	4900
Caracas *Venezuela*	4100
Belo Horizonte *Brazil*	3600
Pórto Alegre *Brazil*	3100
Recife *Brazil*	2500
Brasilia *Brazil*	2400
Salvador *Brazil*	2400

	'000
Fortaleza *Brazil*	2100
Curitiba *Brazil*	2000
Guayaquil *Ecuador*	1700
Cali *Colombia*	1600
Medellin *Colombia*	1600
Montevideo *Uruguay*	1200

Asia	'000
Tōkyō *Japan*	18 100
Shanghai *China*	13 400
Calcutta *India*	11 800
Bombay *India*	11 200
Sŏul *South Korea*	11 000
Beijing *China*	10 800
Tianjin *China*	9400
Jakarta *Indonesia*	9300
Delhi *India*	8800
Manila *Philippines*	8500
Ōsaka *Japan*	8500
Karachi *Pakistan*	7700
Bangkok *Thailand*	7200
Tehrān *Iran*	6800

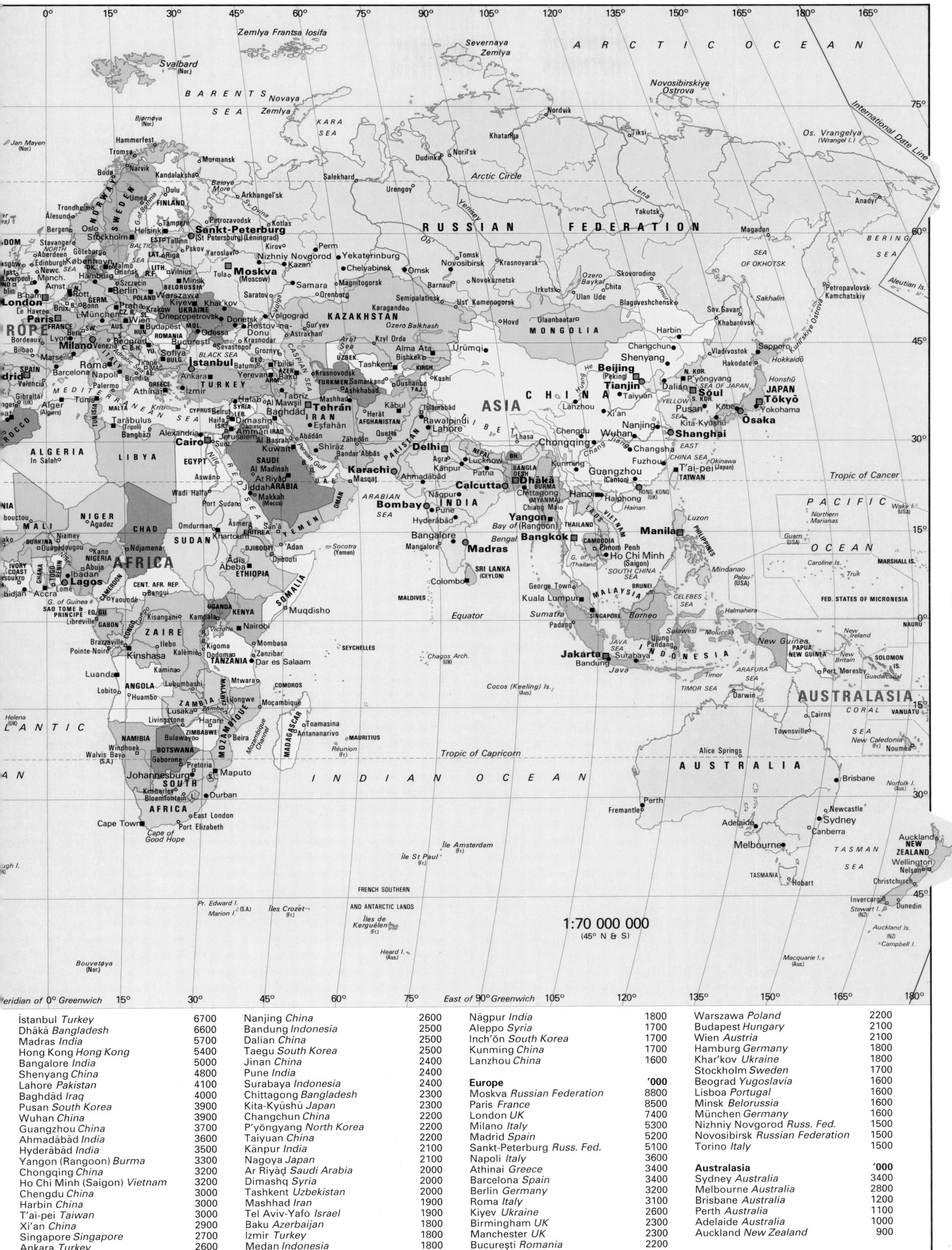

1:70 000 000
(45° N & S)

City		'000	City		'000	City		'000	City		'000
İstanbul	Turkey	6700	Nanjing	China	2600	Nāgpur	India	1800	Warszawa	Poland	2200
Dhākā	Bangladesh	6600	Bandung	Indonesia	2500	Aleppo	Syria	1700	Budapest	Hungary	2100
Madras	India	5700	Dalian	China	2500	Inch'ŏn	South Korea	1700	Wien	Austria	2100
Hong Kong	Hong Kong	5400	Taegu	South Korea	2500	Kunming	China	1700	Hamburg	Germany	1800
Bangalore	India	5000	Jinan	China	2400	Lanzhou	China	1600	Khar'kov	Ukraine	1800
Shenyang	China	4800	Pune	India	2400				Stockholm	Sweden	1700
Lahore	Pakistan	4100	Surabaya	Indonesia	2400	**Europe**		**'000**	Beograd	Yugoslavia	1600
Baghdād	Iraq	4000	Chittagong	Bangladesh	2300	Moskva	Russian Federation	8800	Lisboa	Portugal	1600
Pusan	South Korea	3900	Kita-Kyūshū	Japan	2300	Paris	France	8500	Minsk	Belorussia	1600
Wuhan	China	3900	Changchun	China	2200	London	UK	7400	München	Germany	1600
Guangzhou	China	3700	P'yŏngyang	North Korea	2200	Milano	Italy	5300	Nizhniy Novgorod	Russ. Fed.	1500
Ahmadābād	India	3600	Taiyuan	China	2200	Madrid	Spain	5200	Novosibirsk	Russian Federation	1500
Hyderābād	India	3500	Kānpur	India	2100	Sankt-Peterburg	Russ. Fed.	5100	Torino	Italy	1500
Yangon (Rangoon)	Burma	3300	Nagoya	Japan	2100	Napoli	Italy	3600			
Chongqing	China	3200	Ar Riyāḍ	Saudi Arabia	2000	Athinai	Greece	3400	**Australasia**		**'000**
Ho Chi Minh (Saigon)	Vietnam	3200	Dimashq	Syria	2000	Barcelona	Spain	3400	Sydney	Australia	3400
Chengdu	China	3000	Tashkent	Uzbekistan	2000	Berlin	Germany	3200	Melbourne	Australia	2800
Harbin	China	3000	Mashhad	Iran	1900	Roma	Italy	3100	Brisbane	Australia	1200
T'ai-pei	Taiwan	3000	Tel Aviv-Yafo	Israel	1900	Kiyev	Ukraine	2600	Perth	Australia	1100
Xi'an	China	2900	Baku	Azerbaijan	1800	Birmingham	UK	2300	Adelaide	Australia	1000
Singapore	Singapore	2700	Izmir	Turkey	1800	Manchester	UK	2300	Auckland	New Zealand	900
Ankara	Turkey	2600	Medan	Indonesia	1800	Bucureşti	Romania	2200			

1:35M

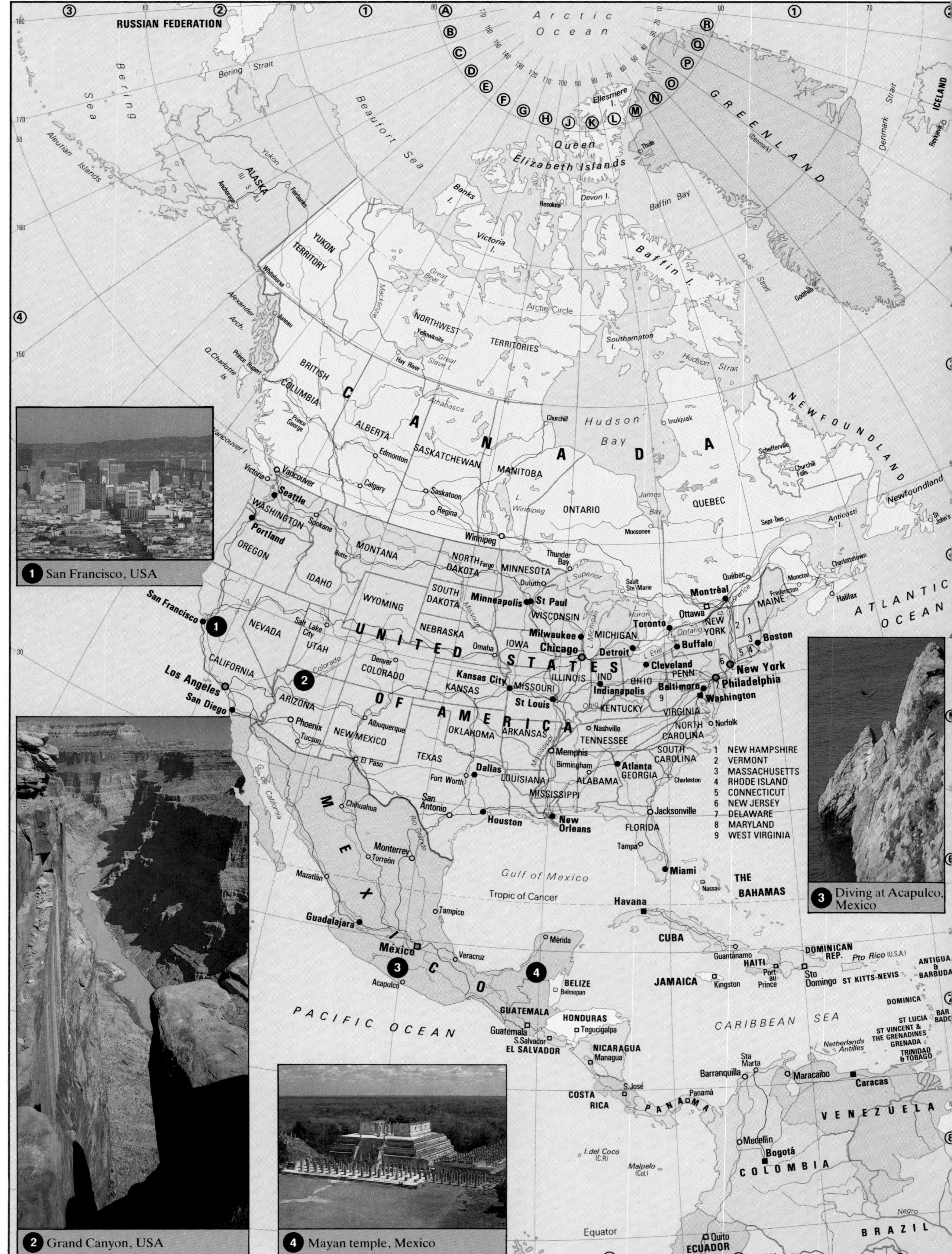

RUSSIAN FEDERATION

1 San Francisco, USA

2 Grand Canyon, USA

4 Mayan temple, Mexico

3 Diving at Acapulco, Mexico

1 NEW HAMPSHIRE
2 VERMONT
3 MASSACHUSETTS
4 RHODE ISLAND
5 CONNECTICUT
6 NEW JERSEY
7 DELAWARE
8 MARYLAND
9 WEST VIRGINIA

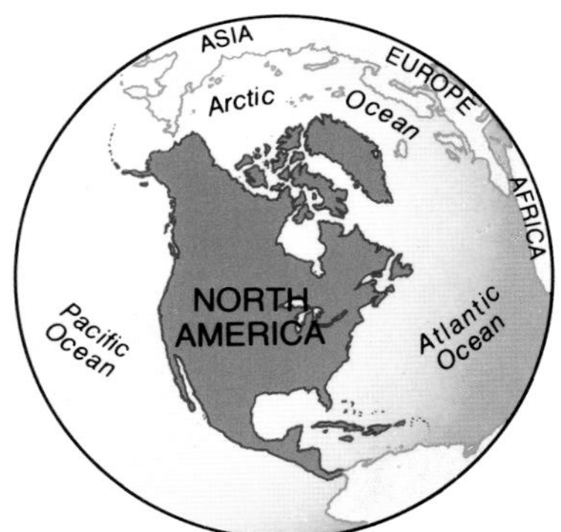

FACTS ABOUT NORTH AMERICA

1 In 1906, the city of San Francisco was almost destroyed by the fires which resulted from an earthquake. The city was hit by another large earthquake in 1989. Beneath the city runs the San Andreas fault, where two of the 'continental plates' which make up the earth's crust slide against one another. When they get jammed together at any point, pressure builds up beneath them, until finally they are forced apart. This causes an earthquake because of the sudden release of so much energy. The longer the plates stay jammed together, the greater the build up of pressure and the greater the strength of the final earthquake: in 1906, land surfaces in San Francisco moved as much as 6metres (20 feet).

2 The huge Grand Canyon in Arizona, USA, was gouged out of the rock by the Colorado River after the land was uplifted. It is as much as 1·6 kilometres (1 mile) deep, a maximum of 29 kilometres (18 miles) from rim to rim and no less than 446 kilometres (277 miles) long! The Grand Canyon is still being carved deeper (though very slowly) by the river.

3 At La Questrada, Acapulco Mexico, divers often swoop 36 m (118 feet) down into the sea. This is the highest dive which people do regularly.

4 The Maya were a people who lived in southern Mexico and Guatemala 1400 years ago. They built great cities with stone temples, public buildings and palaces. The picture shows one of their buildings which can be seen today. It was built without help from any modern machinery.

Cattle	Fruit	Wheat	6 Nickel		
Hogs	Sugar cane	Maize	7 Lead		
Bananas	Timber	Minerals	9 Silver		
Citrus fruit	Tobacco	1 Bauxite	11 Uranium		
Cotton	Coal	3 Copper	12 Zinc		
Fish	Oil	5 Iron	13 Asbestos		

NATURAL VEGETATION/PRODUCTS

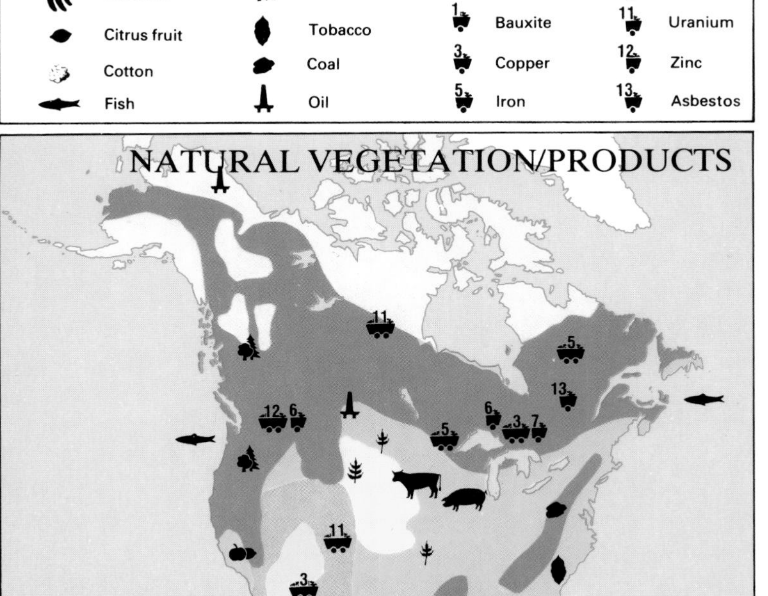
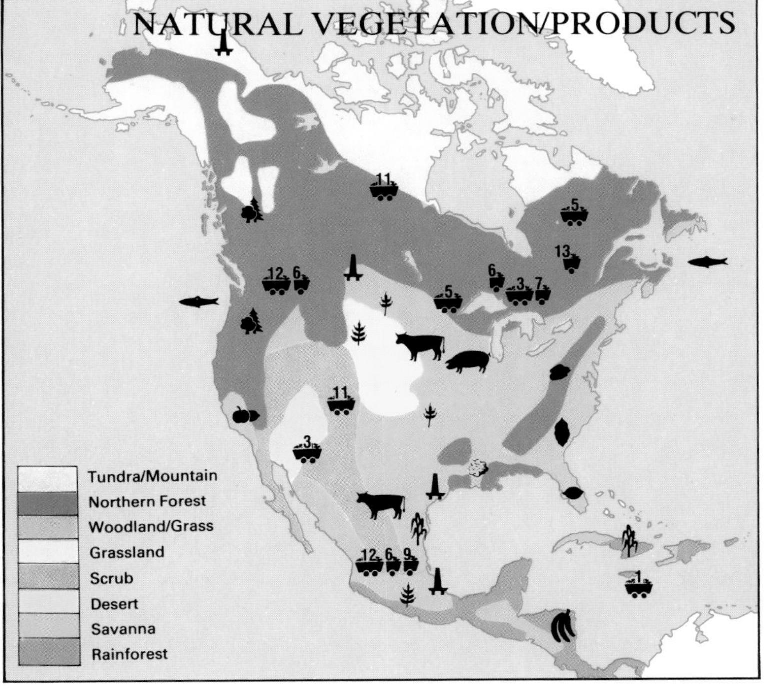

Tundra/Mountain
Northern Forest
Woodland/Grass
Grassland
Scrub
Desert
Savanna
Rainforest

POPULATION

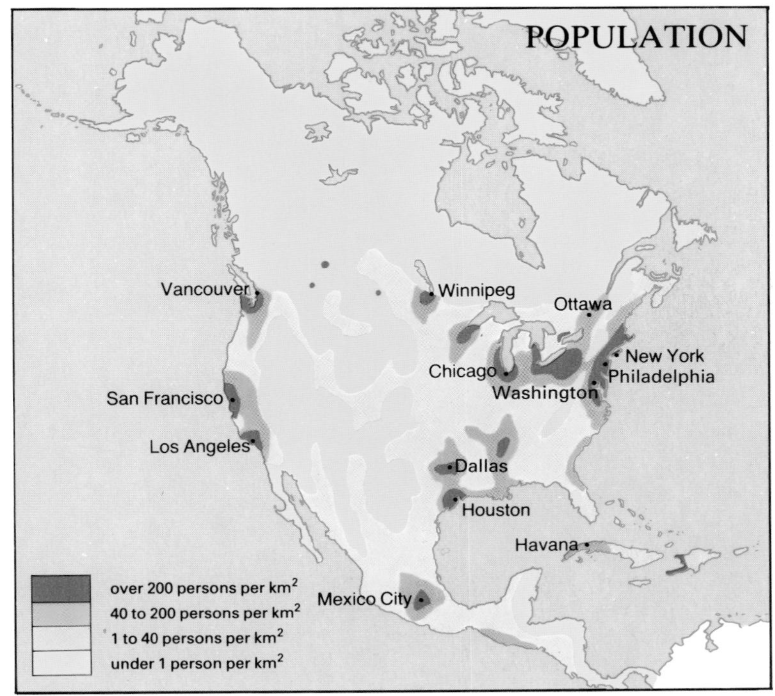

over 200 persons per km²
40 to 200 persons per km²
1 to 40 persons per km²
under 1 person per km²

Vancouver • Winnipeg • Ottawa • New York • Philadelphia • Chicago • Washington • San Francisco • Los Angeles • Dallas • Houston • Havana • Mexico City

---

CANADA

Area: 9 976 147 sq km (3 851 790 sq miles)
Population: 27 300 000
Capital: Ottawa
Languages: English, French
Currency: Canadian Dollar

CUBA

Area: 114 524 sq km (44 218 sq miles)
Population: 10 600 000
Capital: Havana
Language: Spanish
Currency: Cuban Peso

EL SALVADOR

Area: 20 865 sq km (8056 sq miles)
Population: 5 300 000
Capital: San Salvador
Language: Spanish
Currency: Colon

GUATEMALA

Area: 108 888 sq km (42 042 sq miles)
Population: 9 200 000
Capital: Guatemala
Language: Spanish
Currency: Quetzal

JAMAICA

Area: 11 424 sq km (4411 sq miles)
Population: 2 500 000
Capital: Kingston
Language: English
Currency: Jamaican Dollar

MEXICO

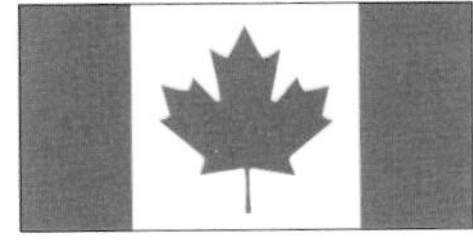
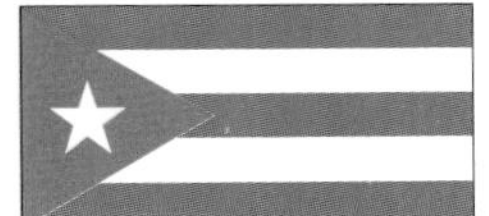

Area: 1 967 180 sq km (759 528 sq miles)
Population: 88 600 000
Capital: Mexico City
Language: Spanish
Currency: Mexican Peso

NICARAGUA

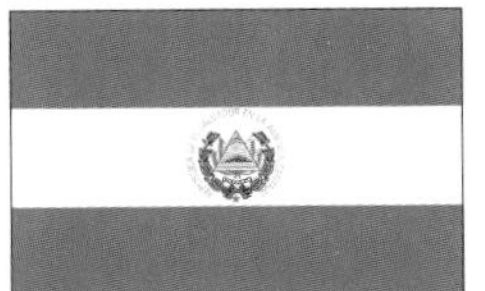
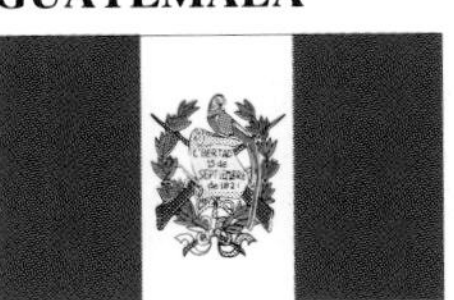

Area: 139 000 sq km (53 668 sq miles)
Population: 3 900 000
Capital: Managua
Language: Spanish
Currency: Cordoba

UNITED STATES OF AMERICA

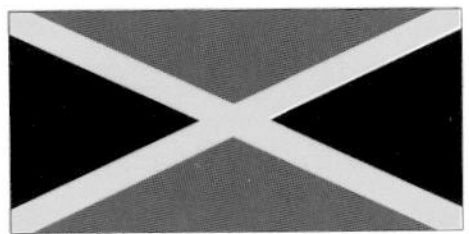
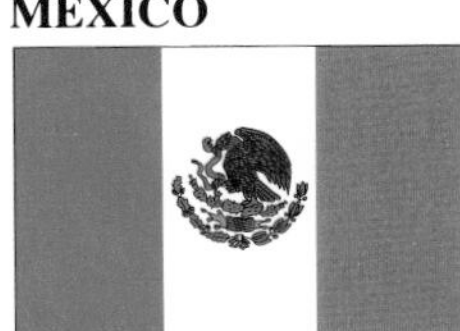
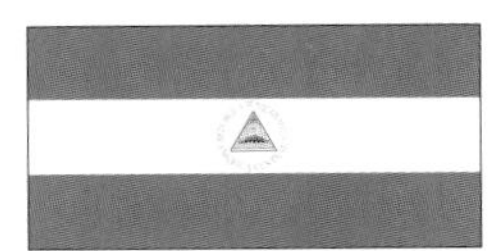
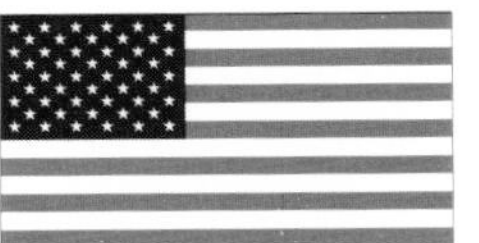

Area: 9 363 130 sq km (3 615 104 sq miles)
Population: 248 700 000
Capital: Washington
Language: English
Currency: U.S. Dollar

SOUTH AMERICA

1:35M

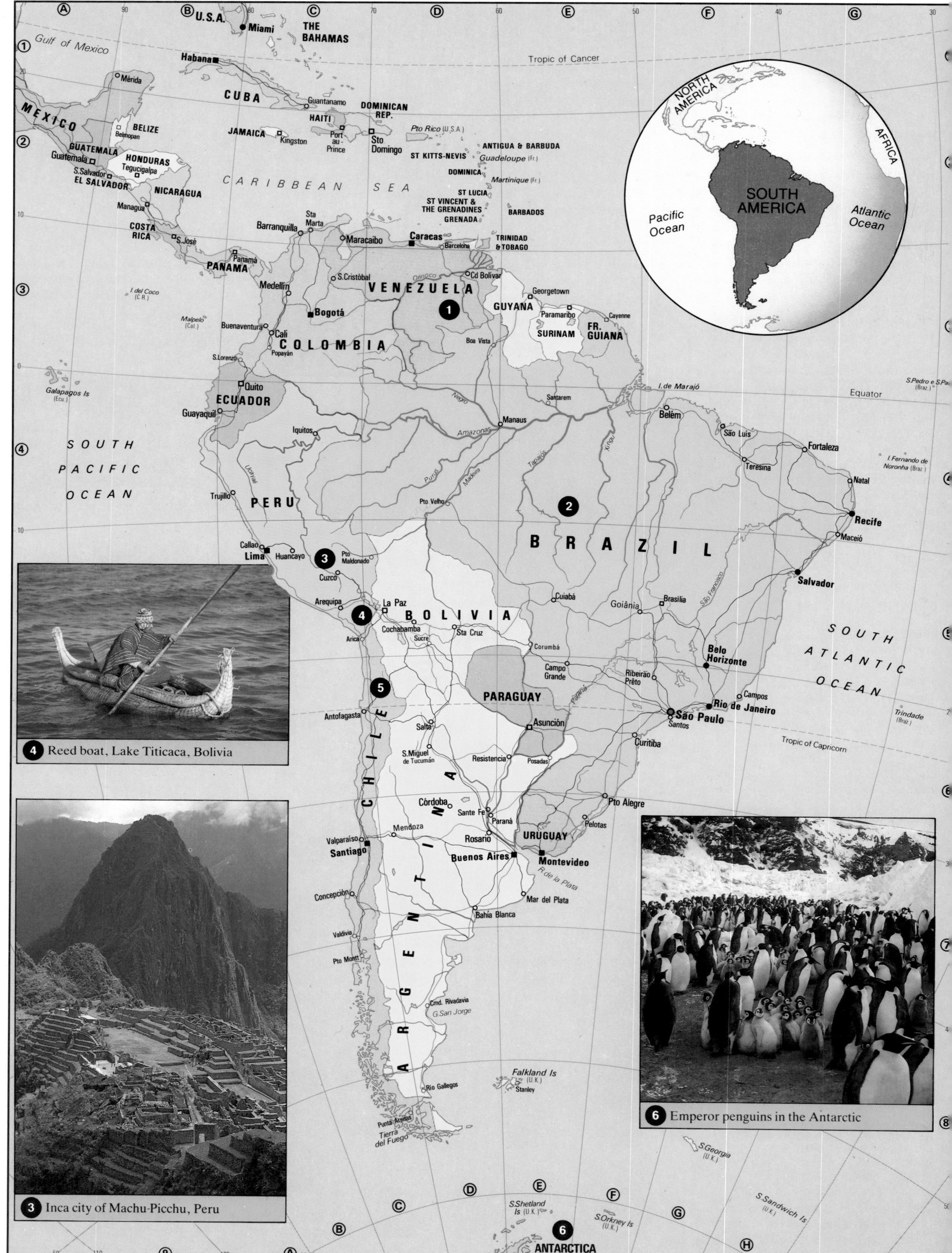

4 Reed boat, Lake Titicaca, Bolivia

3 Inca city of Machu-Picchu, Peru

6 Emperor penguins in the Antarctic

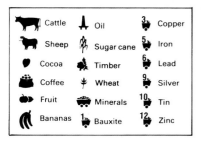

Cattle	Oil	3 Copper
Sheep	Sugar cane	5 Iron
Cocoa	Timber	6 Lead
Coffee	Wheat	9 Silver
Fruit	Minerals	10 Tin
Bananas	Bauxite	12 Zinc

FACTS ABOUT SOUTH AMERICA

1 The Angel Falls, Venezuela, are the highest waterfalls in the world, at 979 m (3212 feet).

2 Deforestation is a major problem in South America. About 1 per cent of the total area of forest is lost each year. Often trees are cut down to clear land for agriculture. On hillsides, the soil soon becomes too poor to grow crops and the land is abandoned. Trees cannot grow again, and so soil is eroded away by rain and wind. Trees are also lost when lakes are made for hydro-electric dams; when new towns are built; and as a result of the way people live – they take too much wood for fuel and timber, allow animals to graze on foliage, and light fires which get out of control.

3 In the Andes Mountains, in the north-west of South America, there are ruins of cities built by the Incas. They ruled the Indians in the area 500 years ago. The Incas had well-developed political and religious systems. They built their cities on terraces engineered from the mountain side. The Spanish, the first Europeans to discover these cities, killed the Incas to seize the gold and silver which they had mined, and their cities were abandoned.

4 The highest navigable lake in the world is Lake Titicaca, on the Peru/Bolivia border. It is no less than 3811 m (12 503 feet) above sea level. The local Indian people make boats from bundles of reeds tied together, to use for fishing. The reeds grow around the edge of the lake.

5 Although in the rain forests of the Amazon Basin it rains every day, in the Atacama Desert, Chile, hundreds of years can pass between one rain storm and the next. A storm in 1971 was the first for 400 years. The desert is the driest place in the world.

6 The Emperor Penguin, found in the Antarctic, does not make a nest. Instead, a single egg is carried on top of the male penguin's feet. It is kept warm by a fold of skin which hangs down and covers it. The penguin does not eat during the two months it takes for the egg to hatch out.

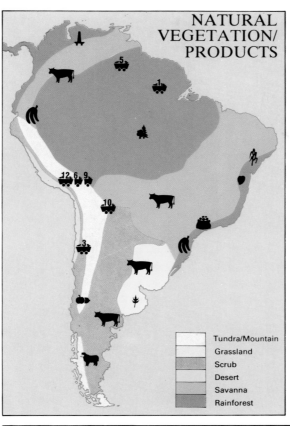

NATURAL VEGETATION/ PRODUCTS

Tundra/Mountain
Grassland
Scrub
Desert
Savanna
Rainforest

POPULATION

Caracas
Bogota
Quito
Manaus
Lima
La Paz
Recife
Brasilia
Rio de Janeiro
São Paulo
Santiago
Montevideo
Buenos Aires

over 200 persons per km²
40 to 200 persons per km²
1 to 40 persons per km²
under 1 person per km²

ARGENTINA

Area: 2 777 815 sq km (1 072 514 sq miles)
Population: 32 300 000
Capital: Buenos Aires
Language: Spanish
Currency: Argentine Peso

BOLIVIA

Area: 1 098 575 sq km (424 160 sq miles)
Population: 7 300 000
Capital: La Paz
Languages: Spanish, Aymara, Quechua
Currency: Bolivian Peso

BRAZIL

Area: 8 511 968 sq km (3 286 471 sq miles)
Population: 150 400 000
Capital: Brasilia
Language: Portuguese
Currency: Cruzeiro

CHILE

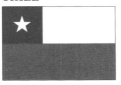

Area: 756 943 sq km (292 256 sq miles)
Population: 13 200 000
Capital: Santiago
Language: Spanish
Currency: Chilean Peso

COLOMBIA

Area: 1 138 907 sq km (439 732 sq miles)
Population: 33 000 000
Capital: Bogota
Language: Spanish
Currency: Colombian Peso

ECUADOR

Area: 455 502 sq km (175 869 sq miles)
Population: 10 600 000
Capital: Quito
Language: Spanish
Currency: Sucre

GUYANA

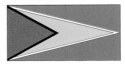

Area: 214 969 sq km (83 000 sq miles)
Population: 800 000
Capital: Georgetown
Language: English
Currency: Guyanese Dollar

PERU

Area: 1 285 215 sq km (496 222 sq miles)
Population: 21 600 000
Capital: Lima
Languages: Spanish, Aymara, Quechua
Currency: Sol

VENEZUELA

Area: 912 047 sq km (352 141 sq miles)
Population: 19 700 000
Capital: Caracas
Language: Spanish
Currency: Bolivar

200   400   600 km
100   200   300 mis

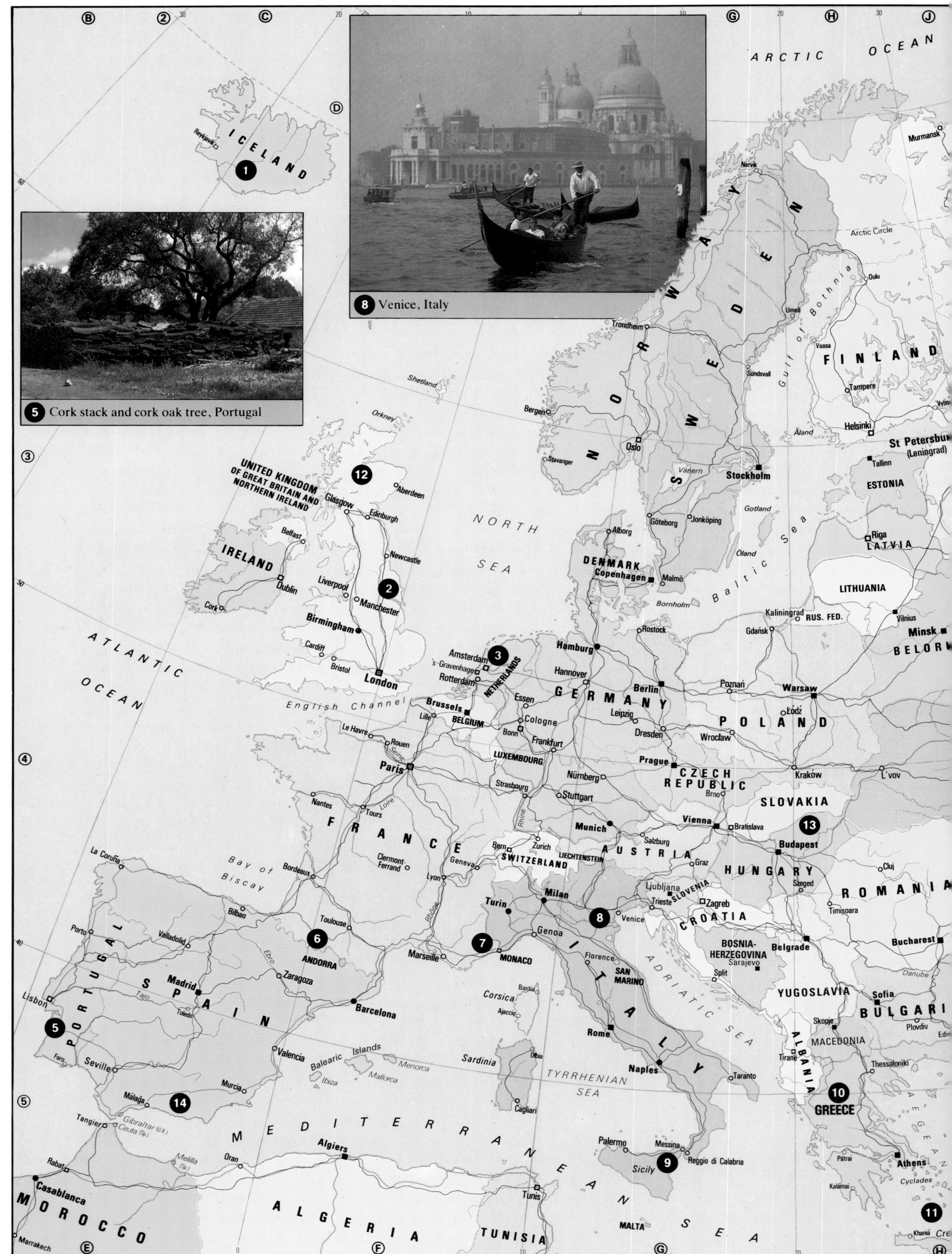

8 Venice, Italy

5 Cork stack and cork oak tree, Portugal

ARCTIC OCEAN

ICELAND
Reykjavík
1

Murmansk
Narvik
Arctic Circle

N O R W A Y
S W E D E N
FINLAND

Trondheim
Bergen
Stavanger
Oslo
Oulu
Umeå
Vaasa
Sundsvall
Tampere
Åland
Helsinki

Gulf of Bothnia

St Petersburg (Leningrad)
Tallinn
ESTONIA

Shetland
Orkney

UNITED KINGDOM OF GREAT BRITAIN AND NORTHERN IRELAND
12
Glasgow
Aberdeen
Edinburgh
Belfast
Newcastle

IRELAND
Dublin
Liverpool
Manchester
2
Cork
Birmingham
Cardiff
Bristol
London

NORTH SEA

Vänern
Stockholm
Göteborg
Jönköping
Gotland
Öland
Riga
LATVIA

DENMARK
Ålborg
Copenhagen
Malmö
Bornholm
Rostock

LITHUANIA
Kaliningrad RUS. FED.
Vilnius
Minsk
BELOR...

Gdańsk
Poznań
Warsaw
Łódź

ATLANTIC OCEAN

English Channel
Le Havre
Rouen
Seine
Lille
Brussels
BELGIUM
Amsterdam
's-Gravenhage
Rotterdam
NETHERLANDS
3
Hamburg
Hannover
Essen
Cologne
Bonn
Frankfurt
LUXEMBOURG
Berlin
Leipzig
Dresden
Wrocław

GERMANY

POLAND

CZECH REPUBLIC
Prague
Brno
Kraków
L'vov

FRANCE
Paris
Nantes
Tours
Loire
Strasbourg
Nürnberg
Stuttgart
Munich
Bern
Zurich
Geneva
SWITZERLAND
LIECHTENSTEIN
Salzburg
Vienna
Bratislava
SLOVAKIA
13
Budapest
Graz
HUNGARY
Cluj
Szeged
ROMANIA
AUSTRIA

Clermont-Ferrand
Lyon
Rhône
Bordeaux
Bay of Biscay
Toulouse
6
ANDORRA
Marseille
Turin
7
MONACO
Milan
Genoa
8
Venice
Trieste
Ljubljana
SLOVENIA
Zagreb
CROATIA
Timişoara

La Coruña
Porto
Bilbao
Valladolid
Zaragoza
Madrid
Barcelona
SPAIN
PORTUGAL
Lisbon
5
Tajo
Toledo
Ebro
Florence
SAN MARINO
Corsica
Ajaccio
Bastia
ITALY
Rome
Naples
ADRIATIC SEA
BOSNIA-HERZEGOVINA
Sarajevo
Split
Belgrade
YUGOSLAVIA
Sofia
BULGARIA
Plovdiv
Danube

Valencia
Murcia
Málaga
14
Seville
Faro
Balearic Islands
Ibiza
Mallorca
Menorca
Sardinia
Cagliari
Obia
TYRRHENIAN SEA
Skopje
MACEDONIA
ALBANIA
Tirane
Thessaloniki
GREECE
10

Tangier
Ceuta (Sp.)
Gibraltar (U.K.)
Melilla (Sp.)
M E D I T E R R A N E A N   S E A
Palermo
Messina
Reggio di Calabria
Sicily
9
Pátrai
Athens
Cyclades
11
Khaniá Cre...

Rabat
Casablanca
Oran
Algiers
Tunis
MALTA
MOROCCO
Marrakech
ALGERIA
TUNISIA

Bay of Biscay

X

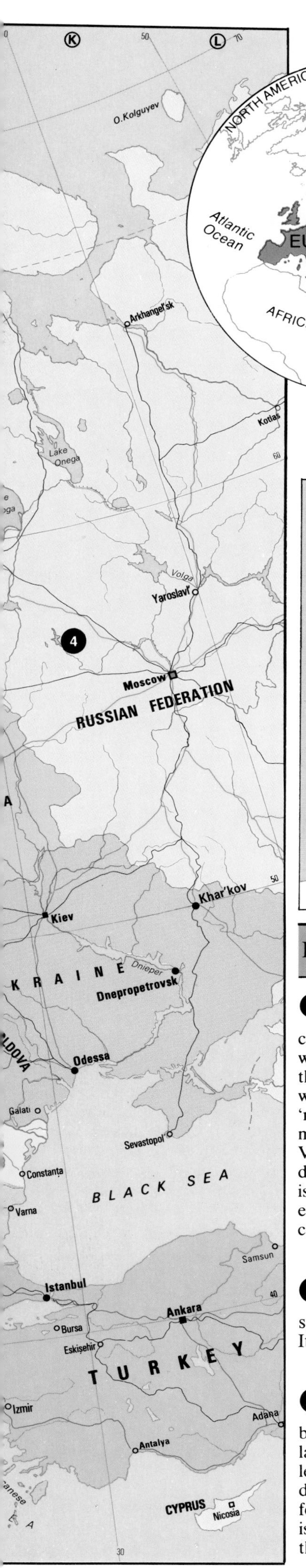

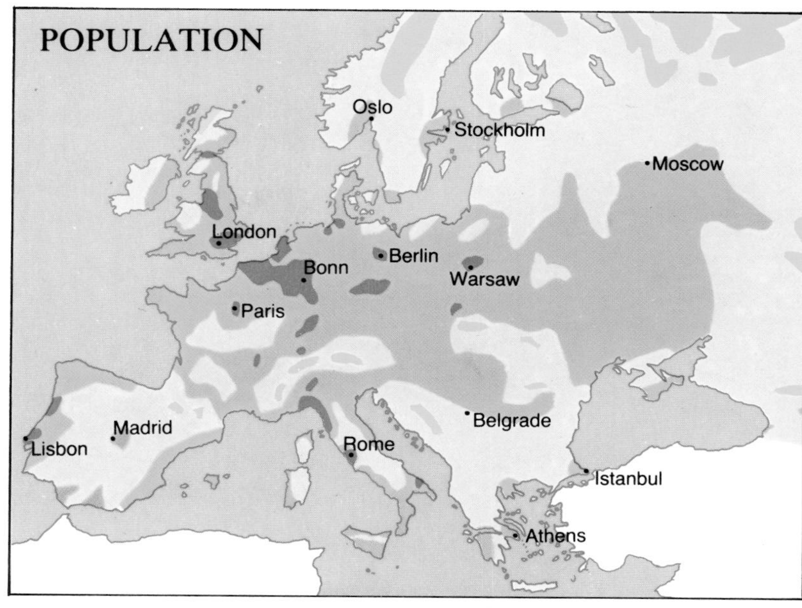

POPULATION

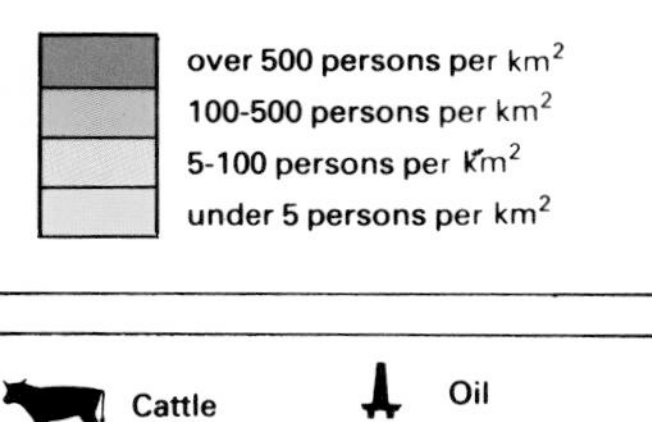

	over 500 persons per km²
	100-500 persons per km²
	5-100 persons per km²
	under 5 persons per km²

NATURAL VEGETATION/ PRODUCTS

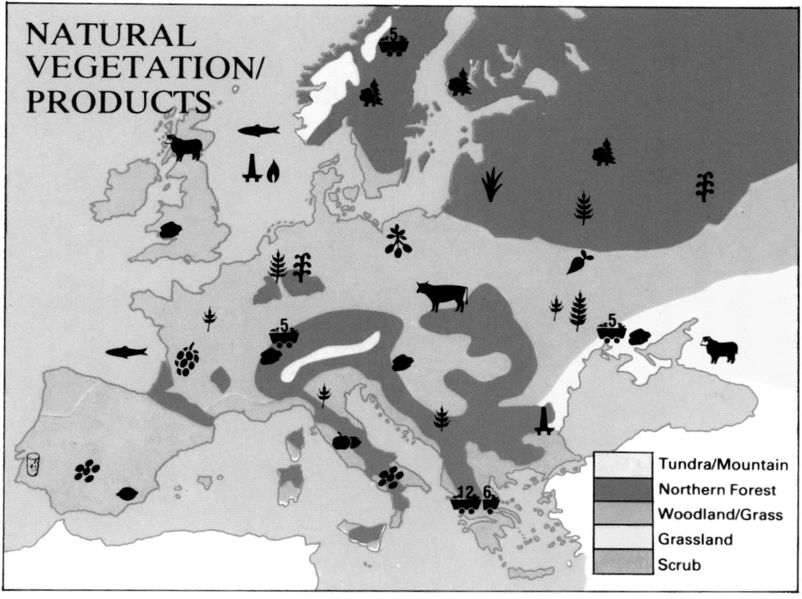

	Tundra/Mountain
	Northern Forest
	Woodland/Grass
	Grassland
	Scrub

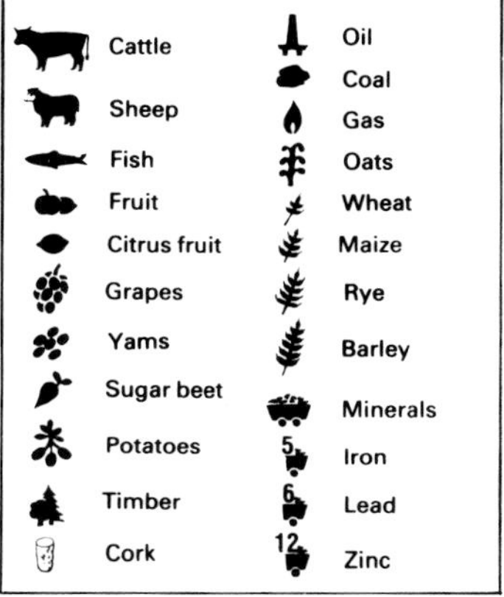

Cattle		Oil	
Sheep		Coal	
Fish		Gas	
Fruit		Oats	
Citrus fruit		Wheat	
Grapes		Maize	
Yams		Rye	
Sugar beet		Barley	
Potatoes		Minerals	
Timber	5	Iron	
Cork	6	Lead	
	12	Zinc	

FACTS ABOUT EUROPE

1 In Iceland, ice and fire exist side by side. Many active volcanoes and geysers (hot springs which shoot a column of water into the air at intervals) can be seen, while glaciers (continually moving 'rivers' of ice) and ice sheets cover much of the land. One volcano – Vatnajokull – is particularly dangerous for an unusual reason: it is underneath a glacier and when it erupts, the ice melts very quickly, causing terrible floods.

2 The Humber Bridge, England, has one of the longest single spans of any bridge in the world. It stretches for 1410 m (4626 feet).

3 More than a third of the land area of the Netherlands has been reclaimed from the sea. These lands (the *polders*) are below sea level and the sea is kept out by dykes. Drainage ditches divide the fertile fields. The water from them is pumped into canals and rivers, then out to sea.

4 The longest river in Europe is the Volga, which runs for 3690 km (2292 miles) from the forests north west of Moscow in Russia all the way to the Caspian Sea.

5 Portugal is an important source of cork, which is actually the bark of a tree. The cork oak produces cork bark up to 15 cm (6 inches) thick and this is stripped off the trees every 10 to 15 years. Cork oaks grow throughout the western and central Mediterranean region.

6 The Pierre Saint Martin Cavern in the Pyrenees mountains, France, is the deepest cave system yet discovered in the world. It goes 1330 m (4364 feet) into the heart of the mountains.

7 The principality of Monaco is one of the most crowded countries in the world: 28 000 people live on 1.9 sq km (467 acres) of land! By contrast, most of Scandinavia has fewer than 40 people per square kilometre.

8 Venice, Italy, is built on no less than 118 islands. Instead of roads, there are canals, and boats are used for transport. Venice is sinking at a rate of 12 inches each century. Some of the reasons for this include water being extracted from wells, and the compression of the mud on the floor of the lagoon.

9 Mount Etna, Sicily, is the highest volcano in Europe (about 3323 m, 10 902 ft) and is still very active. Despite this, many people live on its lower slopes. This is because the soil there is very fertile and grows good produce.

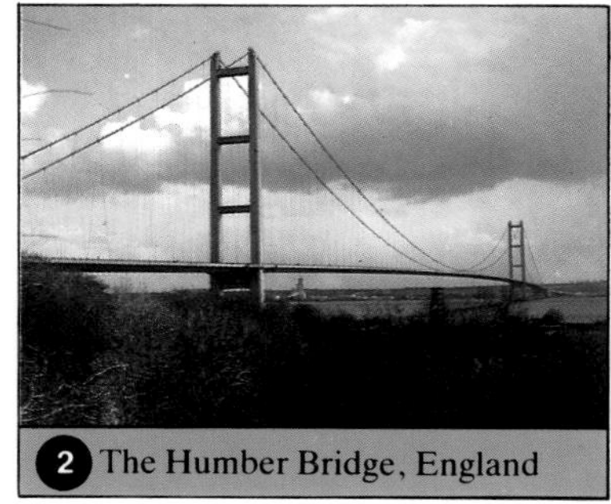

2 The Humber Bridge, England

EUROPE

ALBANIA

Area: 28 748 sq km
(11 079 sq miles)
Population: 3 200 000
Capital: Tirana
Language: Albanian
Currency: Lek

AUSTRIA

Area: 83 848 sq km
(32 374 sq miles)
Population: 7 600 000
Capital: Vienna
Language: German
Currency: Schilling

BELGIUM

Area: 30 512 sq km
(11 781 sq miles)
Population: 9 900 000
Capital: Brussels
Languages: Flemish, French
Currency: Belgian Franc

BELORUSSIA

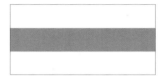

Area: 208 000 sq km
(80 309 sq miles)
Population: 10 278 000
Capital: Minsk
Language: Belorussian
Currency: Rouble

BULGARIA

Area: 110 911 sq km
(42 822 sq miles)
Population: 9 000 000
Capital: Sofia
Language: Bulgarian
Currency: Lev

CZECH REPUBLIC

Area: 78 864 sq km
(30 449 sq miles)
Population: 10 300 000
Capital: Prague
Language: Czech
Currency: Koruna

DENMARK

Area: 43 030 sq km
(16 614 sq miles)
Population: 5 100 000
Capital: Copenhagen
Language: Danish
Currency: Krone

ESTONIA

Area: 45 100 sq km
(17 413 sq miles)
Population: 1 600 000
Capital: Tallinn
Language: Estonian
Currency: Kroon

FINLAND

Area: 337 032 sq km
(130 128 sq miles)
Population: 5 000 000
Capital: Helsinki
Languages: Finnish, Swedish
Currency: Markka

FRANCE

Area: 543 965 sq km
(210 025 sq miles)
Population: 56 100 000
Capital: Paris
Language: French
Currency: French Franc

GERMANY

Area: 356 854 sq km
(137 781 sq miles)
Population: 79 000 000
Capital: Berlin
Language: German
Currency: Deutschmark

GREECE

Area: 131 955 sq km
(50 948 sq miles)
Population: 10 000 000
Capital: Athens
Language: Greek
Currency: Drachma

HUNGARY

Area: 93 030 sq km
(35 919 sq miles)
Population: 10 600 000
Capital: Budapest
Language: Magyar
Currency: Forint

ICELAND

Area: 102 828 sq km
(39 702 sq miles)
Population: 259 577
Capital: Reykjavik
Language: Icelandic
Currency: Króna

IRELAND

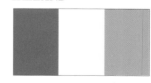

Area: 70 282 sq km
(27 136 sq miles)
Population: 3 700 000
Capital: Dublin
Language: Irish (Gaelic),
English
Currency: Irish Pound (Punt)

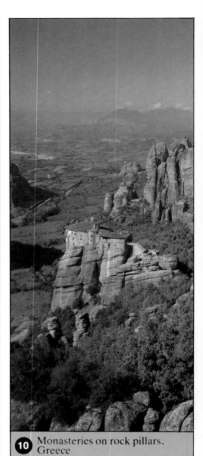

10 Monasteries on rock pillars, Greece

10 Near Kalabaka, Greece, are a group of monasteries built for monks with no fear of heights! They are perched on top of pillars of rock, called meteora, 300 m (1 000 ft) high. The only way up was by ladders or baskets slung on the end of ropes. Now stairways have been constructed so that tourists can visit the buildings.

11 The island of Santorini (Thira) in Greece is the site of the world's largest natural disaster. About 1500 BC this volcanic island erupted leaving a *caldera* (hollow basin shape where the top of the volcano had been) about 13 km (8 miles) across. Many people believe that the destruction of this island is the origin of the story of Atlantis. The people of Atlantis are mentioned by the Greek writer Plato. Crime and corruption spread throughout their island as they became wealthier, until finally the Athenians conquered them. Later the island disappeared into the sea in a single day and night.

7 Monte Carlo, Monaco

XII

12 Loch Ness, in the Highlands of Scotland, is one of the most famous freshwater expanses in the world. Its length and depth are so great that it could accommodate the population of the earth three times over. Its greatest mystery is the world-famous Loch Ness Monster which was first recorded in the 6th century by the Abbot of Iona. 'Nessie', as the monster is affectionately known, has been sighted by many people but evidence of the monster's existence is inconclusive. If it does exist, the most popular theory is that the monster is one of a small colony of unknown creatures which have descended from marine animals trapped in the loch at the end of the last Ice Age 12,000 years ago.

12 Loch Ness, Scotland

13 The stalactite caves of Aggtelek in Hungary form one of the largest cave systems in Europe. They are 23km (14 miles) long and extend over the border into Slovakia. The stalactites and stalagmites in the cave make a spectacular impact. Stalagmites on the floor of the Aggtelek caves bear a clear resemblance to the human form. Others resemble animals, temples, waterfalls, a 'Great Organ' and even a 'Butcher's Shop'.

14 The spectacularly beautiful Alhambra in Spain is situated on a hill overlooking Granada. From the outside, the fortress walls look plain but they belie the complex and colourful interior. Visitors find the intricate stonework, the sumptuous halls and the attractive gardens with their many fountains quite breathtaking. The Palace of the Alhambra was built as a home for the Moorish rulers in the 14th century and is a well-preserved example of the very best of Moorish art.

14 The Alhambra, Spain

ITALY

Area: 301 245 sq km (116 311 sq miles)
Population: 57 100 000
Capital: Rome
Language: Italian
Currency: Lira

NETHERLANDS

Area: 33 940 sq km (13 104 sq miles)
Population: 15 000 000
Capital: Amsterdam & The Hague
Language: Dutch
Currency: Guilder

PORTUGAL

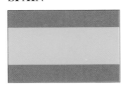

Area: 91 671 sq km (35 394 sq miles)
Population: 10 300 000
Capital: Lisbon
Language: Portuguese
Currency: Escudo

SPAIN

Area: 504 745 sq km (194 882 sq miles)
Population: 39 200 000
Capital: Madrid
Language: Spanish
Currency: Peseta

UKRAINE

Area: 603 700 sq km (233 089 sq miles)
Population: 51 857 000
Capital: Kiev
Languages: Ukrainian, Russian
Currency: Rouble

LATVIA

Area: 63 700 sq km (24 595 sq miles)
Population: 2 700 000
Capital: Riga
Language: Latvian
Currency: Lat

NORWAY

Area: 324 218 sq km (125 180 sq miles)
Population: 4 200 000
Capital: Oslo
Language: Norwegian
Currency: Krone

ROMANIA

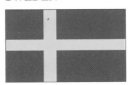

Area: 237 500 sq km (91 699 sq miles)
Population: 23 300 000
Capital: Bucharest
Language: Romanian
Currency: Leu

SWEDEN

Area: 449 791 sq km (173 664 sq miles)
Population: 8 400 000
Capital: Stockholm
Language: Swedish
Currency: Krona

UNITED KINGDOM

Area: 244 104 sq km (94 249 sq miles)
Population: 57 200 000
Capital: London
Language: English
Currency: Pound Sterling

LITHUANIA

Area: 65 200 sq km (25 170 sq miles)
Population: 3 700 000
Capital: Vilnius
Language: Lithuanian
Currency: Litas

POLAND

Area: 312 683 sq km (120 727 sq miles)
Population: 38 400 000
Capital: Warsaw
Language: Polish
Currency: Zloty

RUSSIAN FEDERATION

Area: 17 078 000 sq km (6 593 816 sq miles)
Population: 148 263 000
Capital: Moscow
Language: Russian
Currency: Rouble

SWITZERLAND

Area: 41 287 sq km (15 941 sq miles)
Population: 6 600 000
Capital: Bern
Languages: German, French Italian, Romansch
Currency: Swiss Franc

YUGOSLAVIA

Area: 91 285 sq km (35 245 sq miles)
Population: 10 300 000
Capital: Belgrade
Language: Serbo-Croatian
Currency: Dinar

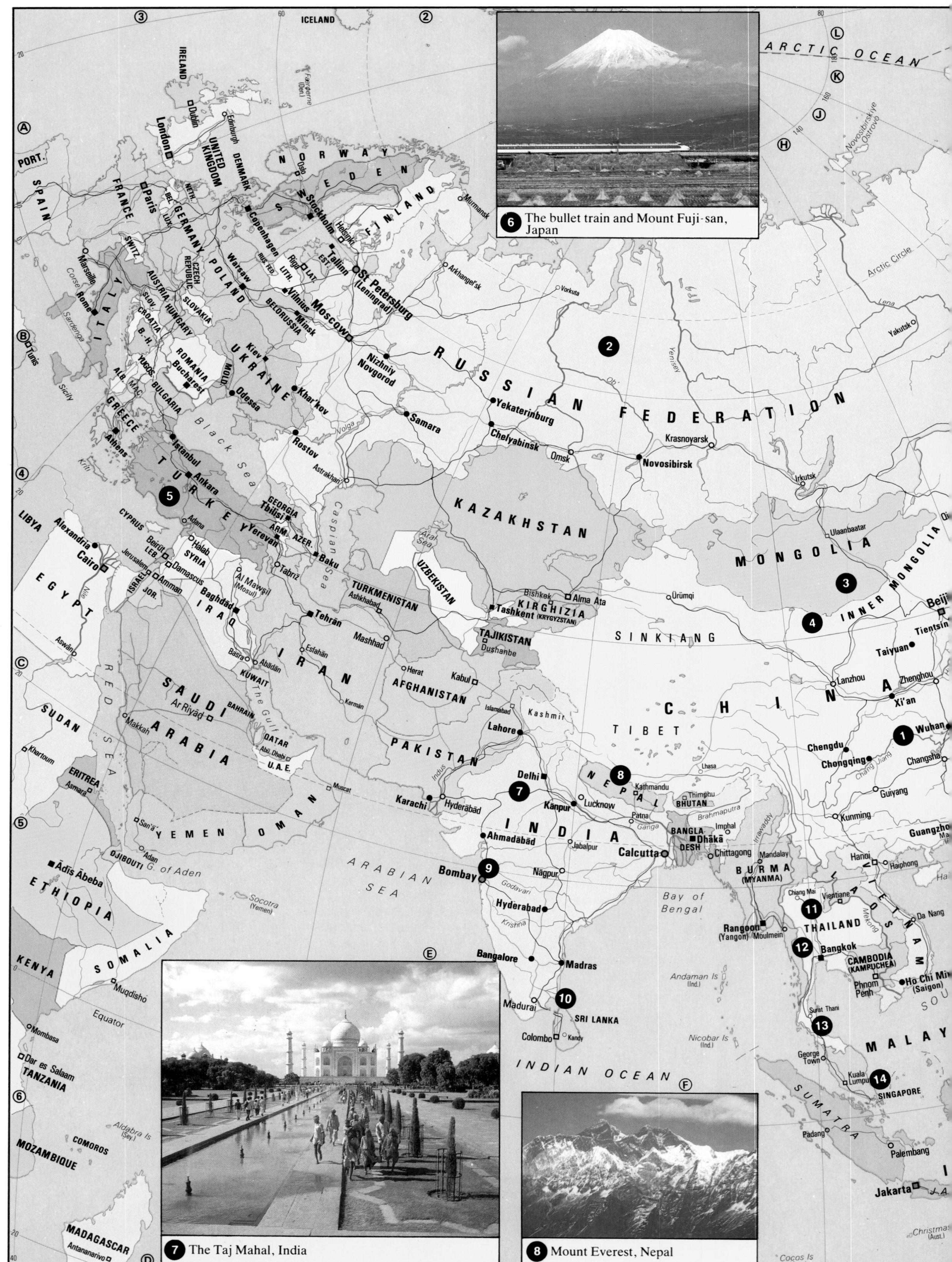

6 The bullet train and Mount Fuji-san, Japan

7 The Taj Mahal, India

8 Mount Everest, Nepal

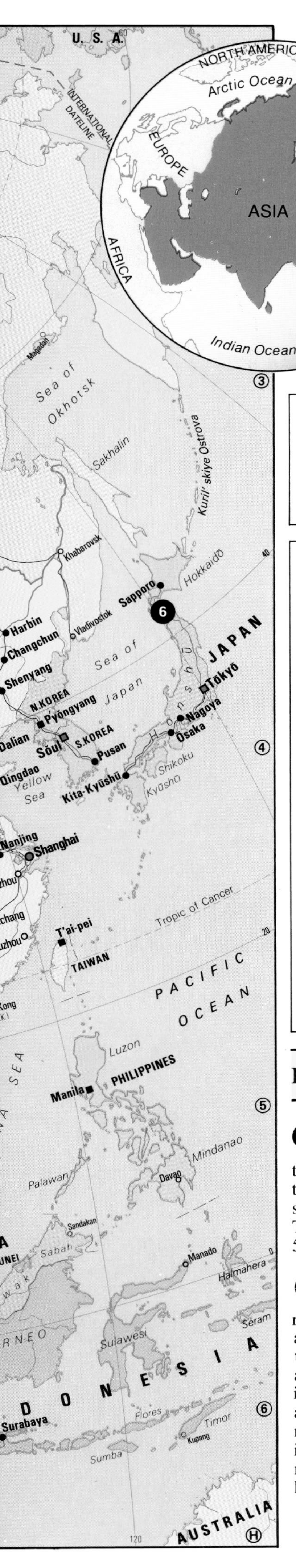

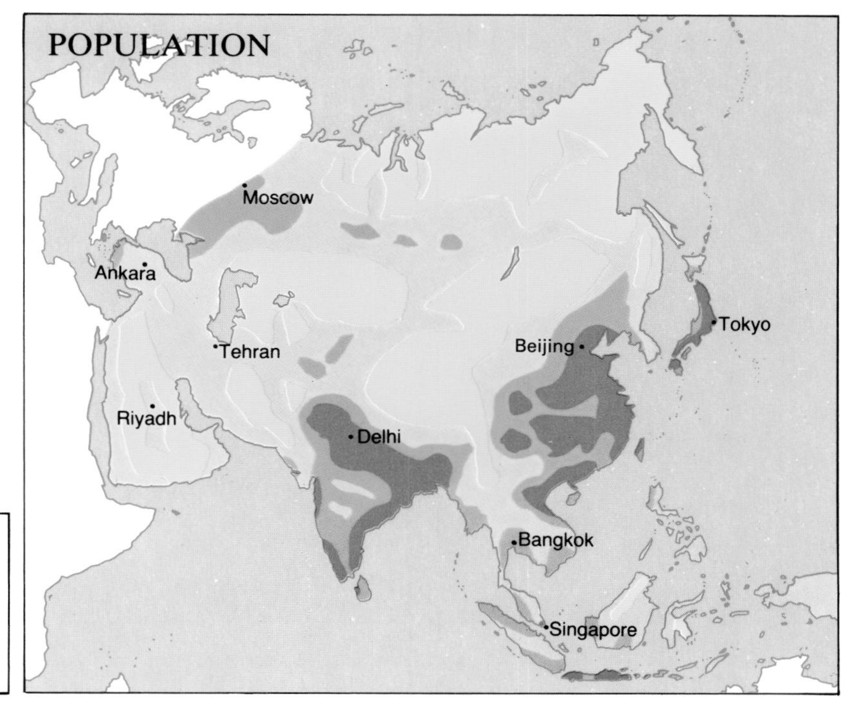

POPULATION

over 500 persons per km²
100-500 persons per km²
5-100 persons per km²
under 5 persons per km²

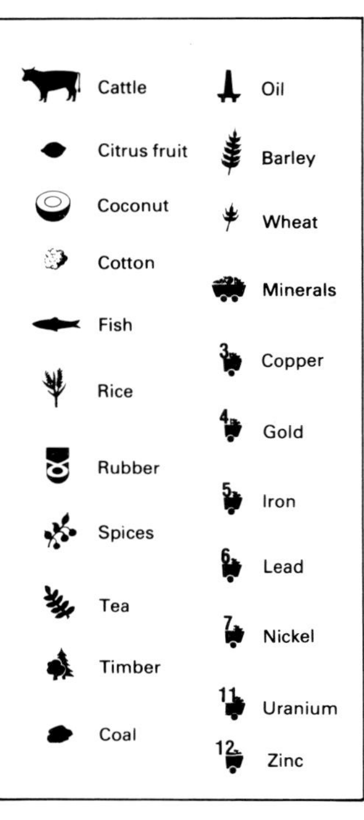

Cattle		Oil	
Citrus fruit		Barley	
Coconut		Wheat	
Cotton		Minerals	
Fish		Copper	3
Rice		Gold	4
Rubber		Iron	5
Spices		Lead	6
Tea		Nickel	7
Timber		Uranium	11
Coal		Zinc	12

NATURAL VEGETATION/PRODUCTS

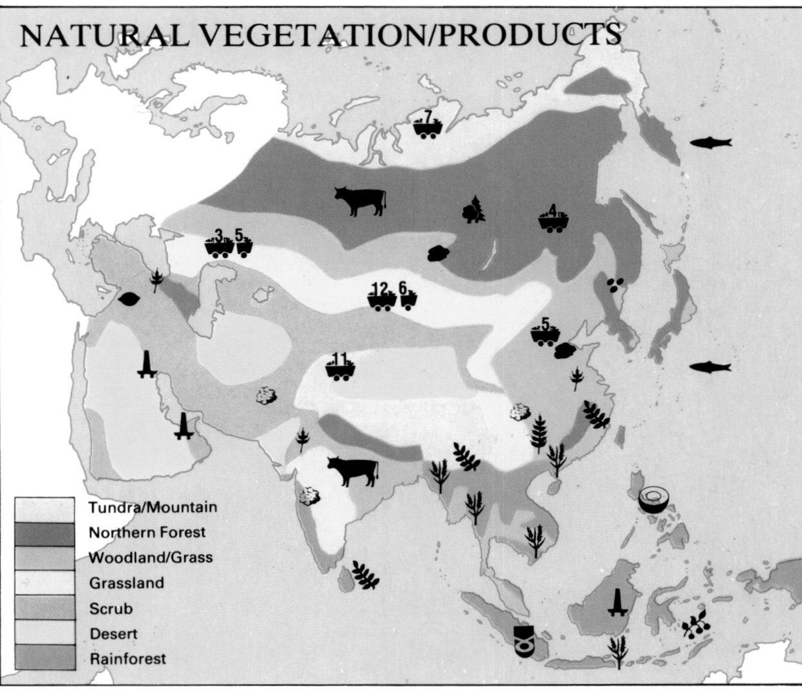

Tundra/Mountain
Northern Forest
Woodland/Grass
Grassland
Scrub
Desert
Rainforest

FACTS ABOUT ASIA

1 The Chang Jiang river (formerly known as the Yangtze Kiang) is the longest river in Asia. Rising in the Tibetan hills, it flows across southern China to the East China Sea. The river has a length of over 5550 km (3450 miles).

2 In Siberia, there is a huge forest called the *taiga*, which makes up a quarter of the total area of forest in the world. The trees are mostly coniferous - pine and larch. Few people used to live in the taiga, as it is a very cold area, but because it is rich in minerals more people are moving into the forest. They live in industrial towns being built deep in its heart, to exploit the minerals.

3 The huge Gobi Desert covers much of Mongolia. The Gobi is a cold, barren region of rocky plains and hills. Water is very scarce and only a few nomads live here. They exist mainly by cattle raising and live in an unusual tent called a *yurt*, which is shaped like an upside-down bowl.

4 The Great Wall of China stretches for 3460 km (2150 miles), making it the longest in the world. It was built for defence in the 3rd century BC and kept in good repair until 400 years ago. Although part of the wall was blown up to make a dam in 1979, the many remaining sections of the wall are still impressive.

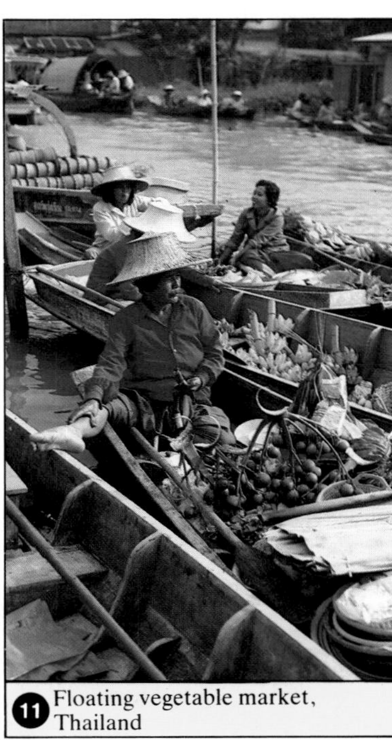

11 Floating vegetable market, Thailand

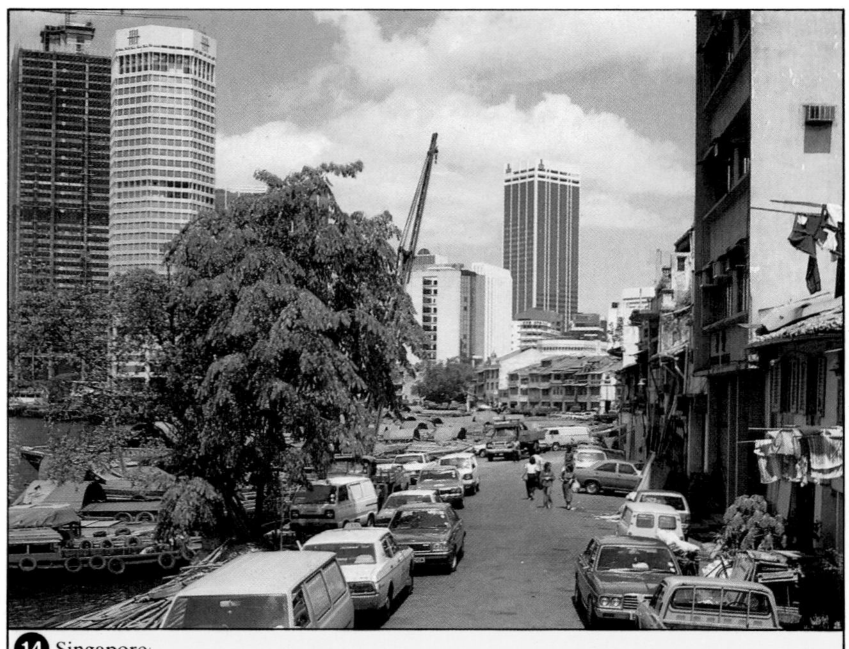
14 Singapore

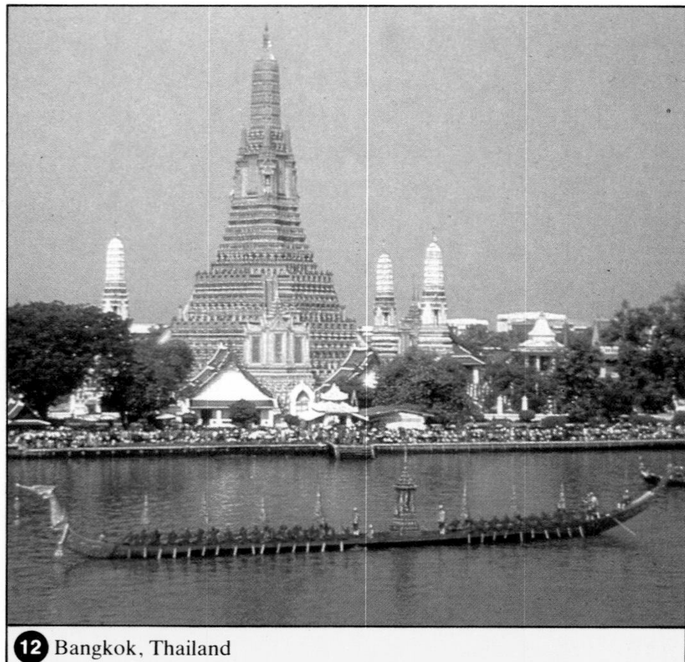
12 Bangkok, Thailand

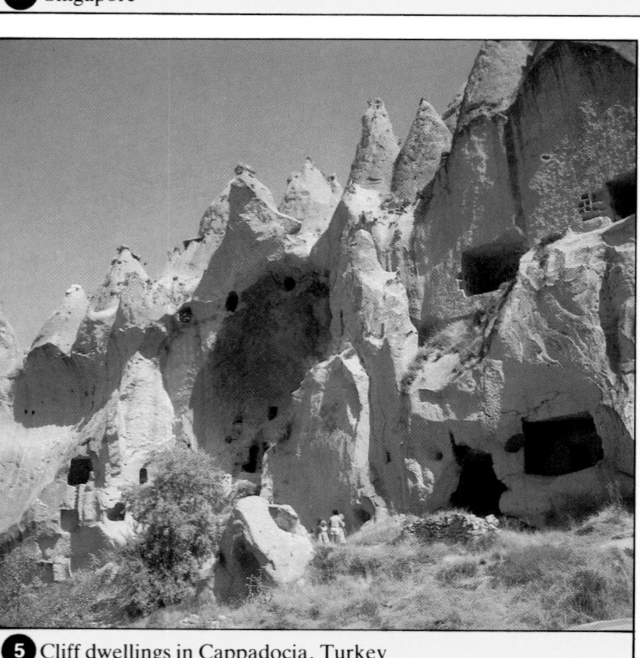
5 Cliff dwellings in Cappadocia, Turkey

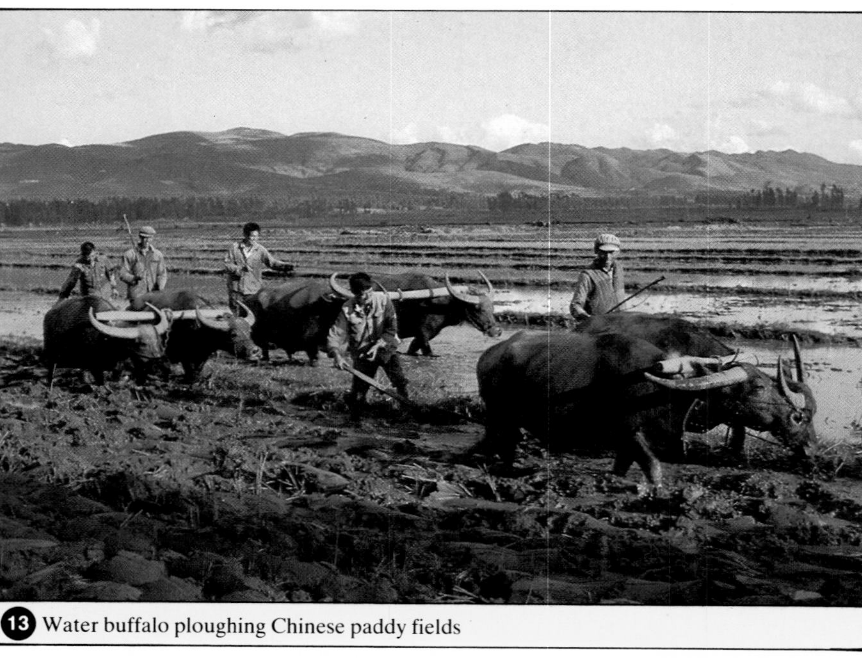
13 Water buffalo ploughing Chinese paddy fields

FACTS ABOUT ASIA

5 In central Turkey, near Urgup in the region called Cappadocia, an extraordinary landscape can be seen. There was once a plateau here, made up of layers of rock, some hard and some much softer. Over thousands of years the softer rocks have been eroded by the weather, by streams and even by men digging out caves to live in. The rocks are now shaped into strange cones, towers and 'mushrooms', with 'hats' of harder rock balancing on top. There are also complete 'villages' of caves connected to each other by passageways cut through the rock. Each cave has 'cupboards' and 'shelves' cut into its walls. Here many centuries ago people hid from religious persecution. Over 300 churches which they dug out of the rock have been found. Some people still live in caves in this region, today.

6 The Seikan Tunnel in Japan is the longest tunnel in the world. It is an underwater tunnel, stretching for 54 km (34 miles). It was built for Japan's famous *bullet train*, the first passenger train to travel at 200 kph.

7 There should have been two Taj Mahals in India – a black one and a white one. In 1648, Emperor Shah Jahan completed the present Taj Mahal. It was a tomb for his wife, and made of white marble. He then began building a tomb of black marble for himself. Before work had got very far, he was overthrown.

8 At 8848 m (29 028 ft) the peak of Mt Everest in the Himalayas is the Earth's highest point. In May 1953, New Zealander Sir Edmund Hillary was the first man to climb Everest. Twenty two years later, in 1975, the first woman to reach the summit was Junko Tabei of Japan.

9 In India cows are sacred animals and are allowed to wander freely, even in the centre of big cities! Drivers are used to going round cows lying peacefully in the middle of the road.

10 Banyan trees can be seen in India and Sri Lanka. They are very unusual to look at, because what seems to be several trees growing close together, is actually just one tree! Aerial roots grow down from the banyan's branches and root in the ground. They become extra 'trunks' and support a huge canopy of leaves, which gives a lot of shade, very useful in such a hot climate.

11 Throughout Asia there are areas where many people live on boats – because there is not enough room for them to live in houses on land (or they cannot afford to) or because they just prefer to live on water. In these places, even the shops are on boats.

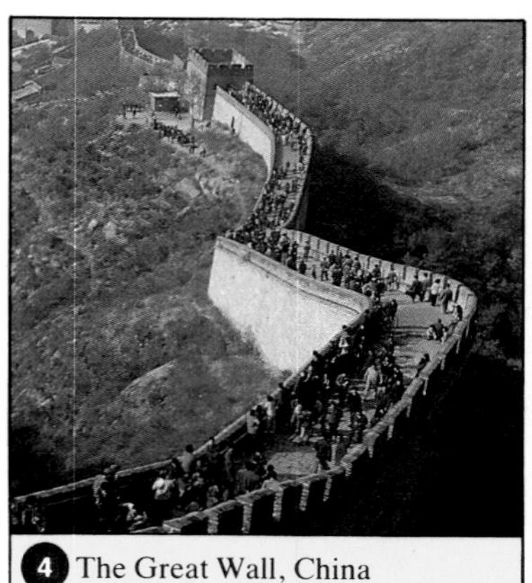
4 The Great Wall, China

10 Banyan tree, India

9 Street in India

12 Bangkok, Thailand, once had many canals, called *klongs*, instead of roads. (The city was called the 'Venice of the East' because the klongs reminded visitors of the canals in Venice, Italy.) They were used for transport and also helped to drain the land during the rainy season. After cars and lorries began to be used for transport, many of the klongs were filled in to make roads. Now Bangkok has problems with flooding when the monsoons come.

13 Paddy fields, the irrigated fields in which rice is grown, get their name from *padi*, the Malayan word for rice. Rice is grown throughout Asia in the fertile lowlands near the equator. Millions of people live in these areas, and rice is very important to them as it yields more food per acre than any other crop.

14 Over half the population of the world lives in Asia – that is 3 113 000 000 people. Some parts of Asia have many people living in a small area. One of the most densely populated countries is Singapore, which has an average of 4 420 people for each square kilometre of ground.

AFGHANISTAN

Area: 674 500 sq km (260 424 sq miles)
Population: 16 600 000
Capital: Kabul
Languages: Pashtu, Dari, Uzbek
Currency: Afghani

CHINA

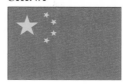

Area: 9 561 000 sq km (3 691 502 sq miles)
Population: 1 118 800 000
Capital: Beijing
Language: Chinese (Mandarin)
Currency: Yuan

INDIA

Area: 3 287 593 sq km (1 269 340 sq miles)
Population: 853 100 000
Capital: Delhi
Languages: Hindi, English
Currency: Indian Rupee

INDONESIA

Area: 1 919 263 sq km (741 027 miles)
Population: 185 000 000
Capital: Jakarta
Language: Bahasa (Indonesian)
Currency: Rupiah

IRAN

Area: 1 648 184 sq km (636 364 sq miles)
Population: 54 600 000
Capital: Tehran
Language: Persian (Farsi)
Currency: Rial

IRAQ

Area: 434 924 sq km (167 924 sq miles)
Population: 18 900 000
Capital: Baghdad
Language: Arabic
Currency: Iraqi Dinar

ISRAEL

Area: 20 770 sq km (8019 sq miles)
Population: 4 600 000
Capital: Jerusalem
Languages: Hebrew, Arabic
Currency: Shekel

JAPAN

Area: 371 000 sq km (143 243 sq miles)
Population: 123 500 000
Capital: Tokyo
Language: Japanese
Currency: Yen

MALAYSIA

Area: 330 669 sq km (127 671 sq miles)
Population: 17 900 000
Capital: Kuala Lumpur
Language: Malay
Currency: Ringgit (Malaysian Dollar)

PAKISTAN

Area: 803 941 sq km (310 402 sq miles)
Population: 122 600 000
Capital: Islamabad
Language: Urdu
Currency: Pakistan Rupee

PHILIPPINES

Area: 299 765 sq km (115 739 sq miles)
Population: 62 400 000
Capital: Manila
Language: Philipino
Currency: Philippine Peso

SAUDI ARABIA

Area: 2 400 930 sq km (927 000 sq miles)
Population: 14 100 000
Capital: Riyadh
Language: Arabic
Currency: Riyal

SINGAPORE

Area: 616 sq km (238 sq miles)
Population: 2 700 000
Capital: Singapore
Languages: Chinese, Malay, Tamil, English
Currency: Singapore Dollar

THAILAND

Area: 513 517 sq km (198 269 sq miles)
Population: 55 700 000
Capital: Bangkok
Languages: Thai, Chinese
Currency: Baht

TURKEY

Area: 780 576 sq km (301 380 sq miles)
Population: 55 900 000
Capital: Ankara
Language: Turkish
Currency: Turkish Lira

1:40M

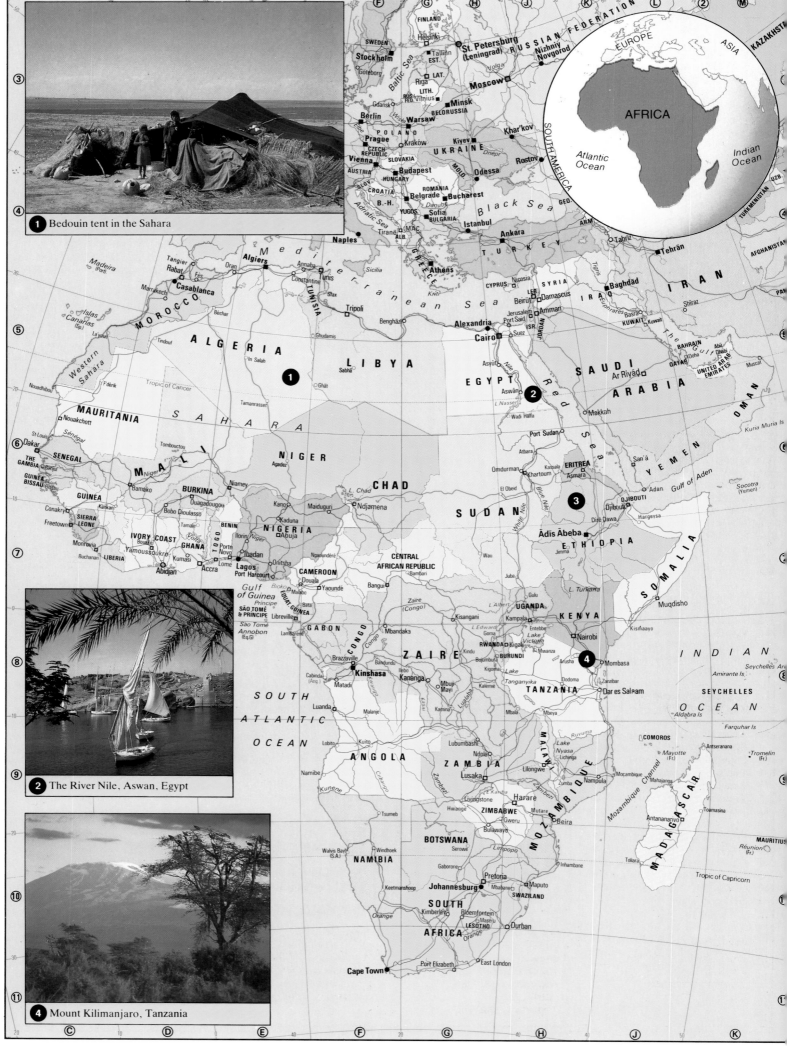

Bedouin tent in the Sahara

2 The River Nile, Aswan, Egypt

4 Mount Kilimanjaro, Tanzania

POPULATION

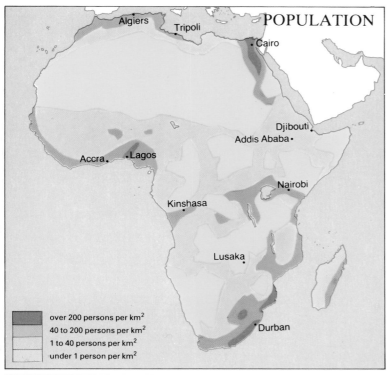

Algiers • Tripoli • Cairo • Djibouti • Addis Ababa • Accra • Lagos • Nairobi • Kinshasa • Lusaka • Durban

over 200 persons per km²
40 to 200 persons per km²
1 to 40 persons per km²
under 1 person per km²

NATURAL VEGETATION/ PRODUCTS

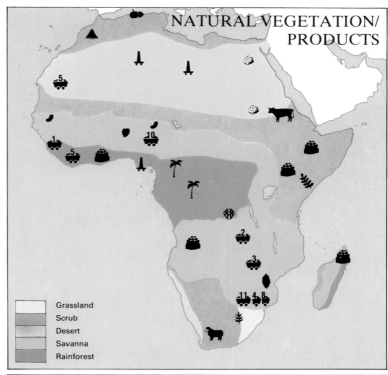

Grassland
Scrub
Desert
Savanna
Rainforest

Cattle	Peanuts	Phosphates	4	Gold
Sheep	Palm oil	Maize	5	Iron
Cocoa	Tea	Minerals	8	Platinum
Coffee	Tobacco	1 Bauxite	10	Tin
Cotton	Diamonds	2 Cobalt	11	Uranium
Fruit	Oil	3 Copper		

FACTS ABOUT AFRICA

1 The largest desert in the world is the Sahara, but only about 30% of it is sand. The rest is rocky waste. People live mainly near oases, where the land is watered by springs rising to the surface and crops can be grown. The desert is very hot and dry, but there are a few plants and animals (like camels) specially adapted to these conditions.

2 The Nile is the longest river in the world and flows for 6650 km (4160 miles) through North Africa to the Mediterranean Sea.

The Nile used to flood its banks each year, but now the High Dam at Aswan controls the floods. When the dam was built, the temples of Abu Simbel (3000 years old) were moved to a higher site to stop them being flooded.

3 Some parts of Africa have had no rain, or very little, for several years. Food crops have failed and many people have died from malnutrition and starvation. A further problem has been wars, which have driven many people from their homes and fields. Even if part of a country can grow food, it is difficult to move that food into areas where none can be grown. There are few lorries and, where people are at war, transporting food may be dangerous. Although western countries have sent food supplies, there is still not enough to feed the hundreds of thousands of people who are starving. Governments are trying to find ways of growing more food and distributing it more quickly.

4 Kilimanjaro (now renamed Uhuru, meaning 'freedom') is the highest mountain in Africa (5895 m; 19 340 feet) and its peaks are always covered in snow.

EGYPT

Area: 1 000 250 sq km (386 197 sq miles)
Population: 52 400 000
Capital: Cairo
Language: Arabic
Currency: Egyptian Pound

ETHIOPIA

Area: 1 104 318 sq km (426 377 sq miles)
Population: 46 626 000
Capital: Addis Ababa
Language: Amharic
Currency: Birr

KENYA

Area: 582 644 sq km (224 959 sq miles)
Population: 24 000 000
Capital: Nairobi
Languages: English, Swahili
Currency: Kenya Shilling

LIBYA
Area: 1 759 530 sq km (679 355 sq miles)
Population: 4 500 000
Capital: Tripoli
Language: Arabic
Currency: Libyan Dinar

NIGERIA

Area: 923 769 sq km (356 667 sq miles)
Population: 108 500 000
Capital: Lagos
Language: English
Currency: Naira

SOUTH AFRICA
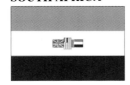
Area: 1 221 038 sq km (471 443 sq miles)
Population: 35 300 000
Capital: Pretoria
Languages: Afrikaans, English
Currency: Rand

SUDAN

Area: 2 505 792 sq km (967 486 sq miles)
Population: 25 200 000
Capital: Khartoum
Language: Arabic
Currency: Sudanese Pound

ZAIRE

Area: 2 344 885 sq km (905 360 sq miles)
Population: 35 600 000
Capital: Kinshasa
Language: French
Currency: Zaire

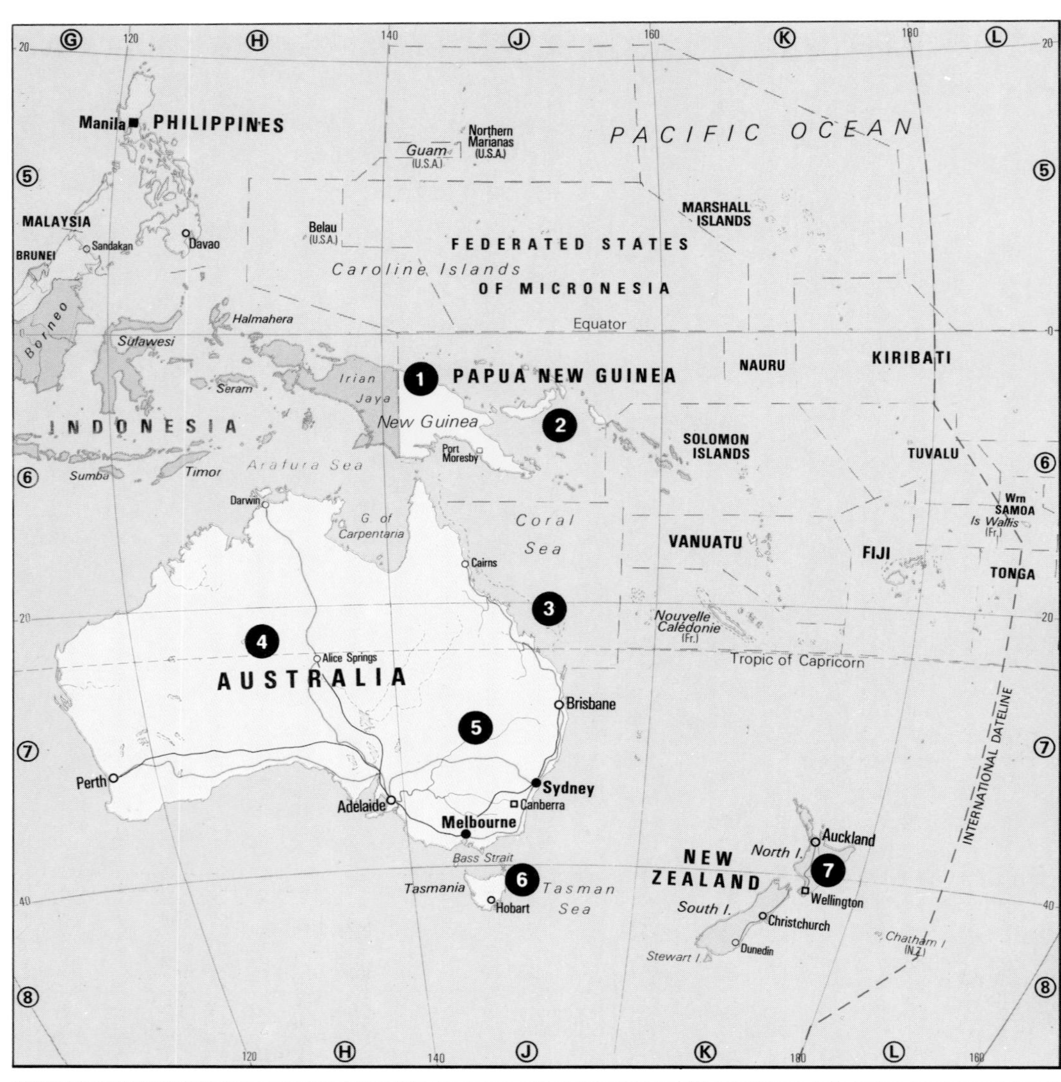

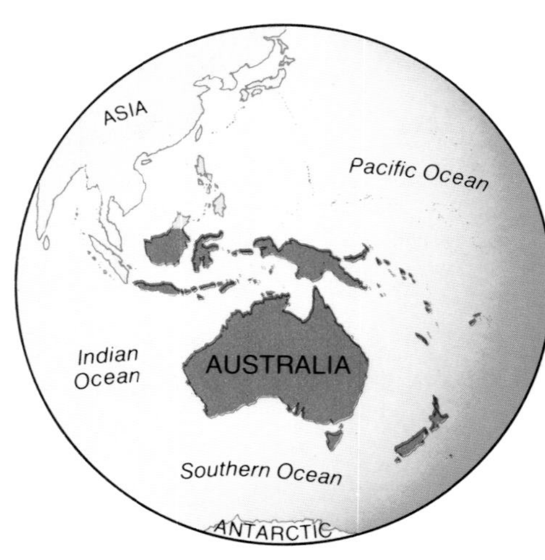

7 Geysers at Whakarewarewa, New Zealand

FACTS ABOUT AUSTRALASIA

1 Over 700 languages are spoken in Papua New Guinea. That is more than a quarter of all the languages spoken in the world. Papua New Guinea's mountains, thick forests and islands meant that different tribes did not mix, so they did not share a common language, but instead each developed its own. Today, Pidgin English and Police Motu have become the languages which the different tribes use to talk to each other.

2 No less than 38 different species of the beautiful Bird of Paradise are to be seen in Papua New Guinea. Another 5 species are found on neighbouring islands and in northern Australia. Their tail feathers are a traditional part of Papua New Guinea tribal costume, although the birds are now protected from hunting to a great extent.

3 Australia's Great Barrier Reef is formed from the shells of millions of tiny sea creatures. It is 2300 km (1430 miles) long and is the world's biggest coral reef. There are many thousands of coral islands or *atolls* in the Pacific region.

4 Ayers Rock is a huge sandstone rock formation which rears up abruptly from the desert in central Australia. The rock is special because it changes colour with the light. To Australia's native *aborigine* people the rock has a very deep spiritual meaning.

5 Australia is a very dry continent. Rainfall is also very unevenly distributed throughout the island: even though some parts of the tropical north receive about 2000 millimetres (79 inches) a year, the central deserts receive less than 150 millimetres (6 inches). Irrigation is very important for agriculture, with rivers and artesian wells being used as sources of water. The Snowy Mountains reservoir and irrigation scheme has brought water from the mountains to irrigate farmland in the east of Australia.

6 A Tasmanian Devil is a little bear-like creature found only in Tasmania. It is just 60 cm (2 ft) long, with a big bushy tail. It has very sharp teeth and eats other

4 Ayers Rock, Australia

6 Tasmanian Devil

POPULATION

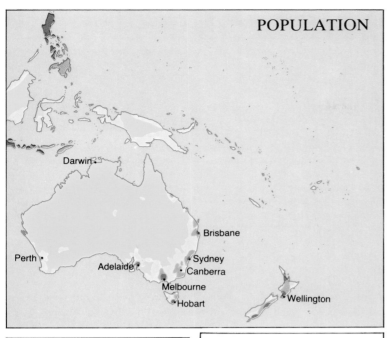

Darwin
Perth
Adelaide
Brisbane
Sydney
Canberra
Melbourne
Hobart
Wellington

	over 500 persons per km²
	100-500 persons per km²
	5-100 persons per km²
	under 5 persons per km²

NATURAL VEGETATION/PRODUCTS

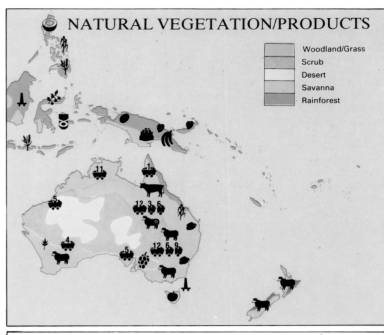

	Woodland/Grass
	Scrub
	Desert
	Savanna
	Rainforest

Sheep	Coffee	Coal	Minerals	6 Lead
Apples	Cocoa	Oil	1 Bauxite	9 Silver
Bananas	Rubber	Spices	3 Copper	11 Uranium
Grapes	Yams	Sugar cane	4 Gold	12 Zinc
Coconut	Rice	Wheat	5 Iron	

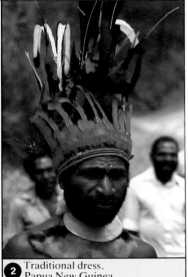

2 Traditional dress, Papua New Guinea

animals and small birds when it comes out at night. The Tasmanian Devil is a *marsupial*. This means it carries its young in a pouch.

7 The tallest geyser ever to have erupted was the Waimangu Geyser in New Zealand. Waimangu geyser played to a height of 490 m (1608 ft) between 1900 and 1904. Today, steam from New Zealand's hot springs and geysers is harnessed to generate electricity.

3 The Great Barrier Reef, Australia

AUSTRALIA
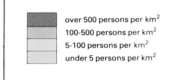

Area: 7 682 300 sq km
(2 966 136 sq miles)
Population: 17 658 700
Capital: Canberra
Language: English
Currency: Australian Dollar

NEW ZEALAND

Area: 268 675 sq km
(103 735 sq miles)
Population: 3 450 000
Capital: Wellington
Language: English
Currency: New Zealand Dollar

TONGA

Area: 699 sq km
(270 sq miles)
Population: 100 000
Capital: Nuku'alofa
Languages: English, Tongan
Currency: Pa'anga

FIJI

Area: 18 272 sq km
(7055 sq miles)
Population: 800 000
Capital: Suva
Languages: English, Fijian
Currency: Fiji Dollar

PAPUA NEW GUINEA

Area: 461 692 sq km
(178 259 sq miles)
Population: 3 900 000
Capital: Port Moresby
Languages: English, Melanesian Pidgin
Currency: Kina

VANUATU

Area: 14 763 sq km
(5700 sq miles)
Population: 160 000
Capital: Vila
Languages: Bislama, English, French
Currency: Australian Dollar, Vatu

KIRIBATI

Area: 800 sq km
(309 sq miles)
Population: 66 000
Capital: Tarawa
Languages: English, I Kiribati
Currency: Australian Dollar

SOLOMON ISLANDS
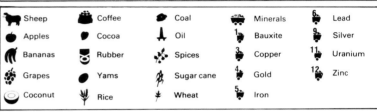

Area: 29 785 sq km
(11 500 sq miles)
Population: 320 000
Capital: Honiara
Languages: English, Pidgin
Currency: Solomon Islands Dollar

WESTERN SAMOA

Area: 2831 sq km
(1093 sq miles)
Population: 170 000
Capital: Apia
Languages: Samoan, English
Currency: Tala

WORLD ENVIRONMENT

The world can be divided into 8 broad 'climatic zones' (these are areas with a particular sort of weather). The natural types of plants and animals found in each zone are different and depend on the weather the zone has. This map shows which parts of the world are in each zone. The colour of the strip at the top of each zone description (for example, Desert, Rainforest) is the same as the colour used for the zone on the big map. The little map beside each zone description pinpoints where that type of habitat is found in the world. (For example, the Desert strip is orange/yellow. The little sketch map shows you where on the big map to look for this colour. You will find this colour in the north of Africa, the west of North America and in parts of Asia and Australia. All these places have deserts. The description tells you what the natural countryside looks like and what plants and animals live there.)

SCRUB OR MEDITERRANEAN

Areas of long, hot, dry summers and short, warm winters. The land used to be covered with trees, but man cleared it for crops and grazed his animals on it. Now there is evergreen scrub – vines and olive trees.

TUNDRA OR MOUNTAIN

Polar areas which are usually frozen over. During the short summers the top layer of soil thaws, creating vast marshes. Compact, wind-resistant plants and lichens and mosses are found here. Animals include lemmings and reindeer.

NORTHERN FOREST (TAIGA)

Forests of conifers growing over a large area. Winters are very cold and long. Summers are short. Trees include spruce and fir. Animals found here include beavers, squirrels and red deer.

WOODLAND AND GRASS

Temperate areas (where the weather is seldom very cold or very hot). Deciduous trees (which lose their leaves in winter) grow in the woodlands. They include oak, beech and maple. Man uses these areas most of all, for farming, building towns and villages, and industry.

GRASSLAND

Hot summers, cold winters and moderate rainfall. Huge area of grassland and 'black' (very fertile) soils. Grain crops grow well, and so does rich pasture for beef cattle. Names for this kind of grassland include steppe, veld, pampas and prairie.

SAVANNA

Tall grasses with thick stems, and flat-topped thorny trees grow here. Animals grazing here include giraffes and zebras. There is a short rainy season. Often it does not rain for a long time (a drought). Fires burn the dried out plants but they have adapted to survive this and grow again.

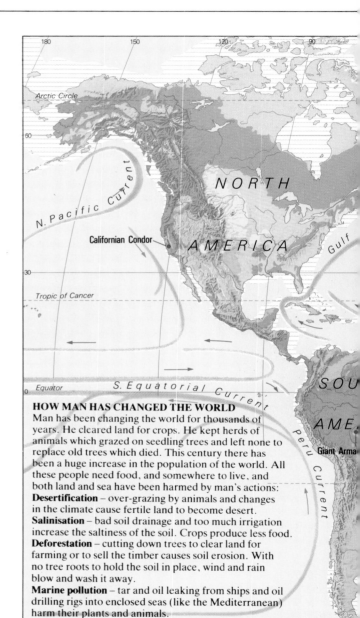

HOW MAN HAS CHANGED THE WORLD

Man has been changing the world for thousands of years. He cleared land for crops. He kept herds of animals which grazed on seedling trees and left none to replace old trees which died. This century there has been a huge increase in the population of the world. All these people need food, and somewhere to live, and both land and sea have been harmed by man's actions:

Desertification – over-grazing by animals and changes in the climate cause fertile land to become desert.

Salinisation – bad soil drainage and too much irrigation increase the saltiness of the soil. Crops produce less food.

Deforestation – cutting down trees to clear land for farming or to sell the timber causes soil erosion. With no tree roots to hold the soil in place, wind and rain blow and wash it away.

Marine pollution – tar and oil leaking from ships and oil drilling rigs into enclosed seas (like the Mediterranean) harm their plants and animals.

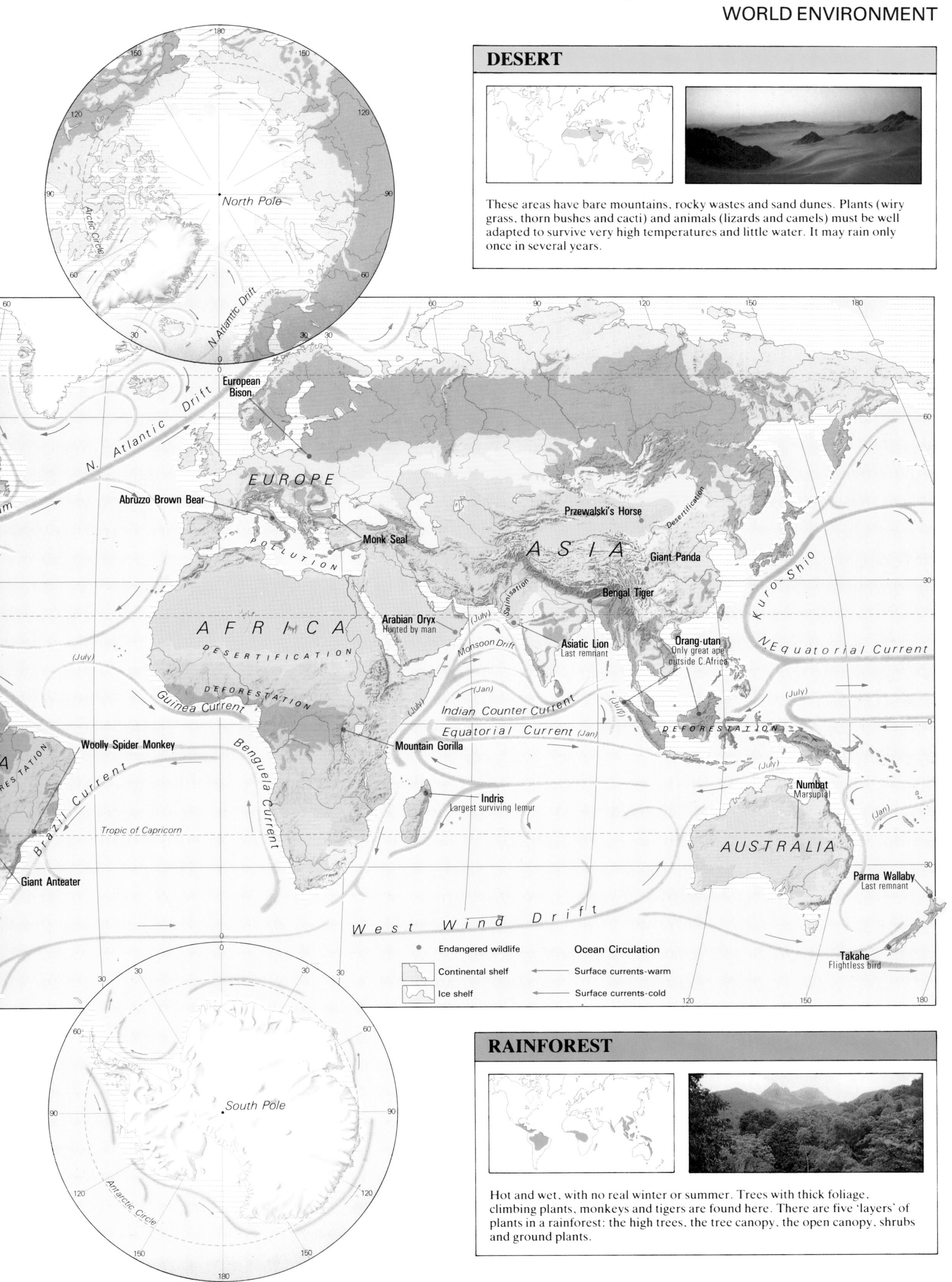

DESERT

These areas have bare mountains, rocky wastes and sand dunes. Plants (wiry grass, thorn bushes and cacti) and animals (lizards and camels) must be well adapted to survive very high temperatures and little water. It may rain only once in several years.

North Pole

Arctic Circle

N Atlantic Drift

N. Atlantic Drift

am

European Bison

EUROPE

Abruzzo Brown Bear

Monk Seal

POLLUTION

ASIA

Przewalski's Horse

Desertification

Giant Panda

Kuro-Shio

Bengal Tiger

AFRICA

DESERTIFICATION

Arabian Oryx
Hunted by man

(July)

Salinisation

Asiatic Lion
Last remnant

Orang-utan
Only great ape
outside C.Africa

N Equatorial Current

DEFORESTATION

Monsoon Drift

Guinea Current

(July)

(July)

DEFORESTATION

(July)

Woolly Spider Monkey

RESTATION

A

Brazil Current

Benguela Current

Mountain Gorilla

Indian Counter Current

Equatorial Current (Jan)

(Jan)

Indris
Largest surviving lemur

Numbat
Marsupial

AUSTRALIA

Tropic of Capricorn

Giant Anteater

Parma Wallaby
Last remnant

West Wind Drift

Takahe
Flightless bird

- Endangered wildlife

Continental shelf

Ice shelf

Ocean Circulation

Surface currents-warm

Surface currents-cold

South Pole

Antarctic Circle

RAINFOREST

Hot and wet, with no real winter or summer. Trees with thick foliage, climbing plants, monkeys and tigers are found here. There are five 'layers' of plants in a rainforest: the high trees, the tree canopy, the open canopy, shrubs and ground plants.

WORLD CLIMATE

World climate has a profound influence upon mankind. Everything is affected by it, from our environment and ability to grow food to our mobility and health. The most important characteristics of climate are rainfall patterns and temperature variations. As the earth revolves around the sun the tilt of its axis causes each hemisphere in turn to be closer than the other to the sun for half a year. The hemisphere facing the overhead sun enjoys a warm summer season while the other experiences winter. Solar radiation, winds, ocean currents, latitude, altitude and land relief also determine types of climate, examples of which are illustrated by the graphs below.

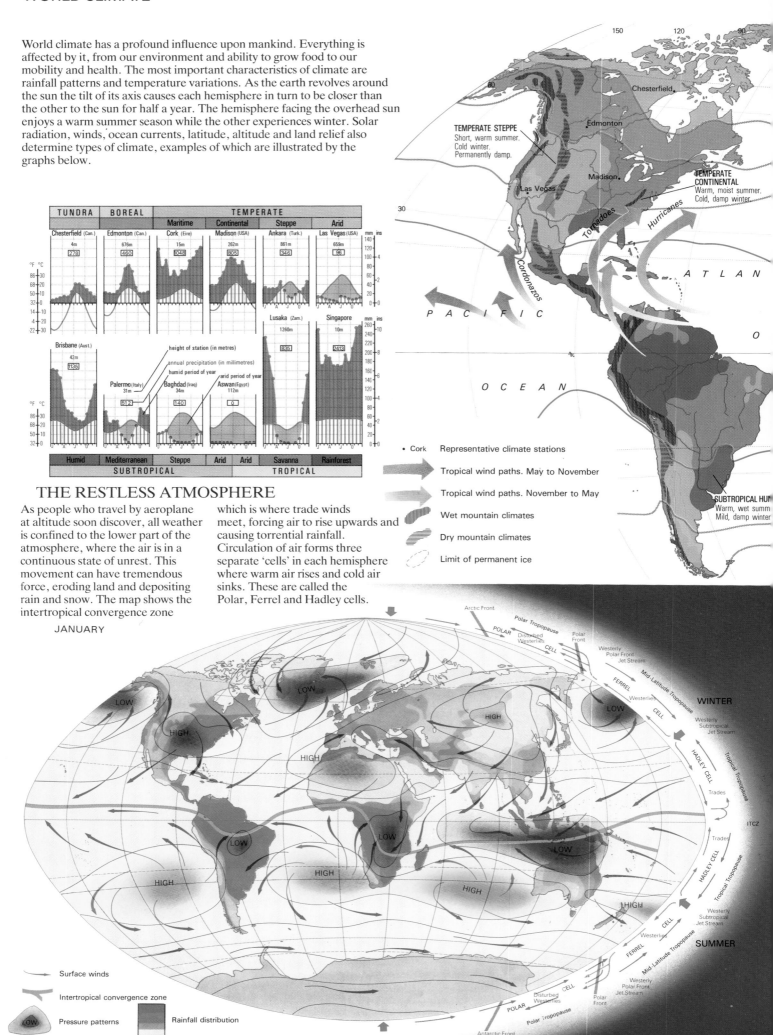

TUNDRA	BOREAL	TEMPERATE				
		Maritime	Continental	Steppe	Arid	
Chesterfield (Can.)	Edmonton (Can.)	Cork (Eire)	Madison (USA)	Ankara (Turk.)	Las Vegas (USA)	
4m 278	676m 460	15m 1048	262m 805	861m 346	659m 96	

Lusaka (Zam.) 1260m 835
Singapore 10m 2413

Brisbane (Aust.) 42m 1135

height of station (in metres)
annual precipitation (in millimetres)
humid period of year
arid period of year

Palermo (Italy) 31m 512
Baghdad (Iraq) 34m 140
Aswan (Egypt) 112m 0

Humid	Mediterranean	Steppe	Arid	Arid	Savanna	Rainforest
SUBTROPICAL				TROPICAL		

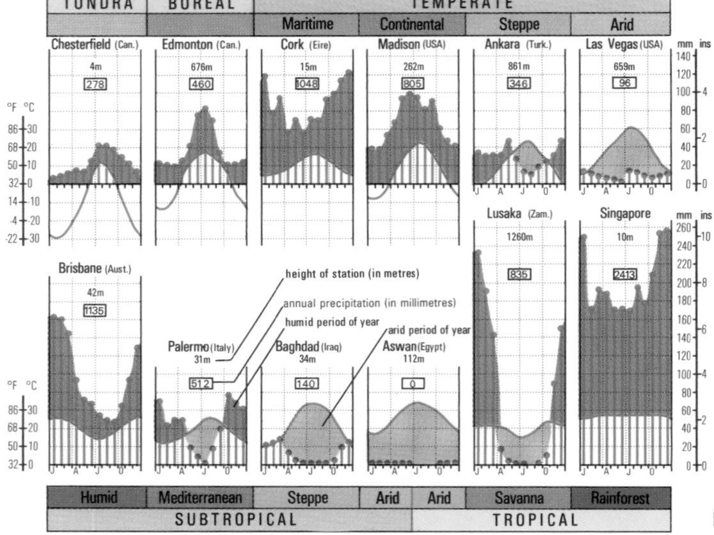

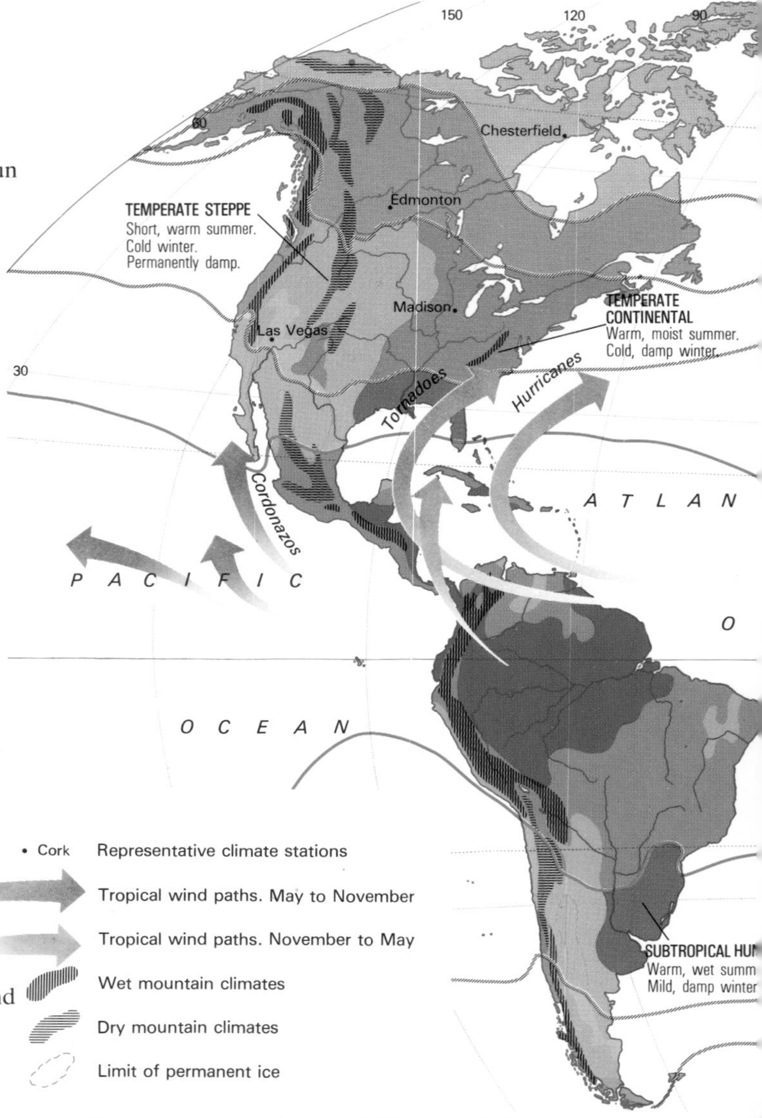

THE RESTLESS ATMOSPHERE

As people who travel by aeroplane at altitude soon discover, all weather is confined to the lower part of the atmosphere, where the air is in a continuous state of unrest. This movement can have tremendous force, eroding land and depositing rain and snow. The map shows the intertropical convergence zone which is where trade winds meet, forcing air to rise upwards and causing torrential rainfall. Circulation of air forms three separate 'cells' in each hemisphere where warm air rises and cold air sinks. These are called the Polar, Ferrel and Hadley cells.

TEMPERATE STEPPE Short, warm summer. Cold winter. Permanently damp.

TEMPERATE CONTINENTAL Warm, moist summer. Cold, damp winter.

SUBTROPICAL HUMID Warm, wet summer. Mild, damp winter.

- Cork   Representative climate stations
- Tropical wind paths. May to November
- Tropical wind paths. November to May
- Wet mountain climates
- Dry mountain climates
- Limit of permanent ice

JANUARY

- Surface winds
- Intertropical convergence zone
- Pressure patterns
- Rainfall distribution

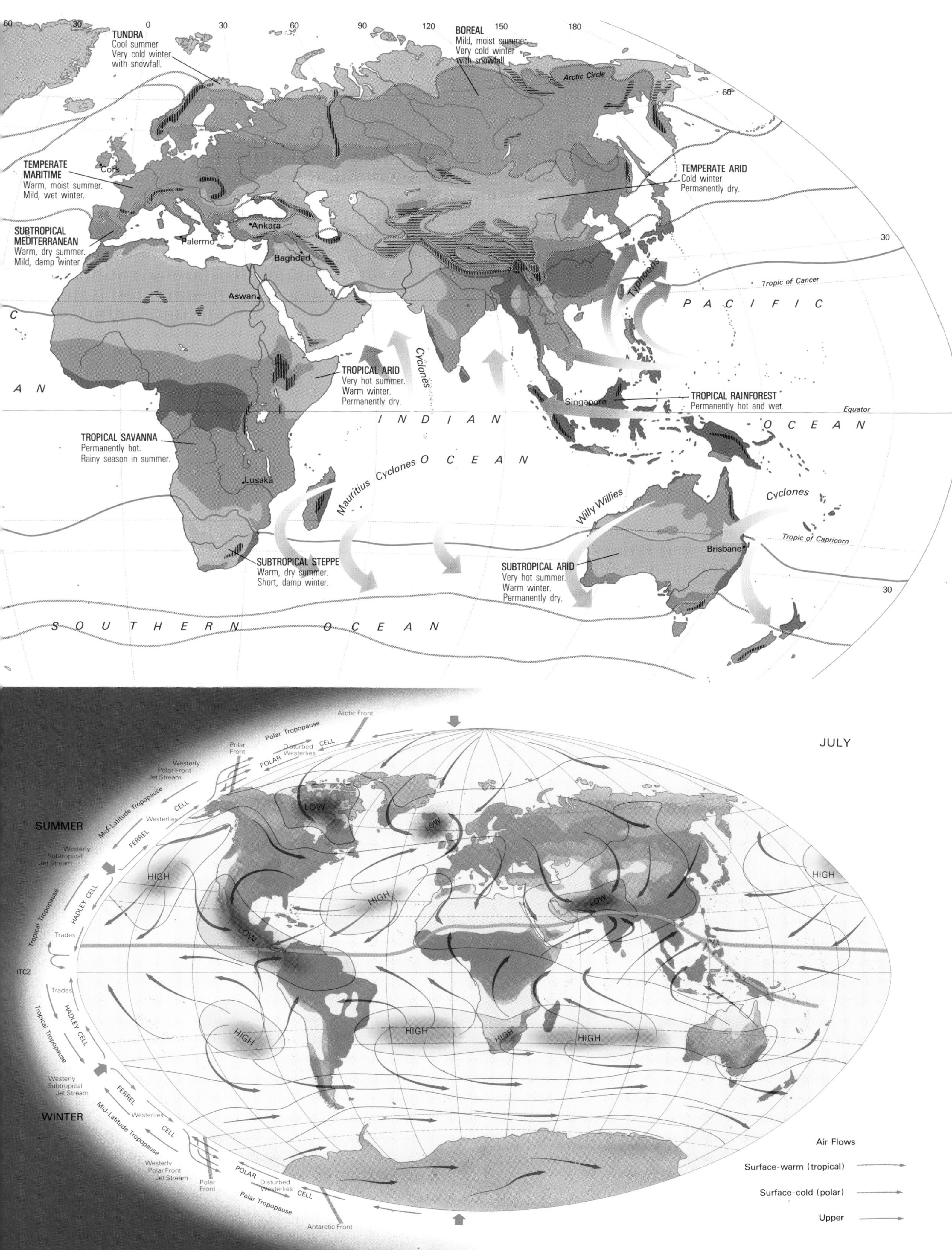

TUNDRA
Cool summer
Very cold winter
with snowfall.

BOREAL
Mild, moist summer.
Very cold winter
with snowfall.

TEMPERATE
MARITIME
Warm, moist summer.
Mild, wet winter.

TEMPERATE ARID
Cold winter.
Permanently dry.

SUBTROPICAL
MEDITERRANEAN
Warm, dry summer.
Mild, damp winter.

TROPICAL ARID
Very hot summer.
Warm winter.
Permanently dry.

TROPICAL RAINFOREST
Permanently hot and wet.

TROPICAL SAVANNA
Permanently hot.
Rainy season in summer.

SUBTROPICAL STEPPE
Warm, dry summer.
Short, damp winter.

SUBTROPICAL ARID
Very hot summer.
Warm winter.
Permanently dry.

Cork
Palermo
Ankara
Baghdad
Aswan
Lusaka
Singapore
Brisbane

PACIFIC
INDIAN OCEAN
Mauritius Cyclones OCEAN
SOUTHERN OCEAN
Cyclones
Typhoons
Willy Willies
Cyclones

Arctic Circle
Tropic of Cancer
Equator
Tropic of Capricorn

JULY

SUMMER
WINTER

Arctic Front
Polar Tropopause
Polar Front
Westerly Polar Front Jet Stream
Disturbed Westerlies
POLAR CELL
Mid Latitude Tropopause
Westerlies
FERREL CELL
Westerly Subtropical Jet Stream
Tropical Tropopause
HADLEY CELL
Trades
ITCZ
Trades
Tropical Tropopause
HADLEY CELL
Westerly Subtropical Jet Stream
FERREL
Westerlies
CELL
Mid Latitude Tropopause
Westerly Polar Front Jet Stream
Polar Front
POLAR Disturbed Westerlies CELL
Polar Tropopause
Antarctic Front

LOW
LOW
HIGH
HIGH
HIGH
LOW
LOW
HIGH
HIGH
HIGH
HIGH

Air Flows

Surface-warm (tropical)

Surface-cold (polar)

Upper

XXV

CLIMATE INDICATORS

Listed from north to south, is selection of places from different climate zones of the world (see p xxiv/xxv), indicating their mean monthly temperatures (in °C and °F) and precipitation (in mm and inches). Also shown are their average temperatures and total precipitation for the year.

REYKJAVIK Iceland 64.1°N 21.9°W TUNDRA

	J	F	M	A	M	J	J	A	S	O	N	D	Year
°C	-0.2	0.2	1.5	3.5	6.7	9.7	11.3	10.8	8.5	5.2	3.0	0.4	5.0
°F	32	32	35	38	44	49	52	51	47	41	37	33	41
mm	89	64	62	56	42	42	50	56	67	94	78	79	779
ins	3.5	2.5	2.4	2.2	1.6	1.6	2.0	2.2	2.6	3.7	3.1	3.1	30.7

ANCHORAGE U.S.A. 61.2°N 150.0°W BOREAL

	J	F	M	A	M	J	J	A	S	O	N	D	Year
°C	-10.4	-7.6	-4.8	2.0	7.7	12.2	14.1	13.1	8.7	1.8	-5.6	-10.2	1.7
°F	13	18	23	36	46	54	57	56	48	35	22	14	29
mm	20	18	13	11	13	25	47	65	63	47	26	24	372
ins	0.8	0.7	0.5	0.4	0.5	1.0	1.8	2.6	2.5	1.8	1.0	0.9	14.6

STOCKHOLM Sweden 59.3°N 18.1°E TEMPERATE Continental

	J	F	M	A	M	J	J	A	S	O	N	D	Year
°C	-3.0	-3.1	-0.5	4.6	10.2	15.0	18.5	16.6	12.3	7.1	2.7	0.0	6.6
°F	27	26	31	40	50	59	65	62	54	45	37	32	44
mm	43	30	25	31	34	45	61	76	60	48	53	48	554
ins	1.7	1.2	1.0	1.2	1.3	1.8	2.4	3.0	2.4	1.9	2.1	1.9	21.8

EDINBURGH U.K. 55.9°N 3.2°W TEMPERATE Maritime

	J	F	M	A	M	J	J	A	S	O	N	D	Year
°C	3.3	3.5	5.1	7.4	9.9	12.9	14.8	14.4	12.5	9.4	6.4	4.6	8.6
°F	38	38	41	45	50	55	59	58	54	49	43	40	47
mm	57	39	39	39	54	47	83	77	57	65	62	57	676
ins	2.2	1.5	1.5	1.5	2.1	1.8	3.3	3.0	2.2	2.6	2.4	2.2	26.6

MOSKVA Russian Federation 55.7°N 37.6°E TEMPERATE Continental

	J	F	M	A	M	J	J	A	S	O	N	D	Year
°C	-12.7	-9.6	-3.8	5.7	13.3	15.8	17.8	16.9	11.8	5.9	-0.9	-7.0	4.4
°F	9	15	25	42	56	60	64	62	53	43	30	19	40
mm	39	38	36	37	53	58	88	71	58	45	47	54	624
ins	1.5	1.5	1.4	1.5	2.1	2.3	3.5	2.8	2.3	1.8	1.8	2.1	24.6

VANCOUVER Canada 49.2°N 123.2°W TEMPERATE Maritime

	J	F	M	A	M	J	J	A	S	O	N	D	Year
°C	2.8	4.1	6.4	9.4	12.6	15.5	17.8	17.2	14.4	10.3	6.3	4.2	10.0
°F	37	39	43	49	55	60	64	63	58	50	43	40	50
mm	214	161	151	90	69	65	39	44	83	172	198	243	1529
ins	8.4	6.3	5.9	3.5	2.7	2.6	1.5	1.7	3.3	6.8	7.8	9.6	60.2

PARIS France 48.8°N 2.3°E TEMPERATE Maritime

	J	F	M	A	M	J	J	A	S	O	N	D	Year
°C	3.4	4.3	7.9	11.0	14.6	17.8	19.5	19.1	16.5	11.7	7.2	4.3	11.5
°F	38	40	46	52	58	64	67	66	62	53	45	40	53
mm	56	46	35	42	57	54	59	64	55	50	51	50	619
ins	2.2	1.8	1.4	1.6	2.2	2.1	2.3	2.5	2.2	2.0	2.0	2.0	24.3

BUCUREŞTI Romania 44.5°N 26.0°E TEMPERATE Steppe

	J	F	M	A	M	J	J	A	S	O	N	D	Year
°C	-4.2	-1.5	6.2	12.4	17.3	21.2	23.5	22.9	18.2	13.0	6.4	0.6	8.2
°F	24	29	43	54	63	70	74	73	65	55	43	33	47
mm	46	26	28	59	77	121	53	45	45	29	36	27	592
ins	1.8	1.0	1.1	2.3	3.0	4.8	2.1	1.8	1.8	1.1	1.4	1.1	23.4

NEW YORK U.S.A. 40.7°N 74.0°W TEMPERATE Continental

	J	F	M	A	M	J	J	A	S	O	N	D	Year
°C	0.7	0.8	4.7	10.5	16.3	21.2	24.1	23.3	19.8	14.3	8.1	2.2	12.2
°F	33	33	40	51	61	70	75	74	68	58	47	36	54
mm	89	74	104	89	91	86	102	119	89	84	89	84	1100
ins	3.5	2.9	4.1	3.5	3.6	3.4	4.0	4.7	3.5	3.3	3.5	3.3	43.3

TŌKYŌ Japan 35.7°N 139.8°E TEMPERATE Continental

	J	F	M	A	M	J	J	A	S	O	N	D	Year
°C	3.3	4.2	7.2	12.5	16.9	20.8	24.7	26.1	22.5	16.7	10.8	5.8	14.4
°F	38	40	45	54	62	69	76	79	72	62	51	42	58
mm	48	74	107	135	147	165	142	152	234	208	96	56	1565
ins	1.9	2.9	4.2	5.3	5.8	6.5	5.6	6.0	9.2	8.2	3.8	2.2	61.6

TANGER Morocco 35.8°N 5.8°W SUBTROPICAL Mediterranean

	J	F	M	A	M	J	J	A	S	O	N	D	Year
°C	11.9	12.5	13.6	14.4	17.2	20.0	22.2	23.0	21.4	18.6	14.7	12.4	16.7
°F	53	54	56	58	63	68	72	73	70	65	58	54	62
mm	114	107	122	89	43	15	2	2	23	99	147	137	897
ins	4.5	4.2	4.8	3.5	1.7	0.6	0.1	0.1	0.9	3.9	5.8	5.4	35.3

JERUSALEM Israel 31.8°N 35.2°E SUBTROPICAL Steppe

	J	F	M	A	M	J	J	A	S	O	N	D	Year
°C	8.9	9.4	13.0	16.4	20.5	22.5	23.9	24.1	23.0	21.1	16.4	11.1	17.2
°F	48	49	55	61	69	72	75	75	73	70	61	52	63
mm	132	132	63	28	2	1	0	0	1	13	71	87	528
ins	5.2	5.2	2.5	1.1	0.1	0.1	0.0	0.0	0.1	0.5	2.8	3.4	20.8

NEW ORLEANS U.S.A. 30.0°N 90.2°W SUBTROPICAL Humid

	J	F	M	A	M	J	J	A	S	O	N	D	Year
°C	12.5	13.9	16.3	19.9	23.5	26.7	27.6	27.7	25.7	21.3	15.5	13.0	20.3
°F	54	57	61	68	74	80	82	82	78	70	60	55	68
mm	97	102	135	114	112	112	170	135	127	71	84	104	1363
ins	3.8	4.0	5.3	4.5	4.4	4.4	6.7	5.3	5.0	2.8	3.3	4.1	53.7

BAHRAIN 26.2°N 50.5°E SUBTROPICAL Arid

	J	F	M	A	M	J	J	A	S	O	N	D	Year
°C	16.9	18.0	20.5	25.0	29.4	31.7	33.3	33.6	31.4	28.0	24.2	18.6	25.8
°F	62	64	69	77	85	89	92	92	88	82	75	65	78
mm	8	18	13	8	1	0	0	0	0	0	18	18	79
ins	0.3	0.7	0.5	0.3	0.1	0.0	0.0	0.0	0.0	0.0	0.7	0.7	3.2

HONG KONG 22.3°N 114.2°E SUBTROPICAL Humid

	J	F	M	A	M	J	J	A	S	O	N	D	Year
°C	15.5	15.0	17.5	21.7	25.5	27.5	28.0	28.0	27.2	25.0	20.8	17.5	22.5
°F	60	59	63	71	78	81	82	82	81	77	69	63	72
mm	33	46	74	137	292	394	381	361	256	114	43	30	2161
ins	1.3	1.8	2.9	5.4	11.5	15.5	15.0	14.2	10.1	4.5	1.7	1.2	85.1

MIAMI U.S.A. 25.8°N 80.3°W TROPICAL Savanna

	J	F	M	A	M	J	J	A	S	O	N	D	Year
°C	19.3	19.9	21.4	23.4	25.3	27.1	27.6	27.9	27.4	25.4	22.4	20.1	23.9
°F	67	68	70	74	77	81	82	82	81	78	72	68	75
mm	51	48	58	99	163	188	170	178	241	208	71	43	1518
ins	2.0	1.9	2.3	3.9	6.4	7.4	6.7	7.0	9.5	8.2	2.8	1.7	59.8

BANGKOK Thailand 13.7°N 100.5°E TROPICAL Savanna

	J	F	M	A	M	J	J	A	S	O	N	D	Year
°C	25.8	27.5	28.9	30.0	29.4	28.6	28.3	28.3	28.0	27.5	26.4	25.3	27.7
°F	78	81	84	86	85	83	83	83	82	81	79	77	82
mm	8	20	36	58	198	160	160	175	305	206	66	5	1397
ins	0.3	0.8	1.4	2.3	7.8	6.3	6.3	6.9	12.0	8.1	2.6	0.2	55.0

COLOMBO Sri Lanka 6.9°N 79.9°E TROPICAL Rainforest

	J	F	M	A	M	J	J	A	S	O	N	D	Year
°C	26.1	26.4	27.2	27.7	28.0	27.2	27.2	27.2	27.2	26.6	26.1	25.8	26.9
°F	79	80	81	82	82	81	81	81	81	80	79	78	80
mm	89	69	147	231	371	223	135	109	160	348	315	147	2344
ins	3.5	2.7	5.8	9.1	14.6	8.8	5.3	4.3	6.3	13.7	12.4	5.8	92.3

NAIROBI Kenya 1.3°S 36.8°E TROPICAL Savanna

	J	F	M	A	M	J	J	A	S	O	N	D	Year
°C	18.6	19.4	19.4	19.2	17.7	16.4	15.5	16.1	17.5	18.6	18.3	18.0	18.0
°F	65	67	67	67	64	61	60	61	63	65	65	64	64
mm	38	63	124	211	157	46	15	23	30	53	109	86	958
ins	1.5	2.5	4.9	8.3	6.2	1.8	0.6	0.9	1.2	2.1	4.3	3.4	37.7

LIMA Peru 12.1°S 77.0°W TROPICAL Arid

	J	F	M	A	M	J	J	A	S	O	N	D	Year
°C	23.3	23.8	23.6	21.9	19.4	17.2	16.7	16.1	16.9	18.0	19.4	21.1	20.0
°F	74	75	74	71	67	63	62	61	62	64	67	70	68
mm	1	1	1	1	5	5	8	8	8	2	2	1	41
ins	0.1	0.1	0.1	0.1	0.2	0.2	0.3	0.3	0.3	0.1	0.1	0.1	1.6

RIO DE JANEIRO Brazil 22.9°S 43.2°W TROPICAL Savanna

	J	F	M	A	M	J	J	A	S	O	N	D	Year
°C	25.8	26.1	25.3	23.6	21.9	21.1	20.5	21.1	21.1	21.9	23.0	24.7	23.0
°F	78	79	77	74	71	70	69	70	70	71	73	76	73
mm	124	122	130	107	79	53	41	43	66	79	104	137	1085
ins	4.9	4.8	5.1	4.2	3.1	2.1	1.6	1.7	2.6	3.1	4.1	5.4	42.6

JOHANNESBURG S. Africa 26.2°S 28.1°E SUBTROPICAL Steppe

	J	F	M	A	M	J	J	A	S	O	N	D	Year
°C	20.0	19.7	18.3	16.1	12.5	10.3	10.5	13.0	15.8	18.3	18.9	19.7	16.1
°F	68	67	65	61	54	50	51	55	60	65	66	67	61
mm	114	109	89	38	25	8	8	8	23	56	107	124	709
ins	4.5	4.3	3.5	1.5	1.0	0.3	0.3	0.3	0.9	2.2	4.2	4.9	27.9

PERTH Australia 31.9°S 115.8°E SUBTROPICAL Mediterranean

	J	F	M	A	M	J	J	A	S	O	N	D	Year
°C	23.3	23.3	21.7	19.2	16.1	13.9	13.0	13.3	14.7	16.4	19.2	21.7	17.8
°F	74	74	71	66	61	57	55	56	58	61	66	71	64
mm	8	10	20	43	130	180	170	145	86	56	20	13	881
ins	0.3	0.4	0.8	1.7	5.1	7.1	6.7	5.7	3.4	2.2	0.8	0.5	34.7

WELLINGTON New Zealand 41.3°S 174.8°E TEMPERATE Maritime

	J	F	M	A	M	J	J	A	S	O	N	D	Year
°C	16.9	16.9	15.8	13.9	11.4	9.7	8.6	9.2	10.8	12.2	13.6	15.8	12.8
°F	62	62	60	57	52	49	47	48	51	54	56	60	55
mm	81	81	81	97	117	117	137	117	97	102	89	89	1205
ins	3.2	3.2	3.2	3.8	4.6	4.6	5.4	4.6	3.8	4.0	3.5	3.5	47.4

Civilisation depends on trade for growth and travel makes this possible.
Shipping is the most important method of world transport but economic
progress and moblity are constantly being improved by the
development of new routes and new modes of transport.

ROAD AND RAIL

Integrated road and rail networks are the basis of
industrial society. Extended highway systems and
improved containerisation techniques have made the
whole road and rail system much more flexible.

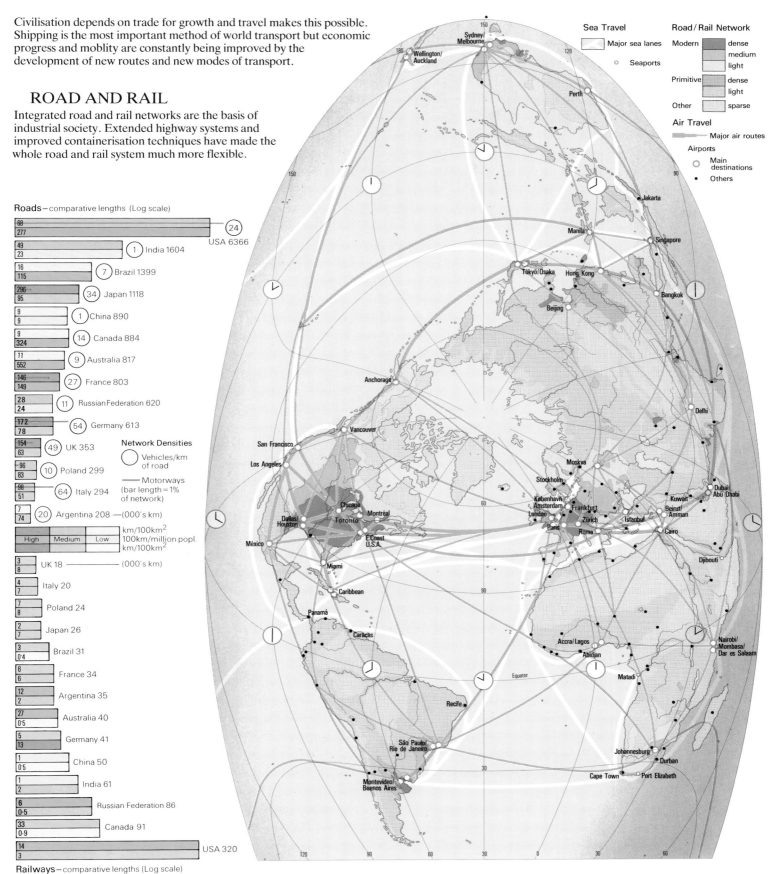

Roads – comparative lengths (Log scale)

68 / 277	(24) USA 6366
49 / 23	(1) India 1604
16 / 115	(7) Brazil 1399
296 / 95	(34) Japan 1118
9 / 9	(1) China 890
9 / 324	(14) Canada 884
11 / 552	(9) Australia 817
146 / 149	(27) France 803
28 / 24	(11) Russian Federation 620
172 / 78	(54) Germany 613
154 / 63	(49) UK 353
96 / 83	(10) Poland 299
98 / 51	(64) Italy 294
7 / 74	(20) Argentina 208 —(000's km)

Network Densities

○ Vehicles/km of road

— Motorways (bar length = 1% of network)

High	Medium	Low	km/100km²

100km/million popl.
km/100km²

3 / 8	UK 18 —(000's km)
4 / 7	Italy 20
7 / 8	Poland 24
2 / 7	Japan 26
3 / 0·4	Brazil 31
6 / 6	France 34
12 / 2	Argentina 35
27 / 0·5	Australia 40
5 / 13	Germany 41
1 / 0·5	China 50
1 / 2	India 61
6 / 0·5	Russian Federation 86
33 / 0·9	Canada 91
14 / 3	USA 320

Railways – comparative lengths (Log scale)

Sea Travel
□ Major sea lanes
○ Seaports

Road / Rail Network
Modern — dense / medium / light
Primitive — dense / light
Other — sparse

Air Travel
— Major air routes

Airports
○ Main destinations
• Others

JOURNEY TIME

The Suez canal cuts 3600 miles off the
London-Singapore route, while Concorde
halves the London-New York journey time.

AIR AND SEA ROUTES

A complex network of primary air routes
centred on the Northern Hemisphere
provides rapid transit across the world for
mass travel, mail and urgent freight. Ships
also follow these principal routes, plying
the oceans between major ports and
transporting the commodities of world
trade in bulk.

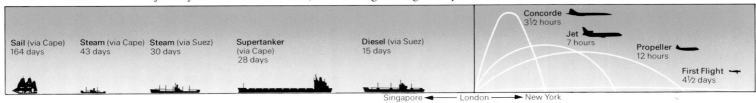

Sail (via Cape) 164 days

Steam (via Cape) 43 days

Steam (via Suez) 30 days

Supertanker (via Cape) 28 days

Diesel (via Suez) 15 days

Concorde 3½ hours

Jet 7 hours

Propeller 12 hours

First Flight 4½ days

Singapore ← London → New York

1:60M

600   1200   1800   2400 km
0
0   600   1200 mls

40 20 Ⓐ 0 Ⓑ 20 Ⓒ 40 Ⓓ 60 Ⓔ 80 Ⓕ 100 Ⓖ 120 Ⓗ 140 Ⓙ 16

Barents Sea

① Arctic Circle

Norwegian Basin

ICELAND

60

North Sea

② E U R O P E   A S I A

Black Sea   *Aral Sea*

Caspian Sea

40

Mediterranean Sea   *Huang He*   *Sea of Okhotsk*   Sakhalin

Sea of Japan

③   *Chang Jiang*   J A P A N   *Kuril Trench*   *Vityaz Depth 10542*

The Gulf   *Ganga*   *Japan Trench*

Red Sea   TAIWAN

20   *Arabian Sea*   *Bay of Bengal*   Hainan   S. Honshu Ridge

Mekong   Mariana Is

Kyushu-Palau Ridge   Guam   M I C R O

Arabian Basin   Andaman Is.   PHILIPPINES   *11022 Challenger Depth*

Raas Caseyr   SRI LANKA (CEYLON)   C. Johnson Depth 10497   *Mariana Trench*

④ A F R I C A   MALDIVES   Nicobar Is   Belau   Caroline Is

Carlsberg Ridge   *South China Sea*   *Philippine Trench*   6920

Somali Basin   *Maldives Ridge*   Borneo   *Celebes Sea*   M E L

SEYCHELLES   Chagos Arch.   Celebes   New Guinea   *Planet Deep 9140*

0   *Mascarene Ridge*   *Sumatra*   I N D O N E S I A

COMOROS   *Mid Indian Basin*   Java   *Arafura Sea*

⑤   *Ninety-East Ridge*   *Java Trench* •7450   Timor   *Coral Sea Basin*

Mozambique Channel   I N D I A N   Christmas I.   •1737

MADAGASCAR   Cocos Is   *West Australian Basin*

Réunion   MAURITIUS   O C E A N   •1924

20   *Mid-Indian Ridge*   *W. Australian Ridge*   Tropic of Capricorn

Madagascar Basin   A U S T R A L I A

S. Madagascar Ridge   2067•   •7102

Natal Basin   T a s m

⑥   *South West Indian Ridge*   *South Australia Basin*

C. Agulhas   •1198   *Crozet Basin*   I.Amsterdam   Tasmania   *Tasman Sea*

Agulhas Plateau   I.St Paul   *Indian-Antarctic Ridge*

40   *Agulhas Basin*   Îs Crozet   Îs Kerguelen   1922•

Pr. Edward Is   *Kerguelen Ridge*   Macquarie

⑦   *Atlantic-Indian Ridge*   Heard I.   *Indian-Antarctic Basin*

Banzare Seamount 186

60   *Atlantic-Indian Antarctic Basin*

⑧   A N T A R C T I C A

40 20 Ⓐ 0 Ⓑ 20 Ⓒ 40 Ⓓ 60 Ⓔ 80 Ⓕ 100 Ⓖ 120 Ⓗ 140 Ⓙ

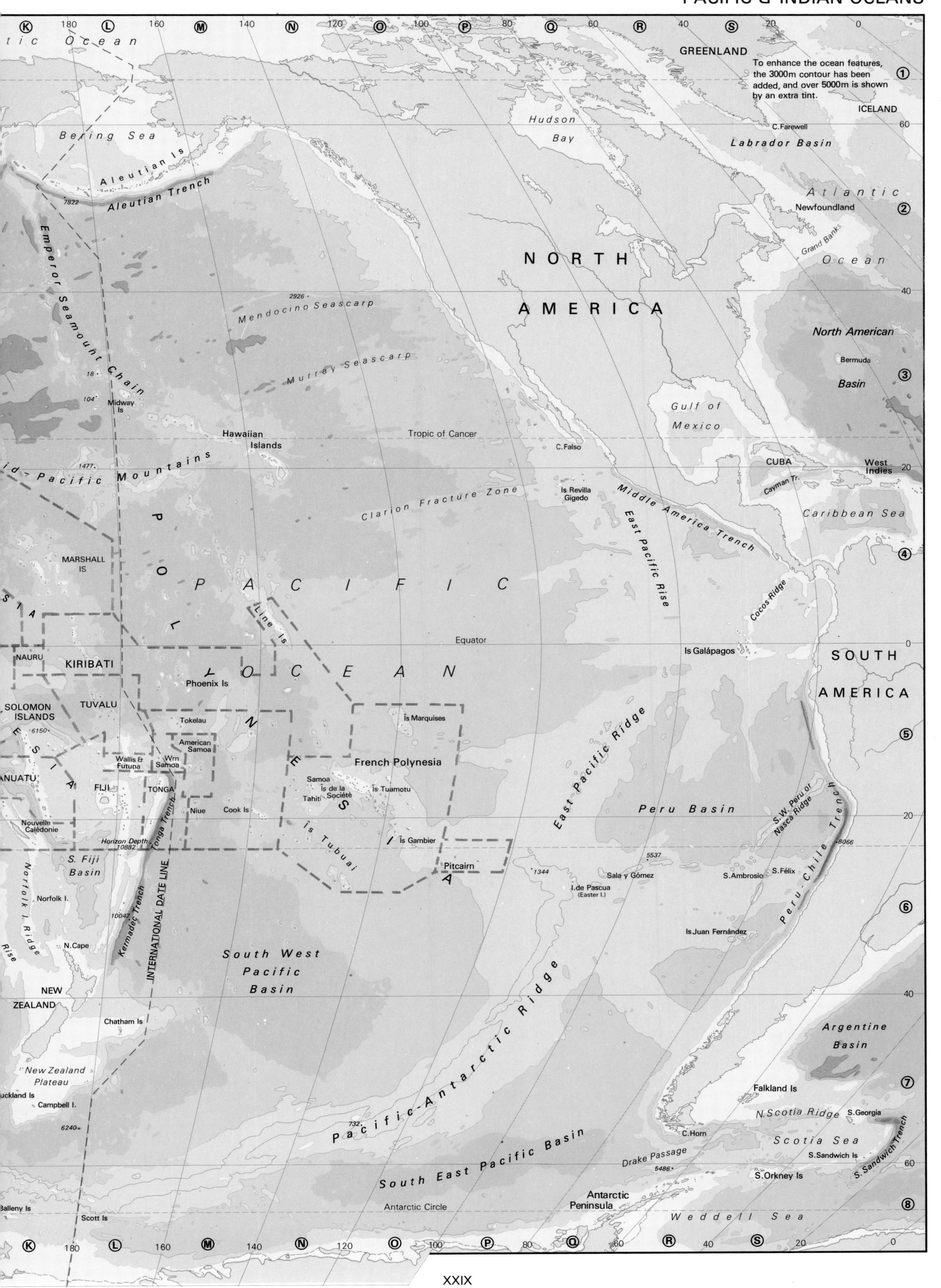

To enhance the ocean features, the 3000m contour has been added, and over 5000m is shown by an extra tint.

GREENLAND

ICELAND

C.Farewell

Hudson Bay

Labrador Basin

Bering Sea

Atlantic

Aleutian Is

Newfoundland

Aleutian Trench

7822

Grand Banks

Ocean

Emperor Seamount Chain

NORTH

AMERICA

North American

Bermuda

Basin

Mendocino Seascarp

2926

Murray Seascarp

Gulf of Mexico

Midway Is

18

104

Hawaiian Islands

Tropic of Cancer

C.Falso

CUBA

West Indies

id-Pacific Mountains

1477

Clarion Fracture Zone

Is Revilla Gigedo

Middle America Trench

Cayman Tr.

Caribbean Sea

P

MARSHALL IS

O

PACIFIC

Line Is

East Pacific Rise

Is Galápagos

SOUTH

Cocos Ridge

NAURU

L

Equator

AMERICA

KIRIBATI

Y

O

Phoenix Is

TUVALU

N

CEAN

Is Marquises

East Pacific Ridge

SOLOMON ISLANDS

Tokelau

E

French Polynesia

Peru Basin

6150

American Samoa

S

Samoa

Is de la Société

Is Tuamotu

S.W. Peru or Nasca Ridge

ANUATU

Wallis & Futuna

Wrn Samoa

Tahiti

FIJI

TONGA

Niue

Cook Is

I

Is Gambier

5537

S.Félix

Nouvelle Calédonie

Horizon Depth 10882

Is Tubuai

A

Pitcairn

1344

Sala y Gómez

S.Ambrosio

Norfolk I. Ridge

S. Fiji Basin

Norfolk I.

I.de Pascua (Easter I.)

10047

Is Juan Fernández

N.Cape

INTERNATIONAL DATE LINE

Kermadec Trench

Tonga Trench

Peru-Chile Trench

8066

Rise

NEW

South West Pacific Basin

Argentine Basin

ZEALAND

Chatham Is

40

New Zealand Plateau

Falkland Is

uckland Is

Campbell I.

N.Scotia Ridge

S.Georgia

6240

Pacific-Antarctic Ridge

732

Scotia Sea

Balleny Is

S.Sandwich Is

S. Sandwich Trench

Scott Is

South East Pacific Basin

Drake Passage

5486

S.Orkney Is

C.Horn

Antarctic Circle

Antarctic Peninsula

Weddell Sea

ATLANTIC OCEAN

600 1200 1800 2400 km

600 1200 mils

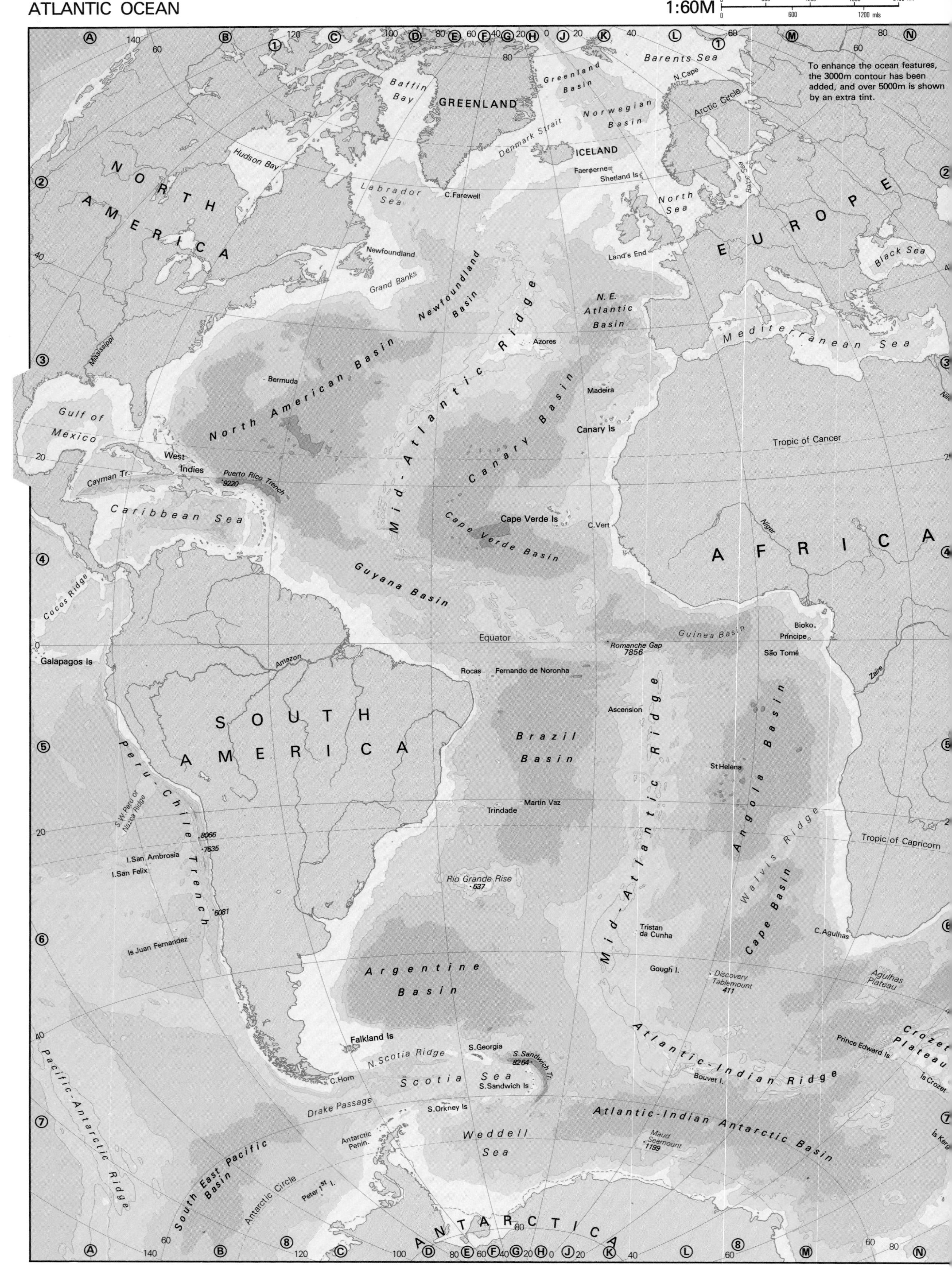

To enhance the ocean features,
the 3000m contour has been
added, and over 5000m is shown
by an extra tint.

Barents Sea

Greenland
Basin

Baffin
Bay

GREENLAND

Norwegian
Basin

N.Cape

Arctic Circle

Denmark Strait

ICELAND

Faeroerne

Shetland Is

Labrador
Sea

C.Farewell

North
Sea

Hudson Bay

N O R T H

A M E R I C A

Newfoundland

Grand Banks

Newfoundland
Basin

N. E.
Atlantic
Basin

Land's End

E U R O P E

Black Sea

Azores

Mediterranean Sea

North American Basin

Bermuda

Mid-Atlantic Ridge

Madeira

Canary Basin

Canary Is

Tropic of Cancer

Gulf of
Mexico

Mississippi

West
Indies

Puerto Rico Trench
9220

C.Vert

Cayman Tr.

Caribbean Sea

Cape Verde Is

Cape Verde Basin

A F R I C A

Cocos Ridge

Guyana Basin

Niger

Guinea Basin

Bioko
Príncipe

São Tomé

Galapagos Is

Equator

Romanche Gap
7856

Zaire

Rocas
Fernando de Noronha

S O U T H

Amazon

Ascension

Brazil
Basin

Mid-Atlantic Ridge

Angola Basin

Peru-Chile Trench

A M E R I C A

St Helena

S.W.Peru or
Nazca Ridge

Martin Vaz

8066

Trindade

7635

I.San Ambrosia

Rio Grande Rise
637

Walvis Ridge

Tropic of Capricorn

I.San Felix

Cape Basin

C.Agulhas

6081

Is Juan Fernandez

Argentine

Tristan
da Cunha

Agulhas
Plateau

Basin

Gough I.

Discovery
Tablemount
411

Crozet
Plateau

Falkland Is

S.Georgia

Prince Edward Is

Atlantic-Indian Ridge

Is Crozet

N.Scotia Ridge

S.Sandwich Tr.
8264

Bouvet I.

C.Horn

Scotia   Sea

S.Sandwich Is

Pacific-Antarctic Ridge

Drake Passage

S.Orkney Is

Atlantic-Indian Antarctic Basin

Is Kerg

South East Pacific
Basin

Antarctic Circle

Peter 1st I.

Weddell
Sea

Maud
Seamount
1199

Antarctic
Penin.

A N T A R C T I C A

MOUNTAIN HEIGHTS

Metres	Feet		Metres	Feet	
8848	29 028	Everest (Qomolangma Feng) *Nepal-Tibet*	6870	22 541	Bonete *Bolivia*
8611	28 250	K2 (Godwin Austen) *Kashmir-Sinkiang*	6800	22 310	Tupungato *Argentina-Chile*
8586	28 168	Kangchenjunga *Nepal-India*	6770	22 211	Mercedario *Argentina*
8475	27 805	Makalu *Tibet-Nepal*	6768	22 205	Huascarán *Peru*
8172	26 810	Dhaulagiri *Nepal*	6723	22 057	Llullaillaco *Argentina-Chile*
8126	26 660	Nanga Parbat *Kashmir*	6714	22 028	Kangrinboqê Feng (Kailas) *Tibet*
8078	26 504	Annapurna *Nepal*	6634	21 765	Yerupaja *Peru*
8068	26 470	Gasherbrum *Kashmir*	6542	21 463	Sajama *Bolivia*
8013	26 291	Xixabangma Feng (Gosainthan) *Tibet*	6485	21 276	Illampu *Bolivia*
7890	25 885	Distaghil Sar *Kashmir*	6425	21 079	Coropuna *Peru*
7820	25 656	Masherbrum *Kashmir*	6402	21 004	Illimani *Bolivia*
7817	25 645	Nanda Devi *India*	6388	20 958	Ancohuma *Bolivia*
7780	25 550	Rakaposhi *Kashmir*	6310	20 702	Chimborazo *Ecuador*
7756	25 447	Kamet *India-Tibet*	6194	20 320	McKinley *USA*
7756	25 447	Namcha Barwa *Tibet*	6050	19 850	Logan *Canada*
7728	25 355	Gurla Mandhata *Tibet*	5895	19 340	Kilimanjaro *Tanzania*
7723	25 338	Muztag (Ulugh Muztagh) *Sinkiang*	5700	18 700	Citlaltepetl *Mexico*
7719	25 325	Kongur Shan (Kungur) *Sinkiang*	5642	18 510	El'bruz *Russian Federation*
7690	25 230	Tirich Mir *Pakistan*	5452	17 887	Popocatepetl *Mexico*
7590	24 903	Gongga Shan (Minya Konka) *China*	5199	17 057	Kirinyaga (Kenya) *Kenya*
7546	24 757	Muztagata (Muztagh Ata) *Sinkiang*	5165	16 946	Ararat *Turkey*
7495	24 590	Pik Kommunizma *Tajikistan*	5140	16 864	Vinson Massif *Antarctica*
7439	24 407	Pik Pobedy (Tomur Feng) *Kirghizia-Sinkiang*	5110	16 763	Stanley *Zaire-Uganda*
7313	23 993	Chomo Lhari *Bhutan-Tibet*	5030	16 500	Jaya (Carstensz) *Indonesia*
7134	23 406	Pik Lenina *Kirghizia-Tajikistan*	4808	15 774	Mont Blanc *France*
6960	22 834	Aconcagua *Argentina*	4508	14 790	Wilhelm *Papua New Guinea*
6908	22 664	Ojos del Salado *Chile-Argentina*	4201	13 784	Mauna Kea *USA*

RIVER LENGTHS

Km	Miles		Km	Miles	
6695	4160	Nile *Africa*	2850	1770	Danube *Europe*
6570	4080	Amazon *South America*	2820	1750	Salween *Asia*
6380	3964	Yangtze *Asia*	2780	1730	São Francisco *South America*
6020	3740	Mississippi-Missouri *North America*	2655	1650	Zambezi *Africa*
5410	3360	Ob-Irtysh *Asia*	2570	1600	Nelson-Saskatchewan *North America*
4840	3010	Huang He (Yellow River) *Asia*	2510	1560	Ganges *Asia*
4630	2880	Zaïre (Congo) *Africa*	2430	1510	Euphrates *Asia*
4500	2796	Paraná *South America*	2330	1450	Arkansas *North America*
4440	2760	Irtysh *Asia*	2330	1450	Colorado *North America*
4416	2745	Amur *Asia*	2285	1420	Dnieper *Europe*
4400	2730	Lena *Asia*	2090	1300	Irrawaddy *Asia*
4240	2630	Mackenzie *North America*	2060	1280	Orinoco *South America*
4180	2600	Mekong *Asia*	2000	1240	Negro *South America*
4100	2550	Niger *Africa*	1870	1160	Don *Europe*
4090	2540	Yenisey *Asia*	1859	1155	Orange *Africa*
3969	2466	Missouri *North America*	1799	1118	Pechora *Europe*
3779	2348	Mississippi *North America*	1609	1000	Marañón *South America*
3750	2330	Murray-Darling *Australia*	1410	876	Dniester *Europe*
3688	2292	Volga *Europe*	1320	820	Rhine *Europe*
3240	2013	Madeira *South America*	1183	735	Donets *Europe*
3058	1900	St. Lawrence *North America*	1159	720	Elbe *Europe*
3030	1880	Rio Grande *North America*	1094	680	Gambia *Africa*
3020	1870	Yukon *North America*	1080	671	Yellowstone *North America*
2960	1840	Brahmaputra *Asia*	1014	630	Vistula *Europe*
2896	1800	Indus *Asia*	1006	625	Tagus *Europe*

LAKE AND INLAND SEA AREAS

Areas are average and some are subject to seasonal variations.

Sq. Km	Sq. Miles		Sq. Km	Sq. Miles	
371 000	142 240	Caspian *Central Asia (salt)*	22 490	8680	Nyasa (Malawi) *Malawi-Mozambique*
82 900	32 010	Superior *USA-Canada*	19 400	7490	Ontario *USA-Canada*
68 800	26 560	Victoria *Kenya-Uganda-Tanzania*	18 390	7100	Ladoga *Russian Federation*
59 580	23 000	Huron *USA-Canada*	17 400	6700	Balkhash *Kazakhstan*
58 020	22 480	Michigan *USA*	10-26 000	4-10 000	Chad *Nigeria-Niger-Chad-Cameroon*
36 500	14 100	Aral *Central Asia (salt)*	9600	3710	Onega *Russian Federation*
32 900	12 700	Tanganyika *Tanzania-Zambia-Zaire-Burundi*	0-8900	0-3430	Eyre *Australia*
31 330	12 100	Great Bear *Canada*	8340	3220	Titicaca *Peru-Bolivia*
30 500	11 800	Baykal *Russian Federation*	8270	3190	Nicaragua *Nicaragua*
28 570	11 030	Great Slave *Canada*	6410	2470	Turkana (Rudolf) *Kenya-Ethiopia*
25 680	9910	Erie *USA-Canada*	5780	2230	Torrens *Australia (salt)*
24 390	9420	Winnipeg *Canada*	5580	2160	Vänern *Sweden*

GREATEST OCEAN DEPTHS

Metres	Feet	Location	Metres	Feet	Location
		PACIFIC OCEAN			ATLANTIC OCEAN
11 022	36 160	Marianas Trench	9220	30 249	Puerto Rico Trench
10 882	35 702	Tonga Trench	8264	27 113	South Sandwich Trench
10 542	34 586	Kuril Trench	7856	25 774	Romanche Gap
10 497	34 439	Philippine Trench	7500	24 600	Cayman Trench
10 047	32 962	Kermadec Trench			
9810	32 185	Izu-Bonin Trench			INDIAN OCEAN
9165	30 069	New Hebrides Trench	7450	24 442	Java Trench
9140	29 987	South Solomon Trench	7440	24 409	Weber Basin
8412	27 598	Japan Trench	7102	23 300	Diamantina Trench
8066	26 463	Peru-Chile Trench			
7822	25 662	Aleutian Trench			ARCTIC OCEAN
6662	21 857	Middle America	5570	18 274	Nansen Fracture Zone

STATES AND DEPENDENCIES

COUNTRY	Area (sq. km)	Population ('000)	Capital
North and Central America			
Anguilla (UK)	91	7	The Valley
Antigua and Barbuda	442	76	St. John's
The Bahamas	13 864	253	Nassau
Barbados	430	255	Bridgetown
Belize	22 965	187	Belmopan
Bermuda (UK)	53	58	Hamilton
Canada	9 976 147	27 296	Ottawa
Cayman Is. (UK)	259	25	George Town
Costa Rica	50 899	3 015	San José
Cuba	114 524	10 608	La Habana (Havana)
Dominica	751	82	Roseau
Dominican Republic	48 441	7 170	Santo Domingo
El Salvador	20 865	5 252	San Salvador
Grenada	344	85	St. George's
Guadeloupe (Fr.)	1 779	343	Basse Terre
Guatemala	108 888	9 197	Guatemala
Haiti	27 749	6 513	Port-au-Prince
Honduras	112 087	5 138	Tegucigalpa
Jamaica	11 425	2 456	Kingston
Martinique (Fr.)	1 101	341	Fort-de-France
Mexico	1 967 180	107 233	Mexico
Montserrat (UK)	102	12	Plymouth
Netherlands Antilles (Neth.)	993	188	Willemstad
Nicaragua	139 000	3 871	Managua
Panama	75 648	2 418	Panamá
Puerto Rico (USA)	8 897	3 480	San Juan
St. Kitts-Nevis	260	44	Basseterre
St. Lucia	616	150	Castries
St. Vincent	389	116	Kingstown
Trinidad and Tobago	5 128	1 281	Port of Spain
United States of America	9 363 130	248 700	Washington
South America			
Argentina	2 777 815	32 322	Buenos Aires
Bolivia	1 098 575	7 314	La Paz
Brazil	8 511 968	150 368	Brasília
Chile	756 943	13 173	Santiago
Colombia	1 138 907	32 978	Bogotá
Ecuador	455 502	10 587	Quito
French Guiana (Fr.)	91 000	98	Cayenne
Guyana	214 969	796	George Town
Paraguay	406 750	4 277	Asunción
Peru	1 285 215	21 550	Lima
Surinam	163 820	422	Paramribo
Uruguay	186 925	3 094	Montevideo
Venezuela	912 047	19 735	Caracas
Europe			
Albania	28 752	3 245	Tiranë (Tirana)
Andorra	453	47	Andorra-la-Vella
Austria	83 848	7 583	Wien (Vienna)
Belgium	30 512	9 845	Bruxelles (Brussels)
Belorussia (Belarus)	207 600	10 278	Minsk
Bosnia-Herzegovina	51 130	4 400	Sarajevo
Bulgaria	110 911	9 010	Sofiya (Sofia)
Croatia	56 540	4 700	Zagreb
Cyprus	9 251	701	Nicosia
Czech Republic	78 864	10 300	Praha (Prague)
Denmark	43 030	5 143	København (Copenhagen)
Estonia	45 100	1 573	Tallinn
Faroes (Den.)	1 399	47	Tórshavn
Finland	337 032	4 975	Helsinki
France	551 000	56 138	Paris
Germany	356 854	79 070	Berlin
Gibraltar (UK)	6	30	Gibraltar
Great Britain and N. Ireland, see United Kingdom			
Greece	131 955	10 047	Athinai (Athens)
Greenland (Den.)	2 175 600	56	Godthåb
Hungary	93 030	10 552	Budapest
Iceland	102 828	260	Reykjavik
Ireland	70 282	3 720	Dublin
Italy	301 245	57 061	Roma (Rome)
Latvia	63 700	2 681	Riga
Liechtenstein	161	28	Vaduz
Lithuania	65 200	3 690	Vilnius
Luxembourg	2 587	373	Luxembourg
Macedonia	25 713	2 090	Skopje
Malta	316	353	Valletta
Moldova	33 700	4 341	Kishinev
Monaco	1.8	28	Monaco
Netherlands	33 940	14 951	Amsterdam/'s-Gravenhage
Norway	324 218	4 212	Oslo
Poland	312 683	38 423	Warszawa (Warsaw)
Portugal	91 671	10 285	Lisboa (Lisbon)
Romania	237 500	23 272	Bucuresti (Bucharest)
Russian Federation	17 075 000	148 263	Moskva (Moscow)
San Marino	61	23	San Marino
Slovakia	49 035	5 300	Bratislava
Slovenia	7 815	1 900	Ljubljana
Spain	504 745	39 187	Madrid
Sweden	449 791	8 444	Stockholm
Switzerland	41 287	6 609	Bern
Ukraine	603 700	51 857	Kiyev
United Kingdom	244 104	57 237	London
Vatican City	.4	1	Vatican City
Yugoslavia	255 803	23 807	Beograd (Belgrade)
Asia			
Afghanistan	674 500	16 557	Kabul
Armenia	29 800	3 283	Yerevan
Azerbaijan	86 600	7 029	Baku
Bahrain	660	516	Al Manāmah
Bangladesh	144 020	115 593	Dhaka (Dacca)
Bhutan	46 620	1 516	Thimphu
Brunei	5 765	266	Bandar Seri Begawan
Burma (Myanma)	678 031	41 675	Yangon (Rangoon)
Cambodia	181 035	8 246	Phnom Penh
China	9 561 000	1 118 760	Beijing (Peking)
Georgia	69 700	5 449	Tbilisi
Hong Kong (UK)	1 062	5 851	
India	3 287 593	853 094	New Delhi
Indonesia	1 919 263	185 020	Jakarta
Iran	1 648 184	54 607	Tehrān
Iraq	434 924	18 920	Baghdād
Israel	20 770	4 600	Jerusalem
Japan	371 000	123 460	Tōkyō
Jordan	97 740	4 009	Amman
Kazakhstan	2 717 300	16 538	Alma Ata
Kirghizia (Kyrgyzstan)	198 500	4 291	Bishkek (Frunze)
Korea, North	121 248	21 773	P'yŏngyang
Korea, South	98 447	42 793	Sŏul (Seoul)
Kuwait	24 300	2 039	Kuwait
Laos	236 798	4 139	Vientiane
Lebanon	10 399	2 701	Beirut
Macau (Port)	16	479	Macao
Malaysia	330 669	17 891	Kuala Lumpur
Maldives	298	215	Malé
Mongolia	1 565 000	2 190	Ulaanbaatar (Ulan Bator)
Nepal	141 414	19 143	Kathmandu
Oman	212 379	1 502	Masqat (Muscat)
Pakistan	803 941	122 626	Islamabad
Philippines	299 765	62 413	Manila
Qatar	11 437	368	Ad Dawḥah
Saudi Arabia	2 400 930	14 134	Ar Riyāḍ
Singapore	616	2 723	Singapore
Sri Lanka	65 610	17 217	Colombo
Syria	185 179	12 530	Dimashq (Damascus)
Taiwan	35 980	20 300	T'ai-pei
Tajikistan	143 100	5 112	Dushanbe
Thailand	513 517	55 702	Bangkok
Turkey	780 576	55 868	Ankara
Turkmenistan	488 100	3 534	Ashkhabad
United Arab Emirates	83 600	1 589	Abū Ẓabī
Uzbekistan	447 400	19 906	Tashkent
Vietnam	329 566	66 693	Hanoi
Yemen	528 038	11 687	San'ā'
Africa			
Algeria	2 381 731	24 960	Alger (El Djezair)
Angola	1 246 694	10 020	Luanda
Benin	112 622	4 630	Porto Novo
Botswana	582 000	1 304	Gaborone
Burkina	274 122	8 996	Ouagadougou
Burundi	27 834	5 472	Bujumbura
Cameroon	475 499	11 833	Yaoundé
Cape Verde	4 033	370	Praia
Central African Republic	622 996	3 039	Bangui
Chad	1 284 000	5 678	N'Djamena
Comoros	1 862	550	Moroni
Congo	342 000	2 271	Brazzaville
Djibouti	21 699	409	Djibouti
Egypt	1 000 250	52 426	Cairo
Equatorial Guinea	28 051	352	Malabo
Eritrea	117 600	2 614	Āsmera (Asmara)
Ethiopia	1 104 318	46 626	Ādis Ābeba
Gabon	267 667	1 172	Libreville
The Gambia	10 688	861	Banjul
Ghana	238 538	15 028	Accra
Guinea	245 855	5 755	Conakry
Guinea-Bissau	36 125	964	Bissau
Ivory Coast	322 463	11 997	Yamoussoukro
Kenya	582 644	24 031	Nairobi
Lesotho	30 344	1 774	Maseru
Liberia	111 370	2 575	Monrovia
Libya	1 759 530	4 545	Tripoli
Madagascar	587 042	12 004	Antananarivo
Malawi	94 100	8 754	Lilongwe
Mali	1 240 142	9 214	Bamako
Mauritania	1 030 700	2 024	Nouakchott
Mauritius	1 865	1 082	Port Louis
Morocco	459 000	25 061	Rabat
Mozambique	784 961	15 656	Maputo
Namibia	824 293	1 781	Windhoek
Niger	1 267 000	7 731	Niamey
Nigeria	923 769	108 542	Abuja
Réunion (Fr.)	2 510	598	Saint-Denis
Rwanda	26 338	7 237	Kigali
São Tomé and Principe	964	121	São Tomé
Senegal	196 722	7 327	Dakar
Seychelles	443	69	Victoria
Sierra Leone	71 740	4 151	Freetown
Somalia	637 539	7 497	Muqdisho (Mogadishu)
South Africa	1 221 038	35 282	Pretoria/Cape Town
Sudan	2 505 792	25 203	Khartoum
Swaziland	17 366	788	Mbabane
Tanzania	942 000	27 318	Dodoma
Togo	56 785	3 531	Lomé
Tunisia	164 148	8 180	Tunis
Uganda	236 036	18 794	Kampala
Western Sahara	266 000	178	-
Zaire	2 344 885	35 568	Kinshasa
Zambia	752 617	8 452	Lusaka
Zimbabwe	390 308	9 709	Harare
Oceania			
American Samoa (USA)	197	38	Fagatogo
Australia	7 682 300	17 659	Canberra
Fiji	18 272	764	Suva
French Polynesia (Fr.)	4 198	206	Papeete
Guam (USA)	549	118	Agaña
Kiribati	800	66	Tarawa
Marshall Islands	181	40	Dalap-Uliga-Darrit
Nauru	21	9	Yaren
New Caledonia (Fr.)	19 104	167	Nouméa
New Zealand	268 675	3 450	Wellington
Niue (NZ)	259	3	Alofi
Federated States of Micronesia	1 300	99	Kolonia
Papua New Guinea	461 692	3 874	Port Moresby
Solomon Islands	29 785	320	Honiara
Tonga	699	95	Nuku'alofa
Tuvalu	25	9	Funafuti
Vanuatu	14 763	158	Vila
Western Samoa	2 831	168	Apai

This page explains the main symbols, lettering style and height/depth colours used on the reference maps on pages 2 to 79. The scale of each map is indicated at the top of each page. Abbreviations used on the maps appear at the beginning of the index.

BOUNDARIES

————————	International
— — — — —	International under Dispute
··········	Cease Fire Line
————————	Autonomous or State
————————	Administrative
— — — —	Maritime (National)
— — — — —	International Date Line

COMMUNICATIONS

————————	Motorway/Express Highway
==========	Under Construction
————————	Major Highway
————————	Other Roads
— — — — —	Under Construction
— — — — —	Track
→⇒·——⇐	Road Tunnel
— — — — —	Car Ferry
————————	Main Railway
————————	Other Railway
— — — — —	Under Construction
→—·——←—	Rail Tunnel
— — — — —	Rail Ferry
┴─┴─┴─┴	Canal
⊕	International Airport
✈	Other Airport

LAKE FEATURES

	Freshwater
	Saltwater
	Seasonal
	Salt Pan

LANDSCAPE FEATURES

	Glacier, Ice Cap
	Marsh, Swamp
	Sand Desert, Dunes

OTHER FEATURES

	River
	Seasonal River
⇉	Pass, Gorge
	Dam, Barrage
	Waterfall, Rapid
→·——·	Aqueduct
	Reef
▲ 4231	Summit, Peak
. 217	Spot Height, Depth
‿	Well
Δ	Oil Field
▲	Gas Field
Gas / Oil ———	Oil/Natural Gas Pipeline
Gemsbok Nat. Pk	National Park
∴ UR	Historic Site

LETTERING STYLES

CANADA	Independent Nation
FLORIDA	State, Province or Autonomous Region
Gibraltar (U.K.)	Sovereignty of Dependent Territory
Lothian	Administrative Area
LANGUEDOC	Historic Region
Loire **Vosges**	Physical Feature or Physical Region

TOWNS AND CITIES

Square symbols denote capital cities. Each settlement is given a symbol according to its relative importance, with type size to match.

▣	◉	**New York**	Major City
■	●	**Dallas**	City
▢	○	Memphis	Small City
■	●	Oakland	Large Town
▢	○	Boise	Town
▫	∘	Durango	Small Town
▫	∘	Marshfield	Village
			Built-up-area

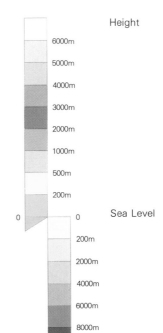

	Height
6000m	
5000m	
4000m	
3000m	
2000m	
1000m	
500m	
200m	
0 ... 0	Sea Level
200m	
2000m	
4000m	
6000m	
8000m	
	Depth

1:35M

250 500 750 1000 1250 km
250 500 750 mls

③ ② ① Ⓐ Ⓡ ①
RUS. FED. Ⓑ Ⓠ
Ⓒ Ⓟ
Ⓓ Ⓞ
Ⓔ Ⓝ
Ⓕ Ⓖ Ⓜ

Arctic Ocean

Bering Strait

ICELAND
Reykjavik

Ⓐ

Bering Sea

Aleutian Islands

A l a s k a
Yukon
Anchorage
Fairbanks

Beaufort Sea

Ellesmere I.
Thule
Queen Elizabeth Islands
Banks I.
Victoria I.
Resolute
Devon I.
Baffin Bay

G R E E N L A N D
(KALAALLIT NUNAAT)
(Denmark)

Denmark Strait

④

Alexander Arch.
Q. Charlotte Is.
Prince Rupert
Juneau

Whitehorse

Mackenzie
Great Bear L.
Yellowknife
Great Slave L.

Arctic Circle

Southampton I.

Baffin I.

Gothåb (Nuuk)

Davis Strait

⑤

Vancouver I.
Victoria
Vancouver
Seattle
Portland

Prince George

Edmonton
Calgary
Saskatoon
Regina

C A N A D A
Athabasca

Hay River
L. Winnipeg

L. Athabasca

James Bay

Churchill
Hudson Bay
Inukjuak
Moosonee

Hudson Strait

Schefferville
Churchill Falls

Newfoundland

San Francisco

Salt Lake City

Spokane
Butte

Winnipeg
Thunder Bay
Fargo
Duluth
L. Superior
Sault Ste Marie

Minneapolis St Paul
Milwaukee
Chicago
L. Michigan
Huron
Detroit
L. Erie
Cleveland
Ohio

Québec
Montréal
Ottawa
L. Ontario
Toronto
Buffalo

St Lawrence
Fredericton
Moncton
Halifax
Charlottetown

Sept-Îles
Anticosti I.
St John's

Boston

⑥

Los Angeles
San Diego

Denver
Colorado

Omaha
Kansas City
St Louis

U N I T E D   S T A T E S
O F   A M E R I C A

Indianapolis
Baltimore
Washington
Norfolk
Philadelphia
New York

A T L A N T I C
O C E A N

Bermuda (U.K)

Phoenix
Tucson
Albuquerque
El Paso

Nashville
Memphis
Birmingham
Dallas
Fort Worth

Mississippi

Atlanta
Charleston

Guadalupe (Mex.)

G. de California
Chihuahua
Rio Grande

San Antonio
Houston
New Orleans
Jacksonville

Tropic of Cancer

M E X I C O

Monterrey
Torreón

Gulf of Mexico

Tampa
Miami

Nassau
THE BAHAMAS

⑦

Is Revilla Gigedo (Mex.)

Mazatlán
Guadalajara
México
Acapulco

Tampico
Veracruz
Mérida

Habana

CUBA

Guantánamo
HAITI
Port-au-Prince
Kingston
JAMAICA

DOMINICAN REP.
Pto Rico (U.S.A)
Sto Domingo
ST KITTS-NEVIS
ANTIGUA & BARBUDA
DOMINICA
ST LUCIA
BARBADOS
ST VINCENT & THE GRENADINES
GRENADA
TRINIDAD & TOBAGO

P A C I F I C

BELIZE
Belmopan
GUATEMALA
Guatemala
S.Salvador
EL SALVADOR
HONDURAS
Tegucigalpa
NICARAGUA
Managua

CARIBBEAN SEA

Netherlands Antilles

⑧

O C E A N

Clipperton (Fr.)

I.del Coco (C.R)

Malpelo (Col.)

COSTA RICA
S.José
PANAMA
Panamá

Sta Marta
Barranquilla
Maracaibo
Caracas

VENEZUELA

Medellín
Bogotá
C O L O M B I A

Negro

B R A Z I L

Equator

Galapagos Is (Ecu.)

Quito
ECUADOR
PERU

G 110 H 100 J 90 K 80 L 70 M

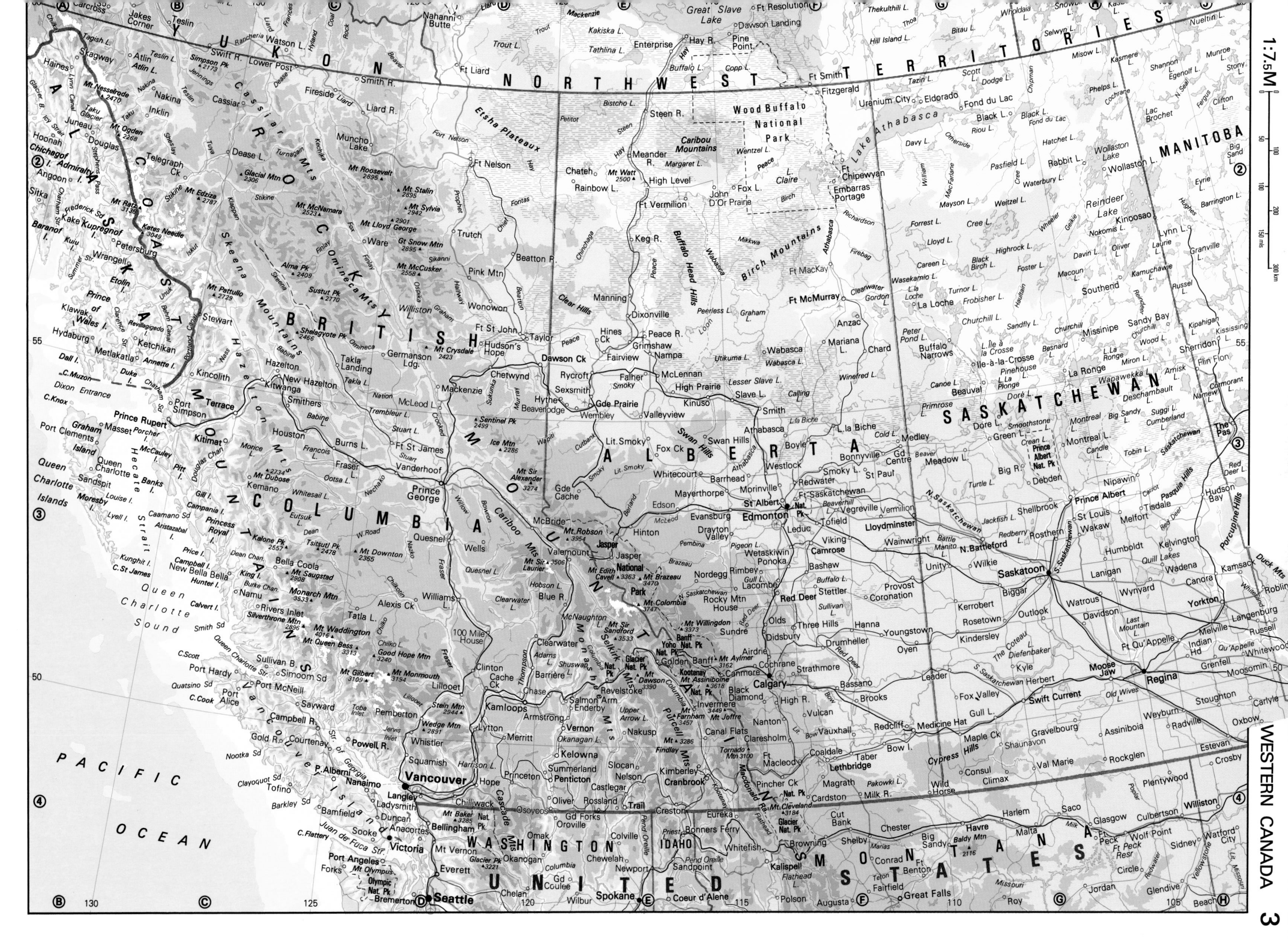

1:7.5M

100   200   300 km
50   100   150 mls

0   100   200   300 km
0   50   100   150 mls

MANITOBA

ONTARIO

Q

HUDSON

BAY

JAMES

Bay

MINNESOTA

WISCONSIN

MICHIGAN

IOWA

ILLINOIS

UNITED STATES

NEW YORK

LAKE SUPERIOR

LAKE MICHIGAN

LAKE HURON

LAKE ERIE

LAKE ONTARIO

Georgian Bay

Lake Winnipeg

Lake Winnipegosis

Lake Manitoba

Lake of the Woods

Lake Nipigon

Reindeer Lake

Cedar Lake

Belcher Islands

Sleeper Islands

King George Islands

Nastapoka Islands

Akimiski Island

Winnipeg
St. Paul
Minneapolis
Milwaukee
Chicago
Detroit
Cleveland
Buffalo
Toronto
Ottawa
Thunder Bay
Duluth
Sudbury
Madison
Grand Rapids
Rochester
Syracuse
Sault Ste. Marie

Polar Bear Provincial Park

Quetico Provincial Park

Algonquin Prov. Park

Churchill

Povungnituk
Ottawa Is.
Inukjuak
Kuujjuarapik

Ungava Bay
Akpatok I.
C. Chidley
Killinek I.
Killiniq
N. Aulatsivik I.
Torngat Mts.
Mt. Caubvick 1729
Kangirsuk
Aupalak
Kangiqsualujjuaq
Tasiujaq
Kuujjuaq
Saglek Bay
C. Uivak
Hebron
Cod I.
Nutak
C. Kiglapatt
S. Aulatsivik I.
Pyramid Hills
Nain
Kamatsuk
Tunungayualok I.
C. Harrigan
Davis Inlet
Hopedale
Makkovik
C. Harrison
Indian Harbour
Groswater Bay
Rigolet
Labrador Sea
NEWFOUNDLAND
Labrador
Smallwood Resr.
Schefferville
Attikamagen Lake
North West River
Goose Bay
Happy Valley
Mealy Mountains
Cartwright
Sandwich Bay
Domino
I. of Ponds
Stony I.
C. Bluff
George's Cove
Seal Bight
St. Lewis Sound
Battle Harbour
Port Hope Simpson
Mary's Harbour
Belle Isle
Churchill
Labrador City
Wabush
Red Bay
L'Anse au Loup
Blanc Sablon
Strait of Belle Isle
C. Bauld
St. Anthony
Hare Bay
Grandois
Grey Islands
Roddickton
Englee
Harbour Deep
Fleur-de-Lys
C. St. John
Baie Verte
Notre Dame Bay
Fogo
Fogo I.
C. Freels
Wesleyville
Twillingate
Sop's Arm
Springdale
Lewisporte
Gander
Bonavista Bay
C. Bonavista
Bonavista
Gros Morne Nat. Park
Long Range Mountains
White Bay
Trout River
Bay of Islands
Deer Lake
Grand Lake
Windsor
Buchans
Grand Falls
Gambo
Corner Brook
Newfoundland
Trans Canada Highway
Clarenville
Trinity Bay
Grates Pt.
Carbonear
Harbour Grace
St. John's
Port au Port
Stephenville
St. George's Bay
St. Fintan's
Blue Hills of Couteau
St. Albans
Terrenceville
Argentia
Placentia
Avalon Pen.
Trepassey
C. Race
C. Pine
Rose Blanche
Burgeo
Belloram
Fortune Bay
Marystown
Burin Pen.
Placentia Bay
St. Mary's B.
C. St. Mary's
Grand Bank
Saint Pierre & Miquelon (Fr.)
C. Ray
Channel Port-aux-Basques
Cabot Strait
Q U E B E C
Résr. Caniapiscau
La Grande Résr. 4
Nitchequon
Monts Otish 1128
Gagnon
Résr. Manicouagan
Mistassini Provincial Park
L. Mistassini
Chibougamau
Sept Îles
Havre St. Pierre
Mingan
Sheldrake
Natashquan
Aguanish
Mutton Bay
C. Mécatina
Harrington Harbour
St. Augustin-Saguenay
Shekalika Bay
Détroit de Jacques Cartier
Port Menier
Î. d'Anticosti
Anticosti Prov. Park
Pointe de l'Est
Port Cartier
Rivière Pentecôte
Pointe aux Anglais
Détroit d'Honguedo
Baie Comeau
Hauterive
Godbout
Mont Louis
Grande Vallée
Mt. Jacques Cartier 1268
Gaspésie Prov. Park
Gaspé
C. de Gaspé
Monts Notre Dame
Péninsule de Gaspé
Matane
Mont Joli
Rimouski
Amqui
Chandler
Grande Cascapédia
Paspébiac
Grande Rivière
Miscou I.
B. des Chaleurs
Gulf of St. Lawrence
Îles de la Madeleine (Québec)
St. Lawrence
Chicoutimi
Jonquière
Alma
Dolbeau
Roberval
Tadoussac
Trois Pistoles
Rivière-du-Loup
Laurentides Provincial Park
La Tuque
Québec
Lévis
Charlesbourg
Trois-Rivières
Shawinigan
Drummondville
Sherbrooke
Granby
Montréal
Laval
Valleyfield
Dalhousie
Campbellton
Bathurst
Shippegan
Tracadie
Miramichi Bay
Big Bald Mtn. 672
Newcastle
Chatham
Richibucto
NEW BRUNSWICK
Edmundston
Madawaska
Grand Falls
Fredericton
Moncton
Saint John
St. Stephen
Bay of Fundy
PRINCE EDWARD I.
Tignish
Alberton
Summerside
Charlottetown
Georgetown
Montague
Souris
Northumberland Strait
C. North
Chéticamp
C. Breton Highlands
New Waterford
Glace Bay
Sydney
C. Breton Island
Port Hawkesbury
Canso
NOVA SCOTIA
Amherst
New Glasgow
Truro
Shubenacadie
Windsor
Kentville
Middleton
Bridgetown
Digby
Dartmouth
Halifax
Mahone B.
Bridgewater
Liverpool
Shelburne
Lockeport
Yarmouth
Wedgeport
Port Maitland
C. Sable
Sable I. (Nova Scotia)
Sheet Harbour
Minas Basin
Minas Ch.
Chignecto B.
Grand Manan I.
MAINE
Presque Isle
Caribou
Houlton
Millinocket
Bangor
Old Town
Machias
Waterville
Augusta
Rockland
Lewiston
Auburn
Portland
Biddeford
Bingham
Rumford
Belfast
VERMONT
NEW HAMPSHIRE
Burlington
Lake Champlain
Montpelier
St. Johnsbury
Concord
Manchester
Nashua
Portsmouth
Dover
MASSACHUSETTS
Boston
Cambridge
Lowell
Lawrence
Worcester
Springfield
Pittsfield
Brockton
Fall River
Providence
Hartford
C. Cod
Cape Cod Bay
Albany
Troy
Schenectady
Amsterdam
Saratoga Springs
Glens Falls
Rutland
ATLANTIC OCEAN

1:15M

200   400   600 km
100   200   300 mls

ARCTIC OCEAN

BEAUFORT SEA

BERING SEA

Gulf of Alaska

PACIFIC OCEAN

ALASKA U.S.A.

Brooks Range

Alaska Range

Aleutian Ra.

Kodiak Island

YUKON TERRITORY

NORTHWEST TERRITORIES

Mackenzie Mountains

Selwyn Mountains

Great Bear Lake

Great Slave Lake

Lake Athabasca

BRITISH COLUMBIA

ALBERTA

SASKATCHEWAN

MANITOBA

COAST MOUNTAINS

Queen Charlotte Islands

Vancouver Island

Vancouver
Victoria
Seattle
Tacoma
Olympia
Portland
Salem
Eugene

WASHINGTON
OREGON
IDAHO
MONTANA
WYOMING
NORTH DAKOTA
SOUTH DAKOTA

U.S.

Edmonton
Calgary
Red Deer
Lethbridge
Medicine Hat
Saskatoon
Regina
Moose Jaw
Prince Albert
Winnipeg
Brandon

Whitehorse
Dawson
Yellowknife
Fort Smith
Uranium City
Fort McMurray

Rocky Mountains

Caribou Mountains

Wood Buffalo Nat. Pk.

Reindeer Lake

Cambridge Bay

Banks Island

Victoria Island

Prince of Wales Island

Melville Island

Parry Islands

Spokane
Missoula
Helena
Butte
Boise
Idaho Falls
Pocatello
Billings
Bismarck
Fargo
Pierre
Rapid City
Sioux Falls

Nome
Fairbanks
Anchorage
Juneau
Sitka
Ketchikan
Prince Rupert
Kitimat
Prince George
Kamloops
Kelowna

Names underlined indicate Province/State capitals

GREENLAND
(KALAALLIT NUNAAT)
(Denmark)
ICELAND
Reykjavík
Akureyri
DENMARK STRAIT
BAFFIN BAY
Baffin Island
DAVIS STRAIT
Labrador Sea
HUDSON STRAIT
HUDSON BAY
James Bay
Ungava Bay
Foxe Basin
Foxe Channel
Lancaster Sound
Devon Island
Ellesmere Island
Melville Peninsula
Southampton Island
Cumberland Sound
Frobisher Bay
NEWFOUNDLAND
Labrador
QUEBEC
ONTARIO
Gulf of Saint Lawrence
ATLANTIC OCEAN
LAKE SUPERIOR
L. HURON
L. MICHIGAN
L. Ontario
L. Erie
NOVA SCOTIA
NEW BRUNSWICK
PRINCE EDWARD I.
MAINE
VERMONT
NEW HAMPSHIRE
MASS.
CONN.
NEW YORK
MICHIGAN
WISCONSIN
MINNESOTA
Thule
Upernavik
Godthåb
Angmagssalik
Scoresby Sd
Kap Farvel (C. Farewell)
Arctic Circle
Iqaluit
Pangnirtung
Cape Dorset
Igloolik
Repulse Bay
Chesterfield Inlet
Rankin Inlet
Churchill
York Factory
Fort Severn
Inukjuak
Kuujjuaq
Kuujjuarapik
Chisasibi
Nain
Hebron
Hopedale
Goose Bay
Schefferville
Labrador City
Churchill Falls
Sept-Iles
Gaspé
St John's
Gander
Corner Brook
Halifax
Sydney
Charlottetown
Fredericton
Saint John
Moncton
Québec
Montréal
Ottawa
Toronto
Hamilton
Buffalo
Detroit
Boston
Providence
Hartford
Portland
Thunder Bay
Sault Ste Marie
Sudbury
Timmins
Duluth
St Paul
Milwaukee
Madison

1:12.5M

0 100 200 300 400 500 km
0 100 200 300 mls
BRITISH COLUMBIA
ALBERTA
SASKATCHEWAN
MANITOBA
WASHINGTON
OREGON
IDAHO
MONTANA
WYOMING
NEVADA
UTAH
COLORADO
ARIZONA
NEW MEXICO
NORTH DAKOTA
SOUTH DAKOTA
NEBRASKA
KANSAS
OKLAHOMA
TEXAS
CALIFORNIA
UNITED STATES
MEXICO
BAJA CALIFORNIA
PACIFIC OCEAN
Golfo de California
ROCKY MOUNTAINS
SIERRA NEVADA
CASCADE RANGE
SIERRA MADRE OCCIDENTAL
Sierra Madre Oriental
Great Basin
Colorado Plateau
Sonoran Desert
Llano Estacado
Edwards Plateau
Vancouver Island
Tropic of Cancer
Vancouver
Seattle
Portland
Spokane
Boise
Salt Lake City
Reno
Sacramento
San Francisco
San Jose
Fresno
Los Angeles
San Diego
Las Vegas
Phoenix
Tucson
Albuquerque
Denver
Cheyenne
Helena
Billings
Calgary
Edmonton
Regina
Saskatoon
El Paso
Cd Juárez
Chihuahua
Hermosillo
Monterrey
Durango
Mazatlán
San Antonio
Corpus Christi
Laredo
Lubbock
Amarillo
Oklahoma City
Wichita
Lincoln
Omaha
Bismarck
Pierre
Names underlined indicate Province/State capitals

James Bay
Q U E B E C
O N T A R I O
LAKE SUPERIOR
L. MICHIGAN
LAKE HURON
L. ONTARIO
LAKE ERIE
Gulf of Saint Lawrence
NEW BRUNSWICK
NOVA SCOTIA
PRINCE EDWARD I.
MAINE
VERMONT
NEW HAMPSHIRE
MASS.
CONN.
R.I.
NEW YORK
N.J.
PENNSYLVANIA
MD
DEL.
OHIO
INDIANA
ILLINOIS
WISCONSIN
MICHIGAN
MINNESOTA
IOWA
MISSOURI
KENTUCKY
WEST VIRGINIA
VIRGINIA
NORTH CAROLINA
SOUTH CAROLINA
TENNESSEE
GEORGIA
ALABAMA
MISSISSIPPI
ARKANSAS
LOUISIANA
FLORIDA
APPALACHIAN MOUNTAINS
Ozark Plateau
ATLANTIC OCEAN
GULF OF MEXICO
THE BAHAMAS
CUBA
Straits of Florida
Montréal
Québec
Ottawa
Toronto
Halifax
Thunder Bay
Sault Ste Marie
Sudbury
Hamilton
Buffalo
Boston
Providence
Hartford
New York
Newark
Philadelphia
Baltimore
Washington D.C.
Richmond
Norfolk
Pittsburgh
Cleveland
Detroit
Chicago
Milwaukee
Minneapolis
St Paul
Duluth
Indianapolis
Cincinnati
Columbus
Louisville
St Louis
Kansas City
Nashville
Memphis
Knoxville
Charlotte
Raleigh
Atlanta
Birmingham
Montgomery
Jackson
Savannah
Charleston
Jacksonville
Tallahassee
Pensacola
Mobile
New Orleans
Baton Rouge
Shreveport
Houston
Galveston
Orlando
Tampa
St Petersburg
Miami
Miami Beach
West Palm Beach
Ft Lauderdale
Key West
Nassau
Habana (Havana)
Camagüey
Holguín
Sta Clara
Cienfuegos
Mt Mitchell 2037
Mt Washington 1916

1:10M

0 100 200 300 400 km

0 100 200 mls

Beaufort Sea

Arctic Ocean

Chukchi Sea

Bering Sea

Gulf of Alaska

Bristol Bay

Norton Sound

Kotzebue Sd

Bering Strait

Anadyrskiy Zaliv

INTERNATIONAL DATE LINE

RUSSIAN FEDERATION

Chukotskiy Poluostrov

NORTHWEST TERRITORIES

YUKON TERRITORY

BRITISH COLUMBIA

Alexander Archipelago

Aleutian Islands

Fox Islands

Rat Islands

Near Islands

Shumagin Islands

Pribilof Is

St Lawrence I.

Nunivak I.

Kodiak I.

Unimak I.

Brooks Range

Alaska Range

Mackenzie Mountains

British Mountains

Richardson Mts

Ogilvie Mountains

Wrangell Mts

Chugach Mountains

St Elias Mountains

Kuskokwim Mts

Kilbuck Mts

Seward Peninsula

Kenai Peninsula

Alaska Peninsula

North Slope

Fairbanks

Anchorage

Juneau

Nome

Barrow

Prudhoe Bay

Kotzebue

Bethel

Dillingham

Valdez

Seward

Kodiak

Sitka

Ketchikan

Whitehorse

Dawson

Inuvik

Tuktoyaktuk

Aklavik

Prince Rupert

Mt McKinley 6194

Mt Logan 6050

Mt St Elias 5489

Mt Blackburn 5036

Mt Sanford 4940

1:5M

50   100   150   200 km
50   100 mls

States/Provinces: ONTARIO, MANITOBA, SASKATCHEWAN, MINNESOTA, WISCONSIN, IOWA, NORTH DAKOTA, SOUTH DAKOTA, NEBRASKA, MONTANA, WYOMING

Water bodies: L. SUPERIOR, Lake of the Woods, Lake Manitoba, Lake Winnipeg, Lac Seul, Lake Sakakawea, Lake Oahe, Fort Peck Reservoir, Apostle Is., Upper Red L., Lower Red L., Leech L., Cass L., Mille Lacs, Devils L.

Rivers: Missouri, Mississippi, Minnesota, Yellowstone, Little Missouri, Big Sioux, James, Red, Souris, Cheyenne, Moreau, Cannonball, Heart, Milk, Assiniboine, N. Loup, Niobrara, Belle Fourche, White, Bighorn, Powder, Tongue, N. Platte, Sweetwater, Medicine Bow, Frenchman, Qu'Appelle

Selected cities and towns:

Thunder Bay, Kakabeka Falls, Grand Marais, Silver Bay, Two Harbors, Duluth, Superior, Proctor, Cloquet, Ashland, Bayfield, Washburn, Hurley, Glidden, Prentice, Ladysmith, Chippewa Falls, Eau Claire, Menomonie, Durand, La Crosse, Onalaska, Winona, Sparta, Tomah, Westby, Viroqua, Prairie du Chien, Platteville, Dubuque, Bettendorf, Davenport, Rock Island, Muscatine, Cedar Rapids

Kenora, Fort Frances, International Falls, Baudette, Warroad, Bemidji, Grand Rapids, Hibbing, Virginia, Chisholm, Keewatin, Babbitt, Ely, Cook, Floodwood, Moose Lake, Sandstone, Hinckley, Mora, Cambridge, Pine City, Cumberland, Spooner, Rice Lake, Barron, Hayward

Winnipeg, St Boniface, Steinbach, Emerson, Pembina, St Vincent, Hallock, Karlstad, Warren, Thief River Falls, Crookston, East Grand Forks, Grand Forks, Bagley, Mahnomen, Fosston, Erskine, Ada, Detroit Lakes, Moorhead, Fargo, Fergus Falls, Alexandria, Glenwood, Morris, Wheaton, Breckenridge, Wahpeton, Elbow Lake, Browerville, Wadena, Park Rapids, Walker, Long Prairie, Sauk Centre, Melrose, Paynesville, Willmar, Litchfield, St Cloud, Monticello, Elk River, Anoka, Minneapolis-St Paul, Bloomington, Hastings, Red Wing, Stillwater, Northfield, Faribault, Owatonna, Rochester, Austin, Albert Lea, Mason City, Waterloo, Cedar Falls, Marshalltown, Ames, Des Moines, Boone, Fort Dodge, Webster City, Iowa Falls, Newton, Grinnell, Iowa City, Washington

Portage la Prairie, Brandon, Neepawa, Minnedosa, Souris, Boissevain, Deloraine, Melita, Virden, Oxbow, Estevan, Weyburn, Regina, Moose Jaw, Swift Current, Assiniboia, Willow Bunch, Radville, Carlyle, Broadview

Devils Lake, Rugby, Cando, Langdon, Cavalier, Grafton, Mayville, Northwood, Cooperstown, Valley City, Jamestown, Carrington, Harvey, Minot, Velva, Drake, Garrison, New Town, Williston, Watford City, Dickinson, Belfield, Beach, Bowman, Hettinger, Lemmon, Mott, Elgin, Mandan, Bismarck, Hebron, Hallidayo, Marmarth, Ekalaka, Baker, Glendive, Sidney, Culbertson, Plentywood, Scobey, Wolf Point, Glasgow, Malta, Harlem, Fort Peck, Circle, Terry, Miles City, Forsyth, Rosebud, Ashland, Broadus, Hardin, Lodge Grass, Sheridan, Buffalo, Story, Clearmont, Gillette, Newcastle, Sundance, Moorcroft, Upton, Osage, Spearfish, Lead, Deadwood, Sturgis, Rapid City, Custer, Hot Springs, Edgemont

Sioux Falls, Sioux City, Brookings, Watertown, Aberdeen, Huron, Mitchell, Yankton, Pierre, Fort Pierre, Chamberlain, Winner, Mission, Valentine, Wall, Wounded Knee, Pine Ridge, Martin, Kadoka, Murdo, Presho, Gettysburg, Mobridge, McLaughlin, Eagle Butte, Faith, Dupree, Selby, Redfield, Miller, Blunt, Highmore, Wessington Springs, Plankinton, Parkston, Freeman, Platte, Gregory, Bonesteel, Norfolk, Neligh, O'Neill, Ainsworth, Burwell, Ord, Alliance, Chadron, Crawford, Rushville, Merriman, Thedford, Hyannis, Scottsbluff, Gering, Bayard, Bridgeport, Broadwater, Casper, Douglas, Glenrock, Wheatland, Torrington, Chugwater, Rawlins, Saratoga, Lamont, Medicine Bow, Rock River

Physical features: Black Hills, Bighorn Mts, Laramie Mts, Riding Mountain Nat. Park, Voyageurs Nat. Park, White Butte 1076, Cloud Peak 4016, Medicine Bow Peak 3661, Elk Mtn 3400

1:5M

0 50 100 150 200 km
0 50 100 mls

Ⓐ Ⓑ Ⓒ ① ② ③ 90 85 45 40

Nipigon
Long L.
Dog L.
Nipigon B.
Schreiber
Terrace Bay
Marathon
Black B.
St Ignace I.
Kabinakagami L.
Iroquois Falls
Littlefork
Kakabeka Falls
Thunder Bay
Pie I.
Northern Light L.
White River
Wabatongushi L.
Missinaibi L.
Ansonville
Timmins
S.Porcupine
Mathes
Nighthawk L.
Pelican L.
Little Fork
Vermilion L.
Ely
Birch L.
Chisholm
Buhl
Babbitt
Virginia
Keewatin
Hibbing
Hoyt L.
Grand Rapids
Isle Royale Nat. Pk
Grand Marais
Michipicoten
Wawa
Dog L.
Manitowik L.
Foleyet
Kirkland Lake
Matachewan
Chapleau
Gogama
Michipicoten I.
MINNESOTA
LAKE SUPERIOR
ONTARIO
CA
Silver Bay
Copper Harbor
Floodwood
Two Harbors
Apostle Is.
Keweenaw Pen.
Keweenaw Bay
Proctor
Duluth
Superior
Cloquet
Houghton
Hancock
Bayfield
Chequamegon Bay
Washburn
Ashland
Coppermine Pt
653 Bathawana Mtn
Biscotasi L.
Moose Lake
Mille Lacs L.
Bessemer
Rockland
Whitefish Pt
Rocky I. L.
Onaping L.
L. Temagami
Spanish
Sandstone
Solon Springs
Hurley
Wakefield
Ironwood
Ishpeming
Marquette
Hinckley
Mora
St Croix
Watersmeet
Munising
Sault Ste Marie
Sault Ste Marie
Echo Bay
Elliot Lake
Webbwood
Sudbury
Coniston
Wanapitei L.
Pine City
Spooner
Chippewa L.
Glidden
Hayward
Iron River
Thessalon
Blind River
Copper Cliff
Cumberland
Park Falls
Crystal Falls
Rapid River
Rudyard
St Joseph
North Channel
Drummond I.
Massey
Espanola
L. Nipissing
Cambridge
Rice Lake
Chippewa
Three Lakes
Iron Mtn
Kingsford
Niagara
Gladstone
Manistique
Straits of Mackinac
Mackinaw City
St Ignace
Bois Blanc I.
Cheboygan
Manitoulin I.
Ladysmith
St Croix Falls
Barron
Prentice
Tomahawk
Rhinelander
Escanaba
Garden Pen.
Beaver I.
Key Harbour
Georgian Bay
Stillwater
Stephenson
Green Bay
Gills Rock
Petoskey
Rogers City
South Baymouth
Fitzwilliam I.
Main Chan.
Tobermory
C. Hurd
Parry Sound
St Paul
Menomonie
Chippewa Falls
Merrill
Antigo
Wolf
Menominee
Peshtigo
Charlevoix
Manitou Is.
Hastings
Durand
Eau Claire
Abbotsford
Wausau
Mosinee
Marinette
Oconto
Gaylord
Alpena
North Pt
Bruce Pen.
Red Wing
Osseo
Augusta
Marshfield
Shawano
Mancelona
Lake City
Whitehall
Neillsville
WISCONSIN
Sturgeon Bay
Atlanta
Zumbrota
Black River Falls
Wisconsin Rapids
Stevens Point
Waupaca
Green Bay
Elberta
Traverse City
Harrisville
Wiarton
Owen Sound
Rochester
Winona
Appleton
Kewaunee
Manistee
Stewartville
Chatfield
Onalaska
Tomah
Petenwell
Neenah
Menasha
Two Rivers
Manistee
East Lake
Au Sable
Southampton
Port Elgin
Collingwood
Root
La Crosse
Sparta
Oshkosh
L. Chilton
Winnebago
Cadillac
Tawas City
Austin
Preston
Caledonia
Mauston
Fond du Lac
Manitowoc
Ludington
Reed City
Standish
Saginaw Bay
Port Austin
Pt Clark
Kincardine
Westby
Viroqua
Wisconsin Dells
Fox
Sheboygan
Clare
Coleman
Walkerton
Orangeville
Osage
Cresco
Decorah
Portage
Waupun
Big Rapids
Harbor Beach
Goderich
Sauk City
Columbus
Sun Prairie
Beaver Dam
Mt Pleasant
Midland
Essexville
New Hampton
Shelby
Wapsipinicon
Wisconsin
Port Washington
Watertown
Menomonee Falls
Muskegon
Bay City
Guelph
Kitchener
Cedar
Elkader
Prairie du Chien
Madison
Brookfield
Wauwatosa
Alma
Saginaw
Vassar
Carsonville
Stratford
Guttenberg
Oelwein
Dodgeville
Waukesha
Milwaukee
Muskegon
Grand Haven
Howard City
Woodstock
Cambridge
Cedar Falls
Whitewater
W. Allis
Greenfield
Grand Rapids
St Johns
Flint
Forest
London
Brantford
Waterloo
Independence
Platteville
Monroe
Janesville
Holland
Kentwood
Wyoming
Grand
Owosso
Burton
Port Huron
Sarnia
Dubuque
Galena
Beloit
Lake Geneva
Racine
Saugatuck
Lansing
St Clair
Sterling Heights
Ingersoll
IOWA
Monticello
Bellevue
Freeport
Woodstock
Kenosha
Otsego
Charlotte
Holt
Pontiac
St Thomas
Vinton
Tama
Anamosa
Rockford
Belvidere
Waukegan
Arlington Heights
Des Plaines
Skokie
Kalamazoo
Battle Creek
Royal Oak
Warren
L. St Clair
St Clair Shores
West Lorne
Iowa
Cedar Rapids
Clinton
Fulton
Rochelle
De Kalb
Elgin
Evanston
S.Haven
Benton Harbor
St Joseph
Hartford
Marshall
Albion
Jackson
Ann Arbor
Livonia
Dearborn
Detroit
Windsor
Chatham
Brooklyn
Bettendorf
Dixon
Chicago
Iowa City
Kalona
Muscatine
Davenport
Rock
Sterling
Aurora
Three Rivers
Coldwater
Adrian
Taylor
Lincoln Park
Wyandotte
Conneaut
Ashtabula
Girard
Washington
Rock Island
Moline
East Moline
Princeton
Mendota
Oak Lawn
East Chicago
Michigan City
Niles
Elkhart
Angola
Sturgis
Hudson
Monroe
Pelee I.
LAKE ERIE
Painesville
Ottumwa
Peru
Ottawa
Joliet
Gary
Hammond
La Porte
Mishawaka
South Bend
Montpelier
Sylvania
Toledo
Oregon
Port Clinton
Mentor
Meadville
Mt Pleasant
Keewanee
La Salle
Park Forest
Chicago Heights
Merrillville
Plymouth
Auburn
St Joseph
Maumee
Perrysburg
Bowling Green
Fremont
Lorain
Lakewood
Euclid
Cleveland
Burlington
Monmouth
Galesburg
Streator
Kankakee
Winamac
Maumee
Sandusky
Elyria
Parma
Fort Madison
Illinois
Kankakee
Fort Wayne
Findlay
Norwalk
Cuyahoga Falls
Warren
Farrell
Kahoka
Macomb
Peoria
El Paso
Pontiac
Gilman
Kentland
Huntington
Van Wert
Tiffin
Barberton
Youngstown
Akron
Boardman
New Castle
Keokuk
Canton
Pekin
Normal
Logansport
Wabash
Decatur
Lima
Carey
Ashland
Massillon
Canton
Canton
Bloomington
ILLINOIS
Havana
Rantoul
Lafayette
Kokomo
Marion
Celina
Kenton
Mansfield
Marion
Wooster
East Liverpool
Rushville
Lincoln
Champaign
Urbana
Attica
Frankfort
Elwood
Portland
Sidney
Delaware
Mt Vernon
Dover
New Philadelphia
Weirton
Aliquippa
Palmyra
Quincy
Hannibal
Beardstown
Springfield
Danville
Crawfordsville
Anderson
Muncie
Piqua
Urbana
Troy
OHIO
Steubenville
Beaver
Washington
Monroe City
Jacksonville
Pittsfield
Sangamon
Decatur
Tuscola
INDIANA
Indianapolis
Rockville
New Castle
Greenville
Richmond
Vandalia
Worthington
Cambridge
Newark
Martins Ferry
Wheeling
Moundsville
Bowling Green
Taylorville
Mattoon
Charleston
Dayton
Springfield
Fairborn
Xenia
Columbus
Zanesville
Barnesville
MISSOURI
Mexico
Carlinville
Marshall
Greencastle
Connersville
Kettering
Scioto
Lancaster
Illinois
Jerseyville
Litchfield
Pana
Effingham
Greenup
Terre Haute
Franklin
Shelbyville
Middletown
Washington C.H.
Circleville
Fairmont
Missouri
St Charles
Alton
Edwardsville
Vandalia
Spencer
Bloomington
Columbus
Fairfield
Hamilton
Norwood
Cincinnati
Hillsboro
Chillicothe
Athens
Marietta
Vienna
Belpre
Williamstown
Clarksburg
Grafton
St Louis
Collinsville
East St Louis
Belleville
Lawrenceville
Olney
Bloomfield
Bedford
Seymour
Aurora
Covington
Newport
Waverly
Jackson
Parkersburg
Washington
Kirkwood
Webster Groves
Kaskaskia
Salem
Centralia
Mt Vernon
White
Vincennes
Washington
Madison
Paoli
Ripley
Ripley
Portsmouth
Point Pleasant
New Boston
Ironton
Weston
WEST VIRGINIA
St James
Sullivan
Meramec
Festus
Crystal City
Rend L.
Wabash
Grayville
Carmi
Oakland City
Jasper
New Albany
Ohio
Carrollton
Maysville
Huntington
Sutton
Rolla
Desloge
Du Quoin
Chester
Huntingburg
Jeffersonville
La Grange
Georgetown
Licking
Grayson
Ashland
Nitro
St Albans
Charleston
Elk
Flat River
Ozark
Plateau
West Frankfort
Evansville
Shively
Louisville
Frankfort
Paris
Morehead
Louisa
Marmet
Ansted
Bunker
Fredericktown
Carbondale
Marion
Harrisburg
Henderson
Owensboro
Pleasure Ridge Park
Radcliff
Lexington
Winchester
W. Liberty
Paintsville
St Francis
Jackson
Cape Girardeau
Anna
Vienna
Mound City
Sturgis
Bardstown
Elizabethtown
Danville
Richmond
Salyersville
Williamson
Beckley
Chaffee
L. Wappapello
Charleston
Metropolis
Paducah
Benton
Madisonville
Beaver Dam
Green
Mammoth Cave Nat. Pk
KENTUCKY
Campbellsville
Greensburg
Berea
Mount Vernon
Pikeville
Welch
Bluefield
Princeton
Narrows
Salem
Poplar Bluff
Sikeston
Mayfield
Princeton
Hopkinsville
Glasgow
Somerset
Hazard
Manchester
Richlands
Blacksburg
Doniphan
Malden
Bowling Green
Russellville
Cumberland
London
Corbin
CUMBERLAND PLATEAU
ALLEGHENY
Wytheville
Radford
Pulaski
Hardy
Piggott
Current
Fulton
Murray
L. Barkley
Guthrie
Clarksville
Albany
Harlan
Big Stone Gap
Mountains
Galax
Hillsville
Walnut Ridge
Kennett
Union City
Martin
Paris
TENNESSEE
Middlesboro
Abingdon
Mt Rogers 1743
ARKANSAS
Paragould
Caruthersville
Kentucky Lake
Gallatin
Hendersonville
Norris L.
Clinch
Clinch
Holston
Kingsport
Bristol
Elizabethton
Jonesboro
Blytheville
Dyersburg
Milan
Nashville
Dickson
Lebanon
Cookeville
Livingston
Johnson City
NORTH

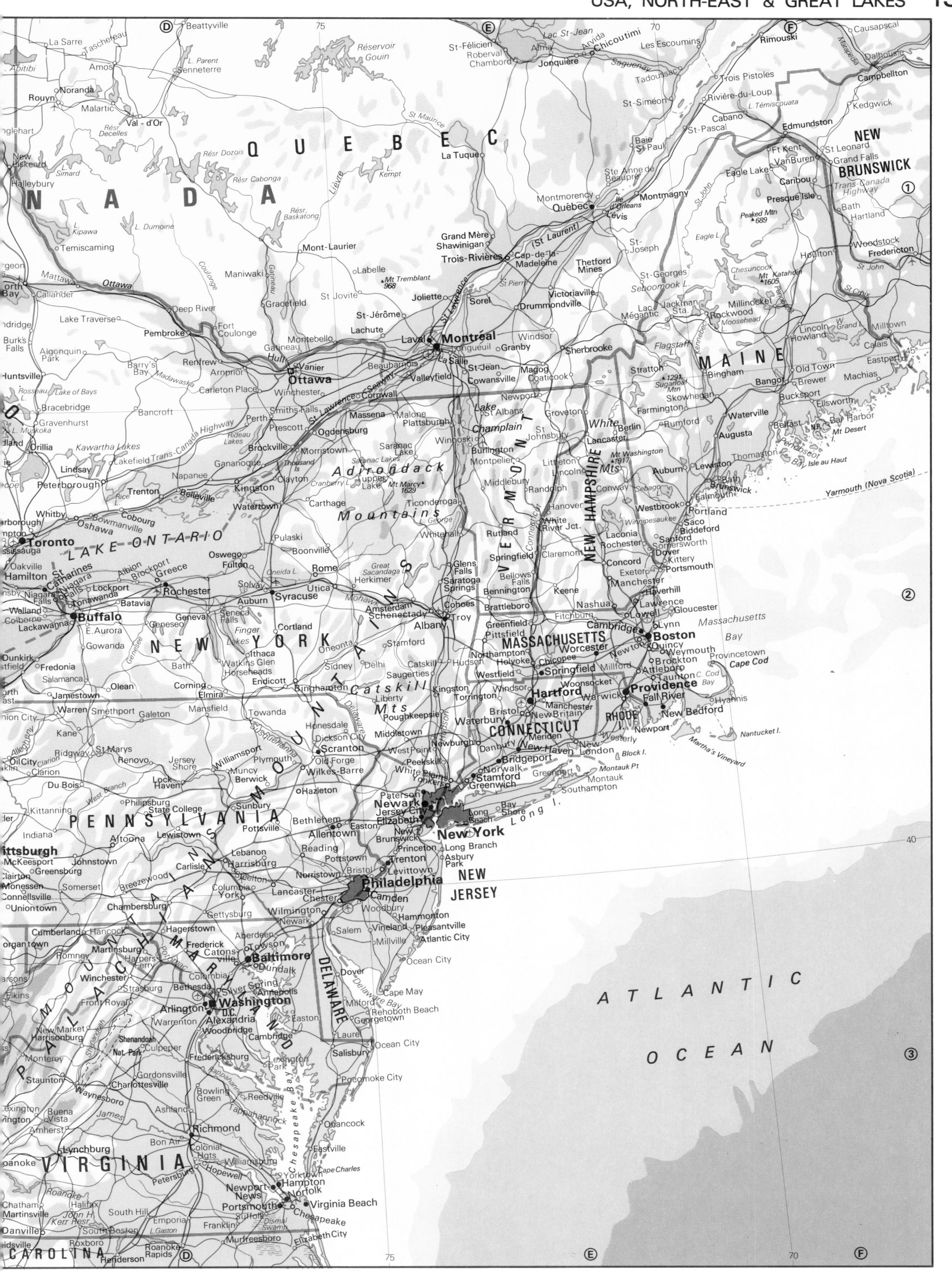
QUEBEC
CANADA
NEW BRUNSWICK
MAINE
VERMONT
NEW HAMPSHIRE
MASSACHUSETTS
RHODE I.
CONNECTICUT
NEW YORK
NEW JERSEY
PENNSYLVANIA
DELAWARE
MARYLAND
VIRGINIA
CAROLINA
LAKE ONTARIO
Adirondack Mountains
Catskill Mts
APPALACHIAN MOUNTAINS
ATLANTIC OCEAN
Montréal
Ottawa
Québec
Toronto
Buffalo
Boston
Providence
Hartford
New York
Philadelphia
Baltimore
Washington D.C.
Richmond
Norfolk
Virginia Beach
Cape Cod
Long I.
Chesapeake Bay
Delaware Bay
Trans-Canada Highway
St Lawrence Seaway

1:2.5M

50 100 150 200 km
50 100 mls

ATLANTIC OCEAN

GULF OF MEXICO

Straits of Florida

KENTUCKY

TENNESSEE

NORTH CAROLINA

SOUTH CAROLINA

GEORGIA

ALABAMA

MISSISSIPPI

FLORIDA

Memphis · Nashville · Knoxville · Chattanooga · Atlanta · Birmingham · Montgomery · Mobile · New Orleans · Jackson · Charlotte · Raleigh · Columbia · Charleston · Savannah · Jacksonville · Orlando · Tampa · Miami · Key West

at the same scale

50 100 150 200 km
50 100 mls

COLORADO
NEW MEXICO
KANSAS
TEXAS
NEBRASKA
OKLAHOMA
MEXICO
CHIHUAHUA
COAHUILA

Uinta Mts, Kings Peak 4114, Manila, Vernal, Roosevelt, Dinosaur, Rangely, Meeker, Craig, Hayden, Steamboat Springs, Yampa, Baggs, Flaming Gorge Resr, Medicine Bow Pk 3661, Bridger Peak 3662, Medicine Bow Mts, Laramie, Foxpark, Pine Bluffs, Cheyenne, Wellington, Fort Collins, Loveland, Greeley, Broadwater, Oshkosh, Kimball, Sidney, Potter, Chappell, Ovid, Julesburg, L. McConaughy, Ogallala, Big Springs, Paxton, Sutherland, North Platte, Stapleton, Ansley, Broken Bow, St Paul, Gothenburg, Cozad, Lexington, Maywood, Imperial, Arapahoe, Holdrege, Kearney, Gibbon, Grand Island, Hastings

Roan Plateau, Grand Valley, Rifle, Eagle, Minturn, Glenwood Springs, Kremmling, Granby, Rocky Mtn. Nat. Park, Fall River Pass, Estes Park, Longs Peak 4345, Longmont, Lafayette, Boulder, Idaho Springs, Loveland Pass, Berthoud Pass, Denver, Lakewood, Aurora, Englewood, Littleton, Byers, Brush, Fort Morgan, Otis, Sterling, Holyoke, Wray, Cope, Benkelman, McCook, Culbertson, Norton, Oberlin, Phillipsburg, Alma, Red Cloud, Lebanon, Stockton, Republican

Green River, Brendel, Mack, Fruita, Palisade, Grand Junction, Colorado, Delta, Montrose, Uncompahgre Plateau, Moab, Mt Peale 3857, Monticello, Abajo Mts, Blanding, Bluff, Mexican Hat, Dove Creek, Cortez, Mesa Verde N.P., Durango, Shiprock, Aztec, Bloomfield, Farmington, Tohatchi, Ganado

Leadville, Mt Elbert 4399, Mt Harvard 4378, Sawatch Mts, Buena Vista, Monarch Pass, Gunnison, Saguache, Ouray, Silverton, Mt Wilson 4342, San Juan Mts, Wolf Creek Pass, South Fork, Monte Vista, Blanca Peak 4364, Alamosa, Antonito, Chama, Pagosa Springs, Tierra Amarilla, Canjilon, Caliente, Taos, Wheeler Peak 4011

Salida, Canon City, Florence, Pueblo, Boone, Ordway, Rocky Ford, Fowler, La Junta, Walsenburg, Delhi, Trinidad, Raton, Des Moines, Cimarron, Springer, Clayton, Manitou Springs, Pikes Peak 4301, Colorado Springs, Castle Rock, Simla, Limon, Burlington, Kanorado, Goodland, Oakley, Cheyenne Wells, Kit Carson, St Francis, Colby, Hill City, Wa Keeney, Russell, Wilson, Hays, Smoky Hills, Ness City, Great Bend, Hosington, Tribune, Scott City, Jetmore, Larned, Sterling, Garden City, Lakin, Syracuse, Montezuma, Dodge City, Kinsley, Lewis, Pratt, Greensburg, Ulysses, Hugoton, Plains, Meade, Ashland, Red Hills, Medicine Lodge, Liberal, Hooker, Forgan, N. Canadian, Boise City, Guymon, Texhoma, Morgan, Alva, Cherokee, Fort Supply, Woodward, Fairview, Seiling

Gallup, Mentmore, Ft Wingate, Thoreau, Zuni Mts, Zuni, Grants, Mt Taylor 3444, St Johns, Springerville, Alpine, Glenwood, Quemado, Laguna, Albuquerque, Bernalillo, Los Lunas, Belen, Moriarty, Los Alamos, Espanola, Jemez Pueblo, Santa Fe, Las Vegas, Watrous, Mosquero, Conchas L., Logan, Tucumcari, Santa Rosa, Newkirk, San Jon, Adrian, Vega, Dalhart, Hartley, Dumas, Stratford, Cactus, Stinnett, Borger, Pampa, L. Meredith, Canadian, Perryton, Spearman, Panhandle, Groom, Shamrock, Amarillo, Canyon, Hereford, Friona, Tulia, Wellington, Memphis, Mangum, Hollis, Childress, Woodward, Arnett, Weston, Weatherford, Clinton, Hinton, Fort Cobb Resr, Anadarko, Sayre, Wichita Mts, Hobart, Altus, Lawton, Frederick, Quanah, Vernon

Rio Grande, Sacramento Mts, Socorro, Magdalena, San Antonio, South Baldy 3288, Carrizozo, Vaughn, Corona, Ft Sumner, Fort Sumner, Clovis, Farwell, Muleshoe, Earth, Portales, Kenna, Roswell, Hondo, Dexter, Tatum, Lovington, Artesia, L. McMillan, Hobbs, Eunice, Malaga, Jal, Carlsbad, Carlsbad Caverns N.P., Red Bluff L., Levelland, Littlefield, Morton, Plainview, Floydada, Dickens, Paducah, Guthrie, Brownfield, Lubbock, Post, Aspermont, Tahoka, Lamesa, Seminole, Andrews, Snyder, Anson, Merkel, Sweetwater, Abilene, Colorado City, Big Spring, Midland, Odessa, Kermit, Monahans, Crane, San Angelo, Sterling City, Colorado, Coleman, Ballinger, Eden, Brady, Goldthwaite

Truth or Consequences, Caballo Resr, Salinas Peak, San Andres Mts, Tularosa, Mayhill, Alamogordo, Elephant Butte Resr, Hillsboro, Silver City, Central, Bayard, Tyrone, Gila, Lordsburg, Deming, Fairacres, Las Cruces, University Park, Anthony, Columbus, Animas Peak 2597, El Paso, Ciudad Juárez, Senecu, Fort Hancock, Guadalupe Pk 2667, Guadalupe Mtns N.P., Sierra Blanca, Van Horn, Kent, Toyah, Pecos, Balmorhea, McCamey, Big Lake, Barnhart, Fort Stockton, Sheffield, Eldorado, Ozona, Sonora, Junction

Lag. de Guzmán, Guadalupe, El Porvenir, Lucero, Villa Ahumada, Lag. de Sta María, Nueva Casas Grandes, Buenaventura, El Sueco, Gallego, Galeana, Madera, Matachic, Aldama, Chihuahua, Ojinaga, Presidio, Chinati Pk 2357, Mt Livermore 2554, Fort Davis, Marfa, Valentine, Alpine, Marathon, Sanderson, Rockspings, Sonora, Del Rio, Ciudad Acuña, Brackettville, Uvalde, San Antonio de Bravo, Eagle Peak, Emory Pk 2389, Big Bend Nat. Park, Boquillas, Manuel Benavides, Amistad Resr, Devils L., Jiménez, Langtry, Comstock, Rio Grande, Rio Bravo del Norte, Pecos, Edwards Plateau, Sierra del Burro, Ciudad Acuña, Kerrville, Comfort, New Braunfels, Schertz, Leakey, Medina L., L. Buchanan, Llano, San Saba, Lampasas, Brownwood, Comanche, Stephenville, Cisco, Tuscola, Breckenridge, Haskell, Stamford, Seymour, Olney, Jacksboro, Wichita Falls, Henrietta

TEXAS

at the same scale

MISSOURI

KENTUCKY

TENNESSEE

ARKANSAS

MISSISSIPPI

ALABAMA

LOUISIANA

1:5M

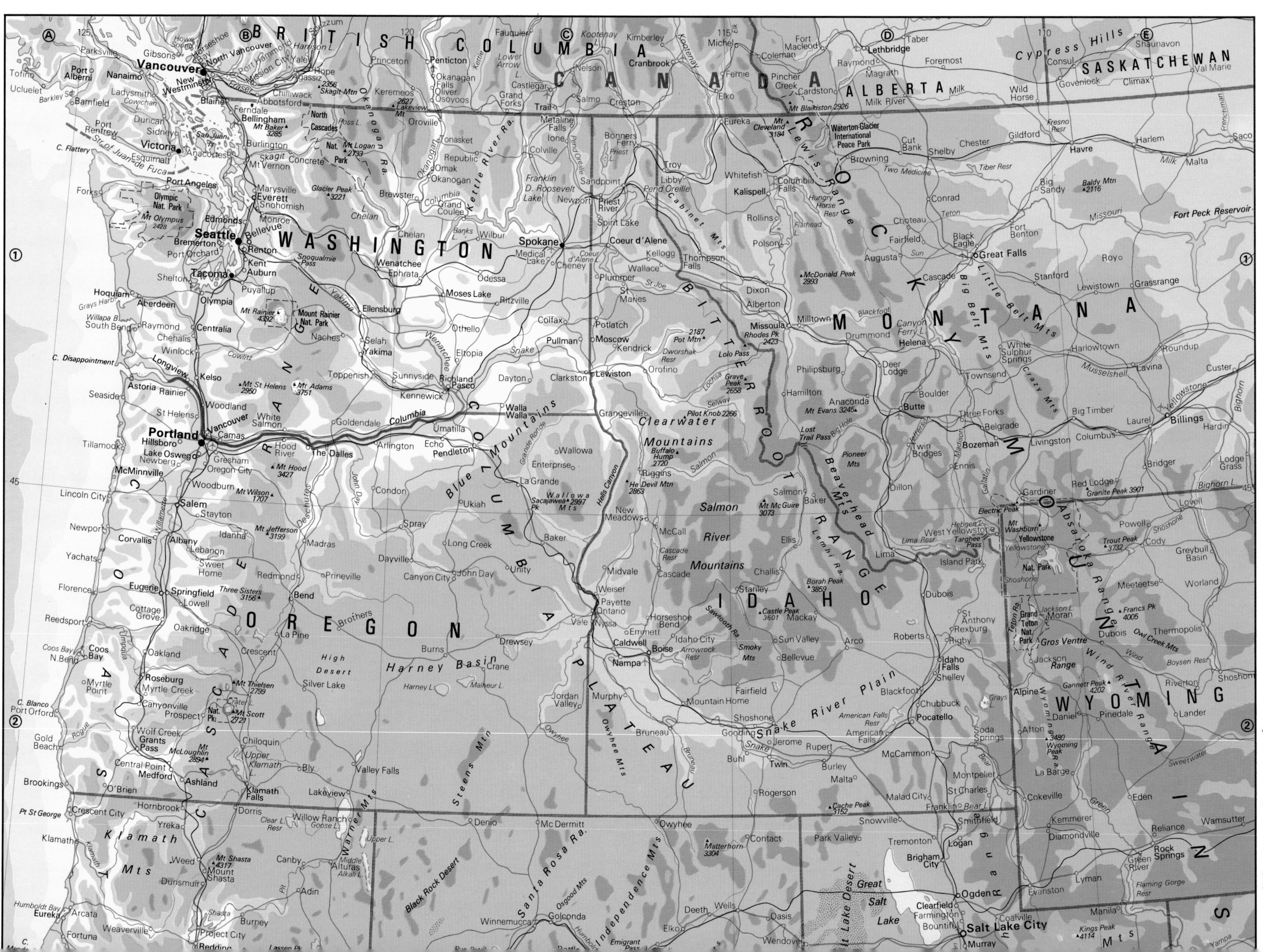

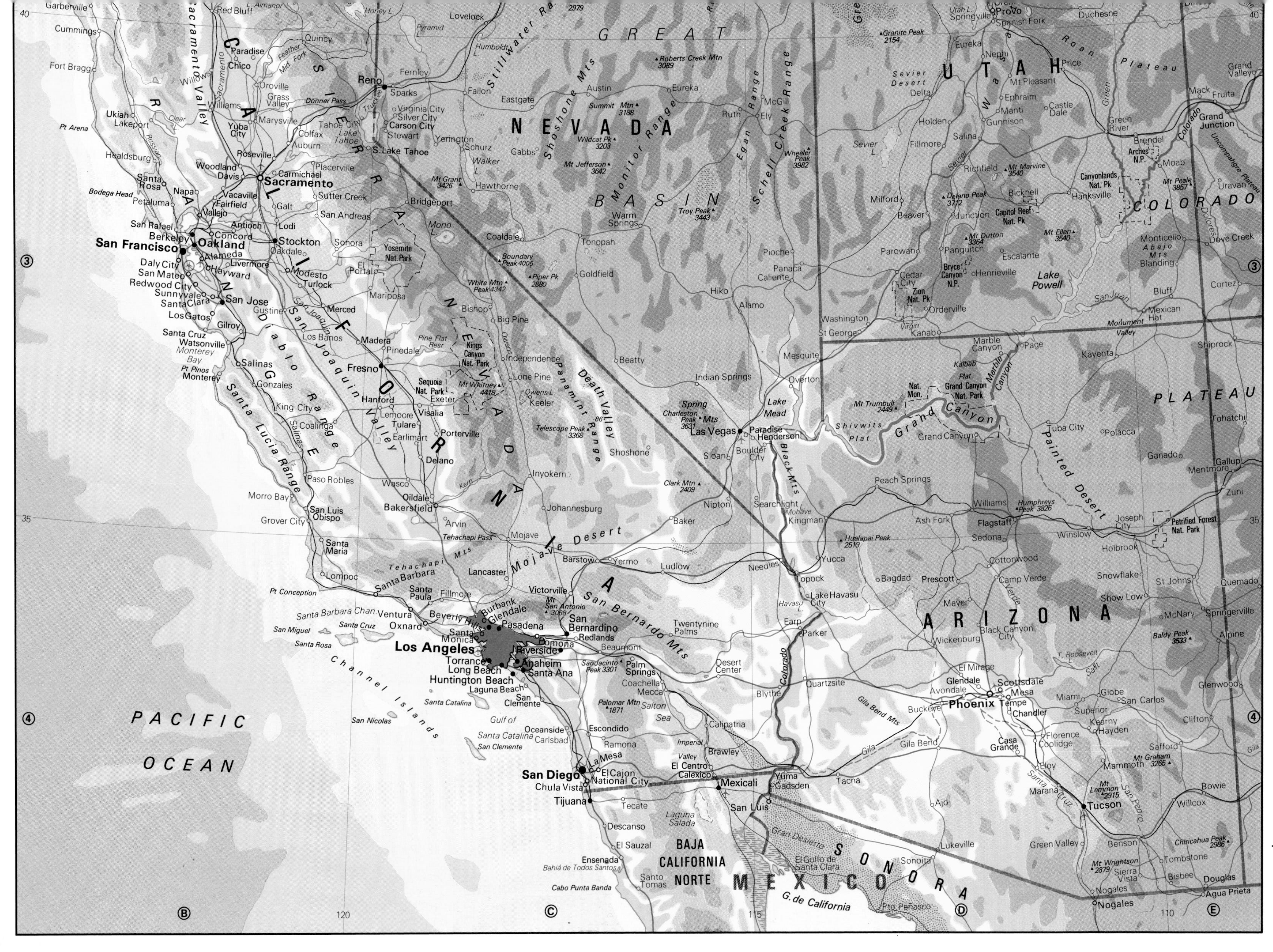
UTAH
NEVADA
CALIFORNIA
ARIZONA
COLORADO
PLATEAU
GREAT BASIN
SIERRA NEVADA
Mojave Desert
SONORA
MEXICO
BAJA CALIFORNIA NORTE
PACIFIC OCEAN
Sacramento Valley
San Joaquin Valley
Diablo Range
Santa Lucia Range
Death Valley
Panamint Range
San Bernardino Mts
Painted Desert
Grand Canyon
Lake Mead
Lake Powell
Channel Islands
G. de California
Salton Sea
San Francisco
Oakland
San Jose
Sacramento
Stockton
Fresno
Bakersfield
Los Angeles
Long Beach
San Diego
Tijuana
Mexicali
Las Vegas
Reno
Carson City
Phoenix
Tucson
Flagstaff
Yuma
Provo
Santa Barbara
Monterey
Santa Cruz
Palm Springs
San Bernardino
Riverside
Anaheim
Santa Ana
Pasadena
Barstow
Kingman
Needles
Prescott
Mesa
Scottsdale
Tempe
Nogales
Ensenada

1:2.5M
0 25 50 75 100 km
0 25 50 mls
NEVADA
SIERRA NEVADA
COAST RANGES
San Joaquin Valley
Diablo Ra.
Santa Lucia Range
Temblor Ra.
La Panza Ra.
Santa Cruz Mts
Gabilan Ra.
Sierra Madre Mts
San Rafael Mts
Santa Ynez Mts
Tehachapi Mts
San Gabriel Mts
White Mts
Inyo Mts
Panamint Ra.
Argus Ra.
Wassuk Ra.
Excelsior Mts
Cedar Mts
Gabbs Valley Ra.
Silver Peak Range
Mojave Desert
Yosemite National Park
Kings Canyon National Park
Sequoia National Park
Death Valley National Monument
PACIFIC OCEAN
Channel Islands
Santa Barbara Channel
San Pedro Channel
Gulf of Santa Catalina
Outer Santa Barbara Channel
Monterey Bay
Morro Bay
Santa Monica Bay
San Francisco
Oakland
San Jose
Sacramento
Stockton
Modesto
Fresno
Bakersfield
Los Angeles
San Diego
Santa Barbara
San Luis Obispo
Riverside
San Bernardino
Lake Tahoe
Mono Lake
Mt Whitney 4418
Mt Dana 3978
Mt Lyell 3997
Mt Goddard 4132
Mt Humphreys 4263
White Mtn Peak 4342
Boundary Pk 4005
Mt Hamilton 1284
Mt Diablo 1173
Mt Pinos 2692
Mt San Antonio 3068
Telescope Pk 3368
Santa Catalina
San Clemente
Santa Cruz
Santa Rosa
San Miguel
USA, HAWAII
1:5M
0 50 100 150 200 km
0 50 100 mls
Kauai
Niihau
Oahu
Molokai
Lanai
Maui
Kahoolawe
Hawaii
Honolulu
Pearl City
Hilo
Mauna Kea 4201
Mauna Loa 4169
Kilauea Crater 1243
Hawaii Volcanoes Nat. Park
Kauai Channel
Kaiwi Channel
Pailolo Chan.
Kealaikahiki Chan.
Alenuihaha Channel
Ka Lae (South Cape)
PACIFIC OCEAN

200   400   600 km
100   200   300 mls

Major Regions and Bodies of Water

GULF OF MEXICO

CARIBBEAN SEA

PACIFIC OCEAN

Straits of Florida

Yucatan Channel

Bahía de Campeche

Golfo de Tehuantepec

Golfo de Panamá

Bay of California / Golfo de California

Countries and States

UNITED STATES

TENNESSEE
GEORGIA
SOUTH CAROLINA
NORTH CAROLINA
ALABAMA
MISSISSIPPI
LOUISIANA
ARKANSAS
OKLAHOMA
TEXAS
NEW MEXICO
ARIZONA
FLORIDA

MEXICO

Sierra Madre Occidental
Sierra Madre Oriental
Sierra Madre del Sur
Baja California

THE BAHAMAS
CUBA
JAMAICA

BELIZE
GUATEMALA
EL SALVADOR
HONDURAS
NICARAGUA
COSTA RICA
PANAMA

Selected Cities

Wilmington, C. Fear, Florence, Columbia, Charleston, Savannah, Brunswick, Jacksonville, St Augustine, Daytona Beach, Melbourne, C. Canaveral, Orlando, Tampa, St Petersburg, Clearwater, Ft Myers, Ft Lauderdale, Hollywood, Miami, Miami Beach, W Palm Beach, Ft Pierce, Key West

Atlanta, Athens, Augusta, Macon, Columbus, Albany, Valdosta, Tallahassee, Gainesville, Ocala, Chattanooga, Huntsville, Birmingham, Tuscaloosa, Montgomery, Dothan, Pensacola, Mobile, Biloxi, Gulfport, New Orleans, Baton Rouge, Lafayette, Lake Charles, Beaumont, Pt Arthur, Orange, Houston, Galveston

Memphis, Little Rock, Hot Springs, Pine Bluff, Greenville, Greenwood, Jackson, Vicksburg, Natchez, Meridian, Monroe, Shreveport, Alexandria

Fort Smith, McAlester, Muskogee, Oklahoma City, Ardmore, Durant, Denison, Sherman, Dallas, Fort Worth, Waco, Austin, San Antonio, Corpus Christi, Victoria, Beeville, Kingsville, Brownsville, McAllen, Laredo, Del Rio, Eagle Pass

El Reno, Chickasha, Lawton, Wichita Falls, Abilene, Sweetwater, San Angelo, Big Spring, Midland, Odessa, Snyder, Lubbock, Plainview, Amarillo, Clovis, Roswell, Carlsbad, Artesia, Alpine, Pecos, El Paso, Cd Juárez

Albuquerque, Las Cruces, Alamogordo, Lordsburg, Douglas, Nogales, Tucson, Phoenix, Mesa, Casa Grande, Yuma, San Diego, Tijuana, Mexicali, Ensenada

Matamoros, Reynosa, Nuevo Laredo, Piedras Negras, Nueva Rosita, Sabinas, Monclova, Cd Camargo, Chihuahua, Delicias, Ojinaga, Cd Cuauhtémoc, Hidalgo del Parral, Sta Bárbara, Gómez Palacio, Torreón, Durango, Fresnillo, Zacatecas, San Luis Potosí, Cd Victoria, Cd Madero, Tampico, Poza Rica, Tuxpan, Veracruz

Monterrey, Saltillo, Matehuala, Aguascalientes, León, Guanajuato, Querétaro, Celaya, Irapuato, Morelia, Guadalajara, Tepic, Mazatlán, Culiacán, Los Mochis, Ciudad Obregón, Navojoa, Guaymas, Hermosillo, Nogales

México, Toluca, Cuernavaca, Pachuca, Puebla, Orizaba, Córdoba, Jalapa, Oaxaca, Acapulco, Chilpancingo, Colima, Manzanillo, Uruapan, Lázaro Cárdenas

Coatzacoalcos, Minatitlán, Villahermosa, Tuxtla Gutiérrez, San Cristóbal, Tapachula, Tehuantepec, Salina Cruz, Comitán, Quezaltenango

Campeche, Cd del Carmen, Frontera, Chetumal, Progreso, Mérida, Ticul, Peto, Valladolid, Cozumel

Havana (Habana), Matanzas, Cárdenas, Cienfuegos, Sancti Spíritus, Santa Clara, Ciego de Ávila, Camagüey, Holguín, Victoria de las Tunas, Manzanillo, Santiago de Cuba, Guantánamo, Pinar del Río

Nassau, Freeport

Montego Bay, Kingston, Spanish Town

Belize, Belmopan, Flores

Guatemala, Sta Rosa, Escuintla, San José

San Salvador, Sta Ana, Sonsonate, San Miguel, Unión

San Pedro Sula, Tela, La Ceiba, Comayagua, Tegucigalpa, Choluteca

Chinandega, León, Managua, Masaya, Granada, Matagalpa, Bluefields, Pto Cabezas

San José, Puntarenas, Limón, Cartago, Alajuela, Liberia

David, Panamá, Colón, La Chorrera, Santiago, Chitré

Islands and Points

Little Cayman, Grand Cayman, I. de la Juventud, Cayo Romano, I. de Providencia, I. de San Andrés, I. del Maíz, Bahama Bank, Great Bahama Bank

Tropic of Cancer

1:5M

0 50 100 150 200 km
0 50 100 mls
GULF OF MEXICO
Bahía de Campeche
Golfo de Tehuantepec
Tropic of Cancer
NUEVO LEÓN
TAMAULIPAS
SAN LUIS POTOSÍ
ZACATECAS
DURANGO
SINALOA
NAYARIT
GUANAJUATO
QUERÉTARO
HIDALGO
JALISCO
COLIMA
MICHOACÁN
GUERRERO
MORELOS
MÉXICO
PUEBLA
OAXACA
VERACRUZ
TABASCO
TLAXCALA
AGS.
Istmo de Tehuantepec
Sierra Madre Oriental
Sierra Madre Occidental
Sierra Madre del Sur
México
Guadalajara
Puebla
Veracruz
Acapulco
Oaxaca
San Luis Potosí
Querétaro
León
Aguascalientes
Zacatecas
Durango
Mazatlán
Tepic
Morelia
Toluca
Cuernavaca
Pachuca
Tampico
Cd Madero
Cd Victoria
Jalapa
Orizaba
Coatzacoalcos
Minatitlán
Tehuantepec
Juchitán
Chilpancingo
Colima
Manzanillo
Puerto Vallarta
Poza Rica
Tuxpan
Celaya
Irapuato
Salamanca
Uruapan
Fresnillo
Matehuala
Tlaxcala
Cd Mante
Cd Valles
Tres Marías

100 200 300 400 km
100 200 mls

Inset maps:

TRINIDAD 1:2.5M
Galera Pt, Matura Bay, St Joseph, Pt Radix, Cocos Bay, Matelot, Northern Range, Arima, Upper Manzanilla, Tunapuna, Princes Town, Guayaguayare, Moruga, Rio Claro, Debe, Siparia, Pt of Spain, San Juan, Chaguanas, San Fernando, Point Fortin, Fullarton, Gulf of Paria

TOBAGO 1:2.5M
Charlotteville, Speyside, Scarborough, Canaan, Crown Pt

Q DOMINICA 1:2.5M
C. Melville, Marigot, Anse Diablotin, Portsmouth 1530, Rosalie, Roseau, 61°30′

R BARBADOS 1:2.5M
North Pt, Speightstown, Mt Hillaby, Blackman's, Ragged Pt, Bridgetown, Holetown, South Pt 59°30′, 13°15′

P ST LUCIA 1:2.5M
Gros Islet, Cap Pt, Castries, Soufrière, Mt Gimie, Vieux Fort, Dennery, 14, 61

N ST VINCENT 1:2.5M
Porter Pt, Soufrière 1234, Georgetown, Barrouallie, Kingstown, 13°15′, 6°15′

M GRENADA 1:2.5M
Mt St Catherine 840, Sauteurs, Grenville, St George's, Pt Salines, Prickly Pt, 12, 6°45′

JAMAICA 1:2.5M
Pt Antonio, Blue Mtn Pk 2256, Morant Bay, Morant Pt, St Ann's Bay, Ocho Rios, Annotto Bay, Moneague, Blue Mts, Kingston, Port Royal, Falmouth, Montego Bay, Cambridge, The Cockpit Country, Mt Denham 986, Wakefield, Dry Harbour Mts, Spanish Town, Chapelton, May Pen, Mandeville, Salt River, Long Bay, S. Negril Point, Savanna la Mar, Southfield, Black River

Main map labels:

ATLANTIC OCEAN

THE BAHAMAS — Grand Bahama, Freeport, Marsh Harbour, Great Abaco, Nassau, New Providence, Andros, Eleuthera, Cat, Long, Great Exuma, Rum Cay, San Salvador, Acklins, Mayaguana, Crooked, Great Inagua, Matthew Town, Little Inagua, Turks Is. (U.K.), Caicos Is. (U.K.)

FLORIDA — Miami, Palm Beach, L. Worth, Delray Beach, Pompano Beach, Ft Lauderdale, Hollywood, Naples, The Everglades, Key West, Florida Keys, Tropic of Cancer

CUBA — Habana, Pinar del Río, Matanzas, Cárdenas, Santa Clara, Cienfuegos, Nueva Gerona, I. de la Juventud (I. de Pinos), Sagua la Grande, Morón, Ciego de Ávila, Camagüey, Victoria de las Tunas, Holguín, Nuevitas, Manzanillo, Bayamo, Santiago de Cuba, Guantánamo, Banes, Baracoa

CAYMAN ISLANDS (U.K.) — Grand Cayman, Little Cayman, Cayman Brac

JAMAICA — Montego Bay, Mandeville, Spanish Town, Kingston, Savanna la Mar

HAITI — Cap-Haïtien, Gonaïves, Port-de-Paix, Port-au-Prince, La Selle 2680, Jacmel, Les Cayes, Anse d'Hainault, I. de la Gonâve, Massif de la Hotte

DOMINICAN REPUBLIC — Puerto Plata, Santiago, S. Francisco, Monte Cristi, La Romana, Santo Domingo, Samaná, Miches, Cordillera Central, Hispaniola

PUERTO RICO (U.S.A.) — San Juan, Caguas, Arecibo, Aguadilla, Mayagüez, Ponce, Cerro de Punta 1338, Mona

Virgin Is. (U.S.A. & U.K.), Anguilla (U.K.), St Martin (Fr. & Neth.), St Croix (U.S.A.), St Barthélemy

LEEWARD ISLANDS — ANTIGUA & BARBUDA (U.K.), Barbuda, ST KITTS NEVIS, Montserrat (U.K.), GUADELOUPE (Fr.), Pointe-à-Pitre, Basse Terre, Marie Galante, DOMINICA, Roseau, MARTINIQUE (Fr.), Fort-de-France

WINDWARD ISLANDS — ST LUCIA, Castries, ST VINCENT & THE GRENADINES, Kingstown, BARBADOS, Bridgetown, GRENADA, St George's

LESSER ANTILLES

GREATER ANTILLES

CARIBBEAN SEA

PUERTO RICO TRENCH

CAYMAN TRENCH

Windward Passage, Jamaica Channel, Mona Passage

TRINIDAD AND TOBAGO — Port of Spain, San Fernando, Tobago, Scarborough

VENEZUELA — Caracas, Maiquetía, Maracay, Valencia, Barcelona, Cumaná, Maturín, Pto la Cruz, Pto Cabello, Coro, Maracaibo, Cabimas, Lago de Maracaibo, Mérida, Barinas, San Cristóbal, Barquisimeto, Valera, Trujillo, Guanare, La Asunción, Isla Margarita, Los Testigos, La Tortuga, I. la Orchila, I. Blanquilla (Ven.), Los Roques, La Guaira, Guiria, Carúpano, Pico Bolívar 5007, Guri, Cd Guayana, Cd Bolívar, El Tigre, Anaco, Coloradito

Bonaire (Neth.), Curaçao (Neth.), Aruba (Neth.), Willemstad

COLOMBIA — Barranquilla, Cartagena, Sta Marta, Ciénaga, Riohacha, Valledupar, Sincelejo, Montería, Golfo del Darién, Pen. de la Guajira, Sierra Nevada de Sta Marta 5775

PANAMA — Panamá, Colón, Panama Canal, David, La Chorrera, Arch. de las Perlas

COSTA RICA — San José, Alajuela, Heredia, Cartago, Limón, Pto Armuelles

NICARAGUA — Bluefields, Puerto Cabezas, Río Grande, San Juan del Norte, Cabo Gracias á Dios, Cayos Miskito, I. de San Andrés (Col.), I. de Providencia (Col.), Swan I. (Hond.)

HONDURAS — Trujillo, Bonanza, Caratasca, Bus Laguna, G. de los Mosquitos

1:35M

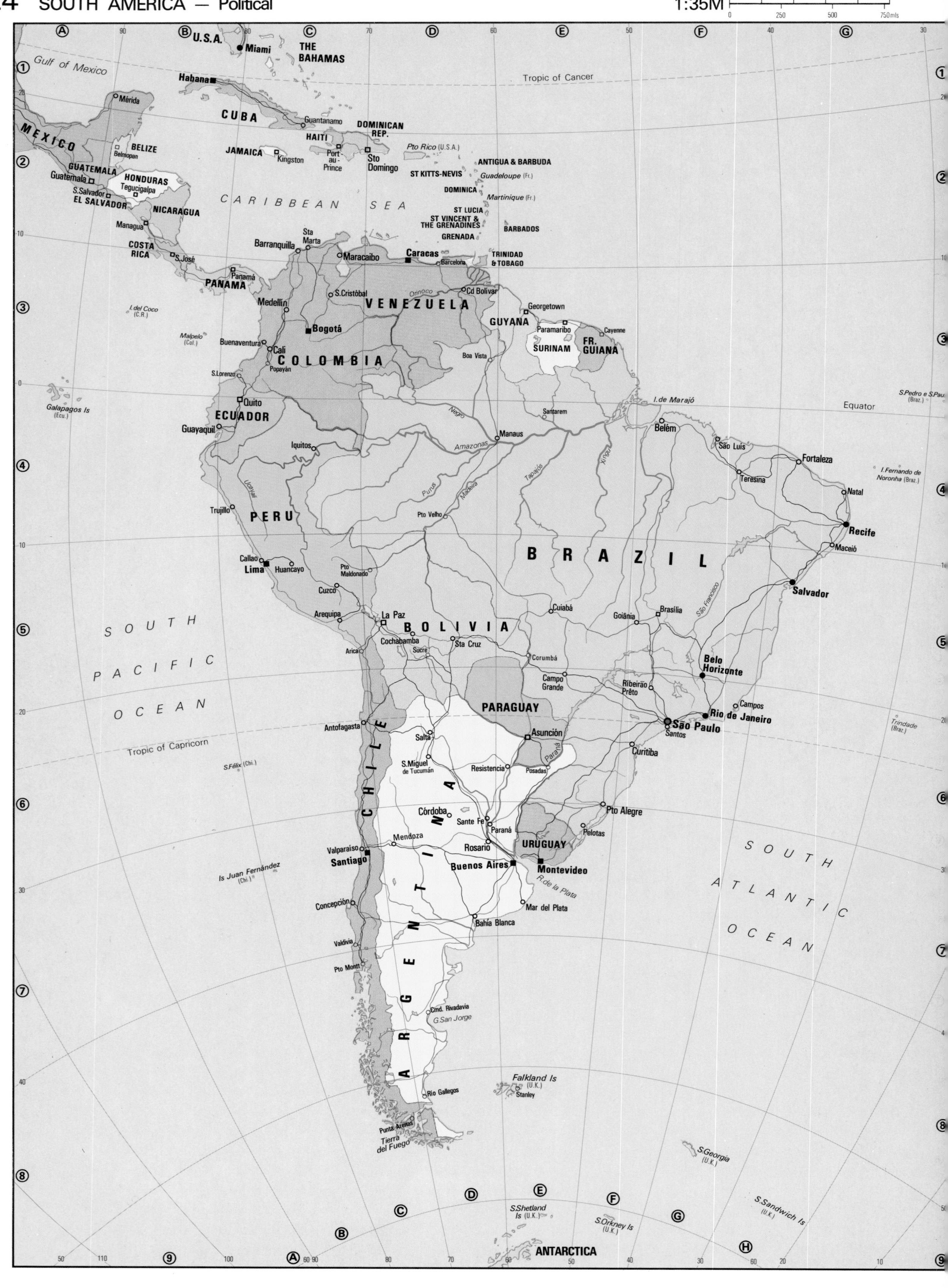

Gulf of Mexico

Ⓐ 90 Ⓑ U.S.A. 80 Miami Ⓒ THE BAHAMAS 70 Ⓓ 60 Ⓔ 50 Ⓕ 40 Ⓖ 30

① Tropic of Cancer

Habana

CUBA

Mérida

MEXICO

BELIZE
Belmopan

GUATEMALA
Guatemala

HONDURAS
Tegucigalpa

EL SALVADOR
S.Salvador

NICARAGUA
Managua

COSTA RICA
S.José

PANAMA
Panamá

Guantanamo

HAITI
Port-au-Prince

JAMAICA
Kingston

DOMINICAN REP.
Sto Domingo

Pto Rico (U.S.A.)

CARIBBEAN SEA

ANTIGUA & BARBUDA
ST KITTS-NEVIS   Guadeloupe (Fr.)
DOMINICA
ST LUCIA   Martinique (Fr.)
ST VINCENT & THE GRENADINES
GRENADA   BARBADOS

Sta Marta
Barranquilla
Maracaibo   Caracas   Barcelona   TRINIDAD & TOBAGO

I. del Coco (C.R.)

S.Cristóbal   VENEZUELA   Cd Bolivar
Medellín   Georgetown
Malpelo (Col.)   Bogotá   GUYANA   Paramaribo   Cayenne
Buenaventura   Cali   SURINAM   FR. GUIANA
S.Lorenzo   COLOMBIA   Popayán   Boa Vista

Galapagos Is (Ecu.)   Quito
ECUADOR
Guayaquil

Equator   Orinoco   Negro   Santarem   I. de Marajó   S.Pedro e S.Pau (Braz.)

Iquitos   Manaus   Belém   São Luis   Fortaleza   I.Fernando de Noronha (Braz.)

Amazonas   Purus   Madeira   Tapajós   Xingu   Teresina   Natal

PERU   Trujillo

Pto Velho   B R A Z I L   Recife   Maceió

Callao   Lima   Huancayo   Pto Maldonado

Cuzco   São Francisco   Salvador

Arequipa   La Paz   Cuiabá   Brasília   Goiânia

SOUTH   Arica   Cochabamba   Sta Cruz   Corumbá   Belo Horizonte
BOLIVIA   Sucre

PACIFIC   Campo Grande   Ribeirão Prêto   Campos

OCEAN   S.Félix (Chi.)   PARAGUAY   Rio de Janeiro
Antofagasta   Asunción   São Paulo   Santos   Trindade (Braz.)

Tropic of Capricorn   Salta   Curitiba

CHILE   S.Miguel de Tucumán   Resistencia   Posadas

Is Juan Fernández (Chi.)   Córdoba   Paraná   Pto Alegre   SOUTH

Valparaíso   Mendoza   Sante Fe   Pelotas   ATLANTIC

Santiago   Rosario   URUGUAY   OCEAN
Buenos Aires   Montevideo

ARGENTINA   R.de la Plata

Concepción   Mar del Plata

Bahía Blanca

Valdivia

Pto Montt

Cmd. Rivadavia
G.San Jorge

Falkland Is (U.K.)
Stanley

Río Gallegos

Punta Arenas
Tierra del Fuego

S.Georgia (U.K.)

S.Shetland Is (U.K.)   S.Orkney Is (U.K.)   S.Sandwich Is (U.K.)

ANTARCTICA

1:15M

200   400   600 km
100   200   300 mls

BOLIVIA

BRAZIL

MATO GROSSO DO SUL

MINAS GERAIS

SÃO PAULO

PARAGUAY

PARANÁ

SANTA CATARINA

RIO GRANDE DO SUL

GRAN CHACO

URUGUAY

ARGENTINA

La Pampa

Mendoza

Buenos Aires

CORDILLERA PATAGONICA

Río Negro

Chubut

Santa Cruz

ATLANTIC OCEAN

Ilo
Pta Coles
Tacna
Arica
Tropic of Capricorn
Iquique
Tocopilla
Pedro de Valdivia
Mejillones
Antofagasta
Taltal
Chañaral
Caldera
Copiapó
Huasco
Vallenar
La Serena
Coquimbo
Ovalle
Punitaqui
Illapel
Los Vilos
Quillota
Viña del Mar
Valparaíso
S.Antonio
Santiago
S.Bernardo
Rancagua
Pichilemu
S.Fernando
Curicó
Constitución
Talca
Linares
Cauquenes
S.Carlos
Chillán
Tomé
Talcahuano
Concepción
Coronel
Lebu
Los Ángeles
Angol
Carahue
Temuco
Toltén
Loncoche
Villarrica
Valdivia
La Unión
Osorno
Pto Varas
Puerto Montt
Ancud
I.de Chiloé
Castro
Achao
Archipiélago de las Chones
Pto Aisen
Coihaique
Pen. de Taitao
G.de Peñas
Madre de Dios
Hanover
Pto Natales
Punta Arenas
Ushuaia
Río Grande
Isla Grande de Tierra del Fuego
Tierra del Fuego
C.de Hornos (C.Horn)

Oruro
Aiquile
Huanuni
Sucre
Potosí
Uyuni
Tupiza
La Quiaca
Jujuy
Orán
Salta
Metán
Tucumán
Catamarca
La Rioja
S.Juan
Mendoza
San Luis
San Rafael
Córdoba
Río Cuarto
Santiago del Estero
Rafaela
Santa Fe
Paraná
Rosario
San Nicolás
Pergamino
Junín
Lincoln
Rufino
Venado Tuerto
Mercedes
Chivilcoy
Buenos Aires
Avellaneda
La Plata
Chascomús
Dolores
Azul
Tandil
Las Flores
Ayacucho
Mar del Plata
Miramar
Necochea
Tres Arroyos
Balcarce
Bahía Blanca
Punta Alta
Neuquén
Gral Roca
Río Colorado
Viedma
Carmen de Patagones
San Antonio Oeste
Valcheta
Maquinchao
S.Carlos de Bariloche
El Bolsón
Esquel
Trelew
Rawson
Gaimán
Pto Madryn
Pto Pirámides
Comodoro Rivadavia
Caleta Olivia
Colonia Las Heras
Sarmiento
Deseado
Río Gallegos
Río Turbio
Bahía Grande
Calafate

Santa Cruz
Valle Grande
San José de Chiquitos
Corumbá
Pto Suárez
Campo Grande
Aquidauana
Dourados
Pto Murtinho
Concepción
Asunción
Formosa
Resistencia
Corrientes
Posadas
Encarnación
Foz do Iguaçu
Curitiba
Paranaguá
Florianópolis
Joinville
Blumenau
Itajaí
São Francisco do Sul
Passo Fundo
Caxias do Sul
Canoas
Pôrto Alegre
Pelotas
Rio Grande
Montevideo
Maldonado
Punta del Este

Campo Grande
Uberlândia
Uberaba
Franca
Ribeirão Prêto
Belo Horizonte
Divinópolis
São Paulo
Campinas
Jundiaí
Sorocaba
Santos
São Vicente
Rio de Janeiro
Volta Redonda

FALKLAND ISLANDS (ISLAS MALVINAS) (U.K.)
West Falkland
East Falkland
Stanley
Jason Is
C.Dolphin
Weddell
Beauchene Is

ATLANTIC OCEAN

South Georgia (U.K.)
Grytviken
Shag Rocks

1:15M

200 400 600 km
100 200 300 mils

PACIFIC OCEAN

NICARAGUA
Siguatepeque, Comayagua, Tegucigalpa, San Miguel, Somoto, La Unión, Choluteca, Chinandega, Estelí, Matagalpa, León, Managua, Granada, Masaya, Rivas, S. Carlos, Alajuela, Heredia, Limón, San José, Cartago, Puntarenas, Pen. de Nicoya, G. de Nicoya, B. de Coronado

Coco (Segovia), Pto Cabezas, I. de Providencia (Col.), I. de San Andrés (Col.), Bluefields, L. de Nicaragua, San Juan, G. del Papagaya

COSTA RICA
Santiago, David, Barú, Chitré, G. de Chiriquí, Armuelles, G. Dulce, Pen. de Azuero, I. Coiba, Pta Mariato, Chirripó Grande 3815

PANAMÁ
Colón, Panamá, La Chorra, La Palma, Arch. de las Perlas, G. de Panamá, G. de San Miguel

Malpelo (Col.), I. del Coco (C.R.), Malpelo (Col.)

COLOMBIA
Barranquilla, Cartagena, Sta Marta, Ciénaga, Ríohacha, Maicao, Valledupar, S. Jacinto, Sincelejo, El Banco, Magangué, Montería, Ocaña, Caucasia, Turbo, Pto Berrio, Yarumal, Bello, Barbosa, Itagüi, Medellín, Manizales, Quibdó, C. Corrientes, Pereira, Cartago, Armenia, Bogotá, Tuluá, Ibagué, Buga, Girardot, Villavicencio, Palmira, Buenaventura, Cali, Granada, Santander, Neiva, Popayán, Vol. Puracé 4700, Pitalito, Pto Rico, Florencia, Tumaco, El Diviso, Pasto, Belén, S. Lorenzo, Ipiales, Mocoa, Pto Asís, Calamar, Mitú, Leguizamo

ECUADOR
Esmeraldas, Ibarra, Otavalo, Tulcán, Quito, Cotopaxi 5896, Chone, Coca, Tena, Manta, Ambato, Chimborazo 6310, Jipijapa, Guaranda, Babahoyo, Riobamba, Guayaquil, Milagro, Macas, La Libertad, Playas, Azogues, I. Puná, Cuenca, Guálaceo, G. de Guayaquil, Tumbes, Machala, Zaruma, Loja, Zamora

PERU
Talara, Negritos, Sullana, Paita, Chulucanas, Huancabamba, Piura, Catacaos, Jaén, Yurimaguas, Moyobamba, Tarapoto, Lambayeque, Ferreñafe, Chachapoyas, Chiclayo, Chepén, Cajamarca, Cajabamba, Pacasmayo, Huamachuco, Otusco, Pomabamba, Pucallpa, Trujillo, Huallanca, Tingo Maria, Huascarán 6768, Chimbote, Huaráz, La Unión, Casma, Huánuco, Huarmey, Oxapampa, Cerro de Pasco, La Merced, Pativilca, Barranca, Tarma, Huacho, La Oroya, Jauja, Acobamba, Ancón, Callao, Huancayo, Lima, Huancavelica, Ayacucho, Parque Nac. de Manu, Chincha Alta, Pisco, Ica, Andahuaylas, Abancay, Cuzco, Machu Picchu, Quillabamba, Nazca, Sicuani, Chala, Ayaviri, Coropuna 6425, Juliaca, Camaná, Arequipa, Misti 5822, Puno, Matarani, Mollendo, Moquegua, Ilo, Tacna, Arica, Pta Coles

VENEZUELA
Neth. Antilles, Aruba, Curaçao (Neth), Bonaire, Willemstad, Pta Gallinas, Pen. de Guajira, Coro, Pto Fijo, G. de Venezuela, Riecito, Tucuyo, Pto Cabello, Maracaibo, Cabimas, Cd Ojeda, Machiques, Valencia, Maracay, Caracas, Barquisimeto, San Cristóbal, Cúcuta, Pamplona, Bucaramanga, Mérida, Valera, Trujillo, Barinas, Guanare, V. de la Pascua, Acarigua, Sogamoso, Tunja, Chocontá, Orocué, Vichada, Pto Carreño, Pto Ayacucho, San Fernando, Cd Bolívar, Cd Guayana, Upata, El Tigre, Maturin, Cumaná, Barcelona, La Asunción, I. de Margarita, Carúpano, Güiria, Trinidad, Port of Spain, Anaco, Zaraza, Ventuari, El Dorado, La Paragua, Sa Pacaraima

BOLIVIA
La Paz, Cochabamba, Santa Cruz, Oruro, Sucre, Potosí, Trinidad, Rurrenabaque, Riberalta, Cobija, Guayaramerín, L. Rogaguado, L. Titicaca, Ancohuma 6388, Sajama 6542, Coroico, Chulumani, Aiquile, Huanuni, Villa Grande, Camiri, Villamontes, Tarija, Yacuiba, Bermejo, Tupiza, Uyuni, Camargo

BRASIL / AMAZONAS / SELVAS
Boa Vista, Manacapuru, Tefé, Iquitos, Leticia, Tabatinga, Caxias, Cruzeiro do Sul, Feijó, Bôca do Acre, Pôrto Velho, Rio Branco, Sena Madureira, Brasiléia, Cobija, Guajará-Mirim, RONDÔNIA, RORAIMA, ACRE, Humaitá

CHILE / ARGENTINA
Iquique, Tocopilla, Chuquicamata, Calama, Antofagasta, Mejillones, Salar de Atacama, Vol. Ollagüe 5870, Llullaillaco 6723, Salta, Jujuy, Orán, Embarcación, Tropic of Capricorn

Inset (bottom left):
at the same scale
ISLAS GALÁPAGOS (ARCHIPIÉLAGO DO COLÓN) (Equ.)
Culpepper, Wenman, Pinta, Marchena, Genovesa, Fernandina, San Salvador, Santa Cruz, San Cristóbal, Isabela, Baquerizo Moreno, Santa Maria, Española

Inset (bottom center):
at the same scale
Islas Juan Fernández (Chile)
Alejandro Selkirk, Robinson Crusoe, Sta Clara

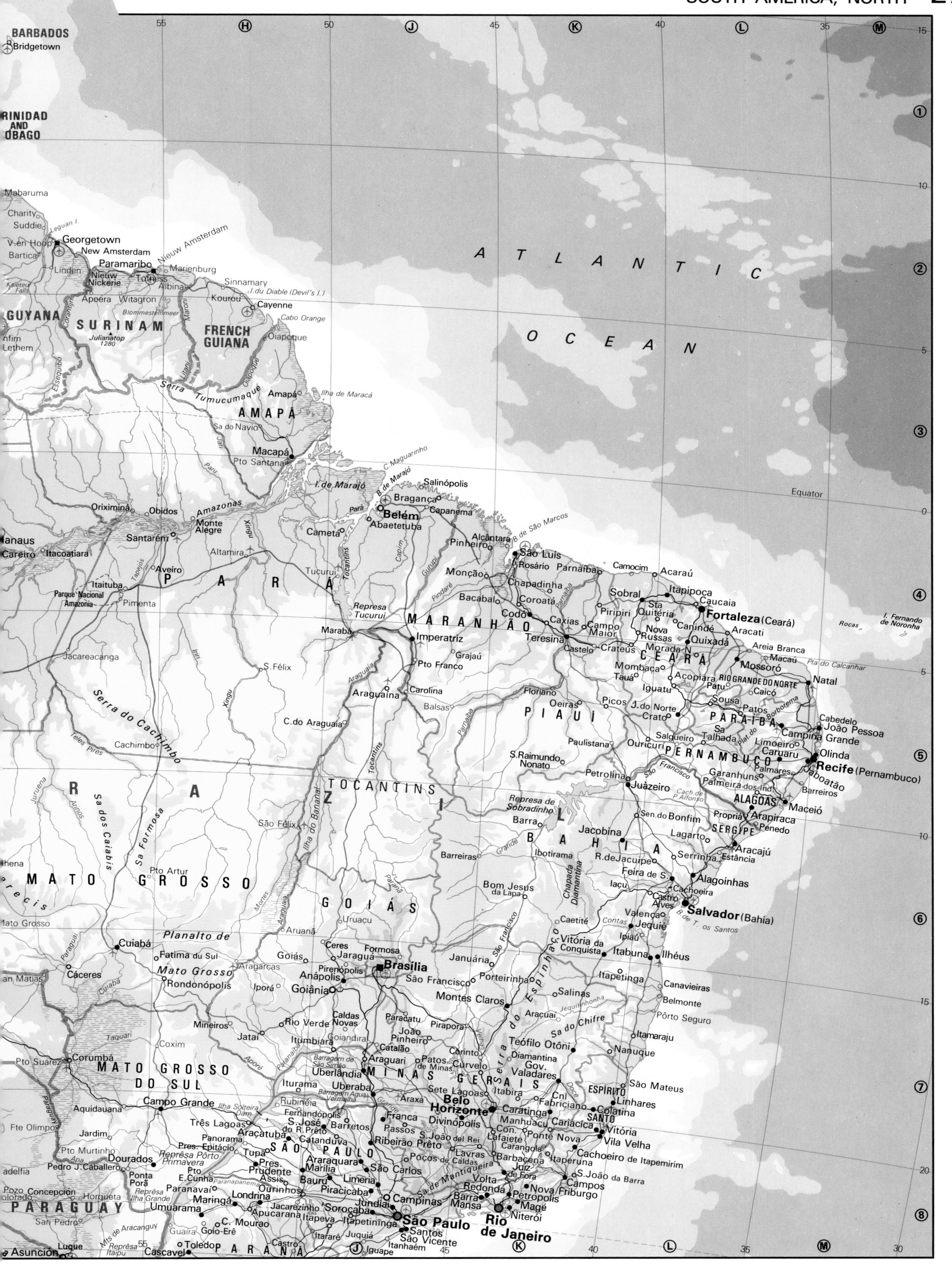
ATLANTIC OCEAN
BARBADOS
Bridgetown
TRINIDAD AND TOBAGO
GUYANA
SURINAM
FRENCH GUIANA
Georgetown
New Amsterdam
Paramaribo
Cayenne
AMAPÁ
Macapá
PARÁ
Belém
Santarém
MARANHÃO
São Luís
Teresina
PIAUÍ
CEARÁ
Fortaleza (Ceará)
RIO GRANDE DO NORTE
Natal
PARAÍBA
João Pessoa
PERNAMBUCO
Recife (Pernambuco)
ALAGOAS
Maceió
SERGIPE
Aracajú
BAHIA
Salvador (Bahia)
TOCANTINS
GOIÁS
Brasília
Goiânia
MATO GROSSO
Cuiabá
MATO GROSSO DO SUL
Campo Grande
MINAS GERAIS
Belo Horizonte
ESPÍRITO SANTO
Vitória
SÃO PAULO
São Paulo
Rio de Janeiro
PARANÁ
PARAGUAY
Asunción
Equator
Serra do Cachimbo
Planalto de Mato Grosso
Serra do Espinhaço
I. de Marajó
Amazonas
Represa de Sobradinho
Manaus
I. Fernando de Noronha

100   200   300 km
50   100   150 mls

B R A Z I L

U R U G U A Y

A R G E N T I N A

C H I L E

ATLANTIC OCEAN

PACIFIC OCEAN

Major cities and places:
Porto Alegre, Rio Grande, Pelotas, Bagé, Montevideo, Buenos Aires, Avellaneda, La Plata, Mar del Plata, Bahía Blanca, Rosario, Santa Fe, Paraná, Córdoba, Corrientes, Resistencia, Santiago del Estero, Catamarca, La Rioja, San Juan, Mendoza, San Luis, Santiago, Valparaíso, Viña del Mar, Rancagua, Concepción, Temuco, Valdivia, Osorno, Neuquén, Río Negro, La Pampa, Buenos Aires

Provinces: Misiones, Corrientes, Chaco, Santa Fe, Entre Ríos, Santiago del Estero, Córdoba, Catamarca, La Rioja, San Juan, Mendoza, San Luis, Neuquén, Río Negro, La Pampa

ATLANTIC
OCEAN
Tropic of Capricorn
BAHIA
MINAS GERAIS
ESPÍRITO SANTO
RIO DE JANEIRO
SÃO PAULO
PARANÁ
GOIÁS
MATO GROSSO
MATO GROSSO DO SUL
DISTRITO FEDERAL
BRAZIL
PARAGUAY
BOLIVIA
ARGENTINA
ARG.
Salvador (Bahia)
Rio de Janeiro
São Paulo
Belo Horizonte
Brasília
Vitória
Goiânia
Campo Grande
Cuiabá
Curitiba
Asunción
Santos
Campinas
Uberlândia
Uberaba
Ribeirão Prêto
Montes Claros
Juiz de Fora
Niterói
Londrina
Corumbá
Cáceres
Dourados
Ilhéus
Itabuna
Jequié
Vitória da Conquista
Teófilo Otôni
Gov. Valadares
Linhares
Colatina
Campos
Petrópolis
Anápolis
Sorocaba
Taubaté
Joinville
Cascavel
Maringá
Pres. Prudente
Marília
Bauru
Araçatuba
Franca
Patos de Minas
Sete Lagoas
Três Lagoas
Foz do Iguaçu
Concepción
Pedro Gomes
Coxim
Aquidauana
Rio Verde
Jataí
Itumbiara
Catalão
Paracatu
Unaí
Formosa
Pirenópolis
Pôrto Artur
Lucas
Diamantino
Paranaguá
Guarapuava
Ponta Grossa
Umuarama
Serra do Espinhaço
Sa da Mantiqueira
Serra Geral de Goiás
Pantanal
Planalto
Tropic of Capricorn

1:15M

200   400   600 km
0   100   200   300 mls

A   40   B   2   30   C   20   70   D   10   E   0   F   10   G

Greenland
(Den.)
Kap Farvel

ARCTIC

Jan Mayen
(Nor.)

Vesterålen
Narvik
Lofoten

ICELAND
Reykjavík

Arctic Circle

N O R W E G I A N

S E A

Trondheim

Sundsi

Bergen

Stavanger   Oslo

Stockho

Vänern

Göteborg   Jönköping   Gotla

NORTH

Ålborg   Öland

DENMARK

Faerøerne
(Den.)

København   Malmö

Shetland   Bornholm

Balti

Orkney   SEA

UNITED KINGDOM
OF GREAT BRITAIN AND
NORTHERN IRELAND   Aberdeen

Glasgow   Rostock   Gdań

Edinburgh

Belfast   Poznań

IRELAND   Newcastle   Hamburg

Dublin   Liverpool   Manchester   Amsterdam   Berlin

Cork   's-Gravenhage   Hannover

Birmingham   Rotterdam   NETHERLANDS   GERMANY   P O

Cardiff   Essen   Leipzig   Wrocław

Bristol   London   Bruxelles   Köln   Dresden

English Channel   BELGIUM   Bonn   Frankfurt   Praha   CZECH

Le Havre   Lille   LUXEMBOURG   REPUBLIC

Rouen   Nürnberg   Brno

A T L A N T I C   Seine   Paris   Strasbourg   Wien   SL

Stuttgart   Bratislav

O C E A N   Nantes   Loire   München   Salzburg   AUSTRIA   Graz   HUN

Tours   Bern   Zürich   Ljubljana

F R A N C E   Genève   SWITZERLAND   LIECHTENSTEIN   SLOVENIA

Clermont-   Lyon   Torino   Milano   Trieste   Zagreb

La Coruña   Bay of   Ferrand   Rhône   Venezia   CROATIA

Biscay   Bordeaux   Genova   I   BOSNIA-

Porto   Bilbao   Marseille   MONACO   Firenze   HERZEGOVI

PORTUGAL   Valladolid   ANDORRA   T   Sarajev

Toulouse   SAN   A   Split

Madrid   Zaragoza   Corse   MARINO   L

Lisboa   SPAIN   Barcelona   Bastia   Roma   Y

Toledo   Ajaccio

Faro   Valencia   Balearic Islands   Sardegna   Olbia   Napoli

Sevilla   Menorca   TYRRHENIAN   Taranto

Murcia   Ibiza   Mallorca   SEA

Málaga   Cagliari   Palermo   Messina

Tanger   Gibraltar (U.K.)   Reggio di Calabria

Ceuta (Sp.)   M E D I T E R R A N E A N   Sicilia

Madeira   Melilla   Alger

(Port.)   Casablanca   Rabat   (Sp.)   Oran   Tunis

MOROCCO   A L G E R I A   TUNISIA   MALTA   S E A

Islas Canarias   Marrakech

(Sp.)

D   10   E   0   F   10   G

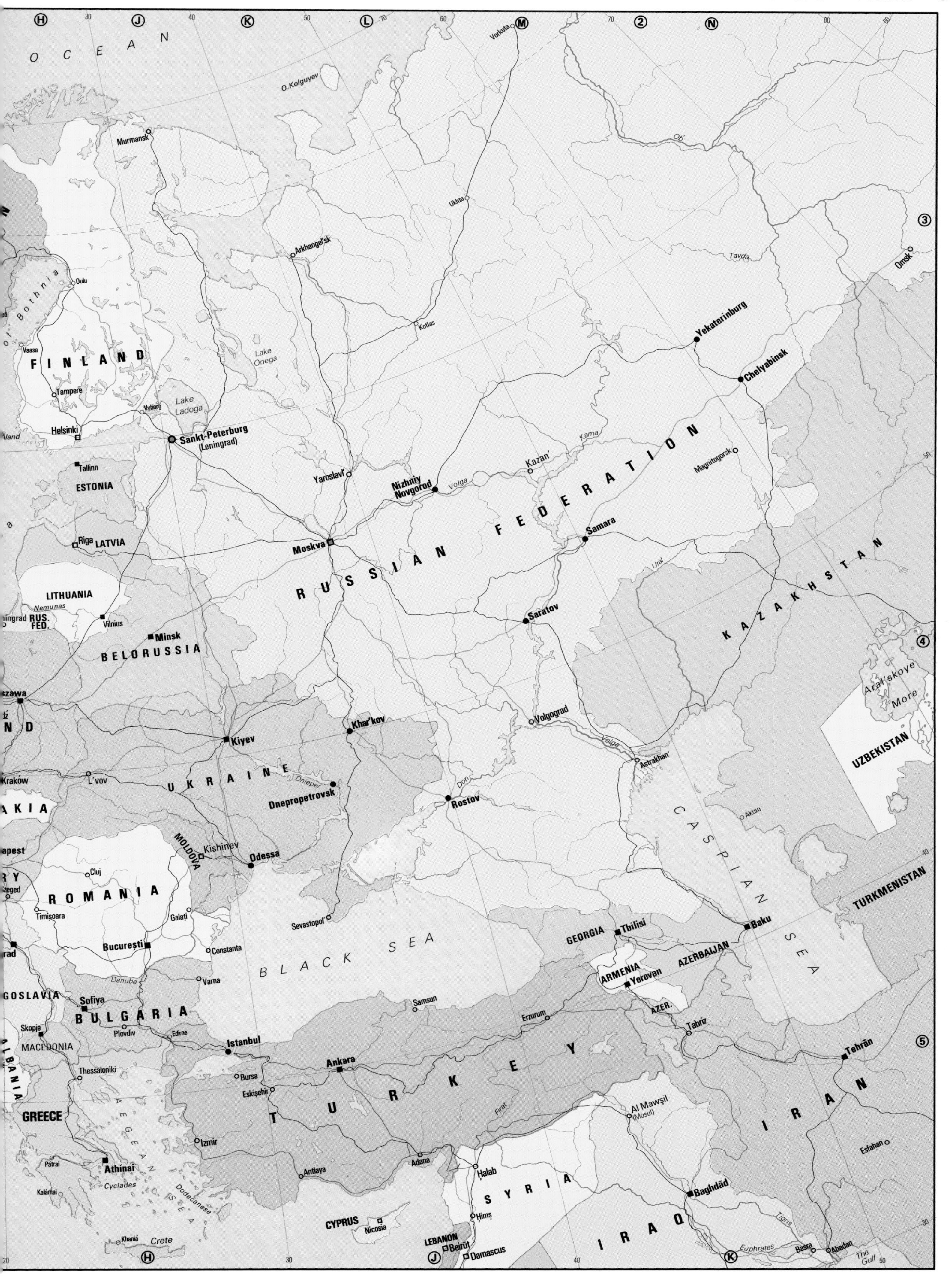
OCEAN
O.Kolguyev
Vorkuta
Murmansk
Ukhta
Arkhangel'sk
Oulu
Bothnia
Vaasa
FINLAND
Tampere
Helsinki
Vyborg
Lake Ladoga
Lake Onega
Kotlas
Ob'
Tavda
Omsk
Yekaterinburg
Chelyabinsk
Sankt-Peterburg (Leningrad)
Tallinn
ESTONIA
Riga
LATVIA
LITHUANIA
Nemunas
Vilnius
RUS. FED.
Minsk
BELORUSSIA
Yaroslavl'
Nizhniy Novgorod
Volga
Kazan'
Kama
Magnitogorsk
Moskva
RUSSIAN FEDERATION
Samara
Ural
Saratov
KAZAKHSTAN
Aral'skoye More
UZBEKISTAN
Kiyev
Khar'kov
Volgograd
Astrakhan'
Kraków
L'vov
UKRAINE
Dnieper
Dnepropetrovsk
Don
Rostov
Aktau
CASPIAN SEA
MOLDOVA
Kishinev
Odessa
Cluj
ROMANIA
Timişoara
Galaţi
Bucureşti
Constanta
Sevastopol'
BLACK SEA
GEORGIA
Tbilisi
Baku
TURKMENISTAN
ARMENIA
Yerevan
AZERBAIJAN
AZER.
Danube
Varna
Sofiya
BULGARIA
Plovdiv
Edirne
Samsun
Erzurum
Tabrīz
Tehrān
Skopje
MACEDONIA
Istanbul
Thessaloniki
Bursa
Ankara
Eskişehir
TURKEY
GREECE
AEGEAN SEA
Izmir
Firat
Al Mawşil (Mosul)
IRAN
Esfahan
Pátrai
Athínai
Antlaya
Adana
Halab
SYRIA
Baghdād
Kalámai
Cyclades
Dodecanese
Hims
IRAQ
Tigris
CYPRUS
Nicosia
LEBANON
Beirut
Damascus
Euphrates
Basra
Abadan
The Gulf
Khaniá
Crete
H J K L M N

1:7.5M

0 100 200 300 km
0 50 100 150 mls
ICELAND
Arctic Circle
Grimsey
Bolungarvik
Ísafjörður
Siglufjörður
Olafsfjörður
Húsavík
Dalvík
Sauðárkrókur
Akureyri
Blönduós
Bakkaflói
Njarðvík
Seyðisfjörður
Neskaupstaður
Eskifjörður
Biargtangar
Breiðafjörður
Stykkishólmur
Faxaflói
Akranes
Reykjavík
Kópavogur
Hafnarfjörður
Keflavík
Grindavík
Selfoss
Vestmannaeyjar
Surtsey
Langjökull
Hofsjökull
Vatnajökull
Mýrdalsjökull
Ingólfshöfði
Öræfajökull 2119
Snæfell 1833
at the same scale
Føroyar (Den.)
Streymoy
Vágar
Tórshavn
Sandoy
Suduroy
at the same scale
ARCTIC OCEAN
BARENTS SEA
NORWEGIAN SEA
NORWAY
SWEDEN
FINLAND
Lappland
Lofoten
Vesterålen
Nordkapp
Honningsvåg
Hammerfest
Vardø
Vadsø
Kirkenes
Alta
Lakselv
Karasjok
Kautokeino
Tromsø
Finnsnes
Andenes
Harstad
Narvik
Kiruna
Gällivare
Bodø
Mo-i-Rana
Mosjøen
Luleå
Boden
Haparanda
Tornio
Kemi
Rovaniemi
Oulu
Murmansk
Kandalaksha
Apatity
Monchegorsk
Kol'skiy poluostrov
Trondheim
Kristiansund
Molde
Ålesund
Bergen
Stavanger
Haugesund
Oslo
Drammen
Lillehammer
Kristiansand
Östersund
Sundsvall
Umeå
Skellefteå
Vaasa
Gulf of Bothnia
Gävle
Uppsala
Stockholm
Västerås
Örebro
Norrköping
Linköping
Jönköping
Göteborg
Malmö
Helsingborg
Karlskrona
Kalmar
Gotland
Åland
Turku
Helsinki (Helsingfors)
Tampere
Jyväskylä
Kuopio
Lahti
Pori
Gulf of Finland
Sankt-Peterburg (Leningrad)
Tallinn
ESTONIA
Tartu
Pärnu
Gulf of Riga
Riga
LATVIA
Liepāja
Daugavpils
LITHUANIA
Šiauliai
Klaipėda
Kaunas
Vilnius
RUSSIAN FEDERATION
Pskov
Novgorod
Lake Ladoga
Minsk
BELORUSSIA
BALTIC SEA
Skagerrak
Kattegat
North Sea
DENMARK
København
Ålborg
Århus
Odense
Esbjerg
Bornholm (Den.)
Kaliningrad
RUS. FED.
Gulf of Gdańsk
Gdańsk
Gdynia
POLAND
Szczecin
Bydgoszcz
Toruń
Warszawa
Poznań
Białystok
Brest
GERMANY
Kiel
Lübeck
Hamburg
Bremen
Rostock
Hannover
Berlin
Harwich

1:5M

50   100   150   200 km
50   100 mls

NORWAY

Herma Ness
Unst
Isbister   Fetlar
St Magnus B.   Yell   Shetland
Whalsay
Foula   Lerwick
Sumburgh Hd

Nordhordland
Dale
Bergen
Sunnhordland   Stord
Leirvik   Haugtjørn
Bømlo
Skjold
Karmøy   Boknafj

Stavanger
Sandnes

Fair Isle

Westray
Rousay   Sanday
N.Rona   Sule Skerry   Stronsay
Stromness   Kirkwall
Stack Skerry   Hoy   Scapa Flow   **Orkney**
Duncansby Hd

Flannan Is
Butt of Lewis   C.Wrath
Thurso
Ben Hope 927   Wick
Stornoway   Ben More Assynt 998   Helmsdale
Lewis   Ullapool   Dornoch   Dornoch Firth
St Kilda   Harris   Dingwall   Moray Firth   Elgin   Banff   Fraserburgh
N.Uist   Inverness   Spey   Peterhead
Portree   Skye   Kyle of Lochalsh   L.Ness   Ben Macdui 1309   Buchan Ness
S.Uist   Fort Augustus   Dee   Aberdeen
Barra   Rum   Mallaig   **SCOTLAND**   Don
Fort William   Braemar   Stonehaven
Ben Nevis 1344   Ben Lawers 1214   Pitlochry   Montrose
Coll   Grampian Mts   Arbroath
Tiree   Mull   Oban   L.Awe   Perth   Dundee   St Andrews
L.Lomond   F.of Tay
Colonsay   Jura   L.Lomond   Stirling   Kirkcaldy
F.of Lorn   Greenock   Glasgow   Edinburgh   F.of Forth
Islay   Paisley   Motherwell   St Abbs Hd
Irvine   Kilmarnock   Galashiels   Berwick-upon-Tweed
Campbeltown   Arran   Ayr   White Coomb 822   Holy I.
Malin Hd   F.of Clyde   Merrick 843   Moffat   Hawick   Alnwick
Tory I.   Rathlin I.   Girvan   Nith   Cheviots   Morpeth   Blyth
Aran I.   Errigal 752   Coleraine   Stranraer   Dumfries   Newcastle upon Tyne
Rossan Pt   Londonderry   **N.IRELAND**   Larne   Kirkcudbright   Carlisle   Gateshead   S.Shields
Donegal   Ballymena   Bangor   Luce B.   Solway Firth   Pennines   Sunderland
Erris Hd   Donegal B.   L.Neagh   Belfast   Penrith   Durham   Hartlepool
Enniskillen   Omagh   Portadown   Isle of Man   Scafell Pike 977   Darlington   Middlesbrough
L.Erne   Armagh   Douglas   Kendal   Yorkshire Moors   Scarborough
Sligo B.   Sligo   Monaghan   Newry   Barrow-in-Furness   Flamborough Hd
Achill I.   L.Conn   Ballina   Cavan   Dundalk   Morecambe   Lancaster   Ouse   York
Clew B.   Castlebar   Boyle   Roscommon   Longford   Blackpool   Harrogate   Hull
L.Mask   Boyle   L.Allen   Drogheda   **IRISH SEA**   Preston   Bradford   Leeds   Spurn Hd
Slyne Hd   L.Corrib   Mullingar   L.Ree   Bolton   Huddersfield   Grimsby
Galway   Athlone   **Dublin**   Liverpool   **Manchester**   Doncaster   Humber
Aran Is   Galway B.   Monasterevin   (Baile Atha Cliath)   Birkenhead   Warrington   Sheffield   Lincoln
Ennis   L.Derg   **REP. OF**   Dun Laoghaire   Anglesey   Chester   Stoke-on-Trent   The Wash
Kilrush   Nenagh   **IRELAND**   Bray   Bangor   Crewe   Derby   Nottingham
Dingle   Tralee   Tipperary   Carlow   Wicklow   Snowdon 1085   Dee   Shrewsbury   Trent   King's Lynn
Dingle B.   Clonmel   Kilkenny   Arklow   Pwllheli   Cambrian Mts   Leicester   Norwich   Great Yarmouth
Carrauntoohill 1041   Waterford   Wexford   Cardigan Bay   Aberystwyth   **WALES**   **Birmingham**   Wolverhampton   Coventry   Peterborough   Lowestoft
Killarney   Blackwater   Rosslare   Builth Wells   Worcester   Northampton   Bedford   Cambridge   Ipswich   Felixstowe
Cork   Dungarvan   St George's Chan.   St David's Hd   Brecon   Wye   Milton Keynes   Newmarket   Colchester   Harwich
Bantry   Youghal   Fishguard   Carmarthen   Gloucester   Luton   Chelmsford
Bantry B.   Old Hd of Kinsale   Pembroke   Swansea   Newport   Oxford   **London**   Southend-on-Sea
C.Clear   Lundy I.   Cardiff   Swindon   **Bristol**   Windsor   Reading   Maidstone   Thames   Canterbury
Bristol Chan.   Bath   Weston-super-Mare   Guildford   Crawley   Dover   Str.of Dover
Barnstaple   Taunton   Salisbury   Winchester   Hastings   Folkestone
Bude   Southampton   Brighton   Eastbourne
Newquay   Exeter   Bournemouth   Portsmouth   Isle of Wight
Truro   Dartmoor   Weymouth
Penzance   Plymouth   Torquay   **English Channel**
Land's End   Falmouth   Prawle Pt
Isles of Scilly   Lizard Pt   C.de la Hague   Pte de Barfleur

NORTH SEA

NETHERLANDS
Den Helder
Alkmaar
Texel
Vlieland
Haarlem
Leiden
's-Gravenhage (Den Haag)
Rotterdam   Dordrecht
Esbjerg   Vlissingen   Zeebrugge   **Antwerpen**   Brugge
Oostende   Gent   **BELGIUM**   Mechelen
Dunkerque   Kortrijk   **Bruxelles (Brussel)**
Calais   Tourcoing   Roubaix   Soignies
St-Omer   **Lille**   Tournai   Mons
Boulogne   Béthune   Lens   Valenciennes   Charleroi
Douai   Denain   Maubeuge
Montreuil   Arras   Cambrai   Fourmies
Le Tréport   Abbeville   St-Quentin
Dieppe   Amiens   Laon
Fécamp   Neufchâtel   Montdidier   Compiègne   Oise   Aisne   Reims
Le Havre   Bolbec   Beauvais   Soissons   Senlis   Château-Thierry   Épernay
Cherbourg   Deauville   Rouen   Elbeuf   Louviers   Cergy   Pontoise   Meaux   Sézanne
Alderney   Bayeux   Seine   Louviers   Mantes   ÎLE-DE-FRANCE   Provins   Romilly-s.-S.
Guernsey   Sark   Valognes   Lisieux   Evreux   Versailles   **Paris**   Melun   Troyes
Channel Is (To U.K.)   Jersey   St Helier   St-Lô   Caen   Eure   Dreux   Rambouillet   Étampes   Fontainebleau
Golfe de St-Malo   Coutances   Orne   Argentan   Chartres   Sens
Granville   Mont-St-Michel   Domfront   Mayenne   **FRANCE**   Alençon
Roscoff   St-Malo   Fougères
Morlaix   Dinan
Brest   St-Brieuc   Carhaix-Plouguer
I.d'Ouessant

1:2.5M

0   25   50   75   100 km
0   25   50 mls

Inset (Shetland/Orkney area)

Tórshavn-Seydhisfjördhur
Hanstholm-Bergen
Norway
U.K.
at the same scale

Shetland
Herma Ness
Unst
Yell
Fetlar
Whalsay
Muckle Roe
Brae
St. Magnus Bay
Hillswick
Isbister
The Faither
Scalloway
Lerwick
Bressay
Noss
Gruthess
Papa Stour
Foula
Fair Isle
Fitful Hd
Sumburgh Hd
Aberdeen
Fair Isle
Stromness

Main map

DOGGER BANK
NORTH SEA
Devil's Hole
Long Forties
Buchan Deep
Farne Deep

Esbjerg-Göteborg
Bergen-Stavanger
Aberdeen
Fair Isle

Cod △
Josephine △
Albuskjell △
Duncan △
Argyll △
Lomond ▲
Clyde △
Fulmar △
Auk △
Buchan △
Montrose △
Piper △
Petronella △
Claymore △
Tartan △
Scapa △
Highlander △
S. E. Forties
Forties
Beatrice △

Orkney
N. Ronaldsay
Sanday
Stronsay
Eday
Papa Westray
Westray
Rousay
Shapinsay
Kirkwall
Birsay
Mainland
Stromness
Scapa Flow
S. Ronaldsay
Burray
Hoy
Duncansby Hd
John o' Groats
Dunnet Hd
Pentland Firth
Lerwick

Highland / Scotland mainland
C. Wrath
Durness
Ben Hope 927
Tongue
Ben Kilbreck 961
Ben Loyal
Thurso
Wick
Lybster
Helmsdale
Brora
Golspie
Loth
Dornoch
Dornoch Firth
Tain
Tarbat Ness
Cromarty
Cromarty Firth
Moray Firth
Nairn
Forres
Elgin
Lossiemouth
Buckie
Keith
Huntly
Banff
Deveron
Fraserburgh
Kinnairds Hd
Buchan Ness
Peterhead
Aberdeen
Girdle Ness
Stonehaven
Inverurie
Ythan
Don
Dufftown
Grantown-on-Spey
Spey
Aviemore
Cairngorms
Ben Macdui 1310
Braemar
Lochnagar 1155
Ballater
Dee
Banchory
Brechin
N. Esk
S. Esk
Forfar
Montrose
Arbroath
Kirriemuir
Blairgowrie
Sidlaw Hills
Dundee
Tay
Perth
St Andrews
Fife Ness
Cupar
Firth of Forth
Glenrothes
Kirkcaldy
Methil
North Berwick
Dunfermline
Edinburgh
Livingston
Falkirk
Coatbridge
Motherwell
Hamilton
Glasgow
Paisley
Greenock
Helensburgh
Dumbarton
Stirling
Callander
Crieff
Auchterarder
Kinross
Loch Leven
Pentland Hills

Sule Skerry
Stack Skerry
N. Rona
Sula Sgeir
Flannan Is
St Kilda

Western Isles / Outer Hebrides
Butt of Lewis
Lewis
Stornoway
Loch Roag
Harris
Tarbert
Scalpay
Taransay
Scarp
Sd of Harris
North Uist
Benbecula
South Uist
Lochmaddy
Lochboisdale
Eriskay
Barra
Castlebay
Barra Hd
Monach Is
Pabbay
Sd of Barra

Inner Hebrides / West coast
Little Minch
The Minch
North Minch
Rubha Hunish
Uig
Portree
Isle of Skye
Cuillin Hills
L. Snizort
Raasay
Sd of Raasay
Broadford
Kyle of Lochalsh
L. Bracadale
Canna
Rum
Eigg
Muck
Coll
Tiree
Mull
Iona
Staffa
Ulva
Tobermory
Ardnamurchan Pt
Mallaig
Arisaig
L. Morar
L. Shiel
Loch nan Uamh
Fort William
Ben Nevis 1344
Loch Linnhe
L. Sunart
Morvern
Oban
L. Etive
L. Awe
Firth of Lorn
Colonsay
Jura
Islay
Sd of Jura
Port Askaig
Port Ellen
The Oa
Mull of Oa
Gigha
Kintyre
Campbeltown
Mull of Kintyre
Sanda I.
Sd of Bute
Rothesay
Bute
Arran
Brodick
Lamlash
Ardrossan
Largs
Firth of Clyde
Arrochar
Inveraray
Ardrishaig
Lochgilphead
Tarbert
Crinan

Ben More Assynt 998
Lochinver
Ben Dearg 1084
Ullapool
Enard Bay
Eddrachillis Bay
Loch Broom
L. Maree
Gairloch
Torridon
L. Torridon
Applecross
Ben Wyvis 1045
Dingwall
Beauly
Inverness
Loch Ness
Fort Augustus
Ben Attow 1031
Kyle of Lochalsh
Loch Lochy
Loch Oich
Kingussie
Newtonmore
Monadhliath Mts
Drumochter
Blair Atholl
Pitlochry
Aberfeldy
Ben Lawers 1214
L. Tay
L. Rannoch
L. Ericht
L. Tummel
Killin
Crianlarich
Ben Lomond
Loch Lomond
Loch Fyne
Loch Awe

GRAMPIAN
HIGHLAND
TAYSIDE
CENTRAL
FIFE
LOTHIAN
STRATHCLYDE
BORDERS
DUMFRIES AND GALLOWAY
NORTHUMBERLAND
TYNE AND WEAR
Grampian Mountains
S C O T L A N D
Cheviot Hills

Borders / Southern Scotland
Kelso
Jedburgh
Hawick
Selkirk
Galashiels
Peebles
Moffat
Lammermuir Hills
Moorfoot Hills
Haddington
Duns
Berwick-upon-Tweed
St Abb's Hd
Eyemouth
Holy I.
Tweed
Coldstream
Lauder
Innerleithen
Tweedsmuir Hills
Broad Law
Ettrick
Yarrow
Newcastleton
Langholm
Lockerbie
Annan
Dumfries
Castle Douglas
Kirkcudbright
New Galloway
Newton Stewart
Merrick 843
Rhins of Kells
Wigtown
Stranraer
Corsewall Pt
Mull of Galloway
Portpatrick
Luce Bay
Girvan
Ballantrae
Maybole
Ayr
Prestwick
Troon
Irvine
Kilmarnock
Cumnock
Dean

Northern England / North East
Alnwick
Amble
Morpeth
Newcastle upon Tyne
Tynemouth
Sth Shields
Gateshead
Sunderland
Blyth
Whitley Bay
Hexham
Haltwhistle
Alston
Carlisle
Longtown
Eden
Cheviot 816
Northumberland Nat. Park
Kielder

Northern Ireland
Donegal
Errigal 752
Blue Stack Mts
L. Swilly
Malin Hd
Inishowen
Buncrana
Carndonagh
Sheep Haven
Dunfanaghy
Letterkenny
Lifford
Strabane
Sperrin Mts
Londonderry
Coleraine
Portrush
Portstewart
Limavady
Magherafelt
Cookstown
Omagh
Tyrone
Ballymoney
Ballycastle
Rathlin I.
Fair Hd
Antrim Hills
Ballymena
Larne
Bann
Newtown Stewart
Antrim

Stanton Banks

North Channel

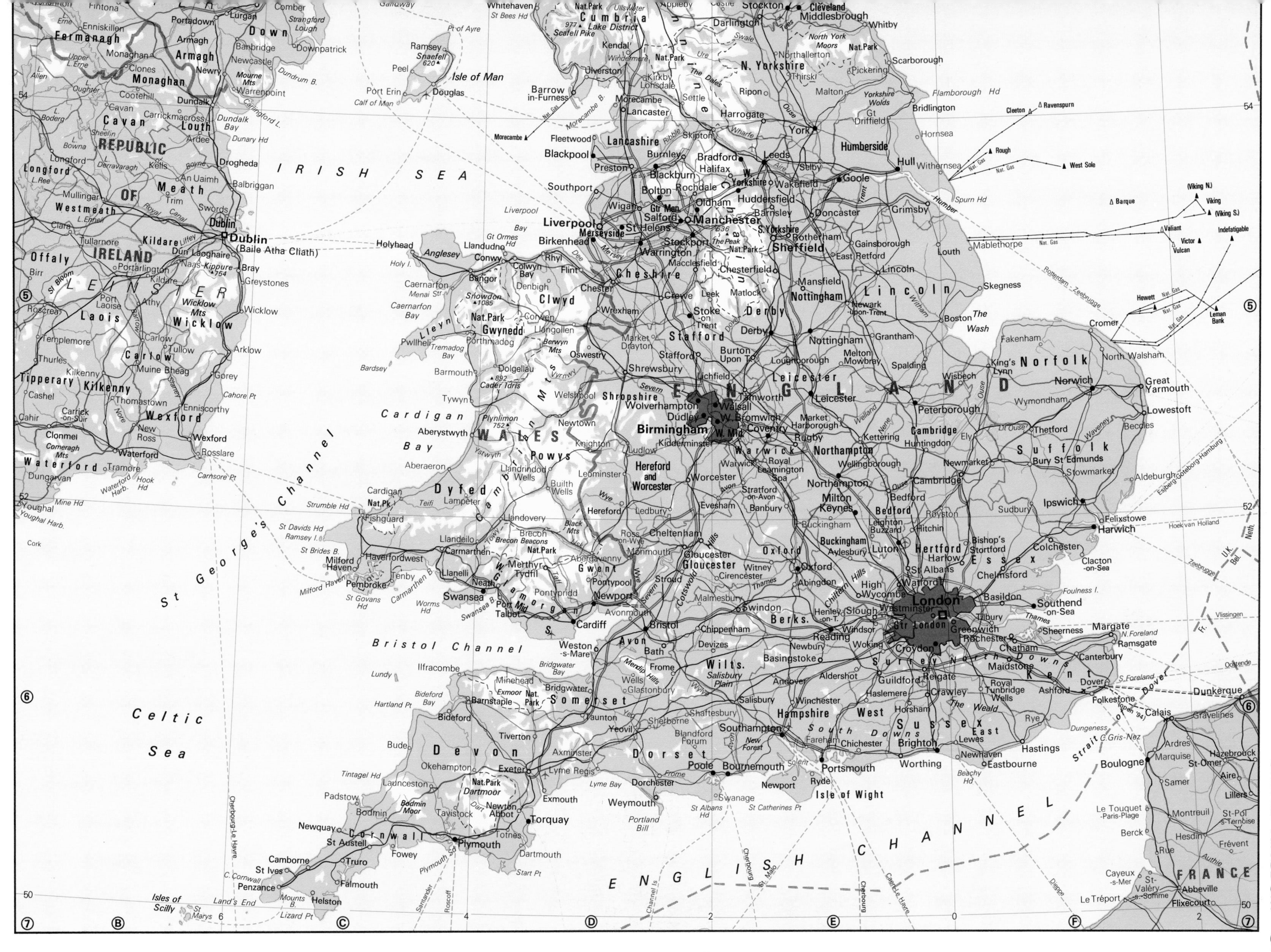
IRISH SEA
ENGLISH CHANNEL
Celtic Sea
St George's Channel
Bristol Channel
Cardigan Bay
Isle of Man
Isle of Wight
Isles of Scilly
REPUBLIC OF IRELAND
LEINSTER
FRANCE
ENGLAND
WALES
London
Gtr London
Birmingham
Manchester
Liverpool
Leeds
Sheffield
Bristol
Cardiff
Swansea
Newport
Nottingham
Leicester
Northampton
Cambridge
Norwich
Ipswich
Peterborough
Oxford
Southampton
Portsmouth
Brighton
Plymouth
Exeter
Torquay
Dublin (Baile Atha Cliath)
Hull
York
Bradford
Preston
Blackpool
Coventry
Stoke on Trent
Derby
Lincoln
Gloucester
Worcester
Hereford
Shrewsbury
Chester
Wrexham
Lancaster
Humberside
Cleveland
Middlesbrough
Stockton
Cumbria
Lancashire
Merseyside
Cheshire
Derby
Nottingham
Lincoln
Norfolk
Suffolk
Essex
Kent
Surrey
West Sussex
East
Hampshire
Dorset
Devon
Cornwall
Somerset
Wilts.
Avon
Berks.
Oxford
Buckingham
Bedford
Hertford
Northampton
Leicester
Warwick
Stafford
Shropshire
Hereford and Worcester
Gloucester
Clwyd
Gwynedd
Powys
Dyfed
Gwent
N. Yorkshire
S. Yorkshire
W. Yorkshire
Fermanagh
Armagh
Down
Monaghan
Cavan
Louth
Meath
Westmeath
Longford
Offaly
Kildare
Laois
Wicklow
Carlow
Kilkenny
Tipperary
Wexford
Waterford
Dover
Folkestone
Calais
Boulogne
Dunkerque
Abbeville
Snowdon 1085
Cader Idris 892
Plynlimon 752
Scafell Pike 977
Snaefell 620
Kippure 754
Bodmin Moor
Dartmoor
Exmoor
The Wash
Humber
Thames
Severn
Trent
Wye
Strait of Dover
Cherbourg-Le Havre

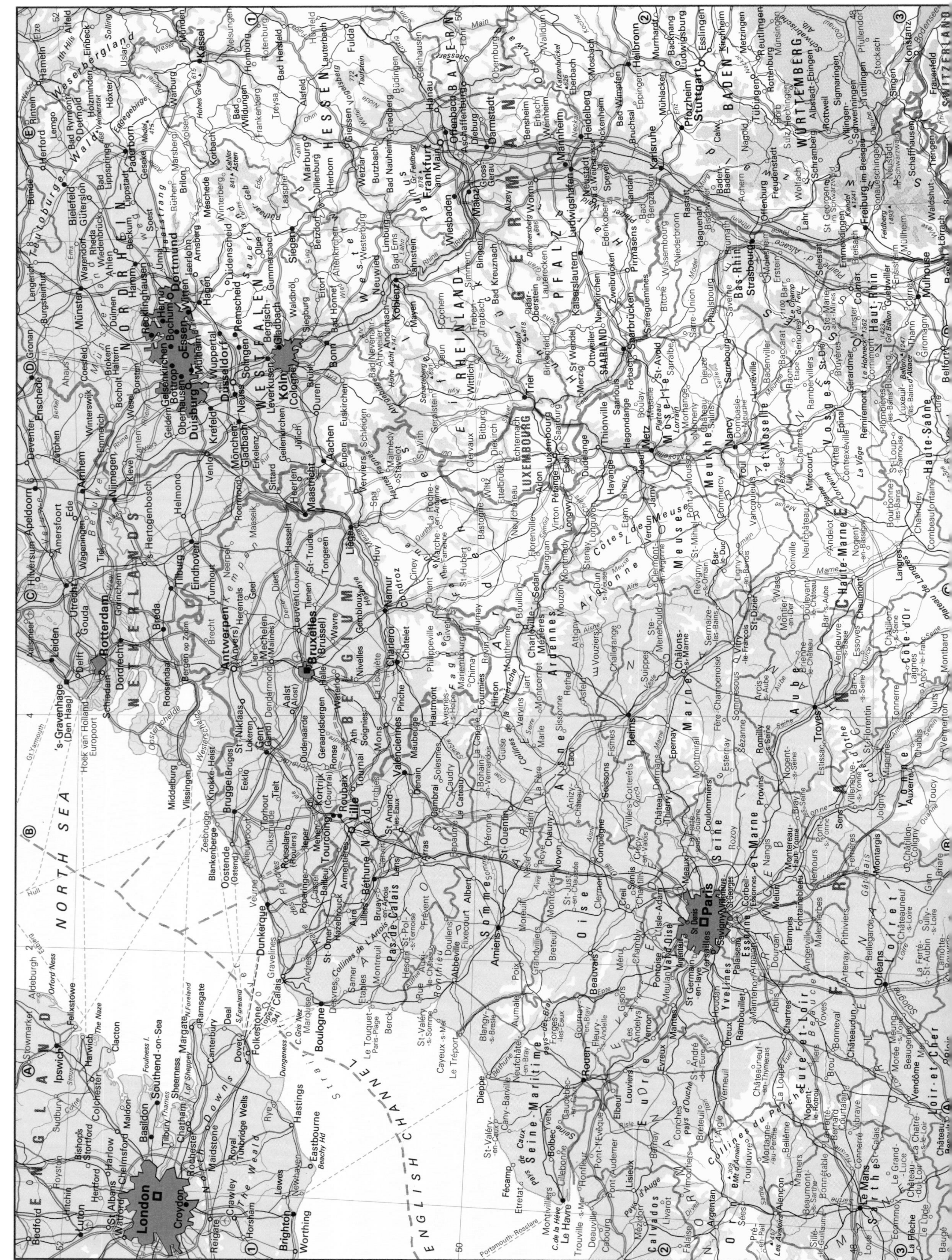

AUSTRIA
SWITZERLAND
LIECHTENSTEIN
SLOVENIA
CROATIA
MONACO
SAN MARINO
LOMBARDIA
PIEMONTE
VENETO
TRENTINO
EMILIA ROMAGNA
TOSCANA
LIGURIA
MARCHE
UMBRIA
FRIULI
VENEZIA GIULIA
VALLE D'AOSTA
VORALBERG
SALZBURG
TIROL
KÄRNTEN
PROVENCE
ADRIATIC SEA
LIGURIAN SEA
Golfo di Venezia
Golfo di Genova
Côte d'Azur
Milano (Milan)
Torino (Turin)
Genova (Genoa)
Venezia (Venice)
Bologna
Firenze (Florence)
Verona
Padova (Padua)
Trieste (Trient)
Bolzano (Bozen)
Innsbruck
Bern (Berne)
Zürich
Basel (Bâle)
Luzern (Lucerne)
Lausanne
Genève (Geneva)
Grenoble
Marseille
Nice
Toulon
Dijon
Besançon
Chambéry
Annecy
Brescia
Bergamo
Parma
Modena
Ravenna
Rimini
Ancona
Pisa
Livorno
Lucca
Perugia
La Spezia
Alessandria
Cuneo
Novara
Como
Trento
Vicenza
Udine
Klagenfurt
Corse (Fr.)

1:5M

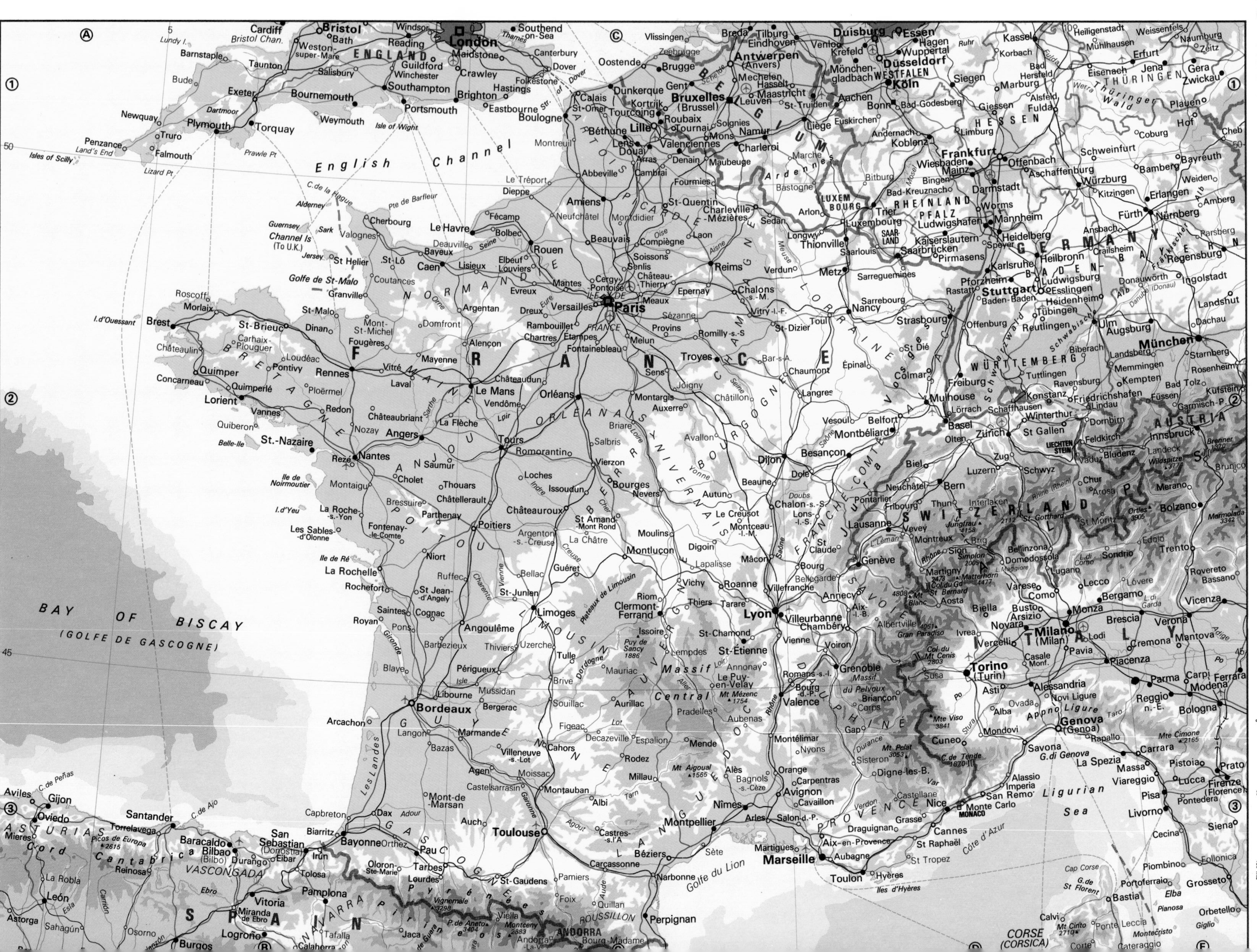

BAY OF BISCAY
(G. DE GASCOGNE)
BALEARIC ISLANDS
(ISLAS BALEARES)
(Sp.)
M E D I T E R R A N E A N S E A
F R A N C E
A L G E R I A
MOROCCO
P O R T U G A L
S P A I N
CASTILLA LA VIEJA
CASTILLA LA NUEVA
ARAGÓN
CATALUÑA
NAVARRA
VASCONGADAS
ASTURIAS
GALICIA
LEÓN
EXTREMADURA
ANDALUCIA
MURCIA
VALENCIA
ROUSSILLON
GASCOGNE
Pyrénées
Pirineos
Cordillera Cantabrica
Sierra Morena
La Mancha
Sa Nevada
Sa de Guadarrama
Sa de Gredos
Montes de Toledo
Serrana de Cuenca
Sa de Albarracín
Sa de Gudar
Sa de Segura
Sa de Alcaraz
Sa de los Filabres
Golfo de Valencia
Golfo de Cádiz
Costa de la Luz
Costa del Sol
Costa Blanca
Costa Brava
Golfe du Lion
Str. of Gibraltar
Massif de l'Ouarsenis
Mts du Hodna
Plat. du Sersou
Dahra
Rif
Madrid
Barcelona
Valencia
Sevilla
(Seville)
Zaragoza
Bilbao
Málaga
Córdoba
Granada
Murcia
Alicante
Cartagena
Valladolid
Salamanca
Toledo
Burgos
Santander
Oviedo
Gijón
León
La Coruña
Vigo
Lisboa
(Lisbon)
Porto
(Oporto)
Coimbra
Palma
de Mallorca
Mallorca
Menorca
Ibiza
Formentera
Marseille
Toulouse
Montpellier
Perpignan
Toulon
Nîmes
Béziers
Carcassonne
Bayonne
Biarritz
Pau
Tarbes
Lourdes
Alger
(Algiers)
Oran
Blida
Sidi-bel-Abbès
Mostaganem
Tanger
(Tangiers)
Tetouan
Ceuta (Sp.)
Melilla (Sp.)
Gibraltar (U.K.)
Algeciras
Cádiz
Huelva
Badajoz
Mérida
Cáceres
Albacete
Cuenca
Teruel
Huesca
Lérida
(Lleida)
Tarragona
Gerona
(Girona)
Pamplona
Vitoria
Logroño
San Sebastian
(Donostia)
ANDORRA
Almeria
Jaén
Ciudad Real
Guadalajara
Segovia
Avila
Soria
Zamora
Palencia
Lugo
Orense
(Ourense)
Pontevedra
Santiago de C.
Faro
Évora
Setúbal
Ebro
Duero
Tajo
Guadiana
Guadalquivir
Júcar
P. de Aneto
3404
Mulhacén
3482
P. de Almanzor
2592

1:5M

0 50 100 150 200 km

0 50 100 mls

FRANCE
SWITZERLAND
GERMANY
AUSTRIA
SLOVENIA
CROATIA
BOSNIA
ITALIA
CORSE (CORSICA)
SARDEGNA (SARDINIA)
SICILIA (SICILY)
MALTA
ALGERIA
TUNISIA
Ligurian Sea
TYRRHENIAN SEA
ADRIATIC
MEDITERRANEAN
Strait of Bonifacio
Sicilian Channel
Malta Channel
Str. de Messina
Roma (Rome)
Milano (Milan)
Torino (Turin)
Genova (Genoa)
Firenze (Florence)
Venezia (Venice)
Napoli (Naples)
Palermo
Cagliari
Tunis
Wien
München
Zagreb
Ljubljana
Marseille
Lyon

Budapest
Miskolc
Nyíregyháza
Debrecen
Eger
Salgótarján
Gyöngyös
Esztergom
Győr
Tatabánya
Székesfehérvár
Szolnok
Kecskemét
Cegléd
Karcag
Berettyóújfalu
Hajdúböszörmény
Békéscsaba
Orosháza
Hódmezővásárhely
Szeged
Makó
Kiskunhalas
Szekszárd
Baja
Pécs
Kaposvár
Dombóvár
Paks
Siófok
Veszprém
Dunaújváros
Kiskunfélegyháza
Nagykőrös
Mátészalka
Újfehértó
Satu Mare
Baia Mare
Carei
Marghita
Zalău
Oradea
Salonta
Cluj-Napoca
Turda
Dej
Bistrița
Reghin
Tîrgu Mureș
Mediaș
Sighișoara
Alba Iulia
Sebeș
Sibiu
Făgăraș
Brașov
Deva
Orăștie
Hunedoara
Arad
Lipova
Timișoara
Lugoj
Caransebeș
Reșița
Oravița
Tîrgu Jiu
Rîmnicu Vîlcea
Pitești
Tîrgoviște
Ploiești
București
(Bucharest)
Craiova
Slatina
Caracal
Alexandria
Giurgiu
Roșiori de Vede
Turnu Măgurele
Corabia
Calafat
Băilești
Dobreta-Turnu-Severin
Filiași
Suceava
Fălticeni
Pașcani
Iași
Roman
Piatra-Neamț
Bacău
Vaslui
Onești
Focșani
Galați
Brăila
Buzău
Rîmnicu Sărat
Tulcea
Babadag
Constanța
Medgidia
Mangalia
Călărași
Fetești
Slobozia
Hîrșova
Urziceni
Mizil
Sulina
Kishinev
(Chișinău)
Tiraspol'
Bendery
Odessa
Belgorod Dnestrovskiy
Komrat
Kagul
Bîrlad
Izmail
Reni
Kiliya
Vilkovo
Bolgrad
Artsiz
Sarata
MOLDOVA
UKRAINE
ROMANIA
HUNGARY
Carpații Meridionali
(Transylvanian Alps)
Novi Sad
Subotica
Sombor
Zrenjanin
Vršac
Pančevo
Beograd
(Belgrade)
Šabac
Smederevo
Smed. Palanka
Kragujevac
Čačak
Kraljevo
Kruševac
Niš
Leskovac
Pirot
Vranje
Zaječar
Bor
Paraćin
Ćuprija
Užice
Valjevo
Loznica
Novi Pazar
Priština
Mitrovica
Peć
Prizren
Uroševac
Dakovica
Podgorica
Nikšić
Kotor
Budva
Bar
Ulcinj
Dubrovnik
Trebinje
Mostar
Sarajevo
Zenica
Tuzla
Doboj
Bijeljina
Osijek
Vukovar
Vinkovci
Našice
Dakovo
YUGOSLAVIA
SERBIA
MONTENEGRO
Kosovo
Vojvodina
Sofiya
Pernik
Plovdiv
Pazardzhik
Stara Zagora
Kazanlŭk
Sliven
Yambol
Burgas
Varna
Shumen
Ruse
Razgrad
Dobrich
Silistra
Pleven
Lovech
Vidin
Lom
Mikhaylovgrad
Vratsa
Gabrovo
Veliko Tŭrnovo
Haskovo
Dimitrovgrad
Kŭrdzhali
Smolyan
Blagoevgrad
Kyustendil
Sandanski
Stanke Dimitrov
Botevgrad
Troyan
Karlovo
Asenovgrad
Elkhovo
Michurin
BULGARIA
Stara Planina
Rodopi Planina
Skopje
Kumanovo
Tetovo
Gostivar
Kičevo
Titov Veles
Prilep
Bitola
Ohrid
Strumica
Kavadarci
Gevgelija
MACEDONIA
Tiranë
Durrës
Shkodër
(Scutari)
Elbasan
Fier
Berat
Vlorë
Korçë
Gjirokastër
Sarandë
Lezhë
Lushnjë
Kavajë
ALBANIA
Thessaloníki
(Salonica)
Kavála
Dráma
Sérrai
Xánthi
Komotiní
Alexandroúpolis
Kilkís
Véroia
Edhessa
Flórina
Kastoría
Kozáni
Kateríni
Lárisa
Vólos
Tríkala
Kardhítsa
Ioánnina
Árta
Préveza
Lamía
Agrínion
Mesolóngion
Pátrai
Aíyion
Kórinthos
Árgos
Tripolis
Kalámai
Pírgos
Spartí
Athínai
(Athens)
Piraiévs
Khalkís
Thívai
Kérkira
(Corfu)
Kefallinía
Zákinthos
Lésvos
Khíos
Sámos
Límnos
Thásos
Samothráki
Náxos
Rhódos
Kárpathos
Crete
(Kríti)
Iráklion
Khaniá
Réthimnon
Sitía
Ierápetra
Kíthira
Cyclades
(Kikládhes)
Dodecanese
GREECE
Ólimbos
(Olympus)
2917
Ionian Islands
Istanbul
Üsküdar
Kartal
Edirne
Kırklareli
Lüleburgaz
Çorlu
Tekirdağ
Keşan
Gelibolu
(Gallipoli)
Çanakkale
Bursa
Balıkesir
İzmir
Manisa
Aydın
Denizli
Muğla
Bodrum
Milas
Söke
Akhisar
Soma
Bergama
Ayvalık
Edremit
Nazilli
Ödemiş
Alaşehir
Salihli
Turgutlu
TURKEY
Sea of Marmara
Bosporus
BLACK SEA
AEGEAN SEA
IONIAN SEA
Sea of Crete
Mirtoan Sea
Strait of Otranto
Brindisi
Lecce
Otranto
Gallipoli
Maglie
Manduria
C. Sta Maria di Leuca
20
25
45
40
35
E
F
G
1
2
3
4

1:5M

NORTH SEA
DENMARK
SWEDEN
NETHERLANDS
BELGIUM
LUXEMBOURG
GERMANY
FRANCE
SWITZERLAND
LIECHTENSTEIN
AUSTRIA
CZECH REPUBLIC
SLOVENIA
ITALY
Kattegat
BALT
København (Copenhagen)
Amsterdam
's-Gravenhage (Den Haag)
Bruxelles (Brussel)
Luxembourg
Berlin
Praha (Prague)
Wien (Vienna)
Ljubljana
Zagreb
Bratislava
Hamburg
Bremen
Hannover
Köln
Frankfurt
Stuttgart
München (Munich)
Dresden
Leipzig
Milano (Milan)
Torino (Turin)
Lyon
Genève
Zürich
Bern
Basel
Göteborg
Malmö
Szczecin
Poznań
Wrocław
NIEDERSACHSEN
NORDRHEIN-WESTFALEN
HESSEN
RHEINLAND-PFALZ
SAARLAND
BADEN-WÜRTTEMBERG
BAYERN
THÜRINGEN
SACHSEN
SACHSEN-ANHALT
BRANDENBURG
MECKLENBURG-VORPOMMERN
SCHLESWIG-HOLSTEIN
Venezia (Venice)
Golfo di Venezia

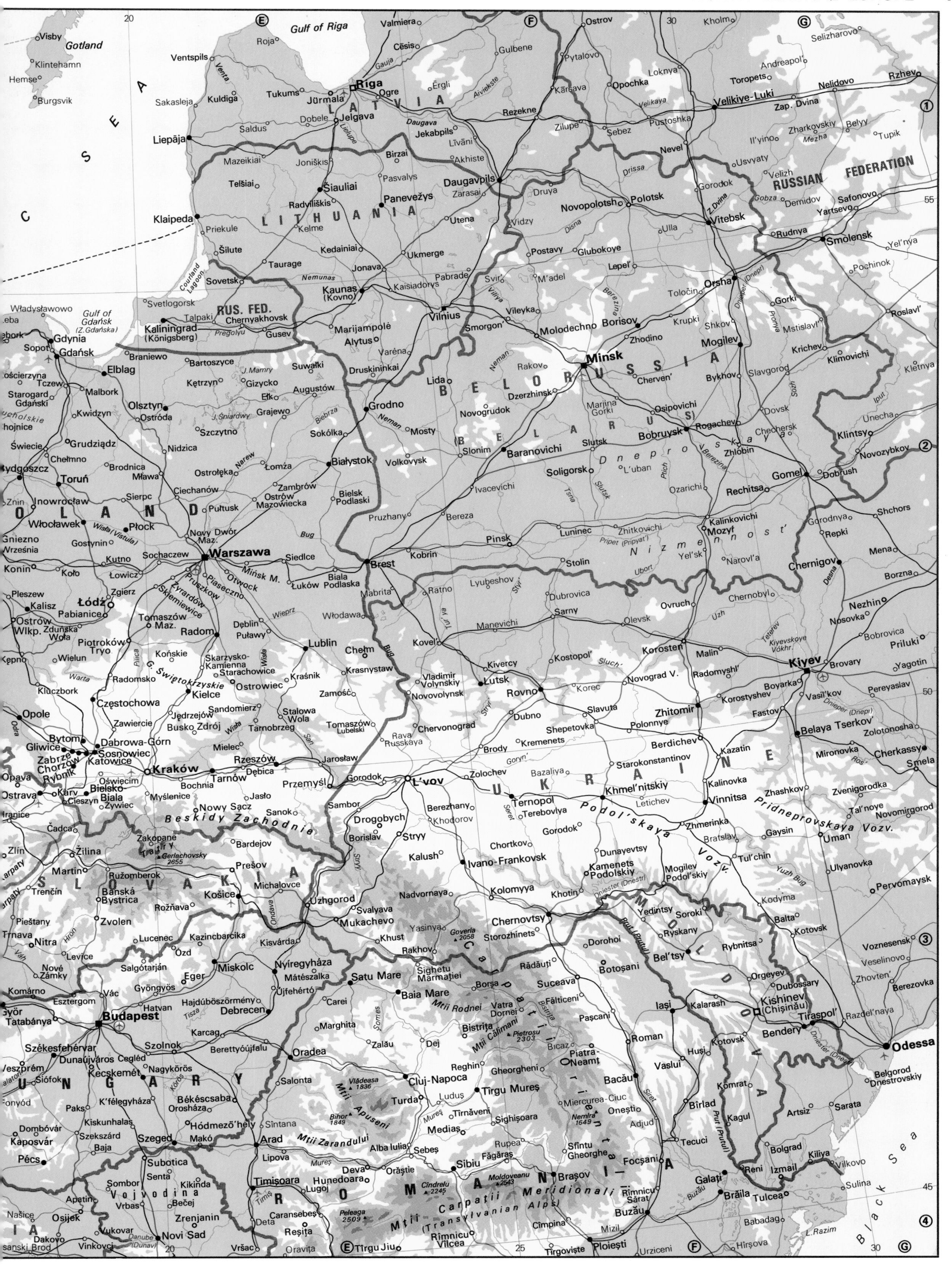
Visby
Gotland
Klintehamn
Hemse
Burgsvik
Gulf of Riga
Roja
Ventspils
Valmiera
Cēsis
Gulbene
Ostrov
Kholm
Selizharovo
Pytalovo
Andreapol'
Rzhev
Riga
Ērgli
Opochka
Loknya
Toropets
Nelidovo
Sakasleja
Kuldiga
Tukums
Jūrmala
Ogre
Kārsava
Velikiye-Luki
Zap. Dvina
LATVIA
Jelgava
Dobele
Rezekne
Pustoshka
Saldus
Daugava
Jekabpils
Zilupe
Sebez
Il'yino
Zharkovskiy
Belyy
Tupik
Liepāja
Līvāni
Nevel
Usvyaty
Mazeikiai
Joniškis
Birzai
Akhiste
Velizh
RUSSIAN FEDERATION
Telšiai
Šiauliai
Pasvalys
Daugavpils
Drissa
Gorodok
Radviliškis
Panevežys
Zarasai
Druya
Novopolotsk
Polotsk
Gobza
Demidov
Safonovo
Yartsevo
Klaipeda
LITHUANIA
Utena
Vidzy
Disna
Vitebsk
Priekule
Kelme
Ulla
Rudnya
Smolensk
Yel'nya
Šilute
Kedainiai
Postavy
Glubokoye
Ukmerge
Lepel'
Pochinok
Taurage
Jonava
Courland Lagoon
Nemunas
Pabrade
Svir'
M'adel
Orsha
Sovetsk
Kaunas (Kovno)
Kaisiadorys
Toločin
Dnepr
Gorki
Władysławowo
Gulf of Gdańsk (Z. Gdańska)
Svetlogorsk
RUS. FED.
Talpaki
Chernyakhovsk
Vilnius
Vileyka
Berezina
Krupki
Shkov
Pronya
Roslavl'
Kaliningrad (Königsberg)
Pregolya
Gusev
Marijampolė
Smorgon'
Molodechno
Borisov
Mstislavl'
Gdynia
Sopot
Gdańsk
Alytus
Varėna
Zhodino
Mogilev
Krichev
Braniewo
Bartoszyce
Druskininkai
Minsk
Klimovichi
Elbląg
Suwałki
Rakov
RUSSIA
Kletnya
Kościerzyna
Tczew
Kętrzyn
Giżycko
J. Mamry
Lida
BELORUSSIA
Cherven'
Bykhov
Slavgorod
Starogard Gdański
Malbork
Ełk
Augustów
Dzerzhinsk
Osipovichi
Olsztyn
Ostróda
Kwidzyn
Grajewo
Grodno
Novogrudok
Marjina Gorki
Iput
Unecha
Chojnice
J. Śniardwy
Biebrza
Neman
Mosty
Rogachev
Dovsk
Szczytno
Sokółka
BELARUS
Bobruysk
Chechersk
Klintsy
Świecie
Grudziądz
Nidzica
Slonim
Baranovichi
Slutsk
Dnepro
Zhlobin
Novozybkov
Chełmno
Białystok
Volkovysk
Soligorsk
L'uban
Bydgoszcz
Toruń
Brodnica
Mława
Ostrołęka
Narew
Łomża
Zambrów
Ptich
Gomel
Dobrush
Ciechanów
Ostrów Mazowiecka
Bielsk Podlaski
Ivacevichi
Ozarichi
Rechitsa
Znin
Inowrocław
Sierpc
POLAND
Pułtusk
Pruzhany
Bereza
Shchors
Włocławek
Płock
Wisła (Vistula)
Nowy Dwór Maz.
Bug
Luninec
Zhitkovichi
Kalinkovichi
Mozyr
Gorodnya
Repki
Gniezno
Gostynin
Pinsk
Pripet (Pripyat')
Nizmennost'
Września
Kutno
Sochaczew
Warszawa
Siedlce
Brest
Kobrin
Stolin
Yel'sk
Narovl'a
Mena
Konin
Koło
Łowicz
Mińsk M.
Biała Podlaska
Łuków
Ubort
Chernigov
Desna
Borzna
Pleszew
Łódź
Zgierz
Otwock
Piaseczno
Pruszków
Żyrardów
Skierniewice
Mabrita
Ratno
Lyubeshov
Styr'
Dubrovica
Chernobyl
Nezhin
Kalisz
Pabianice
Tomaszów Maz.
Dęblin
Wieprz
Włodawa
Sarny
Ovruch
Uzh
Nosovka
Ostrów Wlkp.
Zduńska Wola
Radom
Puławy
Manevichi
Olevsk
Teterev
Kiyevskoye Vdkhr.
Bobrovica
Piotrków Tryb.
Lublin
Chełm
Kovel'
Korosten
Malin
Priluki
Kępno
Wieluń
Końskie
Skarzysko-Kamienna
Starachowice
Kraśnik
Krasnystaw
Kivercy
Kostopol'
Sluch'
Kiyev
Brovary
Yagotin
Pilica
G. Świętokrzyskie
Radomsko
Warta
Ostrowiec
Zamość
Vladimir Volynskiy
Lutsk
Rovno
Novograd V.
Radomyshl'
Kluczbork
Częstochowa
Kielce
Novovolynsk
Korec
Boyarka
Vasil'kov
Pereyaslav
Opole
Odra
Jędrzejów
Sandomierz
Stalowa Wola
Tomaszów Lubelski
Dubno
Slavuta
Zhitomir
Korostyshev
Fastov
Dnieper (Dnepr)
Zawiercie
Busko Zdrój
Tarnobrzeg
San
Rava Russkaya
Chervonograd
Shepetovka
Polonnye
Belaya Tserkov'
Zolotonosha
Bytom
Dąbrowa-Górn.
Gliwice
Zabrze
Chorzów
Sosnowiec
Katowice
Mielec
Jarosław
Brody
Kremenets
Berdichev
Kazatin
Mironovka
Cherkassy
Smela
Ros'
Rybnik
Kraków
Rzeszów
Tarnów
Dębica
Goryn'
Starokonstantinov
UKRAINE
Opava
Oświęcim
Bochnia
Przemyśl
Gorodok
L'vov
Zolochev
Bazaliya
Kalinovka
Zhashkov
Zvenigorodka
Ostrava
Karv.
Bielsko-Biała
Cieszyn
Żywiec
Myślenice
Jasło
Ternopol
Khmel'nitskiy
Letichev
Vinnitsa
Tal'noye
Novomirgorod
Frýdek
Nowy Sącz
Sanok
Sambor
Berezhany
Terebovlya
Seret
Podol'skaya Vozv.
Pridneprovskaya Vozv.
Beskidy Zachodnie
Drogobych
Khodorov
Gorodok
Zhmerinka
Gaysin
Uman
Čadca
Zakopane
Tatry
Gerlachovsky 2655
Bardejov
Borislav
Stryy
Chortkov
Dunayevtsy
Bratslav
Zlín
Žilina
Kalush
Ivano-Frankovsk
Kamenets Podolskiy
Tul'chin
Ulyanovka
Martin
Ružomberok
Prešov
Mogilev Podol'skiy
Yuzh Bug
Pervomaysk
Trenčín
Banská Bystrica
SLOVAKIA
Michalovce
Košice
Uzhgorod
Nadvornaya
Kolomyya
Khotin
Dniester (Dnestr)
Kodyma
Piešťany
Rožňava
Svalyava
Mukachevo
Ondava
Chernovtsy
Yedintsy
Soroki
Balta
Trnava
Zvolen
Hron
Yasinya
Goverla 2058
Storozhinets
Kotovsk
Nitra
Lučenec
Kazincbarcika
Kisvárda
Khust
Rakhov
Prut (Prutul)
Ryskany
Rybnitsa
Voznesensk
Levice
Ózd
Nyíregyháza
Dorohoi
Bel'tsy
Veselinovo
Nové Zámky
Salgótarján
Eger
Miskolc
Mátészalka
Sighetu Marmației
Rădăuți
Botoșani
MOLDOVA
Orgeyev
Zhovten'
Berezovka
Komárno
Gyöngyös
Satu Mare
Borșa
Dubossary
Vác
Esztergom
Hajdúböszörmény
Ujfehértó
Carei
Baia Mare
Suceava
Fălticeni
Kishinev (Chișinău)
Győr
Tatabánya
Budapest
Hatvan
Tisza
Debrecen
Mtii Rodnei
Vatra Dornei
Bistrița
Iași
Kalarash
Tiraspol'
Razdel'naya
Marghita
Someș
Pașcani
Bendery
Odessa
Karcag
Bistrița
Mtii Călimani
Pietrosu 2303
Roman
Székesfehérvár
Szolnok
Berettyóújfalu
Zalău
Dej
Bicaz
Piatra-Neamț
Kotovsk
Dniester (Dnestr)
Veszprém
Dunaújváros
Cegléd
Nagykörös
Oradea
Reghin
Gheorgheni
Huși
Vaslui
Belgorod Dnestrovskiy
Siófok
HUNGARY
Kecskemét
Körös
Salonta
Vlădeasa 1836
Cluj-Napoca
Bacău
Fonyód
K'félegyháza
Békéscsaba
Turda
Luduș
Tîrgu Mureș
Komrat
Paks
Orosháza
Mtii Apuseni
Miercurea-Ciuc
Onești
Bîrlad
Kiskunhalas
Bihor 1849
Mureș
Tîrnăveni
Sighișoara
Nemira 1649
Siret
Artsiz
Sarata
Dombóvár
Kaposvár
Szekszárd
Hódmezővásárhely
Síntana
Mediaș
Adjud
Kagul
Baja
Szeged
Makó
Arad
Mtii Zarandului
Alba Iulia
Sebeș
Rupea
Sfîntu Gheorghe
Tecuci
Prut (Prutul)
Bolgrad
Black Sea
Pécs
Subotica
Lipova
Făgăraș
Focșani
Reni
Izmail
Kiliya
Vilkovo
Senta
Kikinda
Sombor
Timișoara
Hunedoara
Deva
Orăștie
Sibiu
Brașov
Galați
Sulina
Vojvodina
Lugoj
Cîndrelu 2245
Moldoveanu 2543
Rîmnicu Sărat
Brăila
Tulcea
Apatin
Vrbas
Bečej
Timiș
Caransebeș
ROMANIA
Carpații Meridionali
Buzău
Nasice
Osijek
Zrenjanin
Deta
Reșița
Peleaga 2509
Mtii (Transylvanian Alps)
Cîmpina
Babadag
L. Razim
Vukovar
Novi Sad
Dakovo
Vinkovci
Danube (Dunav)
Vršac
Oravița
Tîrgu Jiu
Rîmnicu Vîlcea
Tîrgoviște
Ploiești
Mizil
Urziceni
Hîrșova
Carpathian Mountains
Oriental
Carpații
BALTIC SEA
E
F
G
1
2
3
4
20
25
30
45
50
55

1:10M

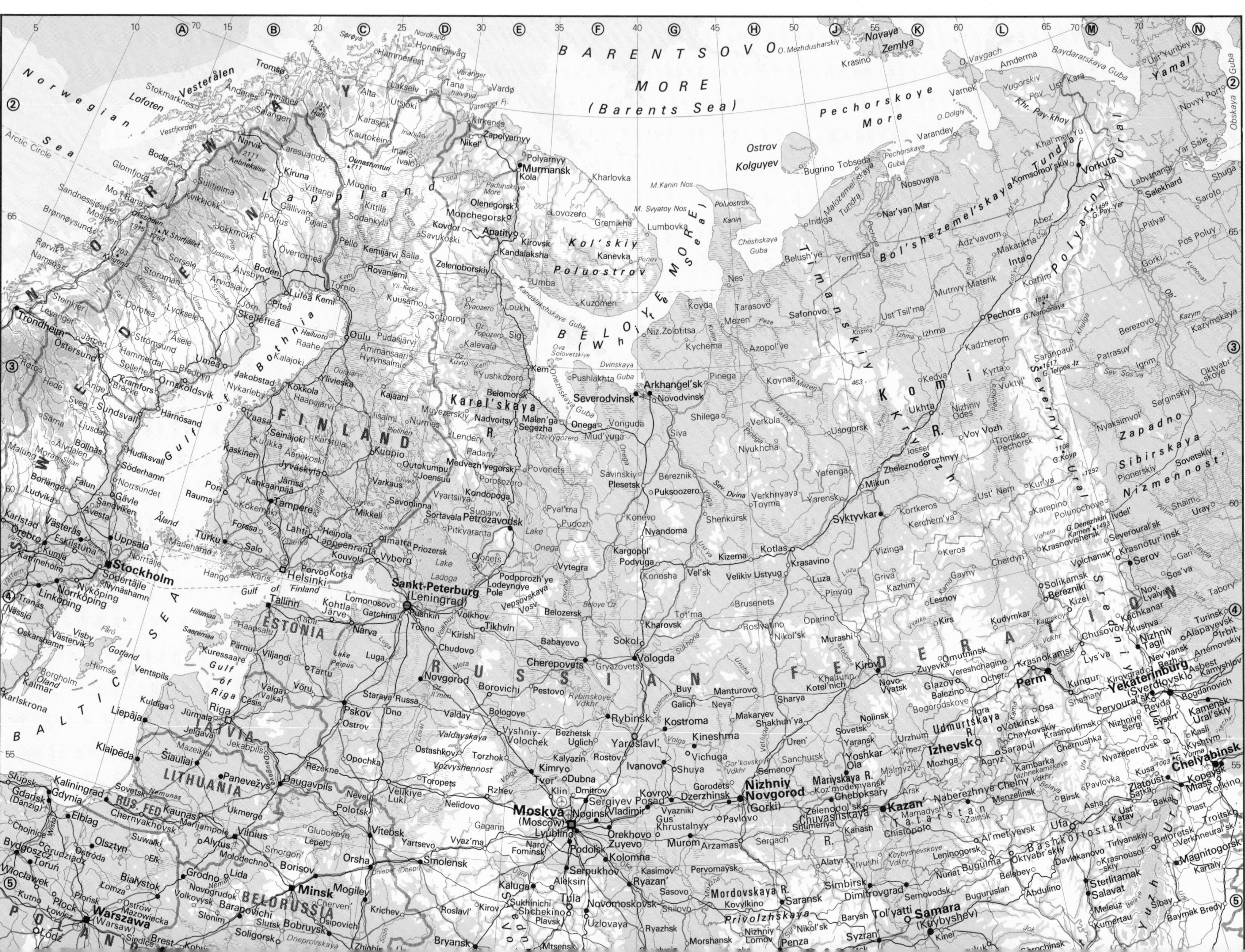
0 100 200 300 400 km
0 100 200 mls
BARENTSOVO MORE
(Barents Sea)
Norwegian Sea
Pechorskoye More
BELOYE MORE
(White Sea)
Ostrov Kolguyev
Novaya Zemlya
Kol'skiy Poluostrov
Moskva
(Moscow)
Sankt-Peterburg
(Leningrad)
Nizhniy Novgorod
(Gorki)
Samara
(Kuybyshev)
Yekaterinburg
(Sverdlovsk)
Arkhangel'sk
Murmansk
Kazan'
Perm
Chelyabinsk
Helsinki
Stockholm
Tallinn
Riga
Minsk
Warszawa
(Warsaw)
FINLAND
ESTONIA
LATVIA
LITHUANIA
BELORUSSIA
RUSSIAN FEDERATION
Gulf of Finland
Gulf of Riga
Gulf of Bothnia
BALTIC SEA
Arctic Circle

1 Severo-Osetinskaya R.
2 Adzharskaya R.
3 Checheno-Ingushskaya R.
4 Kabardino-Balkarskaya R.
5 Nakhichevanskaya R. (to Azerbaijan)
BLACK SEA
CASPIAN SEA
Sea of Azov (Azovskoye More)
Mediterranean Sea
Aegean Sea
Sea of Crete
UKRAINE
KAZAKHSTAN
ROMANIA
MOLDOVA
BULGARIA
GREECE
HUNGARY
SLOVAKIA
TURKEY
SYRIA
IRAQ
IRAN
ARMENIA
AZERBAIJAN
GEORGIA
UZBEKISTAN
TURKMENISTAN
CYPRUS
Caspian Depression
Ustyurt Plato
Dagestanskaya R.
Kalmytskaya R.
Krym
Anadolu Dağları
Toros Dağları
Reshteh ye Alborz (Elburz Mts)

400   800   1200   1600 km
400   800 mls

ARCTIC OCEAN

Greenland (Den.)

ICELAND

IRELAND
Edinburgh
Dublin
London
UNITED KINGDOM
DENMARK
NORWAY
SWEDEN
Oslo
Stockholm
København
FINLAND
Helsinki
Tallinn
EST.
Riga
LAT.
LITH.
Vilnius
Faðerne (Den.)
Barents Sea
Murmansk
Svalbard (Nor.)
Zemlya Frantsa Iosifa
Severnaya Zemlya
Novaya Zemlya
Novosibirskiye Ostrova

PORT.
SPAIN
FRANCE
Paris
Marseille
Corse (Fr.)
Roma
ITALY
Sardegna
Tunis
Sicilia

NETH.
BEL.
LUX.
GERMANY
SWITZ.
AUSTRIA
CZECH REPUBLIC
POLAND
Warszawa
SLOVAKIA
HUNGARY
SLOV.
CROATIA
BOSNIA HERZ.
YUGOSLAVIA
ROMANIA
Bucuresti
MOLD.
BELORUSSIA
Minsk
Moskva
Kiyev
UKRAINE
Odessa
BULGARIA
ALB.
MAC.
GREECE
Athínai
Crete

Sankt-Peterburg (Leningrad)
Arkhangel'sk
Vorkuta
Nizhniy Novgorod
Khar'kov
Rostov
Astrakhan'
Volga

RUSSIAN FEDERATION

Yekaterinburg
Chelyabinsk
Omsk
Ob'
Yenisey
Krasnoyarsk
Novosibirsk
Irkutsk
Lena
Yakutsk

Samara

Black Sea
Istanbul
Ankara
TURKEY
Adana
CYPRUS
Beirut
LEB.
Halab
SYRIA
Damascus
Jerusalem
ISRAEL
JOR.
Amman
Baghdad
IRAQ
Basra
Al Mawsil (Mosul)

GEORGIA
Tbilisi
ARM.
Yerevan
AZER.
Baku
Caspian Sea
Aral Sea
Tabriz
Tehrán
Esfahán
IRAN
Kermán
Ábádán
Mashhad
Herat
Kabul

KAZAKHSTAN

TURKMENISTAN
Ashkhabad
UZBEKISTAN
Tashkent
Bishkek
Alma Ata
KIRGHIZIA (KYRGYZSTAN)
TAJIKISTAN
Dushanbe
AFGHANISTAN

MONGOLIA
Ulaanbaatar
INNER MONGOLIA
Ürümqi
Qiqihar
SINKIANG
Beijing
Taiyuan
Tianjin
Lanzhou
Zhengzhou
Xi'an
CHINA

LIBYA
Alexandria
Cairo
EGYPT
Aswân
Nile

SAUDI ARABIA
Ar Riyád
Makkah
BAHRAIN
QATAR
Abú Dhabi
U.A.E.
KUWAIT
The Gulf
Muscat
OMAN
YEMEN
San'á
Aden
G. of Aden
Socotra (Yemen)

SUDAN
Khartoum
ERITREA
Asmera
DJIBOUTI
Adis Abeba
ETHIOPIA
SOMALIA
Muqdisho
KENYA
Mombasa
Dar es Salaam
TANZANIA
Equator

RED SEA

PAKISTAN
Islamabad
Kashmir
Lahore
Karachi
Hyderábád
Delhi
NEPAL
Kathmandu
Thimphu
BHUTAN
Kánpur
Lucknow
Patna
Ganga
BANGLADESH
Dhaka
Chittagong
Ahmadábád
Jabalpur
Calcutta
Bombay
Nágpur
Godávari
Hyderabad
Krishna
INDIA
TIBET
Lhasa
Brahmaputra
Imphal
Mandalay
BURMA (MYANMA)
Irrawaddy
Yangon (Rangoon)
Moulmein
Chiang Mai
THAILAND
Bangkok
LAOS
Vientiane
Hanoi
Haiphong
VIETNAM
Da Nang
CAMBODIA
Phnom Penh
Ho Chi Minh (Saigon)
Surat Thani

Chengdu
Chongqing
Wuhan
Changsha
Guiyang
Kunming
Guangzhou
Chang Jiang

ARABIAN SEA
Bangalore
Madras
Madurai
Lakshadweep (Ind.)
SRI LANKA
Colombo
Kandy
MALDIVES
Bay of Bengal
Andaman Is (Ind.)
Nicobar Is (Ind.)

INDIAN OCEAN
SEYCHELLES
Aldabra Is (Sey.)
COMOROS
MOZAMBIQUE
MADAGASCAR
Antananarivo
Chagos Arch. (U.K.)
Cocos Is (Aust.)
Christmas (Aust.)

George Town
Kuala Lumpur
SINGAPORE
MALAY
SUMATERA
Padang
Palembang
Jakarta

Arctic Circle

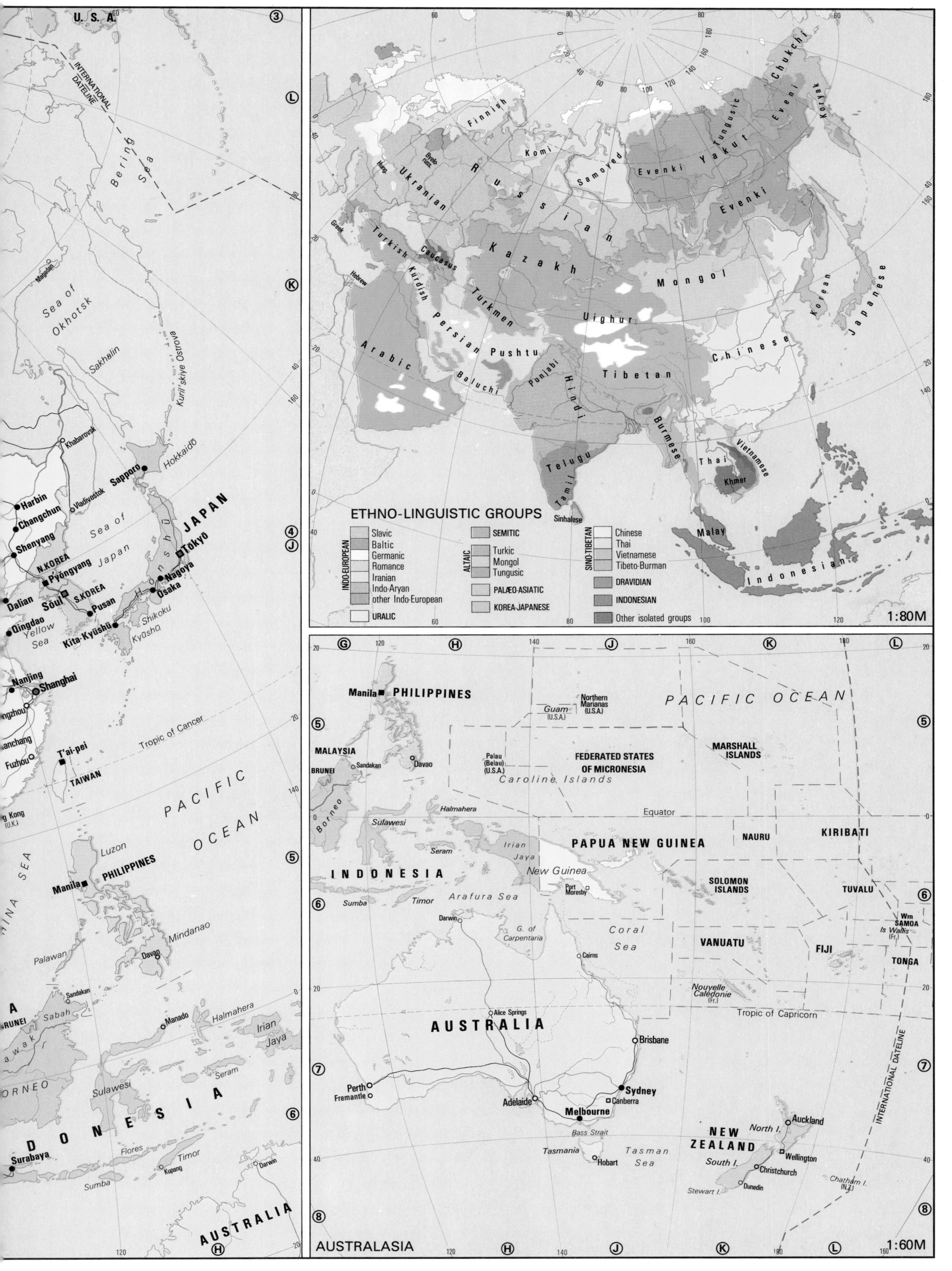

Main map (left)

U.S.A.

INTERNATIONAL DATELINE

Bering Sea

Sea of Okhotsk

Sakhalin

Kuril'skiye Ostrova

Magadan

Khabarovsk

Vladivostok

Hokkaidō

Sapporo

JAPAN

Harbin

Changchun

Shenyang

N.KOREA

Pyŏngyang

Dalian

Sŏul

S.KOREA

Pusan

Sea of Japan

Honshū

Tōkyō

Nagoya

Osaka

Shikoku

Kyūshū

Kita-Kyūshū

Qingdao

Yellow Sea

Nanjing

Shanghai

nchangchou

Fuzhou

T'ai-pei

TAIWAN

Hong Kong (U.K.)

CHINA SEA

PACIFIC OCEAN

Tropic of Cancer

Luzon

PHILIPPINES

Manila

Mindanao

Palawan

Davao

Sandakan

Sabah

BRUNEI

Manado

Halmahera

Irian Jaya

BORNEO

Sarawak

INDONESIA

Sulawesi

Seram

Surabaya

Flores

Sumba

Timor

Kupang

Darwin

AUSTRALIA

Ethno-Linguistic map (top right)

Finnish

Komi

Karel.

Byelo-russ.

Ukranian

Russian

Samoyed

Evenki

Yakut

Tungusic

Chukchi

Evenki

Koryak

Evenki

Greek

Turkish

Caucasus

Kazakh

Mongol

Korean

Japanese

Hebrew

Kurdish

Turkmen

Uighur

Chinese

Persian

Pushtu

Tibetan

Arabic

Baluchi

Punjabi

Hindi

Telugu

Burmese

Thai

Vietnamese

Khmer

Tamil

Sinhalese

Malay

Indonesian

ETHNO-LINGUISTIC GROUPS

INDO-EUROPEAN
- Slavic
- Baltic
- Germanic
- Romance
- Iranian
- Indo-Aryan
- other Indo-European

URALIC

ALTAIC
- SEMITIC
- Turkic
- Mongol
- Tungusic
- PALÆO-ASIATIC
- KOREA-JAPANESE

SINO-TIBETAN
- Chinese
- Thai
- Vietnamese
- Tibeto-Burman
- DRAVIDIAN
- INDONESIAN
- Other isolated groups

1:80M

Australasia map (bottom right)

Manila **PHILIPPINES**

MALAYSIA

BRUNEI

Sandakan

Davao

Borneo

Sulawesi

Halmahera

Seram

INDONESIA

Sumba

Timor

Irian Jaya

Guam (U.S.A.)

Northern Marianas (U.S.A.)

PACIFIC OCEAN

Palau (Belau) (U.S.A.)

FEDERATED STATES OF MICRONESIA

Caroline Islands

MARSHALL ISLANDS

Equator

PAPUA NEW GUINEA

New Guinea

Port Moresby

NAURU

KIRIBATI

SOLOMON ISLANDS

TUVALU

Darwin

G. of Carpentaria

Coral Sea

VANUATU

FIJI

Wm SAMOA

Is Wallis (Fr.)

TONGA

Cairns

Nouvelle Calédonie (Fr.)

Tropic of Capricorn

Alice Springs

AUSTRALIA

Brisbane

Perth

Fremantle

Adelaide

Canberra

Sydney

Melbourne

Bass Strait

Tasmania

Hobart

Tasman Sea

NEW ZEALAND

North I.

Auckland

Wellington

South I.

Christchurch

Dunedin

Stewart I.

Chatham I. (N.Z.)

INTERNATIONAL DATELINE

AUSTRALASIA

1:60M

200 400 600 800 km
200 400 mls

Legend (bottom left):

RUSSIAN FEDERATION
1 Chuvashskaya R.
2 Checheno-Ingushskaya R.
3 Severo-Osetinskaya R.
4 Kabardino- Balkarskaya R.
GEORGIA
5 Abkhazskaya R.
6 Adzharskaya R.
AZERBAIJAN
7 Nakhichevanskaya R.

Major labels:

NORWEGIAN SEA
BARENTS SEA
KARA SEA
ARCTIC
SVALBARD (SPITSBERGEN)
ZEMLYA FRANTSA JOSIFA (FRANZ-JOSEF-LAND)
NOVAYA ZEMLYA
NORTH SEA
BALTIC SEA
BLACK SEA
CASPIAN SEA
Aral Sea (Aral'skoye More)

SCOTLAND · U.K. · DENMARK · GERMANY · POLAND · SWEDEN · NORWAY · FINLAND · LATVIA · LITHUANIA · UKRAINE · GEORGIA · ARMENIA · AZERBAIJAN · TURKEY · IRAQ · IRAN · TURKMENISTAN · UZBEKISTAN · KAZAKHSTAN · KIRGHIZIA (KYRGYZSTAN) · TAJIKISTAN · AFGHANISTAN · SINKIANG

RUSSIAN Zapadno Sibirskaya Nizmennost'

Glasgow, Edinburgh, Aberdeen, Inverness, Bergen, Trondheim, Oslo, Stockholm, København, Hamburg, Berlin, Warszawa, Kraków, Minsk, Kiyev, Moskva (Moscow), Sankt-Peterburg (Leningrad), Helsinki, Riga, Tallinn, Kharkov, Odessa, Donetsk, Dnepropetrovsk, Rostov-na-Donu, Volgograd, Saratov, Samara (Kuybyshev), Nizhniy Novgorod, Kazan, Ufa, Yekaterinburg (Sverdlovsk), Chelyabinsk, Magnitogorsk, Perm, Kirov, Omsk, Novosibirsk, Barnaul, Tomsk, Karaganda, Alma Ata (Almaty), Tashkent (Toshkent), Samarkand, Bishkek, Baku (Baky), Tbilisi, Yerevan, Tehran, Mashhad, Ashkhabad, Dushanbe, Kabul, Herat

ARCTIC OCEAN

SEVERNAYA ZEMLYA (NORTH LAND)
Ostrov Komsomolets
Ostrov Bol'shevik
Ostrov Oktyabr'skoy Revolyutsii
O. Russkiy

NOVOSIBIRSKYE OSTROVA (NEW SIBERIAN ISLANDS)
Ostrova De-Longa
O. Bennetta
O. Novaya Sibir'
O. Bol'shoy Lyakhovskiy
O. Kotel'nyy

LAPTEV SEA

EAST SIBERIAN SEA

CHUKCHI SEA

BERING SEA
Bering Str.

Poluostrov Taymyr
Gory Byrranga
Ozero Taymyr

RUSSIAN FEDERATION

Verkhoyanskiy Khrebet
Khrebet Cherskogo
Khrebet Orulgan
Yakutsk
Lena
Aldan
Stanovoy Khrebet
Aldanskoye Nagor'ye
Sredne Sibirskoye Ploskogor'ye

KAMCHATKA
Petropavlovsk-Kamchatskiy
Sredinnyy Khrebet
Koryakskoye Nagor'ye

SEA OF OKHOTSK
Magadan
Okhotsk

SAKHALIN
Yuzhno-Sakhalinsk
Komsomol'sk-na-Amure
Khabarovsk

Kuril'skiye Ostrova (Kuril Islands)

HOKKAIDO
Sapporo
Hakodate

SEA OF JAPAN

JAPAN
HONSHU
TOKYO
Yokohama
Nagoya
Kyoto
Osaka
Sendai
Niigata
Akita
Aomori
KYUSHU
SHIKOKU
Fukuoka
Nagasaki
Kagoshima

MONGOLIA
Ulaanbaatar
ALTAI MTS.

INNER MONGOLIA
Hohhot
Baotou

CHINA
Beijing (Peking)
Tianjin (Tientsin)
Jinan
Taiyuan
Shijiazhuang
Qingdao

MANCHURIA
Harbin
Changchun
Shenyang
Dalian
Qiqihar
Mudanjiang
Vladivostok
Ussuriysk
Nakhodka

NORTH KOREA
P'yongyang

SOUTH KOREA
Seoul
Pusan
Taegu
Inch'on

YELLOW SEA

Baykal
Irkutsk
Ulan Ude
Chita
Bratsk
Krasnoyarsk
Angarsk
Abakan
Kyzyl

GREAT WALL

1:20M

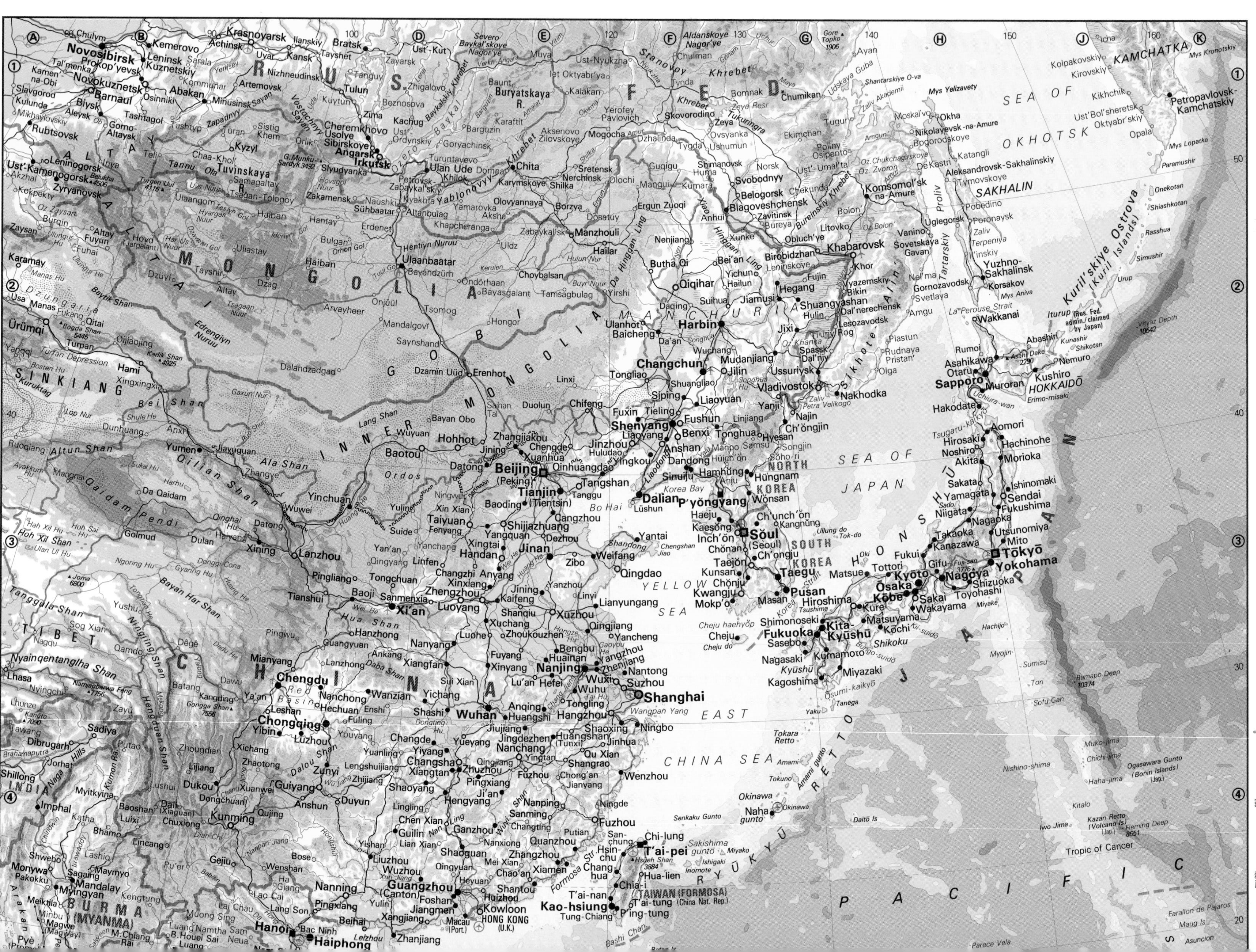

0 200 400 600 800 km
0 200 400 mls
SEA OF OKHOTSK
SEA OF JAPAN
YELLOW SEA
EAST CHINA SEA
PACIFIC
KAMCHATKA
SAKHALIN
HOKKAIDŌ
HONSHŪ
SHIKOKU
KYŪSHŪ
JAPAN
NORTH KOREA
SOUTH KOREA
MONGOLIA
INNER MONGOLIA
MANCHURIA
GOBI
ALTAI
CHINA
SINKIANG
TIBET
BURMA (MYANMAR)
INDIA
TAIWAN (FORMOSA) (China Nat. Rep.)
Kuril'skiye Ostrova (Kuril Islands)
RYŪKYŪ RETTO
Tropic of Cancer
Beijing (Peking)
Tianjin (Tientsin)
Shanghai
Nanjing
Wuhan
Chongqing
Chengdu
Guangzhou (Canton)
HONG KONG (U.K.)
Xi'an
Harbin
Shenyang
Dalian
P'yŏngyang
Sŏul (Seoul)
Pusan
Tōkyō
Yokohama
Nagoya
Ōsaka
Kyōto
Kōbe
Sapporo
Vladivostok
Khabarovsk
Irkutsk
Ulaanbaatar
Novosibirsk
Krasnoyarsk
Ürümqi
Lhasa
Hanoi
Haiphong
Mandalay
T'ai-pei
Kao-hsiung

PAPUA NEW GUINEA

IRIAN JAYA

PHILIPPINES

FEDERATED STATES OF MICRONESIA

CAROLINE ISLANDS

MARIANA

Northern Marianas

PACIFIC OCEAN

MINDANAO

LUZON

MOLUCCAS

CELEBES SEA

CERAM SEA

BANDA SEA

ARAFURA SEA

CORAL SEA

AUSTRALIA

Arnhem Land

TIMOR SEA

SOUTH CHINA SEA

SULU SEA

SABAH

SARAWAK

BORNEO

KALIMANTAN

MALAYSIA

INDONESIA

JAVA SEA

FLORES SEA

SULAWESI (CELEBES)

THAILAND

CAMBODIA

INDO-CHINA

PENINSULAR MALAYSIA

SUMATRA

JAVA (JAWA)

INDIAN OCEAN

ANDAMAN SEA

Gulf of Thailand

Manila
Quezon City
Cebu
Davao
Zamboanga
Bacolod
Iloilo
Cagayan de Oro
General Santos

Jakarta
Bandung
Surabaya
Semarang
Yogyakarta
Surakarta

Kuala Lumpur
SINGAPORE
Johor Bharu
Kota Bharu
Ipoh
George Town
Medan
Palembang
Padang
Pontianak
Banjarmasin
Balikpapan
Samarinda
Ujung Pandang (Makassar)
Kupang
Manado
Kuching
Bandar Seri Begawan
BRUNEI
Kota Kinabalu

Bangkok (Krung Thep)
Phnom Penh
Vientiane
Ho Chi Minh (Saigon)
Da Nang
Yangon (Rangoon)

Port Moresby
Jayapura
Darwin

SPRATLY ISLANDS
Palau (U.S.A.)
Guam (U.S.A.)

1:10M

MONGOLIA

NEI MONGGOL

Gobi

QINGHAI

Lanzhou

Xining

Ningxia

Yinchuan

Baotou

Hohhot

Datong

Beijing (Peking)

Tianjin (Tientsin)

Hebei

Shijiazhuang

Taiyuan

Shanxi

SHAANXI

Xi'an (Sian)

Xianyang

Baoji

Qin Ling

Henan

Zhengzhou

Luoyang

Kaifeng

Shandong

Jinan (Tsinan)

Qingdao (Tsingtao)

Weifang

Zibo

Yantai

Weihai

Xuzhou

Jiangsu

Nanjing (Nanking)

Shanghai

Suzhou

Wuxi

Changzhou

Zhenjiang

Yangzhou

Hefei

Anhui

Bengbu

Huainan

Wuhu

Ma'anshan

Hangzhou

Zhejiang

Ningbo

Shaoxing

Wenzhou

CHINA

SICHUAN

Chengdu

Chongqing (Chungking)

Hubei

Wuhan

Yichang

Shashi

Huangshi

Jiangxi

Nanchang

Jingdezhen

Jiujiang

Hunan

Changsha

Zhuzhou

Xiangtan

Hengyang

Shaoyang

Guizhou

Guiyang

Yunnan

Kunming

Guangxi

Nanning

Guilin

Liuzhou

Wuzhou

Guangdong

Guangzhou (Canton)

Foshan

Shenzhen

Kowloon

HONG KONG (U.K.)

Macao (Port.)

Shantou (Swatow)

Zhanjiang

Maoming

Beihai

Haikou

Hainan

Fujian

Fuzhou (Foochow)

Xiamen (Amoy)

Quanzhou

TAIWAN

T'ai-pei

T'ai-chung

Chang-hua

Chia-i (Nat. Rep. China)

T'ai-nan

Kao-hsiung

Ping-tung

FORMOSA STRAIT (TAIWAN HAI-HSIA)

YELLOW SEA (HUANG HAI)

BOHAI

KOREA BAY

Dalian

Shenyang

Liaoning

Changchun

Jilin

Fushun

Anshan

Jinzhou

SOUTH CHINA SEA

GULF OF TONGKIN

VIETNAM

Hanoi

Haiphong

LAOS

Huang He

Yangtze

Chang Jiang

100 200 300 400 km
100 200 mls

RUS. FED.

Yerofey Pavlovich · Urusha · Skovorodino · Never · Solov'yevsk · Zeya · Ovsyanka · Udskoye
Shika · Gulian · Mangui · Dzhalinda · Talden · Urkan · Khrebet Dzhagdy · Uda · Udskoye
Yudi Shan 1054 · Magdagachi · Tygda · Ushumun · Yasnyy · Shevli · Tugur
Jiliu He · Fengshui Shan 1398 · Amur · Zeya · Selemdzhinsk · Tokur · Ekimchan · Peliny Osipenko · Tugur
Huma He · Shimanovsk · Zavitinsk · Selemdzha · Turana · Norsk · Fevral'skoye · Kerbi · Bichi
Bishui · Linhai · Xiao'ergou · Nemor He · Huma · Kumara · Svobodnyy · Blagoveshchensk · Aihui · Belogorsk · Raychikhinsk · Novobureyskiy · Progress · Arkhara · Obluch'ye · Bira · Izvestkovyy · Smidovich · Fuyuan · Korfovskiy

Zaliv Akademii · Litke · Sakhalinskiy Zaliv · Moskal'vo · Kolendo · Okha · Vostochnyy · Neftegorsk

OKHOTSKOYE MORE (SEA OF OKHOTSK)

SAKHALIN

Nikolayevsk-na-Amure · Val · Nogliki · Katangli · G. Lopatina 1609 · Tymovskoye · Pobedino · Smirnykh · Buyukly · Leonidovo · Poronaysk · Zaliv Terpeniya · Makarov · Vostochnyy · Krasnogorsk · Il'inskiy · Tomari · Chekhov · Bykov · Dolinsk · Nevel'sk · Yuzhno-Sakhalinsk · Kholmsk · Korsakov · Ozerskiy · Gornozavodsk · Shebunino · Zaliv Aniva · Novikovo

Kuril'skiye Ostrova (Rus. Fed. admin./claimed by Japan)
Kuril'sk · O. Iturup · O. Kunashir · Yuzhno-Kuril'sk · Golovnino · Habomai Shoto

NEI MONGGOL
Bugt · Butha Qi · Nianzishan · Longjiang · Qiqihar · aicheng · Qian Gorlos · Tongyu · Da'an · Songyuan

HEILONGJIANG
Nehe · Keshan · Yi'an · Baiquan · Hailun · Suihua · Bei'an · Anda · Zhaodong · Hulan · Bayan · Mulan · Tonghe · Fangzheng · Yilan · Boli · Huanan · Baoqing · Jixi · Mishan · Hulin
Harbin · Acheng · Shuangcheng · Wuchang · Shulan

CHINA
Hegang · Jiamusi · Shuangyashan · Qitaihe

JILIN
Changchun · Jilin · Yongji · Jiaohe · Dunhua · Huadian · Panshi · Liaoyuan
Siping · Gongzhuling

LIAONING
Shenyang · Fushun · Benxi · Anshan · Liaoyang · Dandong · Sinuiju

NORTH KOREA
P'yŏngyang · Namp'o · Sariwŏn · Kaesŏng · Wŏnsan · Hamhŭng · Hŭngnam · Ch'ŏngjin · Kimch'aek · Nanam · Hyesan · Kanggye

SOUTH KOREA
Sŏul (Seoul) · Inch'ŏn · Suwŏn · Wŏnju · Ch'unch'ŏn · Taejŏn · Chŏnju · Kwangju · Mokp'o · Taegu · Pusan · Ulsan · Masan · Chinju · Chinhae · Yŏsu

YELLOW SEA (HUANG HAI)

SEA OF JAPAN

HOKKAIDŌ
Sapporo · Otaru · Yūbari · Asahikawa · Abashiri · Kitami · Muroran · Tomakomai · Hakodate · Kushiro · Obihiro · Nemuro · Nayoro · Bibai

HONSHŪ
Aomori · Hachinohe · Towada · Hirosaki · Morioka · Akita · Miyako · Kamaishi · Sendai · Yamagata · Fukushima · Niigata · Nagaoka · Nagano · Matsumoto · Toyama · Kanazawa · Fukui · Tokyo · Kawasaki · Yokohama · Chiba · Nagoya · Kyoto · Osaka · Kobe · Himeji · Okayama · Hiroshima · Shimonoseki · Fuji-san 3776 · Matsue · Tottori · Yamaguchi

SHIKOKU
Takamatsu · Tokushima · Matsuyama · Kōchi · Uwajima

KYŪSHŪ
Kita-Kyūshū · Fukuoka · Sasebo · Nagasaki · Kumamoto · Ōita · Beppu · Miyazaki · Kagoshima · Kanoya · Nobeoka

PACIFIC OCEAN

JAPAN

125 130 135 140 145

1:5M

50 100 150 200 km
50 100 mls

Major regions
- **JAPAN**
- **HOKKAIDŌ**
- **KYŪSHŪ**
- **SHIKOKU**
- **NORTH KOREA**
- **SOUTH KOREA**
- **CHINA**
- SEA OF JAPAN
- PACIFIC OCEAN
- KOREA STRAIT
- TSUSHIMA-KAIKYŌ

continued on inset
145 at the same scale

Selected cities and places

Hakodate, Aomori, Hachinohe, Morioka, Miyako, Kamaishi, Ōfunato, Kesennuma, Ishinomaki, Shiogama, Sendai, Akita, Odate, Noshiro, Yamagata, Tsuruoka, Sakata, Niigata, Nagaoka, Wakamatsu, Aizu, Kōriyama, Fukushima, Iwaki, Hitachi, Mito, Utsunomiya, Nikkō, Takasaki, Maebashi, Kumagaya, Ōmiya, Tokyo, Chiba, Kawasaki, Yokohama, Yokosuka, Odawara, Fuji, Shizuoka, Hamamatsu, Toyohashi, Nagoya, Toyota, Gifu, Yokkaichi, Tsu, Ōtsu, Kyōto, Ōsaka, Kōbe, Sakai, Nara, Wakayama, Himeji, Okayama, Kurashiki, Fukuyama, Onomichi, Hiroshima, Kure, Iwakuni, Yamaguchi, Ube, Shimonoseki, Kita-Kyūshū, Fukuoka, Kurume, Ōmuta, Saga, Karatsu, Sasebo, Nagasaki, Ōita, Beppu, Kumamoto, Kagoshima, Takamatsu, Tokushima, Matsuyama, Kōchi, Uwajima

Sapporo, Otaru, Asahikawa, Kushiro, Obihiro, Muroran, Tomakomai, Ebetsu, Wakkanai

Sōul (Seoul), Inch'ŏn, Suwŏn, Taejŏn, Taegu, Pusan, Kwangju, Chŏnju, Ulsan, Masan, Chinju, Cheju, Kangnŭng, P'ohang

P'yŏngyang, Namp'o, Kaesŏng, Wŏnsan, Hamhŭng, Hŭngnam, Ch'ŏngjin, Najin, Sinŭiju, Kanggye, Hyesan, Kimch'aek, Tanch'ŏn

Tsushima, Tok-do (Take-shima) (Liancourt Rocks), Ullŭng-do, Cheju-do, Sado-shima, Oki-shotō, Hachijō-jima

BURMA (MYANMAR)
Mandalay
Myingyan
Meiktila
Yamethin
Pyinmana
Toungoo
Magwe (Magway)
Thayetmyo
Pyè (Prome)
Henzada
Yangon (Rangoon)
Bassein (Pathein)
Pegu (Bago)
Moulmein (Mawlamyine)
Tavoy (Dawei)
Mergui
Bay of Bengal
Mouths of the Irrawaddy
G. of Martaban
ANDAMAN SEA
Mergui Archipelago
NICOBAR ISLANDS (India)
Little Nicobar
Great Nicobar
THAILAND
Chiang Mai
M. Lampang
M. Phitsanulok
M. Nakhon Sawan
Lop Buri
Ayutthaya
Bangkok
Thon Buri
M. Samut Prakan
Chon Buri
Nakhon Ratchasima
Ubon Ratchathani
Udon Thani
Nong Khai
Muang Khon Kaen
Bight of Bangkok
Chumphon
Isthmus of Kra
Ranong
Surat Thani
Nakhon Si Thammarat
Phuket
Songkhla
Ban Hat Yai
Pattani
Narathiwat
LAOS
Vientiane (Viangchan)
Luang Prabang
Savannakhet
Pakse
CAMBODIA
Phnom Penh
Battambang
Siem Reap
ANGKOR
Tonle Sap
Kompong Cham
Kompong Thom
Sihanoukville
GULF OF THAILAND
VIETNAM
Hanoi
Haiphong
Thanh Hoa
Vinh
Dong Hoi
Hue
Da Nang
Quang Ngai
Qui Nhon
Nha Trang
Cam Ranh
Da Lat
Ho Chi Minh (Saigon)
Vung Tau
My Tho
Can Tho
Mouths of the Mekong
Gulf of Tongkin
CHINA
Nanning
Zhanjiang
Haikou
HAINAN
Paracel Islands (claimed by China & Vietnam)
SOUTH CHINA SEA
MALAYSIA
PENINSULAR MALAYSIA
Kota Bharu
Alor Setar
George Town
Butterworth
Ipoh
Kuala Trengganu
Kuantan
Kuala Lumpur
Kelang
Seremban
Melaka
Johor Bharu
SINGAPORE
Strait of Malacca
Kep. Anambas
Bunguran
SARAWAK (Malaysia)
Kuching
BORNEO
Pontianak
INDONESIA
SUMATERA
Banda Aceh
Medan
Pematangsiantar
Sibolga
Pekanbaru
Padang
Jambi
Bangka
Nias
Siberut
Kep. Riau
Kep. Lingga
Equator

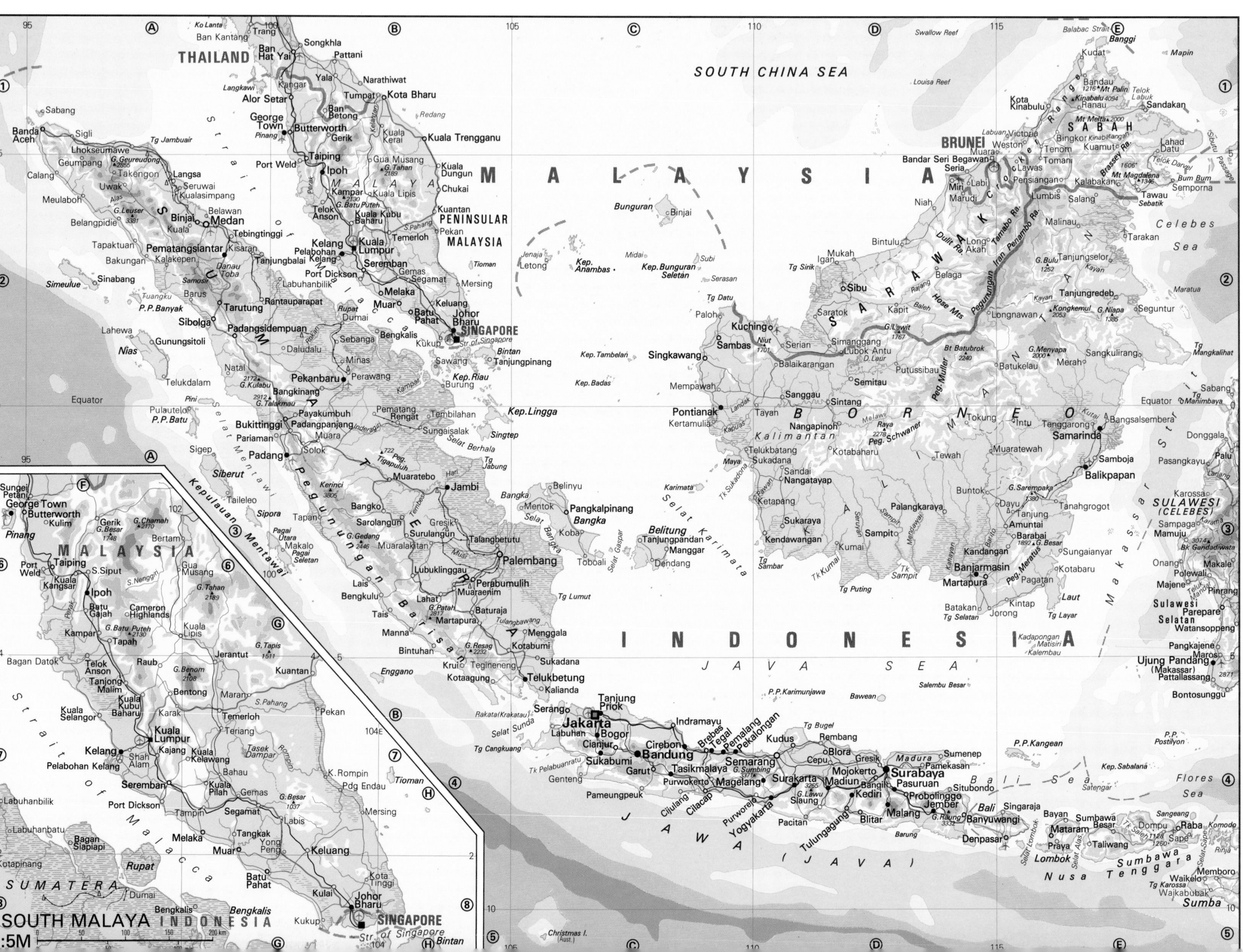

1:10M

SOUTH CHINA SEA

MALAYSIA

BRUNEI

SABAH

SARAWAK

BORNEO

KALIMANTAN

INDONESIA

Celebes Sea

SULAWESI (CELEBES)

Flores Sea

JAVA SEA

PENINSULAR MALAYSIA

THAILAND

SINGAPORE

SUMATERA

Straits of Malacca

JAVA (DJAWA)

Madura

Bali

Lombok

Sumbawa

Nusa Tenggara

SOUTH MALAYA
1:5M

INDONESIA

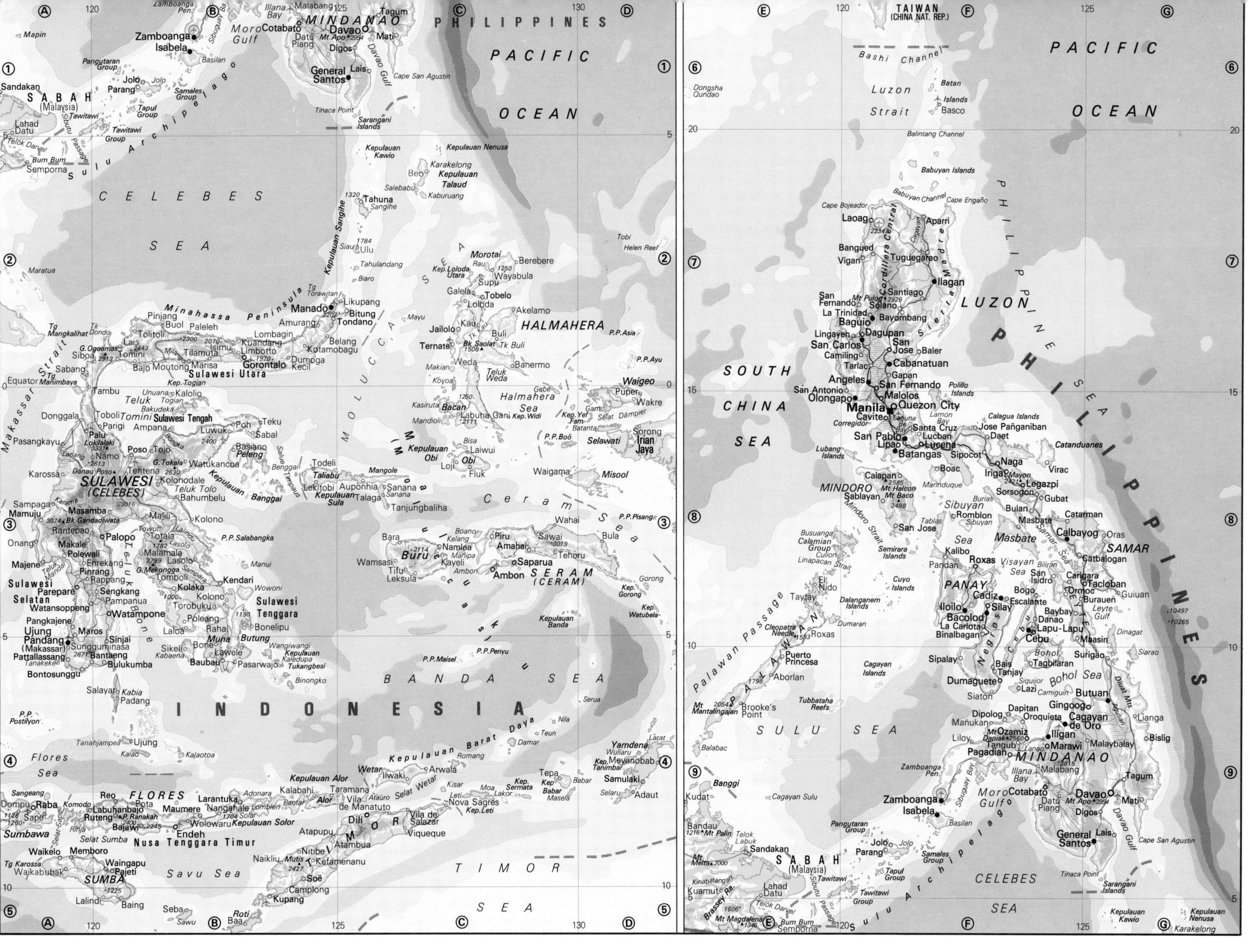
PACIFIC OCEAN
PHILIPPINES
PHILIPPINE SEA
LUZON
SOUTH CHINA SEA
SULU SEA
CELEBES SEA
MINDANAO
SAMAR
PANAY
MINDORO
PALAWAN
TAIWAN (CHINA NAT. REP.)
Luzon Strait
Bashi Channel
Manila
Quezon City
Cebu
Davao
Zamboanga
SABAH (Malaysia)
Sulu Archipelago
INDONESIA
HALMAHERA
MOLUCCA SEA
Halmahera Sea
SULAWESI (CELEBES)
Sulawesi Utara
Sulawesi Tengah
Sulawesi Selatan
Sulawesi Tenggara
Minahassa Peninsula
Makassar Strait
SERAM (CERAM)
Ceram Sea
Buru
BANDA SEA
Irian Jaya
TIMOR
TIMOR SEA
Savu Sea
Flores Sea
FLORES
SUMBA
Nusa Tenggara Timur
Kepulauan Barat Daya

1:20M

200 400 600 800 km
200 400 mls

A ROMANIA · MOL · **B** · **C** · **D** · 60 · **E**

Beograd · Sarajevo · Sibiu · Meridionali · Galati · Zaporozh'ye · Donetsk · Volgograd · Temir · Chelkar · KAZA · Dzhezkazgan
Split · B.-H. · YUGOS · Carpatii · Nikolayev · Mariupol' · Rostov-na-Donu · Shakhty · Simlyanskoye Vokhr. · Gur'yev · Kul'sary · Be
Dubrovnik · Nis · Ploiesti · Odessa · Melitopol · Taganrog · RUS. FED. · Astrakhan' · Dossor · Aral'sk

① Shkodër · Skopie · BULGARIA · Ruse · Bucuresti · Kerch · Krasnodar · Maykop · Kropotkin · Kalmykskaya · Ft Shevchenko · Novokazalinsk · Kzyl-Orda
Tiranë · Sofiya · Constanta · Sevastopol' · Krym · Sea of Azov · Stavropol' · Divnoye R. · Aktau · Aral Sea (Aral'skoye More) · Chimbay · Kyzyl-Kum · Sy Darya
MACEDONIA · Rodopi Pl. · Plovdiv · Varna · Simferopol · Novorossiysk · Sochi · Kislovodsk · Groznyy · Makhachkala · Plato Ustyurt · Nukus · Tashauz · Urgench · Turtkul · UZBEKISTAN
Trikkala · Olimbos · Thessaloniki · Burgas · Elbrus 5642 · Vladikavkaz · Dagestanskaya R. · Zaliv Kara-Bogaz Gol · Krasnovodsk

② GREECE · Athinai · Edirne · Istanbul · Zonguldak · Sinop · Samsun · Trabzon · Batumi · Sukhumi · Kutaisi · Tbilisi · GEORGIA · Gvandzha · Baku (Baky) · Nebit-Dag · TURKMENISTAN · Chardzhou · Bukhara
Peloponnisos · Uskudar · Sea of Marmara · Bursa · Eskisehir · Kizil Irmak · Sivas · Erzurum · Yerevan · ARMENIA · AZERBAIJAN · Karakumy · Kizyl'-Arvat · Ashkhabad (Ashgabat) · Kerki · Karshi
Kalamai · Izmir · Aydin · Ankara · Kayseri · Kizil · Buyuk Agri D. 5165 · Nakhichevan · Lenkoran' · Rasht · Bojnurd · Kopet Dag · Tedzhen · Mary · Termez · Andkhui · Mazar-i Sharif
Kriti · Rodhos · Denizli · Konya · Toros Daglari · Malatya · Diyarbakir · Van · Van Golu · Khvoy · Tabriz · Ardabil · Babol · Kushka · Daulat Yar · Meymaneh
Aegean Sea · Afyon · Adana · Gaziantep · TURKEY · Murat R. · Kurtalan · 4168 · Zanjan · Elburz · Mashhad · Herat · AFGHANIS
Antalya · Ak Dag · Ercives D. 3916 · Kurtalan · Orumiyeh (Urmia) · Qazvin · 5601 Damavand · Shahrud · Sabzevar

MEDITERRANEAN SEA · Nicosia · CYPRUS · Al Ladhiqiyah · Halab · Al Hasakah · Al Mawsil (Mosul) · Arbil · As Sulaymaniyah · Kermanshah · Tehran · Hamadan · Qom · D. Namak · Dasht-e-Kavir · Birjand · Farah · Girishk
Darnah · Famagusta · Hamah · SYRIA · Dayr az Zawr · Kirkuk · Samarra · Qom · Kashan · Yazd · Bafq · Kuh-i-Taftan 4042
Tobruq · LEBANON · Hims · Tudmur · Euphrates R. · Baghdad · Arak · Esfahan · Zaranj · Zahedan · Nushki
Beirut · Damascus · Dar'a · Ar Ramadi · Karbala · An Najaf · Ad Diwaniyah · Dezful · Ahvaz · Kerman · Kuh-e-Hazaran · Shur Gaz · Bam · Baluchistan
LIBYA · Haifa · Tel Aviv · ISRAEL · Amman · Ar Rutbah · Ar · IRAQ · Al Amarah · Basra · Abadan · Bandar Khomeyni · Shiraz · Sa'idabad · Kerman · Kuh-e-Taftan · PA
Alexandria · Matruh · Dumyat · Port Said · JORDAN · Jerusalem · Ma'an · Badanah · Kuwait · KUWAIT · Bushehr · Lar · Hamun-e Jaz Murian · Ormara · Hyde

③ Cairo · Tanta · Ismailiya · El 'Arish · Aqaba · An Nafud · Ha'il · Buraydah · Safaniya · Dhahran · BAHRAIN · Manamah · QATAR · Dubai · Bandar 'Abbas · Str. of Hormuz · Turbat · Karach
El Faiyum · Suez · Sinai · Tabuk · Tayma' · Shaqra · Dukhan · Abu Dhabi · Doha · Gulf of Oman · Jask · Chah Bahar · Gwadar
Beni Suef · Al Wajh · Unayzah · Ar Riyad · As Salamiyah · UNITED ARAB EMIRATES · Al Khaburah · Muscat · Ormara
EGYPT · El Minya · Farafra Oasis · Yanbu al Bahr · Medina · Al Hufuf · Al Liwa · Suhar · Nazwa · Sur · Muscat
Asyut · Hurghada · Bur Safaga · Rabigh · SAUDI ARABIA · Layla · The Gulf · Al Hadd

Qattara Depression · Siwa · Al Khaga · Luxor · El-Kharga Oasis · Jiddah · Makkah · At Ta'if · Rub' al Khali · OMAN · Masirah · Gulf of Masirah · Tropic of Cancer · ARABIA
Libyan Desert · Aswan · L. Nasser · El Lith · Al Qunfidhah · Qal'at Bishah · Abha · Ra's al Madrakah · SEA

④ Wadi Halfa · Nubian Desert · Dongola · Port Sudan · Suakin · Sabya · Jizan · Sa'dah · Salalah · Sayhut · Ash Shihr · Al Mukalla
Berber · Merowe · Ed Damer · Al Luhayyah · San'a · Nisab · Hadramawt · Ra's Fartak · Socotra (Sugutra) (Yemen) · Hadjboh
Omdurman · Khartoum · Kassala · Mits'iwa (Massawa) · ERITREA · Ta'izz · YEMEN · Aden · ARABIA
Atbara · Wad Medani · Asmera · Adigrat · Al Hudaydah · Al Mukha · Adan (Aden) · Gulf of Aden · Raas Caseyr · Raas Xaafuun
SUDAN · Ed Dueim · El Obeid · Sennar · Singa · Adan · Bab el Mandeb · Djibouti · Berbera · Ceerigaabo
En Nahud · Kosti · Ras Dashan 4620 · Gonder · L. Tana · Aseb · DJIBOUTI · Hargeysa · Somali Basin

⑤ Malakal · Sudd · ETHIOPIA · Dendi 3077 · Nazret · Dire Dawa · Harer · SOMALIA · Carlsberg
Rumbek · Adis Abeba · Debre Markos · Jima · Batu 4307 · Ginir · Berbera
ZAIRE · L. Albert · Nimule · Juba · Dolo Odo · Baraawe · Marka · Muqdisho (Mogadishu)
UGANDA · Kampala · Jinja · Mt Elgon 4321 · KENYA · Wajir · Shebele · Hobyo · INDIA
L. Kyoga · Entebbe · Eldoret · Kirinyaga (Mt Kenya) 5199 · Garissa · Juba (Giuba)

⑥ RWANDA · Kigali · Mbale · Kisumu · Nakuru · Nanyuki · Nairobi · Baraawe · Kismaayo · Equator
BURUNDI · Butare · Bukoba · Lake Victoria · TANZANIA · Kilimanjaro 5896 · Meru 4565 · Moshi · Tana
Bujumbura · Gitega · L. Eyasi · Arusha

A · 40 · **B** · 50 · **C** · **D** · 60 · **E**

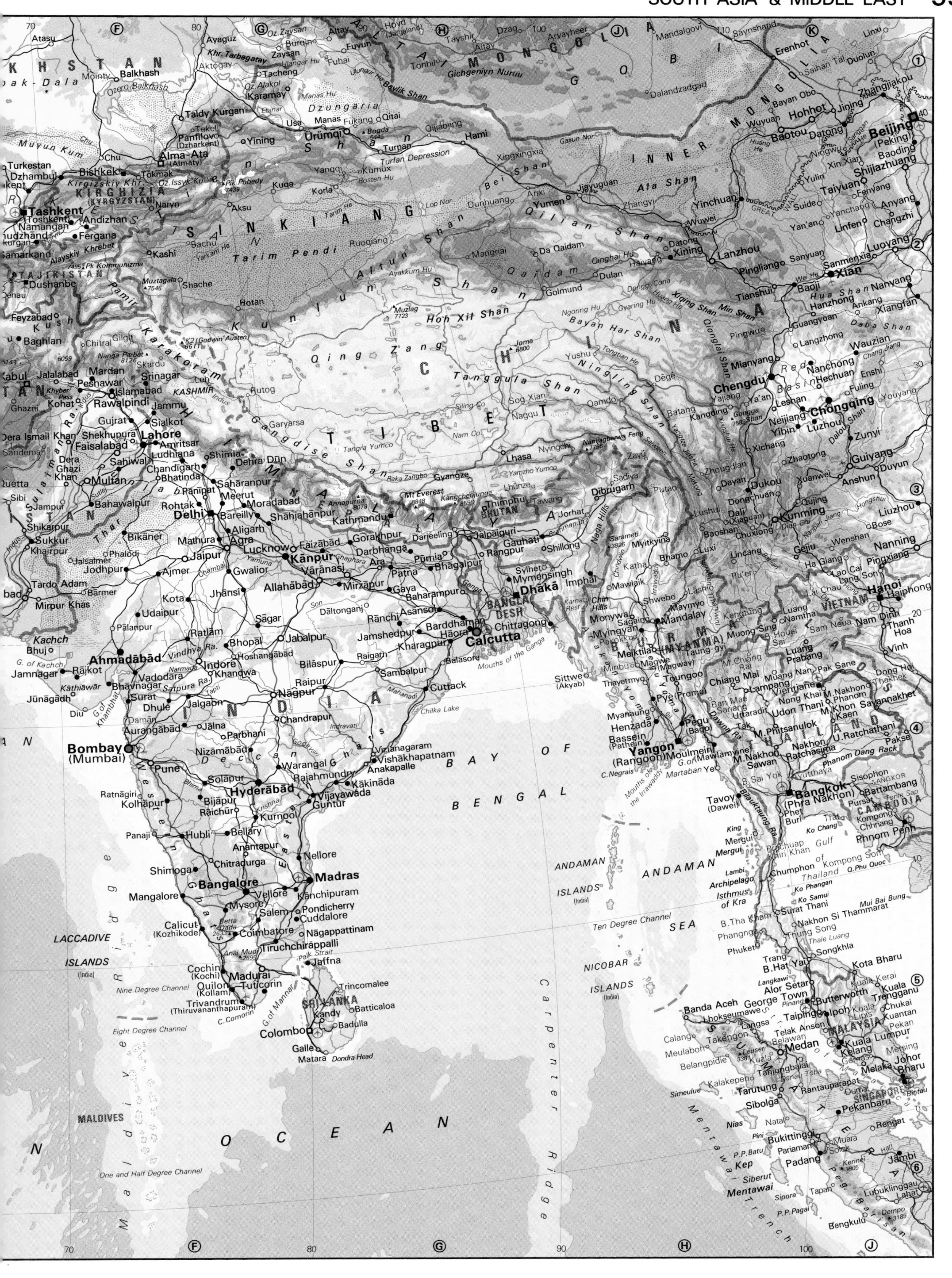

Atasu
Balkhash
Taldy Kurgan
Alma-Ata
(Almaty)
Bishkek
Tokmak
KIRGHIZIA
(KYRGYZSTAN)
Naryn
Tashkent
Andizhan
Namangan
Fergana
Samarkand
Kashi
Dushanbe
Feyzabad
Baghlan
Chitral
Gilgit
Jalalabad
Mardan
Peshawar
Islamabad
Rawalpindi
Kohat
Ghazni
Srinagar
Jammu
KASHMIR
Sialkot
Gujrat
Lahore
Faisalabad
Amritsar
Ludhiana
Shekhupura
Dera Ismail Khan
Sahiwal
Multan
Chandigarh
Shimla
Dehra Dun
Bhatinda
Saharanpur
Meerut
Panipat
Rohtak
Delhi
Moradabad
Bareilly
Shahjahanpur
Bahawalpur
Sukkur
Shikarpur
Khairpur
Bikaner
Aligarh
Agra
Mathura
Jaipur
Jodhpur
Ajmer
Gwalior
Lucknow
Kanpur
Faizabad
Gorakhpur
Darbhanga
Varanasi
Allahabad
Mirzapur
Patna
Gaya
Ara
Purnia
Bhagalpur
Kathmandu
Darjeeling
Jalpaiguri
Thimphu
BHUTAN
Gauhati
Shillong
Rangpur
Dibrugarh
Jorhat
Mymensingh
Sylhet
Dhaka
Imphal
BANGLADESH
Chittagong
Calcutta
Haora
Barddhaman
Asansol
Ranchi
Jamshedpur
Kharagpur
Balasore
Mouths of the Ganga
Mirpur Khas
Barmer
Kota
Jhansi
Udaipur
Sagar
Jabalpur
Ratlam
Bhopal
Kachch
Bhuj
Ahmadabad
Rajkot
Jamnagar
Vadodara
Bhavnagar
Indore
Khandwa
Bilaspur
Raigarh
Sambalpur
Raipur
Cuttack
Surat
Dhule
Jalgaon
Nagpur
INDIA
Chandrapur
Chilka Lake
Diu
Daman
Aurangabad
Jalna
Parbhani
Bombay
(Mumbai)
Nizamabad
Pune
Warangal
Vizianagaram
Vishakhapatnam
Anakapalle
Solapur
Hyderabad
Rajahmundry
Kakinada
Ratnagiri
Kolhapur
Bijapur
Raichur
Vijayawada
Guntur
Kurnool
Panaji
Hubli
Bellary
Anantapur
Nellore
Shimoga
Chitradurga
Bangalore
Madras
Mangalore
Vellore
Kanchipuram
Mysore
Salem
Pondicherry
Cuddalore
Calicut
(Kozhikode)
Coimbatore
Nagappattinam
Tiruchchirappalli
Cochin
(Kochi)
Madurai
Tuticorin
Quilon
(Kollam)
Trivandrum
(Thiruvananthapuram)
C. Comorin
Jaffna
Trincomalee
SRI LANKA
Kandy
Batticaloa
Colombo
Badulla
Galle
Matara
Dondra Head
LACCADIVE
ISLANDS
(India)
Nine Degree Channel
Eight Degree Channel
MALDIVES
One and Half Degree Channel
OCEAN
BAY OF BENGAL
ANDAMAN ISLANDS
(India)
ANDAMAN SEA
Ten Degree Channel
NICOBAR ISLANDS
(India)
Carpenter Ridge
Tarim Pendi
SINKIANG
Urumqi
Turpan
Turfan Depression
Hami
Kuqa
Korla
Aksu
Hotan
Kunlun Shan
Altun Shan
Qaidam Pendi
Golmund
Da Qaidam
Dunhuang
Yumen
Jiayuguan
Qilian Shan
Xining
Lanzhou
Yinchuan
Wuwei
Ala Shan
Hoh Xil Shan
Bayan Har Shan
Qing Zang
Tanggula Shan
TIBET
Lhasa
Gangdise Shan
Gyangze
Mt Everest
CHINA
HIMALAYA
Chengdu
Chongqing
Leshan
Yibin
Neijiang
Luzhou
Zunyi
Guiyang
Duyun
Anshun
Kunming
Dali
Dukou
Xichang
Qujing
Nanning
Gejiu
Hanoi
Haiphong
VIETNAM
Vinh
Luang Prabang
Vientiane
Chiang Mai
Lampang
Udon Thani
Nong Khai
Nakhon Ratchasima
Bangkok
(Phra Nakhon)
Phnom Penh
CAMBODIA
Battambang
Sisophon
Kompong Som
Gulf of Thailand
THAILAND
Myitkyina
Bhamo
Lashio
Mandalay
Sagaing
Monywa
Shwebo
Meiktila
Magwe
Minbu
Taunggyi
Toungoo
Prome
Pegu
Yangon
(Rangoon)
Bassein
(Pathein)
Henzada
Myanaung
Moulmein
(Mawlamyine)
Sittwe
(Akyab)
BURMA
(MYANMAR)
Tavoy
(Dawei)
Mergui
Chumphon
Isthmus of Kra
Surat Thani
Nakhon Si Thammarat
Phuket
Songkhla
Kota Bharu
Alor Setar
George Town
Butterworth
Ipoh
Kuala Trengganu
Kuantan
Kuala Lumpur
MALAYSIA
Johor Bharu
SINGAPORE
Melaka
Banda Aceh
Medan
Tanjungbalai
Sibolga
Pekanbaru
Bukittinggi
Padang
Jambi
Bengkulu
Simeulue
Nias
Siberut
Mentawai
Mentawai Trench
Beijing
(Peking)
Tianjin
Baoding
Shijiazhuang
Taiyuan
Datong
Baotou
Hohhot
Jining
Zhangjiakou
Erenhot
INNER MONGOLIA
GOBI
MONGOLIA
Altai
Luoyang
Xian
Baoji
Hanzhong
Ankang
Xiangfan
Nanchong
Mianyang
Lanzhou
Tianshui
Pingliang
Yan'an
Linfen
Changzhi
Anyang

1:7.5M

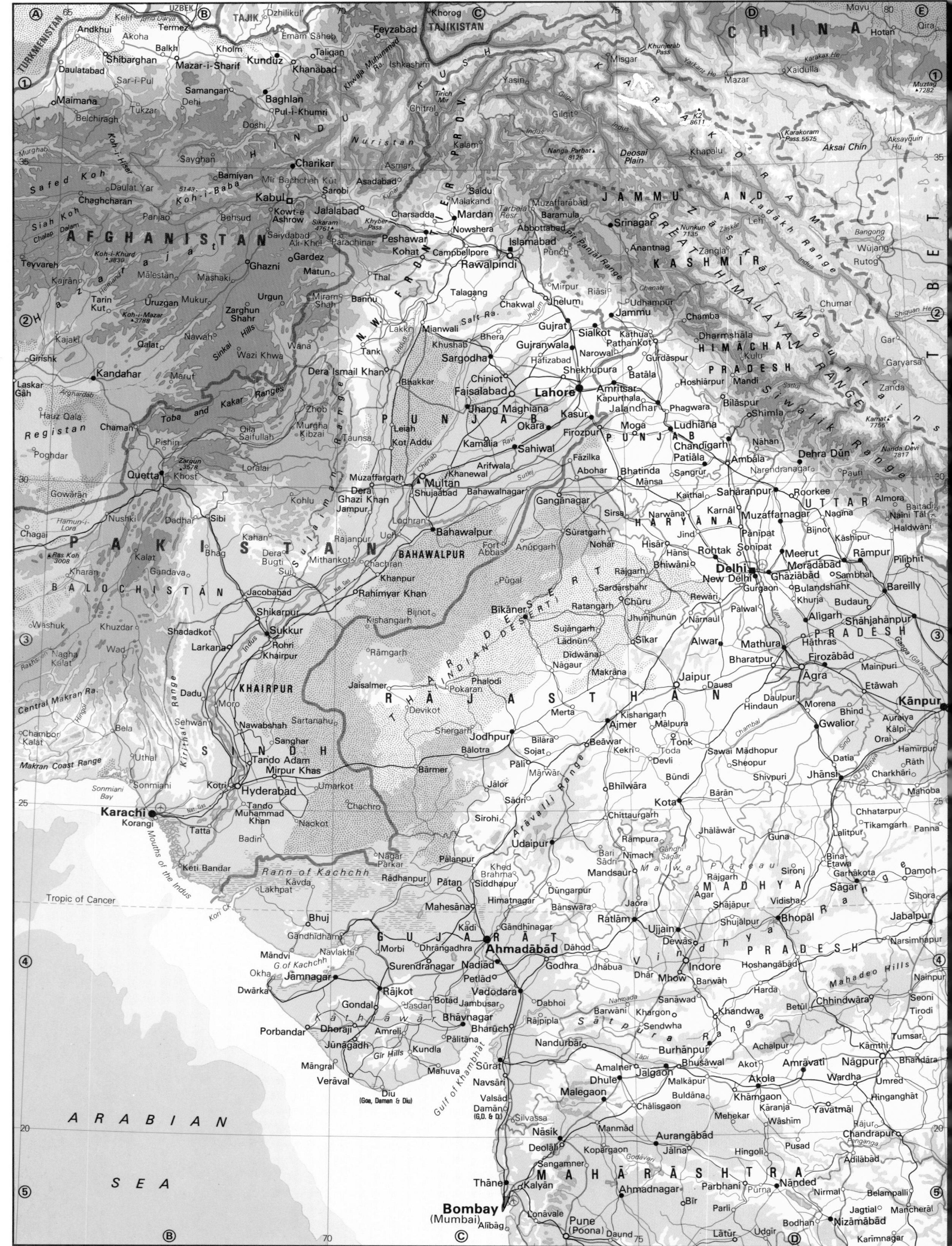

CHINA
TAJIKISTAN
UZBEK.
TAJIK.
TURKMENISTAN
AFGHANISTAN
PAKISTAN
JAMMU AND KASHMĪR
HIMĀCHAL PRADESH
PUNJAB
HARYĀNA
UTTAR PRADESH
RĀJASTHĀN
GUJARĀT
MADHYA PRADESH
MAHĀRĀSHTRA
SINDH
BALOCHISTĀN
KHAIRPUR
BAHAWALPUR
N.W. FRONTIER PROV.
TIBET
HINDU KUSH
KARAKORAM
GREAT HIMALAYAN RANGE
Siwalik Range
Ladākh Range
Zāskār Mountains
Pir Panjal Range
Salt Ra.
Sulaiman Range
Toba and Kakar Ranges
Central Makran Ra.
Makran Coast Range
Kirthar Range
Arāvalli Range
Sātpura Range
Vindhya Range
Mahadeo Hills
Malwa Plateau
Gir Hills
Kāthiāwār
Rann of Kachchh
THAR or INDIAN DESERT
Registan
Aksai Chin
Deosai Plain
Hazarajat
Siah Koh
Safed Koh
Koh-i-Baba
Koh-i-Hisar
Sinkai Hills
ARABIAN SEA
Tropic of Cancer
Mouths of the Indus
G. of Kachchh
Gulf of Khambhat
Sonmiani Bay
Nanga Parbat 8126
K2 8611
Nunkun 7135
Nanda Devi 7817
Kamet 7756
Tirich Mir
Muztag 7282
Karakoram Pass 5575
Khunjerab Pass
Khyber Pass
Sikaram 4761
Kabul
Islamabad
Rawalpindi
Peshawar
Lahore
Delhi
New Delhi
Karachi
Hyderabad
Quetta
Multan
Faisalabad
Srinagar
Amritsar
Jaipur
Ahmadābād
Bombay (Mumbai)
Pune (Poona)
Kānpur
Āgra
Indore
Bhopāl
Nāgpur
Jodhpur
Bīkāner
Ajmer
Udaipur
Kota
Gwalior
Jhānsi
Sūrat
Vadodara
Rājkot
Jāmnagar
Bhuj
Nāsik
Aurangābād
Ahmadnagar
Thāne
Kandahar
Ghazni
Jalalabad
Charikar
Bamiyan
Mazar-i-Sharif
Kunduz
Baghlan
Feyzabad
Sukkur
Bahawalpur
Sargodha
Sialkot
Gujranwala
Jammu
Shimla
Dehra Dūn
Chandīgarh
Ludhiāna
Jalandhar
Meerut
Morādābād
Bareilly
Alīgarh
Mathura
Ujjain
Jabalpur
Akola
Amrāvati
Jalgaon
Dhule
Malegaon
Bhāvnagar
Porbandar
Jūnāgadh
Diu (Goa, Daman & Diu)
Damān (G.D. & D.)
Silvassa

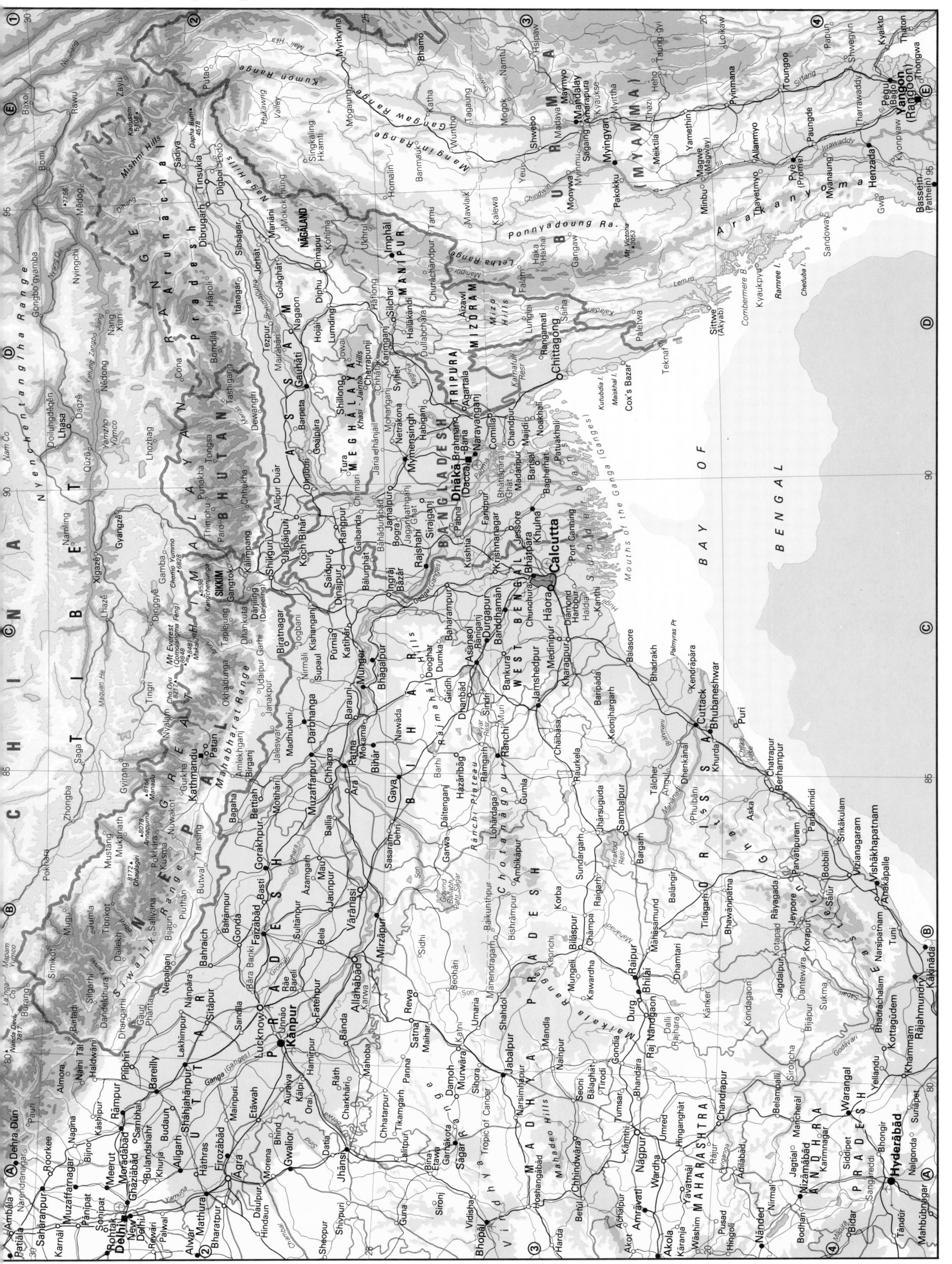
CHINA
TIBET
NEPAL
BHUTAN
SIKKIM
BANGLADESH
BURMA
MYANMAR
ARUNACHAL PRADESH
ASSAM
MEGHALAYA
NAGALAND
MANIPUR
MIZORAM
TRIPURA
WEST BENGAL
BIHAR
UTTAR PRADESH
MADHYA PRADESH
ORISSA
ANDHRA PRADESH
MAHARASHTRA
BAY OF BENGAL
GREAT HIMALAYAN RANGE
Mahabharat Range
Siwalik Range
Chota Nagpur
Nyenchentanglha Range
Mishmi Hills
Naga Hills
Arakan Yoma
Mouths of the Ganga (Ganges)
Delhi
Kathmandu
Thimphu
Lhasa
Dhaka (Dacca)
Calcutta
Shillong
Imphal
Chittagong
Mandalay
Yangon (Rangoon)
Hyderabad
Kanpur
Lucknow
Patna
Varanasi
Allahabad
Agra
Nagpur
Bhubaneshwar
Cuttack
Vishakhapatnam
Guwahati
Mt Everest
Kangchenjunga

1:7.5M

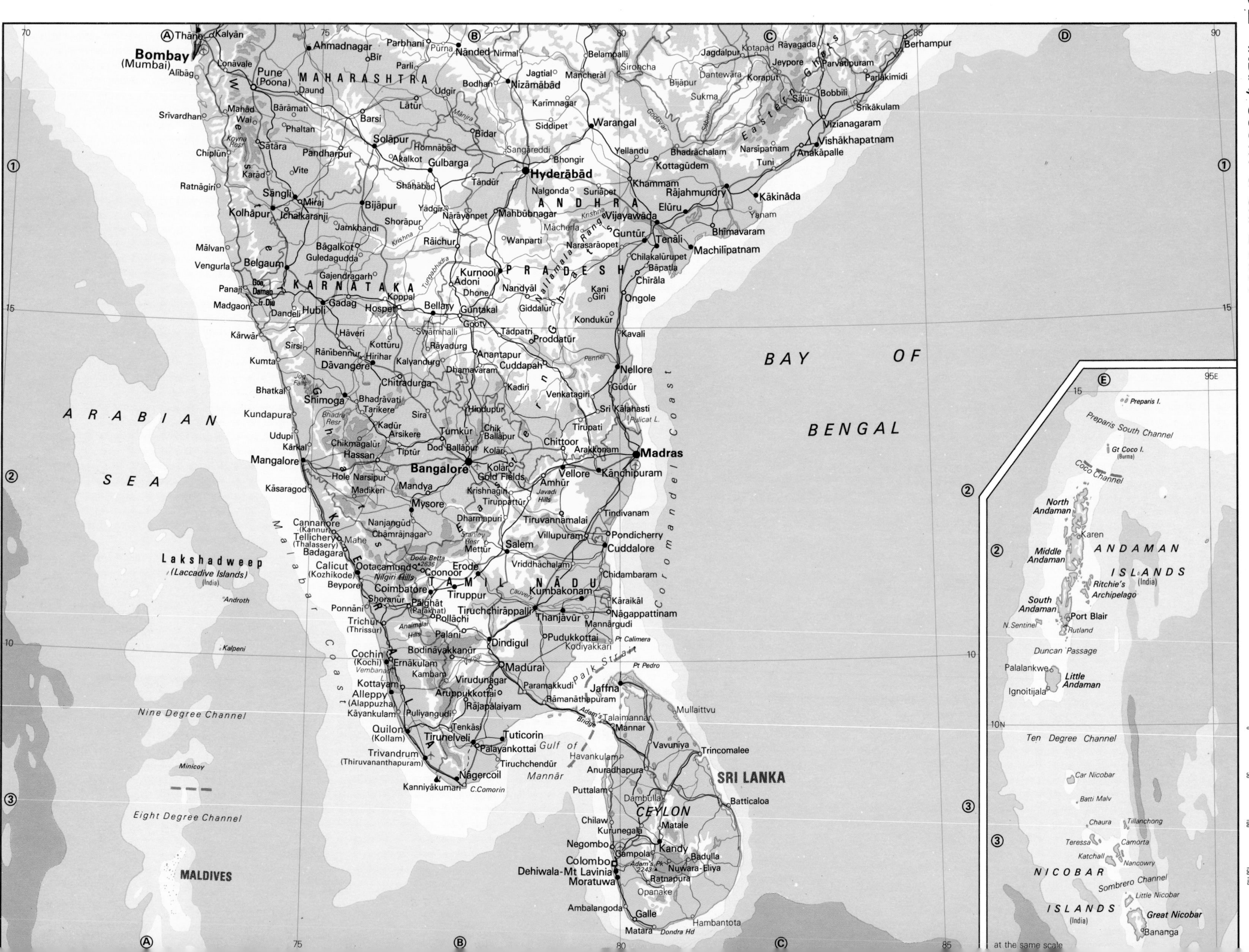
0 100 200 300 km
0 50 100 150 mls
BAY OF BENGAL
ARABIAN SEA
SRI LANKA
CEYLON
ANDAMAN ISLANDS (India)
NICOBAR ISLANDS (India)
Lakshadweep (Laccadive Islands) (India)
MALDIVES
MAHARASHTRA
KARNATAKA
ANDHRA PRADESH
TAMIL NADU
KERALA
Coromandel Coast
Malabar Coast
Palk Strait
Gulf of Mannār
Adam's Bridge
Nine Degree Channel
Eight Degree Channel
Ten Degree Channel
Duncan Passage
Preparis South Channel
Coco Channel
Sombrero Channel
North Andaman
Middle Andaman
South Andaman
Little Andaman
Ritchie's Archipelago
Port Blair
Car Nicobar
Great Nicobar
Little Nicobar
at the same scale
Bombay (Mumbai)
Pune (Poona)
Hyderābād
Madras
Bangalore
Mysore
Mangalore
Calicut (Kozhikode)
Cochin (Kochi)
Quilon (Kollam)
Trivandrum (Thiruvananthapuram)
Madurai
Tiruchchirāppalli
Coimbatore
Salem
Vellore
Pondicherry
Cuddalore
Nellore
Guntūr
Vijayawāda
Rājahmundry
Kākināda
Vishākhapatnam
Vizianagaram
Srīkākulam
Berhampur
Warangal
Kurnool
Belgaum
Hubli
Gulbarga
Bijāpur
Solāpur
Kolhāpur
Sāngli
Jaffna
Trincomalee
Batticaloa
Kandy
Colombo
Dehiwala-Mt Lavinia
Moratuwa
Galle
Matara
Anurādhapura
Vavuniya
Hambantota
Nuwara-Eliya
Badulla
Tuticorin
Tirunelveli
Nāgercoil
C.Comorin
Dindigul
Thanjāvūr
Kumbakonam
Nāgappattinam
Erode
Tiruppur
Ootacamund
Shimoga
Dāvangere
Bellary
Anantapur
Cuddapah
Tirupati
Chittoor
Kolār Gold Fields
Ongole
Machilīpatnam
Nizāmābād
Nānded
Ahmadnagar
Ratnāgiri
Panaji
Madgaon
Kārwār
Udupi
Kāsaragod
Cannanore (Kannur)
Tellichery (Thalassery)
Trichur (Thrissur)
Alleppey (Alappuzha)
Kottayam
Pālghāt
Pt Pedro
Pt Calimera
Dondra Hd
Adam's Pk 2243

100   200   300 km
50   100   150 mls

Countries / regions:
GEORGIA, ARMENIA, AZERBAIJAN, AZER., IRAN, TURKEY, SYRIA, IRAQ, SAUDI ARABIA, KUWAIT, JORDAN, ISRAEL, LEBANON, CYPRUS, GREECE, EGYPT

Seas / waters:
BLACK SEA, Mediterranean Sea, Caspian Sea, Sea of Marmara, Gulf of Suez, Gulf of Aqaba, Van Gölü, Tuz Gölü

Selected cities and towns:
Baku (Bakı), Sumqait, Shemakha, Bilajary, Ali Bayramli, Tbilisi, Rustavi, Telavi, Kutaisi, Batumi, Yerevan, Nakhichevan, Tabriz, Marand, Maragheh, Urumiyeh, Mahabad, Miandowab, Zanjan, Qazvin, Hamadan, Malayer, Boruĵerd, Khorramabad, Sanandaj, Kermanshah, Nahavand, Kangavar, Dezful, Ahvaz, Khorramshahr, Abadan, KUWAIT, Al Ahmadi, Basra, Az Zubayr, An Nasiriyah, As Samawah, Al Amarah, Al Kut, Baghdad, Ba'qubah, Al Fallujah, Karbala, An Najaf, Al Hillah, Ad Diwaniyah, Samarra', Tikrit, Kirkuk, Arbil, Al Mawsil (Mosul), Zakho, Al Amadiyah, Tall Afar, Sinjar, Al Hasakah, Al Qamishli, Nusaybin, Mardin, Dayr az Zawr, Ar Raqqah, Manbij, Al Bab, Halab (Aleppo), Idlib, Hamah, Hims, Tudmur, Ar Rutbah, Damascus (Dimashq), Az Zarqa, Amman, Irbid, As Suwayda, Beirut (Beyrouth), Tripoli (Tarabulus), Tartus, Al Ladhiqiyah, Tyr, Haifa, Nazareth, Tel Aviv Yafo, Jerusalem, Hebron, Gaza, Beersheba, Elat, Aqaba, Tabuk, Sakakah, Rafha, Hafar al Batin

Turkey:
Istanbul, Üsküdar, İzmit, Adapazarı, Bursa, İzmir, Manisa, Aydın, Denizli, Muğla, Antalya, Isparta, Burdur, Konya, Karaman, Mersin, Tarsus, Adana, İskenderun, Antakya, Gaziantep, Kilis, Şanlıurfa, Diyarbakır, Batman, Siirt, Cizre, Hakkari, Van, Bitlis, Muş, Bingöl, Elazığ, Malatya, Adıyaman, Kahramanmaraş, Kayseri, Niğde, Nevşehir, Kırşehir, Ankara, Eskişehir, Kütahya, Afyon, Uşak, Balıkesir, Çanakkale, Edirne, Tekirdağ, Zonguldak, Karabük, Kastamonu, Sinop, Samsun, Ordu, Giresun, Trabzon, Rize, Bayburt, Erzurum, Erzincan, Sivas, Yozgat, Tokat, Amasya, Çorum, Kars, Ardahan, Ağrı, Iğdır, Doğubayazıt, Erciş

Physical features:
Kuzey Anadolu Dağları, Toros Dağları, Munzur Silsilesi, Nafud, An Nafud, Ad Dibdibah, Widyan ash Sham, Badiyat ash Sham, Al Hamad, Wadi Sirhan, Libyan Plateau, Sinai, Negev, Karkheh, Tigris, Euphrates, Nile, Suez Canal

Cyprus: Nicosia, Famagusta, Limassol, Larnaca

Egypt: Cairo, El Giza, Alexandria (El Iskandariya), Port Said, Suez, Ismailia, El Mansura, Tanta, Damanhur, Zagazig, Beni Suef, El Minya, El Faiyum

0   25   50   75   100 km
0   25   50 mls

CYPRUS

C.A.Andreas
Yialousa
Rizokaipaso
C. Kormakiti   Lapithos   Akanthou   Leonarisso
Morphou   Kyrenia   Kythrea   Trikomo   C.Elea
Bay   Morphou   ATTILA LINE   Lefkoniko   Salamis   Famagusta Bay
Khrysokhou   Karayostasi   Nicosia   Famagusta
Bay   C. Arnauti   Polis   Dhali   Athna
Pedhoulas   IDALION
Mt Olympus   Paleokhorio   C. Greco
Troodos   1951   Larnaca
Paphos   Range   Platres   Lefkara   C. Kiti
Episkopi   Zyyi
Episkopi B.   Limassol
C. Zevgari   Akrotiri Bay
C. Gata

SYRIA

Serai
Jisr ash Shughūr
Al Baylūlīyah   Al Haffah   Ma'arrat an Nu'mān
Ra's Ibn Hāni'   Silinfah   Shathah Tahtā   Khān Shaykhūn
Al Lādhiqīyah   (Latakia)   Al Qardāhah   SAHYŪN
Jablah   Suqaylibīyah   Dayr Shumayyil
'Arab al Mulk   (Orontes)   Sūrān
Bāniyās   Al Qadmūs   Hamāh
QAL'AT AL MARQAB   Maşyāf   Kafr Behūm   Birīn
Ţarţūs   Duraykīsh   Kafrūn Bashūr   Ar Rastan
Arwad   Şāfītā   An Naşirah   Tall Bīsah
Dil   Qal'at al Hisn   Ḩimş (Homs)
(KRAK-DES CHEVALIERS)
Tall Kalakh   Shinshār

Tripoli
(Tarābulus esh Sham)   El Mīna   Al Ḩermel   Jūsīyah
Zghorta   Hamīdīyah   Al Quşayr   Hisyah
Batroun   Qoubayāt
LEBANON   Amioune   Bcharre   Qornet es Saouda 3086   Laboue   Jabal Halīmah 2464
Jubail   Rhazir   Deir el Ahmar   Kartaba   Sh a
BYBLOS   Ba'albek   2559   Dayr 'Aţīyah
Jounié   An Nabk
Baie de St Georges   Bikfaya 2628   Yabrūd
Beirut (Beyrouth)   Ba'abda   Zahle   Rayak   Qutayfah
Aley   Az Zabdānī   Dūmā 'Adhrā   Dumayr
Damour   Beit ed Dine   Machghârab   1910   'Ayn al Fījah   At Tall   Dayr 'Alī
Saïda (Sidon)   Jezzine   Rachaya   **Damascus** (Dimashq)
Hâsbaiya   Barada
Tyr   Marjayoun   Jash Shaykh   A'waj Al Ḩijānah
(Tyre, Sour)   Q.Shemona   (Mt Hermon)   Al Kiswah   Dayr 'Alī
Litâni   Jouai'ya   Baniyas   Al Qunayţirah   As Sanamayn   Khabab
Enn Nâqoûra   Yesud   Mas'ada   CEASE FIRE LINES 1974   Ghabāghib   Burāq
Bennt   1208   Hamā-Ala   Mismīyah
Naharîya   J.Jbail   Har Meron   Khushnīyah   Al Lajāh   Shaqqā
Ma'alot   Tarshīhā   Zefat (Safad)   Nawa   Izra'   Shahbā
'Akko   Rama   863   Tasil   Shaykh Miskīn   Jabal al 'Arab 1735
(Acre)   Q. Yam   Shefar'am   Tiberias   Fīq   Buşrā ash Shām
B. of Haifa   (Yam Kinneret)   (Sea of Galilee)   Dar'a   Şalkhad   Tīsīyah
Haifa (Hefa)   Q. Ata   Nazareth   Ma'agan   Irbid   W. az Zaydī   Sabhā
'Atlit   528 Mt Carmel   Afula   Husn   Er Rummān   Es Samrā
Zikhron Ya'aqov   Deir Abu Sa'id   Ajlūn   Mafraq
MEGIDDO ARMAGEDDON   Beyt Shean   J. Um ed Daraj 1247   Jarash   Qa el Khanna
CAESAREA   Pardes Hanna   Jenin   Tubas   Salt   Suweileh   Zarqa
Hadera   Qabaţiya   Fār'a   Karama   Marka   **Amman**
Netanya   Tulkarm   Sabastiya   Wadi es Sir   Sahāb
ISRAEL   Sabastiya   Nablus   Zarqa
Herzliyya   Kefar Sava   Ba'al Hazor 1016   Ramallah   Naur   Jiza   Qasr el Kharana
Ramat Gan   Bat Yam   Petah Tiqwa   Sarida   Jericho (Arīhā)   Qasr 'Amra
Tel Aviv   Lod   Latrun   Jerusalem (El Quds)   Mādabā   Dab'a
Yafo (Jaffa)   Ramla   Beit Jala   (Yerushalayim)   Jebel Mudeisisat   Wad dhah
Rishon le Ziyyon   Bethlehem (Bayt Lahm)   Dhībān   Khan ez Zabib
Rehovot   Qiryat   Bet Guvrin   Hebron (El Khalil)   Mazra
Ashdod   Gat   LACHISH   Dura   En Gedi   Rabba   Qatrāna
Ashqelon   Yatta   Karak 1253   Qā el Ḩafīra
Sederot   Gerar   Edh Dhahiriya   T.el Meise   Manzil
Gaza   Sedom   Mazār   Khan ez Zabīb
Gaza Strip   Bīr Sheva   MEZADA   MAMSHIT   Safi   **JORDAN**
Khan Yunis   Beersheba   Nevatim   Arad   Ed Dabab   Ḩasā   Qa el Jinz
Rafah   (Be'er Sheva)   Sedom   Tafila   Jurf ed Darāwīsh
Ofaqim   Zeelim   Dimona   1305   Rashādīya   Dana   1641   J.el Atā'ita   1082
Revivim   Yeroham   Oron   PETRA   Wādi Mūsā
Qeziot   SHIVTA   Sede Boqer   Hazeva   Nijil   Jum Suwwāna   Ābū el Jurdhān
NIZANA   AVEDAT   Mizpe Ramon   1356   Qasred Deir   Taiyiba   El Jafr
El Quseima   N e g e v   Ein Yahav   1727   J.Mubrak   Ma'an
Har Ramon   Negarot   J.Ḩārūn   Shaubak
G.Araif el Naqa 934   Har Hakippa 467   Nabi Menuha   Taiyiba 1727   El Jafr
1006   Har Saggi   J.el Atā'ita
El Quntilla   Vahel   Yotvata   1242   J.Qatim   1420   J. Harad 1274   El Kabid
Naqb Ishtar   Beer Ora   Tuwayilel Hāj 1095   W. Qa'ish Shubak
Elat   1592   Bāqir   1754   J. Um Ishrin   Ras en Naqb
Aqaba   Ram   1216   J. Um al Hashim

MEDITERRANEAN SEA

EGYPT

Rās el Barr   Masabb Dumyāt
Dumyât (Damietta)
Kafr Sa'd   Bahra el Manzala
Fâriskûr   Port Said (Bûr Saïd)   Rās Burûn
El Matarîya   Bûr Fu'ad   Ras el Barr
Shirbîn   El Zarqa   El Manzala   Suez Canal   Sabkhet el Bardawîl   El 'Arîsh
Talkha   Mit el Nasâra   El Tîna   Khalig el Tîna
El Mansûra   Dîkirnis   PELUSIUM   Bîr Lahfan   El Quseima
Samannûd   El Simbillâwein   El Sâlhîya   Români   W.Hareidin
Aga   El Qantara   Ofaqim
Kafr Saqv   Faqûs   Bîr el Duweidâr   Abu 'Aweigila   Zeelim
Mît Ghamr   El Firdân   NIZANA
Abu Kebir Hihya   Ismaîlîya   Talata   W.el Arîsh   Kathîb el Henu 207   Bîr Hasana   G.Libni 463
Zifta   Abu Suweir   Timsâh   G.Maghâra 735   892 G.Halâl   Mizpe Ramon
Zagâzig   Fâyid   Saba'a   1094 G.Yi'allaq   G.Kharîm 704   G.Araif el Naqa
Minya el Qamn   El Abbâsa   Great Bitter Lake   W.el Higâb   W.Hasana   G.Ariaf
Bilbeis   Little Bitter Lake   Giddi Pass   Har Ramon
Shibîn el Qanâtir   Gineifa   840 el Giddi   W.el Brûk
El Khânka   520   El Shallûfa   Mitle Pass   Vahel
El Matarîya   El Kûbri   Suez   Nakhl   El Kuntilla
Heliopolis   G.Ataqa 871   (El Suweis)   W.el Aqaba
Cairo (El Qâ'hira)   El Shatt   Yotvata
El Ma'âdi   Bûr Taufiq   S I N A I   Mikhrot Timna
Bîr Gindali
Helwân   Uyûn Mûsa   Beer Ora
El Tabbin   G.Sinn Bishr 622   G.Buthûa   Elat
El Minya   Râs el Sudr   W.abu Tarfa   Aqaba
El Saff   Sudr   G.Sha'ira 1030   G.Abu Rûtha 1018   1216 J.Um al Hashim
Râs Matarma   W.el Sîq   1080 Râs el Nafas
Gebel el Galâla   Asl   1076   G e b e l   e l   T î h   Râs en Naqb
el Baharîya
Gulf of Suez   'Ain Sukhna   Râs 'el 'Agramîya

J O R D A N

1:7.5M

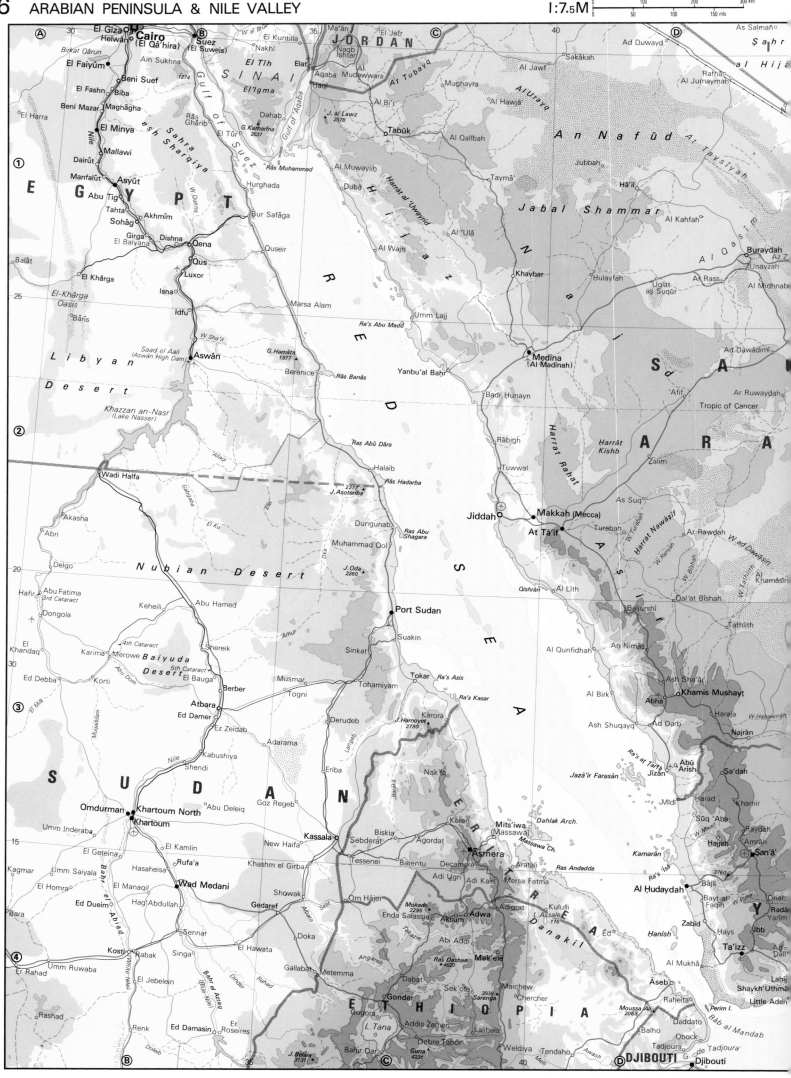

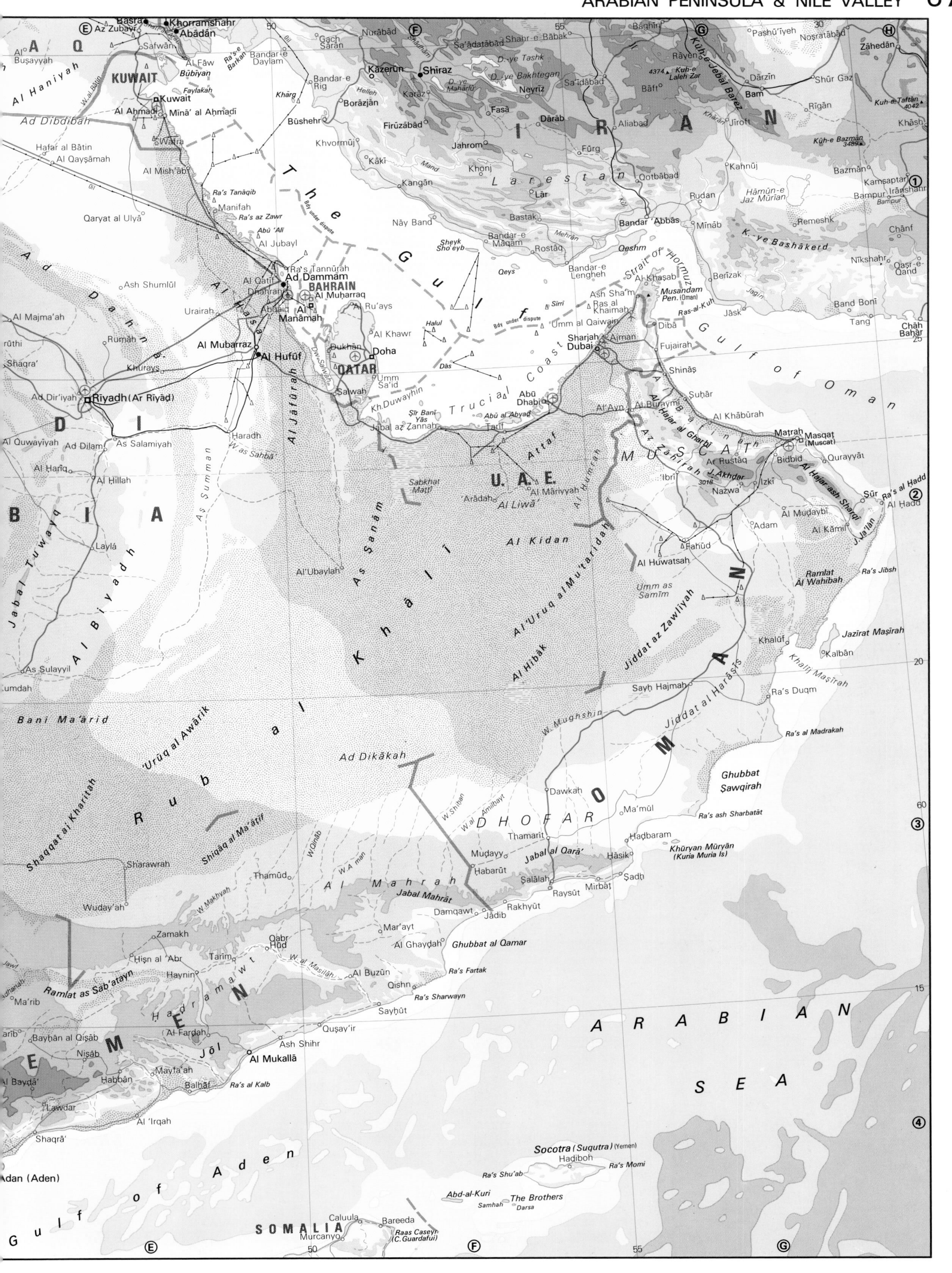

KUWAIT
Kuwait
BAHRAIN
QATAR
Doha
U. A. E.
Abū Dhabi
Dubai
Sharjah
Muscat
Masqat
IRAN
Shiraz
Bandar 'Abbās
The Gulf
Gulf of Oman
Strait of Hormuz
Trucial Coast
MUSCAT
OMAN
SAUDI ARABIA
Riyadh (Ar Riyāḍ)
Ad Dammām
Al Hufūf
Al Mubarraz
Al Manāmah
Rub al Khālī
DHOFAR
Şalālah
YEMEN
Al Mukallā
Hadramawt
ARABIAN SEA
Gulf of Aden
Socotra (Suqutra) (Yemen)
Hadiboh
Abd-al-Kuri
The Brothers
SOMALIA
Raas Caseyr (C. Guardafui)
Ghubbat Şawqirah
Jazīrat Maşīrah
Khūryan Mūryān (Kuria Muria Is)
Ghubbat al Qamar
Ramlat al Wahibah
Jiddat al Harāsīs
Jiddat az Zawlīyah
Al 'Uruq al Mu'tariḍah
Ad Dahnā
Aş Şummān
Abādān
Khorramshahr
Basra
Musandam Pen. (Oman)
Ras al Khaimah
Fujairah
Şuḥār
Şūr
Ra's al Hadd
Nizwā
Ibrī
Al Buraymī
Al 'Ayn

400 800 1200 1600 km
400 800 mls

NORWAY FINLAND SWEDEN Helsinki
Oslo Stockholm Tallinn Sankt Peterburg (Leningrad) Nizhniy Novgorod Magnitogorsk
UNITED KINGDOM North Sea DENMARK Göteborg EST. Riga LAT. Moskva RUSSIAN FEDERATION Samara
IRELAND Edinburgh København Baltic Sea LITH. R.F. Vilnius Minsk BELORUSSIA Volga Ural KAZAKHSTAN Oz. Balkhash
Dublin Hamburg Gdansk Warszawa Kiyev Khar'kov Volgograd Aral Sea Syr-Darya
London NETH. s'Gravenhage Berlin GERMANY POLAND UKRAINE Rostov Don UZBEKISTAN Tashkent KIR.
BELG. Bruxelles Bonn Praha Kraków Odessa Amu-Darya TAJ.
Paris LUX. CZECH REPUBLIC SLOVAKIA MOLD. Bucureşti Volga TURKMENISTAN Ashkhabad
FRANCE Bern München Wien AUSTRIA Budapest HUNGARY ROMANIA Beograd Odessa GEORGIA Tbilisi Baku AZER. Caspian Sea Mashhad
Bay of Biscay SWITZ. Milano SLOV. CROATIA YUGOS. Sofia BULGARIA Istanbul ARM. AFGHANISTAN
Bordeaux Marseille ITALY Adriatic Sea BOSNIA HERZ. Tirana MAC. Ankara Tabrīz Tehrān
Porto Madrid Barcelona Roma Napoli Corse Sardegna ALB. Athinai GREECE TURKEY IRAN
PORTUGAL SPAIN Balearic Islands Sicilia Crete CYPRUS Nicosia SYRIA IRAQ Baghdād Shīrāz PAK.
Lisboa Tanger Rabat Fès Oran Alger Annaba Tunis Constantine Mediterranean Sea Beirut Damascus Euphrates Tigris
Madeira (Port.) Marrakech Casablanca Béchar TUNISIA Sfax Tripoli Benghāzi Jerusalem Port Said Amman Basra KUWAIT The Gulf BAHRAIN Abū Dhabi
Islas Canarias (Sp.) MOROCCO Alexandria Cairo Suez ISR. JORDAN Ar Riyād QATAR UNITED ARAB EMIRATES Muscat
La'yuun ALGERIA LIBYA Ghudāmis Asyūt Nile SAUDI ARABIA OMAN
Nouadhibou Western Sahara Tropic of Cancer In Salah Sabhā EGYPT Aswān Makkah Kuria Muria Is
MAURITANIA Nouakchott SAHARA Ghāt L. Nasser Wadi Halfa Red Sea San'ā YEMEN Socotra (Yemen)
Dakar St-Louis Sénégal Tombouctou Port Sudan Atbara Omdurman Khartoum Kassala ERITREA Asmera Adan Gulf of Aden Aden
THE GAMBIA SENEGAL Banjul MALI Bamako NIGER Agadez El Obeid Blue Nile DJIBOUTI Djibouti Hargeysa
GUINEA BISSAU Kankan BURKINA Ouagadougou Niamey L. Chad CHAD Ndjamena White Nile SUDAN Dire Dawa
GUINEA Conakry Bobo Dioulasso Kano Kaduna Maiduguri Ādīs Ābeba Jimma ETHIOPIA
SIERRA LEONE Freetown Tamale BENIN NIGERIA Abuja Wau SOMALIA
Monrovia IVORY COAST GHANA TOGO Ilorin Niger CENTRAL AFRICAN REPUBLIC Juba L. Turkana
Buchanan LIBERIA Yamoussoukro Kumasi Porto Novo Ibadan Onitsha Bambari Muqdisho
Abidjan Accra Lomé Lagos Port Harcourt CAMEROON Ngaoundéré Bangui Gulu UGANDA KENYA
Gulf of Guinea Bioko Malabo Douala Yaoundé Zaire (Congo) L. Albert Kampala Nairobi
SÃO TOMÉ & PRINCIPE Principe Bata EQUAT. GUINEA Libreville Kisangani L. Edward RWANDA Kigali Lake Victoria Kismaayo
Sao Tomé Annobon (Eq.G) GABON Lambaréné Mbandaka Goma BURUNDI Bujumbura Mwanza Mombasa
Equator CONGO Congo ZAIRE Kindu Kigoma Arusha Dodoma INDIAN
Ascension (U.K.) Brazzaville Bandundu Ilebo Kananga Kalémié Lake Tanganyika Zanzibar TANZANIA Dar es Salaam Seychelles Arch.
Cabinda (Ang.) Kinshasa Mbuji-Mayi Lake Amirante Is SEYCHELLES
Matadi Kwango Kasai Kamina Mbeya Aldabra Is Farquhar Is
Luanda Malanje Luapula Mbala OCEAN
SOUTH Kuito Lubumbashi Lake Nyasa COMOROS Antseranana Tromelin (Fr.)
ATLANTIC ANGOLA Ndola MALAWI Lichinga Mayotte (Fr.)
St Helena (U.K.) Namibe ZAMBIA Lusaka Lilongwe Nampula MADAGASCAR
Namibe Zambezi Livingstone Harare Zumbo Mozambique Channel Mahajanga
OCEAN Kunene Cubango L. Kariba ZIMBABWE Beira Antananarivo Toamasina
Tsumeb Hwange Gweru Mutare MAURITIUS
BOTSWANA Serowe Bulawayo MOZAMBIQUE Réunion (Fr.) Toliara
Tropic of Capricorn Walvis Bay (S.A.) Windhoek Limpopo Inhambane
NAMIBIA Gaborone Pretoria Maputo
Keetmanshoop Johannesburg Mbabane SWAZILAND
Kimberley Bloemfontein Maseru LESOTHO Durban
SOUTH AFRICA Orange East London
Cape Town Port Elizabeth
Tristan da Cunha (U.K.)

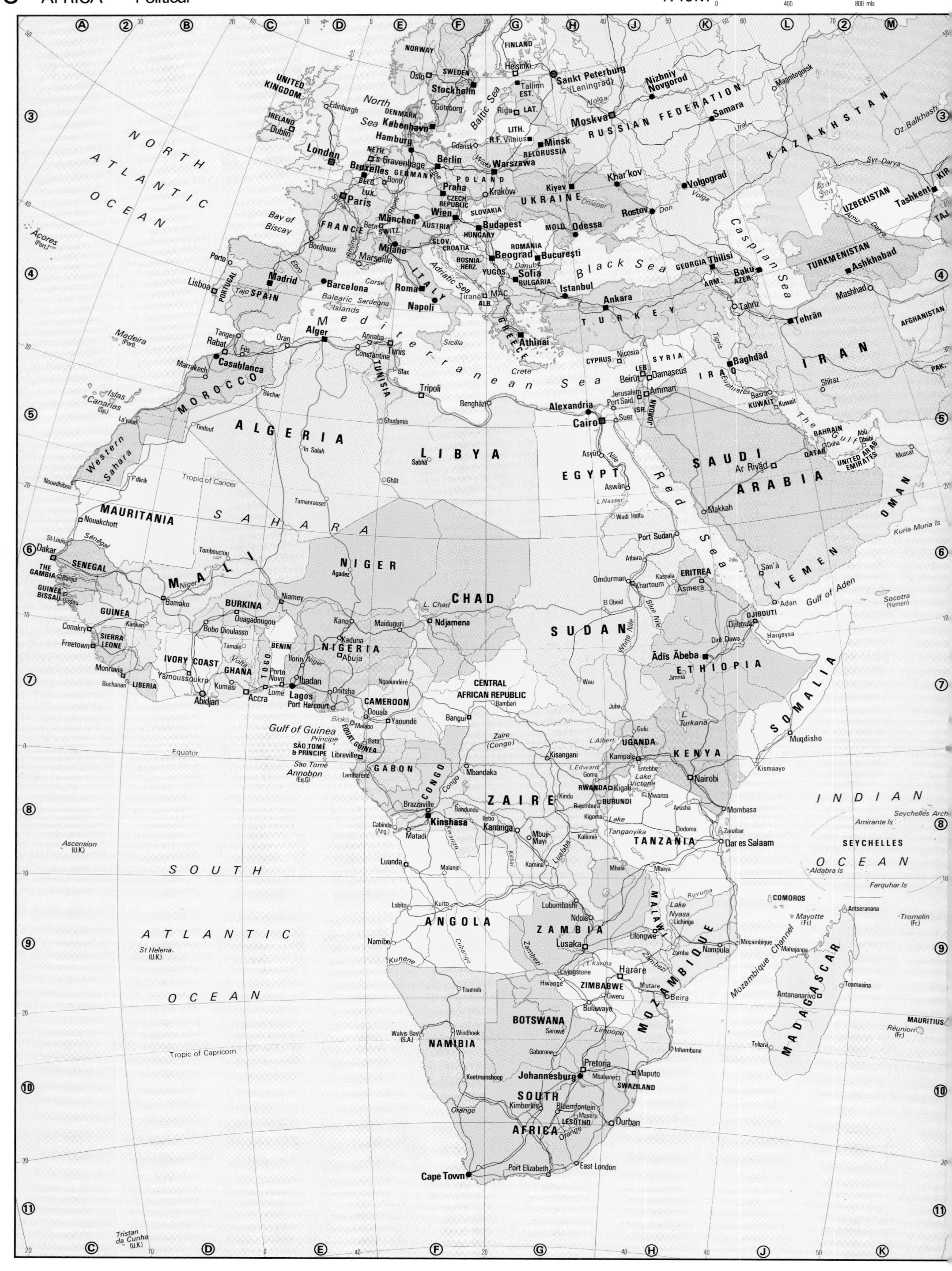

NORTH ATLANTIC OCEAN
Açores (Port.)
Black Sea
Mediterranean Sea
SAHARA
Gulf of Guinea
INDIAN OCEAN

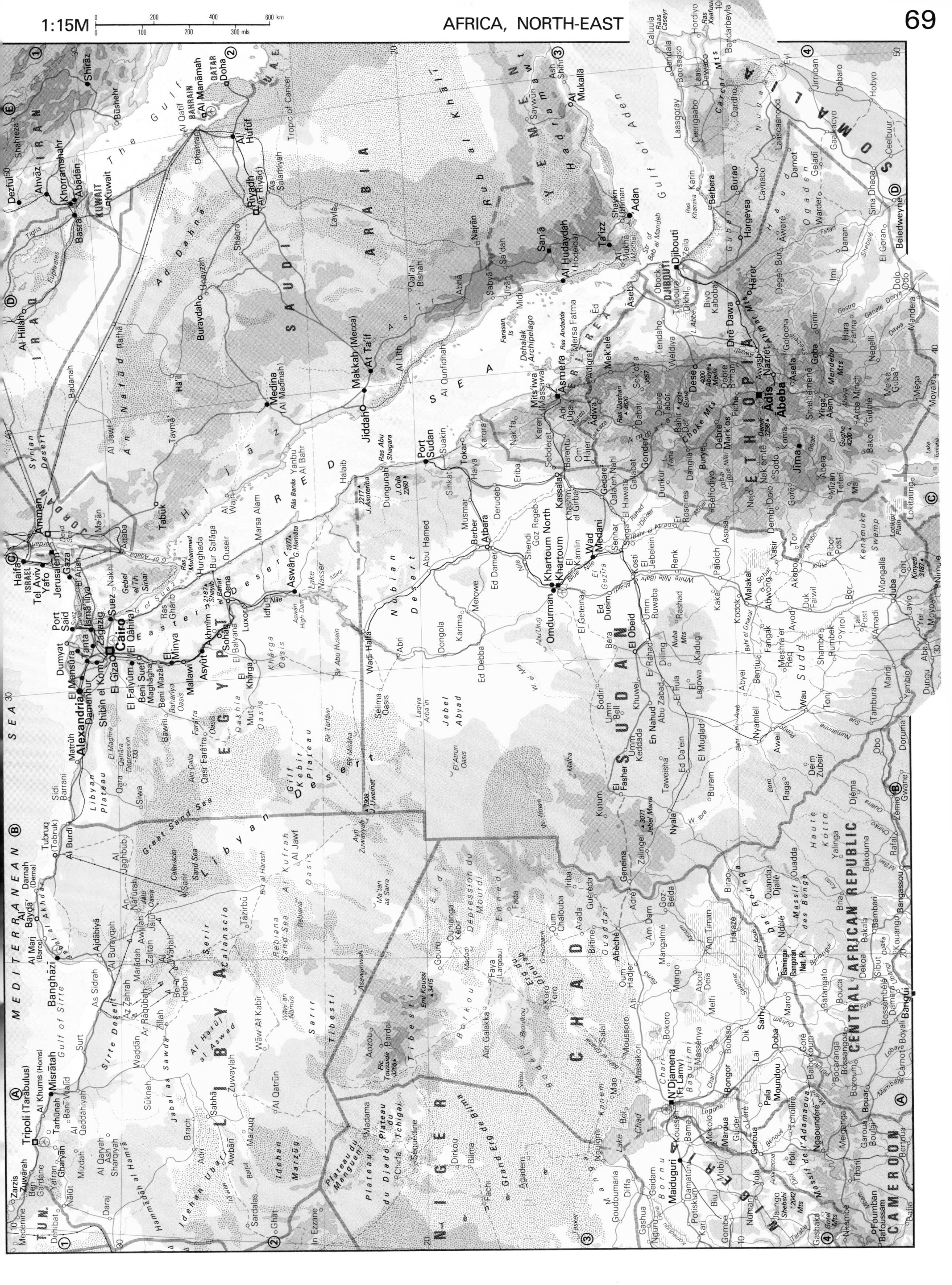
MEDITERRANEAN SEA
LIBYA
EGYPT
SUDAN
CHAD
NIGER
NIGERIA
CAMEROON
CENTRAL AFRICAN REPUBLIC
ETHIOPIA
SOMALIA
DJIBOUTI
ERITREA
YEMEN
SAUDI ARABIA
IRAQ
IRAN
KUWAIT
BAHRAIN
QATAR
U.A.E.
JORDAN
ISRAEL
TUN.
RED SEA
Gulf of Aden
The Gulf
Gulf of Sirte
Libyan Desert
Nubian Desert
Rub al Khali
Tropic of Cancer
Tripoli (Tarābulus)
Banghāzī
Tubruq (Tobruk)
Alexandria
Cairo
El Giza
Port Said
Suez
Aswân
Asyût
Luxor
Wadi Halfa
Port Sudan
Khartoum
Khartoum North
Omdurman
Wad Medani
Kassala
El Obeid
El Fasher
Nyala
Geneina
Abéché
N'Djamena (Ft Lamy)
Maiduguri
Moundou
Bangui
Asmera
Adis Abeba
Dire Dawa
Harer
Djibouti
Aden
Ta'izz
San'ā
Makkah (Mecca)
Jiddah
Medina (Al Madinah)
Riyadh (Ar Riyad)
Amman
Jerusalem
Tel Aviv Yafo
Gaza
Basra
Kuwait
Doha
Al Manāmah
Shīrāz
Lake Chad
Lake Nasser
Tibesti
Emi Koussi 3415
Jebel Marra 3071

Açores (Azores) (Portugal)

Corvo
Flores
São Jorge
Faial · Pico · Terceira
Angra Do Heroismo
Graciosa
São Miguel
Ponta Delgada
Formigas
Santa Maria

at the same scale

PORTUGAL
Lisboa (Lisbon)
Beja
Faro
C. de S. Vincente

SPAIN
Badajoz
Sierra Morena
Ciudad Real
Córdoba
Linares
Albacete
Murcia
Alicante
Cartagena
Sevilla (Seville)
Granada
Huelva
Cádiz
Málaga
Almería
Gibraltar (U.K.)
Str. of Gibraltar
Islas Baleares (Balearic Is.)
Ibiza

MEDITERRANEAN SEA
Sardegna (Sardinia)
Cagliari

Tanger (Tangier)
Ceuta (Sp.)
Tetouan
Melilla (SP.)
Al Hoceima
Oran
Mostaganem
Ech Cheliff
Blida
ALGER (Algiers)
Tizi Ouzou
Bejaïa (Bougie)
Skikda (Philippeville)
Annaba (Bône)
Bizerte
Tunis
La Galite

Kenitra
Rabat
Meknès
Fès
Taza
Oujda
Tlemcen
Sidi-bel-Abbès
Constantine
Souk Ahras
El Kef
Nabeul
Sousse
Kairouan

CASABLANCA (Dar-el-Beida)
El Jadida
Settat
Oued Zem
Beni Mellal
Sétif
Batna
Aurès
Kasserine
El Jem
Mahdia
Sfax
G. de Gabès
I. de Djerba

Safi
Essaouira
Marrakech
Azrou
Midelt
Missour
Bou Saâda
M'sila
Biskra
Gafsa
Kebili
Médenine
Zarzis

MOROCCO
Haut Atlas
Toubkal 4165
Ouarzazate
Agadir
Taroudannt
Er Rachidia
Figuig
Béchar
Laghouat
Berriane
Ghardaïa
El Oued
Touggourt
Hassi-Messaoud
TUNISIA
Tataouine
Nálut

Tiznit
Anti Atlas
Jbel Sarhro
Zagora
Tata
Abadla
Beni Abbès
El Golea
El Gassi
Ghadames
Daraj

Ilhas Selvagens (Port.)
Islas Canarias (Canary Islands) (Spain)
Lanzarote
Arrecife
Santa Cruz De La Palma
La Palma
Gomera
Hierro
Tenerife
Santa Cruz De Tenerife
Gran Canaria
Las Palmas De Gran Canaria
Fuerteventura
Pto Del Rosario
C. Yubi

Madeira (Portugal)
Porto Santo
Funchal
Deserta Grande

Tarfaya
Laâyoune
Tan-Tan
Bou Izakarn
Hamada du Dra
Tindouf
Tabelbala
Kerzaz
Timimoun
Grand Erg Occidental
Plateau du Tademaït
Fort Lallemand
Hamada de Tinrhert
Hammâdah al Hamra

Dakhla
B. de Rio de Oro
Western Sahara
Smara
El Farsia
Hamada Tounassine
Hassi Mdakane
Adrar
In Salah
Bordj Omar Driss
In Amenas
Idehan Ubari

Guelta Zemmur
Bir Moghrein
Erg Iguidi
Bir Ste Marie
Reggane
Aoulef
Plaine du Tidikelt
Arak
Illizi
Tarat
Sardalas
Ghat

Tiris Tir
Ausert
Aguenit
Tichla
Zouérate
Fdérik
Tourine
Erg Chech
Tanezrouft
Mts du Mouydir
Idelès
In Ecker
Hoggar (Ahaggar)
Tabat 2916
In Afaleleh
In Ezzane

Nouadhibou
Ras Nouadhibou
Atar
Chinguetti
Ouadâne
Bir Zreigat
Troudenni
Bidon 5 (Ruins)
Oguilet Khenachich
Abalessa
Tamanrasset
In Ebeggi
Adrar
Tin Tarabine

MAURITANIA
Akjoujt
Bou Naga
El Djouf
El Khenachich
Foum el Alba
Adrar des Iforas
Tessalit
Aguelhok
Tassili du Hoggar
In Guezzam
Ténéré du Tafassasset
Chirfa

Nouakchott
Tidjikja
Tichitt
Araouane
Kidal
Aïr (Azbine)
Timia
Fachi

Rosso
Dagana
Kaédi
Kiffa
Néma
Timbédra
Tombouctou
Gao
Ansongo
Ménaka
Ingal
Agadez
Erg du Ténéré

St-Louis
Louga
Matam
Mbout
Nioro Du Sahel
Nara
Nampala
Bourem
Gourma Rharous
Anéfis
Tahoua
Zinder
Gouré
Goudoumaria
Diffa

Dakar
Thiès
Diourbel
Bakel
Kayes
Diéma
Sokolo
Mopti
Douentza
Niamey
Maradi
Katsina
Kano

SENEGAL
Kaolack
Kaffrine
Tambacounda
Bafoulabé
Kita
Ségou
Djenné
Bandiagara
Ouahigouya
Dori
Niamey
Sokoto
Zaria
Kaduna

THE GAMBIA
Banjul
Georgetown
Kédougou
Bamako
Koulikoro
San
BURKINA
Ouagadougou
Fada N'Gourma
Birnin-Kebbi
Gusau
Kano

GUINEA-BISSAU
Bissau
Bolama
Arquipélago dos Bijagós

GUINEA
Labé
Boké
Dalaba
Mamou
Siguiri
Kankan
Sikasso
Bobo Dioulasso
Bolgatanga
Zaria
Kaduna
Jos
Bauchi
Gombe
NIGERIA
Abuja
Minna

Conakry
Forécariah
SIERRA LEONE
Freetown
Makeni
Kenema
Man
Odienné
Korhogo
Ferkessédougou
Wa
Tamale
Yendi
Ilorin
Ogbomosho
Ibadan

LIBERIA
Monrovia
Buchanan
Greenville
Harper
IVORY COAST
Bouaké
Yamoussoukro
Daloa
Abidjan
GHANA
Kumasi
Accra
Cape Coast
Sekondi
Takoradi

LAGOS
Porto Novo
Cotonou
Benin City
Onitsha
Enugu
Port Harcourt
Calabar
CAMEROON
Douala
Yaoundé

Bight of Benin
Mouths of the R. Niger
Bight of Biafra

GULF OF GUINEA
EQUATORIAL GUINEA
Malabo
Bioko (Fernando Poo)
S. TOME & PRINCIPE
Libreville

CAPE VERDE
Sto Antão
S. Vicente
S. Luzia
S. Nicolau
Sal
Boa Vista
S. Tiago
Praia
Fogo
Brava
Maio

at the same scale

Annobon (Equat. Guinea)
Equator

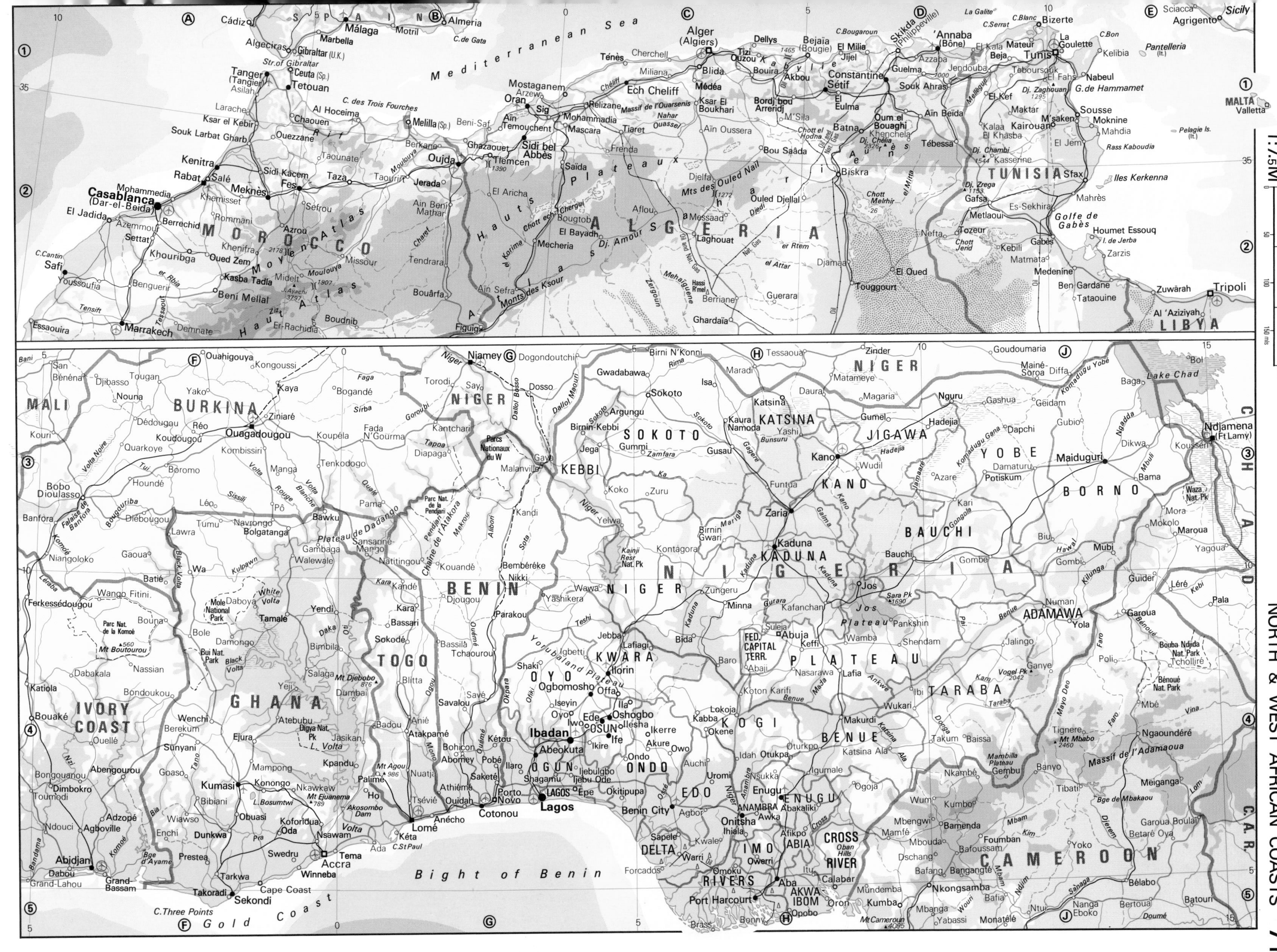

1:15M

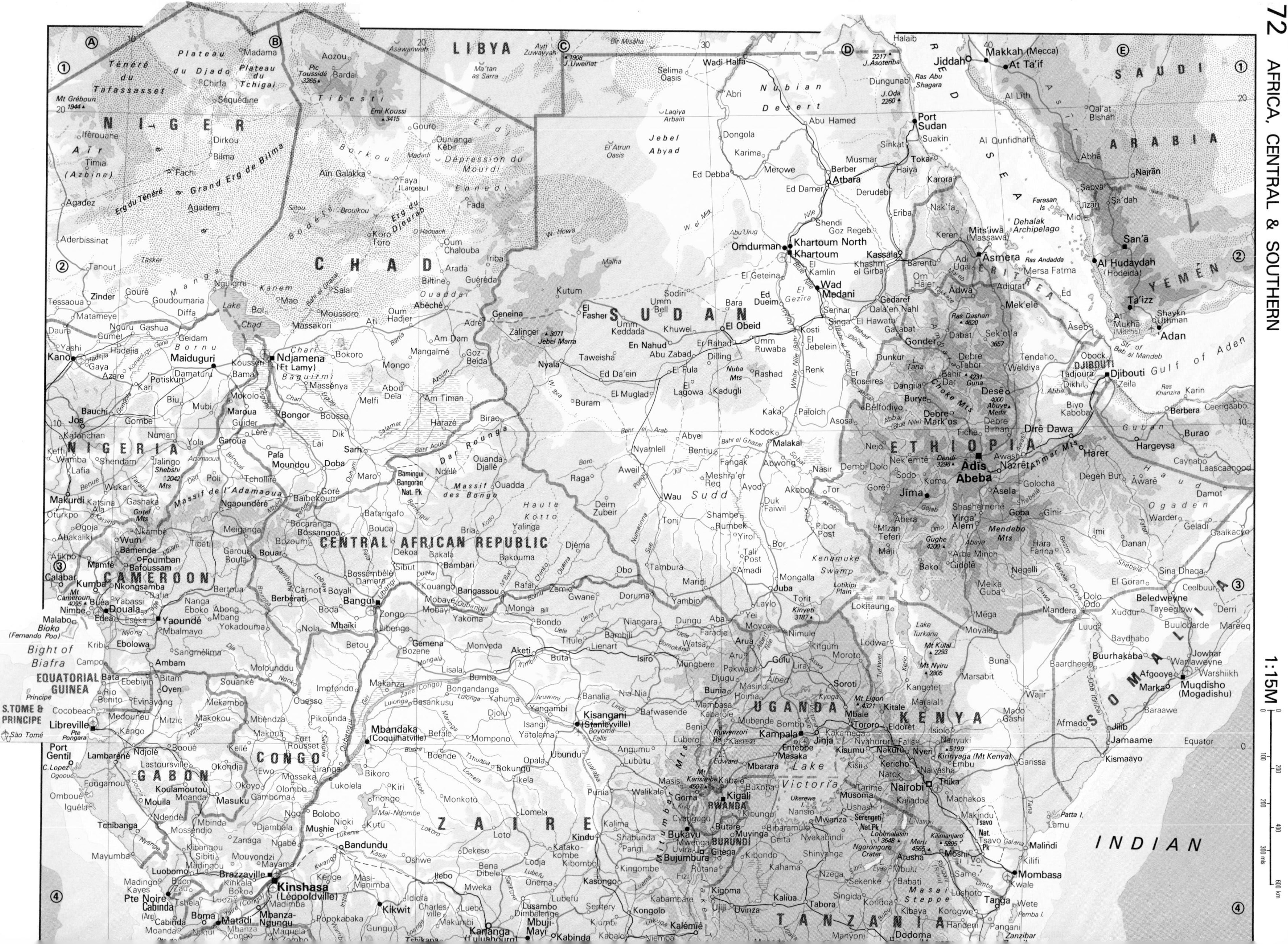
0
200
400
600 km
0
100
200
300 mls
LIBYA
NIGER
CHAD
SUDAN
ETHIOPIA
ERITREA
DJIBOUTI
SAUDI ARABIA
YEMEN
RED SEA
Gulf of Aden
NIGERIA
CAMEROON
CENTRAL AFRICAN REPUBLIC
EQUATORIAL GUINEA
S.TOME & PRINCIPE
GABON
CONGO
ZAIRE
UGANDA
KENYA
RWANDA
BURUNDI
TANZANIA
SOMALIA
INDIAN
Lake Chad
Lake Victoria
Khartoum
Omdurman
Ndjamena (Ft Lamy)
Adis Abeba
Nairobi
Kinshasa (Léopoldville)
Brazzaville
Kampala
Kigali
Bangui
Yaoundé
Libreville
Muqdisho (Mogadishu)
Djibouti
Asmera
San'ā
Jiddah
Makkah (Mecca)
Mombasa

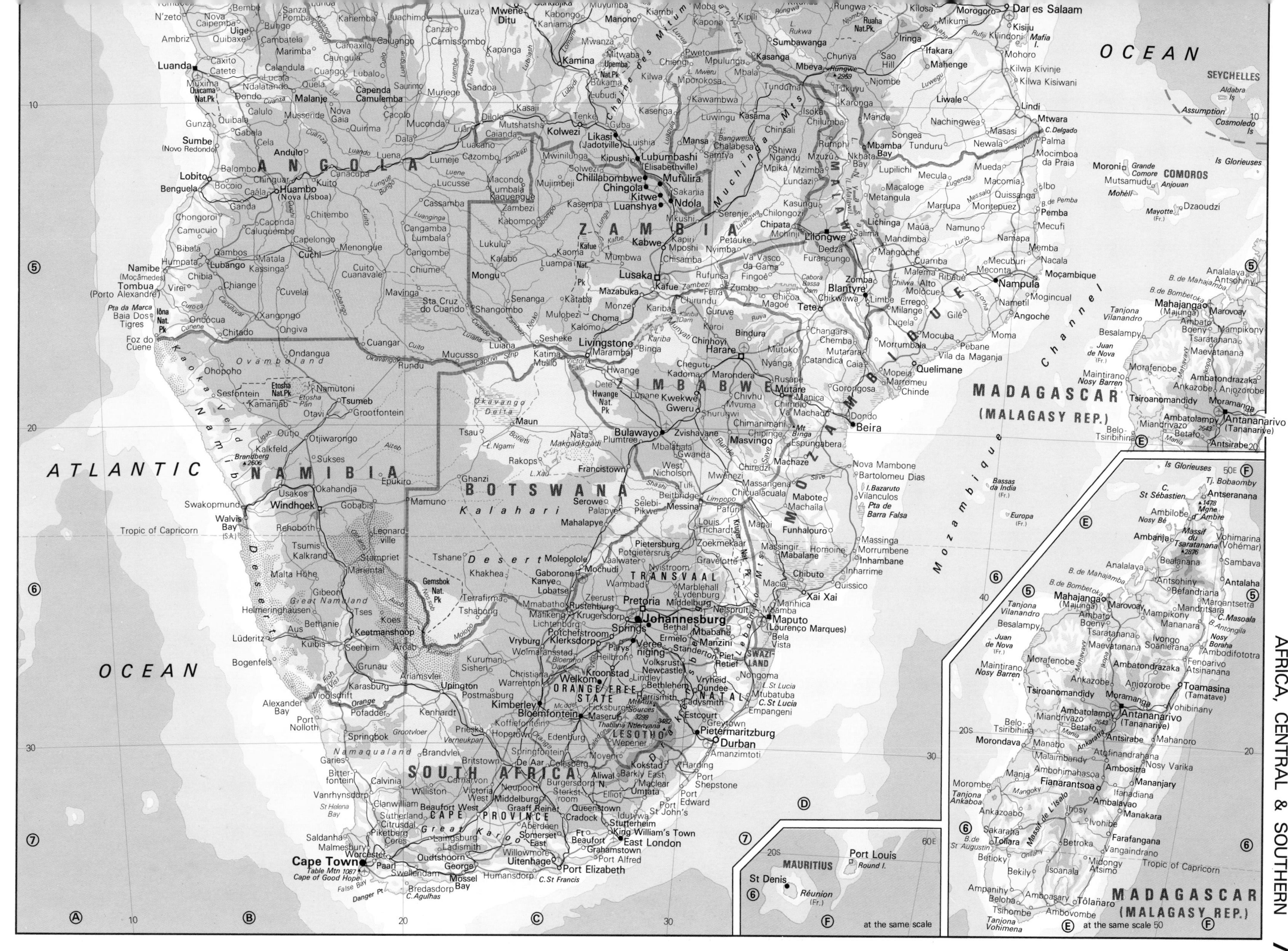
ATLANTIC
OCEAN
OCEAN
ANGOLA
ZAMBIA
NAMIBIA
BOTSWANA
ZIMBABWE
MOZAMBIQUE
MALAWI
SOUTH AFRICA
TRANSVAAL
ORANGE FREE STATE
CAPE PROVINCE
NATAL
LESOTHO
SWAZILAND
MADAGASCAR (MALAGASY REP.)
Mozambique Channel
COMOROS
SEYCHELLES
MAURITIUS
Réunion (Fr.)
Kalahari
Desert
Tropic of Capricorn
Luanda
Lusaka
Harare
Windhoek
Gaborone
Maputo (Lourenço Marques)
Pretoria
Johannesburg
Cape Town
Durban
Port Elizabeth
East London
Bloemfontein
Lilongwe
Blantyre
Beira
Bulawayo
Livingstone (Maramba)
Dar es Salaam
Antananarivo (Tananarive)
Port Louis
St Denis
at the same scale

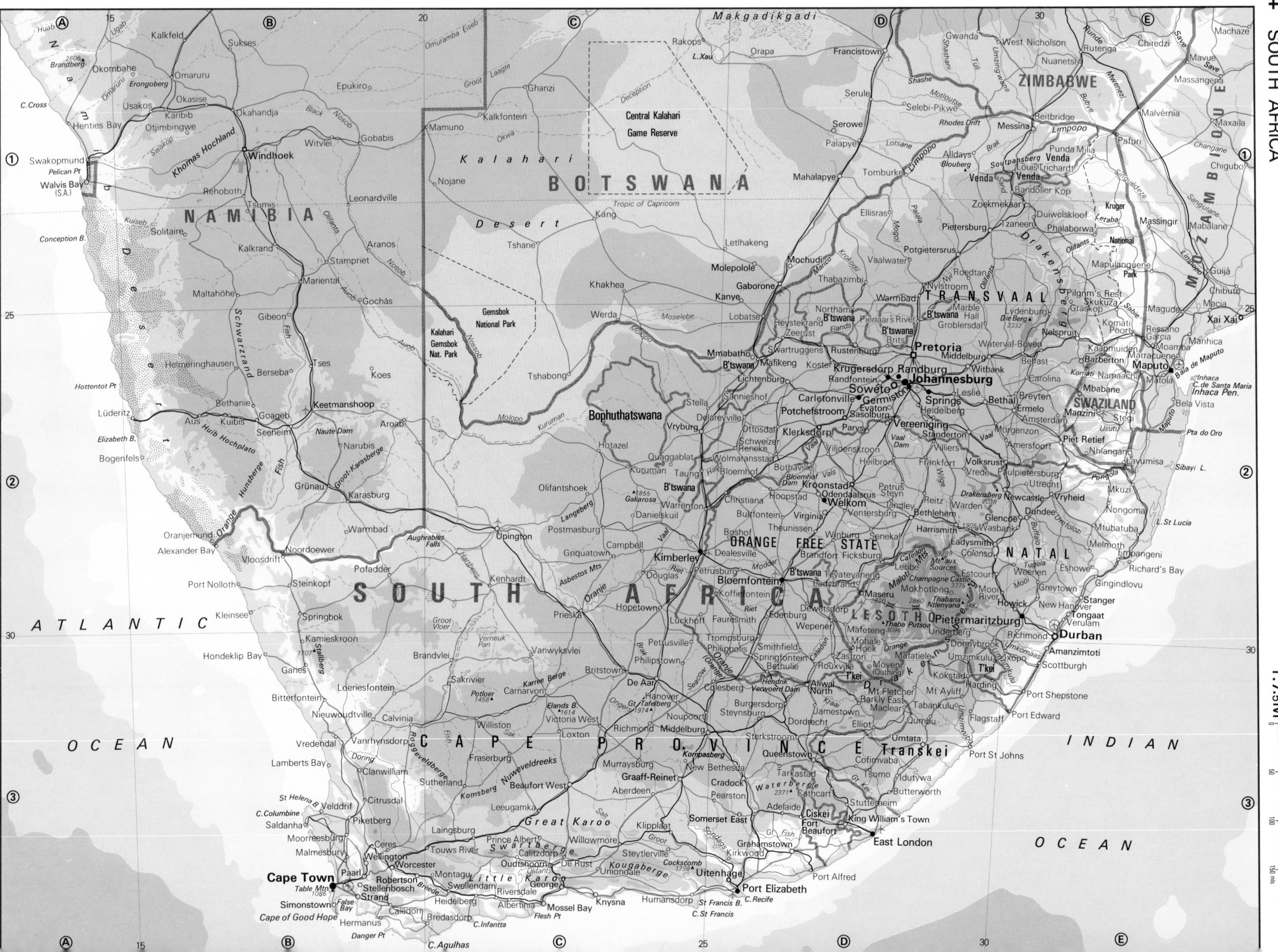

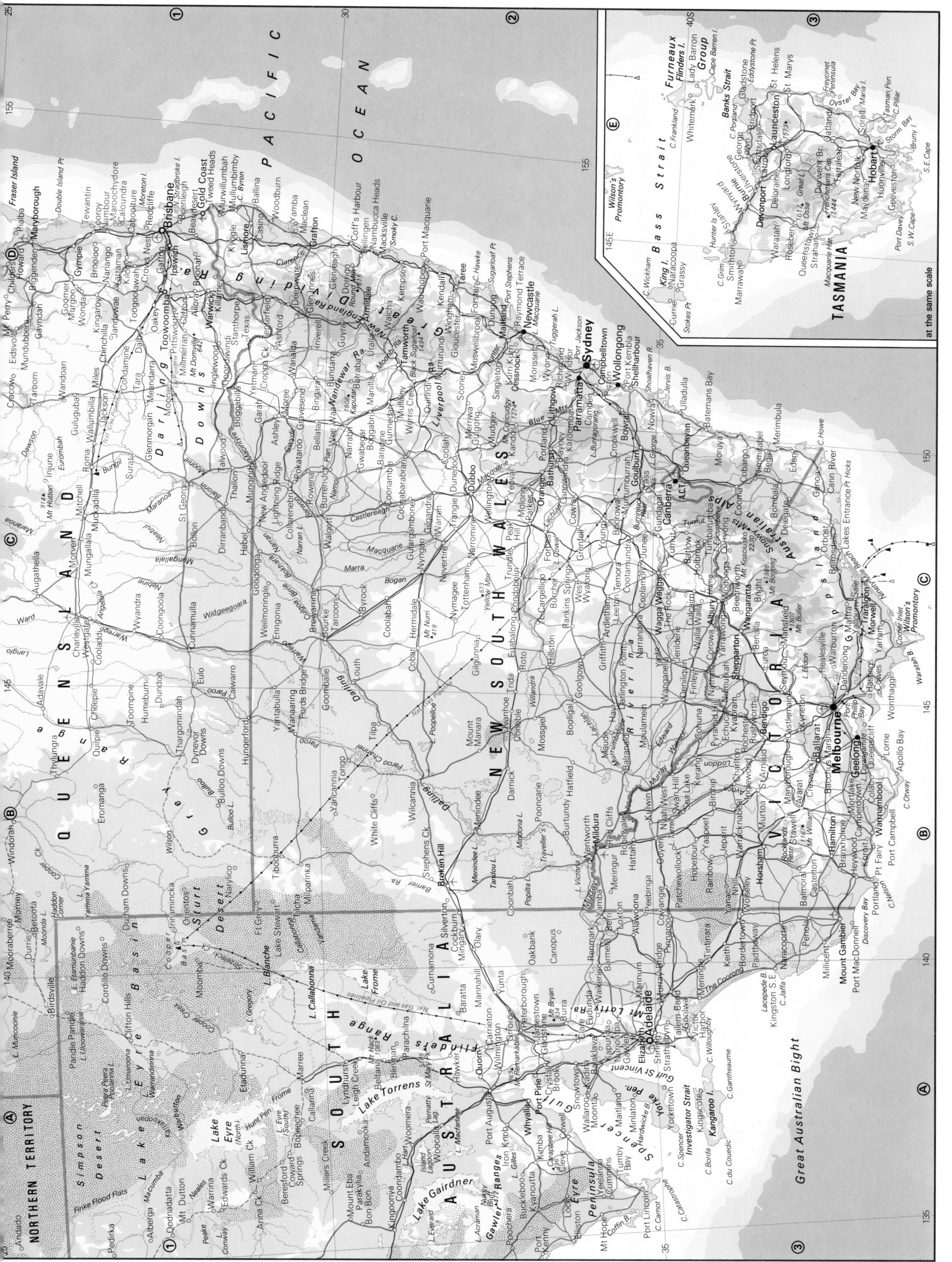

200   400   600   800 km
200   400 mils

BORNEO

Tajungselor
Tanjungredeb
Kelolokan
Samarinda
Balikpapan
Tanjung
Banjarmasin
Kintap
Tg Selatan
Ujung Pandang (Makassar)
Bonthain
Palopo
Parepare
Majene
Donggala
Palu
Poso
Kendari
Watampone
Butung
Kabaena
Baubau
Kep. Tukangbesi

SULAWESI (CELEBES)

Teluk Tomini
Toboli
Gorontalo
Tolitoli
Minahassa Peninsula
Manado
Belang Sea
Tomini
Euwuk
Peleng
Teluk Banggai
Kep. Sula
Taliabu
Obi
Ceram Sea
Piru
Bula
Ambon
Namlea
Buru
Seram

MOLUCCAS
Morotai
Tubelo
Halmahera
Ternate
Weda
Teluk Weda
Sorong
Salawati
Misool
Fakfak
Kaimana

Kep. Asia
Kep. Ayu
P.P. Mapia

Manokwari
Biak
Numfoor
Yapen
Sarmi
Jayapura
Aitape
Wewak

IRIAN JAYA
Pegunungan Maoke
Pk. Jaya 5029
Tanahmerah
Kokonau
Dolak
Digul
Merauke
Daru
Saibai I.

NEW GUINEA
Madang
Mt Hagen
Mendi
Goroka
Sepik
Central Ra.
Mt Wilhelm
Bulolo
Morobe
Lae
Kikori
Kerema
Kokoda
Owen Stanley Ra.
Port Moresby
Kupiano
Gulf of Papua
Popondetta
D'Entrecasteaux
Samarai

PAPUA NEW GUINEA
Talasea
New Britain

Bismarck Archipelago
Admiralty Is
Manus
Schouten Is
Manam
Ninigo Is
Hermit Is
Mussau
Saint Matthias Group
New Hanover
Kavieng
New Ireland
Rabaul

Bismarck Sea

Arafura Sea

Timor Sea
Cartier I.
Scott Reef
Rowley Shoals

INDIAN OCEAN
Java Trench

Bali
Denpasar
Lombok
Mataram
Sumbawa
Sumba
Memberoo
Raba
Reo
Ruteng
Flores
Ende
Waingapu
Kupang
Roti
Sawu
Alor
Dili
Timor
Wetar
Romang

Flores Sea
P.P. Kangean
P.P. Macan

Banda Sea
Kep. Barat Daya
Damar
Kep. Babar
Kep. Leti
Kep. Sermata

Kep. Tanimbar
Kep. Aru
Dobo
Kep. Kai
Kep. Banda

INDONESIA

Melville I.
Bathurst I.
Van Diemen G.
Clarence Str.
Darwin
Rum Jungle
Adelaide River
Burrundie
Pine Creek
Katherine
Cobourg Pen.
Croker I.
Arnhem Land
Nhulunbuy
C. Arnhem
Groote Eylandt
Limmen Bight
Sir Edward Pellew Group

Gulf of Carpentaria
Wessel Is
Weipa
Cape York
Iron Range
Coen
York Peninsula
Mitchell River
Laura
Cooktown
Princess Charlotte B.
C. Grenville
Torres Strait
Pr. of Wales I.
C. York
Somerset

NORTHERN TERRITORY
Wyndham
L. Argyle
Victoria River Downs
Daly Waters
Newcastle Waters
Wave Hill
Powell Creek
Tennant Creek
Barkly Tableland
Barrow Creek
Camooweal
Mount Isa
Cloncurry
Dajarra
Georgina
Selwyn
Winton

QUEENSLAND
Normanton
Croydon
Forsayth
Burketown
Gilbert
Leichhardt
Flinders
Gregory Ra.
Richmond
Hughenden
Longreach
Barcaldine
Blackall
Barcoo
Diamantina
Windorah
Charleville
Quilpie
Roma
Miles
Toowoomba
Cunnamulla
St George
Goondiwindi

Mt Bartle Frere 1612
Cairns
Innisfail
Ravenshoe
Ingham
Palm Is
Townsville
Charters Towers
Ayr
Bowen
Proserpine
Collinsville
Mackay
Sarina
Northumberland Is
Marlboro
Rockhampton
Mount Morgan
Gladstone

Great Barrier Reef
Willis Group
Coringa Is

Great Dividing Range

Broome
Derby
Fitzroy Crossing
Hall's Creek
Halls Creek
Fitzroy
Sturt Ck
King Leopold Ra.
Kimberley Plateau
Mt Ord 936
C. Lévêque
King Sound
C. Londonderry
Joseph Bonaparte Gulf
Pago Mission
Victoria
Birdum
Borroloola
Mornington
Wellesley

Lagrange
Eighty Mile Beach
Great Sandy Desert
Shay Gap
Marble Bar
De Grey
Port Hedland
Roebourne
Dampier
Monte Bello Is
Barrow I.
Onslow
Fortescue
Nullagine
Wittenoom
Hamersley Ra.
Mt Bruce 1226
Paraburdoo
Ashburton
Newman
North West C.
Barlee Ra.
Lyons
Mt Augustus 1106
Gascoyne
Carnarvon
Shark B.
Dirk Hartog I.
L. McLeod
Murchison
Meekatharra
Wiluna
Cue
Sandstone
Mt Magnet
Leonora

WESTERN AUSTRALIA

Great Sandy Desert
L. Mackay
L. Disappointment
Gibson Desert
L. Carnegie
L. Wells
Macdonnell Ranges
Mt Zeil 1510
Alice Springs
Petermann Ra.
Mt Aloysius 987
Tomkinson Ra.
Musgrave Ra.
Mt Woodroffe 1440
Finke
Simpson Desert
Birdsville
Lake Eyre Basin
Oodnadatta
L. Eyre
Coober Pedy
Marree
Milparinka
Tibooburra

Gibson Desert
Great Victoria Desert
Petermann Ra.

SOUTH AUSTRALIA

Ooldea
Tarcoola
Woomera
L. Everard
L. Gairdner
Penong
Ceduna
Streaky Bay
L. Torrens
St Mary Pk 1189
Leigh Ck
L. Frome
Quorn
Port Augusta
Peterborough
Iron Knob
Whyalla
Port Pirie
Wallaroo
Port Lincoln
Eyre Pen.
Spencer Gulf
Gawler Ranges
Renmark
Murray Bridge
Elizabeth
Adelaide
Gulf St Vincent
Kangaroo I.
Victor Harbour
Kingston
Naracoorte
Mount Gambier
Portland
Port Fairy
Warrnambool

Northampton
Mullewa
Geraldton
Dongara
Houtman Abrolhos
Moora
Goomalling
Merredin
Kalgoorlie
Coolgardie
Southern Cross
Bullfinch
Norseman
Eyre
Rawlinna
Forrest
Nullarbor Plain

Great Australian Bight
Flinders I.
C. Pasley
Arch. of the Recherche
Esperance

Perth
Fremantle
Pinjarra
Collie
Narrogin
Wagin
Katanning
Bunbury
Busselton
C. Naturaliste
Augusta
C. Leeuwin
Manjimup
Bluff Knoll 1114
Bunbury
Albany

Mildura
Balranald
Deniliquin
Swan Hill
Kerang
Bendigo
Ballarat
Geelong
Colac
Hamilton
Horsham
Ararat
VICTORIA
Melbourne
Morwell
Sale
Bairnsdale
Wonthaggi
Wilson's Prom.

NEW SOUTH WALES
Broken Hill
Wilcannia
Menindee
Ivanhoe
Cobar
Bourke
Walgett
Moree
Narrabri
Gunnedah
Tamworth
Armidale
Nyngan
Dubbo
Gondobolin
Griffith
Hay
Lachlan
Wagga Wagga
Albury
Cootamundra
Yass
Goulburn
Bathurst
Lithgow
Orange
Cessnock
Maitland
Newcastle
Sydney
Wollongong
Canberra
A.C.T.
Mt Kosciusko 2230
Australian Alps
Bombala
Orbost
C. Howe

King I.
Bass Strait
Furneaux Group
Flinders I.
C. Barren

C. Grim
Smithton
Burnie
Devonport
Launceston
St Mary's
Queenstown
Mt Ossa 1617
Hobart
Geeveston
South West C.
South East C.
TASMANIA

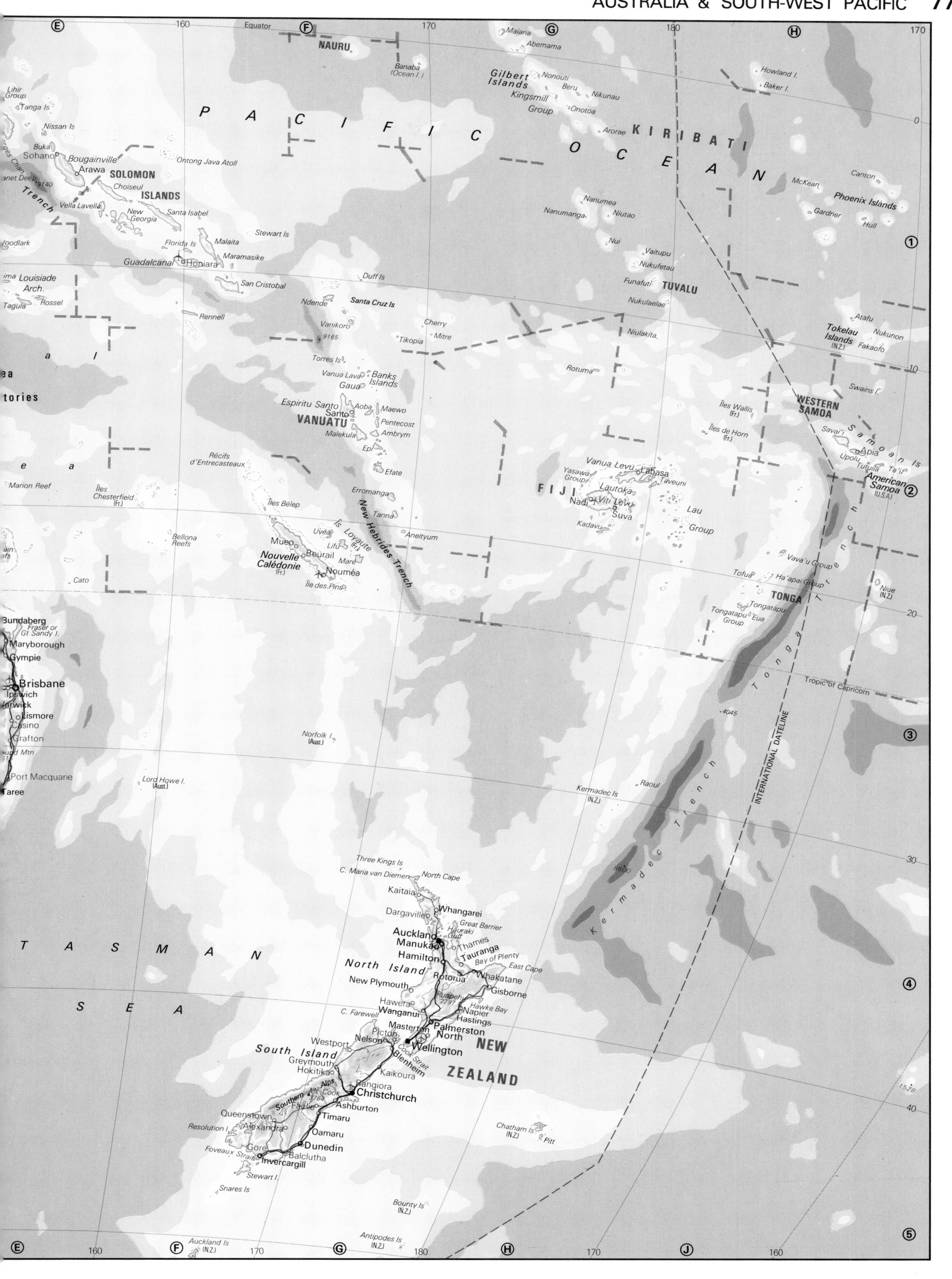
PACIFIC OCEAN
KIRIBATI
NAURU
SOLOMON ISLANDS
TUVALU
VANUATU
FIJI
WESTERN SAMOA
American Samoa (U.S.A.)
TONGA
NEW ZEALAND
North Island
South Island
TASMAN SEA
Nouvelle Calédonie (Fr.)
Nouméa
Santa Cruz Is
Gilbert Islands
Kingsmill Group
Phoenix Islands
Tokelau Islands (N.Z.)
Îles Wallis (Fr.)
Samoan Is
Lau Group
Tonga Trench
Kermadec Trench
New Hebrides Trench
Kermadec Is (N.Z.)
Norfolk I. (Aust.)
Lord Howe I. (Aust.)
Chatham Is (N.Z.)
Bounty Is (N.Z.)
Antipodes Is (N.Z.)
Auckland Is (N.Z.)
INTERNATIONAL DATELINE
Tropic of Capricorn
Equator
Brisbane
Auckland
Wellington
Christchurch
Dunedin
Invercargill
Hamilton
Tauranga
Rotorua
Gisborne
Napier
Hastings
Palmerston North
Wanganui
New Plymouth
Nelson
Blenheim
Timaru
Suva
Apia
Honiara
Bougainville
Guadalcanal
Espiritu Santo
Vanua Levu
Viti Levu

50   100   150   200 km
50   100 mls

Three Kings Is

C. Maria
van Diemen
North
Cape

TASMAN

Ninety Mile Beach
Rangaunu B.
Doubtless B.
Ahipara B.
Tauroa Pt
Kaitaia
Bay of Islands
C. Brett
Russell
Kaikohe
Kawakawa
Hikurangi
Hokianga Har.
Whangarei
Hen & Chickens Is
Bream B.
Dargaville
Little Barrier I.
Great Barrier I.
Kaipara Har.
Wellsford
C. Colville
Manly
Hauraki
Gulf
Mercury Is
Takapuna
Mercury Bay
Auckland
Coromandel
Peninsula
Papatoetoe
Manukau
Papakura
Thames
Pukekohe
Waiuku
Paeroa
Waihi
Mayor I.

NORTH

SEA

Huntly
Te Aroha
Matakana I.
White I.
C. Runaway
Hicks
Bay
Glen Afton
Morrinsville
Tauranga Har.
Ngaruawahia
Cambridge
Tauranga
Te Puke
Bay of
Plenty
East C.
Hamilton
Whakatane
Opotiki
Te Awamutu
Putaruru
Rotorua
Kawerau
Tangatatu
Raukumara Ra.
Kawhia
Otorohanga
Rotorua
Tokomaru
Bay
Waitomo
Mangakino
Tolaga
Bay
Te Kuiti
Murupara

ISLAND

N. Taranaki Bight
Ohura
Taumarunui
Taupo
L. Taupo
Waikaremoana
Gisborne
Waitara
Mt Ngauruhoe
2291
Mt Makorako
1274 Mohaka
Poverty Bay
New Plymouth
Inglewood
Mt Egmont
2518
Stratford
Mt Ruapehu
2797
Wairoa
Mahia Peninsula
C. Egmont
Eltham
Ohakune
Waiouru
Eskdale
Tarawera
Portland I.
Opunake
Raetihi
Kaimanawa Mts
Taradale
Napier
Hawera
Patea
Taihape
Waiouru
Ngaruroro Ra.
Hastings
S. Taranaki Bight
Patea
C. Kidnappers
Havelock North
Wanganui

Marton
Rangitikei
Waipukurau
C. Farewell
Farewell Spit
COOK
Palmerston N.
Dannevirke
Collingwood
Golden
Bay
Feilding
Woodville
Rocks Pt
Separation Pt
C. Stephens
Pahiatua
Foxton
C. Turnagain
Takaka
D'Urville I.
Levin
Eketahuna
Herbertville
Tasman
Mts
Tasman
Bay
Paraparaumu
Otaki
Karamea
The Twins
1826
Motueka
C. Jackson
5291
Hector
Masterton
Karamea
Bight
Nelson
Picton
Porirua
Tawa
Carterton
Seddonville
Richmond
Upper Hutt
Westport
Murchison
Richmond Ra.
Wellington
Wairau
Lower
Hutt
Martinborough
C. Foulwind
Blenheim
Palliser Bay
Mt Ross
983
Reefton
L. Rotoroa
Awatere
C. Campbell
C. Palliser
Runanga
L. Rotoiti
Ra.
Buller
Spenser Mts
Tapuaenuku
2885
Greymouth
Victoria
Ra.
Mt Travers
2338
Kaikoura
Hokitika
Lewis
Pass
Hanmer
Springs
Kaikoura Pen.
Ross
L. Brunner
Waiau
Culverden
Waiau
Hurunui
Cheviot
Arthurs
Pass
L. Sumner
Abut Hd
Puketeraki
Ra.
Waipara
Pegasus
Bay
Franz Josef Gl
Coleridge
Rangiora
Kaiapoi
Rakaia
Waimakariri
Mt Cook
3764
Waimakariri
Hornby
Christchurch
Mt Sefton
3157
Methven
Lyttelton
Hermitage
Rangitata
Lincoln
Banks
Peninsula
Jackson Hd
Pollux
2542
L. Coleridge
Akaroa
Cascade Pt
Geraldine
Ashburton
Ellesmere
L. Tekapo
Awarua Pt
Young Ra.
L. Ohau
Fairlie
Canterbury
Bight
Mt Aspiring
3027
L. Pukaki
Temuka
Milford Sd
Wanaka
L. Pukaki
Milford Sd
Mt Pyramid
2326
L. Hawea
L. Benmore
Timaru
George Sd
Homer
Tunnel
Wanaka
Omarama
Caswell Sd
Arrowtown
L. Aviemore
Waimate
Cromwell
Kurow
Waitaki
Secretary Sd
Queenstown
Clyde
Oamaru
Doubtful
Sd
L. Wakatipu
Alexandra
Ranfurly
Hampden
Breaksea
Sd
Kingston
Roxburgh
Waikouaiti
Resolution
Mt Ward
718
Manapouri
Palmerston
Dusky
Sd
Cromwell
Port Chalmers
L. Hauroko
Lumsden
Herriot
Taieri
Otago Peninsula
Puysegur
Pt
Riversdale
Mosgiel
Dunedin
Cameron Mts
Winton
Gore
Lawrence
Te Waewae
Bay
Ohai
Milton
Balclutha
Solander I.
Edendale
Mataura
Kaitangata
Foveaux
Strait
Riverton
Owaka
Codfish I.
Invercargill
Bluff
Oban
Paterson Inlet
Stewart Island
Mt Allen
730
Shelter Pt
Port Pegasus

SOUTH

ISLAND

SOUTHERN ALPS

Fiordland
Nat. Park

Canterbury
Plains

PACIFIC

OCEAN

35

40

45

170

175

170

175

400 800 1200 1600 km
400 800 mils

Northern Polar Region (Arctic)

Portland
Seattle
Vancouver
Vancouver I.
Prince Rupert
Juneau
Mt McKinley 6194
Yukon
Anchorage
Teller
Vankarem
Bering Str.
Blagoveshchensk
Ayan
CHINA
120
Vaduz
Calgary
Edmonton
Saskatoon
ROCKY MTS
Fairbanks
Dawson
Alaska (U.S.A.)
Chukchi Sea
70
Pevek
Ambarchik
Kolyma
Ust'-Nera
Skovorodino
Chu'man
Amur
Chita
CANADA
L. Athabasca
Flin Flon
Yellowknife
Norman Wells
Inuvik
Mackenzie
Gt Bear L.
Gt Slave L.
Prudhoe Bay
Barrow
O. Vrangelya
Beaufort Sea
E. Siberian Sea
Indigirka
Polyarn'yy
Kazach'ye
Zhigansk
Aldan
Yakutsk
Verkhoyansk
Lena
Ulan-Ude
Oz. Baykal
Irkutsk
90
Churchill
L. Winnipeg
Banks I.
Victoria I.
McClure Str.
80
Novosibirskiye Ostrova
Laptev Sea
Tiksi
Khatanga
Nordvik
Ust'-Kut
9
Hudson Bay
Southampton I.
Foxe Basin
Queen Elizabeth Islands
N. Magnetic Pole (1990)
Resolute
Islands
A
North Pole
A
Severnaya Zemlya
B
Tree Limit
Noril'sk
Turukhansk
Dudinka
Dikson
Yenisey
Krasnoyarsk
90
D
James B.
Chisasibi
Inukjuak
Hudson Str.
Baffin I.
Baffin Bay
Pond Inlet
Nares Str.
Eureka
Thule
Alert
Lincoln Sea
Zemlya Frantsa Iosifa
Novaya Zemlya
Kara Sea
Salekhard
Berezovo
Nadym
Vorkuta
Novosibirsk
Barnaul
3
Scheffervile
Hebron
Nain
Davis Str.
Godhavn
Søndre Strømfjord
Godthåb (Nuuk)
Upernavik
Greenland (Kalaallit Nunaat) (Den.)
Nord
Svalbard (Spitsbergen) (Nor.)
Greenland Sea
Barents Sea
Serov
Salekhard
Tobol'sk
Omsk
Tselinograd
10
Gulf of St Lawrence
30
Newfoundland
Gander
Julianehåb
Angmagssalik
Watkins Bjerge 3700
Scoresbysund
K. Farvel
Denmark Strait
Bjørnøya (Bear I.) (Nor.)
Jan Mayen (Nor.)
Nordkapp
Tromsø
Narvik
Murmansk
Arkhangel'sk
Mezen
Kotlas
Sev. Dvina
Syktyvkar
Kirov
Yekaterinburg
Perm'
Ufa
Magnitogorsk
Uralskiy Khrebet
RUSSIAN FEDERATION
KAZAKHSTAN
Orsk
Aktyubinsk
60
2
ATLANTIC OCEAN
ICELAND
Reykjavik
1
NORWAY
SWEDEN
FINLAND
Oulu
Umeå
Norwegian Sea
Arctic Circle
0
Kazan'
Samara
Yaroslavl'
Nizhniy Novgorod
Sankt-Peterburg (Leningrad)
11
12

Southern Polar Region (Antarctica)

ATLANTIC OCEAN
Falkland Is (U.K.)
Scotia Sea
Orcadas (Arg.) S. Orkney Is (U.K.)
Signy (U.K.)
Georg von Neumayer (Germany)
Sanae (S.A.)
Maitri (India)
Prinsesse Astrid Kyst
Novolazarevskaya (Rus. Fed.)
Asuka (Jap.)
Prinsesse Ragnhild Kyst
Syowa (Jap.)
Molodezhnaya (Rus. Fed.)
Enderby Land
INDIAN
60
ARGENTINA
Tierra del Fuego
CHILE
S. Shetland Is (U.K.)
Weddell Sea
C. Norvegia
Halley (U.K.)
Coats Land
Dronning Maud Land
Mawson (Aust.)
Heard I. (Aust.)
10
Drake Passage
Graham Land
Palmer Arch.
Antarctic Peninsula
Grl Belgrano (Arg.)
Berkner I.
Ronne Ice Shelf
Mac. Robertson Land
+3355
Pr. Charles Mts
C. Darnley
Amery Ice Shelf
Zhongshan (China)
Davis (Aust.)
3
PACIFIC
Palmer Land
Alexander I.
Charcot I.
Bellingshausen Sea
Ellsworth Land
Vinson Massif 5140
Pensacola Mts
GREATER ANTARCTICA
American Highland
90
H
Peter I Øy (Nor.)
Thurston I.
Mt Seelig 3022
Transantarctic Mts
South Pole
Amundsen-Scott (U.S.)
E
F
Queen Mary Land
Mirnyy (Rus. Fed.)
G
90
Walgreen Coast
Amundsen Sea
Siple I.
ANTARCTICA
LESSER ANTARCTICA
Mt Sidley 4181
Marie Byrd Land
Q. Maud Mts
Mt Kirkpatrick 4528
Mt Markham 4351
Ross Ice Shelf
Roosevelt I.
80
Vostok (Rus. Fed.)
Shackleton Ice Shelf
Knox Coast
Casey (Aust.)
C. Poinsett
Wilkes Land
9
C. Colbeck
Scott (N.Z.) McMurdo
Ross Sea
Victoria Land
George V Land
Terre Adélie
Dumont d'Urville (Fr.)
S. Magnetic Pole (1990)
C. Adare
Oates Land
Balleny Is
Scott I.
Sturge I.
70

Antarctic Research Stations
1 Artigas (Uruguay)
2 Teniente Rodolfo Marsh Martin (Chile)
3 Bellingshausen (Rus. Fed.)
4 Chang Cheng (Great Wall) (China)
5 Comandante Ferraz (Brazil)
6 Henryk Arctowski (Poland)
7 Teniente Jubany (Arg.)
8 King Sejong (Korea)
9 Capitán Arturo Prat (Chile)
10 General Bernardo O'Higgins (Chile)
11 Esperanza (Arg.)
12 Vicecomodoro Marambio (Arg.)
13 Palmer (USA)
14 Farady (UK)
15 Rothera
16 General San Martin (Arg.)
17 Václav Voytěch (Czech Rep.)

Abbreviations

Abbreviations used in Reference Map Section

	Full Form	English Form	Language
A			
a.d.	an der	on the	German
Akr.	Ákra, Akrotírion	cape	Greek
Appno	Appennino	mountain range	Italian
Arch.	Archipelago	archipelago	English
B			
B.	1. Baai, Bahía, Baía, Baie, Bay, Bucht, Bukhta, Bugt	bay	Dutch, Spanish, Portuguese, French, English, German, Russian, Danish
	2. Ban	village	Indo-Chinese
	3. Barrage	dam	French
Bol.	Bol'sh/aya, -oy, -oye	big	Russian
Br.	1. Branch	branch	English
	2. Bridge, Brücke	bridge	English, German
	3. Burun	cape	Turkish
Brj	Baraj,-i	dam	Turkish
C			
C.	Cabo, Cap, Cape	cape	Spanish, French, English
Can.	Canal	canal	English
Cd	Ciudad	town	Spanish
Chan.	Channel	channel	English
Ck	Creek	creek	English
Cord.	Cordillera	mountain range	Spanish
D			
D.	1. Dağ, Dāgh, Daği, Daǧlari	mountain, range	Persian, Turkish
	2. Daryācheh	lake	Persian
Dj.	Djebel	mountain	Arabic
E			
E.	East	east	English
Emb.	Embalse	reservoir	Spanish
Escarp.	Escarpment	escarpment	English
Estr.	Estrecho	strait	Spanish
F			
F.	Firth	estuary	Gaelic
Fj.	1. Fjell	mountain	Norwegian
	2. Fjord, Fjorður	fjord	Norwegian, Icelandic
Ft	Fort	fort	English
G			
G.	1. Gebel	mountain	Arabic
	2. Göl, Gölü	lake	Turkish
	3. Golfe, Golfo, Gulf	gulf	French, Italian, Portuguese, Spanish, English
	4. Gora, -gory	mountain, range	Russian
	5. Gunung	mountain	Malay, Indonesian
Gd, Gde	Grand, Grande	grand	English, French
Geb.	Gebirge	mountain range	German
Gl.	Glacier	glacier	French, English
Grl	General	general	Spanish
Gt, Gtr	Great, Groot, -e, Greater	greater	English, Dutch
H			
Har.	Harbour	harbour	English
Hd	Head	head	English
I			
I.	Ile, Ilha, Insel, Isla, Island Isle, Isola, Isole	island	French, Portuguese, German Spanish, English, Italian
In.	1. Indre, Inner	inner	Norwegian, English
	2. Inlet	inlet	English
Is	Iles, Ilhas, Islands, Isles, Islas	islands	French, Portuguese, English, Spanish
Isth.	Isthmus	isthmus	English
J			
J.	Jabal, Jebel, Jibal	mountain	Arabic
K			
K.	1. Kaap, Kap, Kapp	cape	Dutch, German, Norwegian, Swedish
	2. Koh, Kuh, Kuhha	mountain	Persian
	3. Kolpos	gulf	Greek
Kep.	Kepulauan	islands	Indonesian
Khr.	Khrebet	mountain range	Russian
Kör.	Körfez, -i	gulf, bay	Turkish
L			
L.	1. Lac, Lago, Lagoa, Lake, Liman, Limni, Loch, Lough	lake	French, Italian, Spanish, Portuguese, English, Russian, Greek, Gaelic
Lag.	Lagoon, Laguna, -e, Lagôa	lagoon	English, Spanish, French, Portuguese
Ld	Land	land	English
Lit.	Little	little	English
M			
M.	1. Muang	town	Thai
	2. Mys	cape	Russian
m	metre, -s	metre(s)	English, French
Mal.	Mali, -o, -yy	small	Russian
Mf	Massif	mountain group	French
Mgne	Montagne(s)	mountain(s)	French
Mont	Monument	monument	English
Mt	Mont, Mount	mountain	French, English
Mte	Monte	mountain	Italian, Portuguese, Spanish
Mti	Monti	mountain, range	Italian
Mtn	Mountain	mountain	English
Mts	Monts, Mountains Montañas, Montes	mountains	French, English, Spanish, Italian, Portuguese

	Full Form	English Form	Language
N			
N.	1. Neu, Ny	new	German
	2. Nevado	snow capped mtns	Spanish
	3. Noord, Nord, Norte Nørre, North	north	Danish, French, Portuguese, Spanish, Danish, English
Nat.	National	national	English
Nat. Pk	National Park	national park	English
Ndr	Neder, Nieder	lower	Dutch, Swedish, German
N.E.	North East	north east	English
N.M.	National Monument	national monument	English
N.P.	National Park	national park	English
N.W.	North West	north west	English
O			
O.	1. Oost, Ost	east	Dutch, German
	2. Ostrov	island	Russian
Ø	Øy	island	Norwegian
Oz.	Ozero, Ozera	lake(s)	Russian
P			
P.	1. Pass, Passo	pass	English, German, Italian
	2. Pic, Pico, Pizzo	peak	French, Portuguese, Spanish, Italian
	3. Pulau	island	Malay, Indonesian
P.P.	Pulau-pulau	islands	Indonesian
Pass.	Passage	passage	English
Peg.	Pegunungan	mountains	Indonesian
Pen.	Peninsula, Penisola	peninsula	English, Italian
Pk	1. Park	park	English
	2. Peak, Pik	peak	English, Russian
Plat.	Plateau, Planalto	plateau	English, French, Portuguese
Pov	Poluostrov	peninsula	Russian
Pr.	Prince	prince	English
Pres.	President, Presidente	president	English, Spanish, Portuguese
Promy	Promontory	promontory	English
Pt	Point	point	English
Pta	1. Ponta, Punta	point	Portuguese, Italian, Spanish
	2. Puerta	pass	Spanish
Pte	Pointe	point	French
Pto	Porto, Puerto	port	Spanish
R			
R.	1. Rio, River, Rivière,	river	Portuguese, Spanish, English, French
	2. Ría	river mouth	Spanish
Ra.	Range	range	English
Rap.	Rapids	rapids	English
Res.	Reserve, Reservation	reserve, reservation	English
Resr	Reservoir	reservoir	English
Résr	Réservoir	reservoir	French
S			
S.	1. Salar, Salina	salt marsh	Spanish
	2. San, São	saint	Spanish, Portuguese
	3. See	sea, lake	German
	4. South, Sud	south	English, French
s.	sur	on	French
Sa	Serra, Sierra	mountain range	Portuguese, Spanish
Sd	Sound, Sund	sound	English, German, Swedish
S.E.	South East	south east	English
Sev.	Sever, Severnaya	north	Russian
Sp.	Spitze	peak	German
Spr.	Spring,(s)	spring(s)	English
St	Saint	saint	English
Sta	Santa	saint	Spanish
Sta.	Station	station	English
Ste	Sainte	saint	French
Sto	Santo	saint	Portuguese, Spanish
Str.	Strait	strait	English
S.W.	South West	south west	English
T			
T.	Tall, Tel	hill, mountain	Arabic, Hebrew
Tg	Tanjong, Tandjong	cape	Malay, Indonesian
Tk	Têluk, Têlok	bay	Indonesian
Tr.	Trench, Trough	trench, trough	English
U			
U.	Uad	wadi	Arabic
Ug	Ujung	cape	Malay
Upr	Upper	upper	English
V			
V.	1. Val, Valle	valley	French, Italian, Spanish
	2. Ville	town	French
Va	Villa	town	Spanish
Vdkhr.	Vodokhranilishche	reservoir	Russian
Vol.	Volcán, Volcano	volcano	Spanish, English
Vozv.	Vozvyshennost'	upland	Russian
W			
W.	1. Wadi	wadi	Arabic
	2. Water	water	English
	3. Well	well	English
	4. West	west	English
Y			
Yuzh.	Yuzhnaya, Yuzhno, Yuzhnyy	south	Russian
Z			
Z.	Zaliv	gulf, bay	Russian
Zap.	Zapadnyy, -aya, -o, -oye	western	Russian
Zem.	Zemlya	country, land	Russian

Index

Introduction to the index

In the index, the first number refers to the page, and the following letter and number to the section of the map in which the index entry can be found. For example, 38C2 **Paris** means that Paris can be found on page 38 where column C and row 2 meet.

Abbreviations used in the index

Afghan	Afghanistan	Hung	Hungary	Par	Paraguay	Arch	Archipelago
Alb	Albania	Ind	Indonesia	Phil	Philippines	B	Bay
Alg	Algeria	Irish Rep	Irish Republic	Pol	Poland	C	Cape
Ant	Antarctica	Kirgh	Kirghizia	Port	Portugal	Chan	Channel
Arg	Argentina	Leb	Lebanon	Rom	Romania	Gl	Glacier
Aust	Australia	Lib	Liberia	Russian Fed	Russian Federation	I(s)	Island(s)
Bang	Bangladesh	Liech	Liechtenstein	S Africa	South Africa	Lg	Lagoon
Belg	Belgium	Lux	Luxembourg	S Arabia	Saudi Arabia	L	Lake
B-H	Bosnia-Herzegovina	Mac	Macedonia	Scot	Scotland	Mt(s)	Mountain(s)
Bol	Bolivia	Madag	Madagascar	Sen	Senegal	O	Ocean
Bulg	Bulgaria	Malay	Malaysia	Sl	Slovakia	P	Pass
Camb	Cambodia	Maur	Mauritania	Switz	Switzerland	Pass	Passage
Can	Canada	Mor	Morocco	Tanz	Tanzania	Pen	Peninsula
CAR	Central African Republic	Mozam	Mozambique	Thai	Thailand	Plat	Plateau
Cz. R	Czech Republic	Neth	Netherlands	Turk	Turkey	Pt	Point
Den	Denmark	Nic	Nicaragua	USA	United States of America	Res	Reservoir
Dom Rep	Dominican Republic	Nig	Nigeria	Urug	Uruguay	R	River
El Sal	El Salvador	N Ire	Ireland, Northern	Ven	Venezuela	S	Sea
Eng	England	Nor	Norway	Viet	Vietnam	Sd	Sound
Eq Guinea	Equatorial Guinea	NZ	New Zealand	Yugos	Yugoslavia	Str	Strait
Eth	Ethiopia	Pak	Pakistan	Zim	Zimbabwe	V	Valley
Fin	Finland	PNG	Papua New Guinea				

A

42B2 **Aachen** Germany
36C1 **Aalst** Belg
32K6 **Äänekoski** Fin
37C1 **Aarau** Switz
37B1 **Aare** *R* Switz
52A3 **Aba** China
71H4 **Aba** Nig
72D3 **Aba** Zaïre
63B2 **Abādān** Iran
63C2 **Abādeh** Iran
70B1 **Abadla** Alg
29C2 **Abaeté** Brazil
29C2 **Abaeté** *R* Brazil
27J4 **Abaetetuba** Brazil
52D1 **Abagnar Qi** China
71H4 **Abaji** Nig
19E3 **Abajo Mts** USA
71H4 **Abakaliki** Nig
49L4 **Abakan** Russian Fed
70C3 **Abala** Niger
70C2 **Abalessa** Alg
26D6 **Abancay** Peru
63C2 **Abarqū** Iran
53E3 **Abashiri** Japan
53E3 **Abashiri-wan** *B* Japan
22C1 **Abasolo** Mexico
51H7 **Abau** PNG
72D3 **Abaya** *L* Eth
72D2 **Abbai** *R* Eth
72E2 **Abbe** *L* Eth
38C1 **Abbeville** France
17D4 **Abbeville** Louisiana, USA
15C2 **Abbeville** S Carolina, USA
37C2 **Abbiategrasso** Italy
18B1 **Abbotsford** Can
12A2 **Abbotsford** USA
60C2 **Abbottabad** Pak
67F4 **Abd-al-Kuri** *I* Yemen
44J5 **Abdulino** Russian Fed
72C2 **Abéché** Chad
71F4 **Abengourou** Ivory Coast
32F7 **Åbenrå** Den
42B1 **Åbenra** Den
71G4 **Abeokuta** Nig
72D3 **Abera** Eth
35C5 **Aberaeron** Wales
20C2 **Aberdeen** California, USA
13D3 **Aberdeen** Maryland, USA
15B2 **Aberdeen** Mississippi, USA
74C3 **Aberdeen** S Africa
34D3 **Aberdeen** Scot
8D2 **Aberdeen** S Dakota, USA

8A2 **Aberdeen** Washington, USA
6J3 **Aberdeen L** Can
34D3 **Aberfeldy** Scot
35D6 **Abergavenny** Wales
35C5 **Aberystwyth** Wales
44L2 **Abez'** Russian Fed
66D3 **Abhā** S Arabia
63B1 **Abhar** Iran
71H4 **Abia** *State* Nigeria
66C4 **Abi Addi** Eth
71F4 **Abidjan** Ivory Coast
17C2 **Abilene** Kansas, USA
16C3 **Abilene** Texas, USA
35E6 **Abingdon** Eng
12C3 **Abingdon** USA
7K4 **Abitibi** *R* Can
7L5 **Abitibi,L** Can
45G7 **Abkhazskaya** Respublika, Georgia
36A2 **Ablis** France
60C2 **Abohar** India
71G4 **Abomey** Benin
72B3 **Abong Mbang** Cam
57E9 **Aborlan** Phil
72B2 **Abou Deïa** Chad
67E1 **Abqaiq** S Arabia
39A2 **Abrantes** Port
72D1 **'Abri** Sudan
76A3 **Abrolhos** *Is* Aust
8B2 **Absaroka Range** *Mts* USA
67F2 **Abū al Abyad** *I* UAE
67E1 **Abū 'Ali** *I* S Arabia
66D3 **Abū Arish** S Arabia
66B3 **Abū Deleiq** Sudan
67F2 **Abū Dhabi** UAE
66B3 **'Abu Dom** *Watercourse* Sudan
65C3 **Ābū el Jurdhān** Jordan
66B3 **Abu Fatima** Sudan
72D2 **Abu Hamed** Sudan
68E7 **Abuja** Nigeria
65A3 **Abu Kebir Hihya** Egypt
26E5 **Abunã** Brazil
26E6 **Abuna** *R* Bol
64D3 **Abū Sukhayr** Iraq
65B3 **Abu Suweir** Egypt
78B2 **Abut Head** *C* NZ
66B1 **Abu Tig** Egypt
72D2 **Abu'Urug** *Well* Sudan
72D2 **Abuye Meda** *Mt* Eth
72C2 **Abu Zabad** Sudan
72D3 **Abwong** Sudan
42B1 **Åby** Den

65C3 **Aby 'Aweigîla** *Well* Egypt
72C3 **Abyei** Sudan
13F2 **Acadia Nat Pk** USA
21B2 **Acambaro** Mexico
23B5 **Acandi** Colombia
21B2 **Acaponeta** Mexico
21B3 **Acapulco** Mexico
27L4 **Acaraú** Brazil
26E2 **Acarigua** Ven
21C3 **Acatlán** Mexico
22C2 **Acatlan** Mexico
22C2 **Acatzingo** Mexico
22D2 **Acayucan** Mexico
71F4 **Accra** Ghana
28E2 **Aceguá** Urug
60D4 **Achalpur** India
25B6 **Achao** Chile
53B2 **Acheng** China
37D1 **Achensee** *L* Austria
36E2 **Achern** Germany
33A3 **Achill** *I* Irish Rep
49L4 **Achinsk** Russian Fed
40D3 **Acireale** Italy
11D3 **Ackley** USA
23C2 **Acklins** *I* Caribbean
26D6 **Acobamba** Peru
25B4 **Aconcagua** *Mt* Chile
27L5 **Acopiara** Brazil
68B4 **A'cores** *Is* Atlantic O
A Coruna = La Coruna
37C2 **Acqui** Italy
75A2 **Acraman,L** Aust
Acre = 'Akko
26D5 **Acre** *State*, Brazil
20C3 **Acton** USA
22C1 **Actopan** Mexico
71G4 **Ada** Ghana
17C3 **Ada** USA
39B1 **Adaja** *R* Spain
10C6 **Adak** *I* USA
67G2 **Adam** Oman
72D3 **Adama** Eth
29B3 **Adamantina** Brazil
72B3 **Adamaoua** Region, Nig/Cam
71J4 **Adamawa** State, Nigeria
37D1 **Adamello** *Mt* Italy
14D1 **Adams** USA
62B3 **Adam's Bridge** India/Sri Lanka
3E3 **Adams L** Can
8A2 **Adams,Mt** USA
62C3 **Adam's Peak** *Mt* Sri Lanka

67E4 **'Adan** Yemen
45F8 **Adana** Turk
45E7 **Adapazari** Turk
66B3 **Adarama** Sudan
79F7 **Adare,C** Ant
57D4 **Adaut** Indon
75B1 **Adavale** Aust
37C2 **Adda** *R* Italy
67E1 **Ad Dahna'** Region, S Arabia
66D4 **Ad Dāli'** Yemen
67F1 **Ad Damman** S Arabia
66D3 **Ad Darb** S Arabia
66D2 **Ad Dawādimī** S Arabia
67E1 **Ad Dibdibah** Region, S Arabia
67F3 **Ad Dikākah** Region, S Arabia
67E2 **Ad Dilam** S Arabia
67E2 **Ad Dir'iyah** S Arabia
66C4 **Addis Zeman** Eth
64D3 **Ad Dīwanīyah** Iraq
64D3 **Ad Duwayd** S Arabia
11D3 **Adel** USA
76C4 **Adelaide** Aust
6J3 **Adelaide Pen** Can
51G8 **Adelaide River** Aust
20D3 **Adelanto** USA
Aden = 'Adan
58C4 **Aden,G of** Yemen/Somalia
70C3 **Aderbissinat** Niger
65D2 **Adhra** Syria
51G7 **Adi** *I* Indon
40C1 **Adige** *R* Italy
72D2 **Adigrat** Eth
66C4 **Adi Kale** Eth
60D5 **Adilābād** India
18B2 **Adin** USA
13E2 **Adirondack Mts** USA
72D3 **Ādis Abeba** Eth
72D2 **Adi Ugai** Eritrea
64C2 **Adıyaman** Turk
41F1 **Adjud** Rom
10G1 **Admiralty B** USA
6E4 **Admiralty I** USA
7K2 **Admiralty Inlet** *B* Can
76D1 **Admiralty Is** PNG
57B4 **Adonara** *I* Indon
62B1 **Ādoni** India
38B3 **Adour** *R* France
70A2 **Adrar** Region, Maur
70C2 **Adrar** Alg
70A2 **Adrar** *Mts* Alg
70A2 **Adrar Soutouf** Region, Mor
72C2 **Adré** Chad

69A2 **Adri** Libya
37E2 **Adria** Italy
12C2 **Adrian** Michigan, USA
16B2 **Adrian** Texas, USA
40C2 **Adriatic S** Italy/Yugos
72D2 **Adwa** Eth
49P3 **Adycha** *R* Russian Fed
71F4 **Adzopé** Ivory Coast
44K2 **Adz'va** *R* Russian Fed
44K2 **Adz'vavom** Russian Fed
41E3 **Aegean** *S* Greece
58E2 **Afghanistan** Republic, Asia
72E3 **Afgooye** Somalia
66D2 **'Afif** S Arabia
71H4 **Afikpo** Nig
32G6 **Åfjord** Nor
71C2 **Aflou** Alg
72E3 **Afmado** Somalia
70A3 **Afollé** Region, Maur
14C1 **Afton** New York, USA
18D2 **Afton** Wyoming, USA
65C2 **Afula** Israel
45E8 **Afyon** Turk
65A3 **Aga** Egypt
72B2 **Agadem** Niger
70C3 **Agadez** Niger
70B1 **Agadir** Mor
60D4 **Agar** India
61D3 **Agartala** India
18B1 **Agassiz** Can
10A6 **Agattu** *I* USA
10A5 **Agattu Str** USA
71H4 **Agbor** Nig
71F4 **Agboville** Ivory Coast
64E1 **Agdam** Azerbaijan
54C3 **Agematsu** Japan
38C3 **Agen** France
63B2 **Agha Jārī** Iran
45G8 **Ağn** Turk
37D2 **Agno** *R* Italy
66C3 **Agordat** Eth
37E1 **Agordo** Italy
71G4 **Agou,Mt** Togo
38C3 **Agout** *R* France
60D3 **Agra** India
64D2 **Agri** Turk
40D2 **Agri** *R* Italy
40C3 **Agrigento** Italy
41E3 **Agrínion** Greece
28A3 **Agrio** *R* Chile
40C2 **Agropoli** Italy
44J4 **Agryz** Russian Fed
7N3 **Agto** Greenland
29B3 **Agua Clara** Brazil

28B4 Aguada de Guerra Arg
23D3 Aguadilla Puerto Rico
28B4 Aguado Cicilio Arg
22B1 Aguanava R Mexico
5J3 Aguanish Can
5J3 Aguanus R Can
28D1 Aguapey R Arg
21B1 Agua Prieta Mexico
29A3 Aguaray Guazu Par
21B2 Aguascalientes Mexico
22B1 Aguascalientes State, Mexico
29D2 Aguas Formosas Brazil
25G1 Agua Vermelha, Barragem Res Brazil
39A1 Agueda Port
70C3 Aguelhok Mali
70A2 Agüenit Well Mor
39B2 Aguilas Spain
22B2 Aguililla Mexico
xxviiiC7 Agulhas Basin Indian O
73C7 Agulhas,C S Africa
xxviiiC6 Agulhas Plat Indian O
57G9 Agusan R Phil
Ahaggar = Hoggar
45H8 Ahar Iran
78B1 Ahipara B NZ
36D1 Ahlen Germany
60C4 Ahmadābād India
62A1 Ahmadnagar India
72E3 Ahmar Mts Eth
15D1 Ahoskie USA
36D1 Ahr R Germany
36D1 Ahrgebirge Region, Germany
22B1 Ahuacatlán Mexico
22B1 Ahualulco Mexico
32G7 Åhus Sweden
63C1 Åhuvān Iran
63B2 Ahvāz Iran
23A4 Aiajuela Costa Rica
37B1 Aigle Switz
28E2 Aiguá Urug
37B2 Aiguille d'Arves Mt France
37B2 Aiguille de la Grand Sassière Mt France
53B1 Aihui China
54C3 Aikawa Japan
15C2 Aiken USA
52A5 Ailao Shan Upland China
28B1 Aimogasta Arg
29D2 Aimorés Brazil
37A1 Ain R France
71D1 Aïn Beïda Alg
71B2 Aïn Beni Mathar Mor
69B2 Ain Dalla Well Egypt
39C2 Aïn el Hadjel Alg
72B2 Aïn Galakka Chad
71C1 Aïn Oussera Alg
71B2 Aïn Sefra Alg
64B4 'Ain Sukhna Egypt
11C3 Ainsworth USA
71B1 Aïn Temouchent Alg
54B4 Aioi Japan
70B2 Aioun Abd el Malek Well Maur
70B3 Aïoun El Atrouss Maur
26E7 Aiquile Bol
70C3 Aïr Desert Region Niger
3F3 Airdrie Can
36B1 Aire France
35E5 Aire R Eng
36C2 Aire R France
7L3 Airforce I Can
37C1 Airolo Switz
6E3 Aishihik Can
10L3 Aishihik L Can
36B2 Aisne Department, France
38C2 Aisne R France
76D1 Aitape PNG
43F1 Aiviekste R Latvia
52B2 Aixa Zuogi China
38D3 Aix-en-Provence France
37A2 Aix-les-Bains France
61C3 Aiyar Res India
41E3 Aíyion Greece
41E3 Aíyna I Greece
61D3 Āīzawl India
73B6 Aizeb R Namibia
53E4 Aizu-Wakamatsu Japan
40B2 Ajaccio Corse
22C2 Ajalpan Mexico
69B1 Ajdabiyak Libya
37E2 Ajdovščina Slovenia, Yugos
53E3 Ajigasawa Japan
65C2 Ajlūn Jordan
67G1 Ajman UAE
60C3 Ajmer India
19D4 Ajo USA
41F2 Ajtos Bulg
22B2 Ajuchitan Mexico
41F3 Ak R Turk
54D2 Akabira Japan
54C3 Akaishi-sanchi Mts Japan

62B1 Akalkot India
65B1 Akanthou Cyprus
78B2 Akaroa NZ
66B2 Akasha Sudan
54B4 Akashi Japan
71C1 Akbou Alg
45K5 Akbulak Russian Fed
64C2 Akçakale Turk
70A2 Akchar Watercourse Maur
41F3 Ak Dağ Mt Turk
57C2 Akelamo Indon
72C3 Aketi Zaïre
64D1 Akhalkalaki Georgia
64D1 Akhalsikhe Georgia
41E3 Akharnái Greece
10H4 Akhiok USA
64A2 Akhisar Turk
43F1 Akhiste Latvia
69C2 Akhmîm Egypt
45H6 Akhtubinsk Russian Fed
45E5 Akhtyrka Ukraine
54B4 Aki Japan
7K4 Akimiski I Can
53E4 Akita Japan
70A3 Akjoujt Maur
65C2 'Akko Israel
10L2 Aklavik Can
70B3 Aklé Aouana Desert Region Maur
72D3 Akobo Sudan
72D3 Akobo R Sudan
60B1 Akoha Afghan
60D4 Akola India
71G4 Akosombo Dam Ghana
60D4 Akot India
7M3 Akpatok I Can
41E3 Ákra Kafirévs C Greece
41E4 Ákra Líthinon C Greece
41E3 Ákra Maléa C Greece
32A2 Akranes Iceland
41F3 Ákra Sídheros C Greece
41E3 Ákra Spátha C Greece
41E3 Ákra Taínaron C Greece
9E2 Akron USA
65B1 Akrotiri B Cyprus
60D1 Aksai Chin Mts China
45E8 Aksaray Turk
45J5 Aksay Kazakhstan
60D1 Aksayquin Hu L China
64B2 Akşehir Turk
64B2 Akseki Turk
49N4 Aksenovo Zilovskoye Russian Fed
50E1 Aksha Russian Fed
59G1 Aksu China
66C4 Aksum Eth
45J7 Aktau Kazakhstan
48J5 Aktogay Kazakhstan
45K6 Aktumsyk Kazakhstan
45K5 Aktyubinsk Kazakhstan
4F1 Akulivik Can
71H4 Akure Nig
32B1 Akureyri Iceland
10E5 Akutan USA
10E5 Akutan I USA
10E5 Akutan Pass USA
71H5 Akwa Ibom State Nigeria
Akyab = Sittwe
48K5 Akzhal Kazakhstan
9E3 Alabama State, USA
15B2 Alabama R USA
15B2 Alabaster USA
64C2 Ala Dağlari Mts Turk
45G7 Alagir Russian Fed
37B2 Alagna Italy
27L5 Alagoas State, Brazil
27L6 Alagoinhas Brazil
39B1 Alagón Spain
64E4 Al Ahmadi Kuwait
21D3 Alajuela Costa Rica
10F3 Alakanuk USA
48K5 Alakol, Ozero L Russian Fed/Kazakhstan
32L5 Alakurtti Russian Fed
64E3 Al Amārah Iraq
19B3 Alameda USA
22C1 Alamo Mexico
19C3 Alamo USA
16A3 Alamogordo USA
16C4 Alamo Heights USA
16A2 Alamosa USA
32H6 Åland I Fin
45E8 Alanya Turk
15C2 Alapaha R USA
44L4 Alapayevsk Russian Fed
Alappuzha = Alleppey
56A2 Alas R Indon
64A2 Alaşehir Turk
50D3 Ala Shan Mts China
6C3 Alaska State, USA
6D4 Alaska,G of USA
10G4 Alaska Pen USA
6C3 Alaska Range Mts USA
40B2 Alassio Italy
37C3 Alássio Region, Italy

10H2 Alatna R USA
44H5 Alatyr' Russian Fed
75B2 Alawoona Aust
67G2 Al'Ayn UAE
59F2 Alayskiy Khrebet Mts Tajikistan
49R3 Alazeya R Russian Fed
71E2 Al'Azīzīyah Libya
38D3 Alba Italy
64C2 Al Bāb Syria
39B2 Albacete Spain
39A1 Alba de Tormes Spain
64D2 Al Badi Iraq
41E1 Alba Iulia Rom
41D2 Albania Republic, Europe
76A4 Albany Aust
15C2 Albany Georgia, USA
12B3 Albany Kentucky, USA
13E2 Albany New York, USA
8A2 Albany Oregon, USA
4E3 Albany R Can
7K4 Albany R Can
66C4 Albara R Sudan
28B2 Albardón Arg
67G2 Al Batinah Region, Oman
51H8 Albatross B Aust
69B1 Al Baydā Libya
67E4 Al Baydā' Yemen
65C1 Al Baylūlīyah Syria
15C1 Albemarle USA
15D1 Albemarle Sd USA
37C2 Albenga Region, Italy
39B1 Alberche R Spain
75A1 Alberga Aust
36B1 Albert France
6G4 Alberta Province, Can
51H7 Albert Edward Mt PNG
74C3 Albertinia S Africa
72D3 Albert,L Uganda/Zaïre
9D2 Albert Lea USA
72D3 Albert Nile R Uganda
18D1 Alberton USA
5J4 Alberton Can
38D2 Albertville France
38C3 Albi France
17D1 Albia USA
27H2 Albina Suriname
12C2 Albion Michigan, USA
11C3 Albion Nebraska, USA
13D2 Albion New York, USA
64C4 Al Bi'r S Arabia
66B3 Al Birk S Arabia
67E2 Al Biyadh Region, S Arabia
39B2 Alborán I Spain
32G7 Ålborg Den
36E2 Albstadt-Ebingen Germany
64D3 Al Bū Kamāl Syria
37C1 Albula R Switz
8C3 Albuquerque USA
67G2 Al Buraymi Oman
69A1 Al Burayqah
69B1 Al Burdī Libya
76D4 Albury Aust
64E3 Al Buşayyah Iraq
34G3 Albuskjell Oilfield N Sea
67F3 Al Buzūn Yemen
39B1 Alcalá de Henares Spain
40C3 Alcamo Italy
39B1 Alcaniz Spain
27K4 Alcântara Brazil
39B2 Alcaraz Spain
39B2 Alcázar de San Juan Spain
39B2 Alcira Spain
29E2 Alcobaça Brazil
39B1 Alcolea de Pinar Spain
39B2 Alcoy Spain
39C2 Alcudia Spain
68J8 Aldabra Is Indian O
16A4 Aldama Mexico
22C1 Aldama Mexico
49O4 Aldan Russian Fed
49P4 Aldan R Russian Fed
49O4 Aldanskoye Nagor'ye Upland Russian Fed
35F5 Aldeburgh Eng
38B2 Alderney I UK
35E6 Aldershot Eng
70A3 Aleg Maur
29A2 Alegre R Brazil
25E3 Alegrete Brazil
28C2 Alejandro Roca Arg
49O4 Aleksandrovsk Sakhalinskiy Russian Fed
48J4 Alekseyevka Kazakhstan
44F5 Aleksin Russian Fed
42D1 Älem Sweden
29D3 Além Paraíba Brazil
38C2 Alençon France
20E5 Alenuihaha Chan Hawaiian Is
Aleppo = Ḥalab
7M1 Alert Can
38C3 Alès France
40B2 Alessandria Italy
48B3 Ålesund Nor
10B5 Aleutian Is USA

10G4 Aleutian Range Mts USA
xxixL2 Aleutian Trench Pacific O
6E4 Alexander Arch USA
74B2 Alexander Bay S Africa
15B2 Alexander City USA
79G3 Alexander I Ant
78A3 Alexandra NZ
25J8 Alexandra,C South Georgia
7L2 Alexandra Fjord Can
69B1 Alexandria Egypt
9D3 Alexandria Louisiana, USA
9D2 Alexandria Minnesota, USA
9F3 Alexandria Virginia, USA
41F2 Alexandroúpolis Greece
5K3 Alexis R Can
3D3 Alexis Creek Can
65C2 Aley Leb
48K4 Aleysk Russian Fed
64D3 Al Fallūjah Iraq
67E4 Al Fardah Yemen
39B1 Alfaro Spain
41F2 Alfatar Bulg
64E3 Al Fāw Iraq
36E1 Alfeld Germany
29C3 Alfensas Brazil
41E3 Alfiós R Greece
37D2 Alfonsine Italy
29D3 Alfonzo Cláudio Brazil
29D3 Alfredo Chaves Brazil
67E1 Al Furūthi S Arabia
45K6 Alga Kazakhstan
28A1 Algarrobal Chile
28B3 Algarrobo del Águila Arg
39A2 Algeciras Spain
71C1 Alger Alg
70B2 Algeria Republic, Africa
67F3 Al Ghaydah Yemen
40B2 Alghero Sardegna
Algiers = Alger
11D3 Algona USA
13D1 Algonquin Park Can
4F4 Algonquin Prov Park Can
28D2 Algorta Urug
67G2 Al Hadd Oman
64C3 Al Hadithah Iraq
64C3 Al Hadithah S Arabia
64D2 Al Haḍr Iraq
65D1 Al Haffah Syria
67G2 Al Hajar al Gharbī Mts Oman
67G2 Al Hajar ash Sharqī Mts Oman
64C3 Al Hamad Desert Region Jordan/S Arabia
64E4 Al Haniyah Desert Region Iraq
67E2 Al Harīq S Arabia
64C3 Al Harrah Desert Region S Arabia
69A2 Al Harūj al Aswad Upland Libya
67E1 Al Hasa Region, S Arabia
64D2 Al Hasakah Syria
64C4 Al Hawjä' S Arabia
64E3 Al Hayy Iraq
67F2 Al Hibāk Region, S Arabia
65D2 Al Hijānah Syria
64D3 Al Hillah Iraq
67E2 Al Hillah S Arabia
71B1 Al Hoceima Mor
66D4 Al Hudaydah Yemen
67E1 Al Hufūf S Arabia
67F2 Al Humrah Region, UAE
67G2 Al Huwatsah Oman
63B1 Alīābad Iran
63D3 Aliabad Iran
41E2 Aliákmon R Greece
64E3 Alī al Gharbī Iraq
62A1 Alībāg India
71B3 Alibori R Benin
39B2 Alicante Spain
8D4 Alice USA
76C3 Alice Springs Aust
40C3 Alicudi I Italy
60D3 Aligarh India
63B2 Aligūdarz Iran
60B2 Ali-Khel Afghan
41F3 Alimniá I Greece
61C2 Alīpur Duār India
12C2 Aliquippa USA
67E4 Al'Irqah Yemen
64C3 Al'Isawiyah S Arabia
74D3 Aliwal North S Africa
69B2 Al Jaghbūb Libya
64D3 Al Jālamīd S Arabia
69B2 Al Jawf Libya
64C4 Al Jawf S Arabia
45G8 Al Jazirah Iraq
64D2 Al Jazirah Desert Region Syria/Iraq
39A2 Aljezur Port
67E1 Al Jubayl S Arabia
65D4 Al Kabid Desert Jordan
66D1 Al Kahfah S Arabia
67G2 Al Kāmil Oman

64D2 Al Khābūr R Syria
67G2 Al Khābūrah Oman
64D3 Al Khālis Iraq
66D2 Al Khamāsin S Arabia
67G1 Al Khasab Oman
67F1 Al Khawr Qatar
69A1 Al Khums Libya
67F2 Al Kidan Region, S Arabia
65D2 Al Kiswah Syria
42A2 Alkmaar Neth
69B2 Al Kufrah Oasis Libya
64E3 Al Kūt Iraq
64C2 Al Lādhiqīyah Syria
61B2 Allahābād India
65D2 Al Lajāh Mt Syria
10H2 Allakaket USA
55B2 Allanmyo Burma
66B2 'Allaqi Watercourse Egypt
15C2 Allatoona L USA
74D1 Alldays S Africa
13D2 Allegheny R USA
9F3 Allegheny Mts USA
14A2 Allegheny Res USA
15C2 Allendale USA
78A3 Allen,Mt NZ
13D2 Allentown USA
62B3 Alleppey India
38C2 Aller R France
37D1 Allgäu Mts Germany
11B3 Alliance USA
66D2 Al Līth S Arabia
67F2 Al Liwā Region, UAE
75D1 Allora Aust
37B2 Allos France
12C2 Alma Michigan, USA
16C1 Alma Nebraska, USA
59F1 Alma Ata Kazakhstan
39A2 Almada Port
Al Madinah = Medina
51H5 Almagan I Pacific O
67F3 Al Mahrah Region, Yemen
67E1 Al Majma'ah S Arabia
67F1 Al Manāmah Bahrain
64D3 Al Ma'nīyah Iraq
19B2 Almanor,L USA
39B2 Almansa Spain
3C2 Alma Peak Mt Can
67F2 Al Māriyyah UAE
5G4 Alma Can
69B1 Al Marj Libya
Almaty = Alma Ata
39B1 Almazán Spain
36E1 Alme R Germany
29D2 Almenara Brazil
39B2 Almeria Spain
29C2 Almes R Brazil
44J5 Al'met'yevsk Russian Fed
42C1 Älmhult Sweden
66D1 Al Midhnab S Arabia
64E3 Al Miqdādīyah Iraq
79G3 Almirante Brown Base Ant
28A1 Almirante Latorre Chile
41E3 Almirós Greece
67E1 Al Mish'ab S Arabia
39A2 Almodóvar Port
60D3 Almora India
64D2 Al Mawşil Iraq
67E1 Al Mubarraz S Arabia
64C4 Al Mudawwara Jordan
67G2 Al Mudaybi Oman
67F1 Al Muharraq Bahrain
67E4 Al Mukallā Yemen
66D4 Al Mukhā Yemen
64D3 Al Musayyib Iraq
66C1 Al Muwaylih S Arabia
34C3 Alness Scot
64E3 Al Nu'māniyah Iraq
34E4 Alnwick Eng
4B3 Alonsa Can
57B4 Alor I Indon
55C4 Alor Setar Malay
Alost = Aalst
76E2 Alotau PNG
76B3 Aloysius,Mt Aust
28C3 Alpachiri Arg
37D2 Alpe di Succiso Mt Italy
12C1 Alpena USA
37B1 Alpes du Valais Mts Switz
37B2 Alpes Maritimes Mts France
37E1 Alpi Carniche Mts Italy
40C1 Alpi Dolomitiche Mts Italy
37B2 Alpi Graie Mts Italy
19E4 Alpine Arizona, USA
16B3 Alpine Texas, USA
18D2 Alpine Wyoming, USA
37C1 Alpi Orobie Mts Italy
37B2 Alpi Penine Mts Italy
37C1 Alpi Retiche Mts Switz
37D1 Alpi Venoste Mts Italy
40B1 Alps Mts Europe
69A1 Al Qaddāhiyah Libya
65D1 Al Qadmūs Syria
64D3 Al Qā'im Iraq
64C4 Al Qalībah S Arabia

Al Qāmishlī Arad

64D2 **Al Qāmishlī** Syria
65D1 **Al Qardāhah** Syria
69A1 **Al Qaryah Ash Sharqiyah** Libya
64C3 **Al Qaryatayn** Syria
66D1 **Al Qasīm** Region, S Arabia
67E1 **Al Qātif** S Arabia
69A2 **Al Qatrūn** Libya
67E1 **Al Qayṣāmah** S Arabia
65D2 **Al Quatayfah** Syria
39A2 **Alquera** *Res* Port/Spain
64C3 **Al Qunayṭirah** Syria
66D3 **Al Qunfidhah** S Arabia
64E3 **Al Qurnah** Iraq
65D1 **Al Quṣayr** Syria
64C3 **Al Qutayfah** Syria
67E2 **Al Quwayīyah** S Arabia
42B1 **Als** *I* Den
38D2 **Alsace** Region, France
42B2 **Alsfeld** Germany
34D4 **Alston** Eng
32J5 **Alta** Nor
25D4 **Alta Gracia** Arg
23D5 **Altagracia de Orituco** Ven
50B2 **Altai** *Mts* Mongolia
15C2 **Altamaha** *R* USA
27H4 **Altamira** Brazil
22C1 **Altamira** Mexico
40D2 **Altamura** Italy
50D1 **Altanbulag** Mongolia
49M5 **Altanbulag** Russian Fed
51H7 **Altape** PNG
21B2 **Altata** Mexico
48K5 **Altay** China
49L5 **Altay** Mongolia
48K4 **Altay** *Mts* Russian Fed
37C1 **Altdorf** Switz
36D1 **Altenkirchen** Germany
28B3 **Altiplanicie del Payún** *Plat* Arg
37B1 **Altkirch** France
29B2 **Alto Araguaia** Brazil
73D5 **Alto Molócue** Mozam
12A3 **Alton** USA
13D2 **Altoona** USA
28B2 **Alto Pencoso** *Mts* Arg
29B2 **Alto Sucuriú** Brazil
22C2 **Altotonga** Mexico
22B2 **Altoyac de Alvarez** Mexico
59G2 **Altun Shan** *Mts* China
18B2 **Alturas** USA
16C3 **Altus** USA
67F2 **Al'Ubaylah** S Arabia
66C1 **Al'Ulā** S Arabia
28A3 **Aluminé** Arg
64C4 **Al Urayq** *Desert Region* S Arabia
67F2 **Al'Uruq al Mu'taridah** Region, S Arabia
16C2 **Alva** USA
22C2 **Alvarado** Mexico
17C3 **Alvarado** USA
32G6 **Älvdalen** Sweden
28D1 **Alvear** Arg
17C4 **Alvin** USA
32J5 **Alvsbyn** Sweden
69A2 **Al Wāha** Libya
66C1 **Al Wajh** S Arabia
60D3 **Alwar** India
64D3 **Al Widyān** *Desert Region* Iraq/S Arabia
52A2 **Alxa Yougi** China
64E2 **Alyat** Azerbaijan
32J8 **Alytus** Lithuania
36E2 **Alzey** Germany
22C2 **Amacuzac** *R* Mexico
72D3 **Amadi** Sudan
64D2 **Amādīyah** Iraq
7L3 **Amadjuak L** Can
57C3 **Amahai** Indon
53B5 **Amakusa-shotō** *I* Japan
32G7 **Åmål** Sweden
49N4 **Amalat** *R* Russian Fed
41E3 **Amaliás** Greece
60C4 **Amalner** India
29A3 **Amambai** Brazil
29B3 **Amambai** *R* Brazil
50F4 **Amami** *I* Japan
50F4 **Amami gunto** *Arch* Japan
27H3 **Amapá** Brazil
27H3 **Amapá** State, Brazil
4B3 **Amaranth** Can
61E3 **Amarapura** Burma
16B2 **Amarillo** USA
45F7 **Amasya** Turk
22B1 **Amatitan** Mexico
22C1 **Amaulipas** Mexico
Amazonas = Solimões
27H4 **Amazonas** Brazil
26E4 **Amazonas** State, Brazil
24D4 **Amazonas** *R* Brazil
60D2 **Ambāla** India
62C3 **Ambalangoda** Sri Lanka
73E6 **Ambalavao** Madag
72B3 **Ambam** Cam
73E5 **Ambanja** Madag
49S3 **Ambarchik** Russian Fed
26C4 **Ambato** Ecuador
73E5 **Ambato-Boeny** Madag
73E5 **Ambatolampy** Madag
73E5 **Ambatondrazaka** Madag
42C3 **Amberg** Germany
21D3 **Ambergris Cay** *I* Belize
37A2 **Ambérieu** France
61B3 **Ambikāpur** India
73E5 **Ambilobe** Madag
73E6 **Amboasary** Madag
73E5 **Ambodifototra** Madag
73E6 **Ambohimahasoa** Madag
57C3 **Ambon** Indon
57C3 **Ambon** *I* Indon
73E6 **Ambositra** Madag
73E6 **Ambovombe** Madag
73B4 **Ambriz** Angola
77F2 **Ambrym** *I* Vanuatu
10B6 **Amchitka** USA
10B6 **Amchitka** *I* USA
10C6 **Amchitka Pass** USA
72C2 **Am Dam** Chad
44L2 **Amderma** Russian Fed
21B2 **Ameca** Mexico
22A1 **Ameca** *R* Mexico
22C2 **Amecacameca** Mexico
28C2 **Ameghino** Arg
42B2 **Ameland** *I* Neth
14D2 **Amenia** USA
18D2 **American Falls** USA
18D2 **American Falls Res** USA
19D2 **American Fork** USA
79F10 **American Highland** *Upland* Ant
xxixL5 **American Samoa** *Is* Pacific O
15C2 **Americus** USA
42B2 **Amersfoort** Neth
74D2 **Amersfoort** S Africa
11D2 **Amery** USA
79G10 **Amery Ice Shelf** Ant
11D3 **Ames** USA
14E1 **Amesbury** USA
4E4 **Ameson** Can
41E3 **Amfilokhía** Greece
41E3 **Amfissa** Greece
49P3 **Amga** Russian Fed
49P3 **Amgal** *R* Russian Fed
53D2 **Amgu** Russian Fed
10C2 **Amguema** *R* Russian Fed
53D1 **Amgun'** *R* Russian Fed
72D2 **Amhara** *Region* Eth
Amherst = Kyaikkami Burma
7M5 **Amherst** Can
14D1 **Amherst** Massachusetts, USA
13D3 **Amherst** Virginia, USA
62B2 **Amhūr** India
38C2 **Amiens** France
54C3 **Amino** Japan
65C1 **Amioune** Leb
68K8 **Amirante Is** Indian O
3H3 **Amisk L** Can
16B4 **Amistad Res** Mexico
61C2 **Amlekhgan** Nepal
10D6 **Amlia** *I* USA
64C3 **Amman** Jordan
32K6 **Ämmänsaario** Fin
54A3 **Amnyong-dan** *C* N Korea
63C1 **Amol** Iran
7L5 **Amos** Can
Amoy = Xiamen
57B3 **Ampana** Indon
73E6 **Ampanihy** Madag
29C3 **Amparo** Brazil
39C1 **Amposta** Spain
5H4 **Amqui** Can
66D3 **Amrān** Yemen
60D4 **Amrāvati** India
60C4 **Amreli** India
60C2 **Amritsar** India
42A2 **Amsterdam** Neth
74E2 **Amsterdam** S Africa
13E2 **Amsterdam** USA
72C2 **Am Timan** Chad
48H5 **Amu Darya** *R* Uzbekistan
10D6 **Amukta** *I* USA
10D6 **Amukta Pass** USA
7J2 **Amund Ringnes I** Can
6F2 **Amundsen G** Can
79F4 **Amundsen S** Ant
79E **Amundsen-Scott** *Base* Ant
56E3 **Amuntai** Indon
49O4 **Amur** *R* Russian Fed
66C3 **Amur** *Watercourse* Sudan
57B2 **Amurang** Indon
53D1 **Amursk** Russian Fed
53E1 **Amurskiy Liman** *Str* Russian Fed
53C2 **Amurzet** Russian Fed
49N2 **Anabar** *R* Russian Fed
26F2 **Anaco** Ven
8B2 **Anaconda** USA
18B1 **Anacortes** USA
16C2 **Anadarko** USA
49T3 **Anadyr'** Russian Fed
49T3 **Anadyr'** *R* Russian Fed
49U3 **Anadyrskiy Zaliv** *S* Russian Fed
49T3 **Anadyrskoye Ploskogor'ye** *Plat* Russian Fed
41F3 **Anáfi** *I* Greece
29D1 **Anagé** Brazil
64D3 **'Ānah** Iraq
19C4 **Anaheim** USA
62B2 **Anaimalai Hills** India
62C1 **Anakāpalle** India
10J2 **Anaktuvuk P** USA
73E5 **Analalaya** Madag
71H4 **Anambra** *State* Nig
71H4 **Anambra** *R* Nig
12A2 **Anamosa** USA
45E8 **Anamur** Turk
54B4 **Anan** Japan
62B2 **Anantapur** India
60D2 **Anantnag** India
27J7 **Anápolis** Brazil
63D2 **Anār** Iran
63C2 **Anārak** Iran
63E2 **Anardara** Afghan
51H5 **Anatahan** *I* Pacific O
25D3 **Añatuya** Arg
53B4 **Anbyŏn** N Korea
20C4 **Ancapa Is** USA
28B1 **Ancasti** Arg
6D3 **Anchorage** USA
26E7 **Ancohuma** *Mt* Bol
26C6 **Ancón** Peru
40C2 **Ancona** Italy
14D1 **Ancram** USA
25B6 **Ancud** Chile
36C3 **Ancy-le-Franc** France
26D6 **Andabuaylas** Peru
28A3 **Andacollo** Arg
75A1 **Andado** Aust
28B1 **Andagalá** Arg
32F6 **Andalsnes** Nor
39A2 **Andalucia** Region, Spain
15B2 **Andalusia** USA
59H4 **Andaman Is** Burma
59H4 **Andaman S** Burma
75A2 **Andamooka** Aust
29D1 **Andaraí** Brazil
35B5 **Andee** Irish Rep
36C2 **Andelot** France
32H5 **Andenes** Nor
37C1 **Andermatt** Switz
42B2 **Andernach** Germany
12B2 **Anderson** Indiana, USA
17D2 **Anderson** Missouri, USA
15C2 **Anderson** S Carolina, USA
6F3 **Anderson** *R* Can
62B1 **Andhra Pradesh** State, India
41E3 **Andikíthira** *I* Greece
48J5 **Andizhan** Uzbekistan
48H6 **Andkhui** Afghan
53B4 **Andong** S Korea
39C1 **Andorra** Principality, SW Europe
39C1 **Andorra-La-Vella** Andorra
35E6 **Andover** Eng
14E1 **Andover** New Hampshire, USA
14B1 **Andover** New York, USA
29B3 **Andradina** Brazil
10F3 **Andreafsky** USA
10C6 **Andreanof Is** USA
43G1 **Andreapol'** Russian Fed
64B2 **Andreas,C** Cyprus
16B3 **Andrews** USA
40D2 **Andria** Italy
9F4 **Andros** *I* Bahamas
41E3 **Ándros** *I* Greece
62A2 **Androth** *I* India
39B2 **Andújar** Spain
73B5 **Andulo** Angola
71G4 **Anécho** Togo
70C3 **Anéfis** Mali
77F3 **Aneityum** *I* Vanuatu
28B3 **Añelo** Arg
66C4 **Angareb** *Watercourse* Eth
49M4 **Angarsk** Russian Fed
44A3 **Ånge** Sweden
21A2 **Angel de la Guarda** *I* Mexico
57F7 **Angeles** Phil
32G7 **Angelholm** Sweden
75C1 **Angellala Creek** *R* Aust
20B1 **Angels Camp** USA
51G7 **Angemuk** *Mt* Indon
38B2 **Angers** France
36B2 **Angerville** France
55C3 **Angkor** *Hist Site* Camb
33C3 **Anglesey** *I* Wales
17C4 **Angleton** USA
7P3 **Angmagssalik** Greenland
73E5 **Angoche** Mozam
25B5 **Angol** Chile
12C2 **Angola** Indiana, USA
14A1 **Angola** New York, USA
68F9 **Angola** Republic, Africa
73B5 **Angola** Republic, Africa
xxxJ5 **Angola Basin** Atlantic O
10M4 **Angoon** USA
38C2 **Angoulême** France
70A1 **Angra do Heroismo** Açores
29D3 **Angra dos Reis** Brazil
28C3 **Anguil** Arg
23E3 **Anguilla** *I* Caribbean
23B2 **Anguilla Cays** *Is* Caribbean
61C3 **Angul** India
72C4 **Angumu** Zaïre
42C1 **Anholt** *I* Den
52C4 **Anhua** China
52D3 **Anhui** Province, China
29B2 **Anhumas** Brazil
54A3 **Anhŭng** S Korea
10G3 **Aniak** USA
29C2 **Anicuns** Brazil
71G4 **Anié** Togo
16A2 **Animas** *R* USA
16A3 **Animas Peak** *Mt* USA
11D3 **Anita** USA
36B2 **Anizy-le-Château** France
38B2 **Anjou** Republic, France
73E5 **Anjouan** *I* Comoros
73E5 **Anjozorobe** Madag
53B4 **Anju** N Korea
52B3 **Ankang** China
45E8 **Ankara** Turk
73E5 **Ankaratra** *Mt* Madag
73E6 **Ankazoabo** Madag
73E5 **Ankazobe** Madag
11D3 **Ankeny** USA
42C2 **Anklam** Germany
71H4 **Ankwe** *R* Nig
55D3 **An Loc** Viet
52B4 **Anlong** China
52C3 **Anlu** China
12B3 **Anna** USA
68E4 **Annaba** Alg
71D1 **'Annaba** Alg
64C3 **An Nabk** S Arabia
64C3 **An Nabk** Syria
75A1 **Anna Creek** Aust
69B2 **An Nāfūrah** Libya
64D3 **An Najaf** Iraq
34D4 **Annan** Scot
13D3 **Annapolis** USA
61B2 **Annapurna** *Mt* Nepal
12C2 **Ann Arbor** USA
65D1 **An Nāsirah** Syria
64E3 **An Nāsirīyah** Iraq
37B2 **Annecy** France
37B1 **Annemasse** France
3B2 **Annette I** USA
55D3 **An Nhon** Viet
66D3 **An Nimās** S Arabia
52A5 **Anning** China
15B2 **Anniston** USA
70C4 **Annobon, I** Eq Guinea
38C2 **Annonay** France
37B3 **Annot** France
23J1 **Annotto Bay** Jamaica
52D3 **Anqing** China
52B2 **Ansai** China
42C3 **Ansbach** Germany
23C3 **Anse d'Hainault** Haiti
52E1 **Anshan** China
52B4 **Anshun** China
16C1 **Ansley** USA
16C3 **Anson** USA
51F8 **Anson B** Aust
70C3 **Ansongo** Mali
12C1 **Ansonville** Can
12C3 **Ansted** USA
45F8 **Antakya** Turk
73F5 **Antalaha** Madag
45E8 **Antalya** Turk
45E8 **Antalya Körfezi** *B* Turk
73E5 **Antananarivo** Madag
79G1 **Antarctic Circle** Ant
79G3 **Antarctic Pen** Ant
39B2 **Antequera** Spain
16A3 **Anthony** USA
70B1 **Anti-Atlas** *Mts* Mor
37B3 **Antibes** France
7M5 **Anticosti, Î d'** Can
5J4 **Anticosti Prov Park** Can
12B1 **Antigo** USA
23E3 **Antigua** *I* Caribbean
Anti Lebanon = Jebel esh Sharqi
19B3 **Antioch** USA
77G5 **Antipodes Is** NZ
17C3 **Antlers** USA
25B2 **Antofagasta** Chile
29C4 **Antonina** Brazil
16A2 **Antonito** USA
34B4 **Antrim** County, N Ire
34B4 **Antrim** N Ire
14E1 **Antrim** USA
34B4 **Antrim Hills** N Ire
73E5 **Antseranana** Madag
73E5 **Antsirabe** Madag
73E5 **Antsohiny** Madag
55D3 **An Tuc** Viet
28C1 **Añtuya** Arg
36C1 **Antwerpen** Belg
35B5 **An Uaimh** Irish Rep
54A3 **Anui** S Korea
60C3 **Anupgarh** India
62C3 **Anuradhapura** Sri Lanka
Anvers = Antwerpen
6B3 **Anvik** USA
10B6 **Anvil Pk** *Mt* USA
49L5 **Anxi** China
52C2 **Anyang** China
52A3 **A'nyêmaqên Shan** *Upland* China
49S3 **Anyuysk** Russian Fed
37C2 **Anza** *R* Italy
3F2 **Anzac** Can
48K4 **Anzhero-Sudzhensk** Russian Fed
40C2 **Anzio** Italy
77F2 **Aoba** *I* Vanuatu
53E3 **Aomori** Japan
40B1 **Aosta** Italy
70B3 **Aoukar** *Desert Region* Maur
70C2 **Aoulef** Alg
72B1 **Aozou** Chad
25E2 **Apa** *R* Brazil/Par
9E4 **Apalachee B** USA
15C3 **Apalachicola** USA
15B3 **Apalachicola B** USA
22C2 **Apan** Mexico
26D3 **Apaporis** *R* Colombia
29B3 **Aparecida do Taboado** Brazil
57F7 **Aparri** Phil
41D1 **Apatin** Croatia, Yugos
44E2 **Apatity** Russian Fed
21B3 **Apatzingan** Mexico
42B2 **Apeldoorn** Neth
77H2 **Apia** Western Samoa
29C3 **Apiai** Brazil
22B1 **Apizolaya** Mexico
27G2 **Apoera** Suriname
75B3 **Apollo Bay** Aust
57G9 **Apo,Mt** Phil
15C3 **Apopka,L** USA
27H7 **Aporé** *R* Brazil
12A1 **Apostle Is** USA
22B1 **Apozol** Mexico
9E3 **Appalachian Mts** USA
37D2 **Appenino Tosco-Emiliano** *Mts* Italy
40C2 **Appennino Abruzzese** *Mts* Italy
40B2 **Appennino Ligure** *Mts* Italy
40D2 **Appennino Lucano** *Mts* Italy
40D2 **Appennino Napoletano** *Mts* Italy
40C2 **Appennino Tosco-Emilliano** *Mts* Italy
40C2 **Appennino Umbro-Marchigiano** *Mts* Italy
37C1 **Appenzell** Switz
35D4 **Appleby** Eng
11C2 **Appleton** Minnesota, USA
12B2 **Appleton** Wisconsin, USA
45J7 **Apsheronskiy Poluostrov** *Pen* Azerbaijan
4F5 **Apsley** Can
37A3 **Apt** France
25F2 **Apucarana** Brazil
22C1 **Apulco** Mexico
26E2 **Apure** *R* Ven
26D6 **Apurimac** *R* Peru
64C4 **'Aqaba** Jordan
64B4 **'Aqaba,G of** Egypt/S Arabia
63C2 **'Aqdā** Iran
27G8 **Aqidauana** Brazil
22A1 **Aqua Nueva** Mexico
29A3 **Aquidabán** *R* Par
25E2 **Aquidauana** Brazil
29A2 **Aquidauana** *R* Brazil
22B2 **Aquila** Mexico
61B2 **Ara** India
15B2 **Arab** USA
65C1 **'Arab al Mulk** Syria
58E4 **Arabian** *S* Asia/Arabian Pen
xxviiiE4 **Arabian Basin** Indian O
27L6 **Aracajú** Brazil
25E2 **Aracanguy, Mts de** *Mts* Brazil
29A3 **Aracanguy, Mts de** Par
27L4 **Aracati** Brazil
29D1 **Aracatu** Brazil
27H8 **Araçatuba** Brazil
39A2 **Aracena** Spain
27K7 **Araçuai** Brazil
65C3 **Arad** Israel
45C6 **Arad** Rom

Arada Augustów

72C2 Arada Chad
67F2 'Arādah UAE
76C1 Arafura S Indon/Aust
27H7 Aragarças Brazil
45G7 Aragats *Mt* Armenia
39B1 Aragón Region, Spain
39B1 Aragon *R* Spain
29C1 Araguaçu Brazil
27H6 Araguaia *R* Brazil
27J5 Araguaína Brazil
27J7 Araguari Brazil
29C2 Araguari *R* Brazil
54C3 Arai Japan
70C2 Arak Alg
63B2 Arāk Iran
10D3 Arakamchechen, Ostrov *Is* Russian Fed
55A2 Arakan Yoma *Mts* Burma
62B2 Arakkonam India
48G5 Aral Sea Kazakhstan/Uzbekistan
48H5 Aral'sk Kazakhstan
Aral'skoye More = Aral Sea
22C1 Aramberri Mexico
33B2 Aran *I* Irish Rep
33B3 Aran *Is* Irish Rep
39B1 Aranda de Duero Spain
22B1 Arandas Mexico
39B1 Aranjuez Spain
74B1 Aranos Namibia
17F4 Aransas Pass USA
54B4 Arao Japan
70B3 Araouane Mali
16C1 Arapahoe USA
25E4 Arapey *R* Urug
28D2 Arapey Grande *R* Urug
27L6 Arapiraca Brazil
29B3 Araporgas Brazil
25G3 Ararangua Brazil
27J8 Araraquara Brazil
29C3 Araras Brazil
76D4 Ararat Aust
64D2 Ararat Armenia
64D1 Aras *R* Turk
45H8 Aras *R* Azerbaijan/Iran
66C3 Aratali Eth
54D3 Arato Japan
26E2 Arauca *R* Ven
28A3 Arauco Chile
26D2 Arauea Colombia
60C3 Arāvalli Range *Mts* India
77E1 Arawa PNG
27J7 Araxá Brazil
45G8 Araxes *R* Iran
72D3 Arba Minch Eth
40B3 Arbatax Sardegna, Italy
45G8 Arbīl Iraq
37A1 Arbois France
4B3 Arborg Can
32H6 Arbrå Sweden
34D3 Arbroath Scot
37A3 Arc *R* France
37B2 Arc *R* France
38B3 Arcachon France
14A1 Arcade USA
15E4 Arcadia USA
18B2 Arcata USA
20D1 Arc Dome, Mt USA
22B2 Arcelia Mexico
14C2 Archbald USA
20E3 Arches Nat Pk USA
23B2 Archipiélago de Camaguey *Arch* Cuba
25B8 Archipiélago de la Reina Adelaida *Arch* Chile
25B6 Archipiélago de las Chones *Arch* Chile
26C2 Archipiélago de las Perlas *Arch* Panama
36C2 Arcis-sur-Aube France
18D2 Arco USA
29C3 Arcos Brazil
39A2 Arcos de la Frontera Spain
37A1 Arc Senans France
79C1 Arctic Circle
6E3 Arctic Red Can
6E3 Arctic Red River Can
6D3 Arctic Village USA
79G2 Arctowski *Base* Ant
41F2 Arda *R* Bulg
45H8 Ardabīl Iran
45G7 Ardahan Turk
70C2 Ardar des Iforas *Upland* Alg/Mali
63C2 Ardekān Iran
32F6 Ardel Nor
36C2 Ardennes Department, France
42B2 Ardennes Region, Belg
63C2 Ardestan Iran
64C3 Ardh es Suwwan *Desert Region* Jordan
39A2 Ardila *R* Port
75C2 Ardlethan Aust
8D3 Ardmore USA
34B3 Ardnamurchan *Pt* Scot
35F6 Ardres France
36A1 Ardres France
34C3 Ardrishaig Scot
34C4 Ardrossan Scot
23D3 Arecibo Puerto Rico
27L4 Areia Branca Brazil
19B3 Arena,Pt USA
32F7 Arendal Nor
26D7 Arequipa Peru
40C2 Arezzo Italy
37B3 Argens *R* France
40C2 Argenta Italy
38C2 Argentan France
36B2 Argenteuil France
5L4 Argentia Can
24D7 Argentina Republic, S America
xxxF7 Argentine Basin Atlantic O
38C2 Argenton-sur-Creuse France
41F2 Argeşul *R* Rom
60B2 Arghardab *R* Afghan
41E3 Argolikós Kólpos *G* Greece
36C2 Argonne Region, France
41E3 Árgos Greece
41E3 Argostólion Greece
20B3 Arguello,Pt USA
71G3 Argungu Nig
20D3 Argus Range *Mts* USA
76B2 Argyle,L Aust
34G3 Argyll *Oilfield* N Sea
42C1 Århus Den
73C6 Ariamsvlei Namibia
39B1 Arian zón *R* Spain
28C2 Arias Venado Arg
70B3 Aribinda Burkina
25B1 Arica Chile
60C2 Arifwala Pak
Arihā = Jericho
16B2 Arikaree, R USA
23L1 Arima Trinidad
29C2 Arinos Brazil
27G6 Arinos *R* Brazil
22B2 Ario de Rosales Mexico
23L1 Aripo,Mt Trinidad
26F5 Aripuana Brazil
26F5 Aripuanã *R* Brazil
34C3 Arisaig Scot
62B2 Ariskere India
22B1 Arista Mexico
22D2 Arista Mexico
3C3 Aristazabal I Can
28B3 Arizona Arg
8B3 Arizona State, USA
32G7 Årjäng Sweden
49O4 Arka Russian Fed
45G5 Arkadak Russian Fed
17D3 Arkadelphia USA
48H4 Arkalyk Kazakhstan
9D3 Arkansas State, USA
9D3 Arkansas *R* USA
17C2 Arkansas City USA
44G3 Arkhangel'sk Russian Fed
53C2 Arkhara Russian Fed
49K2 Arkipelag Nordenshelda *Arch* Russian Fed
33B3 Arklow Irish Rep
5G5 Arkville USA
37D1 Arlberg P Austria
38C3 Arles France
11C3 Arlington S Dakota, USA
17C3 Arlington Texas, USA
13D3 Arlington Virginia, USA
18B1 Arlington Washington, USA
12B2 Arlington Heights USA
42B3 Arlon Belg
Armageddon = Megido
35B4 Armagh County, N Ire
35B4 Armagh N Ire
41F3 Armagós *I* Greece
36B3 Armançon *R* France
45G7 Armavir Russian Fed
22B2 Armena Mexico
45G7 Armenia
26C3 Armenia Colombia
76E4 Armidale Aust
3E3 Armstrong Can
53D2 Armu *R* Russian Fed
7L3 Arnaud *R* Can
64B2 Arnauti *C* Cyprus
16C2 Arnett USA
42B2 Arnhem Neth
76C2 Arnhem,C Aust
76C2 Arnhem Land Aust
37D3 Arno *R* Italy
20B1 Arnold USA
37E1 Arnoldstein Austria
4B2 Arnot Can
4F4 Arnprior Can
36E1 Arnsberg Germany
74B2 Aroab Namibia
36E1 Arolsen Germany
37C2 Arona Italy
10F3 Aropuk L USA
77G1 Arorae *I* Kiribati
40B1 Arosa Switz
36B2 Arpajon France
29E2 Arquipélago dos Abrolhos *Arch* Brazil
70A3 Arquipélago dos Bijagós *Arch* Guinea-Bissau
29C1 Arraias Brazil
64D3 Ar Ramādī Iraq
34C4 Arran *I* Scot
64C2 Ar Raqqah Syria
69A2 Ar Rāqūbah Libya
38C1 Arras France
66D1 Ar Rass S Arabia
65D1 Ar Rastan Syria
66D2 Ar Rawdah S Arabia
70A2 Arrecife Canary Is
28C2 Arrecifes Arg
22B1 Arriaga Mexico
22D2 Arriaga Mexico
64E3 Ar Rifā't Iraq
64E3 Ar Rihāb *Desert Region* Iraq
Ar Riyād = Riyadh
34C3 Arrochar Scot
28E2 Arroio Grande Brazil
29C1 Arrojado *R* Brazil
18C2 Arrowrock Res USA
78A2 Arrowtown NZ
20B3 Arroyo Grande USA
22C1 Arroyo Seco Mexico
67F1 Ar Ru'ays Qatar
67G2 Ar Rustaq Oman
64D3 Ar Rutbah Iraq
66D2 Ar Ruwaydah S Arabia
53C3 Arsen'yev Russian Fed
37D2 Arsiero Italy
38D2 Arsizio Italy
44H4 Arsk Russian Fed
41E3 Árta Greece
22B2 Arteaga Mexico
53C3 Artem Russian Fed
49L4 Artemovsk Russian Fed
49N4 Artemovskiy Russian Fed
36A2 Artenay France
8C3 Artesia USA
78B2 Arthurs P NZ
32G7 Århus Den
7K2 Artic Bay Can
25E4 Artigas Urug
28D2 Artigas Urug
6H3 Artillery L Can
38C1 Artois Region, France
43F3 Artsiz Ukraine
79G2 Arturo Prat *Base* Ant
45G7 Artvin Turk
72D3 Aru Zaïre
27H6 Aruanã Brazil
23C4 Aruba *I* Caribbean
61C2 Arun *R* Nepal
61D2 Arunāchal Pradesh Union Territory, India
53A2 Arun He *R* China
53A2 Arun Qi China
62B3 Aruppukkottai India
72D4 Arusha Tanz
72C3 Aruwimi *R* Zaïre
16A2 Arvada USA
50D2 Arvayheer Mongolia
37B2 Arve *R* France
7L5 Arvida Can
32H5 Arvidsjaur Sweden
44B2 Arvidsjaur Sweden
32G7 Arvika Sweden
19C3 Arvin USA
65C1 Arwad *I* Syria
57C4 Arwala Indon
44G4 Arzamas Russian Fed
71B1 Arzew Alg
60C2 Asadabad Afghan
54B4 Asahi *R* Japan
53E3 Asahi dake *Mt* Japan
53E3 Asahikawa Japan
54A3 Asan-man *B* S Korea
61C3 Asansol India
69A2 Asawanwah *Well* Libya
44L4 Asbest Russian Fed
74C2 Asbestos Mts S Africa
13E2 Asbury Park USA
xxxH5 Ascension *I* Atlantic O
42B3 Aschaffenburg Germany
42C2 Aschersleben Germany
40C2 Ascoli Piceno Italy
37C1 Ascona Switz
72E2 Āseb Eritrea
70C2 Asedjirad *Upland* Alg
72D3 Asela Eth
32H6 Åsele Sweden
41E2 Asenovgrad Bulg
36C2 Asfeld France
44K4 Asha Russian Fed
15C2 Ashburn USA
77G5 Ashburton NZ
76A3 Ashburton *R* Aust
64B3 Ashdod Israel
17D3 Ashdown USA
15D1 Asheboro USA
4B3 Ashern Can
9E3 Asheville USA
75D1 Ashford Aust
35F6 Ashford Eng
19D3 Ash Fork USA
Ashgabat = Ashkhabad
54D2 Ashibetsu Japan
53D4 Ashikaga Japan
54B4 Ashizuri-misaki *Pt* Japan
48G6 Ashkhabad Turkmenistan
16C2 Ashland Kansas, USA
9E3 Ashland Kentucky, USA
11A2 Ashland Montana, USA
17C1 Ashland Nebraska, USA
12C2 Ashland Ohio, USA
8A2 Ashland Oregon, USA
13D3 Ashland Virginia, USA
11D2 Ashland Wisconsin, USA
75C1 Ashley Aust
11C2 Ashley USA
14C2 Ashokan Res USA
65C3 Ashqelon Israel
64D3 Ash Shabakh Iraq
67G1 Ash Sha'm UAE
66D3 Ash Sh'ār S Arabia
64D2 Ash Sharqāt Iraq
64E3 Ash Shatrah Iraq
67E4 Ash Shihr Yemen
67E1 Ash Shumlul S Arabia
66D3 Ash Shuqayq S Arabia
12C2 Ashtabula USA
7M4 Ashuanipi L Can
5G4 Ashuapmushuan Prov Park Can
45F8 'Āsī *R* Syria
37D2 Asiago Italy
71A1 Asilah Mor
40B2 Asinara *I* Medit S
48K4 Asino Russian Fed
66D2 Asir Region, S Arabia
61B4 Aska India
64D2 Aşkale Turk
32G7 Askersund Sweden
65B4 Asl Egypt
60C1 Asmar Afghan
72D2 Asmera Eth
54B4 Aso Japan
72D2 Asosa Eth
16B3 Aspermont USA
78A2 Aspiring,Mt NZ
37A2 Aspres-sur-Buëch France
64C2 As Sabkhah Syria
67E2 As Salamiyah S Arabia
64C2 As Salamīyah Syria
66D4 Assale,L Eth
64D3 As Salmān Iraq
61D2 Assam State, India
64E3 As Samāwah Iraq
67F2 AsŞanām Region, S Arabia
65D2 As Sanamayn Syria
37B3 Asse *R* France
42B2 Assen Neth
42C1 Assens Den
69A1 As Sidrah Libya
6H5 Assiniboia Can
6G4 Assiniboine,Mt Can
4B4 Assiniboine *R* Can
5G3 Assinica Prov Park Can
37E3 Assisi Italy
64C3 As Sukhnah Syria
64E3 As Sulaymanīyāh Iraq
67E2 As Sulayyil S Arabia
67E2 As Summan Region, S Arabia
73E4 Assumption *I* Seychelles
66D2 As Suq S Arabia
64C3 As Suwaydā' Syria
64D3 As Suwayrah Iraq
64E2 Astara Azerbaijan
40B2 Asti Italy
41F3 Astipálaia *I* Greece
39A1 Astorga Spain
8A2 Astoria USA
45H6 Astrakhan' Russian Fed
39A1 Asturias Region, Spain
25E3 Asunción Par
72D3 Aswa *R* Uganda
66B2 Aswân Egypt
69C2 Aswân High Dam Egypt
69C2 Asyût Egypt
64C3 As Zilaf Syria
77H1 Atafu *I* Tokelau Is
71G4 Atakpamé Togo
57B5 Atambua Indon
7N3 Atangmik Greenland
57B4 Atapupu Indon
70A2 Atar Maur
20B3 Atascadero USA
48J5 Atasu Kazakhstan
57C4 Atauro *I* Indon
72D2 Atbara Sudan
48H4 Atbasar Kazakhstan
9D4 Atchafalaya B USA
9D3 Atchison USA
14C3 Atco USA
71F4 Atebubu Ghana
22B1 Atenguillo Mexico
40C2 Atessa Italy
36B1 Ath Belg
3F3 Athabasca Can
6G4 Athabasca *R* Can
6H4 Athabasca, L Can
Athens = Athínai
15B2 Athens Alabama, USA
9E3 Athens Georgia, USA
12C3 Athens Ohio, USA
14B2 Athens Pennsylvania, USA
15C1 Athens Tennessee, USA
17C3 Athens Texas, USA
71G4 Athiémé Benin
41E3 Athínai Greece
33B3 Athlone Irish Rep
65B1 Athna Cyprus
14D1 Athol USA
41E2 Áthos *Mt* Greece
35B5 Athy Irish Rep
72B2 Ati Chad
7J5 Atikoken Can
5J3 Atikonak L Can
49R3 Atka Russian Fed
10D6 Atka *I* USA
45G5 Atkarsk Russian Fed
17D2 Atkins USA
22C2 Atlacomulco Mexico
9E3 Atlanta Georgia, USA
12C2 Atlanta Michigan, USA
17C1 Atlantic USA
9F3 Atlantic City USA
14C2 Atlantic Highlands USA
xxxH8 Atlantic Indian Basin Atlantic O
xxxH7 Atlantic Indian Ridge Atlantic O
70C1 Atlas Saharien *Mts* Alg
6E4 Atlin Can
6E4 Atlin L Can
65C2 'Atlit Israel
22C2 Atlixco Mexico
9E3 Atmore USA
73E6 Atofinandrahana Madag
10H4 Atognak I USA
17C3 Atoka USA
22B1 Atotonilco Mexico
22C2 Atoyac *R* Mexico
26C2 Atrato *R* Colombia
67F2 Attaf Region, UAE
66D2 At Tā'if S Arabia
65D2 At Tall Syria
15B2 Attalla USA
7K4 Attawapiskat Can
4D3 Attawapiskat L Can
7K4 Attawapiskat *R* Can
64D3 At Taysīyah *Desert Region* S Arabia
12B2 Attica Indiana, USA
14A1 Attica New York, USA
36C2 Attigny France
5H2 Attikamagen L Can
65B1 Attila Line Cyprus
13E2 Attleboro Massachusetts, USA
55D3 Attopeu Laos
10A5 Attu USA
10A5 Attu *I* USA
64C4 At Tubayq *Upland* S Arabia
28B3 Atuel *R* Arg
32H7 Atvidaberg Sweden
20B2 Atwater USA
38D3 Aubagne France
36C2 Aube Department, France
36C2 Aube *R* France
38C3 Aubenas France
10N2 Aubry L Can
15B2 Auburn Alabama, USA
19B3 Auburn California, USA
12B2 Auburn Indiana, USA
13E2 Auburn Maine, USA
17C1 Auburn Nebraska, USA
13D2 Auburn New York, USA
18B1 Auburn Washington, USA
38C3 Auch France
71H4 Auchi Nig
77G4 Auckland NZ
xxixK7 Auckland Is NZ
38C3 Aude *R* France
7K4 Auden Can
37B1 Audincourt France
11D3 Audubon USA
75C1 Augathella Aust
74B2 Aughrabies Falls S Africa
42C3 Augsburg Germany
76A4 Augusta Aust
9E3 Augusta Georgia, USA
17C2 Augusta Kansas, USA
9G2 Augusta Maine, USA
18D1 Augusta Montana, USA
12A2 Augusta Wisconsin, USA
10H4 Augustine I USA
43E2 Augustów Pol

Banes
Beja

21E2 Banes Cuba
3E3 Banff Can
34D3 Banff Scot
6G4 Banff R Can
3E3 Banff Nat Pk Can
71F3 Banfora Burkina
62B2 Bangalore India
71J4 Bangangté Cam
72C3 Bangassou CAR
56E1 Banggi I Malay
55D2 Bang Hieng R Laos
56C3 Bangka I Indon
56B2 Bangkinang Indon
56B3 Bangko Indon
55C3 Bangkok Thai
59H3 Bangladesh Republic, Asia
60D2 Bangong Co L China
9G2 Bangor Maine, USA
34B4 Bangor N Ire
14C2 Bangor Pennsylvania, USA
35C5 Bangor Wales
56E3 Bangsalsembera Indon
55B3 Bang Saphan Yai Thai
57F7 Bangued Phil
72B3 Bangui CAR
73D5 Bangweulu L Zambia
55C4 Ban Hat Yai Thai
55C2 Ban Hin Heup Laos
55C1 Ban Houei Sai Laos
55B3 Ban Hua Hin Thai
70B3 Bani R Mali
70C3 Bani Bangou Niger
67E3 Banī Ma'arid Region, S Arabia
69A1 Banī Walīd Libya
64C2 Bāniyās Syria
65C2 Baniyas Syria
40D2 Banja Luka Bosnia-Herzegovina, Yugos
56D3 Banjarmasin Indon
70A3 Banjul The Gambia
55B4 Ban Kantang Thai
55D2 Ban Khemmarat Laos
55B4 Ban Khok Kloi Thai
77F2 Banks Is Vanuatu
51H8 Banks I Aust
6E4 Banks I British Columbia, Can
6F2 Banks I Northwest Territories, Can
18C1 Banks L USA
78B2 Banks Pen NZ
75E3 Banks Str Aust
61C3 Bankura India
55B2 Ban Mae Sariang Thai
55B2 Ban Mae Sot Thai
61E3 Banmauk Burma
55D3 Ban Me Thuot Viet
34B4 Bann R N Ire
55B4 Ban Na San Thai
60C2 Bannu Pak
28A4 Baños de Chihuio Chile
28A3 Baños Maule Chile
55C2 Ban Pak Neun Laos
55C4 Ban Pak Phanang Thai
55D3 Ban Ru Kroy Camb
55B3 Ban Sai Yok Thai
55C3 Ban Sattahip Thai
43D3 Banská Bystrica Slovakia
60C4 Bānswāra India
57B4 Bantaeng Indon
55B4 Ban Tha Kham Thai
55D2 Ban Thateng Laos
55C2 Ban Tha Tum Thai
33B3 Bantry Irish Rep
33A3 Bantry B Irish Rep
55D3 Ban Ya Soup Viet
71J4 Banyo Cam
56D4 Banyuwangi Indon
xxviiiE7 Banzare Seamount Indian O
52C3 Baofeng China
55C1 Bao Ha Viet
52B3 Baoji China
55D3 Bao Loc Viet
53C2 Baoqing China
50C4 Baoshan China
52C1 Baotou China
62C1 Bāpatla India
36B1 Bapaume France
64D3 Ba'Qūbah Iraq
41D2 Bar Montenegro, Yugos
57C3 Bara Indon
72D2 Bara Sudan
72E3 Baraawe Somalia
56E3 Barabai Indon
61B2 Bāra Banki India
48J4 Barabinsk Russian Fed
48J4 Barabinskaya Step Steppe Kazakhstan/Russian Fed
39B1 Baracaldo Spain
23C2 Baracoa Cuba
65D2 Baradá R Syria
75C2 Baradine Aust
66C3 Baraka Watercourse Eth
62A1 Bārāmati India
60C2 Baramula Pak
60D3 Bārān India
57F8 Barangas Phil
6E4 Baranof I USA
44D5 Baranovichi Belorussia
75A2 Baratta Aust
61C2 Barauni India
27K8 Barbacena Brazil
23F4 Barbados I Caribbean
39C1 Barbastro Spain
74E2 Barberton S Africa
38B2 Barbezieux France
26D2 Barbòsa Colombia
23E3 Barbuda I Caribbean
76D3 Barcaldine Aust
Barce = Al Marj
40D3 Barcellona Italy
39C1 Barcelona Spain
26F1 Barcelona Ven
37B2 Barcelonnette France
76D3 Barcoo R Aust
28B3 Barda del Medio Arg
72B1 Bardai Chad
25C5 Bardas Blancas Arg
61C3 Barddhamān India
43E3 Bardejov Slovakia
37C2 Bardi Italy
37B2 Bardonecchia Italy
35C5 Bardsey I Wales
12B3 Bardstown USA
67F4 Bareeda Somalia
60D3 Bareilly India
44F1 Barentsovo More S Russian Fed
48D2 Barentsøya I Barents S
Barents S = Barentsovo More
72D2 Barentu Eritrea
61B3 Bargarh India
37B2 Barge Italy
49M4 Barguzin Russian Fed
49N4 Barguzin R Russian Fed
13F2 Bar Harbor USA
61C3 Barhi India
40D2 Bari Italy
39D2 Barika Alg
26D2 Barinas Ven
61C3 Baripāda India
66B2 Bâris Egypt
60C4 Bari Sādri India
61D3 Barisal Bang
56D3 Barito R Indon
37B3 Barjols France
69A2 Barjuj Watercourse Libya
52A3 Barkam China
12B3 Barkley,L USA
17E2 Barkley,L USA
3C4 Barkley Sd Can
74D3 Barkly East S Africa
76C2 Barkly Tableland Mts Aust
36C2 Bar-le-Duc France
76A3 Barlee,L Aust
76A3 Barlee Range Mts Aust
40D2 Barletta Italy
60C3 Barmer India
75B2 Barmera Aust
35C5 Barmouth Wales
35E4 Barnard Castle Eng
48K4 Barnaul Russian Fed
14C3 Barnegat USA
14C3 Barnegat B USA
14A2 Barnesboro USA
7L2 Barnes Icecap Can
15C2 Barnesville Georgia, USA
12C3 Barnesville Ohio, USA
16B3 Barnhart USA
35E5 Barnsley Eng
35C6 Barnstaple Eng
71H4 Baro Nig
61D2 Barpeta India
26E1 Barquisimeto Ven
35F5 Barqe Oilfield N Sea
36D2 Barr France
27K6 Barra Brazil
34B3 Barra I Scot
75D2 Barraba Aust
29D1 Barra da Estiva Brazil
22B2 Barra de Navidad Mexico
29D3 Barra de Piraí Brazil
22D2 Barra de Tonalá Mexico
29A2 Barra do Bugres Brazil
29B2 Barra do Garças Brazil
28D2 Barra do Quarai Brazil
28E2 Barra do Ribeiro Brazil
71F4 Barrage d'Ayama Ivory Coast
71J4 Barrage de Mbakaou Dam Cam
27K6 Barragem de Sobradinho Brazil
39A2 Barragem do Castelo do Bode Res Port
39A2 Barragem do Maranhão Port
34B3 Barra Head Pt Scot
27K8 Barra Mansa Brazil
26C6 Barranca Peru
26D2 Barrancabermeja Colombia
26F2 Barrancas Ven
105E3 Barranqueras Arg
26D1 Barranquilla Colombia
34B3 Barra,Sound of Chan Scot
4F4 Barraute Can
14D1 Barre USA
28B3 Barreal Arg
27K6 Barreiras Brazil
39A2 Barreiro Port
27L5 Barreiros Brazil
76D5 Barren,C Aust
10H4 Barren Is USA
27J8 Barretos Brazil
3F3 Barrhead Can
4F5 Barrie Can
3D3 Barrière Can
75B2 Barrier Range Mts Aust
3H2 Barrington L Can
76E4 Barrington,Mt Aust
29C2 Barro Alto Brazil
51G8 Barroloola Aust
12A1 Barron USA
23N2 Barrouaillie St Vincent
6C2 Barrow USA
33B3 Barrow R Irish Rep
35B5 Barrow R Irish Rep
76C3 Barrow Creek Aust
76A3 Barrow I Aust
35D4 Barrow-in-Furness Eng
6C2 Barrow,Pt USA
7J2 Barrow Str Can
13D1 Barry's Bay Can
14C2 Barryville USA
62B1 Barsi India
8B3 Barstow USA
38C2 Bar-sur-Aube France
36C2 Bar-sur-Seine France
27G2 Bartica Guyana
64B1 Bartın Turk
76D2 Bartle Frere,Mt Aust
8D3 Bartlesville USA
11C3 Bartlett USA
73D6 Bartolomeu Dias Mozam
43E2 Bartoszyce Pol
26B2 Barú Panama
56D4 Barung I Indon
56A2 Barus Indon
60D4 Barwāh India
60C4 Barwāni India
75C1 Barwon R Aust
44H5 Barysh Russian Fed
28D1 Basail Arg
20C1 Basalt USA
72B3 Basankusu Zaïre
28D2 Basavilbas Arg
57F6 Basco Phil
36D3 Basel France
40B1 Basel Switz
40D2 Basento R Italy
3F3 Bashaw Can
57F6 Bashi Chan Phil
44J5 Bashkortostan Respsublika, Russian Fed
57B3 Basiano Indon
57F9 Basilan I Phil
35F6 Basildon Eng
28E2 Basilio Brazil
18E2 Basin USA
35E6 Basingstoke Eng
8B2 Basin Region USA
64E3 Basra Iraq
36D2 Bas-Rhin Department, France
55D3 Bassac R Camb
3F3 Bassano Can
40C1 Bassano Italy
37D2 Bassano del Grappa Italy
71G4 Bassari Togo
73D6 Bassas da India I Mozam Chan
55A2 Bassein Burma
23E3 Basse Terre Guadeloupe
11C3 Bassett USA
71G4 Bassila Benin
20C2 Bass Lake USA
76D5 Bass Str Aust
32G7 Båstad Sweden
63C3 Bastak Iran
61B2 Basti India
40B2 Bastia Corse
42B3 Bastogne Belg
17D3 Bastrop Louisiana, USA
17C3 Bastrop Texas, USA
72A3 Bata Eq Guinea
56D3 Batakan Indon
60D2 Batala India
50C3 Batang China
72B3 Batangafo CAR
57F6 Batan Is Phil
57D3 Batanta I Indon
29C3 Batatais Brazil
13D2 Batavia USA
75D3 Batemans Bay Aust
15C2 Batesburg USA
17D2 Batesville Arkansas, USA
17E3 Batesville Mississippi, USA
5H4 Bath Can
35D6 Bath Eng
13F2 Bath Maine, USA
13D2 Bath New York, USA
72B2 Batha R Chad
12C1 Bathawana Mt Can
76D4 Bathurst Aust
7M5 Bathurst Can
6F2 Bathurst,C Can
76C2 Bathurst I Aust
6H2 Bathurst I Can
6H3 Bathurst Inlet B Can
71F4 Batié Burkina
63C2 Bātlāq-e-Gavkhūnī Salt Flat Iran
75C3 Batlow Aust
64D2 Batman Turk
71D1 Batna Alg
9D3 Baton Rouge USA
65C1 Batroun Leb
55C3 Battambang Camb
62C3 Batticaloa Sri Lanka
62E3 Batti Malv I Indian O
3G3 Battle R Can
9E2 Battle Creek USA
7N4 Battle Harbour Can
18C2 Battle Mountain USA
56F6 Batu Gajah Malay
56E2 Batukelau Indon
45G7 Batumi Georgia
55C5 Batu Pahat Malay
56B3 Baturaja Indon
65C2 Bat Yam Israel
76B1 Baubau Indon
71H3 Bauchi Nig
71H3 Bauchi State, Nig
11D2 Baudette USA
37B2 Bauges Mts France
7N4 Bauld,C Can
37B1 Baumes-les-Dames France
49N4 Baunt Russian Fed
27J8 Bauru Brazil
29B2 Baus Brazil
42C2 Bautzen Germany
56D4 Baween I Indon
69B2 Bawîti Egypt
71F3 Bawku Ghana
55B2 Bawlake Burma
75A2 Bawlen Aust
15C2 Baxley USA
61E1 Baxoi China
21E2 Bayamo Cuba
53B2 Bayan China
56E4 Bayan Indon
50D2 Bayandzürh Mongolia
50C3 Bayan Har Shan Mts China
52A1 Bayan Mod China
52B1 Bayan Obo China
11B3 Bayard Nebraska, USA
16A3 Bayard New Mexico, USA
37B2 Bayard P France
10N4 Bayard,Mt Can
49N5 Bayasgalant Mongolia
57F8 Baybay Phil
64D1 Bayburt Turk
9E2 Bay City Michigan, USA
17C4 Bay City Texas, USA
64B2 Bay Dağlari Turk
44M2 Baydaratskaya Guba B Russian Fed
72E3 Baydhabo Somalia
38B2 Bayeaux France
37D1 Bayerische Alpen Mts Germany
42C3 Bayern State, Germany
12A1 Bayfield USA
67E4 Bayhan al Qisāb Yemen
64C3 Bāyir Jordan
49M6 Baykal, Ozero L Kazakhstan
50D1 Baykalskiy Khrebet Mts Russian Fed
49L3 Baykit Russian Fed
49L5 Baylik Shan Mts China/Mongolia
44K5 Baymak Russian Fed
15B2 Bay Minette USA
57F7 Bayombang Phil
38B3 Bayonne France
63E1 Bayram Ali Turkmenistan
42C3 Bayreuth Germany
17E3 Bay St Louis USA
13E2 Bay Shore USA
13D1 Bays,L of Can
66D4 Bayt al Faqīh Yemen
50B2 Baytik Shan Mts China
Bayt Lahm = Bethlehem
17D4 Baytown USA
39B2 Baza Spain
43F3 Bazaliya Ukraine
45H7 Bazar-Dyuzi Mt Azerbaijan
38B3 Bazas France
52B3 Bazhong China
63E3 Bazmān Iran
65D1 Bcharre Leb
11B2 Beach USA
14C3 Beach Haven USA
35F6 Beachy Head Eng
14D2 Beacon USA
73E5 Bealanana Madag
18D2 Bear R USA
12A2 Beardstown USA
Bear I = Bjørnøya
18D2 Bear L USA
4C3 Bearskin Lake Can
20B1 Bear Valley USA
8D2 Beatrice USA
34D2 Beatrice Oilfield N Sea
3D2 Beatton R Can
6F4 Beatton River Can
8B3 Beatty USA
4F4 Beattyville Can
36A2 Beauce Region, France
25E8 Beauchene Is Falkland Is
75D1 Beaudesert Aust
79B5 Beaufort S Can
74C3 Beaufort West S Africa
36A3 Beaugeney France
13E1 Beauharnois Can
34C3 Beauly Scot
19C4 Beaumont California, USA
9D3 Beaumont Texas, USA
36A2 Beaumont-sur-Sarthe France
38C2 Beaune France
4B3 Beauséjour Can
38C2 Beauvais France
3G2 Beauval Can
10J2 Beaver Alaska, USA
19D3 Beaver Utah, USA
4D2 Beaver R Can
3G3 Beaver R Saskatchewan, Can
3C1 Beaver R Yukon, Can
6D3 Beaver Creek Can
10J2 Beaver Creek USA
12B3 Beaver Dam Kentucky, USA
12B2 Beaver Dam Wisconsin, USA
18D1 Beaverhead Mts USA
3F3 Beaverhill L Can
12B1 Beaver I USA
17D2 Beaver L USA
3E2 Beaverlodge Can
60C3 Beawar India
28B2 Beazley Arg
29C3 Bebedouro Brazil
35F5 Beccles Eng
41E1 Bečej Serbia, Yugos
70B1 Béchar Alg
10G4 Becharof L USA
10F4 Bechevin B USA
9E3 Beckley USA
36E1 Beckum Germany
35E5 Bedford County, Eng
35E5 Bedford Eng
12B3 Bedford Indiana, USA
14A3 Bedford Pennsylvania, USA
23M2 Bedford Pt Grenada
14B2 Beech Creek USA
6D2 Beechey Pt USA
75C3 Beechworth Aust
75D1 Beenleigh Aust
65C3 Beer Menuha Israel
65C4 Beer Ora Israel
64B3 Beersheba Israel
Beèr Sheva = Beersheba
65C3 Beér Sheva, R Israel
8D4 Beeville USA
72C3 Befale Zaïre
73E5 Befandriana Madag
75C3 Bega Aust
49N2 Begicheva, Ostrov I Russian Fed
63C2 Behbehān Iran
10M4 Behm Canal Sd USA
63C1 Behshahr Iran
60B2 Behsud Afghan
53B2 Bei'an China
52B5 Beihai China
55D1 Beihai China
52D2 Beijing China
55E1 Beiliu China
52B4 Beipan Jiang R China
52E1 Beipiao China
73D5 Beira Mozam
64C3 Beirut Leb
50C2 Bei Shan Mts China
74E1 Beitbridge Zim
65C2 Beit ed Dīne Leb
65C3 Beit Jala Israel
39A2 Beja Port
71D1 Beja Tunisia

Bejaïa **Birch Mts**

71D1 **Bejaïa** Alg
39A1 **Béjar** Spain
63D2 **Bejestān** Iran
43E3 **Békéscsaba** Hung
73E6 **Bekily** Madag
61B2 **Bela** India
60B3 **Bela** Pak
56D2 **Belaga** Malay
14B3 **Bel Air** USA
62B1 **Belamoalli** India
57B2 **Belang** Indon
56A2 **Belangpidie** Indon
xxviiiH4 **Belau** *I* Pacific O
Belau = Palau
74E2 **Bela Vista** Mozam
29A3 **Béla Vista** Par/Brazil
56A2 **Belawan** Indon
44K4 **Belaya** *R* Ukraine
43G3 **Belaya Tserkov'** Russian Fed
7J2 **Belcher Chan** Can
7L4 **Belcher Is** Can
60B1 **Belchiragh** Afghan
44J5 **Belebey** Russian Fed
72E3 **Beled Weyne** Somalia
27J4 **Belém** Brazil
28B1 **Belén** Arg
26C3 **Belén** Colombia
29A3 **Belén** Par
28D2 **Belén** Urug
8C3 **Belen** USA
28B1 **Belén** *R* Arg
34B4 **Belfast** N Ire
74E2 **Belfast** S Africa
5H5 **Belfast** USA
34B4 **Belfast Lough** *Estuary* N Ire
11B2 **Belfield** USA
72D2 **Bēlfodiyo** Eth
34E4 **Belford** Eng
38D2 **Belfort** France
62A1 **Belgaum** India
42A2 **Belgium** Kingdom, N W Europe
45F5 **Belgorod** Russian Fed
45E6 **Belgorod Dnestrovskiy** Ukraine
Belgrade = Beograd
18D1 **Belgrade** USA
69A2 **Bel Hedan** Libya
56C3 **Belinyu** Indon
56C3 **Belitung** *I* Indon
21D3 **Belize** Belize
21D3 **Belize** Republic, C America
49P2 **Bel'kovskiv, Ostrov** *I* Russian Fed
38C2 **Bellac** France
6F4 **Bella Coola** Can
37C2 **Bellagio** Italy
17C4 **Bellaire** USA
37C1 **Bellano** Italy
62B1 **Bellary** India
75C1 **Bellata** Aust
28D2 **Bella Union** Urug
28D1 **Bella Vista** Arg
37B2 **Belledonne** *Mts* France
14B2 **Bellefonte** USA
8C2 **Belle Fourche** USA
11B3 **Belle Fourche** *R* USA
38D2 **Bellegarde** France
15E4 **Belle Glade** USA
7N4 **Belle I** Can
38B2 **Belle-Ile** *I* France
7N4 **Belle Isle,Str of** Can
36A2 **Bellême** France
5K4 **Belleoram** Can
7L5 **Belleville** Can
12B3 **Belleville** Illinois, USA
17C2 **Belleville** Kansas, USA
18D2 **Bellevue** Idaho, USA
12A2 **Bellevue** Iowa, USA
18B1 **Bellevue** Washington, USA
37A2 **Belley** France
75D2 **Bellingen** Aust
8A2 **Bellingham** USA
79G2 **Bellingshausen** *Base* Ant
79G3 **Bellingshausen S** Ant
40B1 **Bellinzona** Switz
26C2 **Bello** Colombia
77E3 **Bellona Reefs** Nouvelle Calédonie
20B1 **Bellota** USA
13E2 **Bellows Falls** USA
7K3 **Bell Pen** Can
40C1 **Belluno** Italy
25D4 **Bell Ville** Arg
4C5 **Belmond** USA
14B1 **Belmont** USA
27L7 **Belmonte** Brazil
21D3 **Belmopan** Belize
53B1 **Belogorsk** Russian Fed
73E6 **Beloha** Madag
27K7 **Belo Horizonte** Brazil
16C2 **Beloit** Kansas, USA
9E2 **Beloit** Wisconsin, USA
44E3 **Belomorsk** Russian Fed
44K5 **Beloretsk** Russian Fed
44D5 **Belorussia**
73E5 **Belo-Tsiribihina** Madag
44F2 **Beloye More** *S*
44F3 **Beloye Ozero** *L* Russian Fed
44F3 **Belozersk** Russian Fed
12C3 **Belpre** USA
75A2 **Beltana** Aust
17C3 **Belton** USA
43F3 **Bel'tsy** Moldova
48K5 **Belukha** *Mt* Russian Fed
44H2 **Belush'ye** Russian Fed
12B2 **Belvidere** Illinois, USA
14C2 **Belvidere** New Jersey, USA
48J2 **Belyy, Ostrov** *I* Russian Fed
73B4 **Bembe** Angola
71G3 **Bembéréke** Benin
9D2 **Bemidji** USA
15B1 **Bemis** USA
32G6 **Bena** Nor
72C4 **Bena Dibele** Zaïre
75C3 **Benalla** Aust
34C2 **Ben Attow** *Mt* Scot
39A1 **Benavente** Spain
34B3 **Benbecula** *I* Scot
76A4 **Bencubbin** Aust
8A2 **Bend** USA
69E3 **Bendarbeyla** Somalia
34C3 **Ben Dearg** *Mt* Scot
43F3 **Bendery** Moldova
76D4 **Bendigo** Aust
71F3 **Bénéna** Mali
42C3 **Benešov** Czech Republic
40C2 **Benevento** Italy
59G4 **Bengal,B of** Asia
69A1 **Ben Gardane** Libya
71E2 **Ben Gardane** Tunisia
52D3 **Bengbu** China
57B3 **Benggai** *I* Indon
69B1 **Benghāzī** Libya
56B2 **Bengkalis** Indon
56B3 **Bengkulu** Indon
73B5 **Benguela** Angola
71A2 **Benguerir** Mor
64B3 **Benha** Egypt
34C2 **Ben Hope** *Mt* Scot
72C3 **Beni** Zaïre
26E6 **Béni** *R* Bol
70B1 **Beni Abbes** Alg
39C1 **Benicarló** Spain
39B2 **Benidorm** Spain
39C2 **Beni Mansour** Alg
69C2 **Beni Mazar** Egypt
71A2 **Beni Mellal** Mor
70C4 **Benin** Republic, Africa
71H4 **Benin City** Nig
71B1 **Beni-Saf** Alg
69C2 **Beni Suef** Egypt
16B2 **Benkelman** USA
34C2 **Ben Kilbreck** *Mt* Scot
33C2 **Ben Lawers** *Mt* Scot
34D3 **Ben Macdui** *Mt* Scot
34C2 **Ben More Assynt** *Mt* Scot
78B2 **Benmore,L** NZ
49R2 **Bennetta, Ostrov** *I* Russian Fed
34C3 **Ben Nevis** *Mt* Scot
13E2 **Bennington** USA
65C2 **Bennt Jbail** Leb
72B3 **Bénoué** *R* Cam
71J4 **Bénoué Nat Pk** Cam
36E2 **Bensheim** Germany
8B3 **Benson** Arizona, USA
11C2 **Benson** Minnesota, USA
72C3 **Bentiu** Sudan
29A2 **Bento Gomes** *R* Brazil
17D3 **Benton** Arkansas, USA
20C2 **Benton** California, USA
12B3 **Benton** Kentucky, USA
12B2 **Benton Harbor** USA
71H4 **Benue** State, Nig
71H4 **Benue** *R* Nig
34C3 **Ben Wyvis** *Mt* Scot
52E1 **Benxi** China
57C2 **Beo** Indon
41E2 **Beograd** Serbia, Yugos
61B3 **Beohāri** India
53C5 **Beppu** Japan
41D2 **Berat** Alb
72D2 **Berber** Sudan
72E2 **Berbera** Somalia
72B3 **Berbérati** CAR
36A1 **Berck** France
43F3 **Berdichev** Ukraine
45F6 **Berdyansk** Ukraine
12C3 **Berea** USA
57C2 **Berebere** Indon
71F4 **Berekum** Ghana
20B2 **Berenda** USA
66C2 **Berenice** Egypt
4C3 **Berens** *R* Can
6J4 **Berens** *R* Can
6J4 **Berens River** Can
75A1 **Beresford** Aust
11C3 **Beresford** USA
43E3 **Berettyoújfalu** Hung
43E2 **Bereza** Belorussia
43E3 **Berezhany** Ukraine
43F2 **Berezina** *R* Belorussia
44G3 **Bereznik** Russian Fed
44K4 **Berezniki** Russian Fed
45E6 **Berezovka** Ukraine
44L3 **Berezovo** Russian Fed
53D1 **Berezovyy** Russian Fed
64A2 **Bergama** Turk
40B1 **Bergamo** Italy
32F6 **Bergen** Nor
14B1 **Bergen** USA
36C1 **Bergen op Zoom** Neth
38C3 **Bergerac** France
36D1 **Bergisch-Gladbach** Germany
4D4 **Bergland** USA
62C1 **Berhampur** India
49S4 **Beringa, Ostrov** *I* Russian Fed
10K3 **Bering Gl** USA
49T3 **Beringovskiy** Russian Fed
xxixK2 **Bering S** Russian Fed/USA
79C6 **Bering Str** Russian Fed/ USA
63D3 **Berīzak** Iran
39B2 **Berja** Spain
71B2 **Berkane** Mor
8A3 **Berkeley** USA
14A3 **Berkeley Spring** USA
79F2 **Berkner I** Ant
41E2 **Berkovitsa** Bulg
35E6 **Berkshire** County, Eng
14D1 **Berkshire Hills** USA
3E3 **Berland** *R* Can
42C2 **Berlin** Germany
13E2 **Berlin** New Hampshire, USA
14A3 **Berlin** Pennsylvania, USA
42C2 **Berlin** State, Germany
26F8 **Bermejo** Bol
25E3 **Bermejo** *R* Arg
2M5 **Bermuda** *I* Atlantic O
40B1 **Bern** Switz
16A2 **Bernalillo** USA
29B4 **Bernardo de Irigoyen** Arg
14C2 **Bernardsville** USA
28C3 **Bernasconi** Arg
36A2 **Bernay** France
42C2 **Bernburg** Germany
37B1 **Berner Orberland** *Mts* Switz
7K2 **Bernier B** Can
42C3 **Berounka** *R* Czech Republic
71A2 **Berrechid** Mor
75B2 **Berri** Aust
71C2 **Berriane** Alg
38C2 **Berry** Region, France
20A1 **Berryessa,L** USA
9F4 **Berry Is** Bahamas
14B3 **Berryville** USA
74B2 **Berseba** Namibia
56F6 **Bertam** Malay
16A2 **Berthoud P** USA
72B3 **Bertoua** Cam
77G1 **Beru** *I* Kiribati
13D2 **Berwick** USA
34D4 **Berwick-upon-Tweed** Eng
35D5 **Berwyn** *Mts* Wales
73E5 **Besalampy** Madag
38D2 **Besançon** France
43E3 **Beskidy Zachodnie** *Mts* Pol
3G2 **Besnard L** Can
64C2 **Besni** Turk
65C3 **Besor** *R* Israel
15B2 **Bessemer** Alabama, USA
12B1 **Bessemer** Michigan, USA
73E5 **Betafo** Madag
39A1 **Betanzos** Spain
71J4 **Betaré Oya** Cam
65C3 **Bet Guvrin** Israel
74D2 **Bethal** S Africa
74B2 **Bethanie** Namibia
17D1 **Bethany** Missouri, USA
17C2 **Bethany** Oklahoma, USA
6B3 **Bethel** Alaska, USA
14D2 **Bethel** Connecticut, USA
12C2 **Bethel Park** USA
13D3 **Bethesda** USA
65C3 **Bethlehem** Israel
74D2 **Bethlehem** S Africa
13D2 **Bethlehem** USA
74D3 **Bethulie** S Africa
38C1 **Bethune** France
36A2 **Béthune** *R* France
73E6 **Betioky** Madag
75B1 **Betoota** Aust
72B3 **Betou** Congo
59E1 **Betpak Dala** *Steppe* Kazakhstan
73E6 **Betroka** Madag
7M5 **Betsiamites** Can
12A2 **Bettendorf** USA
61B2 **Bettiah** India
10H2 **Bettles** USA
37C2 **Béttola** Italy
60D4 **Bētul** India
36C1 **Betuwe** Region, Neth
60D3 **Betwa** *R* India
36D1 **Betzdorf** Germany
10G4 **Beverley,L** USA
14E1 **Beverly** USA
20C3 **Beverly Hills** USA
70B4 **Beyla** Guinea
62B2 **Beypore** India
Beyrouth = Beirut
64B2 **Beyşehir** Turk
45E8 **Beysehir Gölü** *L* Turk
65C2 **Beyt Shean** Israel
37C1 **Bezan** Austria
44F4 **Bezhetsk** Russian Fed
38C3 **Béziers** France
63D1 **Bezmein** Turkmenistan
50D1 **Beznosova** Russian Fed
61C2 **Bhadgaon** Nepal
62C1 **Bhadrāchalam** India
61C3 **Bhadrakh** India
62B2 **Bhadra Res** India
62B2 **Bhadrāvati** India
60B3 **Bhag** Pak
61C2 **Bhāgalpur** India
60C2 **Bhakkar** Pak
61E3 **Bhamo** Burma
60D4 **Bhandāra** India
60D3 **Bharatpur** India
60C4 **Bharūch** India
61C3 **Bhātiāpāra Ghat** Bang
60C2 **Bhatinda** India
62A2 **Bhatkal** India
61C3 **Bhātpāra** India
60C4 **Bhāvnagar** India
61B4 **Bhawānipatna** India
60C2 **Bhera** Pak
61B2 **Bheri** *R* Nepal
61B3 **Bhilai** India
60C3 **Bhīlwāra** India
62C1 **Bhīmavaram** India
60D3 **Bhind** India
60D3 **Bhiwāni** India
62B1 **Bhongir** India
60D4 **Bhopāl** India
61C3 **Bhubaneshwar** India
60B4 **Bhuj** India
60D4 **Bhusāwal** India
46F4 **Bhutan** Kingdom, Asia
59H3 **Bhutan** Kingdom, Asia
71F4 **Bia** *R* Ghana
51G7 **Biak** *I* Indon
43E2 **Biala Podlaska** Pol
42D2 **Bialograd** Pol
43E2 **Bialystok** Pol
32A1 **Biargtangar** *C* Iceland
63D1 **Bīarjmand** Iran
57C2 **Biaro** *I* Indon
38B3 **Biarritz** France
37C1 **Biasca** Switz
64B4 **Biba** Egypt
53E3 **Bibai** Japan
73B5 **Bibala** Angola
37D3 **Bibbiena** Italy
42B3 **Biberach** Germany
71F4 **Bibiani** Ghana
5H4 **Bic** Can
41F1 **Bicaz** Rom
53D1 **Bichi** *R* Russian Fed
19D3 **Bicknell** USA
71H4 **Bida** Nig
62B1 **Bīdar** India
67G2 **Bidbid** Oman
13E2 **Biddeford** USA
35C6 **Bideford** Eng
35C6 **Bideford B** Eng
70C2 **Bidon 5** Alg
43E2 **Biebrza** Pol
40B1 **Biel** Switz
42D2 **Bielawa** Pol
42B2 **Bielefeld** Germany
37B1 **Bieler See** *L* Switz
40B1 **Biella** Italy
43E2 **Bielsk Podlaski** Pol
55D3 **Bien Hoa** Viet
40C2 **Biferno** *R* Italy
64A1 **Biga** Turk
41F3 **Bigadiç** Turk
5H4 **Big Bald Mt** Can
4D3 **Big Beaver House** Can
16B4 **Big Bend Nat Pk** USA
18D1 **Big Belt Mts** USA
17E3 **Big Black** *R* USA
17C1 **Big Blue** *R* USA
15E4 **Big Cypress Swamp** USA
6D3 **Big Delta** USA
38D2 **Bigent** Germany
3G3 **Biggar** Can
75D1 **Biggenden** Aust
10L4 **Bigger,Mt** Can
18D1 **Big Hole** *R* USA
11A2 **Bighorn** *R* USA
11A2 **Bighorn L** USA
11A3 **Bighorn Mts** USA
55C3 **Bight of Bangkok** *B* Thai
70C4 **Bight of Benin** *B* W Africa
70C4 **Bight of Biafra** *B* Cam
7L3 **Big I** Can
10G4 **Big Koniuji** *I* USA
16B3 **Big Lake** USA
37C1 **Bignasco** Switz
70A3 **Bignona** Sen
19C3 **Big Pine** USA
15E4 **Big Pine Key** USA
20C3 **Big Pine Mt** USA
12B2 **Big Rapids** USA
6H4 **Big River** Can
4B2 **Big Sand** *L* Can
18D1 **Big Sandy** USA
3H3 **Big Sandy L** Can
11C3 **Big Sioux** *R* USA
20D1 **Big Smokey V** USA
8C3 **Big Spring** USA
16B1 **Big Springs** USA
11C2 **Big Stone City** USA
12C3 **Big Stone Gap** USA
4B3 **Bigstone L** Can
20B2 **Big Sur** USA
18E1 **Big Timber** USA
7J4 **Big Trout L** Can
4D3 **Big Trout Lake** Can
7K4 **Big Trout Lake** Can
40D2 **Bihać** Bosnia-Herzegovina, Yugos
61C2 **Bihār** India
61C3 **Bihar** State, India
72D4 **Biharamulo** Tanz
45C6 **Bihor** *Mt* Rom
62B1 **Bijāpur** India
62C1 **Bījāpur** India
63B1 **Bījār** Iran
61B2 **Bijauri** Nepal
41D2 **Bijeljina** Bosnia-Herzegovina, Yugos
52B4 **Bijie** China
60D3 **Bijnor** India
60C3 **Bijnot** Pak
60C3 **Bikāner** India
65C2 **Bikfaya** Leb
53C2 **Bikin** Russian Fed
53D2 **Bikin** *R* Russian Fed
72B4 **Bikoro** Zaïre
53A2 **Bila He** *R* China
60C3 **Bilara** India
60D2 **Bilaspur** India
61B3 **Bilāspur** India
55B3 **Bilauktaung Range** *Mts* Thai
39B1 **Bilbao** Spain
65A3 **Bilbeis** Egypt
Bilbo = Bilbao
42D3 **Bilé** *R* Czech Republic/ Slovakia
41D2 **Bileća** Bosnia-Herzegovina, Yugos
64B1 **Bilecik** Turk
72C3 **Bili** *R* Zaïre
49S3 **Bilibino** Russian Fed
57F8 **Biliran** *I* Phil
8C2 **Billings** USA
72B2 **Bilma** Niger
9E3 **Biloxi** USA
72C2 **Biltine** Chad
71F4 **Bimbita** Ghana
60D4 **Bina-Etawa** India
57F8 **Binalbagan** Phil
73D5 **Bindura** Zim
73C5 **Binga** Zim
73D5 **Binga** *Mt* Zim
75D1 **Bingara** Aust
42B3 **Bingen** Germany
13F1 **Bingham** USA
9F2 **Binghamton** USA
56E1 **Bingkor** Malay
64D2 **Bingöl** Turk
52D3 **Binhai** China
56A2 **Binjai** Indon
56C2 **Binjai** Indon
57B4 **Binongko** *I* Indon
56B2 **Bintan** *I* Indon
56B3 **Bintuhan** Indon
56D2 **Bintulu** Malay
25B5 **Bió Bió** *R* Chile
xxxJ4 **Bioko** *I* Atlantic O
62B1 **Bīr** India
53C2 **Bira** Russian Fed
69B2 **Bīr Abu Husein** *Well* Egypt
69B2 **Bi'r al Harash** *Well* Libya
72C2 **Birao** CAR
61C2 **Biratnagar** Nepal
3F2 **Birch** *R* Can
10J2 **Birch Creek** USA
75B3 **Birchip** Aust
11D2 **Birch L** USA
4C3 **Birch L** Can
6G4 **Birch Mts** Can

Bird **Boutourou,Mt**

7J4 **Bird** Can
76C3 **Birdsville** Aust
76C2 **Birdum** Aust
65A4 **Bîr el 'Agramîya** *Well* Egypt
65B3 **Bir el Duweidâr** *Well* Egypt
61B2 **Birganj** Nepal
65B3 **Bîr Gifgâfa** *Well* Egypt
65A4 **Bîr Gindali** *Well* Egypt
65B3 **Bîr Hasana** *Well* Egypt
29B3 **Birigui** Brazil
65D1 **Bīrīn** Syria
63D2 **Birjand** Iran
64B4 **Birkat Qarun** *L* Egypt
36D2 **Birkenfeld** Germany
35D5 **Birkenhead** Eng
45D6 **Bîrlad** Rom
65B3 **Bir Lahfân** *Well* Egypt
35D5 **Birmingham** Eng
9E3 **Birmingham** USA
69B2 **Bîr Misâha** *Well* Egypt
70A2 **Bir Moghrein** Maur
71H3 **Birnin Gwari** Nig
71G3 **Birnin Kebbi** Nig
71H3 **Birni N'Konni** Nig
53C2 **Birobidzhan** Russian Fed
35B5 **Birr** Irish Rep
39C2 **Bir Rabalou** Alg
75C1 **Birrie** *R* Aust
34D2 **Birsay** Scot
44K4 **Birsk** Russian Fed
69B2 **Bîr Tarfâwi** *Well* Egypt
11B1 **Birtle** Can
65B4 **Bîr Udelb** *Well* Egypt
49L4 **Biryusa** *R* Russian Fed
32J7 **Biržai** Lithuania
70B2 **Bir Zreigat** *Well* Maur
57C3 **Bisa** *I* Indon
19E4 **Bisbee** USA
38A2 **Biscay,B of** Spain/France
15E4 **Biscayne B** USA
37E1 **Bischofshofen** Austria
36D2 **Bischwiller** France
12C1 **Biscotasi L** Can
52B4 **Bishan** China
59F1 **Bishkek** Kirgizia
8B3 **Bishop** USA
35E4 **Bishop Auckland** Eng
35F6 **Bishop's Stortford** Eng
61B3 **Bishrāmpur** India
53A1 **Bishui** China
66C3 **Biskia** Eth
71D2 **Biskra** Alg
57G9 **Bislig** Phil
8C2 **Bismarck** USA
76D1 **Bismarck Arch** PNG
76D1 **Bismarck Range** *Mts* PNG
76D1 **Bismarck S** PNG
63B2 **Bīsotūn** Iran
70A3 **Bissau** Guinea-Bissau
4B3 **Bissett** Can
6G4 **Bistcho L** Can
41F1 **Bistrita** *R* Rom
72B3 **Bitam** Gabon
3G1 **Bitau L** Can
42B3 **Bitburg** Germany
36D2 **Bitche** France
64D2 **Bitlis** Turk
41E2 **Bitola** Macedonia, Yugos
42C2 **Bitterfeld** Germany
74B3 **Bitterfontein** S Africa
64B3 **Bitter Lakes** Egypt
8B2 **Bitteroot Range** *Mts* USA
57C2 **Bitung** Indon
71J3 **Biu** Nig
53D4 **Biwa-ko** *L* Japan
72E2 **Biyo Kaboba** Eth
48K4 **Biysk** Russian Fed
71D1 **Bizerte** Tunisia
39C2 **Bj bou Arréridj** Alg
40D1 **Bjelovar** Croatia, Yugos
70B2 **Bj Flye Ste Marie** Alg
48C2 **Bjørnøya** *I* Barents S
10K2 **Black** *R* USA
17D2 **Black** *R* USA
76D3 **Blackall** Aust
12B1 **Black B** Can
3G2 **Black Birch L** Can
35D5 **Blackburn** Eng
6D3 **Blackburn,Mt** USA
19D4 **Black Canyon City** USA
3F3 **Black Diamond** Can
11D2 **Blackduck** USA
4D2 **Black Duck** *R* Can
18D1 **Black Eagle** USA
18D2 **Blackfoot** USA
18D1 **Blackfoot** *R* USA
6H5 **Black Hills** USA
34C3 **Black Isle** *Pen* Scot
3G2 **Black L** Can
3G2 **Black Lake** Can
23Q2 **Blackman's** Barbados
19D3 **Black Mts** USA
35D6 **Black Mts** Wales
74B1 **Black Nossob** *R* Namibia
35D5 **Blackpool** Eng
23H1 **Black River** Jamaica
4E5 **Black River** USA
12A2 **Black River Falls** USA
8B2 **Black Rock Desert** USA
45D7 **Black S** Europe/Asia
12C3 **Blacksburg** USA
75D2 **Black Sugarloaf** *Mt* Aust
71F4 **Black Volta** *R* Ghana
15B2 **Black Warrior** *R* USA
33B3 **Blackwater** *R* Irish Rep
10O3 **Blackwater L** Can
17C2 **Blackwell** USA
41E2 **Blagoevgrad** Bulg
49O4 **Blagoveshchensk** Russian Fed
18D1 **Blaikiston,Mt** Can
18B1 **Blaine** USA
11C3 **Blair** USA
34D3 **Blair Atholl** Scot
34D3 **Blairgowrie** Scot
15C2 **Blakely** USA
16A2 **Blanca Peak** *Mt* USA
75A1 **Blanche,L** Aust
28A2 **Blanco** *R* Arg
28B1 **Blanco** *R* Arg
22C1 **Blanco** *R* Mexico
8A2 **Blanco,C** USA
7N4 **Blanc Sablon** Can
35D6 **Blandford Forum** Eng
19E3 **Blanding** USA
36A2 **Blangy-sur-Bresle** France
36B1 **Blankenberge** Belg
28D2 **Blanquillo** Urug
73D5 **Blantyre** Malawi
38B2 **Blaye** France
75C2 **Blayney** Aust
77G5 **Blenheim** NZ
37B2 **Bléone** *R* France
71C1 **Blida** Alg
4E4 **Blind River** Can
75A2 **Blinman** Aust
56D4 **Blitar** Indon
71G4 **Blitta** Togo
13E2 **Block I** USA
14E2 **Block Island Sd** USA
74D2 **Bloemfontin** S Africa
74D2 **Bloemhof** S Africa
74D2 **Bloemhof Dam** *Res* S Africa
36A3 **Blois** France
27G3 **Blommesteinmeer** *L* Suriname
32A1 **Blönduós** Iceland
12B3 **Bloomfield** Indiana, USA
17D1 **Bloomfield** Iowa, USA
11C3 **Bloomfield** Nebraska, USA
16A2 **Bloomfield** New Mexico, USA
12B2 **Bloomington** Illinois, USA
12B3 **Bloomington** Indiana, USA
11D3 **Bloomington** Minnesota, USA
14B2 **Bloomsburg** USA
56D4 **Blora** Indon
14B2 **Blossburg** USA
7Q3 **Blosseville Kyst** *Mts* Greenland
74D1 **Blouberg** *Mt* S Africa
42B3 **Bludenz** Austria
9E3 **Bluefield** USA
26B1 **Bluefields** Nic
16C1 **Blue Hill** USA
14A2 **Blue Knob** *Mt* USA
23B3 **Blue Mountain Peak** *Mt* Jamaica
14B2 **Blue Mt** USA
75D2 **Blue Mts** Aust
23J1 **Blue Mts** Jamaica
8A2 **Blue Mts** USA
72D2 **Blue Nile, R** Sudan
6G3 **Bluenose L** Can
15C2 **Blue Ridge** USA
9E3 **Blue Ridge Mts** USA
3E3 **Blue River** Can
34A4 **Blue Stack** *Mt* Irish Rep
78A3 **Bluff** NZ
19E3 **Bluff** USA
5K3 **Bluff,C** Can
76A4 **Bluff Knoll** *Mt* Aust
25G3 **Blumenau** Brazil
38D2 **Blundez** Austria
11C3 **Blunt** USA
18B2 **Bly** USA
10J4 **Blying Sd** USA
34E4 **Blyth** Eng
8B3 **Blythe** USA
9E3 **Blytheville** USA
70A4 **Bo** Sierra Leone
57F8 **Boac** Phil
52D2 **Boading** China
57C3 **Boano** *I* Indon
29D1 **Boa Nova** Brazil
12C2 **Boardman** USA
49M5 **Boatou** China
24D3 **Boa Vista** Brazil
26F3 **Boa Vista** Brazil
70A4 **Boa Vista** *I* Cape Verde
55E1 **Bobai** China
62C1 **Bobbili** India
37C2 **Bóbbio** Italy
71F3 **Bobo Dioulasso** Burkina
43G2 **Bobrovica** Ukraine
44D5 **Bobruysk** Belorussia
15E4 **Boca Chica Key** *I* USA
26E4 **Bõca do Acre** Brazil
29D2 **Bocaiúva** Brazil
22C1 **Boca Jesús Maria** Mexico
72B3 **Bocaranga** CAR
15E4 **Boca Raton** USA
43E3 **Bochnia** Pol
42B2 **Bocholt** Germany
36D1 **Bochum** Germany
73B5 **Bocoio** Angola
72B3 **Boda** CAR
49N4 **Bodaybo** Russian Fed
19B3 **Bodega Head** *Pt* USA
72B2 **Bodélé** *Desert Region* Chad
32J5 **Boden** Sweden
37C1 **Bodensee** *L* Switz/Germany
62B1 **Bodhan** India
62B2 **Bodināyakkanūr** India
35C6 **Bodmin** Eng
35C6 **Bodmin Moor** *Upland* Eng
32G5 **Bodø** Nor
41F3 **Bodrum** Turk
72C4 **Boende** Zaïre
70A3 **Boffa** Guinea
55B2 **Bogale** Burma
17E3 **Bogalusa** USA
75C2 **Bogan** *R* Aust
71F3 **Bogandé** Burkina
64C2 **Boğazlıyan** Turk
44L4 **Bogdanovich** Russian Fed
50B2 **Bogda Shan** *Mt* China
74B2 **Bogenfels** Namibia
75D1 **Boggabilla** Aust
75C2 **Boggabri** Aust
57F8 **Bogo** Phil
75C3 **Bogong,Mt** Aust
56C4 **Bogor** Indon
44J4 **Bogorodskoye** Russian Fed
26D3 **Bogotá** Colombia
49K4 **Bogotol** Russian Fed
61C3 **Bogra** Bang
52D2 **Bo Hai** *B* China
36B2 **Bohain-en-Vermandois** France
52D2 **Bohai Wan** *B* China
37E1 **Boh Bistrica** Slovenia, Yugos
71G4 **Bohicon** Benin
42C3 **Bohmer-wald** *Upland* Germany
57F9 **Bohol** *I* Phil
57F9 **Bohol S** Phil
29B2 **Bois** *R* Brazil
12C1 **Bois Blanc I** USA
8B2 **Boise** USA
16B2 **Boise City** USA
11B2 **Boissevain** Can
70A2 **Bojador,C** Mor
57F7 **Bojeador,C** Phil
63D1 **Bojnūrd** Iran
70A3 **Boké** Guinea
75C1 **Bokhara** *R* Aust
32F7 **Boknafjord** *Inlet* Nor
72B4 **Boko** Congo
55C3 **Bokor** Camb
72B2 **Bokoro** Chad
72C4 **Bokungu** Zaïre
72B2 **Bol** Chad
22B1 **Bolaãnos** Mexico
70A3 **Bolama** Guinea-Bissau
22B1 **Bolanos** *R* Mexico
38C2 **Bolbec** France
71F4 **Bole** Ghana
53D1 **Bolen** Russian Fed
42D2 **Boleslawiec** Pol
71F3 **Bolgatanga** Ghana
45D6 **Bolgrad** Ukraine
53C2 **Boli** China
28C3 **Bolívar** Arg
17D2 **Bolivar** Missouri, USA
17E2 **Bolivar** Tennessee, USA
26E7 **Bolivia** Republic, S America
32H6 **Bollnas** Sweden
75C1 **Bollon** Aust
26D2 **Bollvar** *Mt* Ven
72B4 **Bolobo** Zaire
40C2 **Bologna** Italy
44E4 **Bologoye** Russian Fed
53D2 **Bolon'** Russian Fed
53D2 **Bolon', Ozero** *L* Russian Fed
49M2 **Bol'shevik, Ostrov** *I* Russian Fed
44J2 **Bol'shezemel'skaya Tundra** *Plain* Russian Fed
49S3 **Bol'shoy Anyuy** *R* Russian Fed
53E1 **Bol'shoye Kizi, Ozero** *L* Russian Fed
45H5 **Bol'shoy Irgiz** *R* Russian Fed
53C3 **Bol'shoy Kamen** Russian Fed
49Q2 **Bol'shoy Lyakhovskiy, Ostrov** *I* Russian Fed
45H6 **Bol'shoy Uzen** *R* Kazakhstan
8C4 **Bolson de Mapimi** *Desert* Mexico
35D5 **Bolton** Eng
4B3 **Bolton L** Can
64B1 **Bolu** Turk
32A1 **Bolugarvik** Iceland
64B2 **Bolvadin** Turk
40C1 **Bolzano** Italy
72B4 **Boma** Zaïre
76D4 **Bombala** Aust
62A1 **Bombay** India
72D3 **Bombo** Uganda
61D2 **Bomdila** India
61E2 **Bomi** China
70A4 **Bomi Hills** Lib
27K6 **Bom Jesus da Lapa** Brazil
49O4 **Bomnak** Russian Fed
72C3 **Bomokandi** *R* Zaïre
72C3 **Bomu** *R* CAR/Zaïre
13D3 **Bon Air** USA
23D4 **Bonaire** *I* Caribbean
10K3 **Bona,Mt** USA
21D3 **Bonanza** Nic
7N5 **Bonavista** Can
5L4 **Bonavista B** Can
5L4 **Bonavista,C** Can
75A2 **Bon Bon** Aust
29C2 **Bon Despacho** Brazil
72C3 **Bondo** Zaïre
71F4 **Bondoukou** Ivory Coast
Bône = 'Annaba
57B4 **Bone** Indon
57B3 **Bonelipu** Indon
11C3 **Bonesteel** USA
27G3 **Bonfim** Guyana
72C3 **Bongandanga** Zaïre
57B3 **Bongka** *R* Indon
72B2 **Bongor** Chad
71F4 **Bongouanou** Ivory Coast
17C3 **Bonham** USA
40B2 **Bonifacio** Corse
40B2 **Bonifacio,Str of** *Chan* Medit S
Bonin Is = Ogasawara Gunto
15E4 **Bonita Springs** USA
29A3 **Bonito** Brazil
42B2 **Bonn** Germany
18C1 **Bonners Ferry** USA
36A2 **Bonnétable** France
10M2 **Bonnet Plume** *R* Can
36A2 **Bonneval** France
3F3 **Bonnyville** Can
76A1 **Bonthain** Indon
70A4 **Bonthe** Sierra Leone
57A4 **Bontosunggu** Indon
69D3 **Booaaso** Somalia
75B2 **Booligal** Aust
75D1 **Boonah** Aust
16B2 **Boone** Colorado, USA
11D3 **Boone** Iowa, USA
15C1 **Boone** North Carolina, USA
13D2 **Boonville** USA
75C2 **Boorowa** Aust
7J2 **Boothia,G of** Can
7J2 **Boothia Pen** Can
72B4 **Booué** Gabon
75A1 **Bopeechee** Aust
74C2 **Bophuthatswana** Self governing homeland, S Africa
16B4 **Boquillas** Mexico
72D3 **Bor** Sudan
64B2 **Bor** Turk
41E2 **Bor** Serbia, Yugos
8B2 **Borah Peak** *Mt* USA
32G7 **Borås** Sweden
63C3 **Borāzjān** Iran
75A3 **Borda,C** Aust
38B3 **Bordeaux** France
6G2 **Borden I** Can
7K2 **Borden Pen** Can
14C2 **Bordentown** USA
34D4 **Borders** Region, Scot
75B3 **Bordertown** Aust
37B3 **Bordighera** Italy
70C2 **Bordi Omar Dris** Alg
71C1 **Bordj bou Arreridj** Alg
32K6 **Borgå** Fin
32A2 **Borgarnes** Iceland
8C3 **Borger** USA
32H7 **Borgholm** Sweden
37D3 **Borgo San Lorenzo** Italy
37C2 **Borgosia** Italy
37C2 **Borgo Val di Taro** Italy
37D1 **Borgo Valsugana** Italy
43E3 **Borislav** Ukraine
45G5 **Borisoglebsk** Russian Fed
44D5 **Borisov** Belorussia
45F5 **Borisovka** Russian Fed
29A4 **Borja** Par
72B2 **Borkou** *Desert Region* Chad
32H6 **Borlänge** Sweden
37C2 **Bormida** Italy
37D1 **Bormio** Italy
32H7 **Bornholm** *I* Den
71J3 **Borno** State, Nig
41F3 **Bornova** Turk
72C3 **Boro** *R* Sudan
49P3 **Borogontsy** Russian Fed
71F3 **Boromo** Burkina
20D3 **Boron** USA
44E4 **Borovichi** Russian Fed
76C2 **Borroloola** Aust
41E1 **Borsa** Rom
63B2 **Borūjed** Iran
63C2 **Borūjen** Iran
42D2 **Bory Tucholskie** Region, Pol
43G2 **Borzna** Ukraine
49N4 **Borzya** Russian Fed
52B5 **Bose** China
53E2 **Boshnyakovo** Russian Fed
74D2 **Boshof** S Africa
41D2 **Bosna** *R* Bosnia-Herzegovina, Yugos
40D2 **Bosnia-Herzegovina** *Republic* Europe
54D3 **Bōsō-hantō** *B* Japan
Bosporus = Karadeniz Boğazi
39C2 **Bosquet** Alg
72B3 **Bossangoa** CAR
72B3 **Bossèmbélé** CAR
17D3 **Bossier City** USA
48K5 **Bosten Hu** *L* China
35E5 **Boston** Eng
9F2 **Boston** USA
9D3 **Boston Mts** USA
71F4 **Bosumtwi,L** Ghana
60C4 **Botād** India
41E2 **Botevgrad** Bulg
74D2 **Bothaville** S Africa
44B3 **Bothnia,G of** Sweden/Fin
73C6 **Botletli** *R* Botswana
45D6 **Botosani** Rom
73C6 **Botswana** Republic, Africa
40D3 **Botte Donato** *Mt* Italy
11B2 **Bottineau** USA
36D1 **Bottrop** Germany
29C3 **Botucatu** Brazil
29D1 **Botupora** Brazil
7N5 **Botwood** Can
70B4 **Bouaflé** Ivory Coast
68D7 **Bouaké** Ivory Coast
72B3 **Bouar** CAR
71B2 **Bouârfa** Mor
71J4 **Bouba Ndija Nat Pk** Cam
72B3 **Bouca** CAR
71B2 **Boudnib** Mor
39C2 **Boufarik** Alg
77E1 **Bougainville** *I* PNG
Bougie = Bejaïa
70B3 **Bougouni** Mali
71F3 **Bougouriba** *R* Burkina
71C2 **Bougtob** Alg
36C2 **Bouillon** France
71C1 **Bouira** Alg
70B2 **Bou Izakarn** Mor
36D2 **Boulay-Moselle** France
8C2 **Boulder** Colorado, USA
18D1 **Boulder** Montana, USA
8B3 **Boulder City** USA
20A2 **Boulder Creek** USA
38C1 **Boulogne** France
72B3 **Boumba** *R* CAR
71F4 **Bouna** Ivory Coast
8B3 **Boundary Peak** *Mt* USA
70B4 **Boundiali** Ivory Coast
18D2 **Bountiful** USA
77G5 **Bounty Is** NZ
77F3 **Bourail** Nouvelle Calédonie
36C3 **Bourbonne-les-Bains** France
70B3 **Bourem** Mali
38D2 **Bourg** France
38D2 **Bourg de Péage** France
37A1 **Bourg-en-Bresse** France
38C2 **Bourges** France
38C3 **Bourg-Madame** France
38C2 **Bourgogne** Region, France
37A2 **Bourgoin-Jallieu** France
37B2 **Bourg-St-Maurice** France
75C2 **Bourke** Aust
35E6 **Bournemouth** Eng
71C1 **Bou Saâda** Alg
72B2 **Bousso** Chad
70A3 **Boutilmit** Maur
71F4 **Boutourou,Mt** Ivory Coast

Bouvet I **Busuanga**

xxxJ7 **Bouvet I** Atlantic O
28D2 **Bovril** Arg
3F3 **Bow** *R* Can
11B2 **Bowbells** USA
76D2 **Bowen** Aust
19E4 **Bowie** Arizona, USA
17C3 **Bowie** Texas, USA
3F4 **Bow Island** Can
9E3 **Bowling Green** Kentucky, USA
17D2 **Bowling Green** Missouri, USA
12C2 **Bowling Green** Ohio, USA
13D3 **Bowling Green** Virginia, USA
11B2 **Bowman** USA
13D2 **Bowmanville** Can
75D2 **Bowral** Aust
3D3 **Bowron** *R* Can
52D3 **Bo Xian** China
52D2 **Boxing** China
64B1 **Boyabat** Turk
72B3 **Boyali** CAR
43G2 **Boyarka** Ukraine
6J4 **Boyd** Can
14C2 **Boyertown** USA
3F3 **Boyle** Can
33B3 **Boyle** Irish Rep
35B5 **Boyne** *R* Irish Rep
15E4 **Boynoton Beach** USA
72C3 **Boyoma Falls** Zaïre
18E2 **Boysen Res** USA
41F3 **Bozcaada** *I* Turk
41F3 **Boz Dağlari** *Mts* Turk
8B2 **Bozeman** USA
Bozen = Bolzano
72B3 **Bozene** Zaïre
72B3 **Bozoum** CAR
37B2 **Bra** Italy
40D2 **Brač** *I* Croatia, Yugos
4F4 **Bracebridge** Can
69A2 **Brach** Libya
32H6 **Bräcke** Sweden
16B4 **Brackettville** USA
15E4 **Bradenton** USA
35E5 **Bradford** Eng
14A2 **Bradford** USA
20B3 **Bradley** USA
16C3 **Brady** USA
34E1 **Brae** Scot
34D3 **Braemar** Scot
39A1 **Braga** Port
28C3 **Bragado** Arg
39A1 **Bragana** Port
27J4 **Bragança** Brazil
29C3 **Bragança Paulista** Brazil
61D3 **Brahman-Baria** Bang
61C3 **Brāhmani** *R* India
61D2 **Brahmaputra** *R* India
45D6 **Brăila** Rom
9D2 **Brainerd** USA
74C3 **Brak** *R* S Africa
74D1 **Brak** *R* S Africa
70A3 **Brakna** Region, Maur
6F4 **Bralorne** Can
4F5 **Brampton** Can
26F3 **Branco** *R* Brazil
73B6 **Brandberg** *Mt* Namibia
42C2 **Brandenburg** Germany
42C2 **Brandenburg** State, Germany
74D2 **Brandfort** S Africa
8D2 **Brandon** Can
11C3 **Brandon** USA
74C3 **Brandvlei** S Africa
42C2 **Brandys nad Lebem** Czech Republic
43D2 **Braniewo** Pol
9E2 **Brantford** Can
75B3 **Branxholme** Aust
7M5 **Bras d'Or L** Can
29D2 **Brasíla de Minas** Brazil
26E6 **Brasiléia** Brazil
27J7 **Brasília** Brazil
41F1 **Brasov** Rom
56E2 **Brassay Range** *Mts* Malay
42D3 **Bratislava** Slovakia
49M4 **Bratsk** Russian Fed
43F3 **Bratslav** Ukraine
13E2 **Brattleboro** USA
42C2 **Braunschweig** Germany
70A4 **Brava** *I* Cape Verde
8B3 **Brawley** USA
35B5 **Bray** Irish Rep
7L3 **Bray I** Can
36B2 **Bray-sur-Seine** France
3E3 **Brazeau** *R* Can
3E3 **Brazeau,Mt** Can
24E5 **Brazil** Republic, S America
xxxG5 **Brazil Basin** Atlantic O
8D3 **Brazos** *R* USA
72B4 **Brazzaville** Congo
42C3 **Brdy** *Upland* Czech Republic
78A3 **Breaksea Sd** NZ
78B1 **Bream B** NZ
56C4 **Brebes** Indon
34D3 **Brechin** Scot
36C1 **Brecht** Belg
11C2 **Breckenridge** Minnesota, USA
16C3 **Breckenridge** Texas, USA
42D3 **Břeclav** Czech Republic
35D6 **Brecon** Wales
35D6 **Brecon Beacons** *Mts* Wales
35C5 **Brecon Beacons Nat Pk** Wales
42A2 **Breda** Neth
74C3 **Bredasdorp** S Africa
32H6 **Bredby** Sweden
44B3 **Bredbyn** Sweden
44K5 **Bredy** Russian Fed
74B3 **Breede** *R* S Africa
13D2 **Breezewood** USA
37C1 **Bregenz** Austria
37C1 **Bregenzer Ache** *R* Austria
32A1 **Breiðafjörður** *B* Iceland
36D2 **Breisach** Germany
37C2 **Brembo** Italy
37C2 **Brembo** *R* Italy
15B2 **Bremen** USA
42B2 **Bremen** Germany
42B2 **Bremerhaven** Germany
18B1 **Bremerton** USA
19E3 **Brendel** USA
17C3 **Brenham** USA
38E2 **Brenner** *Mt* Austria
42C3 **Brenner** *P* Austria/Italy
37D2 **Breno** Italy
4F4 **Brent** Can
37D2 **Brenta** *R* Italy
20B2 **Brentwood** USA
40C1 **Brescia** Italy
Breslau = Wrocław
37D1 **Bressanone** Italy
34E1 **Bressay** *I* Scot
38B2 **Bressuire** France
38B2 **Brest** France
43E2 **Brest** Belorussia
38B2 **Bretagne** Region, France
36B2 **Breteuil** France
36A2 **Bretevil** France
15B3 **Breton Sd** USA
14C2 **Breton Woods** USA
78B1 **Brett,C** NZ
15C1 **Brevard** USA
75C1 **Brewarrina** Aust
13F2 **Brewer** USA
14D2 **Brewster** New York, USA
18C1 **Brewster** Washington, USA
15B2 **Brewton** USA
74D2 **Breyten** S Africa
40D1 **Brežice** Slovenia, Yugos
72C3 **Bria** CAR
38D3 **Briancon** France
38C2 **Briare** France
15B2 **Bridgeport** Alabama, USA
19C3 **Bridgeport** California, USA
13E2 **Bridgeport** Connecticut, USA
11B3 **Bridgeport** Nebraska, USA
17C3 **Bridgeport** Texas, USA
20C1 **Bridgeport Res** USA
18E1 **Bridger** USA
16A1 **Bridger Peak** USA
14C3 **Bridgeton** USA
23F4 **Bridgetown** Barbados
5H5 **Bridgetown** Can
7M5 **Bridgewater** Can
14E2 **Bridgewater** USA
35D6 **Bridgwater** Eng
35D6 **Bridgwater B** Eng
35E4 **Bridlington** Eng
75E3 **Bridport** Aust
36C2 **Brienne-le-Château** France
37B1 **Brienzer See** *L* Switz
36C2 **Briey** France
40B1 **Brig** Switz
8B2 **Brigham City** USA
75C3 **Bright** Aust
35E6 **Brighton** Eng
37B3 **Brignoles** France
29A3 **Brilhante** *R* Brazil
36E1 **Brilon** Germany
41D2 **Brindisi** Italy
17D3 **Brinkley** USA
77E3 **Brisbane** Aust
13E2 **Bristol** Connecticut, USA
35D6 **Bristol** Eng
13E2 **Bristol** Pennsylvania, USA
14E2 **Bristol** Rhode Island, USA
9E3 **Bristol** Tennessee, USA
10F4 **Bristol B** USA
35C6 **Bristol Chan** Eng/Wales
6F4 **British Columbia** Province, Can
7K1 **British Empire Range** *Mts* Can
10K2 **British Mts** USA/Can
74D2 **Brits** S Africa
74C3 **Britstown** S Africa
4E4 **Britt** Can
11C2 **Britton** USA
38C2 **Brive** France
42D3 **Brno** Czech Republic
15C2 **Broad** *R* USA
14C1 **Broadalbin** USA
7L4 **Broadback** *R* Can
34B2 **Broad Bay** *Inlet* Scot
34C3 **Broadford** Scot
11A2 **Broadus** USA
11B1 **Broadview** Can
11B3 **Broadwater** USA
6H4 **Brochet** Can
6G2 **Brock I** Can
13D2 **Brockport** USA
14E1 **Brockton** USA
4F5 **Brockville** Can
14A2 **Brockway** USA
7K2 **Brodeur Pen** Can
34C4 **Brodick** Scot
43D2 **Brodnica** Pol
45D5 **Brody** Ukraine
36D1 **Brokem Haltern** Germany
16C1 **Broken Bow** Nebraska, USA
17D3 **Broken Bow** Oklahoma, USA
17D3 **Broken Bow L** USA
76D4 **Broken Hill** Aust
37C2 **Broni** Italy
32G5 **Brønnøysund** Nor
14D2 **Bronx** *Borough* New York, USA
57E9 **Brooke's Point** Phil
17D2 **Brookfield** Missouri, USA
12B2 **Brookfield** Wisconsin, USA
9D3 **Brookhaven** USA
18B2 **Brookings** Oregon, USA
8D2 **Brookings** South Dakota, USA
14E1 **Brookline** USA
11D3 **Brooklyn** USA
14D2 **Brooklyn** *Borough* New York, USA
11D2 **Brooklyn Center** USA
6G4 **Brooks** Can
10G4 **Brooks,L** USA
10E2 **Brooks Mt** USA
6C3 **Brooks Range** *Mts* USA
15C3 **Brooksville** USA
13E2 **Brookton** USA
75D1 **Brooloo** Aust
76B2 **Broome** Aust
34D2 **Brora** Scot
18B2 **Brothers** USA
67F4 **Brothers,The** *Is* Yemen
36A2 **Brou** France
72B2 **Broulkou** *Well* Chad
43G2 **Brovary** Ukraine
11D2 **Browerville** USA
16B3 **Brownfield** USA
3F4 **Browning** USA
8D4 **Brownsville** USA
8D3 **Brownwood** USA
51F8 **Browse** *I* Aust
36B1 **Bruay-en-Artois** France
76A3 **Bruce,Mt** Aust
4E5 **Bruce Pen** Can
36E2 **Bruchsal** Germany
37E1 **Bruck** Austria
42D3 **Bruck an der Mur** Austria
Bruges = Brugge
36B1 **Brugge** Belg
36D1 **Brühl** Germany
29D1 **Brumado** Brazil
36D2 **Brumath** France
18C2 **Bruneau** USA
18C2 **Bruneau** *R* USA
56D2 **Brunei** Sultanate, S E Asia
40C1 **Brunico** Italy
78B2 **Brunner,L** NZ
9E3 **Brunswick** Georgia, USA
13F2 **Brunswick** Maine, USA
17D2 **Brunswick** Mississippi, USA
25B8 **Brunswick,Pen de** Chile
75E3 **Bruny I** Aust
44G3 **Brusenets** Russian Fed
16B1 **Brush** USA
23A3 **Brus Laguna** Honduras
Brussel = Bruxelles
42A2 **Bruxelles** Belg
36D2 **Bruyères** France
8D3 **Bryan** USA
75A2 **Bryan,Mt** Aust
44E5 **Bryansk** Russian Fed
17D3 **Bryant** USA
20D3 **Bryce Canyon Nat Pk** USA
42D2 **Brzeg** Pol
64E4 **Būbīyan** *I* Kuwait/Iraq
72D4 **Bubu** *R* Tanz
74E1 **Bubye** *R* Zim
26D2 **Bucaramanga** Colombia
34E3 **Buchan** *Oilfield* N Sea
70A4 **Buchanan** Lib
16C3 **Buchanan,L** USA
34E3 **Buchan Deep** N Sea
7L2 **Buchan G** Can
33C2 **Buchan Ness** *Pen* Scot
7N5 **Buchans** Can
28C2 **Buchardo** Arg
Bucharest = Bucureşti
20B3 **Buchon, Pt** USA
37C1 **Buchs** Switz
19D4 **Buckeye** USA
35E5 **Buckingham** Eng
10F2 **Buckland** USA
10F2 **Buckland** *R* USA
75A2 **Buckleboo** Aust
13F2 **Bucksport** USA
72B4 **Buco Zau** Congo
5J4 **Buctouche** Can
41F2 **Bucureşti** Rom
43D3 **Budapest** Hung
60D3 **Budaun** India
35C6 **Bude** Eng
17D3 **Bude** USA
45G7 **Budennovsk** Russian Fed
36E1 **Büdingen** Germany
41D2 **Budva** Montenegro, Yugos
72A3 **Buéa** Cam
37A2 **Buech** *R* France
20B3 **Buellton** USA
28B2 **Buena Esperanza** Arg
26C3 **Buenaventura** Colombia
16A4 **Buenaventura** Mexico
16A2 **Buena Vista** Colorado, USA
22B2 **Buenavista** Mexico
13D3 **Buena Vista** Virginia, USA
20C3 **Buena Vista L** USA
28A4 **Bueno** *R* Chile
25E4 **Buenos Aires** Arg
25E5 **Buenos Aires** State, Arg
17D2 **Buffalo** Mississipi, USA
9F2 **Buffalo** New York, USA
11B2 **Buffalo** South Dakota, USA
17C3 **Buffalo** Texas, USA
8C2 **Buffalo** Wyoming, USA
74E2 **Buffalo** *R* S Africa
3E2 **Buffalo Head Hills** *Mts* Can
18C1 **Buffalo Hump** USA
3F3 **Buffalo L** Alberta, Can
3E1 **Buffalo L** Northwest Territories, Can
6H4 **Buffalo Narrows** Can
15C2 **Buford** USA
41F2 **Buftea** Rom
43E2 **Bug** *R* Pol/Ukraine
26C3 **Buga** Colombia
63C1 **Bugdayli** Turkmenistan
44H2 **Bugrino** Russian Fed
53A2 **Bugt** China
44J5 **Bugulma** Russian Fed
44J5 **Buguruslan** Russian Fed
64C2 **Buhayrat al Asad** *Res* Syria
18D2 **Buhl** Idaho, USA
11D2 **Buhl** Minnesota, USA
71F4 **Bui Dam** Ghana
35D5 **Builth Wells** Wales
28A2 **Buin** Chile
37A2 **Buis-les-Baronnies** France
37E2 **Buje** Croatia, Yugos
72C4 **Bujumbura** Burundi
77E1 **Buka** *I* PNG
73C4 **Bukama** Zaïre
72C4 **Bukavu** Zaïre
58E2 **Bukhara** Uzbekistan
56D2 **Bukit Batubrok** *Mt* Indon
56B3 **Bukittinggi** Indon
72D4 **Bukoba** Tanz
57B3 **Buku Gandadiwata** *Mt* Indon
57C2 **Buku Saolat** *Mt* Indon
51G7 **Bula** Indon
57F8 **Bulan** Phil
60D3 **Bulandshahr** India
73C6 **Bulawayo** Zim
41F3 **Buldan** Turk
60D4 **Buldāna** India
10B6 **Buldir I** USA
50D2 **Bulgan** Mongolia
41E2 **Bulgaria** Republic, Europe
57C2 **Buli** Indon
37B1 **Bulle** Switz
78B2 **Buller** *R* NZ
75C3 **Buller,Mt** Aust
76A4 **Bullfinch** Aust
75B1 **Bulloo** *R* Aust
75B1 **Bulloo Downs** Aust
75B1 **Bulloo L** Aust
17D2 **Bull Shoals Res** USA
28A3 **Bulnes** Chile
76D1 **Bulolo** PNG
74D2 **Bultfontein** S Africa
57B4 **Bulukumba** Indon
72C3 **Bumba** Zaïre
56E2 **Bum Bum** *I* Malay
45D8 **Bu Menderes** *R* Turk
55B2 **Bumphal Dam** Thai
72D3 **Buna** Kenya
76A4 **Bunbury** Aust
34B4 **Buncrana** Irish Rep
77E3 **Bundaberg** Aust
75D2 **Bundarra** Aust
60D3 **Būndi** India
75C1 **Bungil** *R* Aust
73B4 **Bungo** Angola
54B4 **Bungo-suidō** *Str* Japan
56C2 **Bunguran** *I* Indon
72D3 **Bunia** Zaïre
17D2 **Bunker** USA
17D3 **Bunkie** USA
15C3 **Bunnell** USA
71H3 **Bunsuru** *R* Nig
56D3 **Buntok** Indon
57B2 **Buol** Indon
65D2 **Burāg** Syria
72C2 **Buram** Sudan
61B1 **Burang** China
72E3 **Burao** Somalia
57G8 **Burauen** Phil
66D1 **Buraydah** S Arabia
19C4 **Burbank** USA
75C2 **Burcher** Aust
63E1 **Burdalyk** Turkmenistan
45E8 **Burdur** Turk
53C1 **Bureinskiy Khrebet** *Mts* Russian Fed
50F2 **Bureya** Russian Fed
53C1 **Bureya** *R* Russian Fed
65B3 **Bûr Fu'ad** Egypt
42C2 **Burg** Germany
41F2 **Burgas** Bulg
15D2 **Burgaw** USA
37B1 **Burgdorf** Switz
5K4 **Burgeo** Can
74D3 **Burgersdorp** S Africa
48K5 **Burgin** China
22C1 **Burgos** Mexico
39B1 **Burgos** Spain
43D1 **Burgsvik** Sweden
41F3 **Burhaniye** Turk
60D4 **Burhānpur** India
57F8 **Burias** *I* Phil
5K4 **Burin Pen** Can
55C2 **Buriram** Thai
29C2 **Buritis** Brazil
3C3 **Burke Chan** Can
76C2 **Burketown** Aust
70B3 **Burkina** Republic, Africa
13D1 **Burk's Falls** Can
8B2 **Burley** USA
4F5 **Burlington** Can
16B2 **Burlington** Colorado, USA
9D2 **Burlington** Iowa, USA
14C2 **Burlington** New Jersey, USA
15D1 **Burlington** North Carolina, USA
9F2 **Burlington** Vermont, USA
18B1 **Burlington** Washington, USA
4D5 **Burlington** Wisconsin, USA
59H3 **Burma** Republic, Asia
16C3 **Burnet** USA
18B2 **Burney** USA
14B2 **Burnham** USA
76D5 **Burnie** Aust
35D5 **Burnley** Eng
18C2 **Burns** USA
6F4 **Burns Lake** Can
59G1 **Burqin** China
75A2 **Burra** Aust
75D2 **Burragorang,L** Aust
34D2 **Burray** *I* Scot
75C2 **Burren Junction** Aust
75C2 **Burrinjuck Res** Aust
51G8 **Burrundie** Aust
45D7 **Bursa** Turk
66B1 **Bur Safâga** Egypt
Bûr Sa'îd = Port Said
65B4 **Bûr Taufiq** Egypt
12C2 **Burton** USA
35E5 **Burton upon Trent** Eng
32J6 **Burtrask** Sweden
75B2 **Burtundy** Aust
57C3 **Buru** Indon
72C4 **Burundi** Republic, Africa
56B2 **Burung** Indon
11C3 **Burwell** USA
49N4 **Buryatskaya** Respublika, Russian Fed
72D2 **Burye** Eth
45J6 **Burynshik** Kazakhstan
35F5 **Bury St Edmunds** Eng
63C3 **Būshehr** Iran
72B4 **Busira** *R* Zaïre
43E2 **Busko Zdrój** Pol
65D2 **Busrā ash Shām** Syria
36D3 **Bussang** France
76A4 **Busselton** Aust
38D2 **Busto** Italy
40B1 **Busto Arsizio** Italy
57E8 **Busuanga** *I* Phil

Cap Serrat Chandrapur

71D1 Cap Serrat C Tunisia
37A3 Cap Sicié C France
70A3 Cap Vert C Sen
26D4 Caquetá R Colombia
41E2 Caracal Rom
26F3 Caracaraí Brazil
26E1 Caracas Ven
29A3 Caracol Brazil
29C3 Caraguatatuba Brazil
25B5 Carahue Chile
29D2 Caraí Brazil
29D3 Carandaí Brazil
29A2 Carandazal Brazil
27K8 Carangola Brazil
41E1 Caransebeş Rom
75A2 Carappee Hill Mt Aust
23A3 Caratasca Honduras
29D2 Caratinga Brazil
39B2 Caravaca Spain
29E2 Caravelas Brazil
28E1 Carazinho Brazil
12B3 Carbondale Illinois, USA
14C2 Carbondale Pennsylvania, USA
7N5 Carbonear Can
40B3 Carbonia Sardegna
6G4 Carcajou Can
69D3 Carcar Mts Somalia
38C3 Carcassonne France
6E3 Carcross Can
22C2 Cardel Mexico
21D2 Cardenas Cuba
22C1 Cárdenas Mexico
22D2 Cárdenas Mexico
35D6 Cardiff Wales
35C5 Cardigan Wales
35C5 Cardigan B Wales
28D2 Cardóna Urug
3F4 Cardston Can
3G2 Careen L Can
41E1 Carei Rom
27G4 Careiro Brazil
28A2 Carén Chile
12C2 Carey USA
38B2 Carhaix-Plouguer France
25D5 Carhué Arg
27K8 Cariacica Brazil
24C2 Caribbean S C America
4B2 Caribou Can
6J4 Caribou Can
13F1 Caribou USA
10N3 Caribou R Can
6G4 Caribou Mts Alberta, Can
6F4 Caribou Mts British Columbia, Can
57F8 Carigara Phil
36C2 Carignan France
36B1 Carin France
29D1 Carinhanha Brazil
29D1 Carinhanha R Brazil
26F1 Caripito Ven
4F4 Carleton Place Can
74D2 Carletonville S Africa
18C2 Carlin USA
12B3 Carlinville USA
34D4 Carlisle Eng
13D2 Carlisle USA
10D5 Carlisle I USA
28C3 Carlos Arg
29D2 Carlos Chagas Brazil
35B5 Carlow County, Irish Rep
35B5 Carlow Irish Rep
19C4 Carlsbad California, USA
8C3 Carlsbad New Mexico, USA
16B3 Carlsbad Caverns Nat Pk USA
xxviiiE4 Carlsberg Ridge Indian O
6H5 Carlyle Can
10L3 Carmacks Can
37B2 Carmagnola Italy
35C6 Carmarthen Wales
35C6 Carmarthen B Wales
20B2 Carmel California, USA
14D2 Carmel New York, USA
65C2 Carmel,Mt Israel
28D2 Carmelo Urug
20B2 Carmel Valley USA
8B4 Carmen I Mexico
25D6 Carmen de Patagones Arg
12B3 Carmi USA
19B3 Carmichael USA
29C2 Carmo do Paranaiba Brazil
39A2 Carmona Spain
76A3 Carnarvon Aust
74C3 Carnarvon S Africa
29E2 Carncacá Brazil
34B4 Carndonagh Irish Rep
76B3 Carnegi,L Aust
34D3 Carngorms Mts Scot
62E3 Car Nicobar I Indian O
72B3 Carnot CAR
75A2 Carnot,C Aust
10N2 Carnwath R Can
15E4 Carol City USA
27J5 Carolina Brazil
74E2 Carolina S Africa
15D2 Carolina Beach USA
xxviiiJ4 Caroline Is Pacific O
45C6 Carpathians Mts E Europe
43F3 Carpatii Orientali Mts Rom
76C2 Carpentaria,G of Aust
59H5 Carpenter Ridge Indian O
38D3 Carpentras France
40C2 Carpi Italy
20C3 Carpinteria USA
15C3 Carrabelle USA
40C2 Carrara Italy
33B3 Carrauntoohill Mt Irish Rep
35B5 Carrickmacross Irish Rep
35B5 Carrick-on-Suir Irish Rep
75A2 Carrieton Aust
6J5 Carrington USA
8D2 Carrington USA
39B1 Carrión R Spain
28A1 Carrizal Bajo Chile
17F4 Carrizo Spring USA
16A3 Carrizozo USA
9D2 Carroll USA
15B2 Carrollton Georgia, USA
12B3 Carrollton Kentucky, USA
17D2 Carrollton Missouri, USA
3H3 Carrot R Can
17E2 Carruthersville USA
45F7 Carsamba Turk
45E8 Carsamba R Turk
8B3 Carson City USA
12C2 Carsonville USA
23B4 Cartagena Colombia
39B2 Cartagena Spain
26C3 Cartago Colombia
21D4 Cartago Costa Rica
20C2 Cartago USA
26D1 Cartegena Colombia
78C2 Carterton NZ
17D2 Carthage Missouri, USA
13D2 Carthage New York, USA
17D3 Carthage Texas, USA
76B2 Cartier I Timor S
7N4 Cartwright Can
27L5 Caruaru Brazil
26F1 Carúpano Ven
15D1 Cary USA
28A2 Casablanca Chile
71A2 Casablanca Mor
29C3 Casa Branca Brazil
8B3 Casa Grande USA
40B1 Casale Monferrato Italy
37D2 Casalmaggiore Italy
28C3 Casares Arg
22C1 Casas Mexico
28E1 Casca Brazil
18D1 Cascade USA
3D4 Cascade Mts Can/USA
78A2 Cascade Pt NZ
8A2 Cascade Range Mts USA
18C2 Cascade Res USA
25F2 Cascavel Brazil
37D3 Casciana Italy
37D3 Cascina Italy
40C2 Caserta Italy
79G9 Casey Base Ant
35B5 Cashel Irish Rep
28C2 Casilda Arg
77E3 Casino Aust
26C5 Casma Peru
20B3 Casmalia USA
39C1 Caspe Spain
8C2 Casper USA
45H6 Caspian Depression Region Kazakhstan
45H7 Caspian S Asia/Europe
13D3 Cass USA
73C5 Cassamba Angola
36B1 Cassel France
11C2 Casselton USA
3C2 Cassiar Can
6E3 Cassiar Mts Can
29B2 Cassilândia Brazil
40C2 Cassino Italy
11D2 Cass Lake USA
20C3 Castaic USA
28B2 Castaño R Arg
37D2 Castelfranco Italy
38D3 Castellane France
28D3 Castelli Arg
39C1 Castellon de la Plana Spain
37D2 Castelnovo ne'Monti Italy
37D2 Castelnuovo di Garfagnana Italy
27K5 Castelo Brazil
39A2 Castelo Branco Port
38C3 Castelsarrasin France
40C3 Castelvetrano Italy
75B3 Casterton Aust
37D3 Castiglion Fiorentino Italy
28A1 Castilla Chile
39B2 Castilla La Nueva Region, Spain
39B1 Castilla La Vieja Region, Spain
28E2 Castillos Urug
33B3 Castlebar Irish Rep
34B3 Castlebay Scot
19D3 Castle Dale USA
34D4 Castle Douglas Scot
18C1 Castlegar Can
75B3 Castlemain Aust
20B3 Castle,Mt USA
18D2 Castle Peak USA
75C2 Castlereagh Aust
16B2 Castle Rock USA
38C3 Castres-sur-l'Agout France
23E4 Castries St Lucia
25B6 Castro Arg
25F2 Castro Brazil
27L6 Castro Alves Brazil
40D3 Castrovillari Italy
20B2 Castroville USA
28D2 Casupa Urug
78A2 Caswell Sd NZ
21E2 Cat I Bahamas
57F8 Catabalogan Phil
26B5 Catacaos Peru
29D3 Cataguases Brazil
17D3 Catahoula L USA
29C2 Catalão Brazil
39C1 Cataluña Region, Spain
25C3 Catamarca Arg
25C3 Catamarca State, Arg
73D5 Catandica Mozam
57F8 Catanduanes I Phil
25G2 Catanduva Brazil
29B4 Catanduvas Brazil
40D3 Catania Italy
28A3 Catan-Lil Arg
40D3 Catanzaro Italy
17F4 Catarina USA
57F8 Catarman Phil
75A2 Catastrophe,C Aust
23C5 Catatumbo R Ven
14B2 Catawissa USA
22C2 Catemaco Mexico
38D3 Cater Corse
40B2 Cateraggio Corse
73B4 Catete Angola
74D3 Cathcart S Africa
28B1 Catinzaco Arg
70A3 Catio Guinea-Bissau
4C3 Cat L Can
4C3 Cat Lake Can
7J4 Cat Lake Can
77E3 Cato I Aust
21D2 Catoche,C Mexico
14B3 Catoctin Mt USA
13D3 Catonsville USA
28C3 Catrilo Arg
13E2 Catskill USA
13E2 Catskill Mts USA
5J2 Caubvick,Mt Can
26D2 Cauca R Colombia
27L4 Caucaia Brazil
26C2 Caucasia Colombia
45G7 Caucasus Mts Georgia
36A2 Caudebec-en-Caux France
36B1 Caudry France
73B4 Caungula Angola
25B5 Cauquenes Chile
13F1 Causapscal Can
62B2 Cauvery R India
38D3 Cavaillon France
29C1 Cavalcanta Brazil
37D1 Cavalese italy
11C2 Cavalier USA
70B4 Cavally R Lib
35B5 Cavan County, Irish Rep
35B5 Cavan Irish Rep
57F8 Cavite Phil
26D4 Caxias Brazil
27K4 Caxias Brazil
25F3 Caxias do Sul Brazil
73B4 Caxito Angola
15C2 Cayce USA
64D1 Çayeli Turk
27H3 Cayenne French Guiana
36A1 Cayeux-sur-Mer France
21E3 Cayman Brac I Caribbean
23A3 Cayman Is Caribbean
23A3 Cayman Trench Caribbean
72E3 Caynabo Somalia
20B3 Cayncos USA
21E2 Cayo Romana I Cuba
21D3 Cayos Mistikos Is Nic
23A2 Cay Sal I Caribbean
14B1 Cayuga L USA
14C1 Cazenovia USA
73C5 Cazombo Angola
5J4 C Breton Highlands Can
Ceará = Fortaleza
27K5 Ceara State, Brazil
28B1 Cebollar Arg
28E2 Cebollati Urug
57F8 Cebu Phil
57F8 Cebu I Phil
14C3 Cecilton USA
40C2 Cecina Italy
37D3 Cecina R Italy
11D3 Cedar R USA
8B3 Cedar City USA
17C3 Cedar Creek Res USA
11D3 Cedar Falls USA
6H4 Cedar L Can
20D1 Cedar Mts USA
9D2 Cedar Rapids USA
15B2 Cedartown USA
22B1 Cedral Mexico
21A2 Cedros I Mexico
76C4 Ceduna Aust
72E3 Ceelbuur Somalia
69D3 Ceerigaabo Somalia
40C3 Cefalù Italy
43D3 Cegléd Hung
73B5 Cela Angola
21B2 Celaya Mexico
Celebes = Sulawesi
51F6 Celebes S S E Asia
12C2 Celina USA
40D1 Celje Slovenia, Yugos
42C2 Celle Germany
35B6 Celtic S UK
51G7 Cendrawasih Pen Indon
37C2 Ceno R Italy
17D3 Center USA
15B1 Center Hill L USA
14D2 Center Moriches USA
37D2 Cento Italy
34C3 Central Region, Scot
16A3 Central USA
72B3 Central African Republic Africa
17C1 Central City Nebraska, USA
14A2 Central City Pennsylvania, USA
12B3 Centralia Illinois, USA
8A2 Centralia Washington, USA
74C1 Central Kalahari Game Res Botswana
63E3 Central Makran Range Mts Pak
18B2 Central Point USA
51H7 Central Range Mts PNG
14B1 Central Square USA
15B2 Centre Point USA
15B2 Centreville Alabama, USA
14B3 Centreville Maryland, USA
56D4 Cepu Indon
Ceram = Seram
51F7 Ceram Sea Indonesia
28C3 Cereales Arg
28C1 Ceres Arg
27J7 Ceres Brazil
74B3 Ceres S Africa
20B2 Ceres USA
38C2 Cergy-Pontoise France
40D2 Cerignola Italy
45D7 Cernavodă Rom
36D3 Cernay France
8C4 Cerralvo I Mexico
22B1 Cerritos Mexico
28B2 Cerro Aconcagua Mt Arg
22C1 Cerro Azul Mexico
28B1 Cerro Boneta Mt Arg
28A3 Cerro Campanario Mt Chile
28C2 Cerro Champaqui Mt Arg
28D2 Cerro Chatto Urug
22B2 Cerro Cuachaia Mt Mexico
22C1 Cerro de Astillero Mexico
28B1 Cerro del Potro Mt Chile/Arg
22C1 Cerro del Tigre Mt Mexico
28B1 Cerro del Toro Mt Chile/Arg
28B2 Cerro de Olivares Mt Arg
26C6 Cerro de Pasco Peru
23D3 Cerro de Punta Mt Puerto Rico
22B2 Cerro El Cantado Mt Mexico
28B3 Cerro El Nevado Arg
28B1 Cerro General M Belgrano Mt Arg
22B2 Cerro Grande Mts Mexico
22A1 Cerro Huehueto Mt Mexico
28A2 Cerro Juncal Mt Arg/Chile
22B1 Cerro la Ardilla Mts Mexico
28A1 Cerro las Tortolas Mt Chile
22B2 Cerro Laurel Mt Mexico
28A2 Cerro Mercedario Mt Arg
28A3 Cerro Mora Mt Chile
23C4 Cerron Mt Ven
28B3 Cerro Payún Mt Arg
22C1 Cerro Peña Nevada Mt Mexico
22C2 Cerro Penón del Rosario Mt Mexico
28B2 Cerro Sosneado Mt Arg
22B2 Cerro Teotepec Mt Mexico
28B2 Cerro Tupungato Mt Arg
22C2 Cerro Yucuyacau Mt Mexico
37E2 Cervia Italy
37C2 Cervo R Italy
40C2 Cesena Italy
44D4 Cēsis Latvia
42C3 České Budějovice Czech Republic
42D3 Českomoravská Vysočina U Czech Republic
41F3 Ceşme Turk
76E4 Cessnock Aust
40D2 Cetina R Croatia, Yugos
71A1 Ceuta N W Africa
64C2 Ceyham Turk
64C2 Ceyhan R Turk
64C2 Ceylanpınar Turk
Ceylon = Sri Lanka
49L4 Chaa-Khol Russian Fed
38C2 Chaâteaudun France
37B1 Chablais Region, France
36B3 Chablis France
28C2 Chacabuco Arg
26C5 Chachapoyas Peru
28B3 Chacharramendi Arg
60C3 Chachran Pak
25D3 Chaco State, Arg
72B2 Chad Republic, Africa
72B2 Chad L C Africa
28B3 Chadileuvu R Arg
8C2 Chadron USA
17E2 Chaffee USA
60A3 Chagai Pak
63E3 Chagai Hills Pak
49P4 Chagda Russian Fed
60B2 Chaghcharan Afghan
xxviiiE5 Chagos Arch Indian O
23L1 Chaguanas Trinidad
63E2 Chahah Burjak Afghan
63E3 Chāh Bahār Iran
54A2 Ch'aho N Korea
55C2 Chai Badan Thai
71G3 Chaîne de l'Atakor Mts Benin
55C3 Chaine des Cardamomes Mts Camb
73C4 Chaine des Mitumba Mts Zaïre
55C2 Chaiyaphum Thai
28D2 Chajari Arg
63E2 Chakhansur Afghan
60C2 Chakwal Pak
26D7 Chala Peru
73D5 Chalabesa Zambia
60A2 Chalap Dalam Mts Afghan
36C3 Chalindrey France
52C4 Chaling China
60D4 Chālisgaon India
10K2 Chalkyitsik USA
36C2 Challerange France
18D2 Challis USA
36C2 Châlons sur Marne France
38C2 Chalon sur Saône France
42C3 Cham Germany
16A2 Chama USA
60B2 Chaman Pak
60D2 Chamba India
60D3 Chambal R India
11C3 Chamberlain USA
10J2 Chamberlin,Mt USA
13D3 Chambersburg USA
38D2 Chambéry France
36B2 Chambly France
13E1 Chambord Can
60A3 Chambor Kalat Pak
22A2 Chamela Mexico
63C2 Chamgordan Iran
28B2 Chamical Arg
37B2 Chamonix France
61B3 Champa India
38C2 Champagne Region, France
74D2 Champagne Castle Mt Lesotho
37A1 Champagnole France
9E2 Champaign USA
55D3 Champassak Laos
9F2 Champlain,L USA
37A1 Champlitte France
62B2 Chāmrājnagar India
25B3 Chañaral Chile
28A3 Chanco Chile
6D3 Chandalar USA
6D3 Chandalar R USA
15B3 Chandeleur Is USA
60D2 Chandīgarh India
5J4 Chandler Can
19D4 Chandler USA
61D3 Chandpur Bang
60D5 Chandrapur India

Chungwa Cooma

54A3 **Chungwa** N Korea
73D4 **Chunya** Tanz
49M3 **Chunya** *R* Russian Fed
54A3 **Ch'unyang** S Korea
23L1 **Chupara Pt** Trinidad
25C2 **Chuquicamata** Chile
40B1 **Chur** Switz
61D3 **Churāchāndpur** India
49P3 **Churapcha** Russian Fed
7J4 **Churchill** Can
7M4 **Churchill** *R* Labrador, Can
7J4 **Churchill** *R* Manitoba, Can
7J4 **Churchill,C** Can
7M4 **Churchill Falls** Can
6H4 **Churchill L** Can
60C3 **Chūru** India
22B2 **Churumuco** Mexico
44K4 **Chusovoy** Russian Fed
44H4 **Chuvashskaya** Respublika, Russian Fed
50C4 **Chuxiong** China
55D3 **Chu Yang Sin** *Mt* Viet
56C4 **Cianjur** Indon
37D2 **Ciano d'Enza** Italy
29B3 **Cianorte** Brazil
43E2 **Ciechanów** Pol
22B2 **Ciedad Altamirano** Mexico
26D1 **Ciedad Ojeda** Ven
21E2 **Ciego de Avila** Cuba
26D1 **Ciénaga** Colombia
21D2 **Cienfuegos** Cuba
43D3 **Cieszyn** Pol
39B2 **Cieza** Spain
64B2 **Cihanbeyli** Turk
22B2 **Cihuatlán** Mexico
56C4 **Cijulang** Indon
56C4 **Cilacap** Indon
16B2 **Cimarron** USA
16C2 **Cimarron** *R* USA
37B3 **Cime du Cheiron** *Mt* France
41F1 **Cîmpina** Rom
39C1 **Cinca** *R* Spain
40D2 **Činčer** *Mt* Bosnia-Herzegovina, Yugos
9E3 **Cincinnati** USA
41E1 **Cindrelu** *Mt* Rom
41F3 **Cine** *R* Turk
36C1 **Ciney** Belg
22D2 **Cintalapa** Mexico
28B3 **Cipolletti** Arg
6D3 **Circle** Alaska, USA
11A2 **Circle** Montana, USA
12C3 **Circleville** USA
56C4 **Cirebon** Indon
35E6 **Cirencester** Eng
16C3 **Cisco** USA
37D2 **Citadella** Italy
22C3 **Citlaltepetl** *Mt* Mexico
74B3 **Citrusdal** S Africa
40C2 **Citta del Vaticano** Italy
40C2 **Città di Castello** Italy
21B2 **Ciudad Acuña** Mexico
26F2 **Ciudad Bolivar** Ven
21B2 **Ciudad Camargo** Mexico
21C3 **Ciudad del Carmen** Mexico
39C2 **Ciudadela** Spain
26F2 **Ciudad Guayana** Ven
21B3 **Ciudad Guzman** Mexico
22B2 **Ciudad Hidalgo** Mexico
21B1 **Ciudad Juárez** Mexico
8C4 **Ciudad Lerdo** Mexico
21C2 **Ciudad Madero** Mexico
22C2 **Ciudad Mendoza** Mexico
21B2 **Ciudad Obregon** Mexico
23C4 **Ciudad Ojeda** Ven
26F2 **Ciudad Piar** Ven
39B2 **Ciudad Real** Spain
39A1 **Ciudad Rodrigo** Spain
21C2 **Ciudad Valles** Mexico
21C2 **Ciudad Victoria** Mexico
37E1 **Cividale del Friuli** Italy
37E3 **Civitanova Marche** Italy
40C2 **Civitavecchia** Italy
64D2 **Cizre** Turk
35F6 **Clacton-on-Sea** Eng
6G4 **Claire,L** Can
13D2 **Clairton** USA
37A1 **Clairvaux** France
15B2 **Clanton** USA
74B3 **Clanwilliam** S Africa
35B5 **Clara** Irish Rep
28D3 **Claraz** Arg
12C2 **Clare** USA
13E2 **Claremont** USA
17C2 **Claremore** USA
75D1 **Clarence** *R* Aust
78B2 **Clarence** *R* NZ
76C2 **Clarence Str** Aust
10M4 **Clarence Str** USA
17D3 **Clarendon** USA
5L4 **Clarenville** Can
7N5 **Clarenville** Can
6G4 **Claresholm** Can
17C1 **Clarinda** USA
11D3 **Clarion** Iowa, USA
13D2 **Clarion** Pennsylvania, USA
21A3 **Clarión** *I* Mexico
13D2 **Clarion** *R* USA
xxixM4 **Clarion Fracture Zone** Pacific O
9E3 **Clark Hill Res** USA
10O3 **Clark,Mt** Can
19C3 **Clark Mt** USA
12C2 **Clark,Pt** Can
12C3 **Clarksburg** USA
9D3 **Clarksdale** USA
10G4 **Clarks Point** USA
18C1 **Clarkston** USA
17D2 **Clarksville** Arkansas, USA
15B1 **Clarksville** Tennessee, USA
29B2 **Claro** *R* Brazil
25E5 **Claromecó** Arg
17C2 **Clay Center** USA
34E2 **Claymore** *Oilfield* N Sea
3C4 **Clayoquot Sd** Can
8C3 **Clayton** New Mexico, USA
13D2 **Clayton** New York, USA
33B3 **Clear** *C* Irish Rep
10J4 **Cleare,C** USA
14A2 **Clearfield** Pennsylvania, USA
18D2 **Clearfield** Utah, USA
3E2 **Clear Hills** *Mts* Can
19B3 **Clear L** USA
11D3 **Clear Lake** USA
18B2 **Clear Lake Res** USA
11A3 **Clearmont** USA
3D3 **Clearwater** Can
9E4 **Clearwater** USA
3F2 **Clearwater** *R* Can
3D3 **Clearwater L** Can
18C1 **Clearwater Mts** USA
8D3 **Cleburne** USA
35F4 **Cleeton** *Oilfield* N Sea
20B1 **Clements** USA
57E8 **Cleopatra Needle** *Mt* Phil
76D3 **Clermont** Aust
36B2 **Clermont** France
36C2 **Clermont-en-Argonne** France
38C2 **Clermont-Ferrand** France
36D1 **Clervaux** Germany
37D1 **Cles** Italy
75A2 **Cleve** Aust
35E4 **Cleveland** County, Eng
17D3 **Cleveland** Mississippi, USA
9E2 **Cleveland** Ohio, USA
15C1 **Cleveland** Tennessee, USA
17C3 **Cleveland** Texas, USA
29B4 **Clevelândia** Brazil
18D1 **Cleveland,Mt** USA
33B3 **Clew** *B* Irish Rep
19E4 **Clifton** Arizona, USA
75D1 **Clifton** Aust
14C2 **Clifton** New Jersey, USA
75A1 **Clifton Hills** Aust
3J2 **Clifton L** Can
3G4 **Climax** Can
15C1 **Clinch** *R* USA
15C1 **Clinch Mts** USA
17D2 **Clinton** Arkansas, USA
6F4 **Clinton** Can
14D2 **Clinton** Connecticut, USA
12A2 **Clinton** Iowa, USA
14E1 **Clinton** Massachusetts, USA
17D3 **Clinton** Mississippi, USA
17D2 **Clinton** Missouri, USA
15D2 **Clinton** N Carolina, USA
14C2 **Clinton** New Jersey, USA
16C2 **Clinton** Oklahoma, USA
6H3 **Clinton-Colden L** Can
21B3 **Clipperton I** Pacific O
26E7 **Cliza** Bol
28C1 **Clodomira** Arg
76D3 **Cloncurry** Aust
35B4 **Clones** Irish Rep
35B5 **Clonmel** Irish Rep
9D2 **Cloquet** USA
29A4 **Clorinda** Arg
11A3 **Cloud Peak** *Mt* USA
10G3 **Cloudy Mt** USA
20A1 **Cloverdale** USA
20C2 **Clovis** California, USA
8C3 **Clovis** New Mexico, USA
45C6 **Cluj** Rom
41E1 **Cluj-Napoca** Rom
37B1 **Cluses** France
37C2 **Clusone** Italy
78A3 **Clutha** *R* NZ
35D5 **Clwyd** County, Wales
7M2 **Clyde** Can
78A3 **Clyde** NZ
14B1 **Clyde** USA
34C4 **Clyde** *R* Scot
19C4 **Coachella** USA
22B2 **Coahuayana** Mexico
16B4 **Coahuila** State, Mexico
10N3 **Coal** *R* Can
22B2 **Coalcomán** Mexico
3F4 **Coaldale** Can
19C3 **Coaldale** USA
19B3 **Coalinga** USA
18D2 **Coalville** USA
29E1 **Coaraci** Brazil
26F5 **Coari** *R* Brazil
15B2 **Coastal Plain** USA
6E4 **Coast Mts** Can
8A2 **Coast Ranges** *Mts* USA
34C4 **Coatbridge** Scot
22C2 **Coatepec** Mexico
14C3 **Coatesville** USA
13E1 **Coaticook** Can
7K3 **Coats I** Can
79F1 **Coats Land** Region, Ant
21C3 **Coatzacoalcas** Mexico
22D2 **Coatzacoalcos** *R* Mexico
7L5 **Cobalt** Can
21C3 **Cobán** Guatemala
76D4 **Cobar** Aust
75C3 **Cobargo** Aust
4C3 **Cobham** *R* Can
26E6 **Cobija** Bol
14C1 **Cobleskill** USA
39B2 **Cobo de Palos** *C* Spain
7L5 **Cobourg** Can
76C2 **Cobourg Pen** Aust
42C2 **Coburg** Germany
26C4 **Coca** Ecuador
15C3 **Coca** USA
29B1 **Cocalinho** Brazil
26E7 **Cochabamba** Bol
36D1 **Cochem** Germany
62B3 **Cochin** India
3F3 **Cochrane** Alberta, Can
7K5 **Cochrane** Ontario, Can
3H2 **Cochrane** *R* Can
75B2 **Cockburn** Aust
14B3 **Cockeysville** USA
23H1 **Cockpit Country,The** Jamaica
74C3 **Cockscomb** *Mt* S Africa
21D3 **Coco** *R* Honduras/Nic
72A3 **Cocobeach** Gabon
62E2 **Coco Channel** Andaman Is
29D1 **Côcos** Brazil
23L1 **Cocos B** Trinidad
xxviiiF5 **Cocos Is** Indian O
xxixP4 **Cocos Ridge** Pacific O
22B1 **Cocula** Mexico
34G3 **Cod** *Oilfield* N Sea
9F2 **Cod,C** USA
78A3 **Codfish I** NZ
7M4 **Cod I** Can
37E2 **Codigoro** Italy
27K4 **Codó** Brazil
37C2 **Codogno** Italy
8C2 **Cody** USA
51H8 **Coen** Aust
42B2 **Coesfeld** Germany
3E4 **Coeur d'Alene** USA
8D3 **Coffeyville** USA
75A2 **Coffin B** Aust
75D2 **Coff's Harbour** Aust
74D3 **Cofimvaba** S Africa
22C2 **Cofre de Perote** *Mt* Mexico
38B2 **Cognac** France
14B1 **Cohocton** USA
14B1 **Cohocton** *R* USA
13E2 **Cohoes** USA
75B3 **Cohuna** Aust
25B7 **Coihaique** Chile
62B2 **Coimbatore** India
39A1 **Coimbra** Port
26B3 **Cojimies** Ecuador
18D2 **Cokeville** USA
76D4 **Colac** Aust
27K7 **Colatina** Brazil
79F6 **Colbeck,C** Ant
16B2 **Colby** USA
35F6 **Colchester** Eng
14D2 **Colchester** USA
37B1 **Col de la Faucille** France
3F3 **Cold L** Can
40B1 **Col du Grand St Bernard** *P* Switz/Italy
37B2 **Col du Lautaret** *P* France
40B1 **Col du Mont Cenis** *P* Italy/France
38D2 **Col du Mt Cenis** *P* Italy
12C2 **Coldwater** USA
4D4 **Coldwell** Can
10K2 **Coleen** *R* USA
18D1 **Coleman** Can
12C2 **Coleman** Michigan, USA
16C3 **Coleman** Texas, USA
74D2 **Colenso** S Africa
34B4 **Coleraine** N Ire
78B2 **Coleridge,L** NZ
74D3 **Colesberg** S Africa
20C1 **Coleville** USA
19B3 **Colfax** California, USA
17D3 **Colfax** Louisiana, USA
18C1 **Colfax** Washington, USA
21B3 **Colima** Mexico
22B2 **Colima** State, Mexico
28A2 **Colina** Chile
34B3 **Coll** *I* Scot
75C1 **Collarenebri** Aust
40B2 **Colle de Tende** *P* Italy/France
37D3 **Colle di Val d'Elsa** Italy
10J3 **College** USA
15C2 **College Park** Georgia, USA
14B3 **College Park** Washington, USA
17C3 **College Station** USA
76A4 **Collie** Aust
76B2 **Collier B** Aust
37D3 **Colline Metallifere** *Mts* Italy
36A1 **Collines de L'Artois** *Mts* France
36B2 **Collines De Thiérache** France
36A2 **Collines du Perche** *Mts* France
4E5 **Collingwood** Can
78B2 **Collingwood** NZ
17E3 **Collins** Mississippi, USA
14A1 **Collins** New York, USA
6H2 **Collinson Pen** Can
76D3 **Collinsville** Aust
12B3 **Collinsville** Illinois, USA
17C2 **Collinsville** Oklahoma, USA
28A3 **Collipulli** Chile
38D2 **Colmar** France
28C1 **Colmena** Arg
36A1 **Colne** *R* Eng
Cologne = Köln
29C3 **Colômbia** Brazil
26D3 **Colombia** Republic, S America
13D3 **Colombia** USA
62B3 **Colombo** Sri Lanka
25E4 **Colón** Arg
21D2 **Colon** Cuba
26C2 **Colón** Panama
25E4 **Colonia** Urug
28D2 **Colonia del Sacramento** Urug
28B3 **Colonia 25 de Mayo** Arg
28C1 **Colonia Dora** Arg
28B3 **Colonia Josefa** Arg
25C7 **Colonia Las Heras** Arg
13D3 **Colonial Heights** USA
34B3 **Colonsay** *I* Scot
23E5 **Coloradito** Ven
8C3 **Colorado** State, USA
8B3 **Colorado** *R* Arizona, USA
25D5 **Colorado** *R* Buenos Aires, Arg
28B1 **Colorado** *R* La Rioja, Arg
8D3 **Colorado** *R* Texas, USA
16B3 **Colorado City** USA
8B3 **Colorado Plat** USA
8C3 **Colorado Springs** USA
22B1 **Colptlán** Mexico
14B3 **Columbia** Maryland, USA
17E3 **Columbia** Mississippi, USA
9D3 **Columbia** Missouri, USA
13D2 **Columbia** Pennsylvania, USA
9E3 **Columbia** S Carolina, USA
9E3 **Columbia** Tennessee, USA
3E3 **Columbia** *R* Can
8A2 **Columbia** *R* USA
18D1 **Columbia Falls** USA
6G4 **Columbia,Mt** Can
18C1 **Columbia Plat** USA
74B3 **Columbine,C** S Africa
9E3 **Columbus** Georgia, USA
12B3 **Columbus** Indiana, USA
9E3 **Columbus** Mississippi, USA
18E1 **Columbus** Montana, USA
8D2 **Columbus** Nebraska, USA
16A3 **Columbus** New Mexico, USA
9E2 **Columbus** Ohio, USA
17C4 **Columbus** Texas, USA
12B2 **Columbus** Wisconsin, USA
18C1 **Colville** USA
6C3 **Colville** *R* USA
78C1 **Colville,C** NZ
6F3 **Colville L** Can
35D5 **Colwyn Bay** Wales
37E2 **Comacchio** Italy
22D2 **Comalcalco** Mexico
16C3 **Comanche** USA
20B1 **Comanche Res** USA
21D3 **Comayagua** Honduras
28A2 **Combarbalá** Chile
35C4 **Comber** N Ire
61D4 **Combermere B** Burma
36C3 **Combeufontaine** France
37E1 **Comeglians** Italy
35B5 **Comeragh** *Mts* Irish Rep
16C3 **Comfort** USA
61D3 **Comilla** Bang
21C3 **Comitán** Mexico
36C2 **Commercy** France
7K3 **Committee B** Can
40B1 **Como** Italy
25C7 **Comodoro Rivadavia** Arg
22B1 **Comonfort** Mexico
62B3 **Comorin,C** India
73E5 **Comoros** *Is* Indian O
38C2 **Compiègne** France
22B1 **Compostela** Mexico
28B2 **Comte Salas** Arg
61D2 **Cona** China
70A4 **Conakry** Guinea
28A1 **Conay** Chile
28B2 **Concarán** Arg
38B2 **Concarneau** France
29E2 **Conceiçao da Barra** Brazil
27J5 **Conceição do Araguaia** Brazil
29D2 **Conceiçao do Mato Dentro** Brazil
28B1 **Concepción** Arg
29A3 **Concepción** Brazil/Par
25B5 **Concepción** Chile
25E2 **Concepción** Par
25E4 **Concepción** *R* Arg
21B2 **Concepcion del Oro** Mexico
28D2 **Concepcion del Uruguay** Arg
74A1 **Conception B** Namibia
8A3 **Conception,Pt** USA
29C3 **Conchas** Brazil
16B2 **Conchas** *L* USA
36A2 **Conches** France
8C4 **Conchos** *R* Mexico
19B3 **Concord** California, USA
9F2 **Concord** New Hampshire, USA
15C1 **Concord** North Carolina, USA
25E4 **Concordia** Arg
22A1 **Concordia** Mexico
8D3 **Concordia** USA
18B1 **Concrete** USA
75D1 **Condamine** Aust
29D1 **Condeuba** Brazil
76D4 **Condobolin** Aust
18B1 **Condon** USA
36C1 **Condroz, Mts** Belg
27H8 **Condrina** Brazil
15B2 **Conecuh** *R* USA
37E2 **Conegliano** Italy
14B1 **Conesus L** USA
29A3 **Confuso** *R* Par
68F8 **Congo** Republic, Africa
68F8 **Congo** *R* Congo
Congo,R = Zaïre,R
12C1 **Coniston** Can
12C2 **Conneaut** USA
9F2 **Connecticut** State, USA
13E2 **Connecticut** *R* USA
13D2 **Connellsville** USA
36A2 **Connerré** France
12B3 **Connersville** USA
75B2 **Conoble** Aust
18D1 **Conrad** USA
17C3 **Conroe** USA
29D3 **Conselheiro Lafaiete** Brazil
55D4 **Con Son** *Is* Viet
Constance,L = Bodensee
45D7 **Constanta** Rom
71D1 **Constantine** Alg
10G4 **Constantine,C** USA
25B5 **Constitución** Chile
28D2 **Constitución** Urug
3G4 **Consul** Can
18D2 **Contact** USA
37E2 **Contarina** Italy
27K6 **Contas** *R* Brazil
22C2 **Contreras** Mexico
36C2 **Contrexéville** France
6H3 **Contwoyto L** Can
9D3 **Conway** Arkansas, USA
13E2 **Conway** New Hampshire, USA
15D2 **Conway** South Carolina, USA
75A1 **Conway,L** Aust
35D5 **Conwy** Wales
76C3 **Coober Pedy** Aust
3C3 **Cook,C** Can
15B1 **Cookeville** USA
6C3 **Cook Inlet** *B* USA
xxixL5 **Cook Is** Pacific O
78B2 **Cook,Mt** NZ
77G5 **Cook Str** NZ
76D2 **Cooktown** Aust
75C2 **Coolabah** Aust
75C1 **Cooladdi** Aust
75C2 **Coolah** Aust
75C2 **Coolamon** Aust
76B4 **Coolgardie** Aust
19D4 **Coolidge** USA
75C3 **Cooma** Aust

Dalou Shan

Digya Nat Pk

52B4 **Dalou Shan** *Mts* China
61B3 **Dāltenganj** India
4E4 **Dalton** Can
15C2 **Dalton** Georgia, USA
14D1 **Dalton** Massachusetts, USA
56B2 **Daludalu** Indon
76C2 **Daly** *R* Aust
19B3 **Daly City** USA
76C2 **Daly Waters** Aust
57F9 **Damaguete** Phil
60C4 **Damān** India
64B3 **Damanhûr** Egypt
76B1 **Damar** *I* Indon
72B3 **Damara** CAR
64C3 **Damascus** Syria
14B3 **Damascus** USA
71J3 **Damaturu** Nig
63C1 **Damavand** Iran
73B4 **Damba** Angola
62C3 **Dambulla** Sri Lanka
63C1 **Damghan** Iran
Damietta = Dumyât
60D4 **Damoh** India
71F4 **Damongo** Ghana
72E3 **Damot** Eth
65C2 **Damour** Leb
76A3 **Dampier** Aust
67F3 **Damqawt** Yemen
65C3 **Danā** Jordan
66D4 **Danakil** Region, Eth
20C2 **Dana,Mt** USA
70B4 **Danané** Lib
55D2 **Da Nang** Viet
57F8 **Danao** Phil
57B3 **Danau Poso** *Mt* Indon
56A2 **Danau Tobu** *L* Indon
57B3 **Danau Tuwuti** *L* Indon
52A3 **Danbu** China
13E2 **Danbury** USA
14D1 **Danby** USA
61B2 **Dandeldhura** Nepal
62A1 **Dandeli** India
75C3 **Dandenong** Aust
53A3 **Dandong** China
74B3 **Danger Pt** S Africa
72D2 **Dangila** Eth
18D2 **Daniel** USA
7N4 **Daniel's Harbour** Can
74C2 **Danielskuil** S Africa
7P3 **Dannebrogs Øy** *I* Greenland
78C2 **Dannevirke** NZ
14B1 **Dansville** USA
62C1 **Dantewāra** India
42C3 **Danube** *R* Aust/Germ
41E2 **Danube** *R* Bulg
41D1 **Danube** *R* Croatia/Serbia
41F2 **Danube** *R* Romania
45G8 **Danuk** Iraq
9E2 **Danville** Illinois, USA
9E3 **Danville** Kentucky, USA
14B2 **Danville** Pennsylvania, USA
9F3 **Danville** Virginia, USA
Danzig = Gdańsk
52C4 **Dao Xian** China
52B4 **Daozhen** China
71J3 **Dapchi** Nig
61E2 **Dapha Bum** *Mt* India
65B3 **Daphnae** *Hist Site* Egypt
57F9 **Dapiak,Mt** Phil
57F9 **Dapitan** Phil
50C3 **Da Qaidam** China
65D2 **Dar'a** Syria
63C3 **Dārāb** Iran
69A1 **Daraj** Libya
63C2 **Dārān** Iran
64C3 **Dar'ā Salkhad** Syria
61C2 **Darbhanga** India
20C1 **Dardanelle** USA
17D2 **Dardanelle,L** USA
73D4 **Dar Es Salaam** Tanz
78B1 **Dargaville** NZ
15C2 **Darien** USA
Darjeeling = Dārjiling
61C2 **Dārjiling** India
76D4 **Darling** *R* Aust
75C1 **Darling Downs** Aust
7L1 **Darling Pen** Can
75B2 **Darlington** Aust
35E4 **Darlington** Eng
15D2 **Darlington** USA
42B3 **Darmstadt** Germany
69B1 **Darnah** Libya
75B2 **Darnick** Aust
6F3 **Darnley B** Can
79G10 **Darnley,C** Ant
39B1 **Daroca** Spain
72C3 **Dar Rounga** Region, CAR
67F4 **Darsa** *I* Yemen
35D6 **Dart** *R* Eng
33C3 **Dartmoor** *Moorland* Eng
35D6 **Dartmoor Nat Pk** Eng
7M5 **Dartmouth** Can
35D6 **Dartmouth** Eng
76D1 **Daru** PNG
40D1 **Daruvar** Croatia, Yugos
63E2 **Darweshan** Afghan
76C2 **Darwin** Aust
63C3 **Daryacheh-ye Bakhtegan** *L* Iran
63C3 **Daryacheh-ye Mahārlū** *L* Iran
63C2 **Daryācheh-ye Namak** *Salt Flat* Iran
63E2 **Daryacheh-ye-Sistan** *Salt Lake* Iran/Afghan
63C3 **Daryacheh-ye Tashk** *L* Iran
45H8 **Daryācheh-ye Urumīyeh** *L* Iran
63D3 **Dārzīn** Iran
67F1 **Das** *I* UAE
52C3 **Dashennonglia** *Mt* China
63D1 **Dasht** Iran
63E3 **Dasht** *R* Pak
63C2 **Dasht-e-Kavir** *Salt Desert* Iran
63D2 **Dasht-e Lut** *Salt Desert* Iran
63E2 **Dasht-e Naomid** *Desert Region* Iran
63E2 **Dasht-i-Margo** *Desert* Afghan
54D2 **Date** Japan
60D3 **Datia** India
52A2 **Datong** China
52C1 **Datong** China
52A2 **Datong He** *R* China
57F9 **Datu Piang** Phil
44D4 **Daugava** *R* Latvia
44D4 **Daugavpils** Latvia
38D2 **Daughiné** Region, France
7M1 **Dauguard Jensen Land** Greenland
60A1 **Daulatabad** Afghan
60D3 **Daulpur** India
36D1 **Daun** Germany
62A1 **Daund** India
6H4 **Dauphin** Can
14B2 **Dauphin** USA
15B2 **Dauphin I** USA
4B3 **Dauphin L** Can
70C3 **Daura** Nig
60D3 **Dausa** India
63E3 **Dāvah Panāh** Iran
62B2 **Dāvangere** India
57G9 **Davao** Phil
57G9 **Davao G** Phil
20A2 **Davenport** California, USA
9D2 **Davenport** Iowa, USA
26B2 **David** Panama
3G3 **Davidson** Can
6D3 **Davidson Mts** USA
3H2 **Davin L** Can
19B3 **Davis** USA
79G10 **Davis** *Base* Ant
7M4 **Davis Inlet** Can
7N3 **Davis Str** Greenland/Can
44K5 **Davlekanovo** Russian Fed
37C1 **Davos** Switz
3G2 **Davy L** Can
72E3 **Dawa** *R* Eth
52A4 **Dawan** China
60B2 **Dawat Yar** Afghan
Dawei = Tavoy
67F1 **Dawḩat Salwah** *B* Qatar/S Arabia
67F3 **Dawkah** Oman
55B2 **Dawna Range** *Mts* Burma
6E3 **Dawson** Can
15C2 **Dawson** Georgia, USA
11C2 **Dawson** N Dakota, USA
76D3 **Dawson** *R* Aust
6F4 **Dawson Creek** Can
3F1 **Dawson Landing** Can
3E3 **Dawson,Mt** Can
10L3 **Dawson Range** *Mts* Can
52A3 **Dawu** China
52C3 **Dawu** China
38B3 **Dax** France
52B3 **Daxian** China
52B5 **Daxin** China
52A3 **Daxue Shan** *Mts* China
28D2 **Dayman** *R* Urug
52C4 **Dayong** China
65D2 **Dayr'Ali** Syria
65D1 **Dayr'Atīyah** Syria
64D2 **Dayr az Zawr** Syria
65D1 **Dayr Shumayyil** Syria
9E3 **Dayton** Ohio, USA
15B1 **Dayton** Tennessee, USA
17D4 **Dayton** Texas, USA
18C1 **Dayton** Washington, USA
9E4 **Daytona Beach** USA
52C4 **Dayu** China
56E3 **Dayu** Indon
52D2 **Da Yunhe** China
52D2 **Da Yunhe** *R* China
18C2 **Dayville** USA
52B3 **Dazhu** China
74C3 **De Aar** S Africa
23C2 **Deadman's Cay** Bahamas
64C3 **Dead S** Israel/Jordan
11B3 **Deadwood** USA
36A1 **Deal** Eng
74D2 **Dealesville** S Africa
3C3 **Dean** *R* Can
3C3 **Dean Chan** Can
28C2 **Deán Funes** Arg
12C2 **Dearborn** USA
3B2 **Dease Lake** Can
3C2 **Dease** *R* Can
6F3 **Dease Arm** *B* Can
8B3 **Death V** USA
20D2 **Death Valley Nat Mon** USA
38C2 **Deauville** France
71F4 **Debakala** Ivory Coast
10F3 **Debauch Mt** USA
3G3 **Debden** Can
23L1 **Débé** Trinidad
43E2 **Dębica** Pol
43E2 **Deblin** Pol
70B3 **Débo,L** Mali
72D3 **Debre Birhan** Eth
43E3 **Debrecen** Hung
72D2 **Debre Mark'os** Eth
72D2 **Debre Tabor** Eth
66C3 **Decamere** Eth
9E3 **Decatur** Alabama, USA
15C2 **Decatur** Georgia, USA
9E3 **Decatur** Illinois, USA
12C2 **Decatur** Indiana, USA
38C3 **Decazeville** France
74C1 **Deception** *R* Botswana
52A4 **Dechang** China
11D3 **Decorah** USA
71F3 **Dedougou** Burkina
53B2 **Dedu** China
73D5 **Dedza** Malawi
34C4 **Dee** *R* Dumfries and Galloway, Scot
35D5 **Dee** *R* Eng/Wales
34D3 **Dee** *R* Grampian, Scot
4F4 **Deep River** Can
14D2 **Deep River** USA
20D2 **Deep Springs** USA
75D1 **Deepwater** Aust
10F5 **Deer I** USA
7N5 **Deer Lake** Can
8B2 **Deer Lodge** USA
26E7 **Deésaguadero** *R* Bol
18C2 **Deeth** USA
28D3 **Defferrari** Arg
4E5 **Defiance** USA
15B2 **De Funiak Springs** USA
50C3 **Dêgê** China
76A3 **De Grey** *R* Aust
66D3 **Dehalak** *Arch* Eritrea
63C2 **Deh Bīd** Iran
60B1 **Dehi** Afghan
70D1 **Dehibat** Tunisia
62B3 **Dehiwala-Mt Lavinia** Sri Lanka
63B2 **Dehlorān** Iran
60D2 **Dehra Dūn** India
61B3 **Dehri** India
53B3 **Dehui** China
72C3 **Deim Zubeir** Sudan
65C2 **Deir Abu Sa'id** Jordan
65D1 **Deir el Ahmar** Leb
45C6 **Dej** Rom
12B2 **De Kalb** Illinois, USA
17D3 **De Kalb** Texas, USA
49Q4 **De Kastri** Russian Fed
72C4 **Dekese** Zaïre
72B3 **Dekoa** CAR
8B3 **Delano** USA
19D3 **Delano Peal** *Mt* USA
74D2 **Delareyville** S Africa
10C6 **Delarof Is** USA
9F3 **Delaware** State, USA
12C2 **Delaware** USA
13D2 **Delaware** *R* USA
9F3 **Delaware B** USA
75C3 **Delegate** Aust
37B1 **Delemont** Switz
73E5 **Delgado** *C* Mozam
66B2 **Delgo** Sudan
16B2 **Delhi** Colorado, USA
60D3 **Delhi** India
13E2 **Delhi** New York, USA
64B1 **Delice** Turk
21B2 **Delicias** Mexico
63C2 **Delījān** Iran
37B1 **Delle** France
11C3 **Dell Rapids** USA
71C1 **Dellys** Alg
20D4 **Del Mar** USA
32F8 **Delmenhorst** Germany
10F2 **De Long Mts** USA
49R2 **De-Longa, Ostrov** *I* Russian Fed
75E3 **Deloraine** Aust
6H5 **Deloraine** Can
15E4 **Delray Beach** USA
8C4 **Del Rio** USA
8B3 **Delta** USA
10J3 **Delta** *R* USA
71H4 **Delta** *State* Nigeria
10J3 **Delta Junction** USA
14C1 **Delta Res** USA
72D3 **Dembī Dolo** Eth
36C1 **Demer** *R* Belg
43G1 **Demidov** Russian Fed
16A3 **Deming** USA
41F2 **Demirköy** Turk
71A2 **Demnate** Mor
37B2 **Demonte** Italy
15B2 **Demopolis** USA
48H4 **Demyanskoya** Russian Fed
38C1 **Denain** France
59E2 **Denau** Uzbekistan
35D5 **Denbigh** Wales
10F3 **Denbigh,C** USA
56C3 **Dendang** Indon
36C1 **Dendermond** Belg
72D3 **Dendi** *Mt* Eth
36B1 **Dèndre** *R* Belg
52B1 **Dengkou** China
52C3 **Deng Xian** China
Den Haag = 's-Gravenhage
23H1 **Denham,Mt** Jamaica
42A2 **Den Helder** Neth
39C2 **Denia** Spain
76D4 **Deniliquin** Aust
18C2 **Denio** USA
11C3 **Denison** Iowa, USA
8D3 **Denison** Texas, USA
10H4 **Denison,Mt** USA
45D8 **Denizli** Turk
32F7 **Denmark** Kingdom, Europe
79C1 **Denmark Str** Greenland/Iceland
23P2 **Dennery** St Lucia
56E4 **Denpasar** Indon
14C3 **Denton** Maryland, USA
8D3 **Denton** Texas, USA
76E1 **D'Entrecasteaux Is** PNG
37B1 **Dents du Midi** *Mt* Switz
8C3 **Denver** USA
4F2 **Denys** *R* Can
72B3 **Déo** *R* Cam
61C3 **Deoghar** India
60C5 **Deolāli** India
60D1 **Deosai Plain** India
14A1 **Depew** USA
14C1 **Deposit** USA
72C2 **Dépression du Mourdi** *Desert Region* Chad
49P3 **Deputatskiy** Russian Fed
17D3 **De Queen** USA
60C3 **Dera** Pak
60B3 **Dera Bugti** Pak
60B2 **Dera Ismail Khan** Pak
45H7 **Derbent** Russian Fed
76B2 **Derby** Aust
14D2 **Derby** Connecticut, USA
35E5 **Derby** County, Eng
35E5 **Derby** Eng
17C2 **Derby** Kansas, USA
45F5 **Dergachi** Ukraine
17D3 **De Ridder** USA
69B1 **Derna** Libya
72E3 **Derri** Somalia
14E1 **Derry** USA
72D2 **Derudeb** Sudan
74C3 **De Rust** S Africa
14C1 **De Ruyter** USA
75E3 **Derwent Bridge** Aust
28B2 **Desaguadero** Arg
28B2 **Desaguadero** *R* Arg
19C4 **Descanso** Mexico
3H3 **Deschambault L** Can
18B2 **Deschutes** *R* USA
72D2 **Desē** Eth
25C7 **Deseado** Arg
25C7 **Deseado** *R* Arg
37D2 **Desenzano** Italy
70A1 **Deserta Grande** *I* Medeira
19C4 **Desert Centre** USA
19D2 **Desert Peak** *Mt* USA
63E2 **Deshu** Afghan
25C2 **Desierto de Atacama** *Desert* Chile
17D2 **Desloge** USA
9D2 **Des Moines** Iowa, USA
16B2 **Des Moines** New Mexico, USA
11D3 **Des Moines** *R* USA
45E5 **Desna** *R* Russian Fed
25B8 **Desolación** *I* Chile
12B2 **Des Plaines** USA
42C2 **Dessau** Germany
10L3 **Destruction Bay** Can
36A1 **Desvres** France
41E1 **Deta** Rom
73C5 **Dete** Zim
36E1 **Detmold** Germany
9E2 **Detroit** USA
5J4 **Détroit d'Honguedo** *Str* Can
5J3 **Détroit de Jacques Cartier** *Str* Can
11C2 **Detroit Lakes** USA
55D3 **Det Udom** Thai
41E1 **Deva** Rom
42B2 **Deventer** Neth
34D3 **Deveron** *R* Scot
60C3 **Devikot** India
20C2 **Devil Postpile Nat Mon** USA
20C3 **Devils Den** USA
20C1 **Devils Gate** *P* USA
34F3 **Devil's Hole** *Region* N Sea
Devil's Island = Isla du Diable
11C2 **Devils L** N Dakota, USA
16B4 **Devils L** Texas, USA
8D2 **Devils Lake** USA
10M4 **Devils Paw** *Mt* Can
35E6 **Devizes** Eng
60D3 **Devli** India
41E2 **Devoll** *R* Alb
37A2 **Dévoluy** *Mts* France
35C6 **Devon** County, Eng
7J2 **Devon I** Can
76D5 **Devonport** Aust
61D2 **Dewangiri** Bhutan
60D4 **Dewās** India
74D2 **Dewetsdorp** S Africa
9E3 **Dewey Res** USA
17D3 **De Witt** USA
17E2 **Dexter** Missouri, USA
16B3 **Dexter** New Mexico, USA
52A3 **Deyang** China
63D2 **Deyhuk** Iran
63B2 **Dezfūl** Iran
52D2 **Dezhou** China
63B1 **Dezh Shāhpūr** Iran
67F1 **Dhahran** S Arabia
61D3 **Dhākā** Bang
65B1 **Dhali** Cyprus
66D4 **Dhamār** Yemen
62B2 **Dhamavaram** India
61B3 **Dhamtari** India
61C3 **Dhanbād** India
61B2 **Dhangarhi** Nepal
61C2 **Dhankuta** Nepal
60D4 **Dhār** India
62B2 **Dharmapuri** India
60D2 **Dharmshāla** India
70B3 **Dhar Oualata** *Desert Region* Maur
61B2 **Dhaulagiri** *Mt* Nepal
61C3 **Dhenkānāi** India
65C3 **Dhibah** Jordan
41F3 **Dhíkti Óri** *Mt* Greece
67F3 **Dhofar** Region, Oman
41E3 **Dhomokós** Greece
62B1 **Dhone** India
60C4 **Dhoraji** India
60C4 **Dhrāngadhra** India
61C2 **Dhuburi** India
60C4 **Dhule** India
20B2 **Diablo,Mt** USA
19B3 **Diablo Range** *Mts* USA
28C2 **Diamante** Arg
28B2 **Diamante** *R* Arg
27K7 **Diamantina** Brazil
76D3 **Diamantina** *R* Aust
29A1 **Diamantino** Brazil
61C3 **Diamond Harbours** India
20B1 **Diamond Springs** USA
18D2 **Diamondville** USA
71G3 **Diapaga** Burkina
67G1 **Dibā** UAE
73C4 **Dibaya** Zaïre
61D2 **Dibrugarh** India
16B3 **Dickens** USA
8C2 **Dickinson** USA
15B1 **Dickson** USA
13D2 **Dickson City** USA
45G8 **Dicle** *R* Turk
3F3 **Didsbury** Can
60C3 **Dīdwāna** India
37A2 **Die** France
74E2 **Die Berg** *Mt* S Africa
71F3 **Diebougou** Burkina
36E2 **Dieburg** Germany
3G3 **Diefenbaker,L** Can
36D2 **Diekirch** Lux
70B3 **Diéma** Mali
55C1 **Dien Bien Phu** Viet
42B2 **Diepholz** Germany
38C2 **Dieppe** France
53B3 **Dier Songhua Jiang** *R* China
36C1 **Diest** Belg
36D2 **Dieuze** France
71J3 **Diffa** Niger
61E2 **Digboi** India
7M5 **Digby** Can
38D3 **Digne** France
38C2 **Digoin** France
57G9 **Digos** Phil
76C1 **Digul** *R* Indon
71F4 **Digya Nat Pk** Ghana

Dihang

Dzavhan Gol

61D2 **Dihang** *R* India
Dijlah = Tigris
37A1 **Dijon** France
72B3 **Dik** Chad
72E2 **Dikhil** Djibouti
65A3 **Dîkirnis** Egypt
36B1 **Diksmuide** Belg
48K2 **Dikson** Russian Fed
71J3 **Dikwa** Nig
63E2 **Dilaram** Afghan
57C4 **Dili** Indon
55D3 **Di Linh** Viet
36E1 **Dillenburg** Germany
17F4 **Dilley** USA
72C2 **Dilling** Sudan
10G4 **Dillingham** USA
8B2 **Dillon** USA
14B2 **Dillsburg** USA
73C5 **Dilolo** Zaïre
22A1 **Dimas** Mexico
Dimashq = Damascus
72C4 **Dimbelenge** Zaïre
71F4 **Dimbokro** Ivory Coast
41F2 **Dimitrovgrad** Bulg
44H5 **Dimitrovgrad** Russian Fed
65C3 **Dimona** Israel
61D2 **Dimpāpur** India
57G8 **Dinagat** *I* Phil
61C2 **Dinajpur** India
38B2 **Dinan** France
36C1 **Dinant** Belg
64B2 **Dinar** Turk
72D2 **Dinder** *R* Sudan
62B2 **Dindigul** India
52B2 **Dingbian** China
61C2 **Dinggyê** China
33A3 **Dingle** Irish Rep
33A3 **Dingle** *B* Irish Rep
70A3 **Dinguiraye** Guinea
34C3 **Dingwall** Scot
52A2 **Dingxi** China
52D2 **Ding Xian** China
55D1 **Dinh Lap** Viet
11D2 **Dinorwic L** Can
16A1 **Dinosaur** USA
20C2 **Dinuba** USA
10E2 **Diomede Is** Russian Fed/ USA
70A3 **Diouloulou** Sen
61D2 **Diphu** India
72E3 **Diredawa** Eth
76A3 **Dirk Hartog** *I* Aust
72B2 **Dirkou** Niger
75C1 **Dirranbandi** Aust
25J8 **Disappointment,C** South Georgia
18B1 **Disappointment,C** USA
76B3 **Disappointment,L** Aust
75B3 **Discovery B** Aust
xxxJ6 **Discovery Tablemount** Atlantic O
37C1 **Disentis Muster** Switz
66B1 **Dishna** Egypt
7N3 **Disko** *I* Greenland
7N3 **Disko Bugt** *B* Greenland
7N3 **Diskofjord** Greenland
13D3 **Dismal Swamp** USA
43F1 **Disna** *R* Belorussia
29C2 **Distrito Federal** Federal District, Brazil
60C4 **Diu** India
57G9 **Diuat Mts** Phil
36A2 **Dives** *R* France
27K8 **Divinópolis** Brazil
45G6 **Divnoye** Russian Fed
64C2 **Divriği** Turk
20B1 **Dixon** California, USA
12B2 **Dixon** Illinois, USA
18D1 **Dixon** Montana, USA
6E4 **Dixon Entrance** *Sd* Can/ USA
3E2 **Dixonville** Can
64E3 **Diyālā** *R* Iraq
45G8 **Diyarbakir** Turk
63E3 **Diz** Pak
63B2 **Diz** *R* Iran
72B3 **Dja** *R* Cam
71C2 **Djadi** *R* Alg
72B1 **Djado,Plat du** Niger
71D2 **Djamaa** Alg
72B4 **Djambala** Congo
70C2 **Djanet** Alg
71C2 **Djebel Amour** *Mts* Alg
39A2 **Djebel Bouhalla** *Mt* Mor
71D1 **Djebel Chambi** *Mt* Tunisia
71D1 **Djebel Chélia** *Mts* Alg
71E1 **Djebel Zaghouan** *Mt* Tunisia
71D2 **Djebel Zrega** *Mt* Tunisia
71G4 **Djebobo** *Mt* Ghana
71C2 **Djelfa** Alg
72C3 **Djéma** CAR
70B3 **Djenné** Mali
71J4 **Djerem** *R* Cam
71F3 **Djibasso** Burkina
70B3 **Djibo** Burkina
72E2 **Djibouti** Djibouti
72E2 **Djibouti** Republic, E Africa
72C3 **Djolu** Zaïre
71G4 **Djougou** Benin
72D3 **Djugu** Zaïre
32C2 **Djúpivogur** Iceland
39C2 **Djurdjura** *Mts* Alg
44F4 **Dmitrov** Russian Fed
Dnepr = Dnieper
45E6 **Dneprodzerzhinsk** Ukraine
45F6 **Dnepropetrovsk** Ukraine
44D5 **Dneprovskaya Nizmennost'** Region, Belorussia
Dnestr = Dniester
45E6 **Dnieper** *R* Ukraine
45C6 **Dniester** *R* Ukraine
44E4 **Dno** Russian Fed
72B3 **Doba** Chad
43E1 **Dobele** Latvia
28C3 **Doblas** Arg
76C1 **Dobo** Indon
41D2 **Doboj** Bosnia-Herzegovina, Yugos
41F2 **Dobrich** Bulg
45E5 **Dobrush** Belorussia
27K7 **Doce** *R* Brazil
25D2 **Doctor R P Peña** Arg
62B2 **Dod** India
62B2 **Doda Betta** *Mt* India
41F3 **Dodecanese** *Is* Greece
8C3 **Dodge City** USA
3G2 **Dodge L** Can
12A2 **Dodgeville** USA
72D4 **Dodoma** Tanz
34G4 **Dogger Bank** *Sand-bank* N Sea
12B1 **Dog L** Can
12C1 **Dog L** Can
54B3 **Dōgo** *I* Japan
70C3 **Dogondoutchi** Niger
64D2 **Doğubayazit** Turk
67F1 **Doha** Qatar
61D2 **Doilungdêqên** China
66C4 **Doka** Sudan
76C1 **Dolak** *I* Indon
11C3 **Doland** USA
7L5 **Dolbeau** Can
38D2 **Dole** France
66B4 **Doleib** *Watercourse* Sudan
35D5 **Dolgellau** Wales
14C1 **Dolgeville** USA
44K2 **Dolgiy, Ostrov** *I* Russian Fed
53E2 **Dolinsk** Russian Fed
37D1 **Dolomitche** *Mts* Italy
72E3 **Dolo Odo** Eth
25E5 **Dolores** Arg
28D2 **Dolores** Urug
16A2 **Dolores** *R* USA
22B1 **Dolores Hidalgo** Mexico
6G3 **Dolphin and Union Str** Can
25E8 **Dolphin,C** Falkland Is
51G7 **Dom** *Mt* Indon
45K5 **Dombarovskiy** Russian Fed
32F6 **Dombas** Nor
36D2 **Dombasle-sur-Meurthe** France
41D1 **Dombóvár** Hung
28A1 **Domeyko** Chile
38B2 **Domfront** France
23E3 **Dominica** *I* Caribbean
23C3 **Dominican Republic** Caribbean
7L3 **Dominion,C** Can
7N4 **Domino** Can
50E1 **Domna** Russian Fed
40B1 **Domodossola** Italy
28E2 **Dom Pedrito** Brazil
56E4 **Dompu** Indon
25B5 **Domuyo** *Mt* Arg
75D1 **Domville,Mt** Aust
34D3 **Don** *R* Scot
45G6 **Don** *R* Russian Fed
34B4 **Donaghadee** N Ire
22B1 **Donato Guerta** Mexico
Donau = Dunav
42C3 **Donau, R** Austria
42C3 **Donau** *R* Germany
36E3 **Donaueschingen** Germany
42C3 **Donauwörth** Germany
39A2 **Don Benito** Spain
35E5 **Doncaster** Eng
73B4 **Dondo** Angola
73D5 **Dondo** Mozam
62C3 **Dondra Head** *C* Sri Lanka
34B4 **Donegal** County, Irish Rep
33B3 **Donegal** Irish Rep
33B3 **Donegal** *B* Irish Rep
34A4 **Donegal** *Mts* Irish Rep
45F6 **Donetsk** Ukraine
71J4 **Donga** *R* Nig
52C4 **Dong'an** China
76A3 **Dongara** Aust
52A4 **Dongchuan** China
55D2 **Dongfang** China
53B3 **Dongfeng** China
76A1 **Donggala** Indon
50C3 **Donggi Cona** *L* China
53A4 **Donggou** China
52C5 **Donghai Dao** *I* China
52A1 **Dong He** *R* China
55D2 **Dong Hoi** Viet
52C5 **Dong Jiang** *R* China
53C2 **Donglanghong** China
53C3 **Dongning** China
72D2 **Dongola** Sudan
52D5 **Dongshan** China
50E4 **Dongsha Qundao** *I* China
52C2 **Dongsheng** China
52E3 **Dongtai** China
52C4 **Dongting Hu** *L* China
52B5 **Dongxing** China
52D3 **Dongzhi** China
17D2 **Doniphan** USA
40D2 **Donji Vakuf** Bosnia-Herzegovina, Yugos
32G5 **Dönna** *I* Nor
19B3 **Donner** *P* USA
36D2 **Donnersberg** *Mt* Germany
74D2 **Donnybrook** S Africa
38B3 **Donostia** Spain
20B2 **Don Pedro Res** USA
10H2 **Doonerak,Mt** USA
57F9 **Dopolong** Phil
52A3 **Do Qu** *R* China
37B2 **Dora Baltea** *R* Italy
38D2 **Dorbirn** Austria
53A2 **Dorbod** China
35D6 **Dorchester** Eng
7L3 **Dorchester,C** Can
38C2 **Dordogne** *R* France
42A2 **Dordrecht** Neth
74D3 **Dordrecht** S Africa
3G3 **Doré L** Can
3G3 **Doré Lake** Can
14D1 **Dorest Peak** *Mt* USA
70B3 **Dori** Burkina
74B3 **Doring** *R* S Africa
36B2 **Dormans** France
42B3 **Dornbirn** Austria
34C3 **Dornoch** Scot
34C3 **Dornoch Firth** *Estuary* Scot
32H6 **Dorotea** Sweden
75D2 **Dorrigo** Aust
18B2 **Dorris** USA
35D6 **Dorset** County, Eng
36D1 **Dorsten** Germany
42B2 **Dortmund** Germany
72C3 **Doruma** Zaïre
49N4 **Dosatuy** Russian Fed
60B1 **Doshi** Afghan
20B2 **Dos Palos** USA
71G3 **Dosso** Niger
48G5 **Dossor** Kazakhstan
9E3 **Dothan** USA
38C1 **Douai** France
72A3 **Douala** Cam
75D1 **Double Island Pt** Aust
5K3 **Double Mer** *B* Can
16B3 **Double Mountain Fork** *R* USA
20C3 **Double Mt** USA
38D2 **Doubs** *R* France
78A3 **Doubtful Sd** NZ
70B3 **Douentza** Mali
3B2 **Douglas** Alaska, USA
8C3 **Douglas** Arizona, USA
35C4 **Douglas** Eng
15C2 **Douglas** Georgia, USA
74C2 **Douglas** S Africa
8C2 **Douglas** Wyoming, USA
10E2 **Douglas,C** USA
3C3 **Douglas Chan** Can
15C1 **Douglas L** USA
10H4 **Douglas,Mt** USA
36C2 **Doulevant-le-Château** France
36B1 **Doullens** France
35B4 **Doun** County, N Ire
27H8 **Dourados** Brazil
29B3 **Dourados** *R* Brazil
36B2 **Dourdan** France
39A1 **Douro** *R* Port
16A2 **Dove Creek** USA
13D3 **Dover** Delaware, USA
35F6 **Dover** Eng
13E2 **Dover** New Hampshire, USA
14C2 **Dover** New Jersey, USA
12C2 **Dover** Ohio, USA
35E5 **Dover** *R* Eng
35F6 **Dover,Str of** Eng/France
43G2 **Dovsk** Belorussia
14C3 **Downington** USA
35C4 **Downpatrick** N Ire
14C1 **Downsville** USA
3D3 **Downton,Mt** Can
14C2 **Doylestown** USA
54B3 **Dōzen** *I* Japan
70A2 **Dr'aa** *R* Mor
37A2 **Drac** *R* France
29B3 **Dracena** Brazil
14E1 **Dracut** USA
38D3 **Draguignan** France
11B2 **Drake** USA
73D6 **Drakensberg** *Mts* S Africa
74D2 **Drakensberg** *Mt* S Africa
xxxE7 **Drake Pass** Pacific/ Atlantic O
41E2 **Dráma** Greece
32G6 **Drammen** Nor
32A1 **Drangajökull** Iceland
22B1 **Dr Arroyo** Mexico
37E1 **Drau** *R* Austria
40D1 **Drava** *R* Slovenia, Yugos
3F3 **Drayton Valley** Can
38C2 **Dreaux** France
42C2 **Dresden** Germany
36A2 **Dreux** France
18C2 **Drewsey** USA
4E4 **Driftwood** Can
14A2 **Driftwood** USA
41E2 **Drin** *R* Alb
41D2 **Drina** *R* Bosnia-Herzegovina/Serbia, Yugos
43F1 **Drissa** *R* Belorussia
35B5 **Drogheda** Irish Rep
43E3 **Drogobych** Ukraine
37A2 **Drôme** *R* France
37B2 **Dronera** Italy
79F12 **Dronning Maud Land** Region, Ant
26F8 **Dr P.P. Pená** Par
6G4 **Drumheller** Can
18D1 **Drummond** USA
12C1 **Drummond I** USA
5G4 **Drummondville** Can
43E2 **Druskininksi** Lithuania
49Q3 **Druzhina** Russian Fed
10L4 **Dry B** USA
11D2 **Dryberry L** Can
7J5 **Dryden** Can
14B1 **Dryden** USA
23H1 **Dry Harbour Mts** Jamaica
71J4 **Dschang** Cam
55B3 **Duang** *I* Burma
66C1 **Dubâ** S Arabia
67G1 **Dubai** UAE
6H3 **Dubawnt** *R* Can
6H3 **Dubawnt L** Can
76D4 **Dubbo** Aust
35B5 **Dublin** County, Irish Rep
35B5 **Dublin** Irish Rep
15C2 **Dublin** USA
44F4 **Dubna** Russian Fed
45D5 **Dubno** Ukraine
18D2 **Dubois** Idaho, USA
13D2 **Du Bois** USA
18E2 **Dubois** Wyoming, USA
3C3 **Dubose,Mt** Can
43F3 **Dubossary** Moldova
43F2 **Dubrovica** Ukraine
41D2 **Dubrovnik** Croatia, Yugos
9D2 **Dubuque** USA
19D2 **Duchesne** USA
15B1 **Duck** *R* USA
3H3 **Duck Mts** Can
20C3 **Ducor** USA
36D2 **Dudelange** Lux
48K3 **Dudinka** Russian Fed
35D5 **Dudley** Eng
49L2 **Dudypta** *R* Russian Fed
70B4 **Duekoué** Ivory Coast
39B1 **Duero** *R* Spain
77F1 **Duff Is** Solomon Is
34D3 **Dufftown** Scot
40C2 **Dugi Otok** *I* Croatia, Yugos
5G2 **Du Gué** *R* Can
42B2 **Duisburg** Germany
74E1 **Duiwelskloof** S Africa
64E3 **Dūkan** Iraq
10M5 **Duke I** USA
72D3 **Duk Faiwil** Sudan
67F1 **Dukhān** Qatar
52A4 **Dukou** China
50C3 **Dulan** China
28C2 **Dulce** *R* Arg
56D2 **Dulit Range** *Mts* Malay
61D3 **Dullabchara** India
36D1 **Dülmen** Germany
9D2 **Duluth** USA
65D2 **Dūmā** Syria
56B2 **Dumai** Indon
57E8 **Dumaran** *I* Phil
8C3 **Dumas** USA
65D2 **Dumayr** Syria
71G4 **Dumbai** Ghana
34C4 **Dumbarton** Scot
34D4 **Dumfries** Scot
34C4 **Dumfries and Galloway** Region, Scot
61C3 **Dumka** India
57B2 **Dumoga Kecil** Indon
13D1 **Dumoine,L** Can
79G8 **Dumont d'Urville** *Base* Ant
69C1 **Dumyât** Egypt
Dunărea = Danube *R* Rom
35B5 **Dunary Head** *Pt* Irish Rep
Dunav = Danube
43F3 **Dunayevtsy** Ukraine
3D4 **Duncan** Can
17C3 **Duncan** USA
4E3 **Duncan,C** Can
4F3 **Duncan L** Can
14B2 **Duncannon** USA
62E2 **Duncan Pass** Andaman Is
34D2 **Duncansby Head** *Pt* Scot
35B4 **Dundalk** Irish Rep
14B3 **Dundalk** USA
35B5 **Dundalk B** Irish Rep
7M2 **Dundas** Greenland
10M5 **Dundas I** Can
6G2 **Dundas Pen** Can
51G8 **Dundas Str** Aust
74E2 **Dundee** S Africa
34D3 **Dundee** Scot
14B1 **Dundee** USA
75B1 **Dundoo** Aust
35C4 **Dundrum** *B* N Ire
77G5 **Dunedin** NZ
15C3 **Dunedin** USA
75C2 **Dunedoo** Aust
34D3 **Dunfermline** Scot
60C4 **Dungarpur** India
35B5 **Dungarvan** Irish Rep
35F6 **Dungeness** Eng
75D2 **Dungog** Aust
72C3 **Dungu** Zaïre
72D1 **Dungunab** Sudan
53B3 **Dunhua** China
50C2 **Dunhuang** China
36B1 **Dunkerque** France
9F2 **Dunkirk** USA
72D2 **Dunkur** Eth
71F4 **Dunkwa** Ghana
33B3 **Dun Laoghaire** Irish Rep
14C2 **Dunmore** USA
23B1 **Dunmore Town** Bahamas
15D1 **Dunn** USA
34D2 **Dunnet Head** *Pt* Scot
11B3 **Dunning** USA
34D4 **Duns** Scot
11B2 **Dunseith** USA
18B2 **Dunsmuir** USA
78A2 **Dunstan Mts** NZ
36C2 **Dun-sur-Meuse** France
52D1 **Duolun** China
11B2 **Dupree** USA
73B4 **Duque de Braganca** Angola
12B3 **Du Quoin** USA
65C3 **Dura** Israel
38D3 **Durance** *R* France
12A2 **Durand** USA
21B2 **Durango** Mexico
39B1 **Durango** Spain
22A1 **Durango** State, Mexico
8C3 **Durango** USA
8D3 **Durant** USA
65D1 **Duraykīsh** Syria
25E4 **Durazho** Urug
74E2 **Durban** S Africa
36D1 **Duren** Germany
61B3 **Durg** India
61C3 **Durgapur** India
34E4 **Durham** County, Eng
34E4 **Durham** Eng
9F3 **Durham** N Carolina, USA
14E1 **Durham** New Hampshire, USA
75B1 **Durham Downs** Aust
41D2 **Durmitor** *Mt* Montenegro, Yugos
34C2 **Durness** Scot
41D2 **Durrës** Alb
75B1 **Durrie** Aust
41F3 **Dursunbey** Turk
78B2 **D'Urville I** NZ
63E1 **Dushak** Turkmenistan
52B4 **Dushan** China
59E2 **Dushanbe** Tajikistan
14B2 **Dushore** USA
78A3 **Dusky Sd** NZ
42B2 **Düsseldorf** Germany
10E5 **Dutch Harbor** USA
19D3 **Dutton,Mt** USA
52B4 **Duyun** China
64B1 **Düzce** Turk
44F2 **Dvinskaya Guba** *B* Russian Fed
60B4 **Dwārka** India
18C1 **Dworshak Res** USA
9E3 **Dyersburg** USA
35C5 **Dyfed** County, Wales
45G7 **Dykh Tau** *Mt* Russian Fed
75B1 **Dynevor Downs** Aust
50C2 **Dzag** Mongolia
50D2 **Dzamīn Uūd** Mongolia
73E5 **Dzaoudzi** Mayotte
50C2 **Dzavhan Gol** *R* Mongolia

Dzerzhinsk
Encruzilhada

44G4 **Dzerzhinsk** Russian Fed
49O4 **Dzhalinda** Russian Fed
48J5 **Dzhambul** Kazakhstan
45E6 **Dzhankoy** Ukraine
Dzharkent = Panfilov
48H5 **Dzehezkazgan** Kazakhstan
60B1 **Dzhilikul'** Tajikistan
48J5 **Dzhungarskiy Alatau** *Mts* Kazakhstan
42D2 **Dzierzoniów** Pol
59G1 **Dzungaria** Basin, China
49L5 **Dzüyl** Mongolia

E

7K4 **Eabamet L** Can
10K3 **Eagle** Alaska, USA
16A2 **Eagle** Colorado, USA
5K3 **Eagle** *R* Can
11B2 **Eagle Butte** USA
18B2 **Eagle L** California, USA
11D2 **Eagle L** Can
13F1 **Eagle L** Maine, USA
13F1 **Eagle Lake** USA
17C3 **Eagle Mountain L** USA
8C4 **Eagle Pass** USA
16A3 **Eagle Peak** *Mt* USA
6E3 **Eagle Plain** Can
10J3 **Eagle River** USA
11D1 **Ear Falls** Can
19C3 **Earlimart** USA
19D4 **Earp** USA
16B3 **Earth** USA
15C2 **Easley** USA
13D2 **East Aurora** USA
15B3 **East B** USA
35F6 **Eastbourne** Eng
14C1 **East Branch Delaware** *R* USA
77G4 **East,C** NZ
10B6 **East C** USA
12B2 **East Chicago** USA
50F3 **East China Sea** China/Japan
61B4 **Eastern Ghats** *Mts* India
4B3 **Easterville** Can
25E8 **East Falkland** *I* Falkland Is
10J2 **East Fork** *R* USA
19C3 **Eastgate** USA
11C2 **East Grand Forks** USA
14D1 **Easthampton** USA
14D2 **East Hampton** USA
12B2 **East Lake** USA
12C2 **East Liverpool** USA
74D3 **East London** S Africa
7L4 **Eastmain** Can
7L4 **Eastmain** *R* Can
15C2 **Eastman** USA
12A2 **East Moline** USA
13D3 **Easton** Maryland, USA
13D2 **Easton** Pennsylvania, USA
14C2 **East Orange** USA
xxixO5 **East Pacific Ridge** Pacific O
xxixO4 **East Pacific Rise** Pacific O
15C2 **East Point** USA
13F2 **Eastport** USA
35E5 **East Retford** Eng
15B1 **East Ridge** USA
9D3 **East St Louis** USA
49R2 **East Siberian S** Russian Fed
35F6 **East Sussex** County, Eng
13D3 **Eastville** USA
20C1 **East Walker** USA
15C2 **Eatonton** USA
11D3 **Eau Claire** USA
51H6 **Eauripik** *I* Pacific O
22C1 **Ebano** Mexico
72B3 **Ebebiyin** Eq Guinea
14A2 **Ebensburg** USA
36E2 **Eberbach** Germany
42C2 **Eberswalde** Germany
54D2 **Ebetsu** Japan
52A4 **Ebian** China
48K5 **Ebinur** *L* China
40D2 **Eboli** Italy
72B3 **Ebolowa** Cam
39B1 **Ebro** *R* Spain
64A1 **Eceabat** Turk
71C1 **Ech Cheliff** Alg
52D2 **Eching** China
18C1 **Echo** USA
Echo Bay = Port Radium
6G3 **Echo Bay** Can
36D2 **Echternach** Lux
75B3 **Echuca** Aust
39A2 **Ecija** Spain
7K2 **Eclipse Sd** Can
36A3 **Ecommoy** France
26C4 **Ecuador** Republic, S America
34D2 **Eday** *I* Scot
72E2 **Ed** Eritrea
34G3 **Edda** *Oilfield* N Sea
72C2 **Ed Da'ein** Sudan
66B4 **Ed Damasin** Sudan
72D2 **Ed Damer** Sudan
72D2 **Ed Debba** Sudan
34C2 **Eddrachillis** *B* Scot
72D2 **Ed Dueim** Sudan
75E3 **Eddystone Pt** Aust
71G4 **Ede** Nig
72A3 **Edea** Cam
75C3 **Eden** Aust
16C3 **Eden** Texas, USA
18E2 **Eden** Wyoming, USA
34D4 **Eden** *R* Eng
74D2 **Edenburg** S Africa
78A3 **Edendale** NZ
36D2 **Edenkoben** Germany
36E1 **Eder** *R* Germany
11C2 **Edgeley** USA
7M3 **Edgell I** Can
11B3 **Edgemont** USA
48D2 **Edgeøya** *I* Barents S
14B3 **Edgewood** USA
65C3 **Edh Dhahiriya** Israel
41E2 **Edhessa** Greece
17F4 **Edinburg** USA
34D3 **Edinburgh** Scot
45D7 **Edirne** Turk
20C3 **Edison** USA
20C3 **Edison** USA
15C2 **Edisto** *R* USA
18B1 **Edmonds** USA
6G4 **Edmonton** Can
11C2 **Edmore** USA
7M5 **Edmundston** Can
17C4 **Edna** USA
10M4 **Edna Bay** USA
71H4 **Edo** *State* Nigeria
40C1 **Edolo** Italy
65C3 **Edom** Region, Jordan
45D8 **Edremit** Turk
41F3 **Edremit Körfezi** *B* Turk
50C2 **Edrengiyn Nuruu** *Mts* Mongolia
6G4 **Edson** Can
28C3 **Eduardo Castex** Arg
10N3 **Eduni,Mt** Can
75B3 **Edward** *R* Aust
72C4 **Edward,L** Zaïre/Uganda
20D3 **Edwards** USA
75A1 **Edwards Creek** Aust
8C3 **Edwards Plat** USA
12B3 **Edwardsville** USA
3B2 **Edziza,Mt** Can
10F3 **Eek** USA
36B1 **Eeklo** Belg
77F2 **Efate** *I* Vanuatu
9E3 **Effingham** USA
19D3 **Egan Range** *Mts* USA
7N3 **Egedesminde** Greenland
10G4 **Egegik** USA
3H2 **Egenolf L** Can
43E3 **Eger** Hung
32F7 **Egersund** Nor
36E1 **Eggegebirge** Region, Germany
14C3 **Egg Harbor City** USA
6G2 **Eglinton I** Can
78B1 **Egmont,C** NZ
78B1 **Egmont,Mt** NZ
64B2 **Eğridir Gölü** *L* Turk
29C1 **Eguas** *R* Brazil
49U3 **Egvekinot** Russian Fed
69B2 **Egypt** Republic, Africa
32K6 **Ehsenvaara** Fin
39B1 **Eibar** Spain
38C2 **Eibeuf** France
75D1 **Eidsvolo** Aust
36D1 **Eifel** Region, Germany
34B3 **Eigg** *I* Scot
59F5 **Eight Degree Chan** Indian O
76B2 **Eighty Mile Beach** Aust
75C3 **Eildon,L** Aust
36E1 **Einbeck** Germany
42B2 **Eindhoven** Neth
37C1 **Einsiedeln** Switz
65C3 **Ein Yahav** Israel
42C2 **Eisenach** Germany
42C3 **Eisenerz** Austria
37E1 **Eisenhut** *Mt* Austria
36D1 **Eitorf** Germany
52A1 **Ejin qi** China
71F4 **Ejuanema,Mt** Ghana
71F4 **Ejura** Ghana
22C2 **Ejutla** Mexico
11B2 **Ekalaka** USA
78C2 **Eketahuna** NZ
48J4 **Ekibastuz** Kazakhstan
49P4 **Ekimchan** Russian Fed
64B3 **Ek Mahalla el Kubra** Egypt
32H7 **Eksjo** Sweden
4D3 **Ekwan** *R* Can
65A3 **El Abbâsa** Egypt
64A3 **El'Alamein** Egypt
74D2 **Elands** *R* S Africa
74C3 **Elands Berg** S Africa
22B1 **El Arenal** Mexico
71B2 **El Aricha** Alg
64B3 **El'Arîsh** Egypt
64B4 **Elat** Israel
72C2 **El' Atrun Oasis** Sudan
71C2 **el Attar** *R* Alg
45F8 **Elazig** Turk
64C3 **El Azraq** Jordan
40C2 **Elba** *I* Italy
69C2 **El Balyana** Egypt
53D1 **El'ban** Russian Fed
26D2 **El Banco** Colombia
41E2 **Elbasan** Alb
66B3 **El Bauga** Sudan
23D5 **El Baúl** Ven
71C2 **El Bayadh** Alg
42C2 **Elbe** *R* Germany
65D1 **El Bega'a** *R* Leb
12B2 **Elberta** USA
8C3 **Elbert,Mt** USA
15C2 **Elberton** USA
36A2 **Elbeuf** France
64C2 **Elbistan** Turk
43D2 **Elblag** Pol
25B6 **El Bolson** Arg
11C2 **Elbow Lake** USA
22B1 **El Bozal** Mexico
45G7 **Elbrus** *Mt* Russian Fed
Elburz Mts = Reshteh-ye Alborz
19C4 **El Cajon** USA
17C4 **El Campo** USA
19C4 **El Centro** USA
39B2 **Elche** Spain
4D4 **Elcho** USA
28B3 **El Cuy** Arg
39B2 **Elda** Spain
49P3 **El'dikan** Russian Fed
26C3 **El Diviso** Colombia
70B2 **El Djouf** *Desert* Region Maur
17D2 **Eldon** USA
29B4 **Eldorado** Arg
9D3 **El Dorado** Arkansas, USA
29C3 **Eldorado** Brazil
3G2 **Eldorado** Can
8D3 **El Dorado** Kansas, USA
21B2 **El Dorado** Mexico
16B3 **Eldorado** Texas, USA
26F2 **El Dorado** Ven
72D3 **Eldoret** Kenya
14A2 **Eldred** USA
65C1 **Elea,C** Cyprus
18D2 **Electric Peak** *Mt* USA
70B2 **El Eglab** Region, Alg
66B2 **Elel** *Watercourse* Egypt
16A3 **Elephant Butte Res** USA
39B1 **El Escorial** Spain
64D2 **Eleşkirt** Turk
71D1 **El Eulma** Alg
9F4 **Eleuthera** *I* Bahamas
71D1 **El Fahs** Tunisia
64B4 **El Faiyûm** Egypt
70B2 **El Farsia** *Well* Mor
72C2 **El Fasher** Sudan
64B4 **El Fashn** Egypt
39A1 **El Ferrol del Caudillo** Spain
65B3 **El Firdân** Egypt
72C2 **El Fula** Sudan
70C1 **El Gassi** Alg
72D2 **El Geteina** Sudan
72D2 **El Gezîra** Region, Sudan
65C3 **El Ghor** *V* Israel/Jordan
9E2 **Elgin** Illinois, USA
11B2 **Elgin** N Dakota, USA
34D3 **Elgin** Scot
64B3 **El Gîza** Egypt
70C1 **El Golea** Alg
19D4 **El Golfo de Santa Clara** Mexico
72D3 **Elgon,Mt** Uganda/Kenya
72E3 **El Goran** Eth
22B2 **El Grullo** Mexico
70B2 **El Guettara** *Well* Mali
70B2 **El Haricha** *Desert Region* Mali
64A4 **El Harra** Egypt
39C2 **El Harrach** Alg
66B4 **El Hawata** Sudan
22C1 **El Hig** Mexico
66B4 **El Homra** Sudan
28A3 **El Huecu** Arg
64B4 **El'Igma** *Desert Region* Egypt
10F3 **Elim** USA
Elisabethville = Lubumbashi
32K6 **Elisenvaara** Russian Fed
El Iskandarîya = Alexandria
45G6 **Elista** Russian Fed
76C4 **Elizabeth** Aust
13E2 **Elizabeth** USA
74B2 **Elizabeth B** Namibia
9F3 **Elizabeth City** USA
14E2 **Elizabeth Is** USA
15C1 **Elizabethton** Tennessee, USA
12B3 **Elizabethtown** Kentucky, USA
15D2 **Elizabethtown** N Carolina, USA
14B2 **Elizabethtown** Pennsylvania, USA
71A2 **El Jadida** Mor
64C3 **El Jafr** Jordan
65D3 **El Jafr** *L* Jordan
72D2 **El Jebelein** Sudan
71E1 **El Jem** Tunisia
43E2 **Elk** Pol
14C3 **Elk** *R* Maryland, USA
12C3 **Elk** *R* W Virginia, USA
11D3 **Elkader** USA
71D1 **El Kala** Alg
72D2 **El Kamlin** Sudan
71D1 **El Kef** Tunisia
20B1 **Elk Grove** USA
El Khalil = Hebron
66B3 **El Khandaq** Sudan
65A3 **El Khânka** Egypt
66B1 **El Khârga** Egypt
66B1 **El-Khârga Oasis** Egypt
12B2 **Elkhart** USA
70B2 **El Khenachich** *Desert* Region Mali
11C3 **Elkhorn** *R* USA
41F2 **Elkhovo** Bulg
13D3 **Elkins** USA
14B2 **Elkland** USA
11A3 **Elk Mt** USA
18C1 **Elko** Can
8B2 **Elko** USA
71B2 **el Korima** *R* Alg
14C3 **Elkton** USA
66B2 **El Ku** *Watercourse* Egypt
65B3 **El Kûbri** Egypt
64B3 **El Kuntilla** Egypt
72C2 **El Lagowa** Sudan
6H2 **Ellef Ringnes I** Can
11C2 **Ellendale** USA
19D3 **Ellen,Mt** USA
8A2 **Ellensburg** USA
14C2 **Ellenville** USA
7K2 **Ellesmere I** Can
78B2 **Ellesmere,L** NZ
14B3 **Ellicott City** USA
74D3 **Elliot** S Africa
7K5 **Elliot Lake** Can
18D2 **Ellis** USA
65C3 **El Lisan** *Pen* Jordan
74D1 **Ellisras** S Africa
13F2 **Ellsworth** USA
79F3 **Ellsworth Land** *Region* Ant
65A4 **El Ma'âdi** Egypt
69B1 **El Maghra** *L* Egypt
66B4 **El Manaqil** Sudan
64B3 **El Mansûra** Egypt
65A3 **El Manzala** Egypt
65A3 **El Matariya** Egypt
65B3 **El Matarîya** Egypt
14C3 **Elmer** USA
70B3 **El Merelé** *Desert Region* Maur
28B2 **El Milagro** Arg
71D1 **El Milia** Alg
66B3 **El Milk** *Watercourse* Sudan
65C1 **El Mîna** Leb
64B4 **El Minya** Egypt
20B1 **Elmira** California, USA
9F2 **Elmira** New York, USA
19D4 **El Mirage** USA
71D2 **el Mitta** *R* Alg
17F4 **El Moral** Mexico
70B2 **El Mreitl** *Well* Maur
42B2 **Elmsborn** Germany
72C2 **El Muglad** Sudan
70B2 **El Mzereb** *Well* Mali
57E8 **El Nido** Phil
72D2 **El Obeid** Sudan
22B2 **El Oro** Mexico
22A1 **Elota** Mexico
71D2 **El Oued** Alg
19D4 **Eloy** USA
8C3 **El Paso** USA
19B3 **El Porta** USA
20C2 **El Portal** USA
16A3 **El Porvenir** Mexico
22B1 **El Potosí** Mexico
39A2 **El Puerto del Sta Maria** Spain
El Qâhira = Cairo
65B3 **El Qantara** Egypt
El Quds = Jerusalem
22A1 **El Quelite** Mexico
65C3 **El Quseima** Egypt
65C4 **El Quwetra** Jordan
8D3 **El Reno** USA
6E3 **Elsa** Can
37D3 **Elsa** *R* Italy
65A4 **El Saff** Egypt
65B3 **El Sâlhîya** Egypt
22A1 **El Salto** Mexico
21D3 **El Salvador** Republic, C America
4E4 **Elsas** Can
19C4 **El Sauzal** Mexico
65B3 **El Shallûfa** Egypt
65B4 **El Shatt** Egypt
65A3 **El Simbillâwein** Egypt
20D4 **Elsinore L** USA
28B3 **El Sosneade** Arg
42C2 **Elsterwerde** Germany
16A4 **El Sueco** Mexico
El Suweis = Suez
65A4 **El Tabbin** Egypt
39A1 **El Teleno** *Mt* Spain
78B1 **Eltham** NZ
65C4 **El Thamad** Egypt
26F2 **El Tigre** Ven
64B4 **El Tîh** *Desert Region* Egypt
65B3 **El Tîna** Egypt
28C2 **El Tio** Arg
18C1 **Eltopia** USA
28A1 **El Toro** Chile
28A1 **El Transito** Chile
22A1 **El Tuito** Mexico
64B4 **El Tûr** Egypt
62C1 **Elūru** India
39A2 **Elvas** Port
26D5 **Elvira** Brazil
6H2 **Elvira,C** Can
28A2 **El Volcán** Chile
12B2 **Elwood** USA
35F5 **Ely** Eng
9D2 **Ely** Minnesota, USA
8B3 **Ely** Nevada, USA
12C2 **Elyria** USA
65A3 **El Zarqa** Egypt
63D1 **Emāmrūd** Iran
60B1 **Emām Sāheb** Afghan
42D1 **Eman** *R* Sweden
45K6 **Emba** Kazakhstan
45K6 **Emba** *R* Kazakhstan
25C5 **Embalse Cerros Colorados** *L* Arg
39B2 **Embalse de Alarcón** *Res* Spain
39A2 **Embalse de Alcántarà** *Res* Spain
39A1 **Embalse de Almendra** *Res* Spain
39A2 **Embalse de Garcia de Sola** *Res* Spain
26F2 **Embalse de Guri** *L* Ven
39B1 **Embalse de Mequinenza** *Res* Spain
39A1 **Embalse de Ricobayo** *Res* Spain
25E4 **Embalse de Rio Negro** *Res* Urug
28B3 **Embalse El Choc1on** *Res* Arg
25C5 **Embalse Ezequil Ramos Mexia** *L* Arg
25C6 **Embalse Florentine Ameghino** *L* Arg
39A1 **Embalse Gabriel y Galan** *Res* Spain
28B1 **Embalse Rio Hondo** *Res* Arg
25D2 **Embarcación** Arg
6G4 **Embarras Portage** Can
37B2 **Embrun** France
72D4 **Embu** Kenya
42B2 **Emden** Germany
52A4 **Emei** China
76D3 **Emerald** Aust
7M4 **Emeril** Can
6J5 **Emerson** Can
18C2 **Emigrant P** USA
72B1 **Emi Koussi** *Mt* Chad
28B3 **Emilo Mitre** Arg
64B2 **Emirdağ** Turk
14C2 **Emmaus** USA
42B2 **Emmen** Neth
36D2 **Emmendingen** Germany
36D1 **Emmerich** Germany
18C2 **Emmett** USA
14B3 **Emmitsburg** USA
10F3 **Emmonak** USA
8C4 **Emory Peak** *Mt* USA
21A2 **Empalme** Mexico
74E2 **Empangeni** S Africa
25E3 **Empedrado** Arg
xxixK2 **Emperor Seamount Chain** Pacific O
37D3 **Empoli** Italy
17C2 **Emporia** Kansas, USA
13D3 **Emporia** Virginia, USA
14A2 **Emporium** USA
42B2 **Ems** *R* Germany
4F4 **Emsdale** Can
34C2 **Enard** *B* Scot
22B1 **Encarnacion** Mexico
25E3 **Encarnación** Par
71F4 **Enchi** Ghana
17F4 **Encinal** USA
20D4 **Encinitas** USA
29D2 **Encruzilhada** Brazil

Encruzilhada do Sul Fetisovo

28E2 **Encruzilhada do Sul** Brazil
66C4 **Enda Salassie** Eth
76B1 **Endeh** Indon
3E3 **Enderby** Can
79G11 **Enderby Land** Region, Ant
11C2 **Enderlin** USA
13D2 **Endicott** USA
10H2 **Endicott Mts** USA
15D1 **Enfield** USA
37D1 **Engadin** *Mts* Switz
57F7 **Engaño,C** Phil
54D2 **Engaru** Japan
65C3 **En Gedi** Israel
37C1 **Engelberg** Switz
56B4 **Enggano** *I* Indon
33C3 **England** Country, UK
7N4 **Englee** Can
15D1 **Englehard** USA
13D1 **Englehart** Can
16B2 **Englewood** USA
11D1 **English** *R* Can
33C3 **English Channel** Eng/ France
4C4 **English River** Can
17C2 **Enid** USA
54D2 **Eniwa** Japan
70B3 **Enji** *Well* Maur
32H7 **Enkoping** Sweden
40C3 **Enna** Italy
72C2 **En Nahud** Sudan
72C2 **Ennedi** *Desert Region* Chad
10C2 **Ennelen** Russian Fed
75C1 **Enngonia** Aust
11B3 **Enning** USA
33B3 **Ennis** Irish Rep
18D1 **Ennis** Montana, USA
17C3 **Ennis** Texas, USA
35B5 **Enniscorthy** Irish Rep
35B4 **Enniskillen** N Ire
65C2 **Enn Nâqoûra** Leb
42C3 **Enns** *R* Austria
57A3 **Enrekang** Indon
32F8 **Enschede** Neth
21A1 **Ensenada** Mexico
52B3 **Enshi** China
36D3 **Ensisheim** France
72D4 **Entebbe** Uganda
15B2 **Enterprise** Alabama, USA
3E1 **Enterprise** Can
18C1 **Enterprise** Oregon, USA
71H4 **Enugu** Nig
71H4 **Enugu** *State* Nig
10D2 **Enurmino** Russian Fed
36E2 **Enz** *R* w Germ
54C3 **Enzan** Japan
71G4 **Epe** Nig
38C2 **Epernay** France
19D3 **Ephraim** USA
14B2 **Ephrata** Pennsylvania, USA
18C1 **Ephrata** Washington, USA
77F2 **Epi** *I* Vanuatu
38D2 **Épinal** France
65B1 **Episkopi** Cyprus
65B1 **Episkopi B** Cyprus
36E2 **Eppingen** Germany
36A2 **Epte** *R* France
74B1 **Epukiro** Namibia
28C3 **Epu pel** Arg
63C2 **Eqlid** Iran
68D7 **Equator**
72A3 **Equatorial Guinea** Republic, Africa
14D1 **Equinox Mt** USA
14C2 **Equinunk** USA
37C2 **Erba** Italy
36E2 **Erbach** Germany
36D2 **Erbeskopf** *Mt* Germany
28A3 **Ercilla** Chile
64D2 **Erciş** Turk
45F8 **Erciyas Daglari** *Mt* Turk
53B3 **Erdaobaihe** China
52C1 **Erdene** Mongolia
50D2 **Erdenet** Mongolia
72C2 **Erdi** *Desert Region* Chad
25F3 **Erechim** Brazil
64B1 **Ereğli** Turk
64B2 **Ereğli** Turk
50E2 **Erenhot** China
39B1 **Eresma** *R* Spain
36D1 **Erft** *R* Germany
42C2 **Erfurt** Germany
64C2 **Ergani** Turk
70B2 **Erg Chech** *Desert Region* Alg
72B2 **Erg du Djourab** *Desert Region* Chad
70D3 **Erg Du Ténéré** *Desert Region* Niger
64A1 **Ergene** *R* Turk
70B2 **Erg Iguidi** *Region* Alg
43F1 **Ērgli** Latvia
72B2 **Erguig** *R* Chad
50E1 **Ergun** *R* China/ Russian Fed
49O4 **Ergun Zuoqi** China
10C2 **Erguveyem** *R* Russian Fed
72D2 **Eriba** Sudan
9F2 **Erie** USA
9E2 **Erie,L** USA/Can
4B3 **Eriksdale** Can
54D2 **Erimo-misaki** *C* Japan
35C4 **Erin Port** Eng
34B3 **Eriskay** *I* Scot
66C3 **Eritrea** Republic, Africa
36D1 **Erkelenz** Germany
42C3 **Erlangen** Germany
17D3 **Erling,L** USA
74D2 **Ermelo** S Africa
62B3 **Ernākulam** India
62B2 **Erode** India
75B1 **Eromanga** Aust
74B1 **Erongoberg** *Mt* Namibia
71B2 **Er Rachidia** Mor
72D2 **Er Rahad** Sudan
73D5 **Errego** Mozam
33B2 **Errigal** *Mt* Irish Rep
33A3 **Erris Head** *Pt* Irish Rep
77F2 **Erromanga** *I* Vanuatu
72D2 **Er Roseires** Sudan
71C2 **er Rtem** *R* Alg
65C2 **Er Rummān** Jordan
11C2 **Erskine** USA
36D2 **Erstein** France
28E2 **Erval** Brazil
42C2 **Erzgebirge** *Upland* Germany
45F8 **Erzincan** Turk
45G8 **Erzurum** Turk
54D2 **Esan-misaki** *C* Japan
38C3 **Esara** *R* Spain
54D2 **Esashi** Japan
42B1 **Esbjerg** Den
19D3 **Escalante** USA
8C4 **Escalón** Mexico
9E2 **Escanaba** USA
21C3 **Escárcega** Mexico
36C2 **Esch** Luxembourg
19C4 **Escondido** USA
21B2 **Escuinapa** Mexico
21C3 **Escuintla** Guatemala
72B3 **Eséka** Cam
39C1 **Esera** *R* Spain
63C2 **Eşfahān** Iran
74E2 **Eshowe** S Africa
65C3 **Esh Sharā** *Upland* Jordan
37E3 **Esino** Italy
78C1 **Eskdale** NZ
32C1 **Eskifjörður** Iceland
32H7 **Eskilstuna** Sweden
6E3 **Eskimo L** Can
7J3 **Eskimo Point** Can
45E8 **Eskisehir** Turk
39A1 **Esla** *R* Spain
26C3 **Esmeraldas** Ecuador
23B2 **Esmerelda** Cuba
25A7 **Esmerelda** *I* Chile
38C3 **Espalion** France
4E4 **Espanola** Can
16A2 **Espanola** USA
76B4 **Esperance** Aust
28C2 **Esperanza** Arg
79G2 **Esperanza** *Base* Ant
29D2 **Espírito Santo** State, Brazil
77F2 **Espiritu Santo** *I* Vanuatu
73D6 **Espungabera** Mozam
25B6 **Esquel** Arg
18B1 **Esquimalt** Can
28D2 **Esquina** Arg
65D2 **Es Samra** Jordan
71A2 **Essaourira** Mor
71E2 **Es-Sekhira** Tunisia
42B2 **Essen** Germany
27G3 **Essequibo** Guyana
35F6 **Essex** County, Eng
12C2 **Essexville** USA
42B3 **Esslingen** Germany
36B2 **Essonne** France
36C2 **Essoyes** France
27L6 **Estância** Brazil
74D2 **Estcourt** S Africa
37D2 **Este** Italy
26A1 **Esteli** Nic
36B2 **Esternay** France
20B3 **Estero B** USA
22C1 **Esteros** Mexico
25D2 **Esteros** Par
28D1 **Esteros del Iberá** *Swamp* Arg
16A1 **Estes Park** USA
6H5 **Estevan** Can
11D3 **Estherville** USA
15C2 **Estill** USA
36B2 **Estissac** France
44C4 **Estonia**
25B8 **Estrecho de Magallanes** *Str* Chile
20B3 **Estrella** *R* USA
39A2 **Estremoz** Port
43D3 **Esztergom** Hung
75A1 **Etadunna** Aust
7L2 **Etah** Can
36C2 **Etam** France
5K3 **Etamamiou** Can
38C2 **Etampes** France
75A1 **Etamunbanie,L** Aust
36A1 **Etaples** France
60D3 **Etāwah** India
72D3 **Ethiopia** Republic, Africa
22C2 **Etla** Mexico
40C3 **Etna** *Mt* Italy
10M4 **Etolin I** USA
10E3 **Etolin Str** USA
73B5 **Etosha Nat Pk** Namibia
73B5 **Etosha Pan** *Salt L* Namibia
15C2 **Etowah** *R* USA
36A2 **Etretat** France
3D2 **Etsha Plateau** Can
36C2 **Ettelbruck** Lux
77H3 **Eua** *I* Tonga
75C2 **Euabalong** Aust
12C2 **Euclid** USA
75C3 **Eucumbene,L** Aust
75A2 **Eudunda** Aust
17C2 **Eufala L** USA
15B2 **Eufaula** USA
8A2 **Eugene** USA
75C1 **Eulo** Aust
17D3 **Eunice** Louisiana, USA
16B3 **Eunice** New Mexico, USA
36D1 **Eupen** Germany
64D3 **Euphrates** *R* Iraq
17E3 **Eupora** USA
36A2 **Eure** Department, France
38C2 **Eure** *R* France
36A2 **Eure-et-Loir** Department, France
18B2 **Eureka** California, USA
7K1 **Eureka** Can
18C1 **Eureka** Montana, USA
8B3 **Eureka** Nevada, USA
11C2 **Eureka** S Dakota, USA
19D3 **Eureka** Utah, USA
7K2 **Eureka Sound** Can
20D2 **Eureka V** USA
75C3 **Euroa** Aust
75C1 **Eurombah** *R* Aust
73E6 **Europa** *I* Mozam Chan
36C1 **Europoort** Neth
42B2 **Euskirchen** Germany
15B2 **Eutaw** USA
3C3 **Eutsuk L** Can
3F3 **Evansburg** Can
7K1 **Evans,C** Can
7L4 **Evans,L** Can
16A2 **Evans,Mt** Colorado, USA
18D1 **Evans,Mt** Montana, USA
7K3 **Evans Str** Can
12B2 **Evanston** Illinois, USA
8B2 **Evanston** Wyoming, USA
9E3 **Evansville** Indiana, USA
11A3 **Evansville** Wyoming, USA
74D2 **Evaton** S Africa
76C4 **Everard,L** Aust
59G3 **Everest,Mt** Nepal/China
14A2 **Everett** Pennsylvania, USA
8A2 **Everett** Washington, USA
14D1 **Everett,Mt** USA
9E4 **Everglades,The** *Swamp* USA
15B2 **Evergreen** USA
35E5 **Evesham** Eng
72B3 **Evinayong** Eq Guinea
32F7 **Evje** Nor
37B1 **Evolène** Switz
39A2 **Évora** Port
38C2 **Evreux** France
41E3 **Évvoia** *I* Greece
72B4 **Ewo** Congo
20C1 **Excelisor Mt** USA
20C1 **Excelsior Mts** USA
17D2 **Excelsior Springs** USA
19C3 **Exeter** California, USA
35D6 **Exeter** Eng
13E2 **Exeter** New Hampshire, USA
35D6 **Exmoor Nat Pk** Eng
35D6 **Exmouth** Eng
39A2 **Extremadura** Region, Spain
21E2 **Exuma Sd** Bahamas
72D4 **Eyasi** *L* Tanz
34D4 **Eyemouth** Scot
69D4 **Eyl** Somalia
76B4 **Eyre** Aust
76C3 **Eyre Creek** *R* Aust
76C3 **Eyre,L** Aust
76C4 **Eyre Pen** Aust
3H2 **Eyrie L** Can
57F8 **Eyte** *I* Phil
22B1 **Ezatlan** Mexico
41F3 **Ezine** Turk
66B3 **Ez Zeidab** Sudan

F

4G3 **Faber L** Can
32F7 **Fåborg** Den
40C2 **Fabriano** Italy
37B2 **Fabrosa** Italy
72B2 **Fachi** Niger
72C2 **Fada** Chad
71G3 **Fada N'Gourma** Burkina
49Q2 **Faddeyevskiy, Ostrov** *I* Russian Fed
40C2 **Faenza** Italy
7N3 **Faeringehavn** Greenland
30E2 **Faeroerne** Is, N Atlantic
72B3 **Fafa** *R* CAR
72E3 **Fafan** *R* Eth
71G3 **Faga** *R* Burkina
41E1 **Făgăraş** Rom
36C1 **Fagnes** Region, Belg
70B3 **Faguibine,L** Mali
67G2 **Fahud** Oman
70A1 **Faiol** *I* Açores
16A3 **Fairacres** USA
6D3 **Fairbanks** USA
12C3 **Fairborn** USA
8D2 **Fairbury** USA
14B3 **Fairfax** USA
19B3 **Fairfield** California, USA
14D2 **Fairfield** Connecticut, USA
18D2 **Fairfield** Idaho, USA
18D1 **Fairfield** Montana, USA
12C3 **Fairfield** Ohio, USA
34B4 **Fair Head** *Pt* N Ire
33C2 **Fair Isle** *I* Scot
78B2 **Fairlie** NZ
11D3 **Fairmont** Minnesota, USA
12C3 **Fairmont** W Virginia, USA
14B1 **Fairport** USA
3E2 **Fairview** Can
16C2 **Fairview** USA
6E4 **Fairweather,Mt** USA
51H6 **Fais** *I* Pacific O
60C2 **Faisalabad** Pak
11B2 **Faith** USA
34E1 **Faither,The** *Pen* Scot
61B2 **Faizābād** India
77H1 **Fakaofo** *I* Tokeau Is
35F5 **Fakenham** Eng
76C1 **Fakfak** Indon
32G7 **Faköping** Sweden
71F3 **Falaise de Banfora** Burkina
61D3 **Falam** Burma
28B4 **Falckner** Arg
21C2 **Falcon Res** USA/Mexico
70A3 **Falémé** *R* Mali/Sen
17F4 **Falfurrias** USA
3E2 **Falher** Can
32G7 **Falkenberg** Sweden
34D4 **Falkirk** Scot
25D8 **Falkland Is** Dependency, S Atlantic
25E8 **Falkland Sd** Falkland Is
20D4 **Fallbrook** USA
8B3 **Fallon** USA
13E2 **Fall River** USA
16A1 **Fall River P** USA
17C1 **Falls City** USA
35C6 **Falmouth** Eng
23H1 **Falmouth** Jamaica
13E2 **Falmouth** Maine, USA
14E2 **Falmouth** Massachusetts, USA
74B3 **False B** S Africa
21A2 **Falso,C** Mexico
42C2 **Falster** *I* Den
41F1 **Fălticeni** Rom
32H6 **Falun** Sweden
64B2 **Famagusta** Cyprus
65B1 **Famagusta B** Cyprus
28B1 **Famatina** Arg
36C1 **Famenne** Region, Belg
4B3 **Family L** Can
20C3 **Famoso** USA
55B2 **Fang** Thai
72D3 **Fangak** Sudan
52E5 **Fang liao** Taiwan
53B2 **Fangzheng** China
40C2 **Fano** Italy
65A3 **Fâqûs** Egypt
79G3 **Faraday** *Base* Ant
72C3 **Faradje** Zaïre
73E6 **Farafangana** Madag
69B2 **Farafra Oasis** Egypt
63E2 **Farah** Afghan
63E2 **Farah** *R* Afghan
51H5 **Farallon de Medinilla** *I* Pacific O
70A3 **Faranah** Guinea
51H6 **Faraulep** *I* Pacific O
35E6 **Fareham** Eng
Farewell,C = Kap Farvel
77G5 **Farewell,C** NZ
78B2 **Farewell Spit** *Pt* NZ
8D2 **Fargo** USA
65C2 **Fari'a** *R* Israel
9D2 **Faribault** USA
61C3 **Faridpur** Bang
63D1 **Farīmān** Iran
65A3 **Fâriskûr** Egypt
13E2 **Farmington** Maine, USA
17D2 **Farmington** Missouri, USA
14E1 **Farmington** New Hampshire, USA
8C3 **Farmington** New Mexico, USA
18D2 **Farmington** Utah, USA
20B2 **Farmington Res** USA
34E4 **Farne Deep** N Sea
3E3 **Farnham,Mt** Can
10M3 **Faro** Can
39A2 **Faro** Port
32H7 **Fåro** *I* Sweden
71J4 **Faro** *R* Cam
68K8 **Farquhar** *Is* Indian O
34C3 **Farrar** *R* Scot
12C2 **Farrell** USA
41E3 **Fársala** Greece
63E2 **Farsi** Afghan
16B3 **Farwell** USA
63C3 **Fasā** Iran
45D5 **Fastov** Ukraine
61B2 **Fatehpur** India
27H7 **Fatima du Sul** Brazil
18C1 **Fauquier** Can
74D2 **Fauresmith** S Africa
37B2 **Faverges** France
4C3 **Fawcett L** Can
7K4 **Fawn** *R* Can
32H6 **Fax** *R* Sweden
32A2 **Faxaflóri** *B* Iceland
72B2 **Faya** Chad
15B2 **Fayette** USA
9D3 **Fayetteville** Arkansas, USA
9F3 **Fayetteville** N Carolina, USA
15B1 **Fayetteville** Tennessee, USA
65B3 **Fâyid** Egypt
64E4 **Faylakah** *I* Kuwait
60C2 **Fāzilka** India
70A2 **Fdérik** Maur
9F3 **Fear,C** USA
19B3 **Feather Middle Fork** *R* USA
36A2 **Fécamp** France
28D2 **Federación** Arg
28D2 **Federal** Arg
71H4 **Federal Capital Territory** Nig
51H6 **Federated States of Micronesia** *Is* Pacific O
42C2 **Fehmarn** *I* Germany
26D5 **Feijó** Brazil
52C5 **Feilai Xai Bei Jiang** *R* China
78C2 **Feilding** NZ
73D5 **Feira** Zambia
27L6 **Feira de Santan** Brazil
64C2 **Feke** Turk
36D3 **Feldberg** *Mt* Germany
42B3 **Feldkirch** Austria
28D2 **Feliciano** *R* Arg
33D3 **Felixstowe** Eng
37D1 **Feltre** Italy
32G6 **Femund** *L* Nor
53A3 **Fengcheng** China
52B4 **Fengdu** China
52D1 **Fenging** China
52B3 **Fengjie** China
53A1 **Fengshui Shan** *Mt* China
52B3 **Feng Xian** China
52C1 **Fengzhen** China
52C2 **Fen He** *R* China
10C6 **Fenimore Pass** USA
73E5 **Fenoarivo Atsinanana** Madag
45F7 **Feodosiya** Ukraine
63D2 **Ferdow** Iran
36B2 **Fère** France
36B2 **Fère-Champenoise** France
59F2 **Fergana** Uzbekistan
3J2 **Fergus** *R* Can
11C2 **Fergus Falls** USA
35B4 **Fermanagh** County, N Ire
37E3 **Fermo** Italy
37D1 **Fern** *Mt* Austria
28C1 **Fernandez** Arg
15C2 **Fernandina Beach** USA
xxxG5 **Fernando de Noronha** *I* Atlantic O
29B3 **Fernandópolis** Brazil
70C4 **Fernando Poo** *I* Eq Guinea
18B1 **Ferndale** USA
18C1 **Fernie** Can
19C3 **Fernley** USA
40C2 **Ferrara** Italy
26C5 **Ferreñafe** Peru
17D3 **Ferriday** USA
36B2 **Ferriéres** France
71A2 **Fès** Mor
5G4 **Festubert** Can
17D2 **Festus** USA
41F2 **Feteşti** Rom
64A2 **Fethiye** Turk
45J7 **Fetisovo** Kazakhstan

Fetlar **Gabe's**

34E1 **Fetlar** *I* Scot
53C1 **Fevral'skoye** Russian Fed
48J6 **Feyzabad** Afghan
28B1 **Fiambalá** Arg
73E6 **Fianarantsoa** Madag
72D3 **Fichē** Eth
74D2 **Ficksburg** S Africa
37D2 **Fidenza** Italy
41D2 **Fier** Alb
37D1 **Fiera Di Primeiro** Italy
34D3 **Fife** Region, Scot
34D3 **Fife Ness** *Pen* Scot
38C3 **Figeac** France
39A1 **Figueira da Foz** Port
39C1 **Figueras** Spain
Figueres = Figueras
71B2 **Figuig** Mor
77G2 **Fiji** *Is* Pacific O
27G8 **Filadelpia** Par
41E2 **Filiaşi** Rom
41E3 **Filiatrá** Greece
40C3 **Filicudi** *I* Italy
19C4 **Fillmore** California, USA
19D3 **Fillmore** Utah, USA
37C2 **Finale Ligure** Italy
34C3 **Findhorn** *R* Scot
9E2 **Findlay** USA
3E3 **Findlay,Mt** Can
13D2 **Finger Lakes** USA
73D5 **Fingoè** Mozam
45E8 **Finike** Turk
76C3 **Finke** *R* Aust
75A1 **Finke Flood Flats** Aust
44C3 **Finland** Republic, N Europe
32J7 **Finland,G of** N Europe
6F4 **Finlay** *R* Can
6F4 **Finlay Forks** Can
75C3 **Finley** Aust
32H5 **Finnsnes** Nor
51H7 **Finschhafen** PNG
37C1 **Finsteraarhorn** *Mt* Switz
42C2 **Finsterwalde** Germany
35B4 **Fintona** N Ire
78A3 **Fiordland Nat Pk** NZ
65C2 **Fiq** Syria
45F8 **Firat** *R* Turk
3F2 **Firebag** *R* Can
20B2 **Firebaugh** USA
40C2 **Firenze** Italy
37D2 **Firenzuola** Italy
3C2 **Fireside** Can
28C2 **Firmat** Arg
60D3 **Firozābād** India
60C2 **Firozpur** India
32H7 **Firspång** Sweden
34C4 **Firth of Clyde** *Estuary* Scot
34D3 **Firth of Forth** *Estuary* Scot
34B3 **Firth of Lorn** *Estuary* Scot
33C2 **Firth of Tay** *Estuary* Scot
63C3 **Firūzābād** Iran
74B2 **Fish** *R* Namibia
74C3 **Fish** *R* S Africa
20C2 **Fish Camp** USA
14D2 **Fishers I** USA
7K3 **Fisher Str** Can
35C6 **Fishguard** Wales
1003 **Fish L** Can
7N3 **Fiskenaesset** Greenland
36B2 **Fismes** France
13E2 **Fitchburg** USA
34E2 **Fitful Head** *Pt* Scot
15C2 **Fitzgerald** USA
3F2 **Fitzgerald** Can
76B2 **Fitzroy** *R* Aust
76B2 **Fitzroy Crossing** Aust
12C1 **Fitzwilliam I** Can
Fiume = Rijeka
72C4 **Fizi** Zaïre
74D3 **Flagstaff** S Africa
8B3 **Flagstaff** USA
13E1 **Flagstaff L** USA
35E4 **Flamborough Head** *C* Eng
8C2 **Flaming Gorge Res** USA
34B2 **Flannan Isles** *Is* Scot
10N3 **Flat** *R* Can
3F4 **Flathead** *R* USA
8B2 **Flathead L** USA
17D2 **Flat River** USA
51H8 **Flattery,C** Aust
8A2 **Flattery,C** USA
35D5 **Fleetwood** Eng
32F7 **Flekkefjord** *Inlet* Nor
50H4 **Fleming Deep** Pacific Oc
14C2 **Flemington** USA
42B2 **Flensburg** Germany
5K3 **Fleur-de-Lys** Can
37B1 **Fleurier** Switz
36A2 **Fleury-sur-Andelle** France
76C4 **Flinders** *I* Aust
76D5 **Flinders** *I* Aust
76D2 **Flinders** *R* Aust
76C4 **Flinders Range** *Mts* Aust
6H4 **Flin Flon** Can
9E2 **Flint** USA
35D5 **Flint** Wales
9E3 **Flint** *R* USA
36B1 **Flixecourt** France
12A1 **Floodwood** USA
15B2 **Florala** USA
Florence = Firenze
9E3 **Florence** Alabama, USA
19D4 **Florence** Arizona, USA
16A2 **Florence** Colorado, USA
17C2 **Florence** Kansas, USA
18B2 **Florence** Oregon, USA
9F3 **Florence** S Carolina, USA
20C2 **Florence,L** USA
26C3 **Florencia** Colombia
36C2 **Florenville** Belg
21D3 **Flores** Guatemala
70A1 **Flores** *I* Açores
76B1 **Flores** *I* Indon
28D3 **Flores** *R* Arg
51E7 **Flores S** Indon
27K5 **Floriano** Brazil
25G3 **Florianópolis** Brazil
21D2 **Florida** State, USA
25E4 **Florida** Urug
15E4 **Florida B** USA
15E4 **Florida City** USA
77E1 **Florida Is** Solomon Is
9E4 **Florida Keys** *Is* USA
9E4 **Florida,Strs of** USA
41E2 **Flórina** Greece
32F6 **Florø** Nor
16B3 **Floydada** USA
37D1 **Fluchthorn** *Mt* Austria
57C3 **Fluk** Indon
76D1 **Fly** *R* PNG
37E2 **Foci del Po** *Delta* Italy
41F1 **Focsani** Rom
40D2 **Foggia** Italy
37E3 **Foglia** *R* Italy
5L4 **Fogo** Can
5L4 **Fogo I** Can
70A4 **Fogo** *I* Cape Verde
38C3 **Foix** France
4E4 **Foleyet** Can
7L3 **Foley I** Can
40C2 **Foligno** Italy
35F6 **Folkestone** Eng
15C2 **Folkston** USA
40C2 **Follonica** Italy
20B1 **Folsom** USA
14C1 **Fonda** USA
6H4 **Fond-du-Lac** Can
9E2 **Fond du Lac** USA
38C2 **Fontainebleau** France
3D2 **Fontas** *R* Can
17D2 **Fontenac** USA
38B2 **Fontenay-le-Comte** France
41D1 **Fonyód** Hung
Foochow = Fuzhou
10H3 **Foraker,Mt** USA
36D2 **Forbach** France
75C2 **Forbes** Aust
71H4 **Forcados** Nig
37A3 **Forcalquier** France
20C3 **Ford City** USA
32F6 **Forde** Nor
75C1 **Fords Bridge** Aust
17D3 **Fordyce** USA
70A4 **Forécariah** Guinea
7P3 **Forel,Mt** Greenland
18D1 **Foremost** Can
12C2 **Forest** Can
15B2 **Forest** USA
11D3 **Forest City** Iowa, USA
14C2 **Forest City** Pennsylvania, USA
15C2 **Forest Park** USA
20A1 **Forestville** USA
36B2 **Forêt d'Othe** France
34D3 **Forfar** Scot
16B2 **Forgan** USA
36A2 **Forges-les-Eaux** France
18B1 **Forks** USA
40C2 **Forli** Italy
39C2 **Formentera** *I* Spain
40C2 **Formia** Italy
70A1 **Formigas** *I* Açores
Formosa = Taiwan
25E3 **Formosa** Arg
27J7 **Formosa** Brazil
25D2 **Formosa** State, Arg
52D5 **Formosa Str** Taiwan/China
29C1 **Formoso** Brazil
29C1 **Formoso** *R* Brazil
37D2 **Fornovo di Taro** Italy
34D3 **Forres** Scot
76B4 **Forrest** Aust
9D3 **Forrest City** USA
3G2 **Forrest L** Can
76D2 **Forsayth** Aust
32J6 **Forssa** Fin
75D2 **Forster** Aust
17D2 **Forsyth** Missouri, USA
11A2 **Forsyth** Montana, USA
60C3 **Fort Abbas** Pak
7K4 **Fort Albany** Can
27L4 **Fortaleza** Brazil
34C3 **Fort Augustus** Scot
74D3 **Fort Beaufort** S Africa
18D1 **Fort Benton** USA
19B3 **Fort Bragg** USA
3F2 **Fort Chipewyan** Can
16C2 **Fort Cobb Res** USA
8C2 **Fort Collins** USA
4F4 **Fort Coulonge** Can
13D1 **Fort Coulonge** Can
16B3 **Fort Davis** USA
23E4 **Fort de France** Martinique
15B2 **Fort Deposit** USA
9D2 **Fort Dodge** USA
76A3 **Fortescue** *R* Aust
7J5 **Fort Frances** Can
6F3 **Fort Franklin** Can
6F3 **Fort Good Hope** Can
75B1 **Fort Grey** Aust
34C3 **Forth** *R* Scot
16A3 **Fort Hancock** USA
7K4 **Fort Hope** Can
34F3 **Forties** *Oilfield* N Sea
28B3 **Fortin Uno** Arg
13F1 **Fort Kent** USA
70C1 **Fort Lallemand** Alg
Fort Lamy = Ndjamena
11B3 **Fort Laramie** USA
9E4 **Fort Lauderdale** USA
3D1 **Fort Liard** Can
6G4 **Fort Mackay** Can
6G5 **Fort Macleod** Can
6G4 **Fort McMurray** Can
6E3 **Fort McPherson** Can
12A2 **Fort Madison** USA
8C2 **Fort Morgan** USA
9E4 **Fort Myers** USA
6F4 **Fort Nelson** Can
3D2 **Fort Nelson** *R* Can
6F3 **Fort Norman** Can
15B2 **Fort Payne** USA
11A2 **Fort Peck** USA
8C2 **Fort Peck Res** USA
9E4 **Fort Pierce** USA
11B3 **Fort Pierre** USA
14C1 **Fort Plain** USA
6G3 **Fort Providence** Can
3H3 **Fort Qu'Appelle** Can
10F4 **Fort Randall** USA
6G3 **Fort Resolution** Can
72B4 **Fort Rousset** Congo
6F4 **Fort St James** Can
3D2 **Fort St John** Can
3F3 **Fort Saskatchewan** Can
17D2 **Fort Scott** USA
6E3 **Fort Selkirk** Can
7K4 **Fort Severn** Can
45J7 **Fort Shevchenko** Kazakhstan
6F3 **Fort Simpson** Can
6G3 **Fort Smith** Can
9D3 **Fort Smith** USA
6F3 **Fort Smith** Region, Can
8C3 **Fort Stockton** USA
16B3 **Fort Sumner** USA
16C2 **Fort Supply** USA
18B2 **Fortuna** California, USA
11B2 **Fortuna** N Dakota, USA
5K4 **Fortune B** Can
6G4 **Fort Vermilion** Can
15B2 **Fort Walton Beach** USA
9E2 **Fort Wayne** USA
34C3 **Fort William** Scot
16A2 **Fort Wingate** USA
8D3 **Fort Worth** USA
10K3 **Fortymile** *R* USA
10J2 **Fort Yukon** USA
52C5 **Foshan** China
7K2 **Fosheim** *Pen* Can
37B2 **Fossano** Italy
37E3 **Fossombrone** Italy
11C2 **Fosston** USA
3G2 **Foster L** Can
10L4 **Foster,Mt** USA
72B4 **Fougamou** Gabon
38B2 **Fougères** France
34D1 **Foula** *I* Scot
35F6 **Foulness I** Eng
78B2 **Foulwind,C** NZ
72B3 **Foumban** Cam
38C1 **Fourmies** France
10E5 **Four Mountains,Is of** USA
41F3 **Foúrnoi** *I* Greece
70A3 **Fouta Djallon** *Mts* Guinea
77F5 **Foveaux Str** NZ
35C6 **Fowey** Eng
16B2 **Fowler** USA
12B2 **Fox** *R* USA
3E3 **Fox Creek** Can
7K3 **Foxe Basin** *G* Can
7K3 **Foxe Chan** Can
7L3 **Foxe Pen** Can
10E5 **Fox Is** USA
3F2 **Fox Lake** Can
16A1 **Foxpark** USA
78C2 **Foxton** NZ
3G3 **Fox Valley** Can
73B5 **Foz do Cuene** Angola
25F3 **Foz do Iquaçu** Brazil
22B1 **Fracisco I Madero** Mexico
14B2 **Frackville** USA
28B2 **Fraga** Arg
14E1 **Framingham** USA
27J8 **Franca** Brazil
38C2 **France** Republic, Europe
10N3 **Frances** *R* Can
4D5 **Francesville** USA
38D2 **Franche Comté** Region, France
74D1 **Francistown** Botswana
3C3 **Francois L** Can
18E2 **Francs Peak** *Mt* USA
36E1 **Frankenberg** Germany
12B2 **Frankfort** Indiana, USA
9E3 **Frankfort** Kentucky, USA
14C1 **Frankfort** New York, USA
42B2 **Frankfurt** Germany
74D2 **Frankfurt** S Africa
36E1 **Frankfurt am Main** Germany
42C2 **Frankfurt-an-der-Oder** Germany
42C3 **Fränkischer Alb** *Upland* Germany
18D2 **Franklin** Idaho, USA
12B3 **Franklin** Indiana, USA
17D4 **Franklin** Louisiana, USA
14E1 **Franklin** Massachusetts, USA
15C1 **Franklin** N Carolina, USA
14E1 **Franklin** New Hampshire, USA
14C2 **Franklin** New Jersey, USA
13D2 **Franklin** Pennsylvania, USA
15B1 **Franklin** Tennessee, USA
13D3 **Franklin** Virginia, USA
6F2 **Franklin B** Can
18C1 **Franklin D Roosevelt** *L* USA
6F3 **Franklin Mts** Can
10G1 **Franklin,Pt** USA
6J2 **Franklin Str** Can
14A1 **Franklinville** USA
4E4 **Franz** Can
78B2 **Franz Josef Glacier** NZ
Franz-Joseph-Land = Zemlya Franza Josifa
4F5 **Fraser** *R* Can
74C3 **Fraserburg** S Africa
34D3 **Fraserburgh** Scot
75D1 **Fraser I** Aust
3C3 **Fraser Lake** Can
5J2 **Fraser** *R* Can
37B1 **Frasne** France
37C1 **Frauenfield** Switz
28D2 **Fray Bentos** Urug
33C2 **Frazerburgh** Scot
14C3 **Frederica** USA
42B1 **Fredericia** Den
13D3 **Frederick** Maryland, USA
16C3 **Frederick** Oklahoma, USA
16C3 **Fredericksburg** Texas, USA
13D3 **Fredericksburg** Virginia, USA
10M4 **Frederick Sd** USA
17D2 **Fredericktown** USA
7M5 **Fredericton** Can
7N3 **Frederikshåb** Greenland
32G7 **Frederikshavn** Den
13D2 **Fredonia** USA
32G7 **Fredrikstad** Nor
14C2 **Freehold** USA
20C1 **Freel Peak** *Mt* USA
5L4 **Freels,C** Can
11C3 **Freeman** USA
23B1 **Freeport** Bahamas
5H5 **Freeport** Can
12B2 **Freeport** Illinois, USA
17C4 **Freeport** Texas, USA
17F4 **Freer** USA
70A4 **Freetown** Sierra Leone
42B3 **Freiburg** Germany
36D2 **Freiburg im Breisgau** Germany
28A1 **Freirina** Chile
42C3 **Freistadt** Austria
37B3 **Fréjus** France
76A4 **Fremantle** Aust
20B2 **Fremont** California, USA
17C1 **Fremont** Nebraska, USA
12C2 **Fremont** Ohio, USA
27H3 **French Guiana** Dependency, S America
11A2 **Frenchman** *R* USA
75E3 **Frenchmans Cap** *Mt* Aust
xxixM5 **French Polynesia** *Is* Pacific O
71C1 **Frenda** Alg
21B2 **Fresnillo** Mexico
8B3 **Fresno** USA
20C2 **Fresno** *R* USA
18D1 **Fresno Res** USA
37A1 **Fretigney** France
36E2 **Freudenstadt** Germany
36B1 **Frévent** France
75E3 **Freycinet Pen** Aust
70A3 **Fria** Guinea
20C2 **Friant** USA
20C2 **Friant Dam** USA
28B1 **Frías** Arg
40B1 **Fribourg** Switz
36E1 **Friedberg** Germany
42B3 **Friedrichshafen** Germany
16C4 **Frio** *R* USA
16B3 **Friona** USA
37E1 **Friuli** Region, Italy
7M3 **Frobisher B** Can
7M3 **Frobisher Bay** Can
6H4 **Frobisher L** Can
45G6 **Frolovo** Russian Fed
35D6 **Frome** Eng
75A1 **Frome** *R* Aust
35D6 **Frome** *R* Eng
76C4 **Frome,L** Aust
21C3 **Frontera** Mexico
13D3 **Front Royal** USA
40C2 **Frosinone** Italy
14A3 **Frostburg** USA
16A2 **Fruita** USA
52C5 **Fuchuan** China
52E4 **Fuding** China
21B2 **Fuerte** *R* Mexico
29A3 **Fuerte Olimpo** Brazil
25E2 **Fuerte Olimpo** Par
70A2 **Fuerteventura** *I* Canary Is
52C2 **Fugu** China
50B2 **Fuhai** China
67G1 **Fujairah** UAE
54C3 **Fuji** Japan
52D4 **Fujian** Province, China
53C2 **Fujin** China
54C3 **Fujinomiya** Japan
53D4 **Fuji-san** *Mt* Japan
54C3 **Fujisawa** Japan
54C3 **Fuji-Yoshida** Japan
54D2 **Fukagawa** Japan
48K5 **Fukang** China
53C4 **Fukuchiyima** Japan
54A4 **Fukue** Japan
54A4 **Fukue** *I* Japan
53D4 **Fukui** Japan
53C5 **Fukuoka** Japan
53E4 **Fukushima** Japan
53C5 **Fukuyama** Japan
11C3 **Fulda** USA
42B2 **Fulda** Germany
42B2 **Fulda** *R* Germany
52B4 **Fuling** China
23L1 **Fullarton** Trinidad
20D4 **Fullerton** USA
12A2 **Fulton** Illinois, USA
12B3 **Fulton** Kentucky, USA
13D2 **Fulton** New York, USA
36C1 **Fumay** France
54D3 **Funabashi** Japan
77G1 **Funafuti** *I* Tuvalu
70A1 **Funchal** Medeira
29D2 **Fundão** Brazil
7M5 **Fundy,B of** Can
73D6 **Funhalouro** Mozam
52B5 **Funing** China
52D3 **Funing** China
71H3 **Funtua** Nig
52D4 **Fuqing** China
73D5 **Furancungo** Mozam
54D2 **Furano** Japan
63D3 **Fürg** Iran
37C1 **Furka** *P* Switz
76D5 **Furneaux Group** *Is* Aust
42C2 **Fürstenwalde** Germany
42C3 **Fürth** Germany
54D2 **Furubira** Japan
53D4 **Furukawa** Japan
7K3 **Fury and Hecla Str** Can
53A3 **Fushun** Liaoning, China
52A4 **Fushun** Sichuan, China
53B3 **Fusong** China
42C3 **Füssen** Germany
52E2 **Fu Xian** China
52E1 **Fuxin** China
52D3 **Fuyang** China
53A2 **Fuyu** China
53C2 **Fuyuan** Heilongjiang, China
52E1 **Fuyuan** Liaoning, China
52A4 **Fuyuan** Yunnan, China
50B2 **Fuyun** China
52D4 **Fuzhou** China
42C1 **Fyn** *I* Den

G

72E3 **Gaalkacyo** Somalia
19C3 **Gabbs** USA
20C1 **Gabbs Valley Range** *Mts* USA
73B5 **Gabela** Angola
71E2 **Gabe's** Tunisia

Gabgaba **Gloucester**

66B2 **Gabgaba** *Watercourse* Egypt
20B2 **Gabilan Range** *Mts* USA
72B4 **Gabon** Republic, Africa
74D1 **Gaborone** Botswana
41F2 **Gabrovo** Bulg
63C2 **Gach Sārān** Iran
15B2 **Gadsden** Alabama, USA
19D4 **Gadsden** Arizona, USA
40C2 **Gaeta** Italy
51H6 **Gaferut** *I* Pacific O
15C1 **Gaffney** USA
71D2 **Gafsa** Tunisia
44E4 **Gagarin** Russian Fed
71H3 **Gagere** *R* Nig
7M4 **Gagnon** Can
45G7 **Gagra** Georgia
61C2 **Gaibanda** India
37E1 **Gailtaler Alpen** *Mts* Austria
25C6 **Gaimán** Arg
15C3 **Gainesville** Florida, USA
15C2 **Gainesville** Georgia, USA
17C3 **Gainesville** Texas, USA
35E5 **Gainsborough** Eng
75A2 **Gairdner,L** Aust
34C3 **Gairloch** Scot
14B3 **Gaithersburg** USA
62B1 **Gajendragarh** India
52D4 **Ga Jiang** *R* China
74C2 **Gakarosa** *Mt* S Africa
72D4 **Galana** *R* Kenya
xxxD4 **Galapagos Is** Pacific O
34D4 **Galashiels** Scot
41F1 **Galați** Rom
12C3 **Galax** USA
16A3 **Galeana** Mexico
57C2 **Galela** Indon
6C3 **Galena** Alaska, USA
12A2 **Galena** Illinois, USA
17D2 **Galena** Kansas, USA
23L1 **Galeota Pt** Trinidad
23L1 **Galera Pt** Trinidad
12A2 **Galesburg** USA
14B2 **Galeton** USA
44G4 **Galich** Russian Fed
39A1 **Galicia** Region, Spain
Galilee,S of = Tiberias,L
23J1 **Galina Pt** Jamaica
66C4 **Gallabat** Sudan
37C2 **Gallarate** Italy
15B1 **Gallatin** USA
18D1 **Gallatin** *R* USA
62C3 **Galle** Sri Lanka
16A4 **Gallego** Mexico
39B1 **Gállego** *R* Spain
Gallipoli = Gelibolu
41D2 **Gallipoli** Italy
44C2 **Gällivare** Sweden
34C4 **Galloway** District
35C4 **Galloway,Mull of** *C* Scot
16A2 **Gallup** USA
71H3 **Galma** *R* Nig
21C2 **Galveston** USA
9D4 **Galveston B** USA
28C2 **Galvez** Arg
38D3 **Galvi** Corse
33B3 **Galway** Irish Rep
33B3 **Galway** *B* Irish Rep
57D3 **Gam** *I* Indon
61C2 **Gamba** China
71F3 **Gambaga** Ghana
10D3 **Gambell** USA
70A3 **Gambia** *R* The Gambia/Sen
70A3 **Gambia,The** Republic, Africa
5L4 **Gambo** Can
72B4 **Gamboma** Congo
73B5 **Gambos** Angola
62C3 **Gampola** Sri Lanka
19E3 **Ganado** USA
72E3 **Ganale Dorya** *R* Eth
4F5 **Gananoque** Can
Gand = Gent
73B5 **Ganda** Angola
73C4 **Gandajika** Zaïre
60B3 **Gandava** Pak
7N5 **Gander** Can
60B4 **Gāndhīdhām** India
60C4 **Gāndhīnagar** India
60D4 **Gāndhi Sāgar** *L* India
39B2 **Gandia** Spain
29E1 **Gandu** Brazil
61C3 **Ganga** *R* India
60C3 **Ganganar** India
61D3 **Gangaw** Burma
61E3 **Gangaw Range** *Mts* Burma
52A2 **Gangca** China
59G2 **Gangdise Shan** *Mts* China
Ganges = Ganga
61C2 **Gangtok** India
52B3 **Gangu** China
53A1 **Gan He** *R* China
57C3 **Gani** Indon
53A2 **Gannan** China
18E2 **Gannett Peak** *Mt* USA
52B2 **Ganquan** China
75A3 **Gantheaume** *C* Aust
32K8 **Gantsevichi** Belorussia
71J4 **Ganye** Nig
52D4 **Ganzhou** China
70C3 **Gao** Mali
52A2 **Gaolan** China
52C2 **Gaoping** China
71F3 **Gaoua** Burkina
70A3 **Gaoual** Guinea
52D3 **Gaoyou Hu** *L* China
52C5 **Gaozhou** China
38D3 **Gap** France
57F7 **Gapan** Phil
60D2 **Gar** China
75C1 **Garah** Aust
27L5 **Garanhuns** Brazil
19B2 **Garberville** USA
29C3 **Garça** Brazil
29B3 **Garcias** Brazil
37D2 **Garda** Italy
37A3 **Gardanne** France
16B2 **Garden City** USA
12B1 **Garden Pen** USA
28D3 **Gardey** Arg
60B2 **Gardez** Afghan
18D1 **Gardiner** USA
14D2 **Gardiners I** USA
14E1 **Gardner** USA
77H1 **Gardner** *I* Phoenix Is
20C1 **Gardnerville** USA
37D2 **Gardone** Italy
10C6 **Gareloi** *I* USA
37D2 **Gargano** Italy
60D4 **Garhākota** India
44L4 **Gari** Russian Fed
74B3 **Garies** S Africa
72D4 **Garissa** Kenya
17C3 **Garland** USA
42C3 **Garmisch-Partenkirchen** Germany
63C1 **Garmsar** Iran
17C2 **Garnett** USA
8B2 **Garnett Peak** *Mt* USA
38C3 **Garonne** *R* France
71J4 **Garoua** Cam
71J4 **Garoua Boulai** Cam
11B2 **Garrison** USA
34C3 **Garry** *R* Scot
6H3 **Garry L** Can
56C4 **Garut** Indon
61B3 **Garwa** India
12B2 **Gary** USA
59G2 **Garyarsa** China
6H3 **Gary L** Can
28C1 **Garza** Arg
17C3 **Garza-Little Elm** *Res* USA
63C1 **Gasan Kuli** Turkmenistan
38B3 **Gascogne** Region, France
17D2 **Gasconade** *R* USA
76A3 **Gascoyne** *R* Aust
72B3 **Gashaka** Nig
63E3 **Gasht** Iran
71J3 **Gashua** Nig
5J4 **Gaspé** Can
5H4 **Gaspésie Prov Park** Can
15C1 **Gastonia** USA
15D1 **Gaston,L** USA
65B1 **Gata,C** Cyprus
44D4 **Gatchina** Russian Fed
34D4 **Gateshead** Eng
17C3 **Gatesville** USA
36B2 **Gâtinais** Region, France
4F4 **Gatineau** Can
4F4 **Gatineau** *R* Can
15C1 **Gatlinburg** USA
75D1 **Gatton** Aust
77F2 **Gaua** *I* Vanuatu
63E2 **Gaud-i-Zirreh** *Salt Desert* Afghan
4B2 **Gauer L** Can
61D2 **Gauháti** India
43E1 **Gauja** *R* Latvia
63F1 **Gaurdak** Turkmenistan
61B2 **Gauri Phanta** India
41E4 **Gavdhos** *I* Greece
29D1 **Gavião** *R* Brazil
20B3 **Gaviota** USA
32H6 **Gävle** Sweden
75A2 **Gawler Ranges** *Mts* Aust
52A1 **Gaxun Nur** *L* China
61B3 **Gaya** India
71G3 **Gaya** Niger
53B3 **Gaya** *R* China
12C1 **Gaylord** USA
75D1 **Gayndah** Aust
44J3 **Gayny** Russian Fed
43F3 **Gaysin** Ukraine
64B3 **Gaza** Israel
64C2 **Gaziantep** Turk
70B4 **Gbaringa** Lib
43D2 **Gdańsk** Pol
43D2 **Gdańsk,G of** Pol
32K7 **Gdov** Russian Fed
43D2 **Gdynia** Pol
57C3 **Gebe** *I* Indon
65C4 **Gebel Abu Rûtha** *Mt* Egypt
65C3 **Gebel Araif el Naqa** *Mt* Egypt
65B4 **Gebel Ataqa** *Mt* Egypt
65B4 **Gebel Budhiya** Egypt
65A4 **Gebel el Galâla Baharîya** *Desert* Egypt
65B3 **Gebel El Giddi** *Mt* Egypt
65B4 **Gebel El Tîh** *Upland* Egypt
65B3 **Gebel Halâl** *Mt* Egypt
66C2 **Gebel Hamata** *Mt* Egypt
64B4 **Gebel Katherina** *Mt* Egypt
65B4 **Gebel Kharim** *Mt* Egypt
65B3 **Gebel Libni** *Mt* Egypt
65B3 **Gebel Maghâra** *Mt* Egypt
65C4 **Gebel Sha'îra** *Mt* Egypt
65B4 **Gebel Sinn Bishr** *Mt* Egypt
65B3 **Gebel Yi'allaq** *Mt* Egypt
71E2 **Gebés** Tunisia
22C1 **Gedad del Maiz** Mexico
66C4 **Gedaref** Sudan
41F3 **Gediz** *R* Turk
42C2 **Gedser** Den
36C1 **Geel** Belg
75B3 **Geelong** Aust
75E3 **Geeveston** Aust
71J3 **Geidam** Nig
3H2 **Geikie** *R* Can
36D1 **Geilenkirchen** Germany
72D4 **Geita** Tanz
52A5 **Gejiu** China
40C3 **Gela** Italy
72E3 **Geladi** Eth
36D1 **Geldern** Germany
41F2 **Gelibolu** Turk
64B2 **Gelidonya Burun** Turk
22B1 **Gelleana** Mexico
36E1 **Gelnhausen** Germany
36D1 **Gelsenkirchen** Germany
32F8 **Gelting** Germany
55C5 **Gemas** Malay
36C1 **Gembloux** Belg
71J4 **Gembut** Nig
72B3 **Gemena** Zaïre
64C2 **Gemerek** Turk
64A1 **Gemlik** Turk
40C1 **Gemona** Italy
37E1 **Gemona del Friuli** Italy
74C2 **Gemsbok Nat Pk** Botswana
72C2 **Geneina** Sudan
28C3 **General Acha** Arg
28C3 **General Alvear** Buenos Aires, Arg
28B2 **General Alvear** Mendoza, Arg
28C2 **General Arenales** Arg
28D3 **General Belgrano** Arg
79F2 **General Belgrano** *Base* Ant
79G2 **General Bernardo O'Higgins** *Base* Ant
28C1 **General Capdevia** Arg
28D3 **General Conesa** Buenos Aires, Arg
28C4 **General Conesa** Rio Negro, Arg
25D2 **General Eugenio A Garay** Arg
26F8 **General Eugenio A Garay** Par
20C2 **General Grant Grove Section** *Region* USA
28D3 **General Guido** Arg
28C3 **General La Madrid** Arg
28D3 **General Lavalle** Arg
28C2 **General Levalle** Arg
28D3 **General Madariaga** Arg
25C3 **General Manuel Belgrano** *Mt* Arg
28D3 **General Paz** Buenos Aires, Arg
28D1 **General Paz** Corrientes, Arg
28C3 **General Pico** Arg
28C2 **General Pinto** Arg
28D3 **General Pirán** Arg
25C5 **General Roca** Arg
22B1 **General San Bolivar** Mexico
57G9 **General Santos** Phil
28C3 **General Viamonte** Arg
28C3 **General Villegas** Arg
13D2 **Genesee** *R* USA
13D2 **Geneseo** USA
Geneva = Genève
17C10 **Geneva** Nebraska, USA
14B1 **Geneva** New York, USA
Geneva,L of = Lac Léman
40B1 **Genève** Switz
39B2 **Genil** *R* Spain
Genoa = Genova
75C3 **Genoa** Aust
40B2 **Genova** Italy
36B1 **Gent** Belg
56C4 **Genteng** Indon
42C2 **Genthin** Germany
45H7 **Geokchay** Azerbaijan
74C3 **George** S Africa
7M4 **George** *R* Can
5J4 **George B** Can
75C2 **George,L** Aust
15C3 **George,L** Florida, USA
13E2 **George,L** New York, USA
5K3 **George's Cove** Can
78A2 **George Sd** NZ
75E3 **George Town** Aust
5J4 **Georgetown** Can
20B1 **Georgetown** California, USA
13D3 **Georgetown** Delaware, USA
27G2 **Georgetown** Guyana
12C3 **Georgetown** Kentucky, USA
55C4 **George Town** Malay
23N2 **Georgetown** St Vincent
15D2 **Georgetown** S Carolina, USA
17C3 **Georgetown** Texas, USA
70A3 **Georgetown** The Gambia
79G8 **George V Land** Region, Ant
17F4 **George West** USA
79F12 **Georg Forster** *Base* Ant
45G7 **Georgia**
15C2 **Georgia** State, USA
4E3 **Georgian B** Can
3D4 **Georgia,Str of** Can
76C3 **Georgina** *R* Aust
45G7 **Georgiyevsk** Russian Fed
42C2 **Gera** Germany
36B1 **Geraardsbergen** Belg
78B2 **Geraldine** NZ
76A3 **Geraldton** Aust
4D4 **Geraldton** Can
65C3 **Gerar** *R* Israel
36D2 **Gérardmer** France
6C3 **Gerdine,Mt** USA
10J3 **Gerdova Peak** *Mt* USA
55C4 **Gerik** Malay
11B3 **Gering** USA
45C6 **Gerlachovsky** *Mt* Pol
3D2 **Germanson Lodge** Can
42B2 **Germany** Republic
74D2 **Germiston** S Africa
36D1 **Gerolstein** Germany
39C1 **Gerona** Spain
36E1 **Geseke** Germany
72E3 **Gestro** *R* Eth
39B1 **Getafe** Spain
5J3 **Gethsémani** Can
14B3 **Gettysburg** Pennsylvania, USA
11C2 **Gettysburg** S Dakota, USA
28E1 **Getúlio Vargas** Brazil
56A2 **Geumpang** Indon
64D2 **Gevaş** Turk
41E2 **Gevgelija** Macedonia, Yugos
37B1 **Gex** France
65D2 **Ghabāghib** Syria
70C1 **Ghadamis** Libya
63C1 **Ghaem Shahr** Iran
61B2 **Ghāghara** *R* India
70B4 **Ghana** Republic, Africa
74C1 **Ghanzi** Botswana
71C2 **Ghardaïa** Alg
69A1 **Gharyan** Libya
69A2 **Ghāt** Libya
71B1 **Ghazaouet** Alg
60D3 **Ghāziābād** India
60C3 **Ghazi Khan** Pak
60B2 **Ghazni** Afghan
41F1 **Gheorgheni** Rom
67F3 **Ghubbat al Qamar** *B* Yemen
67G3 **Ghubbat Sawqirah** *B* Oman
68E4 **Ghudamis** Alg
63E2 **Ghurian** Afghan
40D3 **Giarre** Italy
16C1 **Gibbon** USA
74B2 **Gibeon** Namibia
39A2 **Gibraltar** Colony, SW Europe
39A2 **Gibraltar,Str of** Spain/Africa
76B3 **Gibson Desert** Aust
18B1 **Gibsons** Can
62B1 **Giddalūr** India
65B3 **Giddi P** Egypt
72D3 **Gīdolē** Eth
36B3 **Gien** France
42B2 **Giessen** Germany
15C3 **Gifford** USA
53D4 **Gifu** Japan
34C4 **Gigha** *I* Scot
40C2 **Giglio** *I* Italy
39A1 **Gijon** Spain
19D4 **Gila** *R* USA
19D4 **Gila Bend** USA
19D4 **Gila Bend Mts** USA
76D2 **Gilbert** *R* Aust
77G1 **Gilbert Is** Pacific O
3D3 **Gilbert,Mt** Can
18D1 **Gildford** USA
73D5 **Gilé** Mozam
65C2 **Gilead** Region, Jordan
69B2 **Gilf Kebir Plat** Egypt
75C2 **Gilgandra** Aust
60C1 **Gilgit** Pak
60C1 **Gilgit** *R* Pak
75C2 **Gilgunnia** Aust
7J4 **Gillam** Can
75A2 **Gilles** *L* Aust
11A3 **Gillette** USA
3C3 **Gill I** Can
12B1 **Gills Rock** USA
12B2 **Gilman** USA
4F5 **Gilmour** Can
20B2 **Gilroy** USA
4B3 **Gimli** Can
65B3 **Gineifa** Egypt
74E2 **Gingindlovu** S Africa
57G9 **Gingoog** Phil
72E3 **Gīnīr** Eth
41E3 **Gióna** *Mt* Greece
75C3 **Gippsland** *Mts* Aust
12C2 **Girard** USA
26D3 **Girardot** Colombia
34D3 **Girdle Ness** *Pen* Scot
64C1 **Giresun** Turk
66B1 **Girga** Egypt
60C4 **Gir Hills** India
72B3 **Giri** *R* Zaïre
61C3 **Girīdīh** India
60A2 **Girishk** Afghan
36D3 **Giromagny** France
Girona = Gerona
38B2 **Gironde** *R* France
34C4 **Girvan** Scot
78C2 **Gisborne** NZ
36A2 **Gisors** France
72C4 **Gitega** Burundi
Giuba,R = Juba,R
37E2 **Giulia Region,** Italy
41F2 **Giurgiu** Rom
36C1 **Givet** Belg
49S3 **Gizhiga** Russian Fed
43E2 **Gizycko** Pol
41E2 **Gjirokastër** Alb
6J3 **Gjoatlaven** Can
32G6 **Gjøvik** Nor
7M5 **Glace Bay** Can
3C2 **Glacial Mt** Can
3A2 **Glacier B** USA
10L4 **Glacier Bay Nat Mon** USA
3F4 **Glacier Nat Pk** USA
18B1 **Glacier Peak** *Mt* USA
7K2 **Glacier Str** Can
76E3 **Gladstone** Queensland, Aust
75A2 **Gladstone** S Aust, Aust
75E3 **Gladstone** Tasmania, Aust
12B1 **Gladstone** USA
32A1 **Glama** *Mt* Iceland
32G6 **Glåma** *R* Nor
36D2 **Glan** *R* Germany
37C1 **Glarner** *Mts* Switz
37C1 **Glarus** Switz
17C2 **Glasco** USA
12B3 **Glasgow** Kentucky, USA
11A2 **Glasgow** Montana, USA
34C4 **Glasgow** Scot
14C3 **Glassboro** USA
20C2 **Glass Mt** USA
35D6 **Glastonbury** Eng
44J4 **Glazov** Russian Fed
42D3 **Gleisdorf** Austria
78C1 **Glen Afton** NZ
14B3 **Glen Burnie** USA
74E2 **Glencoe** S Africa
19D4 **Glendale** Arizona, USA
20C3 **Glendale** California, USA
11B2 **Glendive** USA
11B3 **Glendo Res** USA
10J3 **Glenhallen** USA
75D1 **Glen Innes** Aust
75C1 **Glenmorgan** Aust
75D2 **Glenreagh** Aust
14B3 **Glen Rock** USA
17C3 **Glen Rose** USA
14D1 **Glens Falls** USA
17D3 **Glenwood** Arkansas, USA
11C2 **Glenwood** Minnesota, USA
16A3 **Glenwood** New Mexico, USA
16A2 **Glenwood Springs** USA
12A1 **Glidden** USA
32F6 **Glittertind** *Mt* Nor
43D2 **Gliwice** Pol
19D4 **Globe** USA
42D2 **Głogów** Pol
32G5 **Glomfjord** Nor
75D2 **Gloucester** Aust

35D6 Gloucester Eng
14E1 Gloucester USA
14C1 Gloversville USA
43F1 Glubokoye Belorussia
45E5 Glukhov Russian Fed
42D3 Gmünd Austria
42C3 Gmunden Austria
43D2 Gniezno Pol
74B2 Goabeg Namibia
62A1 Goa, Daman and Diu Union Territory, India
61D2 Goālpāra India
71F4 Goaso Ghana
72D3 Goba Eth
74B1 Gobabis Namibia
28C2 Gobernador Crespo Arg
28B3 Gobernador Duval Arg
52B1 Gobi Desert China/Mongolia
54C4 Gobo Japan
43G1 Gobza R Russian Fed
74B1 Gochas Namibia
62B1 Godag India
62C1 Godāvari R India
5H4 Godbout Can
20C2 Goddard,Mt USA
4E5 Goderich Can
7N3 Godhavn Greenland
60C4 Godhra India
28B2 Godoy Cruz Arg
4C2 Gods R Can
7J4 Gods L Can
7N3 Godthåb Greenland
Godwin Austen = K2
14E1 Goffstown USA
4E4 Gogama Can
66C4 Gogora Eth
29C2 Goiandira Brazil
29C2 Goianésia Brazil
29C2 Goiânia Brazil
29B2 Goiás Brazil
27J6 Goiás State, Brazil
29B3 Goio-Erê Brazil
72D3 Gojab R Eth
41F2 Gökçeada I Turk
45F8 Goksu R Turk
64C2 Göksun Turk
49M5 Gol R Mongolia
61D2 Golāghāt India
64C2 Gölbaşi Turk
48K2 Gol'chikha Russian Fed
18C2 Golconda USA
14B2 Gold USA
18B2 Gold Beach USA
75D1 Gold Coast Aust
3E3 Golden Can
78B2 Golden B NZ
18B1 Goldendale USA
20A2 Golden Gate Chan USA
17D4 Golden Meadow USA
19C3 Goldfield USA
4C3 Goldpines Can
20D2 Gold Point USA
4A2 Goldsand L Can
16C3 Goldthwaite USA
42C2 Goleniów Pol
20C3 Goleta USA
40B2 Golfe d'Ajaccio G Corse
71E2 Golfe de Gabes G Tunisia
Golfe de Gascogne = Biscay,Bay of
71E1 Golfe de Hammamet G Tunisia
37B3 Golfe de la Napoule G France
40B2 Golfe de St Florent G Corse
38B2 Golfe de St-Malo B France
38C3 Golfe du Lion G France
25B6 Golfo Corcovado G Chile
39B2 Golfo de Almeira G Spain
25B6 Golfo de Ancud G Chile
21D2 Golfo de Batabano G Cuba
23A2 Golfo de Batano G Cuba
39A2 Golfo de Cadiz G Spain
40B3 Golfo de Cagliari G Sardegna
21A1 Golfo de California G Mexico
21D4 Golfo de Chiriqui G Panama
21D3 Golfo de Fonseca Honduras
23B2 Golfo de Guacanayabo G Cuba
26B4 Golfo de Guayaquil G Ecuador
23B5 Golfo del Darien G Colombia/Panama
26B2 Golfo de los Mosquitos G Panama
26A1 Golfo del Papagaya G Nic
39B2 Golfo de Mazarrón G Spain

26A2 Golfo de Nicoya G Costa Rica
40B3 Golfo de Oristano G Sardegna
21E4 Golfo de Panamá G Panama
21D3 Golfo de Papagayo G Costa Rica
23E4 Golfo de Paria G Ven
26F1 Golfo de Paris G Ven
25B7 Golfo de Penas G Chile
38D3 Golfo de St Florent Corse
39C1 Golfo de San Jorge G Spain
21C3 Golfo de Tehuantepec G Mexico
26C3 Golfo de Torugas G Colombia
26C2 Golfo de Uraba G Colombia
39C2 Golfo de Valencia G Spain
37E2 Golfo di Venezia G Italy
23C4 Golfo de Venezuela G Ven
40B2 Golfo di Genova G Italy
40D3 Golfo di Policastro G Italy
40D3 Golfo di Squillace G Italy
40D2 Golfo di Taranto G Italy
37E2 Golfo di Trieste G Italy
40C1 Golfo di Venezia G Italy
21D4 Golfo Dulce G Costa Rica
25C7 Golfo San Jorge G Arg
25D6 Golfo San Matías G Arg
50C3 Golmud China
72E3 Golocha Eth
10F3 Golovin B USA
53F3 Golovnino Russian Fed
72C4 Goma Zaïre
71J3 Gombe Nig
71J3 Gombi Nig
43G2 Gomel Belorussia
70A2 Gomera I Canary Is
21B2 Gómez Palacio Mexico
49O4 Gonam R Russian Fed
63D1 Gonbad-e Kāvūs Iran
61B2 Gonda India
60C4 Gondal India
61B3 Gondia India
64A1 Gönen Turk
41F3 Gönen R Turk
35B5 Goney Irish Rep
61D1 Gongbo'gyamba China
52A4 Gongga Shan Mt China
52A2 Gonghe China
29D1 Gongogi R Brazil
71J3 Gongola R Nig
20B2 Gonzales California, USA
17C4 Gonzales Texas, USA
22C1 Gonzalez Mexico
28C3 Gonzalez Chaves Arg
74B3 Good Hope,C of S Africa
3D3 Good Hope Mt Can
18D2 Gooding USA
16B2 Goodland USA
10F4 Goodnews Bay USA
75C1 Goodooga R Aust
35E5 Goole Eng
75C2 Goolgowi Aust
75A3 Goolwa Aust
76A4 Goomalling Aust
75C2 Goombalie Aust
75D1 Goomer Aust
75D1 Goomeri Aust
75D1 Goondiwindi Aust
7N4 Goose Bay Can
15D2 Goose Creek USA
5J3 Goose R Can
18B2 Goose L USA
62B1 Gooty India
76D1 Goraka PNG
44K3 Gora Koyp Mt Russian Fed
49M4 Gora Munku Sardyk Mt Mongolia/Russian Fed
44K3 Gora Narodnaya Mt Russian Fed
44L2 Gora Pay-Yer Mt Russian Fed
44K3 Gora Telpos-Iz Mt Russian Fed
41D2 Goražde Bosnia-Herzegovina, Yugos
10K2 Gordon USA
3F2 Gordon L Can
13D3 Gordonsville USA
72B3 Goré Chad
72D3 Gorē Eth
78A3 Gore NZ
49P4 Gore Topko Mt Russian Fed
63C1 Gorgān Iran
37C3 Gorgona I Italy
36C1 Gorinchem Neth
64E2 Goris Armenia
40C1 Gorizia Italy
Gorki = Novogorod

44M2 Gorki Russian Fed
44G4 Gor'kovskoye Vodokhranilishche Res Russian Fed
42C2 Gorlitz Germany
45F6 Gorlovka Ukraine
20C3 Gorman USA
41F2 Gorna Orjahovica Bulg
50B1 Gorno-Altaysk Russian Fed
53E1 Gorno Lopatina Mt Russian Fed
53D2 Gorno Medvezh'ya Mt Russian Fed
53C3 Gorno Oblachnaya Mt Russian Fed
53D2 Gorno Tardoki Yani Mt Russian Fed
53E2 Gornozavodsk Russian Fed
53D1 Gornyy Russian Fed
44K3 Goro Denezhkin Kamen' Mt Russian Fed
44G4 Gorodets Russian Fed
43G2 Gorodnya Ukraine
43F1 Gorodok Belorussia
43E3 Gorodok Ukraine
43F3 Gorodok Ukraine
51H7 Goroka PNG
61B2 Gorokhpur India
57D3 Gorong I Indon
73D5 Gorongosa Mozam
57B2 Gorontalo Indon
71G3 Goroubi R Burkina
44L4 Goro Yurma Mt Russian Fed
29D2 Gorutuba R Brazil
49M4 Goryachinsk Russian Fed
45J7 Gory Akkyr Upland Turkmenistan
49L2 Gory Byrranga Mts Russian Fed
43F3 Goryn' R Ukraine
49L3 Gory Putorana Mts Russian Fed
43E2 Góry Świętokrzyskie Upland Pol
32H8 Gorzów Wielkopolski Pol
20C2 Goshen USA
53E3 Goshogawara Japan
45F8 Gosku R Turk
40D2 Gospić Croatia, Yugos
41E2 Gostivar Macedonia, Yugos
43D2 Gostynin Pol
32G7 Göteborg Sweden
72B3 Gotel Mts Nig
16B1 Gothenburg USA
32H7 Gotland I Sweden
53B5 Gotō-retto I Japan
32H7 Gotska Sandön I Sweden
53C4 Gōtsu Japan
36C1 Gouda Neth
72B2 Goudoumaria Niger
xxxH7 Gough I Atlantic O
75C2 Goulburn Aust
70B3 Goumbou Mali
70B3 Goundam Mali
72B2 Gouré Niger
70B3 Gourma Rharous Mali
36A2 Gournay-en-Bray France
72B2 Gouro Chad
18E1 Govenlock Can
51G8 Gove Pen Aust
45C6 Goverla Mt Ukraine
29D2 Governador Valadares Brazil
28D1 Governador Virasoro Arg
61B3 Govind Ballabh Paht Sāgar L India
14A1 Gowanda USA
60B3 Gowārān Afghan
28D1 Goya Arg
72C2 Goz-Beïda Chad
40C3 Gozo I Medit S
66C3 Goz Regeb Sudan
74C3 Graaff-Reinet S Africa
13D1 Gracefield Can
37E2 Grado Italy
75D1 Grafton Aust
11C2 Grafton N Dakota, USA
12C3 Grafton W Virginia, USA
3D2 Graham R Can
3B3 Graham I Can
3F2 Graham L Can
19E4 Graham,Mt USA
74D3 Grahamstown S Africa
27J5 Grajaú Brazil
43E2 Grajewo Pol
41E2 Grámmos Mt Greece/Alb
34D3 Grampian Region, Scot
34C3 Grampian Mts Scot
26D3 Granada Colombia
26A1 Granada Nic
39B2 Granada Spain
5G4 Granby Can
16A1 Granby USA
70A2 Gran Canaria I Canary Is

25D3 Gran Chaco Region Arg
12B2 Grand R Michigan, USA
17D1 Grand R Missouri, USA
23Q2 Grand B Dominica
9F4 Grand Bahama I Bahamas
36D3 Grand Ballon Mt France
7N5 Grand Bank Can
xxxF1 Grand Banks Atlantic O
71F4 Grand Bassam Ivory Coast
37B2 Grand Bérard Mt France
19D3 Grand Canyon USA
19D3 Grand Canyon Nat Pk USA
23A3 Grand Cayman I Caribbean
3F3 Grand Centre Can
18C1 Grand Coulee USA
28B3 Grande R Arg
27K6 Grande R Bahia, Brazil
29C2 Grande R Minas Gerais/São Paulo, Brazil
3E3 Grande Cache Can
5H4 Grande Cascapédia Can
37A2 Grande Chartreuse Region, France
73E5 Grande Comore I Comoros
3E2 Grande Prairie Can
17C3 Grande Prairie USA
72B2 Grand Erg de Bilma Desert Region Niger
70B2 Grand erg Occidental Mts Alg
70C2 Grand erg Oriental Mts Alg
5J4 Grande Rivière Can
7L4 Grande Rivière de la Baleine R Can
18C1 Grande Ronde R USA
19D4 Gran Desierto USA
5H4 Grande Vallée Can
7M5 Grand Falls New Brunswick, Can
7N5 Grand Falls Newfoundland, Can
18C1 Grand Forks Can
11C2 Grand Forks USA
14C1 Grand Gorge USA
12B2 Grand Haven USA
16C1 Grand Island USA
17E3 Grand Isle USA
16A2 Grand Junction USA
5K4 Grand L Can
17D4 Grand L USA
5H5 Grand Manan I Can
12A1 Grand Marais USA
5G4 Grand Mère Can
5K3 Grandois Can
39A2 Grândola Port
6J4 Grand Rapids Can
12B2 Grand Rapids Michigan, USA
12A1 Grand Rapids Minnesota, USA
37B2 Grand St Bernard P Italy/Switz
8B2 Grand Teton Mt USA
18D2 Grand Teton Nat Pk USA
16A2 Grand Valley USA
36A2 Grandvilliers France
21D1 Grangeburg USA
18C1 Grangeville USA
4B5 Granite Falls USA
18E1 Granite Peak Mt Montana, USA
19D2 Granite Peak Mt Utah, USA
39C1 Granollérs Spain
40B1 Gran Paradiso Mt Italy
37D1 Gran Pilastro Mt Austria/Italy
35E5 Grantham Eng
20C1 Grant,Mt USA
34D3 Grantown-on-Spey Scot
16A2 Grants USA
18B2 Grants Pass USA
38B2 Granville France
14D1 Granville USA
6H4 Granville L Can
29D2 Grão Mogol Brazil
20C3 Grapevine USA
20D2 Grapevine Mts USA
74E1 Graskop S Africa
38D3 Grasse France
18E1 Grassrange USA
19B3 Grass Valley USA
5L4 Grates Pt Can
25F4 Gravatai Brazil
6H5 Gravelbourg Can
36B1 Gravelines France
73D6 Gravelotte S Africa
4F5 Gravenhurst Can
18D1 Grave Peak Mt USA
75D1 Gravesend Aust
10M4 Gravina I USA
37A1 Gray France
10F3 Grayling USA

4E5 Grayling Michigan, USA
18B1 Grays Harbor B USA
18D2 Grays L USA
12C3 Grayson USA
12B3 Grayville USA
42D3 Graz Austria
23H1 Great R Jamaica
9F4 Great Abaco I Bahamas
76B4 Great Australian Bight G Aust
14E1 Great B New Hampshire, USA
14C3 Great B New Jersey, USA
21E2 Great Bahama Bank Bahamas
78C1 Great Barrier I NZ
76D2 Great Barrier Reef Is Aust
14D1 Great Barrington USA
19C2 Great Basin USA
10O2 Great Bear R Can
6F3 Great Bear L Can
16C2 Great Bend USA
65B3 Great Bitter L Egypt
14A3 Great Cacapon USA
62E2 Great Coco I Burma
76D3 Great Dividing Range Mts Aust
35E4 Great Driffield Eng
14C3 Great Egg Harbor B USA
79F10 Greater Antarctic Region, Ant
23B2 Greater Antilles Is Caribbean
35E6 Greater London County, Eng
35D5 Greater Manchester County, Eng
21E2 Great Exuma I Bahamas
18D1 Great Falls USA
74D3 Great Fish R S Africa
34C3 Great Glen V Scot
61C2 Great Himalayan Range Mts Asia
9F4 Great Inagua I Bahamas
74C3 Great Karroo Mts S Africa
74D3 Great Kei R S Africa
75E3 Great L Aust
73B6 Great Namaland Region, Namibia
62E3 Great Nicobar I Indian O
35D5 Great Ormes Head C Wales
14E2 Great Pt USA
9F4 Great Ragged I Bahamas
73D4 Great Ruaha R Tanz
13E2 Great Sacandaga L USA
18D2 Great Salt L USA
18D2 Great Salt Lake Desert USA
69B2 Great Sand Sea Libya/Egypt
76B3 Great Sandy Desert Aust
8A2 Great Sandy Desert USA
Great Sandy I = Fraser I
10C6 Great Sitkin, I USA
6G3 Great Slave L Can
15C1 Great Smoky Mts USA
15C1 Great Smoky Mts Nat Pk USA
3D2 Great Snow Mt Can
14D2 Great South B USA
74C3 Great Tafelberg Mt S Africa
76B3 Great Victoria Desert Aust
52B2 Great Wall China
35F5 Great Yarmouth Eng
65C1 Greco,C Cyprus
41E3 Greece Republic, Europe
13D2 Greece USA
16B1 Greeley USA
7K1 Greely Fjord Can
12B3 Green R Kentucky, USA
19D3 Green R Utah, USA
12B1 Green B USA
12B2 Green Bay USA
48H1 Green Bell, Ostrov I Russian Fed
12B3 Greencastle Indiana, USA
14B3 Greencastle Pennsylvania, USA
14C1 Greene USA
15C1 Greeneville USA
20B2 Greenfield California, USA
20C3 Greenfield California, USA
14D1 Greenfield Massachusetts, USA
12B2 Greenfield Wisconsin, USA
5G4 Greening Can
3G3 Green Lake Can
7O2 Greenland Dependency, N Atlantic
xxxH1 Greenland Basin Greenland S
79B1 Greenland S Greenland
34C4 Greenock Scot
14D2 Greenport USA

Green River Hamburg

19D3 **Green River** Utah, USA
18E2 **Green River** Wyoming, USA
14C3 **Greensboro** Maryland, USA
15D1 **Greensboro** N Carolina, USA
16C2 **Greensburg** Kansas, USA
12B3 **Greensburg** Kentucky, USA
13D2 **Greensburg** Pennsylvania, USA
34C3 **Greenstone** *Pt* Scot
12B3 **Greenup** USA
19D4 **Green Valley** USA
15B2 **Greenville** Alabama, USA
70B4 **Greenville** Lib
17D3 **Greenville** Mississippi, USA
15D1 **Greenville** N Carolina, USA
14E1 **Greenville** N Hampshire, USA
12C2 **Greenville** Ohio, USA
15C2 **Greenville** S Carolina, USA
17C3 **Greenville** Texas, USA
51H8 **Greenville,C** Aust
35F6 **Greenwich** Eng
14D2 **Greenwich** USA
14C3 **Greenwood** Delaware, USA
17D3 **Greenwood** Mississippi, USA
15C2 **Greenwood** S Carolina, USA
17D2 **Greers Ferry L** USA
11C3 **Gregory** USA
75A1 **Gregory,L** Aust
76D2 **Gregory Range** *Mts* Aust
42C2 **Greifswald** Germany
44F2 **Gremikha** Russian Fed
42C1 **Grenå** Den
17E3 **Grenada** USA
23E4 **Grenada** *I* Caribbean
75C2 **Grenfell** Aust
3H3 **Grenfell** Can
38D2 **Grenoble** France
23M2 **Grenville** Grenada
76D2 **Grenville,C** Aust
18B1 **Gresham** USA
56D4 **Gresik** Jawa, Indon
56B3 **Gresik** Sumatera, Indon
17D4 **Gretna** USA
78B2 **Grey** *R* NZ
18E2 **Greybull** USA
10L3 **Grey Hunter Pk** *Mt* Can
7N4 **Grey Is** Can
14D1 **Greylock,Mt** USA
78B2 **Greymouth** NZ
76D3 **Grey Range** *Mts* Aust
35B5 **Greystones** Irish Rep
74E2 **Greytown** S Africa
74C2 **Griekwastad** S Africa
15C2 **Griffin** USA
75C2 **Griffith** Aust
76D5 **Grim,C** Aust
13D2 **Grimsby** Can
35E5 **Grimsby** Eng
32B1 **Grimsey** *I* Iceland
3E2 **Grimshaw** Can
32F7 **Grimstad** Nor
37C1 **Grindelwald** Switz
11D3 **Grinnell** USA
7J2 **Grinnell Pen** Can
7K2 **Grise Fjord** Can
44J3 **Griva** Russian Fed
10O2 **Grizzly Bear** *Mt* Can
32J7 **Grobina** Latvia
74D2 **Groblersdal** S Africa
37E1 **Gröbming** Austria
43E2 **Grodno** Belorussia
61B2 **Gromati** *R* India
42B2 **Groningen** Neth
16B2 **Groom** USA
74C3 **Groot** *R* S Africa
76C2 **Groote Eylandt** *I* Aust
73B5 **Grootfontein** Namibia
74B2 **Groot-Karasberge** *Mts* Namibia
74C1 **Groot Laagte** *R* Botswana
74C2 **Groot Vloer** *Salt L* S Africa
23P2 **Gros Islet** St Lucia
5K4 **Gros Morne Nat Park** Can
36E1 **Grosser Feldberg** *Mt* Germany
40C2 **Grosseto** Italy
36E2 **Gross-Gerau** Germany
42C3 **Grossglockner** *Mt* Austria
37E1 **Gross Venediger** *Mt* Austria
10G4 **Grosvenor,L** USA
18D2 **Gros Ventre Range** *Mts* USA
5K3 **Groswater B** Can
11C2 **Groton** USA
4E4 **Groundhog** *R* Can
15B2 **Grove Hill** USA
20B2 **Groveland** USA
20B3 **Grover City** USA
13E2 **Groveton** USA
45H7 **Groznyy** Russian Fed
43D2 **Grudziądz** Pol
74B2 **Grünau** Namibia
34E2 **Grutness** Scot
45G5 **Gryazi** Russian Fed
44G4 **Gryazovets** Russian Fed
25J8 **Grytviken** South Georgia
29D3 **Guaçuí** Brazil
22B1 **Guadalajara** Mexico
39B1 **Guadalajara** Spain
77E1 **Guadalcanal** *I* Solomon Is
39B2 **Guadalimar** *R* Spain
39B1 **Guadalope** *R* Spain
39B2 **Guadalqivir** *R* Spain
21B2 **Guadalupe** Mexico
20B3 **Guadalupe** USA
2G6 **Guadalupe** *I* Mexico
16C4 **Guadalupe** *R* USA
16B3 **Guadalupe Nat Pk** USA
16B3 **Guadalupe Peak** *Mt* USA
22B1 **Guadalupe Victoria** Mexico
22B1 **Guadarupe** Mexico
23E3 **Guadeloupe** *I* Caribbean
39B2 **Guadian** *R* Spain
39A2 **Guadiana** *R* Port
39B2 **Guadian** *R* Spain
39B2 **Guadix** Spain
29B3 **Guaira** Brazil
26E6 **Guajará Mirim** Brazil
26D1 **Guajira,Pen de** Colombia
26C4 **Gualaceo** Ecuador
37E3 **Gualdo Tadino** Italy
28D2 **Gualeguay** Arg
28D2 **Gualeguaychú** Arg
51H5 **Guam** *I* Pacific O
28C3 **Guamini** Arg
55C5 **Gua Musang** Malay
22B1 **Guanajuato** Mexico
22B1 **Guanajuato** State, Mexico
29D1 **Guanambi** Brazil
26E2 **Guanare** Ven
28B1 **Guandacol** Arg
21D2 **Guane** Cuba
52C5 **Guangdong** Province, China
52A3 **Guanghan** China
52C3 **Guanghua** China
52A4 **Guangmao Shan** *Mt* China
52A5 **Guangnan** China
52B3 **Guangyuan** China
52D4 **Guangze** China
52C5 **Guangzhon** China
46G4 **Guangzhou** China
29D2 **Guanhães** Brazil
26E3 **Guania** *R* Colombia
23E5 **Guanipa** *R* Ven
23B2 **Guantánamo** Cuba
52D1 **Guanting Shuiku** *Res* China
52B5 **Guanxi** Province, China
52A3 **Guan Xian** China
26C2 **Guapa** Colombia
28E1 **Guaporé** Brazil
28E1 **Guaporé** *R* Brazil
26F6 **Guaporé** *R* Brazil/Bol
26E7 **Guaquí** Bol
29D1 **Guará** *R* Brazil
29B4 **Guarapuava** Brazil
29C4 **Guaraqueçaba** Brazil
29C3 **Guaratinguetá** Brazil
39A1 **Guarda** Port
29C2 **Guarda Mor** Brazil
28B1 **Guardia** Chile
28C4 **Guardia Mitre** Arg
28E1 **Guarita** *R* Brazil
8C4 **Guasave** Mexico
37D2 **Guastalla** Italy
21C3 **Guatemala** Guatemala
21C3 **Guatemala** Republic, C America
28C3 **Guatraché** Arg
26D3 **Guavrare** *R* Colombia
29C3 **Guaxupé** Brazil
23L1 **Guayaguayare** Trinidad
26B4 **Guayaquil** Ecuador
21A2 **Guaymas** Mexico
28D2 **Guayquiraro** *R* Arg
73C5 **Guba** Zaïre
49P2 **Guba Buorkhaya** *B* Russian Fed
72E3 **Guban** *Region* Somalia
57F8 **Gubat** Phil
37E3 **Gubbio** Italy
42C2 **Gubin** Pol
71J3 **Gubio** Nig
62B2 **Güdür** India
36D3 **Guebwiller** France
71D1 **Guelma** Alg
4E5 **Guelph** Can
70A2 **Guelta Zemmur** Mor
22C1 **Güemez** Mexico
23A2 **Guenabacoa** Cuba
71C2 **Guerara** Alg
72C2 **Guéréda** Chad
38C2 **Guéret** France
11B3 **Guernsey** USA
38B2 **Guernsey** *I* UK
22B2 **Guerrero** State, Mexico
72D3 **Gughe** *Mt* Eth
49O4 **Gugigu** China
51H5 **Guguan** *I* Pacific O
75C2 **Guiargambone** Aust
28D2 **Guichón** Urug
71J4 **Guider** Cam
52C4 **Guidong** China
70B4 **Guiglo** Ivory Coast
74E1 **Guija** Mozam
52C5 **Gui Jiang** *R* China
35E6 **Guildford** Eng
52C4 **Guilin** China
37B2 **Guillestre** France
52A2 **Guinan** China
20A1 **Guinda** USA
70A3 **Guinea** Republic, Africa
xxxH4 **Guinea Basin** Atlantic O
70A3 **Guinea-Bissau** Republic, Africa
70C4 **Guinea,G of** W Africa
23A2 **Güines** Cuba
70B3 **Guir** *Well* Mali
60C2 **Guiranwala** Pak
29B2 **Guiratinga** Brazil
26F1 **Güiria** Ven
36B2 **Guise** France
57G8 **Guiuan** Phil
52B5 **Gui Xian** China
52B4 **Guiyang** China
52B4 **Guizhou** Province, China
60C4 **Gujarāt** State, India
60C2 **Gujrat** Pak
62B1 **Gulbarga** India
43F1 **Gulbene** Latvia
62B1 **Guledagudda** India
15B2 **Gulfport** USA
58D3 **Gulf,The** S W Asia
75C2 **Gulgong** Aust
53A1 **Gulian** China
52B4 **Gulin** China
10J3 **Gulkana** USA
10J3 **Gulkana** *R* USA
3F3 **Gull L** Can
3G3 **Gull Lake** Can
72D3 **Gulu** Uganda
75C1 **Guluguba** Aust
56F6 **Gulung Chamah** *Mt* Malay
71H3 **Gumel** Nig
36D1 **Gummersbach** Germany
71H3 **Gummi** Nig
61B3 **Gumpla** India
64C1 **Gümüşhane** Turk
64C2 **Gümüşhane** Turk
60D4 **Guna** India
72D2 **Guna** *Mt* Eth
75C3 **Gundagai** Aust
72B4 **Gungu** Zaïre
4B3 **Gunisao** *R* Can
4B3 **Gunisao L** Can
7Q3 **Gunnbjørn Fjeld** *Mt* Greenland
75D2 **Gunnedah** Aust
16A2 **Gunnison** USA
16A2 **Gunnison** *R* USA
62B1 **Guntakal** India
15B2 **Guntersville** USA
15B2 **Guntersville L** USA
62C1 **Guntūr** India
55C5 **Gunung Batu Putch** *Mt* Malay
56G7 **Gunung Benom** *Mt* Malay
56E3 **Gunung Besar** *Mt* Indon
56F6 **Gunung Besar** *Mt* Malay
56G7 **Gunung Besar** *Mt* Malay
56E2 **Gunung Bulu** *Mt* Indon
56B3 **Gunung Gedang** *Mt* Indon
56A2 **Gunung Geureudong** *Mt* Indon
56A2 **Gunung Kulabu** *Mt* Indon
56D2 **Gunung Lawit** *Mt* Malay
56D4 **Gunung Lawu** *Mt* Indon
56A2 **Gunung Leuser** *Mt* Indon
57B3 **Gunung Lokilalaka** *Mt* Indon
57B3 **Gunung Mekongga** *Mt* Indon
56E2 **Gunung Menyapa** *Mt* Indon
56E2 **Gunung Niapa** *Mt* Indon
57B2 **Gunung Ogoamas** *Mt* Indon
56B3 **Gunung Patah** *Mt* Indon
56D4 **Gunung Raung** *Mt* Indon
56B3 **Gunung Resag** *Mt* Indon
56E3 **Gunung Sarempaka** *Mt* Indon
56A2 **Gunungsitoli** Indon
56D4 **Gunung Sumbing** *Mt* Indon
55C5 **Gunung Tahan** *Mt* Malay
56B2 **Gunung Talakmau** *Mt* Indon
56G7 **Gunung Tapis** *Mt* Malay
57B3 **Gunung Tokala** *Mt* Indon
73B5 **Gunza** Angola
52D3 **Guoyang** China
26C4 **Guranda** Ecuador
71H4 **Gurara** Nig
60D2 **Gurdāspur** India
60D3 **Gurgaon** India
61B2 **Gurkha** Nepal
37E1 **Gurktaler Alpen** *Mts* Austria
53D1 **Gurskoye** Russian Fed
64C2 **Gürün** Turk
27J4 **Gurupi** *R* Brazil
73D5 **Guruve** Zim
52A1 **Gurvan Sayhan Uul** *Upland* Mongolia
45J6 **Gur'yev** Kazakhstan
71H3 **Gusau** Nig
43E2 **Gusev** Russian Fed
53A4 **Gushan** China
44G4 **Gus'Khrustalnyy** Russian Fed
10L4 **Gustavus** USA
20B2 **Gustine** USA
42B2 **Gütersloh** Germany
12B3 **Guthrie** Kentucky, USA
17C2 **Guthrie** Oklahoma, USA
16B3 **Guthrie** Texas, USA
22C1 **Gutiérrez Zamora** Mexico
11D3 **Guttenberg** USA
27G3 **Guyana** Republic, S America
xxxF4 **Guyana Basin** Atlantic O
52C1 **Guyang** China
38B3 **Guyenne** Region, France
16B2 **Guymon** USA
75D2 **Guyra** Aust
52B2 **Guyuan** China
63F1 **Guzar** Turkmenistan
61D4 **Gwa** Burma
75C2 **Gwabegar** Aust
71H3 **Gwadabawa** Nig
60D3 **Gwalior** India
74D1 **Gwanda** Zim
72C3 **Gwane** Zaïre
63E3 **Gwardar** Pak
68G9 **Gwelo** Zim
35D6 **Gwent** County, Wales
73C5 **Gweru** Zim
75C1 **Gwydir** *R* Aust
35D4 **Gwynedd** Wales
61C2 **Gyangzê** China
50C3 **Gyaring Hu** *L* China
48J2 **Gydanskiy Poluostrov** *Pen* Russian Fed
61C2 **Gyirong** China
7O3 **Gyldenløves** *Fjord* Greenland
75D1 **Gympie** Aust
43D3 **Gyöngyös** Hung
43D3 **Györ** Hung
4B3 **Gypsumville** Can

H

77H2 **Ha'apai Group** *Is* Tonga
32K6 **Haapajärvi** Fin
44C4 **Haapsalu** Estonia
42A2 **Haarlem** Neth
36D1 **Haarstrang** Region, Germany
21D2 **Habana** Cuba
67F3 **Habarūt** Oman
67E4 **Habbān** Yemen
61D3 **Habiganj** Bang
53F3 **Habomai Shoto** *I* Russian Fed
53D5 **Hachijō-jima** *I* Japan
54C3 **Hachiman** Japan
53E3 **Hachinohe** Japan
54C3 **Hachioji** Japan
14C2 **Hackettstown** USA
75A2 **Hack,Mt** Aust
67G3 **Hadbaram** Oman
34D4 **Haddington** Scot
75B1 **Haddon Corner** Aust
75B1 **Haddon Downs** Aust
71J3 **Hadejia** Nig
71H3 **Hadejia** *R* Nig
65C2 **Hadera** Israel
42B1 **Haderslev** Den
67F4 **Hadiboh** Socotra
6H2 **Hadley B** Can
54A3 **Hadong** S Korea
52B5 **Hadong** Vietnam
67E3 **Haḑramawt** Region, Yemen
42C1 **Hadsund** Den
53B4 **Haeju** N Korea
54A3 **Haeju-man** *B* N Korea
54A4 **Haenam** S Korea
67E1 **Hafar al Bātin** S Arabia
7M2 **Haffners Bjerg** *Mt* Greenland
66B3 **Hafir** Sudan
60C2 **Hafizabad** Pak
61D2 **Hāflong** India
32A2 **Hafnafjörður** Iceland
66B4 **Hag'Abdullah** Sudan
10F4 **Hagemeister** *I* USA
42B2 **Hagen** Germany
14B3 **Hagerstown** USA
54B4 **Hagi** Japan
52A5 **Ha Giang** Vietnam
36D2 **Hagondange** France
36D2 **Haguenan** France
70A2 **Hagunia** *Well* Mor
50H4 **Haha-jima** *I* Japan
50C3 **Hah Xil Hu** *L* China
53A3 **Haicheng** China
55D1 **Hai Duong** Viet
65C2 **Haifa** Israel
65C2 **Haifa,B of** Israel
52D2 **Hai He** *R* China
52C5 **Haikang** China
55E1 **Haikou** China
66D1 **Ha'il** S Arabia
61D3 **Hailākāndi** India
49N5 **Hailar** China
53B3 **Hailong** China
53B2 **Hailun** China
32J5 **Hailuoto** *I* Fin
55D2 **Hainan** *I* China
10L4 **Haines** USA
10L3 **Haines Junction** Can
42D3 **Hainfeld** Austria
52B5 **Haiphong** Vietnam
23C3 **Haiti** Republic, Caribbean
20D2 **Haiwee Res** USA
72D2 **Haiya** Sudan
52A2 **Haiyan** China
52B2 **Haiyuan** China
52D3 **Haizhou Wan** *B* China
43E3 **Hajdúböszörmény** Hung
66D3 **Hajfah** Yemen
54C3 **Hajiki-saki** *Pt* Japan
61D3 **Haka** Burma
20E5 **Hakalau** Hawaiian Is
Hakha = Haka
64D2 **Hakkâri** Turk
53E3 **Hakodate** Japan
54C3 **Hakui** Japan
54C3 **Haku-san** *Mt* Japan
45F8 **Ḥalab** Syria
64E3 **Halabja** Iraq
72D1 **Halaib** Sudan
65D1 **Halba** Leb
50C2 **Halban** Mongolia
42C2 **Halberstadt** Germany
57F8 **Halcon,Mt** Phil
32G7 **Halden** Nor
61C3 **Haldia** India
60D3 **Haldwāni** India
3D2 **Halfway** *R* Can
4F4 **Haliburton** Can
4F4 **Haliburton Highlands** Can
7M5 **Halifax** Can
35E5 **Halifax** Eng
13D3 **Halifax** USA
10H1 **Halkett,C** USA
54A4 **Halla-San** *Mt* S Korea
7M1 **Hall Basin** *Sd* Can/Greenland
7K3 **Hall Beach** Can
36C1 **Halle** Belg
42C2 **Halle** Germany
79F1 **Halley** *Base* Ant
13D1 **Halleybury** Can
10D3 **Hall I** USA
11B2 **Halliday** USA
32F6 **Hallingdal** *R* Nor
11C2 **Hallock** USA
7M3 **Hall Pen** Can
76B2 **Hall's Creek** Aust
14C2 **Hallstead** USA
57C2 **Halmahera** *I* Indon
57C3 **Halmahera S** Indon
32G7 **Halmstad** Sweden
42B2 **Haltern** Germany
32J5 **Haltia** *Mt* Nor
34D4 **Haltwhistle** Eng
67F1 **Halul** *I* Qatar
65C3 **Haluza** *Hist Site* Israel
54B4 **Hamada** Japan
70C2 **Hamada de Tinrhert** *Desert Region* Alg
70B2 **Hamada du Dra** *Upland* Alg
63B2 **Hamadān** Iran
70B2 **Hamada Tounassine** Region, Alg
45F8 **Ḥamāh** Syria
54C4 **Hamamatsu** Japan
32G6 **Hamar** Nor
54D1 **Hama-Tombetsu** Japan
62C3 **Hambantota** Sri Lanka
17D3 **Hamburg** Arkansas, USA
17C1 **Hamburg** Iowa, USA

Hamburg Hilo

14A1 **Hamburg** New York, USA
14C2 **Hamburg** Pennsylvania, USA
42B2 **Hamburg** Germany
14D2 **Hamden** USA
32J6 **Hämeenlinna** Fin
76A3 **Hamersley Range** *Mts* Aust
53B3 **Hamgyong Sanmaek** *Mts* N Korea
53B3 **Hamhŭng** N Korea
50C2 **Hami** China
65C1 **Hamīdīyah** Syria
15B2 **Hamilton** Alabama, USA
75B3 **Hamilton** Aust
4F5 **Hamilton** Can
18D1 **Hamilton** Montana, USA
14C1 **Hamilton** New York, USA
78C1 **Hamilton** NZ
12C3 **Hamilton** Ohio, USA
34C4 **Hamilton** Scot
20B2 **Hamilton,Mt** USA
32K6 **Hamina** Fin
61B2 **Hamirpur** India
54A3 **Hamju** N Korea
42B2 **Hamm** Germany
69A2 **Hammādāh al Hamra** *Upland* Libya
32H6 **Hammerdal** Sweden
32J4 **Hammerfest** Nor
4F5 **Hammond** Can
12B2 **Hammond** Illinois, USA
17D3 **Hammond** Louisiana, USA
11B2 **Hammond** Montana, USA
14C3 **Hammonton** USA
78B3 **Hampden** NZ
35E6 **Hampshire** County, Eng
17D3 **Hampton** Arkansas, USA
11D3 **Hampton** Iowa, USA
14E1 **Hampton** New Hampshire, USA
13D3 **Hampton** Virginia, USA
63D3 **Hāmūn-e Jaz Mūrīan** *L* Iran
60B3 **Hamun-i-Lora** *Salt L* Pak
63E3 **Hamun-i Mashkel** *Salt Plain* Pak
54A3 **Han** *R* S Korea
20E5 **Hana** Hawaiian Is
20E5 **Hanalei** Hawaiian Is
53E4 **Hanamaki** Japan
36E1 **Hanau** Germany
52C2 **Hancheng** China
52C3 **Hanchuan** China
13D3 **Hancock** Maryland, USA
12B1 **Hancock** Michigan, USA
14C2 **Hancock** New York, USA
54C4 **Handa** Japan
52C2 **Handan** China
72D4 **Handeni** Tanz
20C2 **Hanford** USA
52B2 **Hanggin Qi** China
32J7 **Hangö** Fin
52E3 **Hangzhou** China
52E3 **Hangzhou Wan** *B* China
66D4 **Hanīsh** *I* Yemen
11C2 **Hankinson** USA
19D3 **Hanksville** USA
78B2 **Hanmer Springs** NZ
3F3 **Hanna** Can
4E3 **Hannah B** Can
17D2 **Hannibal** USA
42B2 **Hannover** Germany
32G7 **Hanöbukten** *B* Sweden
55D1 **Hanoi** Viet
74C3 **Hanover** S Africa
14B3 **Hanover** USA
25B8 **Hanover** *I* Chile
52B3 **Han Shui** China
52C3 **Han Shui** *R* China
60D3 **Hānsi** India
50D2 **Hantay** Mongolia
52B3 **Hanzhong** China
61C3 **Hāora** India
32J5 **Haparanda** Sweden
54A3 **Hapch'on** S Korea
28D1 **Hapevi** Brazil
61D2 **Hāpoli** India
5J3 **Happy Valley** Can
64C4 **Haql** S Arabia
66D3 **Harad** Yemen
67E2 **Haradh** S Arabia
72E3 **Hara Fanna** Eth
66D3 **Haraja** S Arabia
54D3 **Haramachi** Japan
72E3 **Harar** Eth
73D5 **Harare** Zim
72C2 **Harazé** Chad
53B2 **Harbin** China
12C2 **Harbor Beach** USA
5K3 **Harbour Deep** Can
5L4 **Harbour Grace** Can
60D4 **Harda** India
32F6 **Hardangerfjord** *Inlet* Nor
11A2 **Hardin** USA
36D2 **Hardt** Region, Germany
75A2 **Hardwicke B** Aust
17D2 **Hardy** USA
5K3 **Hare B** Can
72E3 **Harēr** Eth
72E3 **Hargeysa** Somalia
65C3 **Har Hakippa** *Mt* Israel
50C3 **Harhu** *L* China
56B3 **Hari** *R* Indon
67E4 **Harīb** Yemen
54B4 **Harima-nada** *B* Japan
12C3 **Harlan** USA
18E1 **Harlem** USA
42B2 **Harlingen** Neth
17F4 **Harlingen** USA
35F6 **Harlow** Eng
18E1 **Harlowtown** USA
65C2 **Har Meron** *Mt* Israel
18C2 **Harney Basin** USA
18C2 **Harney L** USA
32H6 **Härnösand** Sweden
49L5 **Har Nuur** *L* Mongolia
70B4 **Harper** Lib
20D3 **Harper L** USA
10K3 **Harper,Mt** USA
13D3 **Harpers Ferry** USA
65C3 **Har Ramon** *Mt* Israel
66C1 **Harrāt al 'Uwayrid** *Upland* Region, S Arabia
66D2 **Harrāt Kishb** Region, S Arabia
66D2 **Harrat Nawāāsīf** Region, S Arabia
66D2 **Harrat Rahat** Region, S Arabia
7L4 **Harricana** *R* Can
5J2 **Harrigan,C** Can
15C1 **Harriman** USA
14D1 **Harriman Res** USA
14C3 **Harrington** USA
7N4 **Harrington Harbour** Can
34B3 **Harris** *District* Scot
12B3 **Harrisburg** Illinois, USA
14B2 **Harrisburg** Pennsylvania, USA
74D2 **Harrismith** S Africa
17D2 **Harrison** USA
10H1 **Harrison B** USA
13D3 **Harrisonburg** USA
7N4 **Harrison,C** Can
3D4 **Harrison L** Can
17D2 **Harrisonville** USA
34B3 **Harris,Sound of** *Chan* Scot
12C2 **Harrisville** USA
35E4 **Harrogate** Eng
65C3 **Har Saggi** *Mt* Israel
32H5 **Harstad** Nor
10L3 **Hart** *R* Can
74C2 **Hartbees** *R* S Africa
32F6 **Hårteigen** *Mt* Nor
14D2 **Hartford** Connecticut, USA
12B2 **Hartford** Michigan, USA
11C3 **Hartford** S Dakota, USA
32G6 **Hartkjølen** *Mt* Nor
75A2 **Hart,L** Aust
5H4 **Hartland** Can
35C6 **Hartland Pt** Eng
34E4 **Hartlepool** Eng
16B2 **Hartley** USA
15B2 **Hartselle** USA
17C3 **Hartshorne** USA
15C2 **Hartwell Res** USA
74C2 **Hartz** *R* S Africa
50C2 **Har Us Nuur** *L* Mongolia
63E2 **Harut** *R* Afghan
16A2 **Harvard,Mt** USA
11B2 **Harvey** USA
35F6 **Harwich** Eng
60D3 **Haryāna** State, India
65C3 **Hāsā** Jordan
66B4 **Hasaheisa** Sudan
65C2 **Hāsbaiya** Leb
35E6 **Haselmere** Eng
54C4 **Hashimoto** Japan
63B1 **Hashtpar** Iran
63B1 **Hashtrūd** Iran
67G3 **Hāsik** Oman
16C3 **Haskell** USA
62B2 **Hassan** India
42B2 **Hasselt** Belg
70C2 **Hassi Inifel** Alg
70B2 **Hassi Mdakane** *Well* Alg
70C1 **Hassi Messaoud** Alg
71C2 **Hassi R'mel** Alg
32G4 **Hassleholm** Sweden
75C3 **Hastings** Aust
35F6 **Hastings** Eng
11D3 **Hastings** Minnesota, USA
8D2 **Hastings** Nebraska, USA
78C1 **Hastings** NZ
3H2 **Hatchet L** Can
15B1 **Hatchie** *R* USA
75B2 **Hatfield** Aust
10F2 **Hatham Inlet** USA
60D3 **Hāthras** India
55D2 **Ha Tinh** Viet
75B2 **Hattah** Aust
9F3 **Hatteras,C** USA
17E3 **Hattiesburg** USA
43D3 **Hatvan** Hung
55D3 **Hau Bon** Viet
72E3 **Haud** Region, Eth
32F7 **Haugesund** Nor
78C1 **Hauhungaroa Range** *Mts* NZ
3G2 **Haultain** *R* Can
78B1 **Hauraki G** NZ
78A3 **Hauroko,L** NZ
37C1 **Hausstock** *Mt* Switz
71A2 **Haut Atlas** *Mts* Mor
72C3 **Haute Kotto** Region, CAR
36C2 **Haute-Marne** Department, France
5H4 **Hauterive** Can
36C3 **Haute-Saône** Department, France
36C1 **Hautes Fagnes** *Mts* Belg
37A2 **Hauteville-Lompnès** France
36C1 **Hautmont** Belg
36D3 **Haut-Rhin** Department, France
71B2 **Hauts Plateaux** *Mts* Alg
63E2 **Hauzdar** Iran
60A2 **Hauz Qala** Afghan
12A2 **Havana** USA
Havana = Habana
62B3 **Havankulam** Sri Lanka
19D4 **Havasu L** USA
15D2 **Havelock** USA
78C1 **Havelock North** NZ
35C6 **Haverfordwest** West
14E1 **Haverhill** USA
62B2 **Hāveri** India
14D2 **Haverstraw** USA
42D3 **Havlíčkův Brod** Czech Republic
18E1 **Havre** USA
14B3 **Havre de Grace** USA
7M4 **Havre-St-Pierre** Can
41F2 **Havsa** Turk
20E5 **Hawaii** Hawaiian Is
20E5 **Hawaii Volcanoes Nat Pk** Hawaiian Is
71J3 **Hawal** *R* Nig
78A2 **Hawea,L** NZ
78B1 **Hawera** NZ
20E5 **Hawi** Hawaiian Is
34D4 **Hawick** Scot
78A2 **Hawkdun Range** *Mts* NZ
78C1 **Hawke B** NZ
75D2 **Hawke,C** Aust
75A2 **Hawker** Aust
14C2 **Hawley** USA
55B1 **Hawng Luk** Burma
64D3 **Hawr al Habbaniyah** *L* Iraq
64E3 **Hawr al Hammár** *L* Iraq
20C1 **Hawthorne** USA
75B2 **Hay** Aust
6G3 **Hay** *R* Can
36C2 **Hayange** France
6B3 **Haycock** USA
19D4 **Hayden** Arizona, USA
16A1 **Hayden** Colorado, USA
4C2 **Hayes** *R* Can
7J4 **Hayes** *R* Can
7M2 **Hayes Halvø** *Region* Greenland
10J3 **Hayes,Mt** USA
14B3 **Haymarket** USA
67E3 **Haynin** Yemen
6G3 **Hay River** Can
16C2 **Hays** USA
66D4 **Hays** Yemen
17C2 **Haysville** USA
12A1 **Hayward** Wisconsin, USA
12C3 **Hazard** USA
61C3 **Hazārībāg** India
36B1 **Hazebrouck** France
17D3 **Hazelhurst** USA
6F4 **Hazelton** Can
3C2 **Hazelton Mts** Can
10E3 **Hazen B** USA
7M1 **Hazen L** Can
6G2 **Hazen Str** Can
65C3 **Hazeva** Israel
14C2 **Hazleton** USA
75C3 **Healesville** Aust
10J3 **Healy** USA
xxviiiE7 **Heard I** Indian O
17C3 **Hearne** USA
4E4 **Hearst** Can
11B2 **Heart** *R* USA
17F4 **Hebbronville** USA
52D2 **Hebei** Province, China
75C1 **Hebel** Aust
18D2 **Heber City** USA
18D2 **Hebger L** USA
52C2 **Hebi** China
52C2 **Hebian** China
7M4 **Hebron** Can
65C3 **Hebron** Israel
11B2 **Hebron** N. Dakota, USA
17C1 **Hebron** Nebraska, USA
3B3 **Hecate Str** Can
10M4 **Heceta I** USA
52B5 **Hechi** China
36E2 **Hechingen** Germany
6G2 **Hecla and Griper B** Can
78C2 **Hector,Mt** NZ
32G6 **Hede** Sweden
32H6 **Hedemora** Sweden
18C1 **He Devil Mt** USA
42B2 **Heerenveen** Neth
36C1 **Heerlen** Neth
Hefa = Haifa
52D3 **Hefei** China
52B4 **Hefeng** China
53C2 **Hegang** China
54C3 **Hegura-jima** *I* Japan
61E3 **Heho** Burma
65C3 **Heidan** *R* Jordan
42B2 **Heide** Germany
74C3 **Heidelberg** Cape Province, S Africa
74D2 **Heidelberg** Transvaal, S Africa
42B3 **Heidelberg** Germany
49O4 **Heihe** China
74D2 **Heilbron** S Africa
42B3 **Heilbronn** Germany
42C2 **Heiligenstadt** Germany
53B2 **Heilongjiang** Province, China
53A1 **Heilong Jiang** *R* China
32K6 **Heinola** Fin
52B4 **Hejiang** China
7R3 **Hekla** *Mt* Iceland
55C1 **Hekou** Viet
52A5 **Hekou Yaozou Zizhixian** China
52B2 **Helan** China
52B2 **Helan Shan** *Mt* China
17D3 **Helena** Arkansas, USA
18D1 **Helena** Montana, USA
20D3 **Helendale** USA
57D2 **Helen Reef** *I* Pacific O
34C3 **Helensburgh** Scot
65A3 **Heliopolis** Egypt
63C3 **Helleh** *R* Iran
39B2 **Hellin** Spain
18C1 **Hells Canyon** *R* USA
36D1 **Hellweg** Region, Germany
20B2 **Helm** USA
63E2 **Helmand** *R* Afghan
74B2 **Helmeringhausen** Namibia
36C1 **Helmond** Neth
34D2 **Helmsdale** Scot
53B3 **Helong** China
32G7 **Helsingborg** Sweden
Helsingfors = Helsinki
42C1 **Helsingør** Den
32J6 **Helsinki** Fin
35C6 **Helston** Eng
64B4 **Helwân** Egypt
17C3 **Hempstead** USA
32H7 **Hemse** Sweden
52A3 **Henan** China
52C3 **Henan** Province, China
78B1 **Hen and Chicken Is** NZ
54C2 **Henashi-zaki** *C* Japan
12B3 **Henderson** Kentucky, USA
15D1 **Henderson** N. Carolina, USA
19D3 **Henderson** Nevada, USA
17D3 **Henderson** Texas, USA
15C1 **Hendersonville** N. Carolina, USA
15B1 **Hendersonville** Tennessee, USA
74D3 **Hendrik Verwoerd Dam** S Africa
52E5 **Heng-ch'un** Taiwan
50C4 **Hengduan Shan** *Mts* China
42B2 **Hengelo** Neth
52B2 **Hengshan** China
52D2 **Hengshui** China
55D1 **Heng Xian** China
52C4 **Hengyang** China
55A4 **Henhoaha** Nicobar Is
35E6 **Henley-on-Thames** Eng
14C3 **Henlopen,C** USA
14E1 **Henniker** USA
16C3 **Henrietta** USA
7K4 **Henrietta Maria,C** Can
19D3 **Henrieville** USA
17C2 **Henryetta** USA
7M3 **Henry Kater Pen** Can
74A1 **Henties Bay** Namibia
50D2 **Hentiyn Nuruu** *Mts* Mongolia
55B2 **Henzada** Burma
52B5 **Hepu** China
63E2 **Herat** Afghan
6H4 **Herbert** Can
10D5 **Herbert** *I* USA
78C2 **Herbertville** NZ
36E1 **Herborn** Germany
23A4 **Heredia** Costa Rica
35D5 **Hereford** Eng
16B3 **Hereford** USA
35D5 **Hereford & Worcester** County, Eng
36C1 **Herentals** Belg
37B1 **Héricourt** France
17C2 **Herington** USA
78A3 **Heriot** NZ
37C1 **Herisau** Switz
14C1 **Herkimer** USA
37E1 **Hermagor** Austria
34E1 **Herma Ness** *Pen* Scot
74B3 **Hermanus** S Africa
75C2 **Hermidale** Aust
78B2 **Hermitage** NZ
76D1 **Hermit Is** PNG
Hermon,Mt = Jebel ash Shaykh
21A2 **Hermosillo** Mexico
29B4 **Hernandarias** Par
14B2 **Herndon** USA
36D1 **Herne** Germany
42B1 **Herning** Den
4D4 **Heron Bay** Can
63B1 **Herowābad** Iran
29A4 **Herradura** Arg
28C1 **Herrera** Arg
39B2 **Herrera del Duque** Spain
10L2 **Herschel I** Can
14B2 **Hershey** USA
35E6 **Hertford** County, Eng
65C2 **Herzliyya** Israel
36C1 **Hesbaye** Region, Belg
36A1 **Hesdin** France
52B2 **Heshui** China
20D3 **Hesperia** USA
10M3 **Hess** *R* Can
42B2 **Hessen** State, Germany
20C2 **Hetch Hetchy Res** USA
11B2 **Hettinger** USA
35F5 **Heweth** *Oilfield* N Sea
34D4 **Hexham** Eng
52C5 **He Xian** China
74D2 **Heystekrand** S Africa
52C5 **Heyuan** China
75B3 **Heywood** Aust
52D2 **Heze** China
15E4 **Hialeah** USA
11D2 **Hibbing** USA
15C1 **Hickory** USA
78C1 **Hicks Bay** NZ
75C3 **Hicks,Pt** Aust
17C3 **Hico** USA
54D2 **Hidaka-sammyaku** *Mts* Japan
22C1 **Hidalgo** Mexico
22C1 **Hidalgo** State, Mexico
21B2 **Hidalgo del Parral** Mexico
29C2 **Hidrolândia** Brazil
70A2 **Hierro** *I* Canary Is
54D3 **Higashine** Japan
53B5 **Higashi-suidō** *Str* Japan
18B2 **High Desert** USA
4B2 **High Hill** *R* Can
17D4 **High Island** USA
34C2 **Highland** Region, Scot
20D3 **Highland** USA
20C1 **Highland Peak** *Mt* USA
14C2 **Highland Falls** USA
3E2 **High Level** Can
15C1 **High Point** USA
3E2 **High Prairie** Can
6G4 **High River** Can
3G2 **Highrock L** Can
4A2 **Highrock L** Can
15C3 **High Springs** USA
14C2 **Hightstown** USA
35E6 **High Wycombe** Eng
32J7 **Hiiumaa** *I* Estonia
66C1 **Hijaz** Region, S Arabia
54C4 **Hikigawa** Japan
19C3 **Hiko** USA
54C3 **Hikone** Japan
78B1 **Hikurangi** NZ
8C4 **Hildago del Parral** Mexico
42B2 **Hildesheim** Germany
23Q2 **Hillaby,Mt** Barbados
16C2 **Hill City** USA
42C1 **Hillerød** Den
3G1 **Hill Island L** Can
11C2 **Hillsboro** N. Dakota, USA
14E1 **Hillsboro** New Hampshire, USA
16A3 **Hillsboro** New Mexico, USA
12C3 **Hillsboro** Ohio, USA
18B1 **Hillsboro** Oregon, USA
17C3 **Hillsboro** Texas, USA
4D4 **Hillsport** Can
75C2 **Hillston** Aust
12C3 **Hillsville** USA
34E1 **Hillswick** Scot
20E5 **Hilo** Hawaiian Is

Idah **Is-sur-Tille**

71H4 **Idah** Nig
18D2 **Idaho** State, USA
18C2 **Idaho City** USA
18D2 **Idaho Falls** USA
16A2 **Idaho Springs** USA
18B2 **Idanha** USA
36D2 **Idar Oberstein** Germany
69A2 **Idehan Marzūg** *Desert* Libya
69A2 **Idehan Ubari** *Desert* Libya
70C2 **Idelés** Alg
50C2 **Iderlym Gol** *R* Mongolia
66B2 **Idfu** Egypt
41E3 **Ídhi Óros** *Mt* Greece
41E3 **Ídhra** *I* Greece
72B4 **Idiofa** Zaïre
10G3 **Iditarod** *R* USA
64C2 **Idlib** Syria
37E2 **Idrija** Slovenia, Yugos
32K7 **Idritsa** Russian Fed
74D3 **Idutywa** S Africa
36B1 **Ieper** Belg
41F3 **Ierápetra** Greece
37E3 **Iesi** Italy
73D4 **Ifakara** Tanz
51H6 **Ifalik** *I* Pacific
73E6 **Ifanadiana** Madag
71G4 **Ife** Nig
70C3 **Iférouane** Niger
56D2 **Igan** Malay
29C3 **Igaranava** Brazil
48K3 **Igarka** Russian Fed
29A3 **Igatimi** Par
71G4 **Igbetti** Nig
64E2 **Igdir** Iran
32H6 **Iggesund** Sweden
28B2 **Iglesia** Arg
40B3 **Iglesias** Sardegna
7K3 **Igloolik** Can
4C4 **Ignace** Can
64A1 **Iğneada Burun** *Pt* Turk
62E2 **Ignoitijala** Andaman Is
41E3 **Igoumenítsa** Greece
44J4 **Igra** Russian Fed
44L3 **Igrim** Russian Fed
22C2 **Iguala** Mexico
25G2 **Iguape** Brazil
29C3 **Iguatama** Brazil
29B3 **Iguatemi** Brazil
29A3 **Iguatemi** *R* Brazil
27L5 **Iguatu** Brazil
72A4 **Iguéla** Gabon
71H4 **Igumale** Nig
71H4 **Ihiala** Nig
73E6 **Ihosy** Madag
53D4 **Iida** Japan
54C3 **Iide-san** *Mt* Japan
32K6 **Iisalmi** Fin
54B4 **Iizuka** Japan
71G4 **Ijebulgbo** Nig
71G4 **Ijebu Ode** Nig
42B2 **IJsselmeer** *S* Neth
28E1 **Ijuí** Brazil
28D1 **Ijui** *R* Brazil
41F3 **Ikaría** *I* Greece
53E3 **Ikeda** Japan
72C4 **Ikela** Zaïre
71H4 **Ikerre** Nig
41E2 **Ikhtiman** Bulg
54A4 **Iki** *I* Japan
71G4 **Ikire** Nig
10H4 **Ikolik,C** USA
73E5 **Ikopa** *R* Madag
71G4 **Ila** Nig
57F7 **Ilagan** Phil
63B2 **Ilām** Iran
50C1 **Ilanskiy** Russian Fed
37C1 **Ilanz** Switz
71G4 **Ilaro** Nig
3G2 **Île à la Crosse** Can
3G2 **Île à la Crosse,L** Can
68G8 **Ilebo** Zaire
36B2 **Île De France** Region, France
71E2 **Île de Jerba** *I* Tunisia
38B2 **Ile de Noirmoutier** *I* France
38B2 **Ile de Ré** *I* France
77F3 **Île des Pins** *I* Nouvelle Calédonie
13E1 **Ile d'Orleans** Can
38A2 **Ile d'Ouessant** *I* France
38B2 **Ile d'Yeu** *I* France
45K5 **Ilek** *R* Russian Fed
22A1 **Ile María Cleofas** *I* Mexico
22A1 **Ile María Madre** *I* Mexico
22A1 **Ile María Magdalena** Mexico
22A1 **Ile San Juanico** *I* Mexico
77F2 **Îles Bélèp** Nouvelle Calédonie
77E2 **Îles Chesterfield** Nouvelle Calédonie
77H2 **Îles de Horn** *Is* Pacific O
38D3 **Iles d'Hyères** *Is* France
71G4 **Ilesha** Nig
71E2 **Iles Kerkenna** *Is* Tunisia
4B2 **Ilford** Can
35C6 **Ilfracombe** Eng
64B1 **Ilgaz Dağları** *Mts* Turk
73D6 **Ilha Bazaruto** *I* Mozam
29C3 **Ilha Comprida** *I* Brazil
29E1 **Ilha de Boipeba** *I* Brazil
27H3 **Ilha De Maracá** *I* Brazil
27H4 **Ilha de Marajó** *I* Brazil
29C4 **Ilha de São Francisco** *I* Brazil
29C3 **Ilha de São Sebastião** *I* Brazil
29E1 **Ilha de Tinharé** *I* Brazil
27H6 **Ilha do Bananal** *Region* Brazil
29C4 **Ilha do Cardoso** *I* Brazil
25F2 **Ilha Grande, Reprêsa** *Res* Brazil
29D3 **Ilha Grande** *I* Brazil
29B3 **Ilha Grande ou Sete Quedas** *I* Brazil
29C3 **Ilha Santo Amaro** *I* Brazil
29B3 **Ilha Solteira Dam** Brazil
70A2 **Ilhas Selvegens** *I* Atlantic O
27L6 **Ilhéus** Brazil
48J5 **Ili** *R* Kazakhstan
10G4 **Iliamna L** USA
10H3 **Iliamna V** USA
36A2 **Iliers** France
57F9 **Iligan** Phil
49M4 **Ilim** *R* Russian Fed
49M4 **Ilimsk** Russian Fed
53E2 **Il'inskiy** Russian Fed
41E3 **Iliodhrómia** *I* Greece
14C1 **Ilion** USA
57F9 **Illana B** Phil
28A2 **Illapel** Chile
28A2 **Illapel** *R* Chile
70C3 **Illéla** Niger
37D1 **Iller** *R* Germany
22B1 **Illescas** Mexico
77H2 **Îles Wallis** *Is* Pacific O
12B2 **Illinois** State, USA
12A3 **Illinois** *R* USA
70C2 **Illizi** Alg
44E4 **Il'men, Ozero** *L* Russian Fed
26D7 **Ilo** Peru
57F8 **Iloilo** Phil
32L6 **Ilomantsi** Fin
71G4 **Ilorin** Nig
57C4 **Ilwaki** Indon
43G1 **Il'yino** Russian Fed
54B4 **Imabari** Japan
54C3 **Imalchi** Japan
32L5 **Imandra, Ozero** *L* Russian Fed
54A4 **Imari** Japan
44D3 **Imatra** Fin
25G3 **Imbituba** Brazil
29B4 **Imbituva** Brazil
72E3 **Imi** Eth
54A3 **Imjin** *R* N Korea
18C2 **Imlay** USA
37D1 **Immenstadt** Germany
71H4 **Imo** State, Nig
40C2 **Imola** Italy
27J5 **Imperatriz** Brazil
40B2 **Imperia** Italy
16B1 **Imperial** USA
19C4 **Imperial V** USA
72B3 **Impfondo** Congo
61D3 **Imphāl** India
37D1 **Imst** Austria
10F2 **Imuruk L** USA
54C3 **Ina** Japan
70C2 **In Afahleleh** *Well* Alg
54C4 **Inamba-jima** *I* Japan
70C2 **In Amenas** Alg
32K5 **Inari** Fin
32K5 **Inarijärvi** *L* Fin
54D3 **Inawashiro-ko** *L* Japan
70C2 **In Belbel** Alg
45F7 **Ince Burun** *Pt* Turk
64B2 **Incekum Burun** *Pt* Turk
53B4 **Inch'ŏn** S Korea
70B2 **In Dagouber** *Well* Mali
29C2 **Indais** *R* Brazil
32H6 **Indals** *R* Sweden
35G5 **Indefatigable** *Gasfield* N Sea
20C2 **Independence** California, USA
11D3 **Independence** Iowa, USA
17C2 **Independence** Kansas, USA
17D2 **Independence** Missouri, USA
18C2 **Independence Mts** USA
56B3 **Inderagiri** *R* Indon
45J6 **Inderborskiy** Kazakhstan
59F4 **India** Federal Republic, Asia
12B2 **Indiana** State, USA
13D2 **Indiana** USA
xxviiiF7 **Indian-Antarctic Basin** Indian O
xxviiiF7 **Indian-Antarctic Ridge** Indian O
12B3 **Indianapolis** USA
Indian Desert = Thar Desert
7N4 **Indian Harbour** Can
3H3 **Indian Head** Can
xxviiiE5 **Indian O**
17D1 **Indianola** Iowa, USA
17D3 **Indianola** Mississippi, USA
29C2 **Indianópolis** Brazil
19C3 **Indian Springs** USA
44H2 **Indiga** Russian Fed
49Q3 **Indigirka** *R* Russian Fed
55D2 **Indo China** Region, S E Asia
51F7 **Indonesia** Republic, S E Asia
60D4 **Indore** India
56C4 **Indramayu** Indon
38C2 **Indre** *R* France
60B3 **Indus** *R* Pak
45E7 **Inebdu** Turk
70C2 **In Ebeggi** *Well* Alg
64B1 **Inebolu** Turk
70C2 **In Ecker** Alg
64A1 **Inegöl** Turk
70D2 **In Ezzane** Alg
74C3 **Infante,C** S Africa
70C3 **Ingal** Niger
12C2 **Ingersoll** Can
76D2 **Ingham** Aust
7M2 **Inglefield Land** *Region* Greenland
78B1 **Inglewood** NZ
75D1 **Inglewood** Queensland, Aust
20C4 **Inglewood** USA
75B3 **Inglewood** Victoria, Aust
32B2 **Ingólfshöfði** *I* Iceland
42C3 **Ingolstadt** Germany
61C3 **Ingrāj Bāzār** India
70C3 **In-Guezzam** *Well* Alg
74E2 **Inhaca** *I* Mozam
74E2 **Inhaca Pen** Mozam
73D6 **Inhambane** Mozam
73D6 **Inharrime** Mozam
29C2 **Inhumas** Brazil
26E3 **Inirida** *R* Colombia
34B4 **Inishowen** District, Irish Rep
75C1 **Injune** Aust
3B2 **Inklin** Can
10M4 **Inklin** *R* Can
10G2 **Inland L** USA
37D1 **Inn** *R* Austria
75B1 **Innamincka** Aust
50D2 **Inner Mongolia** Autonomous Region, China
76D2 **Innisfail** Aust
53E2 **Innokent'yevskiy** Russian Fed
10G3 **Innoko** *R* USA
42C3 **Innsbruck** Austria
72B4 **Inongo** Zaïre
43D2 **Inowrocław** Pol
70C2 **In Salah** Alg
54A3 **Insil** S Korea
44L2 **Inta** Russian Fed
37B1 **Interlaken** Switz
77H3 **International Date Line**
11D2 **International Falls** USA
28C1 **Intiyaco** Arg
37C2 **Intra** Italy
56E3 **Intu** Indon
54D3 **Inubo-saki** *C* Japan
7L4 **Inukjuak** Can
6E3 **Inuvik** Can
6E3 **Inuvik** Region, Can
34C3 **Inveraray** Scot
78A3 **Invercargill** NZ
75D1 **Inverell** Aust
3E3 **Invermere** Can
34C2 **Inverness** Scot
34D3 **Inverurie** Scot
75A3 **Investigator Str** Aust
50B1 **Inya** Russian Fed
49Q3 **Inya** *R* Russian Fed
73D5 **Inyanga** Zim
20D3 **Inyokern** USA
20C2 **Inyo Mts** USA
72B4 **Inzia** *R* Zaïre
41E3 **Ioánnina** Greece
17C2 **Iola** USA
63E1 **Iolotan** Turkmenistan
34B3 **Iona** *I* Scot
73B5 **Iôna Nat Pk** Angola
18C1 **Ione** USA
Ionian Is = Iónioi Nísoi
41D3 **Ionian S** Italy/Greece
41E3 **Iónioi Nísoi** *Is* Greece
10D2 **Ioniveyem** *R* Russian Fed
41F3 **Íos** *I* Greece
44J3 **Iosser** Russian Fed
11D3 **Iowa** State, USA
11D3 **Iowa** *R* USA
12A2 **Iowa City** USA
11D3 **Iowa Falls** USA
29C2 **Ipameri** Brazil
29D2 **Ipanema** Brazil
45G6 **Ipatovo** Russian Fed
26C3 **Ipiales** Colombia
29E1 **Ipiaú** Brazil
29B4 **Ipiranga** Brazil
55C5 **Ipoh** Malay
27H7 **Iporá** Brazil
41F2 **Ipsala** Turk
75D1 **Ipswich** Aust
35F5 **Ipswich** Eng
14E1 **Ipswich** USA
43G2 **Iput** *R* Russian Fed
29C3 **Iquape** Brazil
25B2 **Iquique** Chile
26D4 **Iquitos** Peru
28E1 **Irai** Brazil
41F3 **Iráklion** Greece
58D2 **Iran** Republic, S W Asia
63E3 **Irānshahr** Iran
22B1 **Irapuato** Mexico
64D3 **Iraq** Republic, S W Asia
29B4 **Irati** Brazil
69A2 **Irā Wan** *Watercourse* Libya
65C2 **Irbid** Jordan
44L4 **Irbit** Russian Fed
27G3 **Ireng** *R* Guyana
53B4 **Iri** S Korea
51G7 **Irian Jaya** Province, Indon
72C2 **Iriba** Chad
57F8 **Iriga** Phil
73D4 **Iringa** Tanz
50F4 **Iriomote** *I* Japan
23A3 **Iriona** Honduras
27H5 **Iriri** *R* Brazil
35C5 **Irish S** Eng/Irish Rep
10H2 **Irkillik** *R* USA
49M4 **Irkutsk** Russian Fed
75A2 **Iron Knob** Aust
12B1 **Iron Mountain** USA
76D2 **Iron Range** Aust
12B1 **Iron River** USA
12C3 **Irontown** USA
12A1 **Ironwood** USA
4E4 **Iroquois Falls** Can
54C4 **Iro-zaki** *C* Japan
61E4 **Irrawaddy** *R* Burma
55A2 **Irrawaddy,Mouths of the** Burma
48H4 **Irtysh** *R* Russian Fed
39B1 **Irun** Spain
34C4 **Irvine** Scot
17C3 **Irving** USA
71H3 **Isa** Nig
57F9 **Isabela** Phil
20C3 **Isabella Res** USA
6H2 **Isachsen** Can
6H2 **Isachsen,C** Can
7Q3 **Ísafjörður** Iceland
53C5 **Isahaya** Japan
72C3 **Isangi** Zaïre
37D1 **Isar** *R* Germany
37D1 **Isarco** *R* Italy
34E1 **Isbister** Scot
37D1 **Ischgl** Austria
40C2 **Ischia** *I* Italy
54C4 **Ise** Japan
37D2 **Iseo** Italy
37A2 **Isère** *R* France
36D1 **Iserlohn** Germany
40C2 **Isernia** Italy
54C4 **Ise-wan** *B* Japan
71G4 **Iseyin** Nig
50F4 **Ishigaki** *I* Japan
53E3 **Ishikari** *R* Japan
53E3 **Ishikari-wan** *B* Japan
48H4 **Ishim** Russian Fed
48H4 **Ishim** *R* Kazakhstan
53E4 **Ishinomaki** Japan
54D3 **Ishioka** Japan
60C1 **Ishkashim** Afghan
12B1 **Ishpeming** USA
48J4 **Isil'kul'** Russian Fed
57B2 **Isimu** Indon
72D3 **Isiolo** Kenya
72C3 **Isiro** Zaïre
64C2 **Iskenderun** Turk
64C2 **Iskenferun Körfezi** *B* Turk
64B1 **Iskilip** Turk
48K4 **Iskitim** Russian Fed
41E2 **Iskur** *R* Bulg
10M4 **Iskut** *R* Can/USA
22C2 **Isla** Mexico
28D1 **Isla Apipe Grande** Arg
23C3 **Isla Beata** Dom Rep
28C3 **Isla Bermejo** *I* Arg
23E4 **Isla Blanquilla** Ven
26B2 **Isla Coiba** *I* Panama
8B4 **Isla de Cedros** *I* Mexico
25B6 **Isla de Chiloé** *I* Chile
21D2 **Isla de Cozumel** *I* Mexico
23C3 **Isla de la Gonâve** Cuba
23A2 **Isla de la Juventud** *I* Cuba
28D2 **Isla de las Lechiguanas** *I* Arg
2K8 **Isla del Coco** *I* Costa Rica
21D3 **Isla del Maiz** *I* Caribbean
22C1 **Isla de Lobos** *I* Mexico
25D8 **Isla de los Estados** *I* Arg
24F4 **Isla de Marajó** *I* Brazil
xxixO6 **Isla de Pascua** *I* Pacific O
23A4 **Isla de Providencia** *I* Caribbean
23A4 **Isla de San Andres** *I* Caribbean
25G3 **Isla de Santa Catarina** *I* Brazil
27H2 **Isla du Diable** *I* French Guiana
27M4 **Isla Fernando de Noronha** *I* Brazil
25C8 **Isla Grande de Tierra del Fuego** *I* Arg/Chile
23D4 **Isla la Tortuga** *I* Ven
60C2 **Islamabad** Pak
21A2 **Isla Magdalena** *I* Mexico
23E4 **Isla Margarita** Ven
28A3 **Isla Mocha** Chile
15E4 **Islamorada** USA
4C3 **Island L** Can
75A2 **Island Lg** Aust
18D2 **Island Park** USA
5K4 **Islands,B of** Can
78B1 **Islands,B of** NZ
26B1 **Isla Providencia** *I* Colombia
26B4 **Isla Puná** *I* Ecuador
xxxD6 **Isla San Ambrosia** *I* Pacific O
xxxD6 **Isla San Felix** *I* Pacific O
21A2 **Isla Santa Margarita** *I* Mexico
28A3 **Isla Santa Maria** *I* Chile
Islas Baleares = Balearic Is
70A2 **Islas Canarias** *Is* Atlantic O
39C2 **Islas Columbretes** *Is* Spain
21D3 **Islas de la Bahia** *Is* Honduras
23A4 **Islas del Maíz** *Is* Caribbean
26F1 **Islas de Margarita** *Is* Ven
25C9 **Islas Diego Ramírez** *Is* Chile
26N0 **Islas Galapagos** *Is* Pacific O
26Q0 **Islas Juan Fernandez** *Is* Pacific O
26E1 **Islas los Roques** *Is* Ven
Islas Malvinas = Falkland Is
xxixO4 **Islas Revilla Gigedo** *Is* Pacific O
25C9 **Islas Wollaston** *Is* Chile
70A3 **Isla Tidra** *I* Maur
25B7 **Isla Wellington** *I* Chile
34B4 **Islay** *I* Scot
38C2 **Isle** *R* France
xxviiiE6 **Isle Amsterdam** *I* Indian O
13F2 **Isle au Haut** *I* USA
35E6 **Isle of Wight** *I* Eng
12B1 **Isle Royale** *I* USA
12B1 **Isle Royale Nat Pk** USA
xxviiiE6 **Isle St Paul** *I* Indian O
xxviiiD7 **Îsles Crozet** *I* Indian O
xxixM5 **Îsles de la Société** Pacific O
xxixN6 **Îsles Gambier** *Is* Pacific O
73E5 **Îsles Glorieuses** *Is* Madag
xxviiiE7 **Îsles Kerguelen** *Is* Indian O
77F3 **Îsles Loyauté** *Is* Nouvelle Calédonie
xxixN5 **Îsles Marquises** *Is* Pacific O
xxixM5 **Îsles Tuamotu** *Is* Pacific O
xxixM6 **Îsles Tubai** *Is* Pacific O
20B1 **Isleton** USA
64B3 **Ismâ'ilîya** Egypt
66B1 **Isna** Egypt
73E6 **Isoanala** Madag
73D5 **Isoka** Zambia
37C3 **Isola di Capraia** *I* Italy
40C3 **Isola Egadi** *I* Italy
40C2 **Isola Ponziane** *I* Italy
40C3 **Isole Lipari** *Is* Italy
40D2 **Isoles Tremiti** *Is* Italy
54C3 **Isosaki** Japan
64B2 **Isparta** Turk
65C2 **Israel** Republic, S W Asia
39C2 **Isser** *R* Alg
38C2 **Issoire** France
38C2 **Issoudun** France
37A1 **Is-sur-Tille** France

Issyk Kul, Ozero — Johannesburg

59F1 **Issyk Kul, Ozero** *I* Kirgizia
64A1 **İstanbul** Turk
41E3 **Istiáia** Greece
22D2 **Istmo de Tehuantepec** *Isthmus* Mexico
15E4 **Istokpoga,L** USA
40C1 **Istra** *Pen* Croatia, Yugos
41F2 **Istranca Dağlari** *Upland* Turk
29C2 **Itaberai** Brazil
29D2 **Itabira** Brazil
29D3 **Itabirito** Brazil
29E1 **Itabuna** Brazil
29E1 **Itacaré** Brazil
27G4 **Itacoatiara** Brazil
29A3 **Itacurubi del Rosario** Par
26C2 **Itagui** Colombia
25F2 **Itaipu, Reprêsa** *Res* Brazil
27G4 **Itaituba** Brazil
25G3 **Itajaí** Brazil
29C3 **Itajuba** Brazil
40C2 **Italy** Repubic, Europe
29E2 **Itamaraju** Brazil
29D2 **Itamarandiba** Brazil
29D2 **Itambacuri** Brazil
29D2 **Itambe** Brazil
29D2 **Itambé** *Mt* Brazil
61D2 **Itānagar** India
29C3 **Itanhaém** Brazil
29D2 **Itanhém** Brazil
29D2 **Itanhém** *R* Brazil
29D2 **Itaobím** Brazil
29C1 **Itapaci** Brazil
29C3 **Itapecerica** Brazil
29D3 **Itaperuna** Brazil
27K7 **Itapetinga** Brazil
29C3 **Itapetininga** Brazil
29C3 **Itapeva** Brazil
27L4 **Itapipoca** Brazil
29C2 **Itapuranga** Brazil
29C1 **Itaquari** *R* Brazil
28D1 **Itaqui** Brazil
29D2 **Itarantim** Brazil
29C3 **Itararé** Brazil
29C3 **Itararé** *R* Brazil
29D3 **Itaúna** Brazil
26F6 **Iténez** *R* Brazil/Bol
13D2 **Ithaca** USA
36E1 **Ith Hills** *Mts* Germany
72C3 **Itimbiri** *R* Zaïre
29D2 **Itinga** Brazil
29A2 **Itiquira** *R* Brazil
7N3 **Itivdleq** Greenland
32G6 **Itjørdal** Nor
54C4 **Ito** Japan
53D4 **Itoigawa** Japan
36A2 **Iton** *R* France
26F6 **Itonomas** *R* Bol
29C3 **Itu** Brazil
71H4 **Itu** Nig
29E1 **Ituberá** Brazil
29C2 **Itumbiara** Brazil
29B2 **Iturama** Brazil
25C2 **Iturbe** Arg
22C1 **Iturbide** Mexico
53F3 **Iturup, Ostrov** *I* Russian Fed
29C2 **Iturutaba** Brazil
28D1 **Ituzzaingó** Arg
42B2 **Itzehoe** Germany
49U3 **Iul'tin** Russian Fed
43F2 **Ivacevichi** Belorussia
29B3 **Ivai** *R* Brazil
32K5 **Ivalo** Fin
41D2 **Ivangrad** Montenegro, Yugos
75B2 **Ivanhoe** Aust
43E3 **Ivano-Frankovsk** Ukraine
44G4 **Ivanovo** Russian Fed
44L3 **Ivdel'** Russian Fed
72B3 **Ivindo** *R* Gabon
29B3 **Ivinhema** Brazil
29B3 **Ivinhema** *R* Brazil
73E6 **Ivohibe** Madag
73E5 **Ivongo Soanierana** Madag
70B4 **Ivory Coast** Republic, Africa
40B1 **Ivrea** Italy
7L3 **Ivujivik** Can
53E4 **Iwaki** Japan
54D2 **Iwaki** *R* Japan
54D2 **Iwaki-san** *Mt* Japan
53C5 **Iwakuni** Japan
54D2 **Iwamizawa** Japan
53E3 **Iwanai** Japan
71G4 **Iwo** Nig
50H4 **Iwo Jima** *I* Japan
22B1 **Ixcuintla** Mexico
22C1 **Ixmiquilpa** Mexico
22B2 **Ixtapa** Mexico
22C2 **Ixtepec** Mexico
22B1 **Ixtlán** Mexico
54B4 **Iyo** Japan
54B4 **Iyo-nada** *B* Japan
44J4 **Izhevsk** Russian Fed
44J2 **Izhma** Russian Fed
44J2 **Izhma** *R* Russian Fed
10E5 **Izigan,C** USA
67G2 **Izkī** Oman
43F3 **Izmail** Ukraine
64A2 **İzmir** Turk
41F3 **Izmir Körfezi** *B* Turk
64A1 **İzmit** Turk
64A1 **İznik** Turk
41F2 **Iznik Golü** *L* Turk
65D2 **Izra'** Syria
22C2 **Izúcar de Matamoros** Mexico
54A4 **Izuhara** Japan
54C4 **Izumi-sano** Japan
54B3 **Izumo** Japan
53D5 **Izu-shotō** *Is* Japan
53C2 **Izvestkovyy** Russian Fed

J

69B1 **Jabal al Akhdar** *Mts* Libya
65D2 **Jabal al 'Arab** Syria
67F3 **Jabal al Qara'** *Mts* Oman
65D1 **Jabal an Nuşayrīyah** *Mts* Syria
69A2 **Jabal as Sawdā** *Mts* Libya
67F2 **Jabal az Ẓannah** UAE
65D1 **Jabal Halīmah** *Mt* Syria/Leb
67F3 **Jabal Mahrāt** *Mts* Yemen
61B3 **Jabalpur** India
66D1 **Jabal Shammar** Region, S Arabia
67E2 **Jabal Tuwayq** *Mts* S Arabia
65C1 **Jablah** Syria
42D2 **Jablonec nad Nisou** Czech Republic
27L5 **Jaboatão** Brazil
39B1 **Jaca** Spain
22C1 **Jacala** Mexico
27G5 **Jacareacanga** Brazil
27H8 **Jacarezinho** Brazil
29C3 **Jacarie** Brazil
25C4 **Jáchal** Arg
29B2 **Jaciara** Brazil
29D2 **Jacinto** Brazil
3G3 **Jackfish L** Can
13E1 **Jackman Station** USA
16C3 **Jacksboro** USA
14B2 **Jacks Mt** USA
15B2 **Jackson** Alabama, USA
75C1 **Jackson** Aust
20B1 **Jackson** California, USA
12C2 **Jackson** Michigan, USA
11D3 **Jackson** Minnesota, USA
17D3 **Jackson** Mississippi, USA
12B3 **Jackson** Missouri, USA
12C3 **Jackson** Ohio, USA
15B1 **Jackson** Tennessee, USA
18D2 **Jackson** Wyoming, USA
78B2 **Jackson,C** NZ
78A2 **Jackson Head** *Pt* NZ
18D2 **Jackson L** USA
17D3 **Jacksonville** Arkansas, USA
15C2 **Jacksonville** Florida, USA
12A3 **Jacksonville** Illinois, USA
15D2 **Jacksonville** N Carolina, USA
17C3 **Jacksonville** Texas, USA
15C2 **Jacksonville Beach** USA
23C3 **Jacmel** Haiti
60B3 **Jacobabad** Pak
27K6 **Jacobina** Brazil
22B2 **Jacona** Mexico
28E1 **Jacui** *R* Brazil
67F3 **Jādib** Yemen
Jadotville = Likasi
26C5 **Jaén** Peru
39B2 **Jaén** Spain
Jaffa = Tel Aviv Yafo
75A3 **Jaffa** *C* Aust
62B3 **Jaffna** Sri Lanka
14D1 **Jaffrey** USA
61C3 **Jagannathganj Ghat** Bang
62C1 **Jagdalpur** India
53A1 **Jagdaqi** China
63D3 **Jagin** *R* Iran
62B1 **Jagtial** India
29E1 **Jaguaquara** Brazil
28E2 **Jaguarão** Brazil
28E2 **Jaguarão** *R* Brazil
29C3 **Jaguarialva** Brazil
28B1 **Jagüé** Arg
28B1 **Jagüé** *R* Arg
45H8 **Jahan Dāgh** *Mt* Iran
63C3 **Jahrom** Iran
57C2 **Jailolo** Indon
60D5 **Jāina** India
52A2 **Jainca** China
60D3 **Jaipur** India
60C3 **Jaisalmer** India
63D1 **Jajarm** Iran
40D2 **Jajce** Bosnia-Herzegovina, Yugos
56C4 **Jakarta** Indon
3B1 **Jakes Corner** Can
7N3 **Jakobshavn** Greenland
32J6 **Jakobstad** Fin
16B3 **Jal** USA
22C2 **Jalaca** Mexico
53A2 **Jalaid Qi** China
60C2 **Jalalabad** Afghan
60D2 **Jalandhar** India
22C2 **Jalapa** Mexico
29B3 **Jales** Brazil
61C2 **Jaleswar** Nepal
60D4 **Jalgaon** India
71J4 **Jalingo** Nig
22A2 **Jalisco** State, Mexico
39B1 **Jalón** *R* Spain
60C3 **Jālor** India
22B1 **Jalostotitlan** Mexico
61C2 **Jalpāiguri** India
22C1 **Jalpan** Mexico
69B2 **Jālū** Libya
69B2 **Jālū Oasis** Libya
26B4 **Jama** Ecuador
72E3 **Jamaame** Somalia
71H3 **Jamaaré** *R* Nig
23B3 **Jamaica** *I* Caribbean
23B3 **Jamaica Chan** Caribbean
61C3 **Jamalpur** Bang
56B3 **Jambi** Indon
60C4 **Jambussar** India
11C2 **James** *R* N Dakota, USA
13D3 **James** *R* Virginia, USA
7K4 **James B** Can
75A2 **Jamestown** Aust
11C2 **Jamestown** N Dakota, USA
13D2 **Jamestown** New York, USA
14E2 **Jamestown** Rhode Island, USA
74D3 **Jamestown** S Africa
22C2 **Jamiltepec** Mexico
62B1 **Jamkhandi** India
60C2 **Jammu** India
60D2 **Jammu and Kashmir** State, India
60B4 **Jamnagar** India
60C3 **Jampur** Pak
44C3 **Jämsä** Fin
61C3 **Jamshedpur** India
61C2 **Janakpur** Nepal
29D2 **Janaúba** Brazil
63C2 **Jandaq** Iran
75D1 **Jandowae** Aust
12B2 **Janesville** USA
79B1 **Jan Mayen** *I* Norwegian S
29D2 **Januária** Brazil
60D4 **Jaora** India
53 **Japan** Empire, E Asia
53C4 **Japan,S of** S E Asia
xxviiiJ3 **Japan Trench** Pacific O
26E4 **Japurá** *R* Brazil
64C2 **Jarābulus** Syria
29C2 **Jaraguá** Brazil
29B3 **Jaraguari** Brazil
39B1 **Jarama** *R* Spain
65C2 **Jarash** Jordan
29A3 **Jardim** Brazil
39B2 **Jardin** *R* Spain
23B2 **Jardines de la Reina** *Is* Cuba
Jargalant = Hovd
27H3 **Jari** *R* Brazil
61D2 **Jaria Jhānjail** Bang
36C2 **Jarny** France
42D2 **Jarocin** Pol
43E2 **Jaroslaw** Pol
44A3 **Järpen** Sweden
52B2 **Jartai** China
60C4 **Jasdan** India
71G4 **Jasikan** Ghana
63D3 **Jāsk** Iran
43E3 **Jaslo** Pol
25D8 **Jason Is** Falkland Is
15B2 **Jasper** Alabama, USA
17D2 **Jasper** Arkansas, USA
3E3 **Jasper** Can
15C2 **Jasper** Florida, USA
12B3 **Jasper** Indiana, USA
17D3 **Jasper** Texas, USA
3E3 **Jasper Nat Pk** Can
42D2 **Jastrowie** Pol
29B2 **Jatai** Brazil
39B2 **Játiva** Spain
29C3 **Jau** Brazil
26C6 **Jauja** Peru
22C1 **Jaumave** Mexico
61B2 **Jaunpur** India
Java = Jawa
62B2 **Javadi Hills** India
63E1 **Javand** Afghan
Javari = Yavari
51D7 **Java S** Indon
76A2 **Java Trench** Indon
56C4 **Jawa** *I* Indon
51H7 **Jayapura** Indon
65D2 **Jayrūd** Syria
66D3 **Jazá'ir Farasān** *Is* S Arabia
67G2 **Jazīrat Maşīrah** *I* Oman
22B1 **Jazminal** Mexico
71B2 **Jbel Ayachi** *Mt* Mor
70B2 **Jbel Ouarkziz** *Mts* Mor
70B1 **Jbel Sarhro** *Mt* Mor
17D4 **Jeanerette** USA
71G4 **Jebba** Nig
64D2 **Jebel 'Abd al 'Azīz** *Mt* Syria
72C2 **Jebel Abyad** *Desert Region* Sudan
67G2 **Jebel Akhdar** *Mt* Oman
64C4 **Jebel al Lawz** *Mt* S Arabia
65C2 **Jebel ash Shaykh** *Mt* Syria
72D1 **Jebel Asoteriba** *Mt* Sudan
65D1 **Jebel az Zāwīyah** *Upland* Syria
65C4 **Jebel Bāqir** *Mt* Jordan
66C4 **Jebel Belaia** *Mt* Eth
65C3 **Jebel Ed Dabab** *Mt* Jordan
65C3 **Jebel el Ata'ita** *Mt* Jordan
65C4 **Jebel el Harad** *Mt* Jordan
64C3 **Jebel esh Sharqi** *Mts* Leb/Syria
66C3 **Jebel Hamoyet** *Mt* Sudan
65C3 **Jebel Hārūn** *Mt* Jordan
65D3 **Jebel Ithrīyat** *Mt* Jordan
67G2 **Jebel Ja'lan** *Mt* Oman
65C2 **Jebel Liban** *Mts* Leb
65D2 **Jebel Ma'lūlā** *Mt* Syria
72C2 **Jebel Marra** *Mt* Sudan
65C3 **Jebel Mubrak** *Mt* Jordan
65D3 **Jebel Mudeisisat** *Mt* Jordan
66C2 **Jebel Oda** *Mt* Sudan
65C3 **Jebel Qasr ed Deir** *Mt* Jordan
65C4 **Jebel Qatim** *Mt* Jordan
65C4 **Jebel Ram** Jordan
65C2 **Jebel Um ed Daraj** *Mt* Jordan
65C4 **Jebel Um el Hashim** *Mt* Jordan
65C4 **Jebel Um Ishrīn** *Mt* Jordan
72C1 **Jebel Uweinat** *Mt* Sudan
34D4 **Jedburgh** Scot
Jedda = Jiddah
43E2 **Jędrzejów** Pol
11D3 **Jefferson** Iowa, USA
17D3 **Jefferson** Texas, USA
18D1 **Jefferson** *R* USA
9D3 **Jefferson City** USA
8B3 **Jefferson,Mt** USA
12B3 **Jeffersonville** USA
71G3 **Jega** Nig
29A3 **Jejui-Guazú** *R* Par
44D4 **Jekabpils** Latvia
42D2 **Jelena Góra** Pol
44C4 **Jelgava** Latvia
56D4 **Jember** Indon
16A2 **Jemez Pueblo** USA
42C2 **Jena** Germany
56C2 **Jenaja** *I* Indon
37D1 **Jenbach** Austria
71D1 **Jendouba** Tunisia
65C2 **Jenin** Israel
17D3 **Jennings** USA
3B2 **Jennings** *R* Can
42D2 **Jenseniky** *Upland* Czech
7O3 **Jensen Nunatakker** *Mt* Greenland
7K3 **Jens Munk I** Can
75B3 **Jeparit** Aust
27L6 **Jequié** Brazil
29D2 **Jequital** *R* Brazil
29D2 **Jequitinhonha** Brazil
27K7 **Jequitinhonha** *R* Brazil
71B2 **Jerada** Mor
56G7 **Jerantut** Malay
22B1 **Jerez** Mexico
39A2 **Jerez de la Frontera** Spain
39A2 **Jerez de los Caballeros** Spain
65C3 **Jericho** Israel
75C3 **Jerilderie** Aust
18D2 **Jerome** USA
38B2 **Jersey** *I* UK
9F2 **Jersey City** USA
13D2 **Jersey Shore** USA
12A3 **Jerseyville** USA
64C3 **Jerusalem** Israel
75D3 **Jervis B** Aust
3D3 **Jervis Inlet** *Sd* Can
40C1 **Jesenice** Slovenia, Yugos
61C3 **Jessore** Bang
9E3 **Jesup** USA
22D2 **Jesus Carranza** Mexico
28C2 **Jesus Maria** Arg
16C2 **Jetmore** USA
14E2 **Jewett City** USA
62C1 **Jeypore** India
41D2 **Jezerce** *Mt* Alb
43E2 **Jezioro Mamry** *L* Pol
43E2 **Jezioro80Sniardwy** *L* Pol
65C2 **Jezzine** Leb
60C4 **Jhābua** India
60D4 **Jhālāwār** India
60C2 **Jhang Maghiana** Pak
60D3 **Jhānsi** India
61B3 **Jhārsuguda** India
60C2 **Jhelum** Pak
60C2 **Jhelum** *R* Pak
9F3 **J H Kerr L** USA
60D3 **Jhunjhunūn** India
53C2 **Jiamusi** China
52C4 **Ji'an** Jiangxi, China
53B3 **Ji'an** Jilin, China
52D4 **Jiande** China
52B4 **Jiang'an** China
52D4 **Jiangbiancun** China
52A5 **Jiangcheng** China
52B3 **Jiang Jiang** *R* China
52B4 **Jiangjin** China
52C5 **Jiangmen** China
52D3 **Jiangsu** Province, China
52C4 **Jiangxi** Province, China
52A3 **Jiangyou** China
52D1 **Jianping** China
52A5 **Jianshui** China
52D4 **Jian Xi** *R* China
52D4 **Jianyang** China
53B3 **Jiaohe** China
52E2 **Jiaonan** China
52E2 **Jiao Xian** China
52E2 **Jiaozhou Wan** *B* China
52C2 **Jiaozuo** China
52E3 **Jiaxiang** China
53C2 **Jiayin** China
50C3 **Jiayuguan** China
66C2 **Jiddah** S Arabia
67G3 **Jiddat Al Harāsīs** Region, Oman
67G2 **Jiddat az Zawlīyah** Region, Oman
52D3 **Jieshou** China
52C2 **Jiexiu** China
71H3 **Jigawa** *State* Nig
52A3 **Jigzhi** China
42D3 **Jihlava** Czech Republic
71D1 **Jijel** Alg
72E3 **Jilib** Somalia
53B3 **Jilin** China
53B3 **Jilin** Province, China
53A1 **Jiliu He** *R* China
39B1 **Jiloca** *R* Spain
72D3 **Jima** Eth
16B4 **Jiménez** Coahuila, Mexico
22C1 **Jiménez** Tamaulipas, Mexico
52D2 **Jinan** China
60D3 **Jind** India
52B2 **Jingbian** China
52D4 **Jingdezhen** China
55C1 **Jinghong** China
52C3 **Jingmen** China
52B2 **Jingning** China
52B4 **Jing Xiang** China
52D4 **Jinhua** China
52C1 **Jining** Nei Monggol, China
52D2 **Jining** Shandong, China
72D3 **Jinja** Uganda
55C1 **Jinping** China
52A4 **Jinsha Jiang** *R* China
52C4 **Jinshi** China
52E1 **Jinxi** China
52E2 **Jin Xian** China
52E1 **Jinzhou** China
26F5 **Jiparaná** *R* Brazil
26B4 **Jipijapa** Ecuador
22B2 **Jiquilpan** Mexico
63D3 **Jiroft** Iran
69D4 **Jirriban** Somalia
52B4 **Jishou** China
64C2 **Jisr ash Shughūr** Syria
41E2 **Jiu** *R* Rom
52D4 **Jiujiang** China
52A4 **Jiulong** China
52D4 **Jiulong Jiang** *R* China
53B3 **Jiutai** China
63E3 **Jiwani** Pak
53C2 **Jixi** China
65C3 **Jiza** Jordan
66D3 **Jīzan** S Arabia
70A3 **Joal** Sen
29D2 **João Monlevade** Brazil
27M5 **João Pessoa** Brazil
27J7 **João Pinheiro** Brazil
29C2 **João Pirheiro** Brazil
29C3 **Joboticabal** Brazil
28B2 **Jocoli** Arg
60C3 **Jodhpur** India
32K6 **Joensuu** Fin
36C2 **Joeuf** France
3E3 **Joffre,Mt** Can
61C2 **Jogbani** India
62A2 **Jog Falls** India
74D2 **Johannesburg** S Africa

Johannesburg **Karaman**

19C3 **Johannesburg** USA
7L2 **Johan Pen** Can
10H2 **John** *R* USA
18C2 **John Day** USA
18B1 **John Day** *R* USA
3E2 **John d'Or Prairie** Can
13D3 **John H. Kerr Res** USA
16B2 **John Martin Res** USA
34D2 **John O'Groats** Scot
17C2 **John Redmond Res** USA
14A2 **Johnsonburg** USA
14C1 **Johnson City** New York, USA
15C1 **Johnson City** Tennessee, USA
15C2 **Johnston** USA
23N2 **Johnston Pt** St Vincent
14C1 **Johnstown** New York, USA
13D2 **Johnstown** Pennsylvania, USA
55C5 **Johor Bharu** Malay
38C2 **Joigny** France
25G3 **Joinville** Brazil
36C2 **Joinville** France
44J5 **Jok** *R* Russian Fed
32H5 **Jokkmokk** Sweden
67E4 **Jōl** *Mts* Yemen
45H8 **Jolfa** Iran
9E2 **Joliet** USA
7L5 **Joliette** Can
57F9 **Jolo** Phil
57F9 **Jolo** *I* Phil
59H2 **Joma** *Mt* China
43E1 **Jonava** Lithuania
52A3 **Jonê** China
9D3 **Jonesboro** Arkansas, USA
17D3 **Jonesboro** Louisiana, USA
7K2 **Jones Sd** Can
43E1 **Joniškis** Lithuania
32G7 **Jönköping** Sweden
5G4 **Jonquière** Can
9D3 **Joplin** USA
64C3 **Jordan** Kingdom, S W Asia
11A2 **Jordan** Montana, USA
14B1 **Jordan** New York, USA
65C2 **Jordan** *R* Israel
18C2 **Jordan Valley** USA
29B4 **Jordão** *R* Brazil
61D2 **Jorhāt** India
44C2 **Jörn** Sweden
56D3 **Jorong** Indon
32F7 **Jørpeland** Nor
71H4 **Jos** Nig
28E2 **José Batlle y Ordoñez** Urug
57F8 **Jose Pañganiban** Phil
28E2 **José Pedro Varela** Urug
76B2 **Joseph Bonaparte G** Aust
19D3 **Joseph City** USA
34G3 **Josephine** *Oilfield* N Sea
71H4 **Jos Plat** Nig
48B3 **Jotunheimen** *Mt* Nor
65C2 **Jouai'ya** Leb
65C2 **Jounié** Leb
61D2 **Jowal** India
72E3 **Jowhar** Somalia
10M3 **Joy,Mt** Can
27K5 **Juàjeiro** Brazil
22B1 **Juan Aldama** Mexico
6F5 **Juan de Fuca,Str of** USA/Can
73E5 **Juan de Nova** *I* Mozam Chan
28D3 **Juárez** Arg
27L5 **Juazeiro do Norte** Brazil
72D3 **Juba** Sudan
72E3 **Juba** *R* Somalia
65C1 **Jubail** Leb
64D3 **Jubbah** S Arabia
39B2 **Jucar** *R* Spain
22C2 **Juchatengo** Mexico
22B1 **Juchipila** *R* Mexico
22C2 **Juchitán** Mexico
22B1 **Juchitlan** Mexico
42C3 **Judenburg** Austria
26D7 **Juilaca** Peru
52C4 **Juiling Shan** *Hills* China
27K8 **Juiz de Fora** Brazil
25C2 **Jujuy** State, Arg
16B1 **Julesburg** USA
26E7 **Juli** Peru
27G3 **Julianatop** *Mt* Suriname
7O3 **Julianehåb** Greenland
36D1 **Jülich** Germany
37E1 **Julijske Alpen** *Mts* Slovenia, Yugos
28E1 **Júlio de Castilhos** Brazil
61B2 **Jumla** Nepal
65C3 **Jum Suwwāna** *Mt* Jordan
60C4 **Jūnāgadh** India
52D2 **Junan** China
16C3 **Junction** Texas, USA
19D3 **Junction** Utah, USA
8D3 **Junction City** USA
25G2 **Jundiaí** Brazil
6E4 **Juneau** USA
76D4 **Junee** Aust
20C2 **June Lake** USA
40B1 **Jungfrau** *Mt* Switz
14B2 **Juniata** *R* USA
25D4 **Junín** Arg
28A3 **Junín de los Andes** Arg
20B2 **Junipero Serra Peak** *Mt* USA
52A4 **Junlian** China
25G2 **Juquiá** Brazil
72C3 **Jur** *R* Sudan
34C4 **Jura** *I* Scot
38D2 **Jura** *Mts* France
34C3 **Jura,Sound of** *Chan* Scot
65C3 **Jurf ed Darāwīsh** Jordan
48K4 **Jurga** Russian Fed
44C4 **Jūrmala** Latvia
26E4 **Juruá** *R* Brazil
27G6 **Juruena** *R* Brazil
53B2 **Jusheng** China
65D1 **Jūsīyah** Syria
28B2 **Justo Daract** Arg
26E4 **Jutai** *R* Brazil
21D3 **Juticalpa** Honduras
Jutland = Jylland
63D2 **Jūymand** Iran
42B1 **Jylland** *Pen* Den
32K6 **Jyväskyla** Fin

K

59F2 **K2** *Mt* China/India
71H3 **Ka** *R* Nig
63D1 **Kaakhka** Turkmenistan
74E2 **Kaapmuiden** S Africa
76B1 **Kabaena** *I* Indon
70A4 **Kabala** Sierra Leone
72D4 **Kabale** Rwanda
72C4 **Kabalo** Zaïre
72C4 **Kabambare** Zaïre
72D3 **Kabarole** Uganda
71H4 **Kabba** Nig
76B1 **Kabia** *I* Indon
12C1 **Kabinakagami L** Can
4E3 **Kabinakagami** *R* Can
72C4 **Kabinda** Zaïre
65C1 **Kabīr** *R* Syria
63B2 **Kabir Kuh** *Mts* Iran
73C5 **Kabompo** Zambia
73C5 **Kabompo** *R* Zambia
73C4 **Kabongo** Zaïre
60B2 **Kabul** Afghan
57C2 **Kaburuang** *I* Indon
66B3 **Kabushiya** Sudan
60B4 **Kachchh,G of** India
44K4 **Kachkanar** Russian Fed
49M4 **Kachug** Russian Fed
55B3 **Kadan** Burma
56E3 **Kadapongan** *I* Indon
77G2 **Kadavu** *I* Fiji
60C4 **Kadi** India
75A2 **Kadina** Aust
64B2 **Kadınhanı** Turk
62B2 **Kadiri** India
45F6 **Kadiyevka** Ukraine
11B3 **Kadoka** USA
73C5 **Kadoma** Zim
72C2 **Kadugli** Sudan
71H3 **Kaduna** Nig
71H3 **Kaduna** State, Nig
71H3 **Kaduna** *R* Nig
62B2 **Kadūr** India
61E2 **Kadusam** *Mt* China
44K3 **Kadzherom** Russian Fed
54A3 **Kaechon** N Korea
70A3 **Kaédi** Maur
20E5 **Kaena Pt** Hawaiian Is
53B4 **Kaesŏng** N Korea
71H4 **Kafanchan** Nig
70A3 **Kaffrine** Sen
65D1 **Kafr Behum** Syria
65A3 **Kafr Sa'd** Egypt
65A3 **Kafr Saqv** Egypt
65D1 **Kafrūn Bashūr** Syria
73C5 **Kafue** Zambia
73C5 **Kafue** *R* Zambia
73C5 **Kafue Nat Pk** Zambia
53D4 **Kaga** Japan
10C6 **Kagalaska** *I* USA
48H6 **Kagan** Uzbekistan
45G7 **Kağizman** Turk
66B4 **Kagmar** Sudan
53C5 **Kagoshima** Japan
43F3 **Kagul** Moldova
63D1 **Kāhak** Iran
72D4 **Kahama** Tanz
60B3 **Kahan** Pak
56D3 **Kahayan** *R* Indon
73B4 **Kahemba** Zaïre
36E1 **Kahler Asten** *Mt* Germany
63D3 **Kahnūj** Iran
12A2 **Kahoka** USA
20E5 **Kahoolawe** *I* Hawaiian Is
64C2 **Kahramanmaraş** Turk
20E5 **Kahuku Pt** Hawaiian Is
20E5 **Kahului** Hawaiian Is
78B2 **Kaiapoi** NZ
19D3 **Kaibab Plat** USA
27G2 **Kaieteur Fall** Guyana
52C3 **Kaifeng** China
78B1 **Kaikohe** NZ
77G5 **Kaikoura** NZ
78B2 **Kaikoura Pen** NZ
78B2 **Kaikoura Range** *Mts* NZ
52B4 **Kaili** China
20E5 **Kailua** Hawaiian Is
51G7 **Kaimana** Indon
54C4 **Kainan** Japan
71G3 **Kainji Res** Nig
78B1 **Kaipara Harbour** *B* NZ
52C5 **Kaiping** China
71E1 **Kairouan** Tunisia
20C2 **Kaiser Peak** *Mt* USA
38D2 **Kaiserslautern** Germany
42B3 **Kaiserslautern** Germany
53B3 **Kaishantun** China
43E2 **Kaisiadorys** Lithuania
78B1 **Kaitaia** NZ
78A3 **Kaitangata** NZ
60D3 **Kaithal** India
20E5 **Kaiwi Chan** Hawaiian Is
52B3 **Kai Xian** China
52A5 **Kaiyuan** Liaoning, China
53A3 **Kaiyuan** Yunnan, China
10G3 **Kaiyuh Mts** USA
32K6 **Kajaani** Fin
60B2 **Kajaki** Afghan
56F7 **Kajang** Malay
72D4 **Kajiado** Kenya
60B2 **Kajrān** Afghan
72D2 **Kaka** Sudan
12B1 **Kakabeka Falls** Can
72D3 **Kakamega** Kenya
54B4 **Kake** Japan
10M4 **Kake** USA
10H4 **Kakhonak** USA
45E6 **Kakhovskoye Vodokhranilishche** *Res* Ukraine
63C3 **Kākī** Iran
62C1 **Kākināda** India
3E1 **Kakiska L** Can
54B4 **Kakogawa** Japan
10K1 **Kaktovik** USA
54D3 **Kakuda** Japan
71D1 **Kalaa El Khasba** Tunisia
Kalaallit Nunaat = Greenland
57B4 **Kalabahi** Indon
41E3 **Kalabáka** Greece
56E2 **Kalabakan** Malay
73C5 **Kalabo** Zambia
45G5 **Kalach** Russian Fed
45G6 **Kalach-na-Donu** Russian Fed
61D3 **Kaladan** *R* Burma
20E5 **Ka Lae** *C* Hawaiian Is
73C6 **Kalahari Desert** Botswana
74C2 **Kalahari Gemsbok Nat Pk** S Africa
63E1 **Kalai-Mor** Turkmenistan
44C3 **Kalajoki** Fin
49N4 **Kalakan** Russian Fed
56A2 **Kalakepen** Indon
60C1 **Kalam** Pak
41E3 **Kalámai** Greece
9E2 **Kalamazoo** USA
57B4 **Kalao** *I* Indon
57B4 **Kalaotoa** *I* Indon
20E5 **Kalapana** Hawaiian Is
43F3 **Kalarsh** Moldova
60B3 **Kalat** Pak
20E5 **Kalaupapa** Hawaiian Is
67G2 **Kalbān** Oman
64B1 **Kalecik** Turk
57B4 **Kaledupa** *I* Indon
56E3 **Kalembau** *I* Indon
72C4 **Kalémié** Zaïre
44E2 **Kalevala** Russian Fed
61D3 **Kalewa** Burma
10H3 **Kalgin I** USA
76B4 **Kalgoorlie** Aust
61B2 **Kali** *R* India
56C4 **Kalianda** Indon
57F8 **Kalibo** Phil
72C4 **Kalima** Zaïre
56D3 **Kalimantan** Province, Indon
41F3 **Kálimnos** *I* Greece
61C2 **Kālimpang** India
44F4 **Kalinin** Russian Fed
32J8 **Kaliningrad** Russian Fed
45D5 **Kalinkovichi** Belorussia
43F3 **Kalinovka** Ukraine
8B2 **Kalispell** USA
43D2 **Kalisz** Pol
72D4 **Kaliua** Tanz
32J5 **Kalix** *R* Sweden
73B6 **Kalkfeld** Namibia
74C1 **Kalkfontein** Botswana
74B1 **Kalkrand** Namibia
75A1 **Kallakoopah** *R* Aust
32K6 **Kallávesi** *L* Fin
41F3 **Kallonis Kólpos** *B* Greece
32H7 **Kalmar** Sweden
45H6 **Kalmytskaya Respublika**, Russian Fed
57B3 **Kalolio** Indon
73C5 **Kalomo** Zambia
12A2 **Kalona** USA
3C3 **Kalone Peak** *Mt* Can
62A2 **Kalpeni** *I* India
60D3 **Kālpi** India
10F3 **Kalskag** USA
10G3 **Kaltag** USA
44F5 **Kaluga** Russian Fed
32G7 **Kalundborg** Den
43E3 **Kalush** Ukraine
62A1 **Kalyān** India
62B2 **Kalyandurg** India
44F4 **Kalyazin** Russian Fed
71J4 **Kam** *R* Nig
44J3 **Kama** *R* Russian Fed
53E4 **Kamaishi** Japan
60C2 **Kamalia** Pak
78C1 **Kamanawa Mts** NZ
73B5 **Kamanjab** Namibia
49O4 **Kamara** China
66D3 **Kamarān** *I* Yemen
5J2 **Kamarsuk** Can
60D2 **Kamat** *Mt* India
62B3 **Kamban** India
44J4 **Kambarka** Russian Fed
70A4 **Kambia** Sierra Leone
49S4 **Kamchatka** *Pen* Russian Fed
43F3 **Kamenets Podolskiy** Ukraine
44G5 **Kamenka** Russian Fed
48K4 **Kamen-na-Obi** Russian Fed
53C3 **Kamen' Rybolov** Russian Fed
49S3 **Kamenskoya** Russian Fed
44L4 **Kamensk-Ural'skiy** Russian Fed
74B3 **Kamieskroon** S Africa
6H3 **Kamilukuak L** Can
73C4 **Kamina** Zaïre
7J3 **Kaminak L** Can
54D3 **Kaminoyama** Japan
6F4 **Kamloops** Can
64E1 **Kamo** Armenia
54D3 **Kamogawa** Japan
72D3 **Kampala** Uganda
55C5 **Kampar** Malay
56B2 **Kampar** *R* Indon
42B2 **Kampen** Neth
55B2 **Kamphaeng Phet** Thai
55C3 **Kampot** Camb
3H3 **Kamsack** Can
63E3 **Kamsaptar** Iran
44K4 **Kamskoye Vodokhranilishche** *Res* Russian Fed
60D4 **Kāmthi** India
3H2 **Kamuchawie L** Can
45H5 **Kamyshin** Russian Fed
44L4 **Kamyshlov** Russian Fed
7L4 **Kanaaupscow** *R* Can
19D3 **Kanab** USA
10C6 **Kanaga** *I* USA
37E1 **Kanal** Slovenia, Yugos
72C4 **Kananga** Zaïre
44H4 **Kanash** Russian Fed
54C3 **Kanayama** Japan
53D4 **Kanazawa** Japan
62B2 **Kānchipuram** India
60B2 **Kandahar** Afghan
5J3 **Kanairiktok** *R* Can
44E2 **Kandalaksha** Russian Fed
32L5 **Kandalakshskaya Guba** *B* Russian Fed
71G4 **Kandé** Togo
36D2 **Kandel** *Mt* Germany
71G3 **Kandi** Benin
75C2 **Kandos** Aust
62C3 **Kandy** Sri Lanka
13D2 **Kane** USA
7L1 **Kane Basin** *B* Can
72B2 **Kanem** *Desert Region* Chad
20E5 **Kaneohe** Hawaiian Is
44F2 **Kanevka** Russian Fed
37E2 **Kanfanar** Slovenia, Yugos
74C1 **Kang** Botswana
70B3 **Kangaba** Mali
64C2 **Kangal** Turk
7N3 **Kangâmiut** Greenland
63C3 **Kangān** Iran
55C4 **Kangar** Malay
76C4 **Kangaroo I** Aust
7N3 **Kangâtsiaq** Greenland
63B2 **Kangavar** Iran
52C1 **Kangbao** China
59G3 **Kangchenjunga** *Mt* Nepal
52A4 **Kangding** China
7P3 **Kangerdlugssuaq** *B* Greenland
7P3 **Kangerdlugssuatsaiq** *B* Greenland
72D3 **Kangetet** Kenya
53B3 **Kanggye** N Korea
7M4 **Kangiqsualujjuaq** Can
7L3 **Kangiqsujuak** Can
7L3 **Kangirsuk** Can
53B4 **Kangnŭng** S Korea
72B3 **Kango** Gabon
50C4 **Kangto** *Mt* China
52B3 **Kang Xian** China
55D4 **Kanh Hung** Viet
73C4 **Kaniama** Zaïre
62B1 **Kani Giri** India
44G2 **Kanin, Poluostrov** *Pen* Russian Fed
32J6 **Kankaanpää** Fin
12B2 **Kankakee** USA
12B2 **Kankakee** *R* USA
70B3 **Kankan** Guinea
61B3 **Kānker** India
15C1 **Kannapolis** USA
62B3 **Kanniyākuman** India
Kannur = Cannanore
71H3 **Kano** Nig
71H3 **Kano** State, Nig
71H3 **Kano** *R* Nig
16B2 **Kanorado** USA
53C5 **Kanoya** Japan
61B2 **Kānpur** India
8D3 **Kansas** State, USA
17C2 **Kansas** *R* USA
9D3 **Kansas City** USA
52D5 **Kanshi** China
49L4 **Kansk** Russian Fed
54A3 **Kansŏng** S Korea
71G3 **Kantchari** Burkina
61C3 **Kanthi** India
10H3 **Kantishna** USA
10H3 **Kantishna** *R* USA
74D1 **Kanye** Botswana
50E4 **Kao-hsiung** Taiwan
73B5 **Kaoka Veld** *Plain* Namibia
70A3 **Kaolack** Sen
73C5 **Kaoma** Zambia
20E5 **Kapaa** Hawaiian Is
20E5 **Kapaau** Hawaiian Is
73C4 **Kapanga** Zaïre
7O3 **Kap Cort Adelaer** *C* Greenland
7O3 **Kap Dalton** *C* Greenland
32H7 **Kapellskär** Sweden
7O4 **Kap Farvel** *C* Greenland
7P3 **Kap Gustav Holm** *C* Greenland
73C5 **Kapiri** Zambia
4E3 **Kapiskau** *R* Can
56D2 **Kapit** Malay
17D3 **Kaplan** USA
42C3 **Kaplice** Czech Republic
55B4 **Kapoe** Thai
73C4 **Kapona** Zaïre
41D1 **Kaposvár** Hung
7L2 **Kap Parry** *C* Greenland
7O3 **Kap Ravn** *C* Greenland
54A2 **Kapsan** N Korea
56C3 **Kapuas** *R* Indon
75A2 **Kapunda** Aust
60D2 **Kapurthala** India
7K5 **Kapuskasing** Can
12C1 **Kapuskasing** *R* Can
75D2 **Kaputar** *Mt* Aust
45H8 **Kapydzhik** *Mt* Armenia
54A3 **Kapyŏng** S Korea
7M2 **Kap York** *C* Greenland
71G4 **Kara** Togo
71G4 **Kara** *R* Togo
64B1 **Karabük** Turk
41F2 **Karacabey** Turk
60B4 **Karachi** Pak
62A1 **Karād** India
45F7 **Kara Daglari** *Mt* Turk
45D7 **Karadeniz Boğazi** *Sd* Turk
50E1 **Karaftit** Russian Fed
48J5 **Karaganda** Kazakhstan
48J5 **Karagayly** Kazakhstan
49S4 **Karaginskiy, Ostrov** *I* Russian Fed
62B2 **Kāraikāl** India
63C1 **Karaj** Iran
64C3 **Karak** Jordan
56F7 **Karak** Malay
48G5 **Kara Kalpakskaya Respublika**, Uzbekistan
60D1 **Karakax He** *R* China
57C2 **Karakelong** *I* Indon
60D1 **Karakoram** *Mts* India
60D1 **Karakoram** *P* India/China
70A3 **Karakoro** *R* Maur/Sen
63E1 **Karakumskiy Kanal** Turkmenistan
48G6 **Karakumy** *Desert* Russian Fed
65C3 **Karama** Jordan
57A3 **Karama** *R* Indon
45E8 **Karaman** Turk

Karamay Khaskovo

48K5 **Karamay** China
78B2 **Karamea** NZ
78B2 **Karamea Bight** *B* NZ
45E8 **Karanhk** *R* Turk
60D4 **Kāranja** India
64B2 **Karapınar** Turk
48J2 **Kara S** Russian Fed
74B2 **Karasburg** Namibia
32K5 **Karasjok** Nor
48J4 **Karasuk** Russian Fed
64C2 **Karataş** Turk
48H5 **Kara Tau** *Mts* Kazakhstan
55B3 **Karathuri** Burma
53B5 **Karatsu** Japan
48K2 **Karaul** Russian Fed
65B1 **Karavostasi** Cyprus
37E1 **Karawanken** *Mts* Austria
63C3 **Karāz** Iran
64D3 **Karbalā'** Iraq
43E3 **Karcag** Hung
41E3 **Kardhítsa** Greece
44E3 **Karel'skaya** Respublika, Russian Fed
62E2 **Karen** Andaman Is
44K3 **Karepino** Russian Fed
32J5 **Karesvando** Sweden
70B2 **Karet** *Desert Region* Maur
48K4 **Kargasok** Russian Fed
44F3 **Kargopol'** Russian Fed
45G8 **Karh** *R* Turk
71J3 **Kari** Nig
73C5 **Kariba** Zim
73C5 **Kariba** *L* Zim/Zambia
73C5 **Kariba Dam** Zim/Zambia
74B1 **Karibib** Namibia
72D2 **Karima** Sudan
56C3 **Karimata** *I* Indon
61D3 **Karimganj** Bang
62B1 **Karīmnagar** India
72E2 **Karin** Somalia
32J6 **Karis** Fin
72C4 **Karishimbe** *Mt* Zaïre
41E3 **Káristos** Greece
62A2 **Kārkal** India
51H7 **Karkar** *I* PNG
63B2 **Karkheh** *R* Iran
45E6 **Karkinitskiy Zaliv** *B* Ukraine
49L5 **Karlik Shan** *Mt* China
42D2 **Karlino** Pol
40D2 **Karlobag** Croatia, Yugos
40D1 **Karlovac** Croatia, Yugos
41E2 **Karlovo** Bulg
42C2 **Karlovy Vary** Czech Republic
32G7 **Karlshamn** Sweden
32G7 **Karlskoga** Sweden
32H7 **Karlskrona** Sweden
42B3 **Karlsruhe** Germany
32G7 **Karlstad** Sweden
11C2 **Karlstad** USA
10H4 **Karluk** USA
61D3 **Karnafuli Res** Bang
60D3 **Karnal** India
62A1 **Karnataka** State, India
41F2 **Karnobat** Bulg
37E1 **Kärnten** Province, Austria
73C5 **Karoi** Zim
73D4 **Karonga** Malawi
72D2 **Karora** Sudan
57A3 **Karossa** Indon
41F3 **Kárpathos** *I* Greece
7N2 **Karrats Fjord** Greenland
74C3 **Karree Berge** S Africa
45G7 **Kars** Turk
48H5 **Karsakpay** Kazakhstan
43F1 **Kārsava** Latvia
58E2 **Karshi** Uzbekistan
32J6 **Karstula** Fin
65C1 **Kartaba** Leb
41F2 **Kartal** Turk
44L5 **Kartaly** Russian Fed
14A2 **Karthaus** USA
63B2 **Kārūn** *R* Iran
61B2 **Karwa** India
62A2 **Kārwār** India
50E1 **Karymskoye** Russian Fed
72B4 **Kasai** *R* Zaïre
73C5 **Kasaji** Zaïre
73D5 **Kasama** Zambia
73D4 **Kasanga** Tanz
62A2 **Kāsaragod** India
6H3 **Kasba L** Can
71A2 **Kasba Tadla** Mor
10F1 **Kasegaluk Lg** USA
73C5 **Kasempa** Zambia
73C5 **Kasenga** Zaïre
72D3 **Kasese** Uganda
63C2 **Kāshān** Iran
10G3 **Kashegelok** USA
59F2 **Kashi** China
54B4 **Kashima** Japan
60D3 **Kāshipur** India
53D4 **Kashiwazaki** Japan
63D1 **Kashmar** Iran
46E4 **Kashmir** State, India
44G5 **Kasimov** Russian Fed
57C3 **Kasiruta** *I* Indon
12B3 **Kaskaskia** *R* USA
4C2 **Kaskattama** *R* Can
32J6 **Kasko** Fin
44L4 **Kasli** Russian Fed
6G5 **Kaslo** Can
3H2 **Kasmere L** Can
72C4 **Kasonga** Zaïre
73B4 **Kasongo-Lunda** Zaïre
41F3 **Kásos** *I* Greece
Kaspiyskiy = Lagan'
72D2 **Kassala** Sudan
42B2 **Kassel** Germany
71D1 **Kasserine** Tunisia
73B5 **Kassinga** Angola
64B1 **Kastamonou** Turk
41E3 **Kastélli** Greece
64A2 **Kastellorizon** *I* Greece
41E2 **Kastoría** Greece
41F3 **Kástron** Greece
53D4 **Kasugai** Japan
54B3 **Kasumi** Japan
73D5 **Kasungu** Malawi
60C2 **Kasur** Pak
73C5 **Kataba** Zambia
13F1 **Katahdin,Mt** USA
72C4 **Katako-kombe** Zaïre
6D3 **Katalla** USA
49Q4 **Katangli** Russian Fed
76A4 **Katanning** Aust
62E3 **Katchall** *I* Indian O
41E2 **Kateríni** Greece
6E4 **Kates Needle** *Mt* Can/USA
61E3 **Katha** Burma
76C2 **Katherine** Aust
60C4 **Kāthiāwār** *Pen* India
65B3 **Kathib El Henu** Egypt
61C2 **Kathmandu** Nepal
60D2 **Kathua** India
61C2 **Katihār** India
73C5 **Katima Mulilo** Namibia
6C4 **Katmai,Mt** USA
10H4 **Katmai Nat Mon** USA
61B3 **Katni** India
75D2 **Katoomba** Aust
43D2 **Katowice** Pol
32H7 **Katrineholm** Sweden
71H3 **Katsina** Nig
71H3 **Katsina** *Region* Nig
71H3 **Katsina** *State* Nig
71H4 **Katsina Ala** Nig
54D3 **Katsuta** Japan
54D3 **Katsuura** Japan
54C3 **Katsuy** Japan
48H6 **Kattakurgan** Uzbekistan
32G7 **Kattegat** *Str* Denmark/Sweden
36E2 **Katzenbuckel** *Mt* Germany
57C2 **Kau** Indon
20E5 **Kauai** *I* Hawaiian Is
20E5 **Kauai Chan** Hawaiian Is
20E5 **Kaulakahi Chan** Hawaiian Is
20E5 **Kaunakaki** Hawaiian Is
44C5 **Kaunas** Lithuania
71H3 **Kaura Namoda** Nig
32J5 **Kautokeino** Nor
41E2 **Kavadarci** Macedonia, Yugos
41D2 **Kavajë** Alb
53D3 **Kavalerovo** Russian Fed
62B2 **Kavali** India
41E2 **Kavália** Greece
60B4 **Kāvda** India
76E1 **Kavieng** PNG
54C3 **Kawagoe** Japan
54C3 **Kawaguchi** Japan
20E5 **Kawaihae** Hawaiian Is
78B1 **Kawakawa** NZ
73C4 **Kawambwa** Zambia
61B3 **Kawardha** India
13D2 **Kawartha Lakes** Can
53D4 **Kawasaki** Japan
20C2 **Kaweah** *R* USA
78C1 **Kawerau** NZ
78B1 **Kawhia** NZ
71F3 **Kaya** Burkina
10K4 **Kayak I** USA
56E2 **Kayan** *R* Indon
62B3 **Kāyankulam** India
11A3 **Kaycee** USA
57C3 **Kayeli** Indon
19D3 **Kayenta** USA
70A3 **Kayes** Mali
45F8 **Kayseri** Turk
49P2 **Kazach'ye** Russian Fed
64E1 **Kazakh** Azerbaijan
48G5 **Kazakhstan**
44H4 **Kazan'** Russian Fed
41F2 **Kazanlŭk** Bulg
50H4 **Kazan Retto** *Is* Japan
43F3 **Kazatin** Ukraine
45G7 **Kazbek** *Mt* Georgia
63C3 **Kāzerūn** Iran
44J3 **Kazhim** Russian Fed
64E1 **Kazi Magomed** Azerbaijan
43E3 **Kazincbarcika** Hung
44M3 **Kazym** *R* Russian Fed
44M3 **Kazymskaya** Russian Fed
41E3 **Kéa** *I* Greece
20E5 **Kealaikahiki Chan** Hawaiian Is
8D2 **Kearney** USA
19D4 **Kearny** USA
64C2 **Keban Baraji** *Res* Turk
71G3 **Kebbi** *State* Nig
70A3 **Kébémer** Sen
71J4 **Kebi** *R* Chad
71D2 **Kebili** Tunisia
65D1 **Kebīr** *R* Syria/Leb
32H5 **Kebrekaise** *Mt* Sweden
3C2 **Kechika** *R* Can
43D3 **Kecskemet** Hung
43E1 **Kedainiai** Lithuania
5H4 **Kedgwick** Can
53B2 **Kedong** China
70A3 **Kédougou** Sen
44J3 **Kedva** Russian Fed
10N4 **Keechiga** *R* Can
10N3 **Keele** *R* Can
10M3 **Keele Pk** *Mt* Can
19C3 **Keeler** USA
20C3 **Keene** California, USA
13E2 **Keene** New Hampshire, USA
74B2 **Keetmanshoop** Namibia
12B2 **Keewanee** USA
4C4 **Keewatin** Can
12A1 **Keewatin** USA
6J3 **Keewatin** *Region* Can
41E3 **Kefallinía** *I* Greece
57B4 **Kefamenanu** Indon
65C2 **Kefar Sava** Israel
71H4 **Keffi** Nig
32A2 **Keflavik** Iceland
6G4 **Keg River** Can
66B3 **Keheili** Sudan
55B1 **Kehsi Mansam** Burma
75B3 **Keith** Aust
34D3 **Keith** Scot
6F3 **Keith Arm** *B* Can
7M3 **Kekertuk** Can
60D3 **Kekri** India
55C5 **Kelang** Malay
57C3 **Kelang** *I* Indon
55C4 **Kelantan** *R* Malay
71E1 **Kelibia** Tunisia
60B1 **Kelif** Turkmenistan
64C1 **Kelkit** *R* Turk
72B4 **Kellé** Congo
10O3 **Keller L** Can
6F2 **Kellet,C** Can
18C1 **Kellogg** USA
48D3 **Kelloselka** Fin
35B5 **Kells** Irish Rep
34C4 **Kells Range** *Hills* Scot
43E1 **Kelme** Lithuania
6G5 **Kelowna** Can
6F4 **Kelsey Bay** Can
34D4 **Kelso** Scot
18B1 **Kelso** USA
3H3 **Kelvington** Can
44E3 **Kem'** Russian Fed
44E3 **Kem'** *R* Russian Fed
70B3 **Ke Macina** Mali
3C3 **Kemano** Can
48K4 **Kemerovo** Russian Fed
32J5 **Kemi** Fin
32K5 **Kemi** *R* Fin
32K5 **Kemijärvi** Fin
18D2 **Kemmerer** USA
36C1 **Kempen** Region, Belg
16C3 **Kemp,L** USA
23B2 **Kemps Bay** Bahamas
75D2 **Kempsey** Aust
42C3 **Kempten** Germany
10H3 **Kenai** USA
10H4 **Kenai Mts** USA
10H3 **Kenai Pen** USA
72D3 **Kenamuke Swamp** Sudan
35D4 **Kendal** Eng
75D2 **Kendall** Aust
76B1 **Kendari** Indon
56D3 **Kendawangan** Indon
61C3 **Kendrāpāra** India
18C1 **Kendrick** USA
17F4 **Kenedy** USA
70A4 **Kenema** Sierra Leone
72B4 **Kenge** Zaïre
55B1 **Kengtung** Burma
74C2 **Kenhardt** S Africa
70A3 **Kéniéba** Mali
71A2 **Kenitra** Mor
11B2 **Kenmare** USA
16B3 **Kenna** USA
13F1 **Kennebec** *R* USA
14E1 **Kennebunk** USA
14A1 **Kennedy** USA
17D4 **Kenner** USA
17E2 **Kennett** USA
14C3 **Kennett Square** USA
18C1 **Kennewick** USA
6F4 **Kenny Dam** Can
4D3 **Kenogami** *R* Can
7J5 **Kenora** Can
9E2 **Kenosha** USA
35F6 **Kent** County, Eng
16B3 **Kent** Texas, USA
18B1 **Kent** Washington, USA
12B2 **Kentland** USA
12C2 **Kenton** USA
6H3 **Kent Pen** Can
9E3 **Kentucky** State, USA
12C3 **Kentucky** *R* USA
9E3 **Kentucky L** USA
5J4 **Kentville** Can
17D3 **Kentwood** Louisiana, USA
12B2 **Kentwood** Michigan, USA
72D3 **Kenya** Republic, Africa
72D4 **Kenya,Mt** Kenya
12A2 **Keokuk** USA
61B3 **Keonchi** India
61C3 **Keonjhargarh** India
51G7 **Kepaluan Tanimbar** *Arch* Indon
43D2 **Kępno** Pol
57C3 **Kepualuan Widi** *Arch* Indon
57B4 **Kepulauan Alor** *Arch* Indon
56C2 **Kepulauan Anambas** *Arch* Indon
51G7 **Kepulauan Aru** *Arch* Indon
76B1 **Kepulauan Babar** *I* Indon
56C2 **Kepulauan Badas** *Is* Indon
51G7 **Kepulauan Banda** *Arch* Indon
76B1 **Kepulauan Banggai** *I* Indon
76B1 **Kepulauan Barat Daya** *Is* Indon
56C2 **Kepulauan Bunguran Seletan** *Arch* Indon
57D3 **Kepulauan Gorong** *Arch* Indon
51G7 **Kepulauan Kai** *Arch* Indon
57C2 **Kepulauan Kawio** *Arch* Indon
76B1 **Kepulauan Leti** *I* Indon
56B3 **Kepulauan Lingga** *Is* Indon
57C2 **Kepulauan Loloda** *Arch* Indon
56A3 **Kepulauan Mentawi** *Arch* Indon
57C2 **Kepulauan Nenusa** *Arch* Indon
57C3 **Kepulauan Obi** *Arch* Indon
56B2 **Kepulauan Riau** *Arch* Indon
56E4 **Kepulauan Sabalana** *Arch* Indon
57C2 **Kepulauan Sangihe** *Arch* Indon
76B1 **Kepulauan Sermata** *I* Indon
76B1 **Kepulauan Sula** *I* Indon
57C2 **Kepulauan Talaud** *Arch* Indon
56C2 **Kepulauan Tambelan** *Is* Indon
76C1 **Kepulauan Tanimbar** *I* Indon
76B1 **Kepulauan Togian** *I* Indon
76B1 **Kepulauan Tukangbesi** *Is* Indon
57D3 **Kepulauan Watubela** *Arch* Indon
57C3 **Kepulauan Yef Fam** *Arch* Indon
57B4 **Kepulaun Solor** *Arch* Indon
62B2 **Kerala** State, India
75B3 **Kerang** Aust
32J6 **Kerava** Fin
53D1 **Kerbi** *R* Russian Fed
45F6 **Kerch'** Ukraine
44J3 **Kerchem'ya** Russian Fed
76D1 **Kerema** PNG
18C1 **Keremeps** Can
72D2 **Keren** Eritrea
xxviiiE7 **Kerguelen Ridge** Indian O
72D4 **Kericho** Kenya
56B3 **Kerinci** *Mt* Indon
72D3 **Kerio** *R* Kenya
58E2 **Kerki** Turkmenistan
41D3 **Kérkira** Greece
41D3 **Kérkira** *I* Greece
77H3 **Kermadec Is** NZ
77H4 **Kermadec Trench** Pacific O
63D2 **Kerman** Iran
20B2 **Kerman** USA
63B2 **Kermānshāh** Iran
41F3 **Kerme Körfezi** *B* Turk
16B3 **Kermit** USA
19C3 **Kern** *R* USA
20C3 **Kernville** USA
44J3 **Keros** Russian Fed
3G3 **Kerrobert** Can
16C3 **Kerrville** USA
15C2 **Kershaw** USA
56C3 **Kertamulia** Indon
49N5 **Kerulen** *R* Mongolia
70B2 **Kerzaz** Alg
4F3 **Kesagami L** Can
41F2 **Keşan** Turk
53E4 **Kesennuma** Japan
53B2 **Keshan** China
45G7 **Kesir Daglari** *Mt* Turk
32L5 **Kesten'ga** Russian Fed
35D4 **Keswick** Eng
71G4 **Kéta** Ghana
56D3 **Ketapang** Indon
6E4 **Ketchikan** USA
70C3 **Ketia** Niger
60B4 **Keti Bandar** Pak
71G4 **Kétou** Benin
43E2 **Kętrzyn** Pol
35E5 **Kettering** Eng
12C3 **Kettering** USA
4D2 **Kettle** *R* Can
18C1 **Kettle** *R* Can
20C2 **Kettleman City** USA
18C1 **Kettle River Range** *Mts* USA
7L3 **Kettlestone B** Can
14B1 **Keuka L** USA
63D2 **Kevir-i Namak** *Salt Flat* Iran
12B2 **Kewaunee** USA
12B1 **Keweenaw B** USA
12B1 **Keweenaw Pen** USA
4E4 **Key Harbour** Can
15E4 **Key Largo** USA
14A3 **Keyser** USA
9E4 **Key West** USA
49M4 **Kezhma** Russian Fed
41D1 **K'félegháza** Hung
10F3 **Kgun L** USA
65D2 **Khabab** Syria
53D2 **Khabarovsk** Russian Fed
45G8 **Khabur** *R* Syria
60B3 **Khairpur** Pak
60B3 **Khairpur** Region, Pak
74C1 **Khakhea** Botswana
65B3 **Khalig El Tina** *B* Egypt
67G2 **Khalīj Maşirah** *B* Oman
41F3 **Khálki** *I* Greece
41E2 **Khalkidhíki** *Pen* Greece
41E3 **Khalkís** Greece
44L2 **Khal'mer-Yu** Russian Fed
44H4 **Khalturin** Russian Fed
67G2 **Khalūf** Oman
60C4 **Khambhāt,G of** India
60D4 **Khāmgaon** India
66D3 **Khamir** Yemen
66D3 **Khamis Mushayt** S Arabia
55C2 **Kham Keut** Laos
62C1 **Khammam** India
65B3 **Khamsa** Egypt
63B1 **Khamseh** *Mts* Iran
55C2 **Khan** *R* Laos
60B1 **Khanabad** Afghan
64E3 **Khānaqīn** Iraq
60D4 **Khandwa** India
60C2 **Khanewal** Pak
65D3 **Khan ez Zabib** Jordan
55D4 **Khanh Hung** Viet
41E3 **Khaniá** Greece
53C3 **Khanka, Ozero** *L* China
Khankendy = Stepanakert
60C3 **Khanpur** Pak
65D1 **Khān Shaykhūn** Syria
48H3 **Khanty-Mansiysk** Russian Fed
65C3 **Khan Yunis** Egypt
60D1 **Khapalu** India
50E2 **Khapcheranga** Russian Fed
45H6 **Kharabali** Russian Fed
61C3 **Kharagpur** India
63D3 **Khāran** Iran
60B3 **Kharan** Pak
63C2 **Kharānaq** Iran
63C3 **Khārg** *Is* Iran
69C2 **Khârga Oasis** Egypt
60D4 **Khargon** India
45F6 **Khar'kov** Ukraine
44F2 **Kharlovka** Russian Fed
41F2 **Kharmanli** Bulg
44G4 **Kharovsk** Russian Fed
72D2 **Khartoum** Sudan
72D2 **Khartoum North** Sudan
53C3 **Khasan** Russian Fed
63E2 **Khash** Afghan
63E3 **Khāsh** Iran
63E2 **Khash** *R* Afghan
72D2 **Khashm el Girba** Sudan
61D2 **Khasi-Jaīntia Hills** India
41F2 **Khaskovo** Bulg

Khatanga **Komsomolets, Ostrov**

49M2 **Khatanga** Russian Fed
49N2 **Khatangskiy Zaliv** *Estuary* Russian Fed
49T3 **Khatyrka** Russian Fed
55B3 **Khawsa** Burma
66C1 **Khaybar** S Arabia
66B2 **Khazzan an-Nasr** *L* Egypt
55C2 **Khe Bo** Viet
60C4 **Khed Brahma** India
39C2 **Khemis** Alg
71A2 **Khemisset** Mor
71D1 **Khenchela** Alg
71A2 **Khenifra** Mor
39D2 **Kherrata** Alg
45E6 **Kherson** Ukraine
49N4 **Khilok** Russian Fed
41F3 **Khíos** Greece
41F3 **Khíos** *I* Greece
45D6 **Khmel'nitskiy** Ukraine
43E3 **Khodorov** Ukraine
59E1 **Khodzhent** Taji
60B1 **Kholm** Afghan
43G1 **Kholm** Russian Fed
53E2 **Kholmsk** Russian Fed
74B1 **Khomas Hochland, Mts** Namibia
55D3 **Khong** Laos
63C3 **Khonj** Iran
53C2 **Khor** Russian Fed
53D2 **Khor** *R* Russian Fed
63B2 **Khoramshahr** Iran
67F2 **Khōr Duwayhin** *B* UAE
60C1 **Khorog** Tajikistan
63B2 **Khorramābad** Iran
63D2 **Khosf** Iran
60B2 **Khost** Pak
45D6 **Khotin** Ukraine
10G3 **Khotol** *Mt* USA
71A2 **Khouribga** Mor
45D5 **Khoyniki** Belorussia
49Q3 **Khrebet Cherskogo** *Mts* Russian Fed
53B1 **Khrebet Dzhagdy** *Mts* Russian Fed
49P4 **Khrebet Dzhugdzhur** *Mts* Russian Fed
10C2 **Khrebet Iskamen** *Mts* Russian Fed
49O3 **Khrebet Orulgan** *Mts* Russian Fed
44L2 **Khrebet Pay-khoy** *Mts* Russian Fed
53D2 **Khrebet Sikhote Alin'** *Mts* Russian Fed
59G1 **Khrebet Tarbagatay** *Mts* Kazakhstan
49O4 **Khrebet Tukuringra** *Mts* Russian Fed
53C1 **Khrebet Turana** *Upland* Russian Fed
65B1 **Khrysokhou B** Cyprus
44L3 **Khulga** *R* Russian Fed
61C3 **Khulna** Bang
60D1 **Khunjerab** *P* China/India
63C2 **Khunsar** Iran
67E1 **Khurays** S Arabia
61C3 **Khurda** India
60D3 **Khurja** India
67G3 **Khūryan Mūryān** *Is* Oman
60C2 **Khushab** Pak
65C2 **Khushnīyah** Syria
43E3 **Khust** Ukraine
72C2 **Khuwei** Sudan
60B3 **Khuzdar** Pak
63E2 **Khvāf** Iran
45H5 **Khvalynsk** Russian Fed
63D2 **Khvor** Iran
63C3 **Khvormūj** Iran
45G8 **Khvoy** Iran
60C1 **Khwaja Muhammad** *Mts* Afghan
60C2 **Khyber P** Afghan/Pak
73C4 **Kiambi** Zaïre
17C3 **Kiamichi** *R* USA
10F2 **Kiana** USA
72B4 **Kibangou** Congo
72D4 **Kibaya** Tanz
72C4 **Kibombo** Zaïre
72D4 **Kibondo** Tanz
72D4 **Kibungu** Rwanda
41E2 **Kičevo** Macedonia, Yugos
6G4 **Kicking Horse P** Can
70C3 **Kidal** Mali
35D5 **Kidderminster** Eng
70A3 **Kidira** Sen
78C1 **Kidnappers,C** NZ
42C2 **Kiel** Germany
43E2 **Kielce** Pol
42C2 **Kieler Bucht** *B* Germany
Kiev = Kiyev
58E2 **Kifab** Uzbekistan
70A3 **Kiffa** Maur
68H8 **Kigali** Rwanda
5J2 **Kiglapatt,C** Can
10E3 **Kigluaik Mts** USA
72C4 **Kigoma** Tanz
20E5 **Kiholo** Hawaiian Is
54C4 **Kii-sanchi** *Mts* Japan
53C5 **Kii-suido** *B* Japan
49R4 **Kikhchik** Russian Fed
41E1 **Kikinda** Serbia, Yugos
Kikládhes = Cyclades
76D1 **Kikon** PNG
54D2 **Kikonai** Japan
51H7 **Kikori** PNG
72B4 **Kikwit** Zaïre
20E5 **Kilauea Crater** *Mt* Hawaiian Is
6C3 **Kilbuck Mts** USA
53B3 **Kilchu** N Korea
75D1 **Kilcoy** Aust
35B5 **Kildane** County, Irish Rep
35B5 **Kildare** Irish Rep
17D3 **Kilgore** USA
72E4 **Kilifi** Kenya
72D4 **Kilimanjaro** *Mt* Tanz
73D4 **Kilindoni** Tanz
64C2 **Kilis** Turk
43F3 **Kiliya** Ukraine
35B5 **Kilkenny** County, Irish Rep
35B5 **Kilkenny** Irish Rep
41E2 **Kilkís** Greece
75D1 **Killarney** Aust
33B3 **Killarney** Irish Rep
17C3 **Killeen** USA
10H2 **Killik** *R* USA
34C3 **Killin** Scot
5J1 **Killinek I** Can
41E3 **Killíni** *Mt* Greece
34C4 **Kilmarnock** Scot
44J4 **Kil'mez** Russian Fed
73D4 **Kilosa** Tanz
33B3 **Kilrush** Irish Rep
71J4 **Kilunga** *R* Nig
73C4 **Kilwa** Zaïre
73D4 **Kilwa Kisiwani** Tanz
73D4 **Kilwa Kivinje** Tanz
71J4 **Kim** *R* Cam
75A2 **Kimba** Aust
16B1 **Kimball** USA
10K3 **Kimball,Mt** USA
3E4 **Kimberley** Can
74C2 **Kimberley** S Africa
76B2 **Kimberley Plat** Aust
53B3 **Kimch'aek** N Korea
53B4 **Kimch'ŏn** S Korea
54A3 **Kimhae** S Korea
41E3 **Kími** Greece
54A3 **Kimje** S Korea
44F4 **Kimry** Russian Fed
54A3 **Kimwha** N Korea
56E1 **Kinabalu** *Mt* Malay
56E1 **Kinabatangan** *R* Malay
4E5 **Kincardine** Can
3C2 **Kincolith** Can
17D3 **Kinder** USA
3G3 **Kindersley** Can
70A3 **Kindia** Guinea
72C4 **Kindu** Zaïre
44J5 **Kinel'** Russian Fed
44G4 **Kineshma** Russian Fed
75D1 **Kingaroy** Aust
19B3 **King City** USA
6F4 **Kingcome Inlet** Can
10F4 **King Cove** USA
17C2 **Kingfisher** USA
7L4 **King George Is** Can
76D5 **King I** Aust
3C3 **King I** Can
44C4 **Kingissepp** Estonia
76B2 **King Leopold Range** *Mts* Aust
8B3 **Kingman** USA
72C4 **Kingombe** Zaïre
75A2 **Kingoonya** Aust
20C2 **Kingsburg** USA
19C3 **Kings Canyon Nat Pk** USA
75A3 **Kingscote** Aust
76B2 **King Sd** Aust
12B1 **Kingsford** USA
15C2 **Kingsland** USA
35F5 **King's Lynn** Eng
77G1 **Kingsmill Group** *Is* Kiribati
14D2 **Kings Park** USA
8B2 **Kings Peak** *Mt* USA
15C1 **Kingsport** USA
76C4 **Kingston** Aust
7L5 **Kingston** Can
21E3 **Kingston** Jamaica
13E2 **Kingston** New York, USA
78A3 **Kingston** NZ
14C2 **Kingston** Pennsylvania, USA
23E4 **Kingstown** St Vincent
8D4 **Kingsville** USA
5J2 **Kingurutik** *R* Can
34C3 **Kingussie** Scot
6J3 **King William I** Can
74D3 **King William's Town** S Africa
72B4 **Kinkala** Congo
32G7 **Kinna** Sweden
34D3 **Kinnairds Head** *Pt* Scot
54C3 **Kinomoto** Japan
34D3 **Kinross** Scot
72B4 **Kinshasa** Zaïre
16C2 **Kinsley** USA
15D1 **Kinston** USA
56E3 **Kintap** Indon
34C4 **Kintyre** *Pen* Scot
3E2 **Kinuso** Can
72D3 **Kinyeti** *Mt* Sudan
36E1 **Kinzig** *R* Germany
3H2 **Kipahigan L** Can
41E3 **Kiparissía** Greece
41E3 **Kiparissiakós Kólpos** *G* Greece
13D1 **Kipawa,L** Can
73D4 **Kipili** Tanz
10F4 **Kipnuk** USA
35B5 **Kippure** *Mt* Irish Rep
73C5 **Kipushi** Zaïre
36E2 **Kirchheim** Germany
49M4 **Kirensk** Russian Fed
48J5 **Kirgizia**
59F1 **Kirgizskiy Khrebet** *Mts* Kirgizia
72B4 **Kiri** Zaïre
77G1 **Kiribati** *Is* Pacific O
64B2 **Kırıkkale** Turk
44E4 **Kirishi** Russian Fed
60B3 **Kirithar Range** *Mts* Pak
41F3 **Kirkağaç** Turk
45H8 **Kirk Bulāg Dāgh** *Mt* Iran
35D4 **Kirkby** Eng
34D3 **Kirkcaldy** Scot
34C4 **Kirkcudbright** Scot
32K5 **Kirkenes** Nor
7K5 **Kirkland Lake** Can
64A1 **Kırklareli** Turk
79E **Kirkpatrick,Mt** Ant
9D2 **Kirksville** USA
64D2 **Kirkūk** Iraq
34D2 **Kirkwall** Scot
17D2 **Kirkwood** USA
74D3 **Kirkwood** *R* S Africa
44E5 **Kirov** Russian Fed
44H4 **Kirov** Russian Fed
45H7 **Kirovabad** Azerbaijan
64D1 **Kirovakan** Armenia
44K4 **Kirovgrad** Russian Fed
45E6 **Kirovograd** Ukraine
44E2 **Kirovsk** Russian Fed
49R4 **Kirovskiy** Kamchatka, Russian Fed
53C2 **Kirovskiy** Primorskiykray, Russian Fed
44J4 **Kirs** Russian Fed
64B2 **Kirşehir** Turk
42C2 **Kiruna** Sweden
54C3 **Kiryū** Japan
72C3 **Kisangani** Zaïre
57C4 **Kisar** *I* Indon
56A2 **Kisaran** Indon
54C3 **Kisarazu** Japan
61C2 **Kishanganj** India
60C3 **Kishangarh** India
43F3 **Kishinev** Moldova
54C4 **Kishiwada** Japan
72D4 **Kisii** Kenya
73D4 **Kisiju** Tanz
10B6 **Kiska** *I* USA
4B3 **Kiskitto L** Can
43D3 **Kiskunhalas** Hung
45G7 **Kislovodsk** Russian Fed
72E4 **Kismaayo** Somalia
54C3 **Kiso-sammyaku** *Mts* Japan
70B4 **Kissidougou** Guinea
15C3 **Kissimmee,L** USA
3H2 **Kississing L** Can
72D4 **Kisumu** Kenya
43E3 **Kisvárda** Hung
70B3 **Kita** Mali
48H6 **Kitab** Uzbekistan
54D3 **Kitakami** Japan
54D3 **Kitakami** *R* Japan
54D3 **Kitakata** Japan
53C5 **Kita-Kyūshū** Japan
72D3 **Kitale** Kenya
50H4 **Kitalo** *I* Japan
53E3 **Kitami** Japan
54D2 **Kitami-Esashi** Japan
16B2 **Kit Carson** USA
7K5 **Kitchener** Can
4F3 **Kitchigama** *R* Can
72D3 **Kitgum** Uganda
41E3 **Kithira** *I* Greece
41E3 **Kithnos** *I* Greece
65B1 **Kiti,C** Cyprus
6G2 **Kitikmeot** Region, Can
6F4 **Kitimat** Can
32K5 **Kitnen** *R* Fin
54B4 **Kitsuki** Japan
13D2 **Kittanning** USA
13E2 **Kittery** USA
32J5 **Kittilä** Fin
15D1 **Kitty Hawk** USA
73D4 **Kitunda** Tanz
10N4 **Kitwanga** Can
73C5 **Kitwe** Zambia
42C3 **Kitzbühel** Austria
37E1 **Kitzbühler Alpen** *Mts* Austria
42C3 **Kitzingen** Germany
72C4 **Kiumbi** Zaïre
10F2 **Kivalina** USA
43F2 **Kivercy** Ukraine
72C4 **Kivu,L** Zaïre/Rwanda
6B3 **Kiwalik** USA
45E5 **Kiyev** Ukraine
43G2 **Kiyevskoye Vodokhranilishche** *Res* Ukraine
44K4 **Kizel** Russian Fed
44G3 **Kizema** Russian Fed
64C2 **Kizil** *R* Turk
58D2 **Kizyl-Arvat** Turkmenistan
45J8 **Kizyl-Atrek** Turkmenistan
42C2 **Kladno** Czech Republic
42C3 **Klagenfurt** Austria
44C4 **Klaipēda** Lithuania
18B2 **Klamath** USA
8A2 **Klamath** *R* USA
8A2 **Klamath Falls** USA
18B2 **Klamath Mts** USA
3C2 **Klappan** *R* Can
42C3 **Klatovy** Czech Republic
10M4 **Klawak** USA
65C1 **Kleiat** Leb
74B2 **Kleinsee** S Africa
74D2 **Klerksdorp** S Africa
43G2 **Kletnya** Russian Fed
36D1 **Kleve** Germany
43G2 **Klimovichi** Belorussia
44F4 **Klin** Russian Fed
43D1 **Klintehamn** Sweden
45E5 **Klintsy** Russian Fed
74C3 **Klipplaat** S Africa
40D2 **Ključ** Bosnia-Herzegovina, Yugos
42D2 **Kłodzko** Pol
10L3 **Klondike** *R* USA/Can
6D3 **Klondike Plat** USA/Can
42D3 **Klosterneuburg** Austria
10L3 **Kluane** *R* Can
10L3 **Kluane L** Can
10L3 **Kluane Nat Pk** Can
43D2 **Kluczbork** Pol
10L4 **Klukwan** USA
10J3 **Klutina L** USA
10J3 **Knight I** USA
35D5 **Knighton** Wales
40D2 **Knin** Croatia, Yugos
76A4 **Knob,C** Aust
36B1 **Knokke-Heist** Belg
10M5 **Knox,C** Can
79G9 **Knox Coast** Ant
11D3 **Knoxville** Iowa, USA
9E3 **Knoxville** Tennessee, USA
7Q3 **Knud Ramsussens Land** *Region* Greenland
74C3 **Knysna** S Africa
56C3 **Koba** Indon
7O3 **Kobberminebugt** *B* Greenland
53D5 **Kobe** Japan
42C1 **København** Den
37E1 **Kobiard** Slovenia, Yugos
42B2 **Koblenz** Germany
53C1 **Koboldo** Russian Fed
44C5 **Kobrin** Russian Fed
51G7 **Kobroör** *I* Indon
10G2 **Kobuk** *R* USA
41E2 **Kočani** Macedonia, Yugos
54A3 **Kochang** S Korea
54A3 **Koch'ang** S Korea
55C3 **Ko Chang** *I* Thai
61C2 **Koch Bihār** India
37D1 **Kochel** Germany
36E2 **Kocher** *R* Germany
7L3 **Koch I** Can
Kochi = Cochin
53C5 **Kōchi** Japan
10H4 **Kodiak** USA
10H4 **Kodiak I** USA
62B2 **Kodiyakkari** India
72D3 **Kodok** Sudan
54D2 **Kodomari-misaki** *C* Japan
43F3 **Kodyma** Ukraine
20D3 **Koehn L** USA
74B2 **Koes** Namibia
74D2 **Koffiefontein** S Africa
71F4 **Koforidua** Ghana
53D4 **Kōfu** Japan
54C3 **Koga** Japan
5J2 **Kogaluk** *R* Can
32G7 **Køge** Den
71H4 **Kogi** *State* Nig
60C2 **Kohat** Pak
60B2 **Koh-i-Baba** *Mts* Afghan
60B1 **Koh-i-Hisar** *Mts* Afghan
60B2 **Koh-i-Khurd** *Mt* Afghan
61D2 **Kohima** India
60B1 **Koh-i-Mazar** *Mt* Afghan
63E2 **Koh-i-Qaisar** *Mt* Afghan
60B3 **Kohlu** Pak
44D4 **Kohtla Järve** Estonia
54A4 **Kohung** S Korea
54A4 **Kohyon** S Korea
54C3 **Koide** Japan
10K3 **Koidern** Can
55A4 **Koihoa** *Is* Nicobar Is
54A2 **Koin** N Korea
53B5 **Kōje-do** *I* S Korea
54C2 **Ko-jima** *I* Japan
48H4 **Kokchetav** Kazakhstan
32J6 **Kokemaki** *L* Fin
32J6 **Kokkola** Fin
71G3 **Koko** Nig
76D1 **Kokoda** PNG
12B2 **Kokomo** USA
51G7 **Kokonau** Indon
50B2 **Kokpekty** Kazakhstan
54A3 **Koksan** N Korea
7M4 **Koksoak** *R* Can
54A3 **Koksŏng** S Korea
74D3 **Kokstad** S Africa
55C3 **Ko Kut** *I* Thai
44E2 **Kola** Russian Fed
57B3 **Kolaka** Indon
55B4 **Ko Lanta** *I* Thai
62B2 **Kolār** India
62B2 **Kolār Gold Fields** India
70A3 **Kolda** Sen
32F7 **Kolding** Den
53E1 **Kolendo** Russian Fed
44H2 **Kolguyev, Ostrov** *I* Russian Fed
62A1 **Kolhāpur** India
10G4 **Koliganek** USA
42D2 **Kolín** Czech Republic
Kollam = Quilon
42B2 **Köln** Germany
43D2 **Kolo** Pol
20E5 **Koloa** Hawaiian Is
42D2 **Kolobrzeg** Pol
70B3 **Kolokani** Mali
44F4 **Kolomna** Russian Fed
45D6 **Kolomyya** Ukraine
57B3 **Kolono** Indon
57B3 **Kolonodale** Indon
49R4 **Kolpakovskiy** Russian Fed
48K4 **Kolpashevo** Russian Fed
41F3 **Kólpos Merabéllou** *B* Greece
41E2 **Kólpos Singitikós** *G* Greece
41E2 **Kólpos Strimonikós** *G* Greece
41E2 **Kólpos Toronaíos** *G* Greece
44F2 **Kol'skiy Poluostrov** *Pen* Russian Fed
44K2 **Kolva** *R* Russian Fed
32G6 **Kolvereid** Nor
73C5 **Kolwezi** Zaïre
49R3 **Kolyma** *R* Russian Fed
49R3 **Kolymskaya Nizmennost** *Lowland* Russian Fed
49S3 **Kolymskoye Nagor'ye** *Mts* Russian Fed
10D2 **Kolyuchinskaya Guba** *B* Russian Fed
41E2 **Kom** *Mt* Bulg/Serbia
72D3 **Koma** Eth
54D3 **Koma** Japan
71J3 **Komaduga Gana** *R* Nig
71J3 **Komadugu Yobé** *R* Nig
54D2 **Komaga take** *Mt* Japan
49S4 **Komandorskiye Ostrova** *I* Russian Fed
43D3 **Komárno** Slovakia
74E2 **Komati,R** S Africa
74E2 **Komati Poort** S Africa
53D4 **Komatsu** Japan
54B4 **Komatsushima** Japan
71F3 **Kombissiri** Burkina
44J3 **Komi** Respublika, Russian Fed
50B1 **Kommunar** Russian Fed
57A4 **Komodo** *I* Indon
71F4 **Komoé** *R* Ivory Coast
51G7 **Komoran** *I* Indon
54C3 **Komoro** Japan
41F2 **Komotiní** Greece
74C3 **Kompasberg** *Mt* S Africa
55D3 **Kompong Cham** Camb
55C3 **Kompong Chhnang** *Mts* Camb
Kompong Som = Sihanoukville
55D3 **Kompong Thom** Camb
55D3 **Kompong Trabek** Camb
43F3 **Komrat** Moldova
74C3 **Komsberg** *Mts* S Africa
49Li **Komsomolets, Ostrov** *I* Russian Fed

Komsomol'skiy — Kzyl Orda

44L2 **Komsomol'skiy** Russian Fed
49P4 **Komsomol'sk na Amure** Russian Fed
48H4 **Konda** *R* Russian Fed
61B4 **Kondagaon** India
72D4 **Kondoa** Tanz
53D1 **Kondon** Russian Fed
44E3 **Kondopoga** Russian Fed
62B1 **Kondukür** India
10C2 **Konergino** Russian Fed
44F3 **Konevo** Russian Fed
7P3 **Kong Christian IX Land** *Region* Greenland
7O3 **Kong Frederik VI Kyst** *Region* Greenland
54A3 **Kongju** S Korea
48D2 **Kong Karls Land** *Is* Barents S
56E2 **Kongkemul** *Mt* Indon
72C4 **Kongolo** Zaïre
71F3 **Kongoussi** Burkina
32F7 **Kongsberg** Den
32G6 **Kongsvinger** Nor
Königsberg = Kaliningrad
37E1 **Königsee, L** Germany
43D2 **Konin** Pol
41D2 **Konjic** Bosnia-Herzegovina, Yugos
71F4 **Konongo** Ghana
44G3 **Konosha** Russian Fed
54C3 **Konosu** Japan
45E5 **Konotop** Ukraine
43E2 **Końskie** Pol
36E3 **Konstanz** Germany
71H3 **Kontagora** Nig
55D3 **Kontum** Viet
10B2 **Konus** *Mt* Russian Fed
45E8 **Konya** Turk
18C1 **Kootenay** *L* Can
3E4 **Kootenay** *R* Can
60C5 **Kopargaon** India
7R3 **Kópasker** Iceland
32A2 **Kópavogur** Iceland
40C1 **Koper** Slovenia, Yugos
58D2 **Kopet Dag** *Mts* Iran/Turkmenistan
44L4 **Kopeysk** Russian Fed
55C4 **Ko Phangan** *I* Thai
55B4 **Ko Phuket** *I* Thai
32H7 **Köping** Sweden
54A3 **Kopo-ri** S Korea
62B1 **Koppal** India
40D1 **Koprivnica** Croatia, Yugos
60B4 **Korangi** Pak
62C1 **Koraput** India
61B3 **Korba** India
42B2 **Korbach** Germany
41E2 **Korçë** Alb
40D2 **Korčula** *I* Croatia, Yugos
52E2 **Korea B** China/Korea
53B5 **Korea Str** S Korea/Japan
43F2 **Korec** Ukraine
49S3 **Korf** Russian Fed
64B1 **Körğlu Tepesi** *Mt* Turk
70B4 **Korhogo** Ivory Coast
60B4 **Kori Creek** India
41E3 **Korinthiakós Kólpos** *G* Greece
41E3 **Kórinthos** Greece
53E4 **Kōriyama** Japan
44L5 **Korkino** Russian Fed
49R3 **Korkodon** Russian Fed
49R3 **Korkodon** *R* Russian Fed
64B2 **Korkuteli** Turk
59G1 **Korla** China
65B1 **Kormakiti,C** Cyprus
40D2 **Kornat** *I* Croatia, Yugos
45E7 **Köroğlu Tepesi** *Mt* Turk
72D4 **Korogwe** Tanz
75B3 **Koroit** Aust
51G6 **Koror** Palau Is, Pacific O
43E3 **Körös** *R* Hung
45D5 **Korosten** Ukraine
43F2 **Korostyshev** Ukraine
72B2 **Koro Toro** Chad
10F4 **Korovin** *I* USA
53E2 **Korsakov** Russian Fed
32G7 **Korsør** Den
66B3 **Korti** Sudan
44J3 **Kortkeroz** Russian Fed
42A2 **Kortrijk** Belg
49S3 **Koryakskoye Nagor'ye** *Mts* Russian Fed
54A3 **Koryong** S Korea
41F3 **Kós** *I* Greece
10D2 **Kosa Belyaka** *B* Russian Fed
55C4 **Ko Samui** *I* Thai
54A3 **Kosan** N Korea
43D2 **Koscierzyna** Pol
15B2 **Kosciusko** USA
76D4 **Kosciusko** *Mt* Aust
10M4 **Kosciusko I** USA
53B5 **Koshikijima-retto** *I* Japan
43E3 **Kosiče** Slovakia
44J2 **Kosma** *R* Russian Fed
53B4 **Kosong** N Korea
41E2 **Kosovo** *Aut Republic* Serbia, Yugos
70B4 **Kossou** *L* Ivory Coast
74D2 **Koster** S Africa
72D2 **Kosti** Sudan
43F2 **Kostopol'** Ukraine
44G4 **Kostroma** Russian Fed
42C2 **Kostrzyn** Pol
44K2 **Kos'yu** *R* Russian Fed
32H8 **Koszalin** Pol
60D3 **Kota** India
56B4 **Kotaagung** Indon
56D3 **Kotabaharu** Indon
56E3 **Kotabaru** Indon
55C4 **Kota Bharu** Malay
56C3 **Kotabum** Indon
60C2 **Kot Addu** Pak
56E1 **Kota Kinabulu** Malay
57B2 **Kotamobagu** Indon
62C1 **Kotapad** India
56F7 **Kotapinang** *I* Indon
56G8 **Kota Tinggi** Malay
44H4 **Kotel'nich** Russian Fed
45G6 **Kotel'nikovo** Russian Fed
49P2 **Kotel'nyy, Ostrov** *I* Russian Fed
32K6 **Kotka** Fin
44H3 **Kotlas** Russian Fed
10F3 **Kotlik** USA
71H4 **Koton Karifi** Nig
41D2 **Kotor** Montenegro, Yugos
45D6 **Kotovsk** Ukraine
60B3 **Kotri** Pak
37E1 **Kötschach** Austria
62C1 **Kottagüdem** India
62B3 **Kottayam** India
72C3 **Kotto** *R* CAR
62B2 **Kottūru** India
49L3 **Kotuy** *R* Russian Fed
10F2 **Kotzebue** USA
6B3 **Kotzebue Sd** USA
71G3 **Kouande** Benin
72C3 **Kouango** CAR
71F3 **Koudougou** Burkina
74C3 **Kougaberge** *Mts* S Africa
72B4 **Koulamoutou** Gabon
70B3 **Koulikoro** Mali
71F3 **Koupéla** Burkina
71F3 **Kouri** Mali
27H2 **Kourou** French Guiana
70B3 **Kouroussa** Guinea
72B2 **Kousséri** Cam
32K6 **Kouvola** Fin
32L5 **Kovdor** Russian Fed
32L5 **Kovdozero, Ozero** *L* Russian Fed
43E2 **Kovel'** Ukraine
Kovno = Kaunas
44G4 **Kovrov** Russian Fed
44G5 **Kovylkino** Russian Fed
44F3 **Kovzha** *R* Russian Fed
55C4 **Ko Way** *I* Thai
52C5 **Kowloon** Hong Kong
54A3 **Kowŏn** N Korea
60B2 **Kowt-e-Ashrow** Afghan
64A2 **Köyceğiz** Turk
44G2 **Koyda** Russian Fed
62A1 **Koyna Res** India
44H3 **Koynas** Russian Fed
57C2 **Koyoa** *I* Indon
10F3 **Koyuk** USA
10F2 **Koyuk** *R* USA
10G3 **Koyukuk** USA
10G2 **Koyukuk** *R* USA
64C2 **Kozan** Turk
41E2 **Kozańi** Greece
Kozhikode = Calicut
44K2 **Kozhim** Russian Fed
44H4 **Koz'modemyansk** Russian Fed
54C4 **Kōzu-shima** *I* Japan
71G4 **Kpandu** Ghana
74D3 **Kraai** *R* S Africa
32F7 **Kragerø** Nor
41E2 **Kragujevac** Serbia, Yugos
55B3 **Kra,Isthmus of** Burma/Malay
Krakatau = Rakata
65D1 **Krak des Chevaliers** *Hist Site* Syria
43D2 **Kraków = Cracow** Pol
41E2 **Kraljevo** Serbia, Yugos
45F6 **Kramatorsk** Ukraine
32H6 **Kramfors** Sweden
40C1 **Kranj** Slovenia, Yugos
44H3 **Krasavino** Russian Fed
44J1 **Krasino** Russian Fed
43E2 **Kraśnik** Pol
45H5 **Krasnoarmeysk** Russian Fed
45F6 **Krasnodar** Russian Fed
53E2 **Krasnogorsk** Russian Fed
44K4 **Krasnokamsk** Russian Fed
44L4 **Krasnotur'insk** Russian Fed
44K4 **Krasnoufimsk** Russian Fed
44K5 **Krasnousol'-skiy** Russian Fed
44K3 **Krasnovishersk** Russian Fed
45J7 **Krasnovodsk** Turkmenistan
49L4 **Krasnoyarsk** Russian Fed
43E2 **Krasnystaw** Pol
45H5 **Krasnyy Kut** Russian Fed
45F6 **Krasnyy Luch** Ukraine
45H6 **Krasnyy Yar** Russian Fed
55D3 **Kratie** Camb
7N2 **Kraulshavn** Greenland
42B2 **Krefeld** Germany
45E6 **Kremenchug** Ukraine
45E6 **Kremenchugskoye Vodokhranilische** *Res* Ukraine
43F2 **Kremenets** Ukraine
16A1 **Kremming** USA
10E5 **Krenitzin Is** USA
72A3 **Kribi** Cam
44E5 **Krichev** Belorussia
37E1 **Krimml** Austria
32J6 **Krinstinestad** Fin
62B1 **Krishna** *R* India
62B2 **Krishnagiri** India
61C3 **Krishnangar** India
32F7 **Kristiansand** Nor
32G7 **Kristianstad** Sweden
48B3 **Kristiansund** Nor
32G7 **Kristineham** Sweden
Kríti = Crete
45E6 **Krivoy Rog** Ukraine
40C1 **Krk** *I* Croatia, Yugos
74D1 **Krokodil** *R* S Africa
49S4 **Kronotskaya Sopka** *Mt* Russian Fed
7P3 **Kronpris Frederik Bjerge** *Mts* Greenland
32K7 **Kronshtadt** Russian Fed
74D2 **Kroonstad** S Africa
45G6 **Kropotkin** Russian Fed
74E1 **Kruger Nat Pk** S Africa
74D2 **Krugersdorp** S Africa
56B4 **Krui** Indon
41D2 **Kruje** Alb
43F2 **Krupki** Belorussia
10F2 **Krusenstern,C** USA
41E2 **Kruševac** Serbia, Yugos
32K7 **Krustpils** Latvia
10L4 **Kruzof I** USA
45E6 **Krym** *Pen* Ukraine
45F7 **Krymsk** Russian Fed
42D2 **Krzyz** Pol
71C1 **Ksar El Boukhari** Alg
71A2 **Ksar el Kebir** Mor
56A2 **Kuala** Indon
55C5 **Kuala Dungun** Malay
56F6 **Kuala Kangsar** Malay
56G7 **Kuala Kelawang** Malay
55C4 **Kuala Kerai** Malay
55C5 **Kuala Kubu Baharu** Malay
55C5 **Kuala Lipis** Malay
55C5 **Kuala Lumpur** Malay
56G7 **Kuala Pilah** Malay
56F7 **Kuala Selangor** Malay
56A2 **Kualasimpang** Indon
55C4 **Kuala Trengganu** Malay
56E1 **Kuamut** Malay
53A3 **Kuandian** China
55C5 **Kuantan** Malay
45H7 **Kuba** Azerbaijan
51H7 **Kubar** PNG
56D2 **Kuching** Malay
56E1 **Kudat** Malay
56D4 **Kudus** Indon
44J4 **Kudymkar** Russian Fed
42C3 **Kufstein** Austria
10M2 **Kugaluk** *R* Can
10M2 **Kugmallit B** Can
63E3 **Kuhak** Iran
63D2 **Kuh Duren** *Upland* Iran
63D3 **Kūh e Bazmān** *Mt* Iran
63C2 **Kūh-e Dinar** *Mt* Iran
63D1 **Kūh-e-Hazār Masjed** *Mts* Iran
63D3 **Kūh-e Jebāl Barez** *Mts* Iran
63C2 **Kūh-e Karkas** *Mts* Iran
63D3 **Kuh-e Laleh Zar** *Mt* Iran
63B1 **Kūh-e Sahand** *Mt* Iran
63E3 **Kuh e Taftān** *Mt* Iran
45H9 **Kūhhaye Alvand** *Mts* Iran
45H8 **Kūhhaye Sabalan** *Mts* Iran
63B2 **Kūhhā-ye Zāgros** *Mts* Iran
32K6 **Kuhmo** Fin
63C2 **Kūhpāyeh** Iran
63D2 **Kūhpāyeh** *Mt* Iran
63D3 **Kūh ye Bashākerd** *Mts* Iran
63B1 **Kūh ye Sabalan** *Mt* Iran
74B2 **Kuibis** Namibia
74B1 **Kuiseb** *R* Namibia
73B5 **Kuito** Angola
10M4 **Kuiu I** USA
54A3 **Kujang** N Korea
53E3 **Kuji** Japan
54B4 **Kuju-san** *Mt* Japan
10G4 **Kukaklek L** USA
41E2 **Kukës** Alb
10F2 **Kukpowruk** *R* USA
55C5 **Kukup** Malay
63D3 **Kūl** *R* Iran
41F3 **Kula** Turk
56G8 **Kulai** Malay
45K6 **Kulakshi** Kazakhstan
72D3 **Kulal,Mt** Kenya
41E2 **Kulata** Bulg
44C4 **Kuldīga** Latvia
56F6 **Kulim** Malay
44G2 **Kulov** *R* Russian Fed
71F3 **Kulpawn** *R* Ghana
45J6 **Kul'sary** Kazakhstan
60D2 **Kulu** India
64B2 **Kulu** Turk
66D4 **Kululli** Eth
48J4 **Kulunda** Russian Fed
75B2 **Kulwin** Aust
45H7 **Kuma** *R* Russian Fed
54C3 **Kumagaya** Japan
56D3 **Kumai** Indon
45L5 **Kumak** Russian Fed
53C5 **Kumamoto** Japan
54C4 **Kumano** Japan
41E2 **Kumanovo** Macedonia, Yugos
53B1 **Kumara** China
71F4 **Kumasi** Ghana
45G7 **Kumayri** Armenia
72A3 **Kumba** Cam
62B2 **Kumbakonam** India
71J4 **Kumbo** Cam
54A3 **Kümch'ŏn** N Korea
67E2 **Kumdah** S Arabia
44K5 **Kumertau** Russian Fed
54A3 **Kumgang** N Korea
53B4 **Kümhwa** S Korea
32H7 **Kumla** Sweden
54A4 **Kümnyŏng** S Korea
54A4 **Kümo-do** *I* S Korea
61E2 **Kumon Range** *Mts* Burma
62A2 **Kumta** India
59G1 **Kümüx** China
60C2 **Kunar** *R* Afghan
53F3 **Kunashir, Ostrov** *I* Russian Fed
32K7 **Kunda** Estonia
62A2 **Kundāpura** India
60C4 **Kundla** India
60B1 **Kunduz** Afghan
68F9 **Kunene** *R* Angola
10M5 **Kunghit** *I* Can
32G7 **Kungsbacka** Sweden
44K4 **Kungur** Russian Fed
55B1 **Kunhing** Burma
59G2 **Kunlun Shan** *Mts* China
52A4 **Kunming** China
44M3 **Kunovat** *R* Russian Fed
53B4 **Kunsan** S Korea
32K6 **Kuopio** Fin
40D1 **Kupa** *R* Croatia/Bosnia-Herzegovina, Yugos
76B2 **Kupang** Indon
76D2 **Kupiano** PNG
10M4 **Kupreanof I** USA
10G4 **Kupreanof Pt** USA
45F6 **Kupyansk** Ukraine
59G1 **Kuqa** China
53C2 **Kur** *R* Russian Fed
45H8 **Kura** *R* Azerbaijan
54C3 **Kurabe** Japan
53C5 **Kurashiki** Japan
54B3 **Kurayoshi** Japan
63B1 **Kurdistan** Region, Iran
41F2 **Kūrdzhali** Bulg
53C5 **Kure** Japan
49L3 **Kureyka** *R* Russian Fed
48H4 **Kurgan** Russian Fed
Kuria Muria Is = Khūryan Mūryān
32J6 **Kurikka** Fin
Kuril Is = Kuril'skiye Ostrova
53F2 **Kuril'sk** Russian Fed
49Q5 **Kuril'skiye Ostrova** *Is* Russian Fed
xxviiiJ2 **Kuril Trench** Pacific O
45H8 **Kurinskaya Kosa** *Sand Spit* Azerbaijan
62B1 **Kurnool** India
54D2 **Kuroishi** Japan
54D3 **Kuroiso** Japan
78B2 **Kurow** NZ
75D2 **Kurri Kurri** Aust
45F5 **Kursk** Russian Fed
50B2 **Kuruktag** *R* China
74C2 **Kuruman** S Africa
74C2 **Kuruman** *R* S Africa
53C5 **Kurume** Japan
62C3 **Kurunegala** Sri Lanka
48K5 **Kurunktag** *R* China
44K3 **Kur'ya** Russian Fed
44K4 **Kusa** Russian Fed
41F3 **Kuşadasi Körfezi** *B* Turk
41F2 **Kus Golü** *L* Turk
53D5 **Kushimoto** Japan
53E3 **Kushiro** Japan
63E1 **Kushka** Afghan
61C3 **Kushtia** Bang
45J5 **Kushum** *R* Kazakhstan
44K4 **Kushva** Russian Fed
10F3 **Kuskokwim** *R* USA
10F4 **Kuskokwim B** USA
10G3 **Kuskokwim Mts** USA
61B2 **Kusma** Nepal
53E3 **Kussharo-ko** *L* Japan
48H4 **Kustanay** Kazakhstan
45D8 **Kütahya** Turk
56E3 **Kutai** *R* Indon
45G7 **Kutaisi** Georgia
54D2 **Kutchan** Japan
42D3 **Kutná Hora** Czech Republic
43D2 **Kutno** Pol
72B4 **Kutu** Zaïre
61D3 **Kutubdia I** Bang
72C2 **Kutum** Sudan
7M4 **Kuujjuaq** Can
7L4 **Kuujjuarapik** Can
32K5 **Kuusamo** Fin
45K5 **Kuvandyk** Russian Fed
64E4 **Kuwait** Kuwait
58C3 **Kuwait** Sheikdom, S W Asia
54C3 **Kuwana** Japan
48J4 **Kuybyshev** Russian Fed
44H5 **Kuybyshevskoye Vodokhranilishche** *Res* Russian Fed
44E2 **Kuyto, Ozero** *L* Russian Fed
49M4 **Kuytun** Russian Fed
45F7 **Kuzey Anadolu Daglari** *Mts* Turk
44H5 **Kuznetsk** Russian Fed
44F2 **Kuzomen** Russian Fed
44C2 **Kvaenangen** *Sd* Nor
10G4 **Kvichak** USA
10G4 **Kvichak** *R* USA
10G4 **Kvichak B** USA
32G5 **Kvigtind** *Mt* Nor
44B2 **Kvikkjokk** Sweden
72D4 **Kwale** Kenya
71H4 **Kwale** Nig
53B4 **Kwangju** S Korea
72B4 **Kwango** *R* Zaïre
54A3 **Kwangyang** S Korea
54A2 **Kwanmo-bong** *Mt* N Korea
71H4 **Kwara** State, Nig
73C5 **Kwekwe** Zim
10F3 **Kwethluk** USA
10F3 **Kwethluk** *R* USA
43D2 **Kwidzyn** Pol
6B4 **Kwigillingok** USA
51G7 **Kwoka** *Mt* Indon
75C3 **Kyabram** Aust
55B2 **Kyaikkami** Burma
55B2 **Kyaikto** Burma
50D1 **Kyakhta** Russian Fed
75A2 **Kyancutta** Aust
55B1 **Kyaukme** Burma
55B1 **Kyauk-padaung** Burma
55A2 **Kyaukpyu** Burma
61E3 **Kyaukse** Burma
44G2 **Kychema** Russian Fed
3G3 **Kyle** Can
33B2 **Kyle of Lochalsh** Scot
36D1 **Kyll** *R* Germany
75B3 **Kyneton** Aust
72D3 **Kyoga** *L* Uganda
75D1 **Kyogle** Aust
53B4 **Kyōngju** S Korea
54A3 **Kyongsang Sanmaek** *Mts* S Korea
54A2 **Kyŏngsŏng** N Korea
61E4 **Kyonpyaw** Burma
53D4 **Kyoto** Japan
65B1 **Kyrenia** Cyprus
44K3 **Kyrta** Russian Fed
44L4 **Kyshtym** Russian Fed
65B1 **Kythrea** Cyprus
53C5 **Kyūshū** *I* Japan
xxviiiH4 **Kyushu-Palau Ridge** Pacific O
41E2 **Kyustendil** Bulg
49O2 **Kyusyur** Russian Fed
Kyyiv = Kiyev
50C1 **Kyzyl** Russian Fed
48H5 **Kyzylkum** *Desert* Uzbekistan
48H5 **Kzyl Orda** Kazakhstan

Laascaanood La Pesca

L

72E3 **Laascaanood** Somalia
22C1 **La Ascensíon** Mexico
69D3 **Laas Dawaco** Somalia
36E1 **Laasphe** Germany
69D3 **Laasqoray** Somalia
26F1 **La Asunción** Ven
70A2 **Laâyoune** Mor
28C1 **La Banda** Arg
22B1 **La Barca** Mexico
18D2 **La Barge** USA
77G2 **Labasa** Fiji
70A3 **Labé** Guinea
42D2 **Labe** *R* Czech Republic
13E1 **Labelle** Can
15E4 **La Belle** USA
10L3 **Laberge,L** Can
56D2 **Labi** Brunei
45G7 **Labinsk** Russian Fed
56G7 **Labis** Malay
65D1 **Laboué** Leb
28C2 **Laboulaye** Arg
7M4 **Labrador** *Region* Can
7M4 **Labrador City** Can
7N4 **Labrador S** Greenland/Can
26F5 **Lábrea** Brazil
56E1 **Labuan** *I* Malay
57C3 **Labuha** Indon
56C4 **Labuhan** Indon
57B4 **Labuhanbajo** Indon
56F7 **Labuhanbatu** Indon
56B2 **Labuhanbilik** Indon
55A2 **Labutta** Burma
44M2 **Labytnangi** Russian Fed
7L4 **Lac à l'Eau Claire** Can
4F2 **Lac Anuc** *L* Can
36B1 **La Capelle** France
28C2 **La Carlota** Arg
57F8 **La Carlota** Phil
4F4 **Lac au Goéland** *L* Can
5G2 **Lac aux Feuilles** *L* Can
5J2 **Lac aux Goélands** *L* Can
5G2 **Lac Bacquerville** *L* Can
5G2 **Lac Bécard** *L* Can
10N2 **Lac Belot** *L* Can
7L4 **Lac Bienville** *L* Can
3H2 **Lac Brochet** Can
5J3 **Lac Brûlé** *R* Can
4F4 **Lac Bryson** *L* Can
Laccadive Is = **Lakshadweep**
59F4 **Laccadive Is** India
5J2 **Lac Champdoré** *L* Can
5G2 **Lac Châteauguay** *L* Can
5F2 **Lac Chavigny** *L* Can
5H3 **Lac Clairambault** *L* Can
4F1 **Lac Couture** *L* Can
5G3 **Lac Dalmas** *L* Can
37B2 **Lac d'Annecy** *L* France
6G3 **Lac de Gras** *L* Can
37B1 **Lac de Joux** *L* Switz
5G3 **Lac Delorme** *L* Can
37B1 **Lac de Neuchâtel** *L* Switz
22B2 **Lac de Patzcuaro** *L* Mexico
22B2 **Lac de Sayula** *L* Mexico
6F3 **Lac des Bois** *L* Can
4C4 **Lac des Mille Lacs** *L* Can
4F4 **Lac Doda** *L* Can
11C1 **Lac du Bonnet** Can
37A2 **Lac du Bourget** *L* France
21D3 **La Ceiba** Honduras
75A3 **Lacepede B** Aust
5G2 **Lac Faribault** *L* Can
4F3 **Lac Grasset** *L* Can
5J2 **Lac Gruéard** *L* Can
4F2 **Lac Guillaume-Delisle** *L* Can
38C2 **La Châtre** France
36A3 **La Châtre-sur-le-Loir** France
37B1 **La-Chaux-de-Fonds** Switz
65C3 **Lachish** *Hist Site* Israel
76D4 **Lachlan** *R* Aust
5G3 **Lac Holmer** *L* Can
26C2 **La Chorrera** Panama
13E1 **Lachute** Can
37A3 **La Ciotat** France
22A1 **La Ciudad** Mexico
7M4 **Lac Joseph** *L* Can
13D2 **Lackawanna** USA
5G4 **Lac Kempt** *L* Can
4F4 **Lac Kipawa** *L* Can
5G1 **Lac Klotz** *L* Can
3F3 **Lac la Biche** Can
6F3 **Lac la Martre** *L* Can
5H3 **Lac Lapointe** *L* Can
5G2 **Lac La Potherie** *L* Can
6H4 **Lac la Ronge** *L* Can
40B1 **Lac Léman** *L* Switz/France
5F2 **Lac Le Roy** *L* Can
5G2 **Lac Mannessier** *L* Can
7L4 **Lac Manouane** Can
4F4 **Lac Matagami** *L* Can
10N2 **Lac Maunoir** *L* Can
7L4 **Lac Mistassini** *L* Can
4F4 **Lac Muskoka** *L* Can
5G3 **Lac Naocócane** *L* Can
5G3 **Lac Néret** *L* Can
5H3 **Lac Nouveau** *L* Can
28B1 **La Cocha** Arg
3F3 **Lacombe** Can
13E2 **Laconia** USA
5H3 **Lac Opiscotéo** *L* Can
39A1 **La Coruña** Spain
37A2 **La Côte-St-André** France
4F4 **Lac Parent** *L* Can
5F2 **Lac Qilalugalik** *L* Can
5H3 **Lac Rambau** *L* Can
5J2 **Lac Ramusio** *L* Can
9D2 **La Crosse** USA
28D1 **La Cruz** Arg
22A1 **La Cruz** Mexico
5G4 **Lac Saint Jean** *L* Can
4F3 **Lac Sakami** *L* Can
7J4 **Lac Seul** *L* Can
4F4 **Lac Simard** *L* Can
5G3 **Lac Sureau** *L* Can
5G3 **Lac Taffanel** *L* Can
5G2 **Lac Tassialouc** *L* Can
17D2 **La Cygne** USA
60D2 **Ladākh Range** India
63E3 **Lādīz** Iran
60C3 **Lādnūn** India
52B5 **Ladong** China
7K2 **Lady Ann Str** Can
75E3 **Lady Barron** Aust
74D2 **Ladybrand** S Africa
3D4 **Ladysmith** Can
74D2 **Ladysmith** S Africa
12A1 **Ladysmith** USA
76D1 **Lae** PNG
55C3 **Laem Ngop** Thai
42C1 **Laesø** *I* Den
16A2 **Lafayette** Colorado, USA
9E2 **Lafayette** Indiana, USA
9D3 **Lafayette** Louisiana, USA
36B2 **La Fène** France
36A2 **La-Ferté-Barnard** France
36B2 **La Ferté-St-Aubin** France
36B2 **La-Ferté-sous-Jouarre** France
71H4 **Lafia** Nig
71H4 **Lafiagi** Nig
38B2 **La Flèche** France
4E4 **Laforest** Can
71D1 **La Galite** *I* Tunisia
42C1 **Lagan** *R* Sweden
45H6 **Lagan'** Russian Fed
27L6 **Lagarto** Brazil
71C2 **Laghouat** Alg
29D3 **Lagoa de Araruama** Brazil
28E2 **Lagoa de Castillos** *L* Urug
28E2 **Lagoa de Rocha** Urug
25F4 **Lagoa dos Patos** *Lg* Brazil
29D3 **Lagoa Feia** Brazil
26C4 **Lago Agrio** Ecuador
29D2 **Lagoa Juparanã** *L* Brazil
29A2 **Lagoa Mandiore** *L* Brazil
28E2 **Lagoa Mangueira** *L* Brazil
25D4 **Lagoa mar Chiguita** *L* Arg
25F4 **Lagoa Mirim** *L* Urug/Brazil
28E2 **Lagoa Negra** *L* Urug
25B8 **Lago Argentino** *L* Arg
29A2 **Lagoa Uberaba** *L* Brazil
28E1 **Lagoa Vermelha** Brazil
25B7 **Lago Buenos Aries** *L* Arg
25B7 **Lago Cochrane** *L* Chile/Arg
25C7 **Lago Colhué Huapi** *L* Arg
21B2 **Lago de Chapala** *L* Mexico
26B2 **Lago de Chiriqui** *L* Panama
22B2 **Lago de Cuitzeo** *L* Mexico
25B5 **Lago de la Laja** *L* Chile
40B2 **Lago del Coghinas** *L* Sardegna
26D2 **Lago de Maracaibo** *L* Ven
26A1 **Lago de Nicaragua** *L* Nic
26B1 **Lago de Perlas** *L* Nic
22B1 **Lago de Santiaguillo** *L* Mexico
40C2 **Lago di Bolsena** *L* Italy
40C2 **Lago di Bracciano** *L* Italy
40B1 **Lago di Como** *L* Italy
37D2 **Lago d'Idro** *L* Italy
40C1 **Lago di Garda** *L* Italy
37C2 **Lago di Lecco** *L* Italy
37C2 **Lago di Lugano** *L* Italy
37D2 **Lago d'Iseo** *L* Italy
37C2 **Lago d'Orta** *L* Italy
25B7 **Lago General Carrera** *L* Chile
40B1 **Lago Maggiore** *L* Italy
25C7 **Lago Musters** *L* Arg
38B3 **Lagon** France
25B6 **Lago Nahuel Haupi** *L* Arg
25B7 **Lago O'Higgins** *L* Chile
40B2 **Lago Omodeo** *L* Sardegna
26E7 **Lago Poopó** *L* Bol
25B6 **Lago Ranco** *L* Chile
26E6 **Lago Rogaguado** *L* Bol
71G4 **Lagos** Nig
39A2 **Lagos** Port
71G4 **Lagos** State, Nig
25B7 **Lago San Martin** *L* Chile/Arg
21B2 **Lagos de Moreno** Mexico
26E7 **Lago Titicaca** Bol/Peru
37E3 **Lago Trasimeno** *L* Italy
71E1 **La Goulette** Tunisia
25B7 **Lago Viedma** *L* Arg
8B2 **La Grande** USA
4F3 **La Grande Réservoir 2** *Res* Can
5G3 **La Grande Réservoir 3** *Res* Can
5G3 **La Grande Réservoir 4** *Res* Can
76B2 **Lagrange** Aust
9E3 **La Grange** Georgia, USA
12B3 **La Grange** Kentucky, USA
15D1 **La Grange** N Carolina, USA
17C4 **La Grange** Texas, USA
26F2 **La Gran Sabana** *Mts* Ven
37B2 **La Grave** France
38B3 **Lagronño** Spain
16A3 **Laguna** USA
22A1 **Laguna Agua Brava** Mexico
28A3 **Laguna Aluminé** *L* Arg
19C4 **Laguna Beach** USA
28C3 **Laguna Colorada Grande** *L* Arg
57F8 **Laguna de Bay** *Lg* Phil
21D3 **Laguna de Caratasca** *Lg* Honduras
21D4 **Laguna de Chiriqui** *L* Panama
16A3 **Laguna de Guzmán** *L* Mexico
28C4 **Laguna del Abra** *L* Arg
22A1 **Laguna del Caimanero** *L* Mexico
21D3 **Laguna de Managua** *L* Nicaragua
21D3 **Laguna de Nicaragua** *L* Nicaragua
23A4 **Laguna de Perlas** *Lg* Nic
22C1 **Laguna de Pueblo Viejo** *L* Mexico
16A3 **Laguna de Santa Maria** *L* Mexico
21C2 **Laguna de Tamiahua** *Lg* Mexico
21C3 **Laguna de Términos** *Lg* Mexico
22B1 **Laguna de Yuriria** *L* Mexico
28D1 **Laguna Iberá** Arg
28D1 **Laguna Itati** *L* Arg
22C1 **Laguna le Altamira** Mexico
21C2 **Laguna Madre** *Lg* Mexico
17F4 **Laguna Madre** *Lg* USA
28C2 **Laguna Mar Chiquita** *L* Arg
28A4 **Laguna Nahuel Huapi** *L* Arg
10C2 **Laguna Nutauge** *Lg* Russian Fed
28C2 **Laguna Paiva** Arg
28A3 **Laguna Panguipulli** *L* Chile
28A4 **Laguna Puyehue** *L* Chile
28A4 **Laguna Ranco** Chile
28A4 **Laguna Repanco** *L* Chile
19C4 **Laguna Salada** *L* Mexico
8C4 **Laguna Seca** Mexico
22C2 **Laguna Superior** *L* Mexico
10C2 **Laguna Tenkergynpil'gyn** *Lg* Russian Fed
22C1 **Laguna Tortugas** *L* Mexico
28A4 **Laguna Traful** *L* Arg
28D1 **Laguna Trin** *L* Arg
10C2 **Laguna Vankarem** *Lg* Russian Fed
37E2 **Laguna Veneta** *Lg* Italy
28A3 **Laguna Villarrica** *L* Chile
22B1 **Lagund Seca** Mexico
56E1 **Lahad Datu** Malay
56B3 **Lahat** Indon
56A2 **Lahewa** Indon
32J6 **Lahia** Fin
66D4 **Lahij** Yemen
63C1 **Lāhījān** Iran
36D1 **Lahn** *R* Germany
36D1 **Lahnstein** Germany
60C2 **Lahore** Pak
36D2 **Lahr** France
32K6 **Lahti** Fin
22B2 **La Huerta** Mexico
72B3 **Lai** Chad
52B5 **Laibin** China
55C1 **Lai Chau** Viet
36A2 **L'Aigle** France
74C3 **Laingsburg** S Africa
34C2 **Lairg** Scot
56B3 **Lais** Indon
57G9 **Lais** Phil
57C3 **Laiwui** Indon
52E2 **Laiyang** China
52D2 **Laizhou Wan** *B* China
28A3 **Laja** *R* Chile
28E1 **Lajeado** Brazil
25F3 **Lajes** Brazil
20D4 **La Jolla** USA
8C3 **La Junta** USA
11C3 **Lake Andes** USA
75C2 **Lake Cargelligo** Aust
9D3 **Lake Charles** USA
15C2 **Lake City** Florida, USA
11D3 **Lake City** Minnesota, USA
15D2 **Lake City** S Carolina, USA
35D4 **Lake District** *Region* Eng
20D4 **Lake Elsinore** USA
76C3 **Lake Eyre Basin** Aust
13D2 **Lakefield** Can
12B2 **Lake Geneva** USA
14D1 **Lake George** USA
7M3 **Lake Harbour** Can
19D4 **Lake Havasu City** USA
20C3 **Lake Hughes** USA
14C2 **Lakehurst** USA
20C3 **Lake Isabella** USA
17C4 **Lake Jackson** USA
3F3 **Lake la Biche** Can
44F3 **Lake Onega** Russian Fed
15C3 **Lakeland** USA
7J5 **Lake of the Woods** Can
44E3 **Lake Ladoga** Ukraine
18B1 **Lake Oswego** USA
5G5 **Lake Placid** USA
19B3 **Lakeport** USA
17D3 **Lake Providence** USA
78B2 **Lake Pukaki** NZ
4E3 **Lake River** Can
75C3 **Lakes Entrance** Aust
20C2 **Lakeshore** USA
75B1 **Lake Stewart** Aust
4E4 **Lake Superior Prov Park** Can
13D1 **Lake Traverse** Can
8A2 **Lakeview** USA
18B1 **Lakeview Mt** Can
17D3 **Lake Village** USA
15C3 **Lake Wales** USA
20C4 **Lakewood** California, USA
16A2 **Lakewood** Colorado, USA
14C2 **Lakewood** New Jersey, USA
12C2 **Lakewood** Ohio, USA
15E4 **Lake Worth** USA
61B2 **Lakhīmpur** India
60B4 **Lakhpat** India
16B2 **Lakin** USA
60C2 **Lakki** Pak
41E3 **Lakonikós Kólpos** *G* Greece
57C4 **Lakor** *I* Indon
70B4 **Lakota** Ivory Coast
32K4 **Laksefjord** *Inlet* Nor
32K4 **Lakselv** Nor
62A2 **Lakshadweep** *Is* India
28C2 **La Laguna** Arg
66C4 **Lalibela** Eth
26B4 **La Libertad** Ecuador
28A2 **La Ligua** Chile
57B5 **Lalindi** Indon
57B3 **Lalindu** *R* Indon
39A2 **La Linea** Spain
60D4 **Lalitpur** India
57B3 **Laloa** Indon
6H4 **La Loche** Can
3G2 **La Loche,L** Can
36A2 **La Loupe** France
36C1 **La Louvièe** Belg
23A4 **La Luz** Nic
28B1 **La Madrid** Arg
7L5 **La Malbaie** Can
22C2 **La Malinche** *Mt* Mexico
22B1 **La Mancha** Mexico
39B2 **La Mancha** Region, Spain
8C3 **Lamar** Colorado, USA
17D2 **Lamar** Missouri, USA
28B3 **Lamarque** Arg
17C4 **La Marque** USA
72B4 **Lambaréné** Gabon
26B5 **Lambayeque** Peru
79F10 **Lambert Gl** Ant
74B3 **Lamberts Bay** S Africa
14C2 **Lambertville** USA
37C2 **Lambro** *R* Italy
6F2 **Lambton,C** Can
55C2 **Lam Chi** *R* Thai
39A1 **Lamego** Port
37B2 **La Meije** *Mt* France
28B1 **La Merced** Arg
26C6 **La Merced** Peru
16B3 **Lamesa** USA
19C4 **La Mesa** USA
41E3 **Lamía** Greece
34D4 **Lammermuir Hills** Scot
32G7 **Lammhult** Sweden
57F8 **Lamon B** Phil
37D2 **Lamone** *R* Italy
17D1 **Lamoni** USA
20C3 **Lamont** California, USA
11A3 **Lamont** Wyoming, USA
51H6 **Lamotrek** *I* Pacific O
36B3 **Lamotte Beuvron** France
11C2 **La Moure** USA
16C3 **Lampasas** USA
35C5 **Lampeter** Wales
72E4 **Lamu** Kenya
37A2 **La Mure** France
37D1 **Lana** Italy
20E5 **Lanai** *I* Hawaiian Is
20E5 **Lanai City** Hawaiian Is
34D4 **Lanark** Scot
55B3 **Lanbi** *I* Burma
55C1 **Lancang** *R* China
35D5 **Lancashire** County, Eng
19C4 **Lancaster** California, USA
35D4 **Lancaster** Eng
17D1 **Lancaster** Mississippi, USA
13E2 **Lancaster** New Hampshire, USA
14A1 **Lancaster** New York, USA
12C3 **Lancaster** Ohio, USA
9F3 **Lancaster** Pennsylvania, USA
15C2 **Lancaster** S Carolina, USA
7K2 **Lancaster Sd** Can
56C3 **Landak** *R* Indon
36E2 **Landan** Germany
42C3 **Landeck** Austria
8C2 **Lander** USA
28C2 **Landeta** Arg
15C1 **Landrum** USA
42C3 **Landsberg** Germany
6F2 **Lands End** *C* Can
35C6 **Land's End** *Pt* Eng
42C3 **Landshut** Germany
32G7 **Làndskrona** Sweden
15B2 **Lanett** USA
61B1 **La'nga Co** *L* China
11C2 **Langdon** USA
66C3 **Langeb** *Watercourse* Sudan
74C2 **Langeberg** *Mt* S Africa
3H3 **Langenburg** Can
42B2 **Langenhagen** Germany
37B1 **Langenthal** Switz
34D4 **Langholm** Scot
32A2 **Langjökull** *Mts* Iceland
55B4 **Langkawi** *I* Malay
4F4 **Langlade** Can
3D4 **Langley** Can
75C1 **Langlo** *R* Aust
37B1 **Langnau** Switz
38D2 **Langres** France
56A2 **Langsa** Indon
50D2 **Lang Shan** *Mts* China
55D1 **Lang Son** Viet
16B4 **Langtry** USA
38C3 **Languedoc** Region, France
3G3 **Lanigan** Can
25B5 **Lanin** *Mt* Arg
57F9 **Lanoa,L** Phil
14C2 **Lansdale** USA
4D3 **Lansdowne House** Can
7K4 **Lansdowne House** Can
5K3 **L'Anse au Loup** Can
14C2 **Lansford** USA
9E2 **Lansing** USA
37B2 **Lanslebourg** France
70A2 **Lanzarote** *I* Canary Is
52A2 **Lanzhou** China
37B2 **Lanzo Torinese** Italy
57F7 **Laoag** Phil
55C1 **Lao Cai** Viet
52D1 **Laoha He** *R* China
35B5 **Laois** County, Irish Rep
35B5 **Laoise Port** Irish Rep
54A2 **Laoling** China
36B2 **Laon** France
4D4 **Laona** USA
26C6 **La Orova** Peru
55C2 **Laos** Republic, S E Asia
29C4 **Lapa** Brazil
38C2 **Lapalisse** France
70A2 **La Palma** *I* Canary Is
26C2 **La Palmas** Panama
28E2 **La Paloma** Urug
28B3 **La Pampa** State, Arg
20B3 **La Panza Range** *Mts* USA
26F2 **La Paragua** Ven
25E4 **La Paz** Arg
28B2 **La Paz** Arg
26E7 **La Paz** Bol
21A2 **La Paz** Mexico
53E2 **La Perouse Str** Russian Fed/Japan
22C1 **La Pesca** Mexico

Linapacan Str **Lucena**

57E8 **Linapacan Str** Phil
25B5 **Linares** Chile
8D4 **Linares** Mexico
39B2 **Linares** Spain
50C4 **Lincang** China
25D4 **Lincoln** Arg
17C1 **Lincoln** California, USA
35E5 **Lincoln** County, Eng
35E5 **Lincoln** Eng
12B2 **Lincoln** Illinois, USA
13F1 **Lincoln** Maine, USA
8D2 **Lincoln** Nebraska, USA
13E2 **Lincoln** New Hampshire, USA
78B2 **Lincoln** NZ
79A **Lincoln** *S* Greenland
18B2 **Lincoln City** USA
12C2 **Lincoln Park** USA
40B2 **L'Incudine** *Mt* Corse, France
42B3 **Lindau** Germany
27G2 **Linden** Guyana
32F7 **Lindesnes** *C* Nor
73D4 **Lindi** Tanz
72C3 **Lindi** *R* Zaïre
74D2 **Lindley** S Africa
41F3 **Lindos** Greece
4F5 **Lindsay** Can
20C2 **Lindsay** California, USA
11A2 **Lindsay** Montana, USA
xxixM4 **Line Is** Pacific O
52C2 **Linfen** China
55D2 **Lingao** China
57F7 **Lingayen** Phil
42B2 **Lingen** Germany
11B3 **Lingle** USA
52C4 **Lingling** China
52B5 **Lingshan** China
52C2 **Lingshi** China
70A3 **Linguère** Sen
53A1 **Linhai** Heilongjiang, China
52E4 **Linhai** Rhejiang, China
27L7 **Linhares** Brazil
52B1 **Linhe** China
53B3 **Linjiang** China
32H7 **Linköping** Sweden
53C2 **Linkou** China
52D2 **Linqing** China
29C3 **Lins** Brazil
52A2 **Lintao** China
37C1 **Linthal** Switz
11B2 **Linton** USA
50E2 **Linxi** China
52A2 **Linxia** China
42C3 **Linz** Austria
57F8 **Lipa** Phil
40C3 **Lipari** *I* Italy
45F5 **Lipetsk** Russian Fed
41E1 **Lipova** Rom
42B2 **Lippe** *R* Germany
36E1 **Lippstadt** Germany
72D3 **Lira** Uganda
72B4 **Liranga** Congo
72C3 **Lisala** Zaïre
39A2 **Lisboa** Port
Lisbon = Lisboa
11C2 **Lisbon** USA
35B4 **Lisburn** N Ire
10E2 **Lisburne,C** USA
52D4 **Lishui** China
52C4 **Li Shui** *R* China
45F6 **Lisichansk** Ukraine
38C2 **Lisieux** France
45F5 **Liski** Russian Fed
36B2 **L'Isle-Adam** France
37B1 **L'Isle-sur-le-Doubs** France
77E3 **Lismore** Aust
52B5 **Litang** China
65C2 **Lītanī** *R* Leb
27H3 **Litani** *R* Suriname
12B3 **Litchfield** Illinois, USA
11D2 **Litchfield** Minnesota, USA
76E4 **Lithgow** Aust
44C4 **Lithuania**
14B2 **Lititz** USA
53E1 **Litke** Russian Fed
53D2 **Litovko** Russian Fed
17C3 **Little** *R* USA
9F4 **Little Abaco** *I* Bahamas
66D4 **Little Aden** Yemen
62E2 **Little Andaman** *I* Andaman Is
78C1 **Little Barrier I** NZ
18D1 **Little Belt Mts** USA
65B3 **Little Bitter L** Egypt
3F3 **Little Bow** *R* Can
21D3 **Little Cayman** *I* Caribbean
4D3 **Little Current** Can
4E4 **Little Current** Can
14C3 **Little Egg Harbor** *B* USA
11D2 **Little Falls** Minnesota, USA
14C1 **Little Falls** New York, USA
16B3 **Littlefield** USA
11D2 **Littlefork** USA
11D2 **Little Fork** *R* USA
4B3 **Little Grand Rapids** Can
34E2 **Little Halibut Bank** *Sandbank* Scot
23C2 **Little Inagua** *I* Caribbean
74C3 **Little Karroo** *R* S Africa
10G4 **Little Koniuji** *I* USA
20D3 **Little Lake** USA
11B2 **Little Missouri** *R* USA
55A4 **Little Nicobar** *I* Nicobar Is
9D3 **Little Rock** USA
20D3 **Littlerock** USA
10B6 **Little Sitkin** *I* USA
3E3 **Little Smoky** Can
3E3 **Little Smoky** *R* Can
14B3 **Littlestown** USA
10C6 **Little Tanaga** *I* USA
16A2 **Littleton** Colorado, USA
13E2 **Littleton** New Hampshire, USA
53B3 **Liuhe** China
52B5 **Liuzhou** China
41E3 **Livanátais** Greece
43F1 **Līvāni** Latvia
36A2 **Livarot** France
10J2 **Livengood** USA
37E2 **Livenza** *R* Italy
15C2 **Live Oak** USA
19B3 **Livermore** USA
16B3 **Livermore,Mt** USA
7M5 **Liverpool** Can
35D5 **Liverpool** Eng
6E2 **Liverpool B** Can
35D5 **Liverpool B** Eng
7L2 **Liverpool,C** Can
75D2 **Liverpool Range** *Mts* Aust
8B2 **Livingston** Montana, USA
15B1 **Livingston** Tennessee, USA
17D3 **Livingston** Texas, USA
73C5 **Livingstone** Zambia
17C3 **Livingston,L** USA
40D2 **Livno** Bosnia-Herzegovina, Yugos
45F5 **Livny** Russian Fed
12C2 **Livonia** USA
40C2 **Livorno** Italy
29D1 **Livramento do Brumado** Brazil
73D4 **Liwale** Tanz
35C7 **Lizard Pt** Eng
40C1 **Ljubljana** Slovenia, Yugos
32G6 **Ljungan** *R* Sweden
32G7 **Ljungby** Sweden
32H6 **Ljusdal** Sweden
44B3 **Ljusnan** *R* Sweden
35D6 **Llandeilo** Wales
35D6 **Llandovery** Wales
35D5 **Llandrindod Wells** Wales
35D5 **Llandudno** Wales
35C6 **Llanelli** Wales
35D5 **Llangollen** Wales
16C3 **Llano** USA
16C3 **Llano** *R* USA
8C3 **Llano Estacado** *Plat* USA
Z4D2 **Llanos** Region, Colombia/Ven
26F7 **Llanos de Chiquitos** Region, Bol
Lleida = Láerida
22C1 **Llera** Mexico
39A2 **Llerena** Spain
35C5 **Lleyn** *Pen* Wales
68E7 **Llorin** Nigeria
3C2 **Lloyd George,Mt** Can
3G2 **Lloyd L** Can
6H4 **Lloydminster** Can
25C2 **Llullaillaco** *Mt* Chile/Arg
25C2 **Loa** *R* Chile
38C2 **Loan** France
72B4 **Loange** *R* Zaïre
74D2 **Lobatse** Botswana
72B3 **Lobaye** *R* CAR
28D3 **Loberia** Arg
73B5 **Lobito** Angola
28D3 **Lobos** Arg
37B2 **Locano** Italy
37C1 **Locarno** Switz
34C3 **Loch Awe** *L* Scot
34B3 **Lochboisdale** Scot
34B3 **Loch Bracadale** *Inlet* Scot
34C3 **Loch Broom** *Estuary* Scot
34C4 **Loch Doon** *L* Scot
34C3 **Loch Earn** *L* Scot
34C2 **Loch Eriboll** *Inlet* Scot
34C3 **Loch Ericht** *L* Scot
38C2 **Loches** France
34C3 **Loch Etive** *Inlet* Scot
34C3 **Loch Ewe** *Inlet* Scot
34C3 **Loch Fyne** *Inlet* Scot
34C3 **Loch Hourn** *Inlet* Scot
34B4 **Loch Indaal** *Inlet* Scot
34C2 **Lochinver** Scot
34C3 **Loch Katrine** *L* Scot
34D3 **Loch Leven** *L* Scot
34C3 **Loch Linnhe** *Inlet* Scot
34C3 **Loch Lochy** *L* Scot
34C3 **Loch Lomond** *L* Scot
34C3 **Loch Long** *Inlet* Scot
34B3 **Lochmaddy** Scot
34C3 **Loch Maree** *L* Scot
34C3 **Loch Morar** *L* Scot
34D3 **Lochnagar** *Mt* Scot
34C3 **Loch Ness** *L* Scot
34C3 **Loch Rannoch** *L* Scot
34B2 **Loch Roag** *Inlet* Scot
18C1 **Lochsa** *R* USA
34C3 **Loch Sheil** *L* Scot
34C2 **Loch Shin** *L* Scot
34B3 **Loch Snizort** *Inlet* Scot
34C3 **Loch Sunart** *Inlet* Scot
34C3 **Loch Tay** *L* Scot
34C3 **Loch Torridon** *Inlet* Scot
75A2 **Lock** Aust
5H5 **Lockeport** Can
34D4 **Lockerbie** Scot
13D2 **Lock Haven** USA
13D2 **Lockport** USA
55D3 **Loc Ninh** Viet
40D3 **Locri** Italy
65C3 **Lod** Israel
75B3 **Loddon** *R* Aust
44E3 **Lodeynoye Pole** Russian Fed
18E1 **Lodge Grass** USA
60C3 **Lodhran** Pak
40B1 **Lodi** Italy
19B3 **Lodi** USA
72C4 **Lodja** Zaïre
37B1 **Lods** France
72D3 **Lodwar** Kenya
43D2 **Łódź** Pol
74B3 **Loeriesfontein** S Africa
37E1 **Lofer** Austria
32G5 **Lofoten** *Is* Nor
16B2 **Logan** New Mexico, USA
8B2 **Logan** Utah, USA
6D3 **Logan,Mt** Can
10N3 **Logan Mts** Can
12B2 **Logansport** Indiana, USA
17D3 **Logansport** Louisiana, USA
14B2 **Loganton** USA
39B1 **Logroño** Spain
61B3 **Lohārdaga** India
32J6 **Lohja** Fin
36E2 **Lohr** Germany
55B2 **Loikaw** Burma
32J6 **Loimaa** Fin
36B2 **Loing** *R* France
38C2 **Loir** *R* France
36A3 **Loir et Cher** Department, France
38C2 **Loire** *R* France
36B3 **Loiret** Department, France
26C4 **Loja** Ecuador
39B2 **Loja** Spain
57C3 **Loji** Indon
32K5 **Lokan Tekojärvi** *Res* Fin
36B1 **Lokeren** Belg
72D3 **Lokitaung** Kenya
43F1 **Loknya** Russian Fed
71H4 **Lokoja** Nig
72C4 **Lokolo** *R* Zaïre
72C4 **Lokoro** *R* Zaïre
7M3 **Loks Land** *I* Can
42C2 **Lolland** *I* Den
57C2 **Loloda** Indon
18D1 **Lolo P** USA
41E2 **Lom** Bulg
71J4 **Lom** *R* Cam
73C4 **Lomami** *R* Zaïre
70A4 **Loma Mts** Sierra Leone/Guinea
57B2 **Lombagin** Indon
37C2 **Lombardia** Region, Italy
57B4 **Lomblen** *I* Indon
56E4 **Lombok** *I* Indon
71G4 **Lomé** Togo
72C4 **Lomela** Zaïre
72C4 **Lomela** *R* Zaïre
34G3 **Lomond** *Oilfield* N Sea
44D4 **Lomonosov** Russian Fed
37B1 **Lomont** Region, France
19B4 **Lompoc** USA
43E2 **Łomza** Pol
62A1 **Lonāvale** India
25B5 **Loncoche** Chile
7K5 **London** Can
35E6 **London** Eng
12C3 **London** USA
34B4 **Londonderry** County, N Ire
34B4 **Londonderry** N Ire
25B9 **Londonderry** *I* Chile
76B2 **Londonderry,C** Aust
25C3 **Londres** Arg
25F2 **Londrina** Brazil
20D1 **Lone Mt** USA
20C2 **Lone Pine** USA
9F4 **Long** *I* Bahamas
51H7 **Long** *I* PNG
56D2 **Long Akah** Malay
37E1 **Longarone** Italy
28A3 **Longavi** *Mt* Chile
23H2 **Long B** Jamaica
15D2 **Long B** USA
8B3 **Long Beach** California, USA
13E2 **Long Beach** New York, USA
13E2 **Long Branch** USA
52D5 **Longchuan** China
18C2 **Long Creek** USA
75E3 **Longford** Aust
35B5 **Longford** County, Irish Rep
35B5 **Longford** Irish Rep
34E3 **Long Forties** *Region* N Sea
52D1 **Longhua** China
7L4 **Long I** Can
76D1 **Long I** PNG
9F2 **Long I** USA
14D2 **Long Island Sd** USA
53A2 **Longjiang** China
4D4 **Long L** Can
11B2 **Long L** USA
7K5 **Longlac** Can
52B5 **Longlin** China
8C2 **Longmont** USA
56E2 **Longnawan** Indon
36C2 **Longny** France
11D2 **Long Prairie** USA
25B5 **Longquimay** Chile
5K4 **Long Range Mts** Can
76D3 **Longreach** Aust
52A2 **Longshou Shan** *Upland* China
16A1 **Longs Peak** *Mt* USA
34D4 **Longtown** Eng
13E1 **Longueuil** Can
28A3 **Longuimay** Chile
36C2 **Longuyon** France
9D3 **Longview** Texas, USA
8A2 **Longview** Washington, USA
38D2 **Longwy** France
52A3 **Longxi** China
55D3 **Long Xuyen** Viet
52D4 **Longyan** China
52B5 **Longzhou** China
37D2 **Lonigo** Italy
38D2 **Lons-le-Saunier** France
9F3 **Lookout,C** USA
72D4 **Loolmalasin** *Mt* Tanz
3E2 **Loon** *R* Can
55C3 **Lop Buri** Thai
72A4 **Lopez** *C* Gabon
50C2 **Lop Nur** *L* China
39A2 **Lora del Rio** Spain
9E2 **Lorain** USA
60B2 **Loralai** Pak
63C2 **Lordegān** Iran
77E4 **Lord Howe** *I* Aust
xxixK5 **Lord Howe Rise** Pacific O
7J3 **Lord Mayor B** Can
8C3 **Lordsburg** USA
29C3 **Lorena** Brazil
37E2 **Loreo** Italy
22B1 **Loreto** Mexico
38B2 **Lorient** France
75B3 **Lorne** Aust
42B3 **Lörrach** Germany
38D2 **Lorraine** *Region* France
8C3 **Los Alamos** USA
28A2 **Los Andes** Chile
25B5 **Los Angeles** Chile
8B3 **Los Angeles** USA
20C3 **Los Angeles Aqueduct** USA
19B3 **Los Banos** USA
28B2 **Los Cerrillos** Arg
22A1 **Los Corchos** Mexico
19B3 **Los Gatos** USA
40C2 **Lošinj** *I* Croatia, Yugos
28C1 **Los Juries** Arg
28A3 **Los Lagos** Chile
22C1 **Los Laiaderoz** Mexico
28A1 **Los Loros** Chile
16A3 **Los Luncas** USA
28B4 **Los Menucos** Arg
21B2 **Los Mochis** Mexico
20B3 **Los Olivos** USA
28A3 **Los Sauces** Chile
34D3 **Lossiemouth** Scot
28C1 **Los Telares** Arg
23E4 **Los Testigos** *Is* Ven
20C3 **Lost Hills** USA
18D1 **Lost Trail P** USA
25B4 **Los Vilos** Chile
38C3 **Lot** *R* France
28A3 **Lota** Chile
34D4 **Lothian** Region, Scot
72D3 **Lotikipi Plain** Sudan/Kenya
72C4 **Loto** Zaïre
74D1 **Lotsane** *R* Botswana
37B1 **Lötschberg Tunnel** Switz
32K5 **Lotta** *R* Fin/Russian Fed
38B2 **Loudéac** France
70A3 **Louga** Sen
33B3 **Lough Allen** *L* Irish Rep
35E5 **Loughborough** Eng
33B3 **Lough Conn** *L* Irish Rep
33B3 **Lough Corrib** *L* Irish Rep
33B3 **Lough Derg** *L* Irish Rep
6H2 **Lougheed I** Can
35B5 **Lough Ennell** *L* Irish Rep
33B3 **Lough Erne** *L* N Ire
33B2 **Lough Foyle** *Estuary* N Ire/Irish Rep
33B3 **Lough Neagh** *L* N Ire
33B3 **Lough Ree** *L* Irish Rep
35C4 **Lough Strangford** *L* Irish Rep
34B4 **Lough Swilly** *Estuary* Irish Rep
37A1 **Louhans** France
12C3 **Louisa** USA
56D1 **Louisa Reef** *I* S E Asia
10M5 **Louise** *I* Can
10J3 **Louise,L** USA
77E2 **Louisiade Arch** Solomon Is
9D3 **Louisiana** State, USA
74D1 **Louis Trichardt** S Africa
15C2 **Louisville** Georgia, USA
9E3 **Louisville** Kentucky, USA
15B2 **Louisville** Mississippi, USA
44E2 **Loukhi** Russian Fed
11D1 **Lount L** Can
37B3 **Loup** *R* France
16C1 **Loup** *R* USA
38B3 **Lourdes** France
75C2 **Louth** Aust
35B5 **Louth** County, Irish Rep
35E5 **Louth** Eng
Louvain = Leuven
38C2 **Louviers** France
44E4 **Lovat** *R* Russian Fed
41E2 **Lovech** Bulg
16A1 **Loveland** USA
16A2 **Loveland P** USA
18E2 **Lovell** USA
19C2 **Lovelock** USA
40C1 **Lóvere** Italy
16B3 **Lovington** USA
44F2 **Lovozero** Russian Fed
7K3 **Low,C** Can
9F2 **Lowell** Massachusetts, USA
18B2 **Lowell** Oregon, USA
14E1 **Lowell** USA
18C1 **Lower Arrow L** Can
78B2 **Lower Hutt** NZ
20A1 **Lower Lake** USA
10N4 **Lower Post** Can
11C2 **Lower Red L** USA
35F5 **Lowestoft** Eng
43D2 **Łowicz** Pol
75B2 **Loxton** Aust
74C3 **Loxton** S Africa
14B2 **Loyalsock Creek** *R* USA
41D2 **Loznica** Serbia, Yugos
22B2 **loz Reyes** Mexico
48H3 **Lozva** *R* Russian Fed
73C5 **Luacano** Angola
73C4 **Luachimo** Angola
72C4 **Lualaba** *R* Zaïre
73C5 **Luampa** Zambia
73C5 **Luân** Angola
52D3 **Lu'an** China
73B4 **Luanda** Angola
73B5 **Luando** *R* Angola
73C5 **Luanginga** *R* Angola
55C1 **Luang Namtha** Laos
55C2 **Luang Prabang** Laos
73B4 **Luangue** *R* Angola
73D5 **Luangwa** *R* Zambia
52D1 **Luan He** *R* China
52D1 **Luanping** China
73C5 **Luanshya** Zambia
73C5 **Luapula** *R* Zaïre
39A1 **Luarca** Spain
73B4 **Lubalo** Angola
43F2 **L'uban** Belorussia
57F8 **Lubang Is** Phil
73B5 **Lubango** Angola
8C3 **Lubbock** USA
42C2 **Lübeck** Germany
72C4 **Lubefu** Zaïre
72C4 **Lubefu** *R* Zaïre
72C3 **Lubero** Zaïre
37A3 **Lubéron** *R* France
73C4 **Lubilash** *R* Zaïre
43E2 **Lublin** Pol
45E5 **Lubny** Ukraine
56D2 **Lubok Antu** Malay
73C4 **Lubudi** Zaïre
73C4 **Lubudi** *R* Zaïre
56B3 **Lubuklinggau** Indon
73C5 **Lubumbashi** Zaïre
72C4 **Lubutu** Zaïre
29A1 **Lucas** Brazil
57F8 **Lucban** Phil
40C2 **Lucca** Italy
34C4 **Luce** *B* Scot
17E3 **Lucedale** USA
57F8 **Lucena** Phil

Lucenec Malange

43D3 **Lucenec** Slovakia
Lucerne = Luzern
16A3 **Lucero** Mexico
53C2 **Luchegorsk** Russian Fed
52C5 **Luchuan** China
20B2 **Lucia** USA
42C2 **Luckenwalde** Germany
74C2 **Luckhoff** S Africa
61B2 **Lucknow** India
73C5 **Lucusse** Angola
36D1 **Lüdenscheid** Germany
74B2 **Lüderitz** Namibia
60D2 **Ludhiana** India
12B2 **Ludington** USA
19C4 **Ludlow** California, USA
35D5 **Ludlow** Eng
14D1 **Ludlow** Vermont, USA
41F2 **Ludogorie** *Upland* Bulg
15C2 **Ludowici** USA
41E1 **Luduş** Rom
32H6 **Ludvika** Sweden
42B3 **Ludwigsburg** Germany
42B3 **Ludwigshafen** Germany
42C2 **Ludwigslust** Germany
72C4 **Luebo** Zaïre
72C4 **Luema** *R* Zaïre
73C4 **Luembe** *R* Angola
73B5 **Luena** Angola
73C5 **Luene** *R* Angola
52B3 **Lüeyang** China
52D5 **Lufeng** China
9D3 **Lufkin** USA
44D4 **Luga** Russian Fed
44D4 **Luga** *R* Russian Fed
40B1 **Lugano** Switz
73D5 **Lugela** Mozam
73D5 **Lugenda** *R* Mozam
37D2 **Lugo** Italy
39A1 **Lugo** Spain
41E1 **Lugoj** Rom
52A3 **Luhuo** China
73B4 **Lui** *R* Angola
73C5 **Luiana** Angola
73C5 **Luiana** *R* Angola
Luichow Peninsula = Leizhou Bandao
37C2 **Luino** Italy
72B3 **Luionga** *R* Zaïre
52B2 **Luipan Shan** *Upland* China
44D2 **Luiro** *R* Fin
73C5 **Luishia** Zaïre
50C4 **Luixi** China
73C4 **Luiza** Zaïre
28B2 **Luján** Arg
28D2 **Luján** Arg
52D3 **Lujiang** China
72B4 **Lukenie** *R* Zaïre
19D4 **Lukeville** USA
72B4 **Lukolela** Zaïre
43E2 **Luków** Pol
72C4 **Lukuga** *R* Zaïre
73C5 **Lukulu** Zambia
44C2 **Lule** *R* Sweden
32J5 **Luleå** Sweden
41F2 **Lüleburgaz** Turk
52C2 **Lüliang Shan** *Mts* China
17C4 **Luling** USA
26E8 **Lullaillaco** *Mt* Chile
72C3 **Lulonga** *R* Zaïre
Luluabourg = Kananga
73C5 **Lumbala Kaquengue** Angola
9F3 **Lumberton** USA
56E2 **Lumbis** Indon
44G2 **Lumbovka** Russian Fed
61D2 **Lumding** India
73C5 **Lumeje** Angola
78A3 **Lumsden** NZ
32G7 **Lund** Sweden
11C1 **Lundar** Can
73D5 **Lundazi** Zambia
73D6 **Lundi** *R* Zim
35C6 **Lundy** *I* Eng
42C2 **Lüneburg** Germany
36D2 **Lunéville** France
73C5 **Lunga** *R* Zambia
61D3 **Lunglei** India
73B5 **Lungue Bungo** *R* Angola
43F2 **Luninec** Belorussia
20C1 **Luning** USA
53C2 **Luobei** China
72B4 **Luobomo** Congo
52B5 **Luocheng** China
52C5 **Luoding** China
52C3 **Luohe** China
52C3 **Luo He** *R* Henan, China
52B2 **Luo He** *R* Shaanxi, China
52C4 **Luoxiao Shan** *Hills* China
52C3 **Luoyang** China
72B4 **Luozi** Zaïre
73C5 **Lupane** Zim
73D5 **Lupilichi** Mozam
Lu Qu = Tao He
25E3 **Luque** Par
36D3 **Lure** France
35B4 **Lurgan** N Ire
73D5 **Lurio** *R* Mozam
63B2 **Luristan** Region, Iran
73C5 **Lusaka** Zambia
72C4 **Lusambo** Zaïre
41D2 **Lushnjë** Alb
72D4 **Lushoto** Tanz
50C4 **Lushui** China
52E2 **Lüshun** China
11B3 **Lusk** USA
35E6 **Luton** Eng
45D5 **Lutsk** Ukraine
72E3 **Luuq** Somalia
11C3 **Luverne** USA
73C4 **Luvua** *R* Zaïre
73D4 **Luwegu** *R* Tanz
73D5 **Luwingu** Zambia
57B3 **Luwuk** Indon
36D2 **Luxembourg** Grand Duchy, N W Europe
38D2 **Luxembourg** Lux
36D3 **Luxeuil-les-Bains** France
52A5 **Luxi** China
69C2 **Luxor** Egypt
44H3 **Luza** Russian Fed
44H3 **Luza** *R* Russian Fed
40B1 **Luzern** Switz
14D1 **Luzerne** USA
52B5 **Luzhai** China
52B4 **Luzhi** China
52B4 **Luzhou** China
29C2 **Luziânia** Brazil
57F7 **Luzon** *I* Phil
57F6 **Luzon Str** Phil
43E3 **L'vov** Ukraine
34D2 **Lybster** Scot
32H6 **Lycksele** Sweden
73C6 **Lydenburg** S Africa
3B3 **Lyell I** Can
8B3 **Lyell,Mt** USA
14B2 **Lykens** USA
18D2 **Lyman** USA
35D6 **Lyme B** Eng
35D6 **Lyme Regis** Eng
9F3 **Lynchburg** USA
75A2 **Lyndhurst** Aust
13E2 **Lynn** USA
3A2 **Lynn Canal** *Sd* USA
15B2 **Lynn Haven** USA
3H2 **Lynn Lake** Can
4D3 **Lynx** Can
6H3 **Lynx L** Can
38C2 **Lyon** France
10L4 **Lyon Canal** *Sd* USA
15C2 **Lyons** Georgia, USA
14B1 **Lyons** New York, USA
76A3 **Lyons** *R* Aust
37B2 **Lys** *R* Italy
44K4 **Lys'va** Russian Fed
78B2 **Lyttelton** NZ
3D3 **Lytton** Can
20A1 **Lytton** USA
43F2 **Lyubeshov** Ukraine
44F4 **Lyublino** Russian Fed

M

55C1 **Ma** *R* Viet
65C2 **Ma'agan** Jordan
65C2 **Ma'alot Tarshīha** Israel
64C3 **Ma'an** Jordan
52D3 **Ma'anshan** China
65D1 **Ma'arrat an Nu'mān** Syria
36C1 **Maas** *R* Neth
36C1 **Maaseik** Belg
57F8 **Maasin** Phil
42B2 **Maastricht** Neth
74E1 **Mabalane** Mozam
27G2 **Mabaruma** Guyana
35F5 **Mablethorpe** Eng
73D6 **Mabote** Mozam
43E2 **Mabrita** Belorussia
43F2 **M'adel** Belorussia
29D3 **Macaé** Brazil
8D3 **McAlester** USA
8D4 **McAllen** USA
73D5 **Macaloge** Mozam
52C5 **Macao** Dependency, China
27H3 **Macapá** Brazil
29D2 **Macarani** Brazil
26C4 **Macas** Ecuador
27L5 **Macaú** Brazil
29D1 **Macaúbas** Brazil
72C3 **M'Bari** *R* CAR
3D3 **McBride** Can
18C2 **McCall** USA
16B3 **McCamey** USA
18D2 **McCammon** USA
10K3 **McCarthy** USA
3B3 **McCauley I** Can
35D5 **Macclesfield** Eng
7K1 **McClintock B** Can
6H2 **McClintock Chan** Can
14B2 **McClure** USA
20B2 **McClure,L** USA
6G2 **McClure Str** Can
17D3 **McComb** USA
16B1 **McConaughy,L** USA
14B3 **McConnellsburg** USA
8C2 **McCook** USA
7L2 **Macculloch,C** Can
3D2 **McCusker,Mt** Can
6F4 **McDame** Can
18C2 **McDermitt** USA
4D4 **Macdiarmid** Can
18D1 **Mcdonald Peak** *Mt* USA
76C3 **Macdonnell Ranges** *Mts* Aust
39A1 **Macedo de Cavaleiros** Port
41E2 **Macedonia** *Republic* Europe
27L5 **Maceió** Brazil
70B4 **Macenta** Guinea
40C2 **Macerata** Italy
3G2 **Macfarlane** *R* Can
75A2 **Macfarlane,L** Aust
17D3 **McGehee** USA
19D3 **McGill** USA
6C3 **McGrath** USA
18D1 **McGuire,Mt** USA
29C3 **Machado** Brazil
73D6 **Machaíla** Mozam
72D4 **Machakos** Kenya
26C4 **Machala** Ecuador
73D6 **Machaze** Mozam
62B1 **Mācherla** India
65C2 **Machgharab** Leb
13F2 **Machias** USA
4C2 **Machichi** *R* Can
62C1 **Machilīpatnam** India
26D1 **Machiques** Ven
26D6 **Machu-Picchu** *Hist Site* Peru
73D6 **Macia** Mozam
Macias Nguema = Fernando Poo
11B2 **McIntosh** USA
75C1 **MacIntyre** *R* Aust
16A2 **Mack** USA
76D3 **Mackay** Aust
18D2 **Mackay** USA
76B3 **Mackay,L** Aust
77H1 **McKean** *I* Phoenix Is
13D2 **McKeesport** USA
3D2 **Mackenzie** Can
6F3 **Mackenzie** *R* Can
6E3 **Mackenzie B** Can
6G2 **Mackenzie King I** Can
6E3 **Mackenzie Mts** Can
12C1 **Mackinac,Str of** USA
12C1 **Mackinaw City** USA
10H3 **McKinley,Mt** USA
17C3 **McKinney** USA
7L2 **Mackinson Inlet** *B* Can
20C3 **McKittrick** USA
75D2 **Macksville** Aust
18B2 **Mclaoughlin,Mt** USA
11B2 **McLaughlin** USA
75D1 **Maclean** Aust
74D3 **Maclear** S Africa
6G4 **McLennan** Can
3E3 **McLeod** *R* Can
6G3 **McLeod B** Can
76A3 **McLeod,L** Aust
3D2 **McLeod Lake** Can
6E3 **Macmillan** *R* Can
16B3 **McMillan,L** USA
10M3 **Macmillan P** Can
18B1 **McMinnville** Oregon, USA
15B1 **McMinnville** Tennessee, USA
79F7 **McMurdo** *Base* Ant
3C2 **McNamara,Mt** Can
19E4 **McNary** USA
3E3 **McNaughton L** Can
12A2 **Macomb** USA
40B2 **Macomer** Sardegna
73D5 **Macomia** Mozam
38C2 **Mâcon** France
9E3 **Macon** Georgia, USA
17D2 **Macon** Missouri, USA
73C5 **Macondo** Angola
3H2 **Macoun L** Can
17C2 **McPherson** USA
xxviiiJ7 **Macquarie** *Is* Aust
75C2 **Macquarie** *R* Aust
75E3 **Macquarie Harbour** *B* Aust
75D2 **Macquarie,L** Aust
15C2 **McRae** USA
79F11 **Mac Robertson Land** Region, Ant
71E1 **M'saken** Tunisia
71C1 **M'Sila** Alg
6G3 **McTavish Arm** *B* Can
75A1 **Macumba** *R* Aust
37C2 **Macunaga** Italy
6F3 **McVicar Arm** *B* Can
42D3 **M'yaróvár** Hung
71H4 **Mada** *R* Nig
65C3 **Mādabā** Jordan
72C2 **Madadi** *Well* Chad
68J9 **Madagascar** *I* Indian O
xxviiiD6 **Madagascar Basin** Indian O
72B1 **Madama** Niger
76D1 **Madang** PNG
70C3 **Madaoua** Niger
61D3 **Madaripur** Bang
63C1 **Madau** Turkmenistan
5H4 **Madawaska** USA
13D1 **Madawaska** *R* Can
61E3 **Madaya** Burma
70A1 **Madeira** *I* Atlantic O
26F5 **Madeira** *R* Brazil
7M5 **Madeleine, Îles de la** Can
11D3 **Madelia** USA
21B2 **Madera** Mexico
19B3 **Madera** USA
62A1 **Madgaon** India
61C2 **Madhubani** India
61B3 **Madhya Pradesh** State, India
62B2 **Madikeri** India
72B4 **Madimba** Zaïre
72B4 **Madingo Kayes** Congo
72B4 **Madingou** Congo
9E3 **Madison** Indiana, USA
11C2 **Madison** Minnesota, USA
11C3 **Madison** Nebraska, USA
11C3 **Madison** S Dakota, USA
9E2 **Madison** Wisconsin, USA
18D1 **Madison** *R* USA
12B3 **Madisonville** Kentucky, USA
17C3 **Madisonville** Texas, USA
56D4 **Madiun** Indon
4F5 **Madoc** Can
72D3 **Mado Gashi** Kenya
37D1 **Madonna Di Campiglio** Italy
62C2 **Madras** India
18B2 **Madras** USA
25A8 **Madre de Dios** *I* Chile
26E6 **Madre de Dios** *R* Bol
39B1 **Madrid** Spain
39B2 **Madridejos** Spain
56D4 **Madura** *I* Indon
62B3 **Madurai** India
54C3 **Maebashi** Japan
55B3 **Mae Khlong** *R* Thai
55B4 **Mae Nam Lunang** *R* Thai
55C2 **Mae Nam Mun** *R* Thai
55B2 **Mae Nam Ping** *R* Thai
54A3 **Maengsan** N Korea
73E5 **Maevatanana** Madag
77F2 **Maewo** *I* Vanuatu
74D2 **Mafeking** S Africa
74D2 **Mafeteng** Lesotho
75C3 **Maffra** Aust
73D4 **Mafia** *I* Tanz
25G3 **Mafra** Brazil
64C3 **Mafraq** Jordan
49R4 **Magadan** Russian Fed
26D2 **Magargué** Colombia
71H3 **Magaria** Niger
53B1 **Magdagachi** Russian Fed
28D3 **Magdalena** Arg
8B3 **Magdalena** Mexico
16A3 **Magdalena** USA
23C4 **Magdalena** *R* Colombia
56E2 **Magdalena,Mt** Malay
42C2 **Magdeburg** Germany
26D2 **Magdelena** *R* Colombia
27K8 **Magé** Brazil
56D4 **Magelang** Indon
37C1 **Maggia** *R* Switz
64B4 **Maghâgha** Egypt
34B4 **Magherafelt** N Ire
41D2 **Maglie** Italy
44K5 **Magnitogorsk** Russian Fed
17D3 **Magnolia** USA
53E1 **Mago** Russian Fed
5G4 **Magog** Can
13E1 **Magog** Can
22C1 **Magosal** Mexico
5J3 **Magpie** *R* Can
37C2 **Magra** *R* Italy
3F3 **Magrath** Can
20D2 **Magruder Mt** USA
74E2 **Magude** Mozam
7J3 **Maguse River** Can
Magway = Magwe
55B1 **Magwe** Burma
45H8 **Mahābād** Iran
61C2 **Mahabharat Range** *Mts* Nepal
62A1 **Mahād** India
60D4 **Mahadeo Hills** India
14A2 **Mahaffey** USA
73E5 **Mahajanga** Madag
74D1 **Mahalapye** Botswana
61B3 **Mahānadi** *R* India
73E5 **Mahanoro** Madag
14B2 **Mahanoy City** USA
62A1 **Maharashtra** State, India
61B3 **Māhāsamund** India
55C2 **Maha Sarakham** Thai
73E5 **Mahavavy** *R* Madag
62B1 **Mahbūbnagar** India
71E1 **Mahdia** Tunisia
62B2 **Mahe** India
60D4 **Mahekar** India
61B3 **Mahendragarh** India
73D4 **Mahenge** Tanz
60C4 **Mahesāna** India
78C1 **Mahia Pen** NZ
11C2 **Mahnomen** USA
60D3 **Mahoba** India
39C2 **Mahón** Spain
5J5 **Mahone B** Can
10N2 **Mahony L** Can
71E2 **Mahrés** Tunisia
60C4 **Mahuva** India
26D1 **Maicao** Colombia
37B1 **Maîche** France
66C4 **Maichew** Eth
35F6 **Maidstone** Eng
72B2 **Maiduguri** Nig
44B3 **Maigomaj** *R* Sweden
61B3 **Maihar** India
61D3 **Maijdi** Bang
55B3 **Mail Kyun** *I* Burma
60A1 **Maimana** Afghan
36E2 **Main** *R* Germany
4E4 **Main Chan** Can
72B4 **Mai-Ndombe** *L* Zaïre
9G2 **Maine** State, USA
36A3 **Maine** *Region* France
71J3 **Mainé-Soroa** Niger
34D2 **Mainland** *I* Scot
60D3 **Mainpuri** India
36A2 **Maintenon** France
73E5 **Maintirano** Madag
42B2 **Mainz** Germany
70A4 **Maio** *I* Cape Verde
25C4 **Maipó** *Mt* Arg/Chile
28D3 **Maipú** Arg
26E1 **Maiquetía** Ven
37B2 **Maira** *R* Italy
61D2 **Mairābāri** India
61D3 **Maiskhal I** Bang
76E4 **Maitland** New South Wales, Aust
75A2 **Maitland** S Australia, Aust
79F12 **Maitri** *Base* Ant
38D1 **Maiz** Germany
53D4 **Maizuru** Japan
76A1 **Majene** Indon
26D7 **Majes** *R* Peru
72D3 **Maji** Eth
52D2 **Majia He** *R* China
Majunga = Mahajanga
72D2 **Makale** Eth
57A3 **Makale** Indon
56B3 **Makalo** Indon
61C2 **Makalu** *Mt* China/Nepal
44K2 **Makarikha** Russian Fed
53E2 **Makarov** Russian Fed
40D2 **Makarska** Croatia, Yugos
44G4 **Makaryev** Russian Fed
Makassar Ujung Pandang
56E3 **Makassar Str** Indon
45J6 **Makat** Kazakhstan
70A4 **Makeni** Sierra Leone
45F6 **Makeyevka** Ukraine
73C6 **Makgadikgadi** *Salt Pan* Botswana
45H7 **Makhachkala** Russian Fed
64D1 **Makharadze** Georgia
57C2 **Makian** *I* Indon
72D4 **Makindu** Kenya
Makkah = Mecca
7N4 **Makkovik** Can
43E3 **Makó** Hung
72B3 **Makokou** Gabon
78C1 **Makorako,Mt** NZ
72B3 **Makoua** Congo
60C3 **Makrāna** India
60A3 **Makran Coast Range** *Mts* Pak
53D2 **Maksimovka** Russian Fed
63E3 **Maksotag** Iran
71D1 **Maktar** Tunisia
45G8 **Mākū** Iran
72C4 **Makumbi** Zaïre
53C5 **Makurazaki** Japan
71H4 **Makurdi** Nig
10E5 **Makushin V** USA
57F9 **Malabang** Phil
62B2 **Malabar Coast** India
68E7 **Malabo** Bioko
28D1 **Malabrigo** Arg
55C5 **Malacca,Str of** S E Asia
18D2 **Malad City** USA
26D2 **Málaga** Colombia
39B2 **Malaga** Spain
16B3 **Malaga** USA
73E6 **Malaimbandy** Madag
77F1 **Malaita** *I* Solomon Is
72D3 **Malakal** Sudan
60C2 **Malakand** Pak
57B3 **Malamala** Indon
56D4 **Malang** Indon
73B4 **Malange** Angola

Masai Steppe Mexico

72D4 **Masai Steppe** *Upland* Tanz
72D4 **Masaka** Uganda
64E2 **Masally** Azerbaijan
57B3 **Masamba** Indon
53B4 **Masan** S Korea
73D5 **Masasi** Tanz
21D3 **Masaya** Nic
57F8 **Masbate** Phil
57F8 **Masbate** *I* Phil
71C1 **Mascara** Alg
xxviiiD5 **Mascarene Ridge** Indian O
22B1 **Mascota** Mexico
29E2 **Mascote** Brazil
57C4 **Masela** *I* Indon
74D2 **Maseru** Lesotho
60B2 **Mashaki** Afghan
63D1 **Mashhad** Iran
63E3 **Mashkel** *R* Pak
72B4 **Masi-Manimba** Zaïre
72D3 **Masindi** Uganda
72C4 **Masisi** Zaïre
63B2 **Masjed Soleyman** Iran
73F5 **Masoala** *C* Madag
20C1 **Mason** Nevada, USA
16C3 **Mason** Texas, USA
9D2 **Mason City** USA
67G2 **Masqat** Oman
42B2 **Mass** *R* Neth
40C2 **Massa** Italy
9F2 **Massachusetts** State, USA
13E2 **Massachusetts B** USA
72B2 **Massakori** Chad
37D3 **Massa Marittima** Italy
73D6 **Massangena** Mozam
66C3 **Massawa Chan** Eth
13E2 **Massena** USA
72B2 **Massénya** Chad
3B3 **Masset** Can
12C1 **Massey** Can
38C2 **Massif Central** *Mts* France
71C1 **Massif de l'Ouarsenis** *Mts* Alg
72B3 **Massif de l'Adamaoua** *Mts* Cam
23C3 **Massif de la Hotte** *Mts* Haiti
73E6 **Massif de l'Isalo** *Upland* Madag
72C3 **Massif des Bongo** *Upland* CAR
38D2 **Massif du Pelvoux** *Mts* France
73E5 **Massif du Tsaratanana** *Mt* Madag
12C2 **Massillon** USA
70B3 **Massina** Region, Mali
73D6 **Massinga** Mozam
74E1 **Massingir** Mozam
45J6 **Masteksay** Kazakhstan
77G5 **Masterton** NZ
53C5 **Masuda** Japan
72B4 **Masuku** Gabon
64C2 **Maşyāf** Syria
4E4 **Matachewan** Can
16A4 **Matachie** Mexico
72B4 **Matadi** Zaïre
26A1 **Matagalpa** Nic
7L5 **Matagami** Can
8D4 **Matagorda B** USA
17F4 **Matagorda I** USA
78C1 **Matakana I** NZ
73B5 **Matala** Angola
62C3 **Matale** Sri Lanka
70A3 **Matam** Sen
70C3 **Matameye** Niger
21C2 **Matamoros** Mexico
69B2 **Ma'tan as Sarra** *Well* Libya
7M5 **Matane** Can
21D2 **Matanzas** Cuba
13F1 **Matapédia** *R* Can
28A2 **Mataquito** *R* Chile
62C3 **Matara** Sri Lanka
76A1 **Mataram** Indon
26D7 **Matarani** Peru
29E1 **Mataripe** Brazil
39C1 **Mataró** Spain
74D3 **Matatiele** S Africa
78A3 **Mataura** NZ
21B2 **Matehuala** Mexico
37E3 **Matelica** Italy
23L1 **Matelot** Trinidad
40D2 **Matera** Italy
43E3 **Mátészalka** Hung
71D1 **Mateur** Tunisia
20C2 **Mather** USA
12C1 **Matheson** Can
17F4 **Mathis** USA
60D3 **Mathura** India
57G9 **Mati** Phil
22C2 **Matías Romero** Mexico
56E3 **Matisiri** *I* Indon
35E5 **Matlock** Eng
71D2 **Matmatma** Tunisia
27G6 **Mato Grosso** Brazil
27G6 **Mato Grosso** State, Brazil
27G7 **Mato Grosso do Sul** State, Brazil
74E2 **Matola** Mozam
67G2 **Matrah** Oman
37E1 **Matrel im Osttirol** Austria
64A3 **Matrûh** Egypt
53C4 **Matsue** Japan
53E3 **Matsumae** Japan
53D4 **Matsumoto** Japan
53D5 **Matsusaka** Japan
53C5 **Matsuyama** Japan
7K5 **Mattagami** *R* Can
4F4 **Mattawa** Can
5H4 **Mattawamkeag** USA
40B1 **Matterhorn** *Mt* Switz/Italy
18C2 **Matterhorn** *Mt* USA
23C2 **Matthew Town** Bahamas
4E4 **Mattice** Can
14D2 **Mattituck** USA
12B3 **Mattoon** USA
60B2 **Matun** Afghan
23L1 **Matura B** Trinidad
26F2 **Maturin** Ven
61B2 **Mau** India
73D5 **Maúa** Mozam
38C1 **Maubeuge** France
75B2 **Maude** Aust
xxxJ8 **Maud Seamount** Atlantic O
20E5 **Maui** *I* Hawaiian Is
28A3 **Maule** *R* Chile
12C2 **Maumee** USA
12C2 **Maumee** *R* USA
57B4 **Maumere** Indon
73C5 **Maun** Botswana
20E5 **Mauna Kea** *Mt* Hawaiian Is
20E5 **Mauna Loa** *Mt* Hawaiian Is
6F3 **Maunoir,L** Can
37B3 **Maures** *Mts* France
38C2 **Mauriac** France
70A2 **Mauritania** Republic, Africa
68K10 **Mauritius** *I* Indian O
12A2 **Mauston** USA
37E1 **Mauterndorf** Austria
73C5 **Mavinga** Angola
74E1 **Mavue** Mozam
61D3 **Mawlaik** Burma
Mawlamyine = Moulmein
79G10 **Mawson** *Base* Ant
11B2 **Max** USA
74E1 **Maxaila** Mozam
22C1 **Maxcaltzin** Mexico
56C3 **Maya** *I* Indon
49P4 **Maya** *R* Russian Fed
64D2 **Mayādīn** Syria
9F4 **Mayaguana** *I* Bahamas
23D3 **Mayagüez** Puerto Rico
70C3 **Mayahi** Niger
72B4 **Mayama** Congo
63D1 **Mayamey** Iran
57D4 **Mayanobab** Indon
34C4 **Maybole** Scot
9F3 **May,C** USA
75E3 **Maydena** Aust
36D1 **Mayen** Germany
38B2 **Mayenne** France
19D4 **Mayer** USA
3E3 **Mayerthorpe** Can
67E4 **Mayfa'ah** Yemen
12B3 **Mayfield** USA
16A3 **Mayhill** USA
45G7 **Maykop** Russian Fed
48H6 **Maymaneh** Afghan
55B1 **Maymyo** Burma
6E3 **Mayo** Can
14B3 **Mayo** USA
71J4 **Mayo Deo** *R* Cam
57F8 **Mayon** *Mt* Phil
39C2 **Mayor** *Mt* Spain
28C3 **Mayor Buratovich** Arg
78C1 **Mayor I** NZ
25D1 **Mayor P Lagerenza** Par
73E5 **Mayotte** *I* Indian O
23H2 **May Pen** Jamaica
14C3 **May Point,C** USA
37D1 **Mayrhofen** Austria
53B1 **Mayskiy** Russian Fed
14C3 **Mays Landing** USA
3G2 **Mayson L** Can
12C3 **Maysville** USA
72B4 **Mayumba** Gabon
11C2 **Mayville** USA
16B1 **Maywood** USA
73C5 **Mazabuka** Zambia
22B1 **Mazapil** Mexico
60D1 **Mazar** China
65C3 **Mazār** Jordan
40C3 **Mazara del Vallo** Italy
60B1 **Mazar-i-Sharif** Afghan
21B2 **Mazatlán** Mexico
44C4 **Mazeikiai** Lithuania
65C3 **Mazra** Jordan
73D6 **Mbabane** Swaziland
71J4 **Mbabo,Mt** Cam
72B3 **Mbaïki** CAR
73D4 **Mbala** Zambia
73C6 **Mbalabala** Zim
72D3 **Mbale** Uganda
72B3 **Mbalmayo** Cam
72B3 **Mbam** *R* Cam
73D5 **Mbamba Bay** Tanz
72B3 **Mbandaka** Zaïre
72B4 **Mbanza Congo** Angola
72B4 **Mbanza-Ngungu** Zaïre
72D4 **Mbarara** Uganda
71J4 **Mbé** Cam
71J4 **Mbengwi** Cam
72B3 **Mbènza** Congo
72B3 **Mbére** *R* Cam
73D4 **Mbeya** Tanz
72B4 **Mbinda** Congo
71J4 **Mbouda** Cam
70A3 **Mbout** Maur
72C4 **Mbuji-Mayi** Zaïre
71J3 **Mbuli** *R* Nig
72D4 **Mbulu** Tanz
28D1 **Mburucuyá** Arg
70B2 **Mcherrah** Region, Alg
73D5 **Mchinji** Malawi
4C2 **M'Clintock** Can
55D3 **Mdrak** Viet
16B2 **Meade** USA
10G1 **Meade** *R* USA
8B3 **Mead,L** USA
6H4 **Meadow Lake** Can
12C2 **Meadville** USA
54D2 **Me-akan dake** *Mt* Japan
7N4 **Mealy Mts** Can
75C1 **Meandarra** Aust
6G4 **Meander River** Can
35B5 **Meath** Irish Rep
38C2 **Meaux** France
66C2 **Mecca** S Arabia
19C4 **Mecca** USA
14D1 **Mechanicville** USA
48G2 **Mechdusharskiy, Ostrov** *I* Russian Fed
42A2 **Mechelen** Belg
71B2 **Mecheria** Alg
42C2 **Mecklenburger Bucht** *B* Germany
42C2 **Mecklenburg-Vorpommern** State, Germany
73D5 **Meconta** Mozam
73D5 **Mecuburi** Mozam
73E5 **Mecufi** Mozam
73D5 **Mecula** Mozam
56A2 **Medan** Indon
28C3 **Medanos** Arg
28D2 **Médanos** Arg
71C1 **Médéa** Alg
26C2 **Medellín** Colombia
71E2 **Medenine** Tunisia
8A2 **Medford** USA
41F2 **Medgidia** Rom
28B2 **Media Agua** Arg
41E1 **Mediaş** Rom
18C1 **Medical Lake** USA
11A3 **Medicine Bow** USA
16A1 **Medicine Bow Mts** USA
11A3 **Medicine Bow Peak** *Mt* USA
6G5 **Medicine Hat** Can
16C2 **Medicine Lodge** USA
29D2 **Medina** Brazil
11C2 **Medina** N Dakota, USA
14A1 **Medina** New York, USA
66C2 **Medina** S Arabia
39B1 **Medinaceli** Spain
39A1 **Medina del Campo** Spain
39A1 **Medina de Rio Seco** Spain
16C4 **Medina L** USA
61C3 **Medinīpur** India
68E4 **Mediterranean S** Europe
3F3 **Medley** Can
45K5 **Mednogorsk** Russian Fed
49S4 **Mednyy, Ostrov** *I* Russian Fed
61E2 **Mêdog** China
72B3 **Medouneu** Gabon
45G5 **Medvedista** *R* Russian Fed
49S2 **Medvezh'i Ova** *I* Russian Fed
44E3 **Medvezh'yegorsk** Russian Fed
76A3 **Meekatharra** Aust
16A1 **Meeker** USA
60D3 **Meerut** India
18E2 **Meeteetse** USA
72D3 **Mēga** Eth
41E3 **Megalópolis** Greece
41E3 **Mégara** Greece
61D2 **Meghālaya** State, India
61D3 **Meghna** *R* Bang
65C2 **Megido** *Hist Site* Israel
4F4 **Mégiscane** *R* Can
71C2 **Mehaïguene** *R* Alg
10E3 **Mehoryuk** USA
63C3 **Mehran** *R* Iran
63C2 **Mehriz** Iran
29C2 **Meia Ponte** *R* Brazil
72B3 **Meiganga** Cam
55B1 **Meiktila** Burma
37C1 **Meiringen** Switz
52A4 **Meishan** China
42C2 **Meissen** Germany
52D5 **Mei Xian** China
52D5 **Meizhou** China
26D8 **Mejillones** Chile
72B3 **Mekambo** Gabon
4E4 **Mekatina** Can
71C4 **Mek'elē** Eth
71A2 **Meknès** Mor
Mekong = Lancang
55D3 **Mekong, R** Camb
71G3 **Mekrou** *R* Benin
55C5 **Melaka** Malay
xxviiiJ5 **Melanesia** *Region* Pacific O
56D3 **Melawi** *R* Indon
76D4 **Melbourne** Aust
9E4 **Melbourne** USA
8C4 **Melchor Muźguiz** Mexico
44K5 **Meleuz** Russian Fed
72B2 **Melfi** Chad
6H4 **Melfort** Can
71B1 **Melilla** N W Africa
25B6 **Melimoyu** *Mt* Chile
28C2 **Melincué** Arg
28A2 **Melipilla** Chile
11B2 **Melita** Can
45F6 **Melitopol'** Ukraine
7M2 **Meliville Bugt** *B* Greenland
72D3 **Melka Guba** Eth
71D1 **Mellègue** *R* Tunisia
66D4 **Melli** *R* Eth
74E2 **Melmoth** S Africa
28C2 **Melo** Arg
25F4 **Melo** Urug
29A3 **Melo** *R* Brazil
20B2 **Melones Res** USA
10H2 **Melozitna** *R* USA
11D2 **Melrose** USA
37C1 **Mels** Switz
36E1 **Melsungen** Germany
56E1 **Melta,Mt** Malay
35E5 **Melton Mowbray** Eng
38C2 **Melun** France
6H4 **Melville** Can
23Q2 **Melville,C** Dominica
6F3 **Melville Hills** *Mts* Can
76C2 **Melville I** Aust
6G2 **Melville I** Can
7N4 **Melville,L** Can
7K3 **Melville Pen** Can
73E5 **Memba** Mozam
76A1 **Memboro** Indon
42C3 **Memmingen** Germany
56C2 **Mempawan** Indon
9E3 **Memphis** Tennessee, USA
16B3 **Memphis** Texas, USA
17D3 **Mena** USA
43G2 **Mena** Ukraine
35C5 **Menai Str** Wales
70C3 **Ménaka** Mali
12B2 **Menasha** USA
28B4 **Mencué** Arg
56D3 **Mendawai** *R* Indon
38C3 **Mende** France
72D3 **Mendebo** *Mts* Eth
10E4 **Mendenhall,C** USA
76D1 **Mendi** PNG
35D6 **Mendip Hills** *Upland* Eng
18B2 **Mendocino,C** USA
xxixM3 **Mendocino Seascarp** Pacific O
20B2 **Mendota** California, USA
12B2 **Mendota** Illinois, USA
25C4 **Mendoza** Arg
25C5 **Mendoza** State, Arg
41F3 **Menemen** Turk
36B1 **Menen** Belg
52D3 **Mengcheng** China
56C3 **Menggala** Indon
55B1 **Menghai** China
52A5 **Mengla** China
55B1 **Menglian** China
52A5 **Mengzi** China
5H3 **Menihek Lakes** Can
76D4 **Menindee** Aust
75B2 **Menindee L** Aust
75A3 **Meningie** Aust
12B1 **Menominee** USA
12B2 **Menomonee Falls** USA
12A2 **Menomonie** USA
73B5 **Menongue** Angola
39C1 **Menorca** *I* Spain
10K3 **Mentasta Mts** USA
16A2 **Mentmore** USA
56C3 **Mentok** Indon
37B3 **Menton** France
12C2 **Mentor** USA
36B2 **Ménu** France
52A2 **Menyuan** China
44J4 **Menzelinsk** Russian Fed
42B2 **Meppen** Germany
36A3 **Mer** France
56E2 **Merah** Indon
17D2 **Meramec** *R* USA
40C1 **Merano** Italy
76D1 **Merauke** Indon
8A3 **Merced** USA
20B2 **Merced** *R* USA
25B4 **Mercedario** *Mt* Chile
25C4 **Mercedes** Arg
25E4 **Mercedes** Buenos Aires, Arg
25E3 **Mercedes** Corrientes, Arg
25E4 **Mercedes** Urug
78C1 **Mercury B** NZ
78C1 **Mercury Is** NZ
6F2 **Mercy B** Can
7M3 **Mercy,C** Can
16B2 **Meredith,L** *L* USA
55B3 **Mergui** Burma
55B3 **Mergui Arch** Burma
21D2 **Mérida** Mexico
39A2 **Mérida** Spain
26D2 **Mérida** Ven
9E3 **Meridian** USA
75C3 **Merimbula** Aust
75B2 **Meringur** Aust
16B3 **Merkel** USA
72D2 **Merowe** Sudan
76A4 **Merredin** Aust
34C4 **Merrick** *Mt* Scot
12B1 **Merrill** USA
12B2 **Merrillville** USA
14E1 **Merrimack** *R* USA
11B3 **Merriman** USA
3D3 **Merritt** Can
15C3 **Merritt Island** USA
75D2 **Merriwa** Aust
66D4 **Mersa Fatma** Eth
39B2 **Mers el Kebir** Alg
35D5 **Mersey** *R* Eng
35D5 **Merseyside** County, Eng
45E8 **Mersin** Turk
55C5 **Mersing** Malay
60C3 **Merta** India
35D6 **Merthyr Tydfil** Wales
39A2 **Mertola** Port
72D4 **Meru** *Mt* Tanz
45F7 **Merzifon** Turk
36D2 **Merzig** Germany
8B3 **Mesa** USA
16A2 **Mesa Verde Nat Pk** USA
36E1 **Meschede** Germany
64D1 **Mescit Dağ** *Mt* Turk
10G4 **Meshik** USA
72C3 **Meshra'er Req** Sudan
37C1 **Mesocco** Switz
41E3 **Mesolóngion** Greece
19D3 **Mesquite** Nevada, USA
17C3 **Mesquite** Texas, USA
71C2 **Messaad** Alg
73D5 **Messalo** *R* Mozam
40D3 **Messina** Italy
74D1 **Messina** S Africa
41E3 **Messíni** Greece
41E3 **Messiniakós Kólpos** *G* Greece
Mesta = Néstos
41E2 **Mesta, R** Bulg
40C1 **Mestre** Italy
26D3 **Meta** *R* Colombia
44E4 **Meta** *R* Russian Fed
26E2 **Meta** *R* Ven
7L3 **Meta Incognita Pen** Can
17D4 **Metairie** USA
18C1 **Metaline Falls** USA
25D3 **Metán** Arg
73D5 **Metangula** Mozam
40D2 **Metaponto** Italy
37E3 **Metauro** *R* Italy
66C4 **Metemma** Eth
34D3 **Methil** Scot
14E1 **Methuen** USA
78B2 **Methven** NZ
10M4 **Metlakatla** USA
71D2 **Metlaoui** Tunisia
12B3 **Metropolis** USA
62B2 **Mettūr** India
38D2 **Metz** France
36E2 **Metzingen** Germany
56A2 **Meulaboh** Indon
36A2 **Meulan** France
36A3 **Meung-sur-Loire** France
36D2 **Meurthe** *R* France
36D2 **Meurthe-et-Moselle** Department, France
36C2 **Meuse** Department, France
36C1 **Meuse** *R* Belg
38D2 **Meuse** *R* France
17C3 **Mexia** USA
21A1 **Mexicali** Mexico
19E3 **Mexican Hat** USA
21B2 **Mexico** Federal Republic, Central America

México **Monreal del Campo**

21C3 **México** Mexico
22B2 **México** State, Mexico
17D2 **Mexico** USA
21C2 **Mexico,G of** C America
37A2 **Meximieux** France
65C3 **Mezada** *Hist Site* Israel
22C2 **Mezcala** Mexico
22D2 **Mezcalapa** *R* Mexico
44G2 **Mezen'** Russian Fed
44H3 **Mezen'** *R* Russian Fed
43G1 **Mezha** *R* Russian Fed
44J1 **Mezhdusharskiy, Ostrov** *I* Russian Fed
22B1 **Mezquital** Mexico
22B1 **Mezquital** *R* Mexico
53E1 **Mgachi** Russian Fed
60D4 **Mhow** India
22C2 **Miahuatlán** Mexico
19D4 **Miami** Arizona, USA
9E4 **Miami** Florida, USA
17D2 **Miami** Oklahoma, USA
9E4 **Miami Beach** USA
45H8 **Miandowāb** Iran
73E5 **Miandrivazo** Madag
45H8 **Mīāneh** Iran
60C2 **Mianwali** Pak
52A3 **Mianyang** China
52C3 **Mianyang** China
52A3 **Mianzhu** China
52E2 **Miaodao Qundao** *Arch* China
52B4 **Miao Ling** *Upland* China
44L5 **Miass** Russian Fed
43E3 **Michalovce** Slovakia
18D1 **Michel** Can
23D3 **Miches** Dom Rep
9E2 **Michigan** State, USA
12B2 **Michigan City** USA
9E2 **Michigan,L** USA
12C1 **Michipicoten** Can
7K5 **Michipicoten I** Can
22B2 **Michoacan** State, Mexico
41F2 **Michurin** Bulg
45G5 **Michurinsk** Russian Fed
47J5 **Micronesia, Fed. States of** Pacific O
xxviiiJ4 **Micronesia** *Region* Pacific O
56C2 **Midai** *I* Indon
xxxF4 **Mid Atlantic Ridge** Atlantic O
36B1 **Middelburg** Neth
18B2 **Middle Alkali L** USA
xxixO4 **Middle America Trench** Pacific O
62E2 **Middle Andaman** *I* Indian O
14E2 **Middleboro** USA
74C3 **Middleburg** Cape Province, S Africa
14B2 **Middleburg** Pennsylvania, USA
74D2 **Middleburg** Transvaal, S Africa
14B3 **Middleburg** Virginia, USA
14C1 **Middleburgh** USA
13E2 **Middlebury** USA
9E3 **Middlesboro** USA
35E4 **Middlesbrough** Eng
5H5 **Middleton** Can
14D2 **Middletown** Connecticut, USA
14C3 **Middletown** Delaware, USA
13E2 **Middletown** New York, USA
12C3 **Middletown** Ohio, USA
14B2 **Middletown** Pennsylvania, USA
14C1 **Middleville** USA
71B2 **Midelt** Mor
35D6 **Mid Glamorgan** County, Wales
66D3 **Mīdī** Yemen
xxviiiE5 **Mid Indian Basin** Indian O
xxviiiE5 **Mid Indian Ridge** Indian O
7L5 **Midland** Can
12C2 **Midland** Michigan, USA
8C3 **Midland** Texas, USA
73E6 **Midongy Atsimo** Madag
xxixK4 **Mid Pacific Mts** Pacific O
18C2 **Midvale** USA
xxixL3 **Midway Is** Pacific O
11A3 **Midwest** USA
17C2 **Midwest City** USA
64D2 **Midyat** Turk
41E2 **Midžor** *Mt* Serbia, Yugos
43E2 **Mielec** Pol
41F1 **Miercurea-Ciuc** Rom
39A1 **Mieres** Spain
14B2 **Mifflintown** USA
22B1 **Miguel Auza** Mexico
22C1 **Miguihuana** Mexico
54B4 **Mihara** Japan
52D1 **Mijun Shuiku** *Res* China
41E2 **Mikhaylovgrad** Bulg
45G5 **Mikhaylovka** Russian Fed
48J4 **Mikhaylovskiy** Russian Fed
65C4 **Mikhrot Timna** Israel
32K6 **Mikkeli** Fin
3F2 **Mikkwa** *R* Can
41F3 **Míkonos** *I* Greece
42D3 **Mikulov** Czech Republic
73D4 **Mikumi** Tanz
44J3 **Mikun** Russian Fed
53D4 **Mikuni-sammyaku** *Mts* Japan
54C4 **Mikura-jima** *I* Japan
11D2 **Milaca** USA
26C4 **Milagro** Ecuador
Milan = Milano
15B1 **Milan** USA
39C2 **Milana** Alg
73D5 **Milange** Mozam
57B2 **Milango** *R* Indon
40B1 **Milano** Italy
45D8 **Milas** Turk
11C2 **Milbank** USA
76D4 **Mildura** Aust
52A5 **Mile** China
64D3 **Mileh Tharthār** *L* Iraq
76E3 **Miles** Aust
8C2 **Miles City** USA
14D2 **Milford** Connecticut, USA
13D3 **Milford** Delaware, USA
13E2 **Milford** Massachusetts, USA
17C1 **Milford** Nebraska, USA
14E1 **Milford** New Hampshire, USA
14C2 **Milford** Pennsylvania, USA
19D3 **Milford** Utah, USA
35C6 **Milford Haven** Wales
35C6 **Milford Haven** *Sd* Wales
17C2 **Milford L** USA
78A2 **Milford Sd** NZ
71C1 **Miliana** Alg
11A2 **Milk** *R* USA
49R4 **Mil'kovo** Russian Fed
3F4 **Milk River** Can
38C3 **Millau** France
14D2 **Millbrook** USA
15C2 **Milledgeville** USA
11D2 **Mille Lacs L** USA
11C3 **Miller** USA
10K3 **Miller,Mt** USA
45G6 **Millerovo** Russian Fed
14B2 **Millersburg** USA
75A1 **Millers Creek** Aust
14D1 **Millers Falls** USA
14D2 **Millerton** USA
20C2 **Millerton L** USA
75B3 **Millicent** Aust
15B1 **Millington** USA
13F1 **Millinocket** USA
75D1 **Millmerran** Aust
37E1 **Millstätter See** *L* Austria
13F1 **Milltown** Can
18D1 **Milltown** USA
20A2 **Mill Valley** USA
13E3 **Millville** USA
7Q2 **Milne Land** *I* Greenland
20E5 **Milolii** Hawaiian Is
41E3 **Mílos** *I* Greece
76D3 **Milparinka** Aust
14B2 **Milroy** USA
15B2 **Milton** Florida, USA
78A3 **Milton** NZ
14B2 **Milton** Pennsylvania, USA
9E2 **Milwaukee** USA
4D3 **Miminiska L** Can
54D2 **Mimmaya** Japan
20C1 **Mina** USA
39C2 **Mina** *R* Alg
64E4 **Mīnā' al Ahmadī** Kuwait
63D3 **Mīnāb** Iran
57B2 **Minahassa Pen** Indon
4C4 **Minaki** Can
53C5 **Minamata** Japan
56B2 **Minas** Indon
25E4 **Minas** Urug
5J4 **Minas Basin** Can
5J4 **Minas Chan** Can
27J7 **Minas Gerais** State, Brazil
29D2 **Minas Novas** Brazil
21C3 **Minatitlan** Mexico
55A1 **Minbu** Burma
55A1 **Minbya** Burma
28A2 **Mincha** Chile
34B3 **Minch,Little** *Sd* Scot
34B2 **Minch,North** *Sd* Scot
33B2 **Minch,The** *Sd* Scot
10H3 **Minchumina,L** USA
37D2 **Mincio** *R* Italy
57F9 **Mindanao** *I* Phil
17D3 **Minden** Louisiana, USA
20C1 **Minden** Nevada, USA
42B2 **Minden** Germany
75B2 **Mindona L** Aust
57F8 **Mindoro** *I* Phil
57F8 **Mindoro Str** Phil
35D6 **Minehead** Eng
27H7 **Mineiros** Brazil
17C3 **Mineola** USA
22C1 **Mineral de Monte** Mexico
16C3 **Mineral Wells** USA
14B2 **Minersville** USA
5J3 **Mingan** Can
75B2 **Mingary** Aust
45H7 **Mingechaurskoye Vodokhranilische** *Res* Azerbaijan
53B2 **Mingshui** China
52A2 **Minhe** China
37D3 **Minialo** Italy
62A3 **Minicoy** *I* India
52D4 **Min Jiang** *R* Fujian, China
52A4 **Min Jiang** *R* Sichuan, China
20C2 **Minkler** USA
75A2 **Minlaton** Aust
52A2 **Minle** China
71H4 **Minna** Nig
9D2 **Minneapolis** USA
6J4 **Minnedosa** Can
9D2 **Minnesota** State, USA
11C3 **Minnesota** *R* USA
4C4 **Minnitaki L** Can
39A1 **Miño** *R* Spain
8C2 **Minot** USA
52A2 **Minqin** China
52A3 **Min Shan** *Upland* China
44D5 **Minsk** Belorussia
43E2 **Mińsk Mazowiecki** Pol
10J3 **Minto** USA
6G2 **Minto Inlet** *B* Can
7L4 **Minto,L** Can
16A2 **Minturn** USA
50C1 **Minusinsk** Russian Fed
52A3 **Min Xian** China
65A3 **Minyael Qamn** Egypt
4F4 **Miquelon** Can
7N5 **Miquelon** *I* France
20D3 **Mirage L** USA
62A1 **Miraj** India
25E5 **Miramar** Arg
5J4 **Miramichi B** Can
60B2 **Miram Shah** Pak
29A2 **Miranda** *R* Brazil
39B1 **Miranda de Ebro** Spain
29A3 **Mirandia** Brazil
37D2 **Mirandola** Italy
60B2 **Mir Bachchen Kūt** Afghan
67F3 **Mirbāt** Oman
37A1 **Mirebeau** France
36C2 **Mirecourt** France
56D2 **Miri** Malay
63E3 **Miri** *Mt* Pak
70A3 **Mirik,C** Maur
28D1 **Mirinay** *R* Arg
63E3 **Mīrjāveh** Iran
37E2 **Mirna** *R* Croatia, Yugos
49K3 **Mirnoye** Russian Fed
49N3 **Mirnyy** Russian Fed
79G9 **Mirnyy** *Base* Ant
3H2 **Miron L** Can
43G3 **Mironovka** Ukraine
60C2 **Mirpur** Pak
60B3 **Mirpur Khas** Pak
41E3 **Mirtoan S** Greece
53B4 **Miryang** S Korea
61B2 **Mirzāpur** India
22C2 **Misantla** Mexico
5J4 **Miscou I** Can
60C1 **Misgar** Pak
53C2 **Mishan** China
12B2 **Mishawaka** USA
10F2 **Misheguk Mt** USA
54B4 **Mi-shima** *I* Japan
61E2 **Mishmi Hills** India
77E2 **Misima** *I* Solomon Is
25F3 **Misiones** State, Arg
43E3 **Miskolc** Hung
65D2 **Mismīyah** Syria
51G7 **Misoöl** *I* Indon
3H2 **Misow L** Can
69A1 **Misrātah** Libya
7K5 **Missinaibi** *R* Can
12C1 **Missinaibi L** Can
3H2 **Missinipe** Can
11B3 **Mission** S Dakota, USA
17F4 **Mission** Texas, USA
18B1 **Mission City** Can
13D2 **Mississauga** Can
9D3 **Mississippi** State, USA
9D3 **Mississippi** *R* USA
17E3 **Mississippi Delta** USA
8B2 **Missoula** USA
71B2 **Missour** Mor
9D3 **Missouri** State, USA
9D3 **Missouri** *R* USA
11C3 **Missouri Valley** USA
5G4 **Mistassini** Can
5G4 **Mistassini** *R* Can
5G3 **Mistassini Provincial Park** Can
5J2 **Mistastin L** Can
26D7 **Misti** *Mt* Peru
5J2 **Mistinibi L** Can
75C1 **Mitchell** Aust
8D2 **Mitchell** USA
76D2 **Mitchell** *R* Aust
9E3 **Mitchell,Mt** USA
51H8 **Mitchell River** Aust
65A3 **Mit el Nasâra** Egypt
65A3 **Mît Ghamr** Egypt
60B3 **Mithankot** Pak
41F3 **Mitilíni** Greece
22C2 **Mitla** Mexico
65B3 **Mitla P** Egypt
77G2 **Mitre** *I* Solomon Is
10G4 **Mitrofania I** USA
41E2 **Mitrovica** Serbia, Yugos
72D2 **Mits'iwa** Eritrea
37E1 **Mittersill** Austria
26D3 **Mitu** Colombia
72C4 **Mitumbar** *Mts* Zaïre
73C4 **Mitwaba** Zaïre
72B3 **Mitzic** Gabon
54C3 **Miura** Japan
52C3 **Mi Xian** China
50G3 **Miyake** *I* Japan
54C4 **Miyake-jima** *I* Japan
50F4 **Miyako** *I* Japan
53C5 **Miyakonojō** Japan
53C5 **Miyazaki** Japan
54C3 **Miyazu** Japan
53C5 **Miyoshi** Japan
52D1 **Miyun** China
54D2 **Mi-zaki** *Pt* Japan
72D3 **Mīzan Teferī** Eth
69A1 **Mizdah** Libya
41F1 **Mizil** Rom
61D3 **Mizo Hills** India
61D3 **Mizoram** Union Territory, India
65C3 **Mizpe Ramon** Israel
79F11 **Mizuho** *Base* Ant
53E4 **Mizusawa** Japan
32H7 **Mjolby** Sweden
73C5 **Mkushi** Zambia
74E2 **Mkuzi** S Africa
42C2 **Mladá Boleslav** Czech Republic
43E2 **Mława** Pol
41D2 **Mljet** *I* Croatia, Yugos
74D2 **Mmabatho** S Africa
60D2 **Mnadi** India
57C4 **Moa** *I* Indon
70A4 **Moa** *R* Sierra Leone
65C3 **Moab** Region, Jordan
8C3 **Moab** USA
74E2 **Moamba** Mozam
72B4 **Moanda** Congo
72B4 **Moanda** Gabon
73C4 **Moba** Zaïre
54D3 **Mobara** Japan
72C3 **Mobaye** CAR
72C3 **Mobayi** Zaire
9D3 **Moberly** USA
9E3 **Mobile** USA
9E3 **Mobile B** USA
15B2 **Mobile Pt** USA
8C2 **Mobridge** USA
73E5 **Moçambique** Mozam
Moçâmedes = Namibe
55C1 **Moc Chau** Viet
74D1 **Mochudi** Botswana
73E5 **Mocimboa da Praia** Mozam
26C3 **Mocoa** Colombia
29C3 **Mococa** Brazil
28D2 **Mocoreta** *R* Arg
22C1 **Moctezulma** *R* Mexico
22B1 **Moctezuma** Mexico
73D5 **Mocuba** Mozam
37B2 **Modane** France
74D2 **Modder** *R* S Africa
40C2 **Modena** Italy
36D2 **Moder** *R* France
8A3 **Modesto** USA
20B2 **Modesto Res** USA
40C3 **Modica** Italy
42D3 **Mödling** Austria
76D4 **Moe** Aust
37C1 **Moesa** *R* Switz
34D4 **Moffat** Scot
60D2 **Moga** India
68J7 **Mogadiscio** Somalia
61E2 **Mogaung** Burma
29C3 **Mogi das Cruzes** Brazil
43G2 **Mogilev** Belorussia
45D6 **Mogilev Podol'skiy** Ukraine
29C3 **Mogi-Mirim** Brazil
73E5 **Mogincual** Mozam
37E2 **Mogliano** Italy
28B2 **Mogna** Arg
50E1 **Mogocha** Russian Fed
48K4 **Mogochin** Russian Fed
61E3 **Mogok** Burma
74D1 **Mogol** *R* S Africa
39A2 **Moguer** Spain
78C1 **Mohaka** *R* NZ
74D3 **Mohale's Hoek** Lesotho
11B2 **Mohall** USA
71C1 **Mohammadia** Alg
71A2 **Mohammedia** Mor
61D3 **Mohanganj** Bang
19D3 **Mohave,L** USA
14C1 **Mohawk** USA
13E2 **Mohawk** *R* USA
73E5 **Mohéli,I** Comoros
10E3 **Mohican,C** USA
73D4 **Mohoro** Tanz
48J5 **Mointy** Kazakhstan
32G5 **Mo i Rana** Nor
5H3 **Moisie** *R* Can
38C3 **Moissac** France
19C3 **Mojave** USA
20D3 **Mojave** *R* USA
8B3 **Mojave Desert** USA
56D4 **Mojokerto** Indon
66C4 **Mokada** *Mt* Eth
61C2 **Mokama** India
78B1 **Mokau** *R* NZ
20B1 **Mokelumne Aqueduct** USA
20B1 **Mokelumne Hill** USA
20B1 **Mokelumne North Fork** *R* USA
74D2 **Mokhotlong** Lesotho
71E1 **Moknine** Tunisia
61D2 **Mokokchūng** India
72B2 **Mokolo** Cam
53B5 **Mokp'o** S Korea
44G5 **Moksha** *R* Russian Fed
22C1 **Molango** Mexico
41E3 **Moláoi** Greece
32F6 **Molde** Nor
45D6 **Moldova**
41E1 **Moldoveanu** *Mt* Rom
71F4 **Mole Nat Pk** Ghana
74D1 **Molepolole** Botswana
36D2 **Molesheim** France
40D2 **Molfetta** Italy
28A3 **Molina** Chile
37E1 **Möll** *R* Austria
26D7 **Mollendo** Peru
44D5 **Molodechno** Belorussia
79G11 **Molodezhnaya** *Base* Ant
20E5 **Molokai** *I* Hawaiian Is
44H4 **Moloma** *R* Russian Fed
75C2 **Molong** Aust
74C2 **Molopo** *R* S Africa/ Botswana
72B3 **Molounddu** Cam
4B3 **Molson L** Can
76B1 **Molucca S** Indon
51F7 **Moluccas** *Is* Indon
73D5 **Moma** Mozam
27K5 **Mombaca** Brazil
72D4 **Mombasa** Kenya
54D2 **Mombetsu** Japan
72C3 **Mompono** Zaïre
42C2 **Mon** *I* Den
34B3 **Monach** *Is* Scot
38D3 **Monaco** Principality, Europe
34C3 **Monadhliath** *Mts* Scot
35B4 **Monaghan** County, Irish Rep
35B4 **Monaghan** Irish Rep
16B3 **Monahans** USA
23D3 **Mona Pass** Caribbean
3C3 **Monarch Mt** Can
16A2 **Monarch P** USA
6G4 **Monashee Mts** Can
33B3 **Monastereven** Irish Rep
54D2 **Monbetsu** Japan
37B2 **Moncalieri** Italy
27J4 **Monção** Brazil
32L5 **Monchegorsk** Russian Fed
42B2 **Mönchen-gladbach** Germany
21B2 **Monclova** Mexico
7M5 **Moncton** Can
39A1 **Mondego** *R* Port
40B2 **Mondovi** Italy
23H1 **Moneague** Jamaica
13D2 **Monessen** USA
4F4 **Monet** Can
17D2 **Monett** USA
40C1 **Monfalcone** Italy
39A1 **Monforte de Lemos** Spain
72C3 **Monga** Zaïre
72C3 **Mongala** *R* Zaïre
72D3 **Mongalla** Sudan
55D1 **Mong Cai** Viet
72B2 **Mongo** Chad
50C2 **Mongolia** Republic, Asia
73C5 **Mongu** Zambia
19C3 **Monitor Range** *Mts* USA
72C4 **Monkoto** Zaïre
35D6 **Monmouth** Eng
12A2 **Monmouth** USA
3D3 **Monmouth,Mt** Can
71G4 **Mono** *R* Togo
19C3 **Mono L** USA
41D2 **Monopoli** Italy
39B1 **Monreal del Campo** Spain

Mugodzhary **Narssalik**

45K6 **Mugodzhary** *Mts* Kazakhstan
64C4 **Mughayra** S Arabia
64A2 **Muğla** Turk
45K6 **Mugodzhary** *Mts* Kazakhstan
61B2 **Mugu** Nepal
52A3 **Muguaping** China
66C2 **Muhammad Qol** Sudan
64D3 **Muhaywir** Iraq
36E2 **Mühlacker** Germany
42C3 **Mühldorf** Germany
42C2 **Muhlhausen** Germany
32K6 **Muhos** Fin
55C4 **Mui Bai Bung** *C* Camb
35B5 **Muine Bheag** Irish Rep
73C5 **Mujimbeji** Zambia
43E3 **Mukachevo** Ukraine
56D2 **Mukah** Malay
54D2 **Mukawa** Japan
50H4 **Muko-jima** *I* Japan
61B2 **Muktinath** Nepal
60B2 **Mukur** Afghan
53B2 **Mulan** China
17D2 **Mulberry** USA
10G3 **Mulchatna** *R* USA
28A3 **Mulchén** Chile
42C2 **Mulde** *R* Germany
11B3 **Mule Creek** USA
16B3 **Muleshoe** USA
51H8 **Mulgrave I** Aust
39B2 **Mulhacén** *Mt* Spain
36D1 **Mülheim** Germany
36D3 **Mulhouse** France
52A4 **Muli** China
53C3 **Muling** China
53C2 **Muling He** *R* China
34C3 **Mull** *I* Scot
62C3 **Mullaitvu** Sri Lanka
75C2 **Mullaley** Aust
76A3 **Mullewa** Aust
36D3 **Müllheim** Germany
14C3 **Mullica** *R* USA
35B5 **Mullingar** Irish Rep
34C4 **Mull of Kintyre** *Pt* Scot
34B4 **Mull of Oa** *C* Scot
75D1 **Mullumbimby** Aust
73C5 **Mulobezi** Zambia
60C2 **Multan** Pak
57C3 **Muluku** *Is* Indon
Mumbai = Bombay
73C5 **Mumbwa** Zambia
45H6 **Mumra** Russian Fed
57B4 **Muna** *I* Indon
42C3 **München** Germany
3C2 **Muncho Lake** Can
54A3 **Munchŏn** N Korea
12B2 **Muncie** USA
75A1 **Munconnie,L** Aust
14B2 **Muncy** USA
42B2 **Münden** Germany
75D1 **Mundubbera** Aust
75C1 **Mungallala** Aust
75C1 **Mungallala** *R* Aust
72C3 **Mungbere** Zaïre
61B3 **Mungeli** India
61C2 **Munger** India
75C1 **Mungindi** Aust
Munich = München
12B1 **Munising** USA
25B8 **Muñoz Gomero,Pen** Chile
3J2 **Munroe L** Can
54A3 **Munsan** S Korea
36E2 **Münsingen** Germany
36D2 **Munster** France
37C1 **Münster** Switz
42B2 **Münster** Germany
36D1 **Münsterland** Region, Germany
41E1 **Muntii Apuseni** *Mts* Rom
41E1 **Muntii Călimanilor** *Mts* Rom
41E1 **Muntii Carpaţii Meridionali** *Mts* Rom
41E1 **Muntii Rodnei** *Mts* Rom
41E1 **Muntii Zarandului** *Mts* Rom
64C2 **Munzur Silsilesi** *Mts* Turk
48D3 **Muomio** Fin
55C1 **Muong Khoua** Laos
55D3 **Muong Man** Viet
55D2 **Muong Nong** Laos
55C1 **Muong Ou Neua** Laos
55C1 **Muong Sai** Laos
55C2 **Muong Sen** Viet
55C1 **Muong Sing** Laos
55C1 **Muong Son** Laos
32J5 **Muonio** Fin
32J5 **Muonio** *R* Sweden/Fin
66B3 **Muqaddam** *Watercourse* Sudan
72E3 **Muqdisho** Somalia
40C1 **Mur** *R* Austria
53D4 **Murakami** Japan
25B7 **Murallón** *Mt* Chile/Arg
44H4 **Murashi** Russian Fed
64D2 **Murat** *R* Turk
40B3 **Muravera** Sardegna
54D3 **Murayama** Japan
67F4 **Murcanyo** Somalia
63C2 **Murcheh Khvort** Iran
78B2 **Murchison** NZ
76A3 **Murchison** *R* Aust
39B2 **Murcia** Region, Spain
39B2 **Murcia** Spain
11B3 **Murdo** USA
41E1 **Mureş** *R* Rom
41E1 **Muresul** *R* Rom
15B1 **Murfreesboro** USA
15D1 **Murfreesboro** USA
36E2 **Murg** *R* Germany
48H6 **Murgab** *R* Turkmenistan
60B2 **Murgha Kibzai** Pak
75D1 **Murgon** Aust
61C3 **Muri** India
29D3 **Muriaé** Brazil
73C4 **Muriege** Angola
44E2 **Murmansk** Russian Fed
44G4 **Murom** Russian Fed
53E3 **Muroran** Japan
39A1 **Muros** Spain
53C5 **Muroto** Japan
54B4 **Muroto-zaki** *C* Japan
18C2 **Murphy** Idaho, USA
15C1 **Murphy** N Carolina, USA
20B1 **Murphys** USA
12B3 **Murray** Kentucky, USA
18D2 **Murray** Utah, USA
75B2 **Murray** *R* Aust
3D2 **Murray** *R* Can
75A3 **Murray Bridge** Aust
51H7 **Murray,L** PNG
15C2 **Murray,L** USA
74C3 **Murraysburg** S Africa
xxixM3 **Murray Seacarp** Pacific O
36E2 **Murrhardt** Germany
75B2 **Murrumbidgee** *R* Aust
75C2 **Murrumburrah** Aust
75D2 **Murrurundi** Aust
37B1 **Murten** Switz
75B3 **Murtoa** Aust
78C1 **Murupara** NZ
61B3 **Murwāra** India
75D1 **Murwillimbah** Aust
64D2 **Muş** Turk
41E2 **Musala** *Mt* Bulg
53B3 **Musan** N Korea
67G1 **Musandam** *Pen* Oman
Muscat = Masqat
67G2 **Muscat** *Region* Oman
11D3 **Muscatine** USA
76C3 **Musgrave Range** *Mts* Aust
72B4 **Mushie** Zaïre
14E2 **Muskeget Chan** USA
12B2 **Muskegon** USA
12B2 **Muskegon** *R* USA
17C2 **Muskogee** USA
66C3 **Musmar** Sudan
72D4 **Musoma** Tanz
76D1 **Mussau** *I* PNG
18E1 **Musselshell** *R* USA
73B5 **Mussende** Angola
38C2 **Mussidan** France
41F2 **Mustafa-Kemalpasa** Turk
61B2 **Mustang** Nepal
54A2 **Musu-dan** *C* N Korea
75D2 **Muswelibrook** Aust
69B2 **Mut** Egypt
73D5 **Mutarara** Mozam
73D5 **Mutare** Zim
57B4 **Mutis** *Mt* Indon
44K2 **Mutnyy Materik** Russian Fed
73D5 **Mutoko** Zim
73E5 **Mutsamudu** Comoros
73C5 **Mutshatsha** Zaïre
53E3 **Mutsu** Japan
53E3 **Mutsu-wan** *B* Japan
5K3 **Mutton Bay** Can
29C1 **Mutunópolis** Brazil
52B2 **Mu Us Shamo** *Desert* China
73B4 **Muxima** Angola
49N4 **Muya** Russian Fed
44E3 **Muyezerskiy** Russian Fed
72D4 **Muyinga** Burundi
73C4 **Muyumba** Zaïre
59E1 **Muyun Kum** *Desert* Kazakhstan
60C2 **Muzaffarābad** Pak
60C2 **Muzaffargarh** Pak
60D3 **Muzaffarnagar** India
61C2 **Muzaffarpur** India
48H3 **Muzhi** Russian Fed
59G2 **Muzlag** *Mt* China
3B3 **Muzon,C** USA
59F2 **Muztagala** *Mt* China
73D5 **Mvuma** Zim
72D4 **Mwanza** Tanz
73C4 **Mwanza** Zaïre
72C4 **Mweka** Zaïre
73C4 **Mwene Ditu** Zaïre
73D6 **Mwenezi** Zim
72C4 **Mwenga** Zaïre
73C4 **Mweru** *L* Zambia
73C5 **Mwinilunga** Zambia
61E4 **Myanaung** Burma
Myanma = Burma
61E3 **Myingyan** Burma
55B1 **Myingyao** Burma
55B3 **Myinmoletkat** *Mt* Burma
61E3 **Myinmu** Burma
61E2 **Myitkyina** Burma
55B3 **Myitta** Burma
61E3 **Myittha** Burma
61D3 **Mymensingh** Bang
50G3 **Myojin** *I* Japan
54A2 **Myongchon** N Korea
54A2 **Myonggan** N Korea
32F6 **Myrdal** Nor
32B2 **Myrdalsjökur** *Mts* Iceland
15D2 **Myrtle Beach** USA
18B2 **Myrtle Creek** USA
49U3 **Mys Chaplino** *C* Russian Fed
49M2 **Mys Chelyuskin** *C* Russian Fed
10D3 **Mys Chukotskiy** *Pt* Russian Fed
10E2 **Mys Dezhneva** *Pt* Russian Fed
32G7 **Mysen** Nor
44G2 **Mys Kanin Nos** *C* Russian Fed
49S4 **Mys Kronotskiy** *C* Russian Fed
43D3 **Myślenice** Pol
42C2 **Myśliborz** Pol
49R4 **Mys Lopatka** *C* Russian Fed
49T3 **Mys Navarin** *C* Russian Fed
10D2 **Mys Nygchigen** *Pt* Russian Fed
49T4 **Mys Olyutorskiy** *C* Russian Fed
62B2 **Mysore** India
45E7 **Mys Sarych** *C* Ukraine
10D2 **Mys Serdtse Kamen** *Pt* Russian Fed
49T2 **Mys Shelagskiy** *C* Russian Fed
49U3 **Mys Shmidta** Russian Fed
49S4 **Mys Sivuchiy** *C* Kirgizia
44F2 **Mys Svyatoy Nos** *C* Russian Fed
14E2 **Mystic** USA
45J7 **Mys Tyub-Karagan** *Pt* Kazakhstan
49Q4 **Mys Yelizavety** *C* Russian Fed
48H2 **Mys Zhelaniya** *C* Russian Fed
55D3 **My Tho** Viet
18B2 **Mytle Point** USA
73D5 **Mzimba** Malawi
73D5 **Mzuzú** Malawi

N

20E5 **Naalehu** Hawaiian Is
32J6 **Naantali** Fin
35B5 **Naas** Irish Rep
54C4 **Nabari** Japan
44J4 **Naberezhnyye Chelny** Russian Fed
10K3 **Nabesna** *R* USA
71E1 **Nabeul** Tunisia
29A3 **Nabileque** *R* Brazil
65C2 **Nablus** Israel
73E5 **Nacala** Mozam
18B1 **Naches** USA
5H2 **Nachikapau L** Can
73D5 **Nachingwea** Tanz
20B3 **Nacimiento** *R* USA
20B3 **Nacimiento Res** USA
17D3 **Nacogdoches** USA
55A3 **Nacondam** *I* Indian O
21B1 **Nacozari** Mexico
36E1 **Nadel** *Mt* Germany
77G2 **Nadi** Fiji
60C4 **Nadiād** India
39B2 **Nador** Mor
63C2 **Nadūshan** Iran
44E3 **Nadvoitsy** Russian Fed
43E3 **Nadvornaya** Ukraine
42C1 **Naestved** Den
54B4 **Nagahama** Japan
61E2 **Naga Hills** Burma
54C3 **Nagai** Japan
10G5 **Nagai** *I* USA
61D2 **Nāgāland** State, India
53D4 **Nagano** Japan
53D4 **Nagaoka** Japan
61D2 **Nagaon** India
62B2 **Nāgappattinam** India
60C4 **Nagar Parkar** Pak
53B5 **Nagasaki** Japan
54C4 **Nagashima** Japan
54B4 **Nagato** Japan
60C3 **Nāgaur** India
62B3 **Nāgercoil** India
60B3 **Nagha Kalat** Pak
60D3 **Nagīna** India
36E2 **Nagold** Germany
53D4 **Nagoya** Japan
60D4 **Nāgpur** India
59H2 **Nagqu** China
42D3 **Nagykanizsa** Hung
43D3 **Nagykörös** Hung
50F4 **Naha** Japan
60D2 **Nāhan** India
63E3 **Nahang** *R* Iran
6F3 **Nahanni Butte** Can
10N3 **Nahanni Nat Pk** Can
10O3 **Nahanni Range** *Mts* Can
65C2 **Nahariya** Israel
71C1 **Nahar Ouassel** *R* Alg
63B2 **Nahāvand** Iran
36D2 **Nahe** *R* Germany
52D2 **Nahpu** China
28B4 **Nahuel Niyeu** Arg
57B4 **Naikliu** Indon
52E1 **Naimen Qi** China
7M4 **Nain** Can
63C2 **Nā'īn** Iran
60D3 **Naini Tai** India
61B3 **Nainpur** India
34D3 **Nairn** Scot
72D4 **Nairobi** Kenya
63C2 **Najafābād** Iran
66D1 **Najd** Region, S Arabia
53C3 **Najin** N Korea
66D3 **Najrān** S Arabia
54A3 **Naju** S Korea
54A4 **Nakadori-jima** Japan
54B4 **Nakama** Japan
53E4 **Nakaminato** Japan
54B4 **Nakamura** Japan
54C3 **Nakano** Japan
54B3 **Nakano-shima** *I* Japan
53C5 **Nakatsu** Japan
54C3 **Nakatsu-gawa** Japan
66C3 **Nak'fa** Eritrea
45H8 **Nakhichevan** Azerbaijan
65B4 **Nakhl** Egypt
53C3 **Nakhodka** Russian Fed
55C3 **Nakhon Pathom** Thai
55C3 **Nakhon Ratchasima** Thai
55C4 **Nakhon Si Thammarat** Thai
3B2 **Nakina** British Columbia, Can
7K4 **Nakina** Ontario, Can
3B2 **Nakina** *R* Can
10G4 **Naknek** USA
10G4 **Naknek L** USA
32G7 **Nakskov** Den
54A3 **Naktong** *R* S Korea
72D4 **Nakuru** Kenya
3E3 **Nakusp** Can
45G7 **Nal'chik** Russian Fed
62B1 **Nalgonda** India
62B1 **Nallamala Range** *Mts* India
44C2 **Naltia** *Mt* Nor/Fin
69A1 **Nālūt** Libya
74E2 **Namaacha** Mozam
48G6 **Namak** *L* Iran
63D2 **Namakzar-e Shadad** *Salt Flat* Iran
48J5 **Namangan** Uzbekistan
73D5 **Namapa** Mozam
73B7 **Namaqualand** Region, S Africa
75D1 **Nambour** Aust
75D2 **Nambucca Heads** Aust
55D4 **Nam Can** Viet
59H2 **Nam Co** *L* China
55D1 **Nam Dinh** Viet
73D5 **Nametil** Mozam
3H3 **Namew L** Can
53B5 **Namhae-do** *I* S Korea
74A1 **Namib Desert** Namibia
73B5 **Namibe** Angola
73B6 **Namibia** Dependency, Africa
57C3 **Namlea** Indon
61C2 **Namling** China
57B3 **Namo** Indon
75C2 **Namoi** *R* Aust
3E2 **Nampa** Can
18C2 **Nampa** USA
70B3 **Nampala** Mali
55C2 **Nam Phong** Thai
53B4 **Namp'o** N Korea
73D5 **Nampula** Mozam
32G6 **Namsos** Nor
55B1 **Namton** Burma
49O3 **Namtsy** Russian Fed
61E3 **Namtu** Burma
3C3 **Namu** Can
73D5 **Namuno** Mozam
36C1 **Namur** Belg
73B5 **Namutoni** Namibia
53B4 **Namwŏn** S Korea
3D4 **Nanaimo** Can
53B3 **Nanam** N Korea
75D1 **Nanango** Aust
53D4 **Nanao** Japan
54C3 **Nanatsu-jima** *I* Japan
52B3 **Nanbu** China
53B2 **Nancha** China
52D4 **Nanchang** China
52B3 **Nanchong** China
62E3 **Nancowry** *I* Indian O
38D2 **Nancy** France
61B1 **Nanda Devi** *Mt* India
62B1 **Nānded** India
75D2 **Nandewar Range** *Mts* Aust
60C4 **Nandurbar** India
62B1 **Nandyāl** India
72B3 **Nanga Eboko** Cam
57B4 **Nangahale** Indon
60C1 **Nanga Parbat** *Mt* Pak
56D3 **Nangapinoh** Indon
56D3 **Nangatayap** Indon
36B2 **Nangis** France
54A2 **Nangnim** N Korea
53B3 **Nangnim Sanmaek** *Mts* N Korea
61D2 **Nang Xian** China
62B2 **Nanjangūd** India
52D3 **Nanjing** China
Nanking = Nanjing
54B4 **Nankoku** Japan
52C4 **Nan Ling** Region, China
55D1 **Nanliu** *R* China
52B5 **Nanning** China
7O3 **Nanortalik** Greenland
52A5 **Nanpan Jiang** *R* China
61B2 **Nānpāra** India
52D4 **Nanping** China
7J1 **Nansen Sd** Can
72D4 **Nansio** Tanz
38B2 **Nantes** France
14C2 **Nanticoke** USA
3F3 **Nanton** Can
52E3 **Nantong** China
37A1 **Nantua** France
14E2 **Nantucket** USA
14E2 **Nantucket I** USA
14E2 **Nantucket Sd** USA
14A2 **Nanty Glo** USA
77G1 **Nanumanga** *I* Tuvalu
77G1 **Nanumea** *I* Tuvalu
29D2 **Nanuque** Brazil
52C3 **Nanyang** China
52D2 **Nanyang Hu** *L* China
72D3 **Nanyuki** Kenya
53D4 **Naoetsu** Japan
60B4 **Naokot** Pak
20A1 **Napa** USA
10F3 **Napaiskak** USA
13D2 **Napanee** Can
48K4 **Napas** Russian Fed
7N3 **Napassoq** Greenland
55D2 **Nape** Laos
78C1 **Napier** NZ
Naples = Napoli
15E4 **Naples** Florida, USA
14B1 **Naples** New York, USA
17D3 **Naples** Texas, USA
52B5 **Napo** China
26D4 **Napo** *R* Peru/Ecuador
11C2 **Napoleon** USA
40C2 **Napoli** Italy
63B1 **Naqadeh** Iran
65C3 **Naqb Ishtar** Jordan
54C4 **Nara** Japan
70B3 **Nara** Mali
76D4 **Naracoorte** Aust
22C1 **Naranjos** Mexico
62B1 **Narasarāopet** India
55C4 **Narathiwat** Thai
61D3 **Narayanganj** Bang
62B1 **Nārāyenpet** India
38C3 **Narbonne** France
60D2 **Narendranagar** India
7L2 **Nares Str** Can
43E2 **Narew** *R* Pol
54D3 **Narita** Japan
60C4 **Narmada** *R* India
60D3 **Nārnaul** India
44F4 **Naro Fominsk** Russian Fed
72D4 **Narok** Kenya
43F2 **Narovl'a** Belorussia
60C2 **Narowal** Pak
76D4 **Narrabri** Aust
75C1 **Narran** *L* Aust
75C1 **Narran** *R* Aust
75C2 **Narrandera** Aust
76A4 **Narrogin** Aust
75C2 **Narromine** Aust
12C3 **Narrows** USA
14C2 **Narrowsburg** USA
60D4 **Narsimhapur** India
62C1 **Narsīpatnam** India
7O3 **Narssalik** Greenland

Nisutlin **Oban**

10M3 **Nisutlin** *R* Can
7L4 **Nitchequon** Can
27K8 **Niterói** Brazil
34D4 **Nith** *R* Scot
57B4 **Nitibe** Indon
43D3 **Nitra** Slovakia
12C3 **Nitro** USA
77J2 **Niue** *I* Pacific O
77G2 **Niulakita** *I* Tuvalu
56D2 **Niut** *Mt* Malay
77G1 **Niutao** *I* Tuvalu
36C1 **Nivelles** Belg
38C2 **Nivernais** Region, France
32L5 **Nivskiy** Russian Fed
62B1 **Nizāmābād** India
65C3 **Nizana** *Hist Site* Israel
44J4 **Nizhnekamskoye Vodokhranilische** *Res* Russian Fed
50C1 **Nizhneudinsk** Russian Fed
44K4 **Nizhniye Sergi** Russian Fed
44G5 **Nizhniy Lomov** Russian Fed
44G4 **Nizhniy Novgorod** Russian Fed
44J3 **Nizhniy Odes** Russian Fed
44K4 **Nizhniy Tagil** Russian Fed
49L3 **Nizhnyaya Tunguska** *R* Russian Fed
44G2 **Nizhnyaya Zolotitsa** Russian Fed
64C2 **Nizip** Turk
73C5 **Njoko** *R* Zambia
73D4 **Njombe** Tanz
72B3 **Nkambé** Cam
71F4 **Nkawkaw** Ghana
73D5 **Nkhata Bay** Malawi
72B3 **Nkongsamba** Cam
70C3 **N'Konni** Niger
61D3 **Noakhali** Bang
10F2 **Noatak** USA
10G2 **Noatak** *R* USA
53C5 **Nobeoka** Japan
54D2 **Noboribetsu** Japan
29A1 **Nobres** Brazil
37D1 **Noce** *R* Italy
22B1 **Nochistlán** Mexico
22C2 **Nochixtlán** Mexico
17C3 **Nocona** USA
21A1 **Nogales** Sonora, Mexico
19D4 **Nogales** USA
22C2 **Nogales** Veracruz, Mexico
37D2 **Nogara** Italy
54B4 **Nogata** Japan
36C2 **Nogent-en-Bassigny** France
36A2 **Nogent-le-Rotrou** France
36B2 **Nogent-sur-Seine** France
44F4 **Noginsk** Russian Fed
53E1 **Nogliki** Russian Fed
28D2 **Nogoyá** Arg
28D2 **Nogoyá** *R* Arg
60C3 **Nohar** India
54D2 **Noheji** Japan
74C1 **Nojane** Botswana
54C4 **Nojima-zaki** *C* Japan
63E3 **Nok Kundi** Pak
3H2 **Nokomis L** Can
72B3 **Nola** CAR
44H4 **Nolinsk** Russian Fed
14E2 **Nomans Land** *I* USA
22B1 **Nombre de Dioz** Mexico
10E3 **Nome** USA
36D2 **Nomeny** France
52B1 **Nomgon** Mongolia
54A4 **Nomo-saki** *Pt* Japan
6H3 **Nonachol L** Can
53B3 **Nong'an** China
55C2 **Nong Khai** Thai
74E2 **Nongoma** S Africa
77G1 **Nonouti** *I* Kiribati
54A3 **Nonsan** S Korea
74B2 **Noordoewer** Namibia
10F2 **Noorvik** USA
3C4 **Nootka Sd** Can
22C2 **Nopala** Mexico
72B4 **Noqui** Angola
7L5 **Noranda** Can
36B1 **Nord** Department, France
48D2 **Nordaustlandet** *I* Barents S
3E3 **Nordegg** Can
32F6 **Nordfjord** *Inlet* Nor
32F8 **Nordfriesische** *Is* Germany
42C2 **Nordhausen** Germany
32J4 **Nordkapp** *C* Nor
7N3 **Nordre Strømfjord** Greenland
42B2 **Nordrhein Westfalen** State, Germany
32G5 **Nord Stronfjället** *Mt* Sweden
49N2 **Nordvik** Russian Fed
35B5 **Nore** *R* Irish Rep
35F5 **Norfolk** County, Eng
11C3 **Norfolk** Nebraska, USA
13D3 **Norfolk** Virginia, USA
77F3 **Norfolk I** Aust
17D2 **Norfolk L** USA
xxixK5 **Norfolk Ridge** Pacific O
49K3 **Noril'sk** Russian Fed
12B2 **Normal** USA
17C2 **Norman** USA
38B2 **Normandie** Region, France
15C1 **Norman,L** USA
76D2 **Normanton** Aust
10N2 **Norman Wells** Can
44B2 **Norra Storfjället** *Mt* Sweden
15C1 **Norris L** USA
13D2 **Norristown** USA
32H7 **Norrköping** Sweden
32H6 **Norrsundet** Sweden
32H7 **Norrtälje** Sweden
76B4 **Norseman** Aust
53C1 **Norsk** Russian Fed
29A1 **Nortelândia** Brazil
xxxJ2 **North** *S* N W Europe
35E4 **Northallerton** Eng
76A4 **Northam** Aust
74D2 **Northam** S Africa
xxxE3 **North American Basin** Atlantic O
76A3 **Northampton** Aust
35E5 **Northampton** County, Eng
35E5 **Northampton** Eng
13E2 **Northampton** USA
62E2 **North Andaman** *I* Indian O
6G3 **North Arm** *B* Can
15C2 **North Augusta** USA
7M4 **North Aulatsivik I** Can
3G3 **North Battleford** Can
7L5 **North Bay** Can
18B2 **North Bend** USA
34D3 **North Berwick** Scot
14E1 **North Berwick** USA
7M5 **North,C** Can
77G4 **North C** NZ
10D5 **North C** USA
16B2 **North Canadian** *R* USA
4C3 **North Caribou L** Can
9E3 **North Carolina** State, USA
18B1 **North Cascade Nat Pk** USA
4E4 **North Chan** Can
34C4 **North Chan** Ire/Scot
14A1 **North Collins** USA
8C2 **North Dakota** State, USA
35F6 **North Downs** Eng
36A1 **North Downs** *Upland* Eng
13D2 **North East** USA
xxxH1 **North East Atlantic Basin** Atlantic O
10E3 **Northeast C** USA
4B2 **Northern Indian L** Can
33B3 **Northern Ireland** UK
11D2 **Northern Light L** Can
23L1 **Northern Range** *Mts* Trinidad
76C2 **Northern Territory** Aust
34D3 **North Esk** *R* Scot
14D1 **Northfield** Massachusetts, USA
11D3 **Northfield** Minnesota, USA
35F6 **North Foreland** Eng
36A1 **North Foreland** *Pt* Eng
10H3 **North Fork** *R* USA
4E3 **North French** *R* Can
5K3 **North Head** *C* Can
78B1 **North I** NZ
4B2 **North Knife** *R* Can
53B4 **North Korea** Republic, S E Asia
North Land = Severnaya Zemlya
17D3 **North Little Rock** USA
11B3 **North Loup** *R* USA
79B4 **North Magnetic Pole** Can
15E4 **North Miami** USA
15E4 **North Miami Beach** USA
10O3 **North Nahanni** *R* Can
20C2 **North Palisade** *Mt* USA
16B1 **North Platte** USA
8C2 **North Platte** *R* USA
5J4 **North Pt** *C* Can
79A **North Pole** Arctic
23Q2 **North Pt** Barbados
12C1 **North Pt** USA
11D3 **North Raccoon** *R* USA
33B2 **North Rona** *I* Scot
34D2 **North Ronaldsay** *I* Scot
3G3 **North Saskatchewan** *R* Can
33D2 **North Sea** N W Europe
3H2 **North Seal** *R* Can
62E2 **North Sentinel** Andaman Is
10J2 **North Slope** USA
6D3 **North Slope** *Region* USA
75D1 **North Stradbroke** *I* Aust
14B1 **North Syracuse** USA
78B1 **North Taranaki Bight** *B* NZ
14A1 **North Tonawanda** USA
8C3 **North Truchas Peak** *Mt* USA
4F3 **North Twin I** Can
34B3 **North Uist** *I* Scot
34D4 **Northumberland** County, Eng
76E3 **Northumberland Is** Aust
7M5 **Northumberland Str** Can
18B1 **North Vancouver** Can
14C1 **Northville** USA
35F5 **North Walsham** Eng
10K3 **Northway** USA
76A3 **North West C** Aust
60C2 **North West Frontier** Province, Pak
7M4 **North West River** Can
6G3 **North West Territories** Can
11C2 **Northwood** USA
35E4 **North York Moors Nat Pk** Eng
16C2 **Norton** *R* USA
10F3 **Norton B** USA
10F3 **Norton Sd** USA
79F1 **Norvegia,C** Ant
14D2 **Norwalk** Connecticut, USA
12C2 **Norwalk** Ohio, USA
32F6 **Norway** Kingdom, Europe
6J4 **Norway House** Can
7J2 **Norwegian B** Can
xxxH1 **Norwegian Basin** Norewegian S
48B3 **Norwegian S** N W Europe
14D2 **Norwich** Connecticut, USA
35F5 **Norwich** Eng
14C1 **Norwich** New York, USA
14E1 **Norwood** Massachusetts, USA
12C3 **Norwood** Ohio, USA
41F2 **Nos Emine** *C* Bulg
53D3 **Noshiro** Japan
41F2 **Nos Kaliakra** *C* Bulg
44J2 **Nosovaya** Russian Fed
43G2 **Nosovka** Ukraine
34E1 **Noss** *I* Scot
74B1 **Nossob** *R* Namibia
63E3 **Nostrābād** Iran
73E5 **Nosy Barren** *I* Madag
73E5 **Nosy Bé** *I* Madag
73F5 **Nosy Boraha** *I* Madag
73E6 **Nosy Varika** Madag
42D2 **Notéc** *R* Pol
6G4 **Notikewin** Can
40D3 **Noto** Italy
32F7 **Notodden** Nor
54C3 **Noto-hantō** *Pen* Japan
7N5 **Notre Dame B** Can
4E5 **Nottawasaga B** Can
4F3 **Nottaway** *R* Can
35E5 **Nottingham** County, Eng
35E5 **Nottingham** Eng
7L3 **Nottingham I** Can
11A2 **Notukeu Creek** *R* Can
70A2 **Nouadhibou** Maur
70A3 **Nouakchott** Maur
77F3 **Nouméa** Nouvelle Calédonie
71F3 **Nouna** Burkina
74C3 **Noupoort** S Africa
77F3 **Nouvelle Calédonie** *I* S W Pacific O
29C2 **Nova América** Brazil
73B4 **Nova Caipemba** Angola
29B3 **Nova Esperança** Brazil
29D3 **Nova Friburgo** Brazil
73B5 **Nova Gaia** Angola
29C3 **Nova Granada** Brazil
29C3 **Nova Herizonte** Brazil
29D3 **Nova Lima** Brazil
Nova Lisboa = Huambo
29B3 **Nova Londrina** Brazil
73D6 **Nova Mambone** Mozam
37C2 **Novara** Italy
29C1 **Nova Roma** Brazil
57C4 **Nova Sagres** Indon
7M5 **Nova Scotia** Province, Can
20A1 **Novato** USA
29D2 **Nova Venécia** Brazil
45E6 **Novaya Kakhovka** Ukraine
49R2 **Novaya Sibir, Ostrov** *I* Russian Fed
48G2 **Novaya Zemlya** *I* Russian Fed
41F2 **Nova Zagora** Bulg
27K4 **Nove Russas** Brazil
41D1 **Nové Zámky** Slovakia
44E4 **Novgorod** Russian Fed
37E2 **Novigrad** Croatia, Yugos
53E2 **Novikovo** Russian Fed
37C2 **Novi Ligure** Italy
22A1 **Novillero** Mexico
41F2 **Novi Pazar** Bulg
41E2 **Novi Pazar** Serbia, Yugos
41D1 **Novi Sad** Serbia, Yugos
45K5 **Novoalekseyevka** Kazakhstan
45G5 **Novoanninskiy** Russian Fed
53C2 **Novobureyskiy** Russian Fed
45G6 **Novocherkassk** Russian Fed
44G3 **Novodvinsk** Russian Fed
43G2 **Novogorod** Belorussia
45D5 **Novograd Volynskiy** Ukraine
43F2 **Novogrudok** Belorussia
28E1 **Novo Hamburgo** Brazil
48H5 **Novokazalinsk** Kazakhstan
48K4 **Novokuznetsk** Russian Fed
79F12 **Novolazarevskaya** *Base* Ant
40D1 **Novo Mesto** Slovenia, Yugos
43G3 **Novomirgorod** Ukraine
44F5 **Novomoskovsk** Russian Fed
Novo Redondo = Sumbe
45F7 **Novorossiysk** Russian Fed
49M2 **Novorybnoye** Russian Fed
48K4 **Novosibirsk** Russian Fed
49P2 **Novosibirskye Ostrova** *Is* Russian Fed
45K5 **Novotroitsk** Russian Fed
45H5 **Novo Uzensk** Russian Fed
43E2 **Novovolynsk** Ukraine
44H4 **Novo Vyatsk** Russian Fed
45E5 **Novozybkov** Russian Fed
48J3 **Novyy Port** Russian Fed
43E2 **Novy Dwór Mazowiecki** Pol
44L4 **Novyy Lyalya** Russian Fed
44N2 **Novyy Port** Russian Fed
45J7 **Novyy Uzen** Kazakhstan
42D2 **Nowa Sól** Pol
17C2 **Nowata** USA
10H3 **Nowitna** *R* USA
75D2 **Nowra** Aust
63C1 **Now Shahr** Iran
60C2 **Nowshera** Pak
43E3 **Nowy Sącz** Pol
10M4 **Noyes I** USA
36B2 **Noyon** France
71F4 **Nsawam** Ghana
71H4 **Nsukka** Nig
74E1 **Nuanetsi** Zim
74E1 **Nuanetsi** *R* Zim
71G4 **Nuatja** Togo
72D2 **Nuba** *Mts* Sudan
66B2 **Nubian Desert** Sudan
28A3 **Nuble** *R* Chile
8D4 **Nueces** *R* USA
6J3 **Nueltin L** Can
21B1 **Nueva Casas Grandes** Mexico
29A3 **Nueva Germania** Par
23A2 **Nueva Gerona** Cuba
28A3 **Nueva Imperial** Chile
28D2 **Nueva Palmira** Urug
21B2 **Nueva Rosita** Mexico
23B2 **Nuevitas** Cuba
22B1 **Nuevo** State, Mexico
21B1 **Nuevo Casas Grandes** Mexico
22A1 **Nuevo Ideal** Mexico
21C2 **Nuevo Laredo** Mexico
69D4 **Nugaal** Region, Somalia
7N2 **Nûgâtsiaq** Greenland
7N2 **Nûgussuaq** *Pen* Greenland
7N2 **Nûgussuaq** *I* Greenland
77G1 **Nui** *I* Tuvalu
52A5 **Nui Con Voi** *R* Vietnam
36C3 **Nuits** France
61E2 **Nu Jiang** *R* China
75A2 **Nukey Bluff** *Mt* Aust
64D3 **Nukhayb** Iraq
77G1 **Nukufetau** *I* Tuvalu
77G1 **Nukulaelae** *I* Tuvalu
77H1 **Nukunon** *I* Tokelau Is
48G5 **Nukus** Uzbekistan
10G3 **Nulato** USA
76B4 **Nullarbor Plain** Aust
71J4 **Numan** Nig
54C3 **Numata** Japan
72C3 **Numatinna** *R* Sudan
53D4 **Numazu** Japan
51G7 **Numfoor** *I* Indon
75C3 **Numurkah** Aust
10F3 **Nunapitchuk** USA
14A1 **Nunda** USA
10E3 **Nunivak I** USA
60D2 **Nunkun** *Mt* India
10C3 **Nunligran** Russian Fed
53A1 **Nuomin He** *R* China
40B2 **Nuoro** Sardegna
63C2 **Nurābād** Iran
37C2 **Nure** *R* Italy
75A2 **Nuriootpa** Aust
60C1 **Nuristan** *Upland* Afghan
44J5 **Nurlat** Russian Fed
32K6 **Nurmes** Fin
42C3 **Nürnberg** Germany
75C2 **Nurri,Mt** Aust
56E4 **Nusa Tenggara** *Is* Indon
57B4 **Nusa Tenggara Timor** Province, Indon
64D2 **Nusaybin** Turk
10G4 **Nushagak** *R* USA
10G4 **Nushagak B** USA
10G4 **Nushagak Pen** USA
60B3 **Nushki** Pak
7M4 **Nutak** Can
10K3 **Nutzotin Mts** USA
Nuuk = Godthåb
7L3 **Nuvukjuak** Can
61B2 **Nuwakot** Nepal
62C3 **Nuwara-Eliya** Sri Lanka
74C3 **Nuweveldreeks** *Mts* S Africa
45C3 **Nyac** USA
14D2 **Nyack** USA
72D3 **Nyahururu Falls** Kenya
75B3 **Nyah West** Aust
50C3 **Nyaingentanglha Shan** *Mts* China
72D4 **Nyakabindi** Tanz
44L3 **Nyaksimvol'** Russian Fed
72C2 **Nyala** Sudan
61C2 **Nyalam** China
72C3 **Nyamlell** Sudan
73D6 **Nyanda** Zim
44G3 **Nyandoma** Russian Fed
72B4 **Nyanga** *R* Gabon
61D2 **Nyang Qu** China
73D5 **Nyasa L** Malawi/Mozam
55B2 **Nyaunglebin** Burma
44K4 **Nyazepetrovsk** Russian Fed
32G7 **Nyborg** Den
32H7 **Nybro** Sweden
48J3 **Nyda** Russian Fed
7M1 **Nyeboes Land** *Region* Can
61D1 **Nyenchentanglha Range** *Mts* China
72D4 **Nyeri** Kenya
73D5 **Nyimba** Zambia
59H2 **Nyingchi** China
43E3 **Nyíregyháza** Hung
72D3 **Nyiru,Mt** Kenya
32J6 **Nykarleby** Fin
32F7 **Nykøbing** Den
32G8 **Nykøbing** Den
32H7 **Nyköping** Sweden
74D1 **Nyl** *R* S Africa
74D1 **Nylstroom** S Africa
75C2 **Nymagee** Aust
32H7 **Nynäshamn** Sweden
75C2 **Nyngan** Aust
37B1 **Nyon** Switz
72B3 **Nyong** *R* Cam
54A3 **Nyongwol** S Korea
54A3 **Nyongwon** N Korea
38D3 **Nyons** France
42D2 **Nysa** Pol
53E1 **Nysh** Russian Fed
18C2 **Nyssa** USA
44H3 **Nyukhcha** Russian Fed
50F1 **Nyukzha** *R* Russian Fed
49N3 **Nyurba** Russian Fed
72D4 **Nzega** Tanz
70B4 **Nzérékore** Guinea
73B4 **N'zeto** Angola
71F4 **Nzi** *R* Ivory Coast

O

11C3 **Oacoma** USA
11B3 **Oahe,L** *Res* USA
20E5 **Oahu,I** Hawaiian Is
75B2 **Oakbank** Aust
20B2 **Oakdale** USA
11C2 **Oakes** USA
75D1 **Oakey** Aust
19B3 **Oakland** California, USA
11C3 **Oakland** Nebraska, USA
18B2 **Oakland** Oregon, USA
12B3 **Oakland City** USA
12B2 **Oak Lawn** USA
20B2 **Oakley** California, USA
16B2 **Oakley** Kansas, USA
15C1 **Oak Ridge** USA
18B2 **Oakridge** USA
4F5 **Oakville** Can
78B3 **Oamaru** NZ
20D2 **Oasis** California, USA
18D2 **Oasis** Nevada, USA
79F7 **Oates Land** Region, Ant
75E3 **Oatlands** Aust
22C2 **Oaxaca** Mexico
22C2 **Oaxaca** State, Mexico
48H3 **Ob'** *R* Russian Fed
4E4 **Oba** Can
54C3 **Obama** Japan
78A3 **Oban** NZ
34C3 **Oban** Scot

Ostróda Paropamisus

43D2 **Ostróda** Pol
43E2 **Ostrołęka** Pol
44D4 **Ostrov** Russian Fed
43E2 **Ostrowiec** Pol
43E2 **Ostrów Mazowiecka** Pol
43D2 **Ostrów Wielkopolski** Pol
53C5 **Ōsumi-kaikyō** *Str* Japan
53C5 **Ōsumi-shotō** *Is* Japan
71G4 **Osun** *State* Nigeria
39A2 **Osuna** Spain
14B1 **Oswego** USA
14B1 **Oswego** *R* USA
35D5 **Oswestry** Eng
43D3 **Oświęcim** Pol
54C3 **Ota** Japan
78B3 **Otago Pen** NZ
78C2 **Otaki** NZ
53E3 **Otaru** Japan
26C3 **Otavalo** Ecuador
73B5 **Otavi** Namibia
54D3 **Otawara** Japan
14C1 **Otego** USA
18C1 **Othello** USA
3G2 **Otherside** *R* Can
41E3 **Óthris** *Mt* Greece
71G4 **Oti** *R* Ghana
71G4 **Otiki** *R* Nig
16B1 **Otis** Colorado, USA
14D1 **Otis** Massachusetts, USA
14C2 **Otisville** USA
74B1 **Otjimbingwe** Namibia
73B6 **Otjiwarongo** Namibia
52B2 **Otog Qi** China
54D2 **Otoineppu** Japan
78C1 **Otorohanga** NZ
41D2 **Otranto** Italy
41D2 **Otranto,Str of** *Chan* Italy/Alb
12B2 **Otsego** USA
14C1 **Otsego L** USA
4E5 **Otsego Lake** USA
54C3 **Otsu** Japan
32F6 **Otta** Nor
32F7 **Otta** *R* Nor
4F4 **Ottawa** Can
4F4 **Ottawa** *R* Can
12B2 **Ottawa** Illinois, USA
17C2 **Ottawa** Kansas, USA
7K4 **Ottawa Is** Can
7K4 **Otter Rapids** Can
7K1 **Otto Fjord** Can
74D2 **Ottosdal** S Africa
12A2 **Ottumwa** USA
36D2 **Ottweiler** Germany
71H4 **Otukpa** Nig
71H4 **Oturkpo** Nig
26C5 **Otusco** Peru
75B3 **Otway,C** Aust
43E2 **Otwock** Pol
37D1 **Ötz** Austria
37D1 **Otzal** *Mts* Austria
55C1 **Ou** *R* Laos
17D3 **Ouachita** *R* USA
17D3 **Ouachita,L** USA
17D3 **Ouachita Mts** USA
70A2 **Ouadane** Maur
72C3 **Ouadda** CAR
72C2 **Ouaddai** *Desert Region* Chad
71F3 **Ouagadougou** Burkina
71F3 **Ouahigouya** Burkina
72C3 **Ouaka** CAR
70C3 **Oualam** Niger
71G3 **Oualé** *R* Burkina
70C2 **Ouallen** Alg
72C3 **Ouanda Djallé** CAR
36B3 **Ouanne** *R* France
70A2 **Ouarane** Region, Maur
70C1 **Ouargla** Alg
72C3 **Ouarra** *R* CAR
70B1 **Ouarzazate** Mor
39C2 **Ouassel** *R* Alg
72B3 **Oubangui** *R* Congo
36B1 **Oudenaarde** Belg
74C3 **Oudtshoorn** S Africa
39B2 **Oued Tlêlat** Alg
71A2 **Oued Zem** Mor
71F4 **Ouellé** Ivory Coast
72B3 **Ouesso** Congo
71A2 **Ouezzane** Mor
72B3 **Ouham** *R* Chad
71G4 **Ouidah** Benin
4D4 **Ouimet** Can
71B2 **Oujda** Mor
32J6 **Oulainen** Fin
32K5 **Oulu** Fin
32K6 **Oulu** *R* Fin
32K6 **Oulujärvi** *L* Fin
72C2 **Oum Chalouba** Chad
71D1 **Oum el Bouaghi** Alg
71A2 **Oumer Rbia** *R* Mor
72B2 **Oum Hadjer** Chad
72C2 **Oum Haouach** *Watercourse* Chad
32K5 **Ounas** *R* Fin
44C2 **Ounasjoki** *R* Fin
44C2 **Ounastunturi** *Mt* Fin
72C2 **Ounianga Kebir** Chad
36D1 **Our** *R* Germany
16A2 **Ouray** USA
36C2 **Ource** *R* France
Ourense = Orense
36B2 **Ourcq** *R* France
27K5 **Ouricurí** Brazil
29C3 **Ourinhos** Brazil
29D3 **Ouro Prêto** Brazil
36C1 **Ourthe** *R* Belg
35E4 **Ouse** *R* Eng
35F5 **Ouse** *R* Eng
33B2 **Outer Hebrides** *Is* Scot
20C4 **Outer Santa Barbara** *Chan* USA
73B6 **Outjo** Namibia
3G3 **Outlook** Can
32K6 **Outokumpu** Fin
37A2 **Ouvèze** *R* France
75B3 **Ouyen** Aust
37C2 **Ovada** Italy
28A2 **Ovalle** Chile
73B5 **Ovamboland** Region, Namibia
19D3 **Overton** USA
32J5 **Övertorneå** Sweden
16B1 **Ovid** Colorado, USA
14B1 **Ovid** New York, USA
39A1 **Oviedo** Spain
45D5 **Ovruch** Ukraine
49O4 **Ovsyanka** Russian Fed
78A3 **Owaka** NZ
14B1 **Owasco L** USA
54C4 **Owase** Japan
11D3 **Owatonna** USA
14B1 **Owego** USA
20C2 **Owens** *R* USA
12B3 **Owensboro** USA
20D2 **Owens L** USA
4E5 **Owen Sound** Can
76D1 **Owen Stanley Range** *Mts* PNG
71H4 **Owerri** Nig
4C2 **Owl** *R* Can
18E2 **Owl Creek Mts** USA
71H4 **Owo** Nig
12C2 **Owosso** USA
18C2 **Owyhee** USA
18C2 **Owyhee** *R* USA
18C2 **Owyhee Mts** USA
26C6 **Oxampampa** Peru
3H4 **Oxbow** Can
32H7 **Oxelösund** Sweden
35E6 **Oxford** County, Eng
35E5 **Oxford** Eng
14E1 **Oxford** Massachusetts, USA
17E3 **Oxford** Mississippi, USA
14C1 **Oxford** New York, USA
20C3 **Oxnard** USA
53D4 **Oyama** Japan
3F3 **Oyen** Can
72B3 **Oyem** Gabon
34C3 **Oykel** *R* Scot
49Q3 **Oymyakon** Russian Fed
71G4 **Oyo** Nig
37A1 **Oyonnax** France
32F6 **Øyre** Nor
75E3 **Oyster B** Aust
57F9 **Ozamiz** Phil
43F2 **Ozarichi** Belorussia
15B2 **Ozark** USA
17D2 **Ozark Plat** USA
17D2 **Ozarks,L of the** USA
43E3 **Ózd** Hung
53E2 **Ozerskiy** Russian Fed
16B3 **Ozona** USA
22C1 **Ozuluama** Mexico
64D1 **Ozurgeti** Georgia

P

74B3 **Paarl** S Africa
34B3 **Pabbay** *I* Scot
43D2 **Pabianice** Pol
61C3 **Pabna** Bang
43F1 **Pabrade** Lithuania
26C5 **Pacasmayo** Peru
28E2 **Pacheca** Brazil
22B1 **Pacheco** Mexico
22C1 **Pachuca** Mexico
20B1 **Pacific** USA
xxixN7 **Pacific-Antarctic Ridge** Pacific O
20B2 **Pacific Grove** USA
xxixG8 **Pacific O**
56D4 **Pacitan** Indon
29D2 **Pacuí** *R* Brazil
56B3 **Padang** Indon
57B4 **Padang** Indon
56B3 **Padangpanjang** Indon
56A2 **Padangsidempuan** Indon
44E3 **Padany** Russian Fed
42B2 **Paderborn** Germany
6J3 **Padlei** Can
61D3 **Padma** *R* Bang
37D2 **Padova** Italy
8D4 **Padre I** USA
35C6 **Padstow** Eng
75B3 **Padthaway** Aust
Padua = Padova
12B3 **Paducah** Kentucky, USA
16B3 **Paducah** Texas, USA
32L5 **Padunskoye More** *L* Russian Fed
54A2 **Paegam** N Korea
53A4 **Paengnyŏng-do** *I* S Korea
78C1 **Paeroa** NZ
74E1 **Pafuri** Mozam
40C2 **Pag** *I* Croatia, Yugos
57F9 **Pagadian** Phil
56B3 **Pagai Seletan** *I* Indon
56B3 **Pagai Utara** *I* Indon
51H5 **Pagan** *I* Pacific O
56E3 **Pagatan** Indon
19D3 **Page** USA
51F8 **Pago Mission** Aust
41F3 **Pagondhas** Greece
16A2 **Pagosa Springs** USA
4C4 **Paguchi L** Can
4D3 **Pagwa River** Can
20E5 **Pahala** Hawaiian Is
78C2 **Pahiatua** NZ
20E5 **Pahoa** Hawaiian Is
15E4 **Pahokee** USA
71J4 **Pai** *R* Nig
32K6 **Päijänna** *L* Fin
28A4 **Paillaco** Chile
20E5 **Pailola Chan** Hawaiian Is
12C2 **Painesville** USA
19D3 **Painted Desert** USA
12C3 **Paintsville** USA
34C4 **Paisley** Scot
26B5 **Paita** Peru
32J5 **Pajala** Sweden
57B4 **Pajeti** Indon
58E3 **Pakistan** Republic, Asia
55C2 **Pak Lay** Laos
61E3 **Pakokku** Burma
3F4 **Pakowki L** Can
40D1 **Pakrac** Croatia, Yugos
41D1 **Paks** Hung
55C2 **Pak Sane** Laos
55D2 **Pakse** Laos
72D3 **Pakwach** Uganda
72B3 **Pala** Chad
40D2 **Palagruža** *I* Croatia, Yugos
36B2 **Palaiseau** France
Palakhat = Pälghät
74D1 **Palala** *R* S Africa
62E2 **Palalankwe** Andaman Is
49S4 **Palana** Russian Fed
56D3 **Palangkaraya** Indon
62B2 **Palani** India
60C4 **Palanpur** India
74D1 **Palapye** Botswana
15C3 **Palatka** USA
51G6 **Palau Is** Pacific O
55B3 **Palaw** Burma
57E9 **Palawan** *I* Phil
57E9 **Palawan Pass** Phil
62B3 **Palayankottai** India
32J7 **Paldiski** Estonia
57B2 **Paleleh** Indon
56B3 **Palembang** Indon
39B1 **Palencia** Spain
65B1 **Paleokhorio** Cyprus
40C3 **Palermo** Italy
17C3 **Palestine** USA
61D3 **Paletwa** Burma
62B2 **Pälghät** India
60C3 **Päli** India
71G4 **Palimé** Togo
56E1 **Palin,Mt** Malay
16A2 **Palisade** USA
60C4 **Pälitäna** India
62B3 **Palk Str** India/Sri Lanka
45H5 **Pallasovka** Russian Fed
32J5 **Pallastunturi** *Mt* Fin
78B2 **Palliser B** NZ
78C2 **Palliser,C** NZ
73E5 **Palma** Mozam
39C2 **Palma de Mallorca** Spain
27L5 **Palmares** Brazil
28E2 **Palmares do Sul** Brazil
23A5 **Palmar Sur** Costa Rica
29B4 **Palmas** Brazil
70B4 **Palmas,C** Lib
29D1 **Palmas de Monte Alto** Brazil
23B2 **Palma Soriano** Cuba
15C3 **Palm Bay** USA
15E4 **Palm Beach** USA
20C3 **Palmdale** USA
29C4 **Palmeira** Brazil
27L5 **Palmeira dos Indos** Brazil
10J3 **Palmer** USA
79G3 **Palmer** *Base* Ant
79G3 **Palmer Arch** Ant
79F3 **Palmer Land** *Region* Ant
78B3 **Palmerston** NZ
78C2 **Palmerston North** NZ
14C2 **Palmerton** USA
15E4 **Palmetto** USA
40D3 **Palmi** Italy
28E1 **Palmiera das Missões** Brazil
22C1 **Palmillas** Mexico
26C3 **Palmira** Colombia
76D2 **Palm Is** Aust
4E5 **Palms** USA
19C4 **Palm Springs** USA
12A3 **Palmyra** Missouri, USA
14B1 **Palmyra** New York, USA
14B2 **Palmyra** Pennsylvania, USA
61C3 **Palmyras Pt** India
20A2 **Palo Alto** USA
56C2 **Paloh** Indon
72D2 **Paloích** Sudan
22C2 **Palomares** Mexico
19C4 **Palomar Mt** USA
57B3 **Palopo** Indon
57A3 **Palu** Indon
64C2 **Palu** Turk
60D3 **Palwal** India
10B2 **Palyavaam** *R* Russian Fed
71G3 **Pama** Burkina
56D4 **Pamekasan** Indon
56C4 **Pameungpeuk** Indon
38C3 **Pamiers** France
59F2 **Pamir** *Mts* China
48J6 **Pamir** *R* Russian Fed
15D1 **Pamlico** *R* USA
15D1 **Pamlico Sd** USA
16B2 **Pampa** USA
28B2 **Pampa de la Salinas** *Salt pan* Arg
28B3 **Pampa de la Varita** *Plain* Arg
57B3 **Pampanua** Indon
28D2 **Pampeiro** Brazil
26D2 **Pamplona** Colombia
39B1 **Pamplona** Spain
12B3 **Pana** USA
19D3 **Panaca** USA
41E2 **Panagyurishte** Bulg
62A1 **Panaji** India
26C2 **Panamá** Panama
26B2 **Panama** Republic, C America
23B5 **Panama Canal** Panama
15B2 **Panama City** USA
19C3 **Panamint Range** *Mts* USA
20D2 **Panamint V** USA
37D2 **Panaro** *R* Italy
57F8 **Panay** *I* Phil
41E2 **Pancevo** Serbia, Yugos
57F8 **Pandan** Phil
62B1 **Pandharpur** India
75A1 **Pandie Pandie** Aust
43E1 **Panevežys** Lithuania
48K5 **Panfilov** Kazakhstan
55B1 **Pang** *R* Burma
72D4 **Pangani** Tanz
72D4 **Pangani** *R* Tanz
72C4 **Pangi** Zaïre
57A3 **Pangkajene** Indon
56C3 **Pangkalpinang** Indon
7M3 **Pangnirtung** Can
55B1 **Pangtara** Burma
19D3 **Panguitch** USA
57F9 **Pangutaran Group** *Is* Phil
16B2 **Panhandle** USA
60D3 **Panipat** India
60B2 **Panjao** Afghan
63E3 **Panjgur** Pak
10F5 **Pankof,C** USA
71H4 **Pankshin** Nig
53B4 **P'anmunjŏm** N Korea
61B3 **Panna** India
29B3 **Panorama** Brazil
29A2 **Pantanal de São Lourenço** *Swamp* Brazil
29A2 **Pantanal do Rio Negro** *Swamp* Brazil
29A2 **Pantanal do Taquari** *Swamp* Brazil
57B4 **Pantar** *I* Indon
40C3 **Pantelleria** *I* Medit S
22C1 **Pantepec** Mexico
22C1 **Panuco** Mexico
22C1 **Pánuco** *R* Mexico
52A4 **Pan Xian** China
40D3 **Paola** Italy
17D2 **Paola** USA
12B3 **Paoli** USA
42D3 **Papa** Hung
20E5 **Papaikou** Hawaiian Is
78B1 **Papakura** NZ
22C2 **Papaloapan** *R* Mexico
22C1 **Papantla** Mexico
34E1 **Papa Stour** *I* Scot
78B1 **Papatoetoe** NZ
34D2 **Papa Westray** *I* Scot
65B1 **Paphos** Cyprus
76D1 **Papua,G of** PNG
76D1 **Papua New Guinea** Republic, S E Asia
28A2 **Papudo** Chile
55B2 **Papun** Burma
27H4 **Para** State, Brazil
27J4 **Pará** *R* Brazil
76A3 **Paraburdoo** Aust
26C6 **Paracas,Pen de** Peru
29C2 **Paracatu** Brazil
29C2 **Paracatu** *R* Brazil
55E2 **Paracel Is** S E Asia
75A2 **Parachilna** Aust
60C2 **Parachinar** Pak
41E2 **Paracin** Serbia, Yugos
29D2 **Pará de Minas** Brazil
19B3 **Paradise** California, USA
19D3 **Paradise** Nevada, USA
5K3 **Paradise** *R* Can
20D1 **Paradise Peak** *Mt* USA
17D2 **Paragould** USA
26F6 **Paraguá** *R* Bol
26F2 **Paragua** *R* Ven
29D1 **Paraguaçu** *R* Brazil
27G7 **Paraguai** *R* Brazil
29A4 **Paraguari** Par
25E2 **Paraguay** Republic, S America
25E2 **Paraguay** *R* Par
27L5 **Paraiba** State, Brazil
29D3 **Paraíba do Sul** *R* Brazil
22D2 **Paraiso** Mexico
71G4 **Parakou** Benin
75A2 **Parakylia** Aust
62B3 **Paramakkudi** India
27G2 **Paramaribo** Suriname
29D1 **Paramirim** Brazil
49R4 **Paramushir, Ostrov** *I* Russian Fed
29B4 **Paraná** Brazil
25F2 **Paraná** State, Brazil
28C2 **Paraná** Urug
25E4 **Paraná** *R* Arg
27J6 **Paranã** *R* Brazil
29C4 **Paranaguá** Brazil
29B2 **Paranaiba** Brazil
29B2 **Paranaiba** *R* Brazil
29B3 **Paranapanema** *R* Brazil
29B3 **Paranavai** Brazil
57F9 **Parang** Phil
29D2 **Paraope** *R* Brazil
78B2 **Paraparaumu** NZ
29D1 **Paratinga** Brazil
62B1 **Parbhani** India
71G3 **Parc National d'Arly** Burkina
71F4 **Parc National de la Komoé** Ivory Coast
71G3 **Parc National de la Pendjari** Benin
71G3 **Parcs Nationaux du W** Benin
65C2 **Pardes Hanna** Israel
28D3 **Pardo** Arg
29E2 **Pardo** *R* Bahia, Brazil
29B3 **Pardo** *R* Mato Grosso do Sul, Brazil
29C2 **Pardo** *R* Minas Gerais, Brazil
29C3 **Pardo** *R* Sao Paulo, Brazil
42D2 **Pardubice** Czech Republic
50G4 **Parece Vela** *Reef* Pacific O
29A1 **Parecis** Brazil
4G4 **Parent** Can
57A3 **Parepare** Indon
28C3 **Parera** Arg
56B3 **Pariaman** Indon
26F1 **Paria,Pen de** Ven
57B3 **Parigi** Indon
38C2 **Paris** France
12C3 **Paris** Kentucky, USA
15B1 **Paris** Tennessee, USA
17C3 **Paris** Texas, USA
19D4 **Parker** USA
12C3 **Parkersburg** USA
75C2 **Parkes** Aust
14C3 **Parkesburg** USA
12A1 **Park Falls** USA
20B3 **Parkfield** USA
12B2 **Park Forest** USA
11C2 **Park Rapids** USA
11C3 **Parkston** USA
18B1 **Parksville** Can
18D2 **Park Valley** USA
62C1 **Parlākimidi** India
62B1 **Parli** India
37D2 **Parma** Italy
12C2 **Parma** USA
27K4 **Parnaiba** Brazil
27K4 **Parnaiba** *R* Brazil
41E3 **Párnon Óros** *Mts* Greece
44C4 **Pärnu** Estonia
61C2 **Paro** Bhutan
75B1 **Paroo** *R* Aust
75B2 **Paroo Channel** *R* Aust
63E2 **Paropamisus** *Mts* Afghan

Páros Pic Toussidé

41F3 **Páros** *I* Greece
19D3 **Parowan** USA
37B2 **Parpaillon** *Mts* France
28A3 **Parral** Chile
75D2 **Parramatta** Aust
8C4 **Parras** Mexico
7K3 **Parry B** Can
10O1 **Parry,C** Can
6G2 **Parry Is** Can
10O2 **Parry Pen** Can
12C1 **Parry Sound** Can
42C3 **Parsberg** Germany
6F4 **Parsnip** *R* Can
17C2 **Parsons** Kansas, USA
13D3 **Parsons** West Virginia, USA
38B2 **Parthenay** France
40C3 **Partinico** Italy
53C3 **Partizansk** Russian Fed
27H4 **Paru** *R* Brazil
22A1 **Páruco** Mexico
62C1 **Parvatipuram** India
74D2 **Parys** S Africa
17C4 **Pasadena** Texas, USA
20C3 **Pasadena** USA
57A3 **Pasangkayu** Indon
57B4 **Pasarwajo** Indon
55B2 **Pasawing** Burma
17E3 **Pascagoula** USA
41F1 **Paşcani** Rom
18C1 **Pasco** USA
36B1 **Pas-de-Calais** Department, France
32G8 **Pasewalk** Germany
3G2 **Pasfield L** Can
63D3 **Pashū'īyeh** Iran
76B4 **Pasley,C** Aust
63E3 **Pasni** Pak
28D1 **Paso de los Libres** Arg
25E4 **Paso de los Toros** Urug
25B6 **Paso Limay** Arg
20B3 **Paso Robles** USA
5H4 **Paspébiac** Can
3H3 **Pasquia Hills** Can
14C2 **Passaic** USA
42C3 **Passau** Germany
25E3 **Passo de los Libres** Arg
22B1 **Passo del Toro** *Mt* Mexico
37D1 **Passo di Stelvio** *Mt* Italy
37D1 **Passo di Tonale** Italy
28E1 **Passo Fundo** Brazil
29C3 **Passos** Brazil
37B2 **Passy** France
26C4 **Pastaza** *R* Peru
28C3 **Pasteur** Arg
6H4 **Pas,The** Can
26C3 **Pasto** Colombia
10F3 **Pastol B** USA
37D2 **Pasubio** *Mt* Italy
56D4 **Pasuruan** Indon
43E1 **Pasvalys** Lithuania
60C4 **Pātan** India
61C2 **Patan** Nepal
75B3 **Patchewollock** Aust
78B1 **Patea** NZ
78B2 **Patea** *R* NZ
40C3 **Paterno** Italy
14C2 **Paterson** USA
78A3 **Paterson Inlet** *B* NZ
60D2 **Pathankot** India
Pathein = Bassein
11A3 **Pathfinder Res** USA
60D2 **Patiāla** India
26C6 **Pativilca** Peru
41F3 **Pátmos** *I* Greece
61C2 **Patna** India
64D2 **Patnos** Turk
49N4 **Patomskoye Nagor'ye** *Upland* Russian Fed
27L5 **Patos** Brazil
29C2 **Patos de Minas** Brazil
28B2 **Patquia** Arg
41E3 **Pátrai** Greece
44L3 **Patrasuy** Russian Fed
29C2 **Patrocinio** Brazil
72E4 **Patta** *I* Kenya
57A4 **Pattallasang** Indon
55C4 **Pattani** Thai
20B2 **Patterson** California, USA
17D4 **Patterson** Louisiana, USA
10M3 **Patterson,Mt** Can
20C2 **Patterson Mt** USA
14A2 **Patton** USA
3C2 **Pattullo,Mt** Can
27L5 **Patu** Brazil
61D3 **Patuakhali** Bang
21D3 **Patuca** *R* Honduras
22B2 **Patzcuaro** Mexico
38B3 **Pau** France
10O2 **Paulatuk** Can
27K5 **Paulistana** Brazil
74E2 **Paulpietersburg** S Africa
17C3 **Pauls Valley** USA
55B2 **Paungde** Burma
60D2 **Pauri** India
32H5 **Pauskie** Nor
29D2 **Pavão** Brazil
37C2 **Pavia** Italy
48J4 **Pavlodar** Kazakhstan
10F4 **Pavlof V** USA
10F4 **Pavlov B** USA
44K4 **Pavlovka** Russian Fed
44G4 **Pavlovo** Russian Fed
45G5 **Pavlovsk** Russian Fed
37D2 **Pavullo nel Frigano** Italy
56D3 **Pawan** *R* Indon
17C2 **Pawhuska** USA
14A3 **Paw Paw** USA
14E2 **Pawtucket** USA
16B1 **Paxton** USA
56B3 **Payakumbuh** Indon
37B1 **Payerne** Switz
18C2 **Payette** USA
7L4 **Payne,L** Can
11D2 **Paynesville** USA
28D2 **Paysandu** Urug
36A2 **Pays d'Auge** Region, France
36A2 **Pays-de-Bray** Region, France
36A2 **Pays de Caux** Region, France
36A2 **Pays d'Ouche** Region, France
41E2 **Pazardzhik** Bulg
37E2 **Pazin** Croatia, Yugos
3E2 **Peace** *R* Can
15E4 **Peace** *R* USA
3E2 **Peace River** Can
19D3 **Peach Springs** USA
35E5 **Peak District Nat Pk** Eng
75A1 **Peake** *R* Aust
13F1 **Peaked Mt** USA
75C2 **Peak Hill** Aust
51G7 **Peak Mandala** *Mt* Indon
35E5 **Peak,The** *Mt* Eng
19E3 **Peale,Mt** USA
17D3 **Pearl** *R* USA
20E5 **Pearl City** Hawaiian Is
20E5 **Pearl Harbor** Hawaiian Is
17F4 **Pearsall** USA
74D3 **Pearston** S Africa
6H2 **Peary Chan** Can
73D5 **Pebane** Mozam
41E2 **Peć** Serbia, Yugos
29D2 **Peçanha** Brazil
17D4 **Pecan Island** USA
32L5 **Pechenga** Russian Fed
44K2 **Pechora** Russian Fed
44J2 **Pechora** *R* Russian Fed
44J2 **Pechorskaya Guba** *G* Russian Fed
44J2 **Pechorskoye More** *S* Russian Fed
40D3 **Pecoraro** *Mt* Italy
16B3 **Pecos** USA
16B3 **Pecos** *R* USA
43D3 **Pécs** Hung
56G7 **Pedang Endau** Malay
65B1 **Pedhoulas** Cyprus
75A1 **Pedirka** Aust
29D2 **Pedra Azul** Brazil
29C3 **Pedregulho** Brazil
23B3 **Pedro Cays** *Is* Caribbean
25C2 **Pedro de Valdivia** Chile
29B2 **Pedro Gomes** Brazil
29A3 **Pedro Juan Caballero** Par
28C3 **Pedro Luro** Arg
22C1 **Pedro Mentova** Mexico
62C3 **Pedro,Pt** Sri Lanka
28D1 **Pedro R Fernandez** Arg
75B2 **Peebinga** Aust
34D4 **Peebles** Scot
15D2 **Pee Dee** *R* USA
14D2 **Peekskill** USA
35C4 **Peel** Eng
10M2 **Peel** *R* Can
6J2 **Peel Sd** Can
75A1 **Peera Peera Poolanna** *L* Aust
3F2 **Peerless L** Can
51G7 **Peg Arfak** *Mt* Indon
78B2 **Pegasus B** NZ
10B2 **Pegtymel'** *R* Russian Fed
61E4 **Pegu** Burma
56B3 **Pegunungan Barisan** *Mts* Indon
56D2 **Pegunungan Iran** *Mts* Malay Indon
76C1 **Pegunungan Maoke** *Mts* Indon
56E3 **Pegunungan Meratus** *Mts* Indon
56D2 **Pegunungan Muller** *Mts* Indon
56D3 **Pegunungan Schwanet** *Mts* Indon
56B3 **Pegunungan Tigapuluh** *Mts* Indon
55B2 **Pegu Yoma** *Mts* Burma
28C3 **Pehuajó** Arg
32K7 **Peipsi Järv** *L* Estonia
32K7 **Peipus, Lake** *L* Russian Fed
29B1 **Peixe** *R* Mato Grosso, Brazil
29B3 **Peixe** *R* Sao Paulo, Brazil
52D3 **Pei Xian** China
56C4 **Pekalongan** Indon
55C5 **Pekan** Malay
56B2 **Pekanbaru** Indon
12B2 **Pekin** USA
Peking = Beijing
55C5 **Pelabohan Kelang** Malay
71E1 **Pelagie Is** Mediterranean S
57C3 **Pelau Pelau Boö** *Is* Indon
56E4 **Pelau Pelau Kangean** *Is* Indon
56D4 **Pelau Pelau Karimunjawa** *Arch* Indon
57C4 **Pelau Pelau Maisel** *Is* Indon
57C4 **Pelau Pelau Penyu** *Is* Indon
56E4 **Pelau Pelau Postilyon** *Is* Indon
57B3 **Pelau Pelau Salabangka** *Is* Indon
41E1 **Peleaga** *Mt* Rom
49N4 **Peleduy** Russian Fed
12C2 **Pelee I** Can
76B1 **Peleng** *I* Indon
10L4 **Pelican** USA
11D2 **Pelican L** USA
74A1 **Pelican Pt** S Africa
41D2 **Pelješac** *Pen* Croatia, Yugos
28C3 **Pellegrini** Arg
32J5 **Pello** Fin
10M3 **Pelly** *R* Can
7J3 **Pelly Bay** Can
10L3 **Pelly Crossing** Can
10M3 **Pelly Mts** Can
28E2 **Pelotas** Brazil
25F3 **Pelotas** *R* Brazil
65B3 **Pelusium** *Hist Site* Egypt
37B2 **Pelvoux** Region, France
44L3 **Pelym** *R* Russian Fed
56C4 **Pemalang** Indon
56B3 **Pematang** Indon
56A2 **Pematangsiantar** Indon
73E5 **Pemba** Mozam
72D4 **Pemba** *I* Tanz
3D3 **Pemberton** Can
11C2 **Pembina** USA
3E3 **Pembina** *R* Can
4F4 **Pembroke** Can
15C2 **Pembroke** USA
35C6 **Pembroke** Wales
28A3 **Pemuco** Chile
14E1 **Penacook** USA
56E2 **Penambo Range** *Mts* Malay
29B3 **Penápolis** Brazil
39A2 **Peñarroya** Spain
39B1 **Penarroya** *Mt* Spain
39A1 **Peña Trevina** *Mt* Spain
72B3 **Pende** *R* Chad
10N4 **Pendelton,Mt** Can
71G3 **Pendjari** *R* Benin
18C1 **Pendleton** USA
18C1 **Pend Oreille** *R* USA
27L6 **Penedo** Brazil
4F5 **Penetanguishene** Can
60D5 **Penganga** *R* India
52D5 **P'eng hu Lieh tao** *Is* Taiwan
52E2 **Penglai** China
52B4 **Pengshui** China
51G7 **Pengunungan Maoke** *Mts* Indon
5H4 **Peninsule de Gaspé** *Pen* Can
23C4 **Península de la Guajiri** *Pen* Colombia
23E4 **Península de Paria** *Pen* Ven
55C5 **Peninsular Malaysia** Malay
22B1 **Penjamo** Mexico
37E3 **Pennabilli** Italy
62B2 **Penner** *R* India
34D4 **Pennine Chain** *Mts* Eng
14C3 **Penns Grove** USA
9F2 **Pennsylvania** State, USA
14B1 **Penn Yan** USA
7M3 **Penny Highlands** *Mts* Can
13F1 **Penobscot** *R* USA
13F2 **Penobscot B** USA
75B3 **Penola** Aust
76C4 **Penong** Aust
23A5 **Penonomé** Panama
35D4 **Penrith** Eng
15B2 **Pensacola** USA
79E **Pensacola Mts** Ant
56E2 **Pensiangan** Malay
77F2 **Pentecost** *I* Vanuatu
3E4 **Penticton** Can
34D2 **Pentland Firth** *Chan* Scot
34D4 **Pentland Hills** Scot
44H5 **Penza** Russian Fed
35C6 **Penzance** Eng
49S3 **Penzhina** *R* Russian Fed
49S3 **Penzhinskaya Guba** *B* Russian Fed
12B2 **Peoria** USA
56B3 **Perabumulih** Indon
55C5 **Perak** *R* Malay
56B2 **Perawang** Indon
29A3 **Perdido** *R* Brazil
26C3 **Pereira** Colombia
29B3 **Pereira Barreto** Brazil
45G6 **Perelazovskiy** Russian Fed
10H4 **Perenosa B** USA
43G2 **Pereyaslav** Ukraine
53D2 **Pereyaslavka** Russian Fed
28C2 **Pergamino** Arg
37E3 **Pergola** Italy
7L4 **Péribonca** *R* Can
66D4 **Perim** *I* Yemen
38C2 **Périqueux** France
21E4 **Perlas Arch de** *Is* Panama
44K4 **Perm'** Russian Fed
Pernambuco = Recife
27L5 **Pernambuco State,** Brazil
75A2 **Pernatty Lg** Aust
41E2 **Pernik** Bulg
36B2 **Péronne** France
22C2 **Perote** Mexico
38C3 **Perpignan** France
20D4 **Perris** USA
15C2 **Perry** Florida, USA
15C2 **Perry** Georgia, USA
14A1 **Perry** New York, USA
17C2 **Perry** Oklahoma, USA
6H3 **Perry River** Can
12C2 **Perrysburg** USA
16B2 **Perryton** USA
10G4 **Perryville** Alaska, USA
17E2 **Perryville** Missouri, USA
4F5 **Perth** Can
13D2 **Perth** Can
34D3 **Perth** Scot
14C2 **Perth Amboy** USA
37A3 **Pertuis** France
26D6 **Peru** Republic, S America
12B2 **Peru** USA
xxixP5 **Peru Basin** Pacific O
xxxE6 **Peru-Chile Trench** Pacific O
40C2 **Perugia** Italy
28D1 **Perugorria** Arg
40D2 **Perušic** Croatia, Yugos
64D2 **Pervari** Turk
44G5 **Pervomaysk** Russian Fed
45E6 **Pervomaysk** Ukraine
44K4 **Pervoural'sk** Russian Fed
37E3 **Pesaro** Italy
20A2 **Pescadero** USA
Pescadores = P'eng-hu Lieh-tao
40C2 **Pescara** Italy
37D2 **Peschiera** Italy
37D3 **Pescia** Italy
60C2 **Peshawar** Pak
41E2 **Peshkopi** Alb
12B1 **Peshtigo** USA
44F4 **Pestovo** Russian Fed
65C2 **Petah Tiqwa** Israel
19B3 **Petaluma** USA
36C2 **Pétange** Lux
22B2 **Petatlán** Mexico
73D5 **Petauke** Zambia
4F4 **Petawawa** Can
12B2 **Petenwell L** USA
75A2 **Peterborough** Aust
4F5 **Peterborough** Can
35E5 **Peterborough** Eng
14E1 **Peterborough** USA
34E3 **Peterhead** Scot
7M1 **Petermann Gletscher** *Gl* Greenland
76B3 **Petermann Range** *Mts* Aust
25B5 **Peteroa** *Mt* Chile/Arg
3G2 **Peter Pond L** Can
10M4 **Petersburg** Alaska, USA
13D3 **Petersburg** Virginia, USA
4F2 **Petite Rivière de la Baleine** *R* Can
3E2 **Petitot** *R* Can
5H3 **Petitsikapau L** Can
60C4 **Petlād** India
22C2 **Petlalcingo** Mexico
21D2 **Peto** Mexico
28A2 **Petorca** Chile
12C1 **Petoskey** USA
65C3 **Petra** *Hist Site* Jordan
79G2 **Petral** *Base* Ant
49N2 **Petra, Ostrov** *I* Russian Fed
19E3 **Petrified Forest Nat Pk** USA
27K5 **Petrolina** Brazil
48H4 **Petropavlovsk** Kazakhstan
50J1 **Petropavlovsk-Kamchatskiy** Russian Fed
29D3 **Petrópolis** Brazil
45H5 **Petrovsk** Russian Fed
49M4 **Petrovsk Zabakal'skiy** Russian Fed
50D1 **Petrovsk Zabaykal'skiy** Russian Fed
44E3 **Petrozavodsk** Russian Fed
74D2 **Petrus** S Africa
74D2 **Petrusburg** S Africa
74C3 **Petrusville** S Africa
49T3 **Pevek** Russian Fed
44H2 **Peza** *R* Russian Fed
36D2 **Pfälzer Wald** Region, Germany
42B3 **Pforzheim** Germany
60D2 **Phagwara** India
74E1 **Phalaborwa** S Africa
60C3 **Phalodi** India
36D2 **Phalsbourg** France
62A1 **Phaltan** India
55B4 **Phangnga** Thai
55C3 **Phanom Dang** *Mts* Camb
55D3 **Phan Rang** Viet
55D3 **Phan Thiet** Viet
17F4 **Pharr** USA
3H2 **Phelps L** Can
15D1 **Phelps L** USA
15B2 **Phenix City** USA
55B3 **Phet Buri** Thai
55D3 **Phiafay** Laos
17E3 **Philadelphia** Mississippi, USA
14C2 **Philadelphia** Pennsylvania, USA
11B3 **Philip** USA
Philippeville = Skikda
36C1 **Philippeville** Belg
51F5 **Philippine S** Pacific O
51F5 **Philippines** Republic, S E Asia
xxviiiH4 **Philippine Trench** Pacific O
74D3 **Philippolis** S Africa
18D1 **Philipsburg** Montana, USA
13D2 **Philipsburg** Pennsylvania, USA
10J2 **Philip Smith Mts** USA
74C3 **Philipstown** S Africa
57F7 **Phillipine S** Phil
7K1 **Phillips B** Can
16C2 **Phillipsburg** Kansas, USA
14C2 **Phillipsburg** New Jersey, USA
7L2 **Philpots Pen** Can
55C3 **Phnom Penh** Camb
19D4 **Phoenix** Arizona, USA
14B1 **Phoenix** New York, USA
77H1 **Phoenix** *Is* Pacific O
14C2 **Phoenixville** USA
55C1 **Phong Saly** Laos
Phra Nakhon = Bangkok
55C2 **Phu Bia** *Mt* Laos
55D3 **Phu Cuong** Viet
55B4 **Phuket** Thai
61B3 **Phulbāni** India
55C2 **Phu Miang** *Mt* Thai
55D2 **Phu Set** *Mt* Laos
55D1 **Phu Tho** Viet
55D4 **Phu Vinh** Viet
32K6 **Phyäselkä** *L* Fin
37C2 **Piacenza** Italy
75D1 **Pialba** Aust
75C2 **Pian** *R* Aust
37D2 **Pianoro** Italy
40C2 **Pianosa** *I* Italy
40D2 **Pianosa** *I* Italy
43E2 **Piaseczno** Pol
29D1 **Piata** Brazil
41F1 **Piatra-Neamţ** Rom
27K5 **Piaui** State, Brazil
37E2 **Piave** Italy
37E1 **Piave** *R* Italy
72D3 **Pibor** *R* Sudan
72D3 **Pibor Post** Sudan
36B2 **Picardie** Region, France
17E3 **Picayune** USA
37B2 **Pic de Rochebrune** *Mt* France
28A2 **Pichilemu** Chile
28C3 **Pichi Mahuida** Arg
22D2 **Pichucalco** Mexico
35E4 **Pickering** Eng
7J4 **Pickle Lake** Can
70A1 **Pico** *I* Açores
37C1 **Pico Bernina** *Mt* Switz
23C5 **Pico Bolivar** *Mt* Ven
39C1 **Pico de Anito** *Mt* Spain
21B3 **Pico del Infiernillo** *Mt* Mexico
23C3 **Pico Duarte** *Mt* Dom Rep
27K5 **Picos** Brazil
39B1 **Picos de Europa** *Mt* Spain
75D2 **Picton** Aust
78B2 **Picton** NZ
72B1 **Pic Toussidé** *Mt* Chad

Picún Leufú Portland

28A3 **Picún Leufú** *R* Arg
29C3 **Piedade** Brazil
20C2 **Piedra** USA
28B4 **Piedra de Aguila** Arg
20B3 **Piedras Blancas,Pt** USA
21B2 **Piedras Negras** Mexico
12B1 **Pie I** Can
32K6 **Pieksämäki** Fin
32K6 **Pielinen** *L* Fin
37B2 **Piemonte** Region, Italy
74D2 **Pienaarsrivier** S Africa
11B3 **Pierre** USA
43D3 **Pieštany** Slovakia
74E2 **Pietermaritzburg** S Africa
74D1 **Pietersburg** S Africa
37D3 **Pietrasanta** Italy
74E2 **Piet Retief** S Africa
45C6 **Pietrosu** *Mt* Rom
41F1 **Pietrosul** *Mt* Rom
37E1 **Pieve di Cadore** Italy
51H6 **Pigailoe** *I* Pacific O
3F3 **Pigeon L** Can
17D2 **Piggott** USA
28C3 **Pigüé** Arg
22D2 **Pijijapan** Mexico
4C3 **Pikangikum** Can
7J4 **Pikangikum L** Can
16A2 **Pikes Peak** USA
74B3 **Piketberg** S Africa
12C3 **Pikeville** USA
7O3 **Pikiutaleq** Greenland
59F2 **Pik Kommunizma** *Mt* Tajikistan
72B3 **Pikounda** Congo
59G1 **Pik Pobedy** *Mt* China/Kirgizia
28D3 **Pila** Arg
42D2 **Pila** Pol
25E3 **Pilar** Par
25D2 **Pilcomayo** *R* Arg/Par
74E1 **Pilgrim's Rest** S Africa
60D3 **Pīlībhīt** India
43D2 **Pilica** *R* Pol
75E3 **Pillar,C** Aust
41E3 **Pílos** Greece
18C1 **Pilot Knob Mt** USA
20D1 **Pilot Peak** *Mt* USA
10G4 **Pilot Point** USA
10F3 **Pilot Station** USA
17E3 **Pilottown** USA
27G4 **Pimenta** Brazil
55C4 **Pinang** *I* Malay
23A2 **Pinar del Rio** Cuba
28B2 **Pinas** Arg
36C1 **Pinche** Belg
3F4 **Pincher Creek** Can
27J4 **Pindaré** *R* Brazil
41E3 **Píndhos** *Mts* Greece
17D3 **Pine Bluff** USA
16B1 **Pine Bluffs** USA
5L4 **Pine,C** Can
11D2 **Pine City** USA
76C2 **Pine Creek** Aust
14B2 **Pine Creek** *R* USA
20C1 **Pinecrest** USA
20C2 **Pinedale** California, USA
18E2 **Pinedale** Wyoming, USA
4B3 **Pine Falls** Can
20C2 **Pine Flat Res** USA
44G3 **Pinega** Russian Fed
44H3 **Pinega** *R* Russian Fed
14B2 **Pine Grove** USA
15C3 **Pine Hills** USA
3G2 **Pinehouse L** Can
15D1 **Pinehurst** USA
15E4 **Pine I** USA
17D3 **Pineland** USA
15C3 **Pinellas Park** USA
20B3 **Pine Mt** USA
3F1 **Pine Point** Can
11B3 **Pine Ridge** USA
4C4 **Pine River** USA
37B2 **Pinerolo** Italy
17D3 **Pines,Lo'the** USA
17D3 **Pineville** USA
52C3 **Pingdingshan** China
52B5 **Pingguo** China
52B2 **Pingliang** China
52B2 **Pingluo** China
52D4 **Pingtan Dao** *I* China
52E5 **P'ing tung** Taiwan
52A3 **Pingwu** China
52B5 **Pingxiang** Guangxi, China
52C4 **Pingxiang** Jiangxi, China
27J4 **Pinheiro** Brazil
28E2 **Pinheiro Machado** Brazil
56A2 **Pini** *I* Indon
41E3 **Piniós** *R* Greece
57B2 **Pinjang** Indon
76A4 **Pinjarra** Aust
3D2 **Pink Mountain** Can
75B3 **Pinnaroo** Aust
Pinos,I de = Isla de la Juventud
20C3 **Pinos,Mt** USA
19B3 **Pinos,Pt** USA
22C2 **Pinotepa Nacional** Mexico
57A3 **Pinrang** Indon
45D5 **Pinsk** Belorussia
28C1 **Pinto** Arg
44H3 **Pinyug** Russian Fed
19D3 **Pioche** USA
40C2 **Piombino** Italy
49K2 **Pioner, Ostrov** *I* Russian Fed
18D1 **Pioneer Mts** USA
44L3 **Pionerskiy** Russian Fed
43D2 **Piotrków Trybunalski** Pol
34F2 **Piper** *Oilfield* N Sea
20D2 **Piper Peak** *Mt* USA
11C3 **Pipestone** USA
4C3 **Pipestone** *R* Can
28D3 **Pipinas** Arg
5M4 **Pipmudcan, Réservoir** *Res* Can
12C2 **Piqua** USA
29B4 **Piquiri** *R* Brazil
29C2 **Piracanjuba** Brazil
29C3 **Piracicaba** Brazil
29C3 **Piraçununga** Brazil
29C3 **Pirai do Sul** Brazil
41E3 **Piraiévs** Greece
29C3 **Pirajui** Brazil
37E2 **Piran** Slovenia, Yugos
29B2 **Piranhas** Brazil
29D2 **Pirapora** Brazil
28D1 **Piratina** *R* Brazil
28E2 **Piratini** *R* Brazil
41E2 **Pirdop** Bulg
29C2 **Pirenópolis** Brazil
29C2 **Pires do Rio** Brazil
41E3 **Pírgos** Greece
Pirineos = Pyrénées
38B3 **Pirineos** *Mts* Spain
27K4 **Piripiri** Brazil
36D2 **Pirmasens** Germany
41E2 **Pirot** Serbia, Yugos
60C2 **Pīr Panjāl Range** *Mts* Pak
57C3 **Piru** Indon
20C3 **Piru Creek** *R* USA
37D3 **Pisa** Italy
26C6 **Pisco** Peru
14C1 **Piseco** USA
42C3 **Písek** Czech Republic
60B2 **Pishin** Pak
20B3 **Pismo Beach** USA
25C3 **Pissis** *Mt* Arg
37D3 **Pistoia** Italy
39B1 **Pisuerga** *R* Spain
18B2 **Pit** *R* USA
26C3 **Pitalito** Colombia
xxixN6 **Pitcairn** *I* Pacific O
32H5 **Pite** *R* Sweden
32J5 **Piteå** Sweden
41E2 **Piteşti** Rom
49L4 **Pit Gorodok** Russian Fed
36B2 **Pithiviers** France
44E3 **Pitkyaranta** Russian Fed
34D3 **Pitlochry** Scot
44M2 **Pitlyar** Russian Fed
28A3 **Pitrutquén** Chile
77H5 **Pitt** *I* NZ
3C3 **Pitt I** Can
20B1 **Pittsburg** California, USA
17D2 **Pittsburg** Kansas, USA
5G4 **Pittsburg** New Hampshire, USA
13D2 **Pittsburgh** USA
12A3 **Pittsfield** Illinois, USA
14D1 **Pittsfield** Massachusetts, USA
14C2 **Pittston** USA
75D1 **Pittsworth** Aust
20C3 **Piute Peak** *Mt* USA
61B2 **Piuthan** Nepal
53D1 **Pivan'** Russian Fed
20C3 **Pixley** USA
37D1 **Pizzo Redorta** *Mt* Italy
32B2 **Pjórsá** Iceland
26B5 **Pjura** Peru
5L4 **Placentia** Can
7N5 **Placentia B** Can
20B1 **Placerville** USA
36D2 **Plaine d'Alsace** *Plain* France
36B1 **Plaine des Flandres** *Plain* France/Belg
70C2 **Plaine du Tidikelt** *Desert* Region
36C2 **Plaine Lorraine** Region, France
16B2 **Plains** USA
11C3 **Plainview** Nebraska, USA
16B3 **Plainview** Texas, USA
20B2 **Planada** USA
27H7 **Planalto de Mato Grosso** *Plat* Brazil
27L5 **Planalto do Borborema** *Plat* Brazil
26B1 **Planalto do Mato Grosso** *Mts* Brazil
77E1 **Planet Deep** PNG
11C3 **Plankinton** USA
17C3 **Plano** USA
15E4 **Plantation** USA
15C3 **Plant City** USA
39A1 **Plasencia** Spain
44L5 **Plast** Russian Fed
53D3 **Plastun** Russian Fed
71H4 **Plateau** State, Nig
71G3 **Plateau de Dadango** Togo
36C3 **Plateau de Langres** *Plat* France
37A2 **Plateau De St Christol** Region, France
70C2 **Plateau du Tademait** Alg
36D2 **Plateau Lorrain** *Plat* France
38C2 **Plateaux de Limousin** *Plat* France
39C2 **Plateaux du Sersou** *Plat* Alg
23C5 **Plato** Colombia
45J7 **Plato Ustyurt** *Plat* Kazakhstan
65B1 **Platres** Cyprus
11C3 **Platte** USA
16B1 **Platte** *R* USA
12A2 **Platteville** USA
13E2 **Plattsburgh** USA
17C1 **Plattsmouth** USA
42C2 **Plauen** Germany
44F5 **Plavsk** Russian Fed
22B2 **Playa Azul** Mexico
26B4 **Playas** Ecuador
22C2 **Playa Vincente** Mexico
39A1 **Plaza de Moro Almanzor** *Mt* Spain
20B2 **Pleasanton** California, USA
17F4 **Pleasanton** Texas, USA
14C3 **Pleasantville** USA
12B3 **Pleasure Ridge Park** USA
55D3 **Pleiku** Viet
78C1 **Plenty,B of** NZ
11B2 **Plentywood** USA
44G3 **Plesetsk** Russian Fed
43D2 **Pleszew** Pol
7L4 **Pletipi,L** Can
41E2 **Pleven** Bulg
41D2 **Pljevlja** Montenegro, Yugos
41D2 **Ploče** Bosnia-Herzegovina, Yugos
43D2 **Płock** Pol
38B2 **Ploërmel** France
41F2 **Ploieşti** Rom
36D3 **Plombières-les-Bains** France
44C5 **Płońsk** Pol
41E2 **Plovdiv** Bulg
18C1 **Plummer** USA
10G3 **Plummer,Mt** USA
73C6 **Plumtree** Zim
20B1 **Plymouth** California, USA
35C6 **Plymouth** Eng
12B2 **Plymouth** Indiana, USA
14E2 **Plymouth** Massachusetts, USA
14C2 **Plymouth** Pennsylvania, USA
14E2 **Plymouth B** USA
35C6 **Plymouth Sd** Eng
35D5 **Plynlimon** *Mt* Wales
42C3 **Plzeň** Czech Republic
42D2 **Pniewy** Pol
71F3 **Pô** Burkina
37E2 **Po** *R* Italy
71G4 **Pobé** Benin
53E2 **Pobedino** Russian Fed
18D2 **Pocatello** USA
43G2 **Pochinok** Russian Fed
22C2 **Pochutla** Mexico
29D1 **Poções** Brazil
13D3 **Pocomoke City** USA
29A2 **Poconé** Brazil
29C3 **Pocos de Caldas** Brazil
41D2 **Podgorica** Montenegro, Yugos
37D2 **Po di Volano** *R* Italy
49L3 **Podkamennaya Tunguska** *R* Russian Fed
44F4 **Podol'sk** Russian Fed
43F3 **Podol'skaya Vozvyshennost'** *Upland* Ukraine
44E3 **Podporozh'ye** Russian Fed
44G3 **Podyuga** Russian Fed
74B2 **Pofadder** S Africa
37D3 **Poggibonsi** Italy
60A2 **Poghdar** Afghan
53C3 **Pogranichnyy** Russian Fed
57B3 **Poh** Indon
53B4 **P'ohang** S Korea
79G9 **Poinsett,C** Ant
75C2 **Point** Aust
23E3 **Pointe-à-Pitre** Guadeloupe
5H4 **Pointe aux Anglais** Can
38B2 **Pointe de Barfleur** *Pt* France
5J4 **Pointe de l'Est** *C* Can
4F3 **Pointe Louis XIV** *C* Can
72B4 **Pointe Noire** Congo
72A3 **Pointe Pongara** *Pt* Gabon
75B3 **Point Fairy** Aust
23L1 **Point Fortin** Trinidad
10E2 **Point Hope** USA
6G3 **Point L** Can
10F2 **Point Lay** USA
14C2 **Point Pleasant** New Jersey, USA
12C3 **Point Pleasant** W Virginia, USA
37B2 **Point St Bernard** *Mt* France
38C2 **Poitiers** France
38B2 **Poitou** Region, France
36A2 **Poix** France
60C3 **Pokaran** India
75C1 **Pokataroo** Aust
61B2 **Pokhara** Nepal
49O3 **Pokrovsk** Russian Fed
19D3 **Polacca** USA
43D2 **Poland** Republic, Europe
14C1 **Poland** USA
4E3 **Polar Bear Prov Park** Can
45E8 **Polath** Turk
64B2 **Polatli** Turk
57B3 **Poleang** Indon
57A3 **Polewali** Indon
71J4 **Poli** Cam
37A1 **Poligny** France
49P4 **Poliny Osipenko** Russian Fed
65B1 **Polis** Cyprus
41E2 **Políyiros** Greece
62B2 **Pollāchi** India
57F8 **Polollo Is** Phil
43F2 **Polonnye** Ukraine
43F1 **Polotsk** Belorussia
18D1 **Polson** USA
45E6 **Poltava** Ukraine
40D1 **Pölten** Austria
44K3 **Polunochoye** Russian Fed
16A3 **Polvadera** USA
44E2 **Polyarnyy** Murmansk, Russian Fed
49Q2 **Polyarnyy** Yakutskaya, Russian Fed
44L2 **Polyarnyy Ural** *Mts* Russian Fed
xxixL4 **Polynesia** *Region* Pacific O
26C5 **Pomabamba** Peru
29D3 **Pomba** *R* Brazil
20D3 **Pomona** USA
17C2 **Pomona Res** USA
15E4 **Pompano Beach** USA
14C2 **Pompton Lakes** USA
17C2 **Ponca City** USA
23D3 **Ponce** Puerto Rico
15E4 **Ponce de Leon B** USA
62B2 **Pondicherry** India
7L2 **Pond Inlet** Can
5K3 **Ponds,I of** Can
39A1 **Ponferrade** Spain
72C3 **Pongo** *R* Sudan
74E2 **Pongola** *R* S Africa
62B2 **Ponnāni** India
61D3 **Ponnyadoung Range** *Mts* Burma
3F3 **Ponoka** Can
48F3 **Ponoy** Russian Fed
44G2 **Ponoy** *R* Russian Fed
38B2 **Pons** France
29E2 **Ponta da Baleia** *Pt* Brazil
70A1 **Ponta Delgada** Açores
29E1 **Ponta do Mutá** *Pt* Brazil
72B4 **Ponta do Padrão** *Pt* Angola
29D3 **Ponta dos Búzios** *Pt* Brazil
29B4 **Ponta Grossa** Brazil
37A1 **Pontailler-sur-Saône** France
29C3 **Pontal** Brazil
36C2 **Pont-à-Mousson** France
29A3 **Ponta Pora** Brazil
38D2 **Pontarlier** France
37D3 **Pontassieve** Italy
4F3 **Pontax** *R* Can
17D3 **Pontchartrain,L** USA
37A1 **Pont d'Ain** France
29A1 **Ponte de Pedra** Brazil
40C2 **Pontedera** Italy
40B2 **Ponte Lecca** Corse
39A1 **Pontevedra** Spain
12B2 **Pontiac** Illinois, USA
12C2 **Pontiac** Michigan, USA
56C3 **Pontianak** Indon
38B2 **Pontivy** France
36B2 **Pontoise** France
17E3 **Pontotoc** USA
37C2 **Pontremoli** Italy
36B2 **Pont-sur-Yonne** France
35D6 **Pontypool** Wales
35D6 **Pontypridd** Wales
35E6 **Poole** Eng
Poona = Pune
75B2 **Pooncarie** Aust
75B2 **Poopelloe,L** Aust
10G3 **Poorman** USA
26C3 **Popayán** Colombia
36B1 **Poperinge** Belg
75B2 **Popilta L** Aust
11A2 **Poplar** USA
4B3 **Poplar** *R* Can
3G4 **Poplar** *R* USA
17D2 **Poplar Bluff** USA
17E3 **Poplarville** USA
76D1 **Popndetta** PNG
22C2 **Popocatepetl** *Mt* Mexico
10F4 **Popof** *I* USA
72B4 **Popokabaka** Zaïre
51H7 **Popondetta** PNG
41F2 **Popovo** Bulg
29C3 **Poraiba** *R* Brazil
29C1 **Porangatu** Brazil
60B4 **Porbandar** India
3B3 **Porcher I** Can
29C1 **Porcos** *R* Brazil
10K2 **Porcupine** *R* USA/Can
3H3 **Porcupine Hills** Can
37E2 **Pordenone** Italy
40C1 **Poreč** Croatia, Yugos
29B3 **Porecatu** Brazil
32J6 **Pori** Fin
78B2 **Porirua** NZ
32H5 **Porjus** Sweden
53E1 **Poronay** *R* Russian Fed
53E2 **Poronaysk** Russian Fed
44E3 **Porosozero** Russian Fed
37B1 **Porrentruy** Switz
37D3 **Porretta** Italy
32K4 **Porsangen** *Inlet* Nor
32F7 **Porsgrunn** Nor
35B4 **Portadown** N Ire
12B2 **Portage** USA
4B4 **Portage la Prairie** Can
11B2 **Portal** USA
3D4 **Port Alberni** Can
39A2 **Portalegre** Port
16B3 **Portales** USA
74D3 **Port Alfred** S Africa
3C3 **Port Alice** Can
14A2 **Port Allegany** USA
17D3 **Port Allen** USA
18B1 **Port Angeles** USA
23B3 **Port Antonio** Jamaica
35B5 **Portarlington** Irish Rep
17D4 **Port Arthur** USA
34B4 **Port Askaig** Scot
36A2 **Port-Audemer** France
75A2 **Port Augusta** Aust
23C3 **Port-au-Prince** Haiti
12C2 **Port Austin** USA
62E2 **Port Blair** Andaman Is
75B3 **Port Campbell** Aust
61C3 **Port Canning** India
7M5 **Port Cartier** Can
78B3 **Port Chalmers** NZ
15E4 **Port Charlotte** USA
14D2 **Port Chester** USA
3B3 **Port Clements** Can
12C2 **Port Clinton** USA
13D2 **Port Colborne** Can
75E3 **Port Davey** Aust
23C3 **Port-de-Paix** Haiti
55C5 **Port Dickson** Malay
74E3 **Port Edward** S Africa
29D2 **Porteirinha** Brazil
12C2 **Port Elgin** Can
74D3 **Port Elizabeth** S Africa
34B4 **Port Ellen** Scot
23N2 **Porter Pt** St Vincent
20C2 **Porterville** USA
76D4 **Port Fairy** Aust
72A4 **Port Gentil** Gabon
17D3 **Port Gibson** USA
10H4 **Port Graham** USA
18B1 **Port Hammond** Can
68E7 **Port Harcourt** Nigeria
3C3 **Port Hardy** Can
7M5 **Port Hawkesbury** Can
76A3 **Port Hedland** Aust
Port Heiden = Meshik
35C5 **Porthmadog** Wales
7N4 **Port Hope Simpson** Can
20C3 **Port Hueneme** USA
12C2 **Port Huron** USA
39A2 **Portimão** Port
75D2 **Port Jackson** *B* Aust
14D2 **Port Jefferson** USA
14C2 **Port Jervis** USA
75D2 **Port Kembla** Aust
12C2 **Portland** Indiana, USA
13E2 **Portland** Maine, USA
75C2 **Portland** New South Wales, Aust
18B1 **Portland** Oregon, USA
75B3 **Portland** Victoria, Aust

Portland Bight **Puri**

23H2 **Portland Bight** *B* Jamaica
35D6 **Portland Bill** *Pt* Eng
75E3 **Portland,C** Aust
3B2 **Portland Canal** *Sd* USA/Can
78C1 **Portland I** NZ
23H2 **Portland Pt** Jamaica
33B3 **Port Laoise** Irish Rep
17F4 **Port Lavaca** USA
36A2 **Port-l'Evêque** France
75A2 **Port Lincoln** Aust
70A4 **Port Loko** Sierra Leone
73F6 **Port Louis** Mauritius
75B3 **Port MacDonnell** Aust
3C3 **Port McNeill** Can
75D2 **Port Macquarie** Aust
5H5 **Port Maitland** Can
14A2 **Port Matilda** USA
5J4 **Port Menier** Can
10F4 **Port Moller** USA
76D1 **Port Moresby** PNG
4C2 **Port Nelson** Can
74B2 **Port Nolloth** S Africa
14C3 **Port Norris** USA
39A1 **Porto** Port
25F4 **Pôrto Alegre** Brazil
Porto Alexandre = Tombula Angola
23A5 **Porto Armuelles** Panama
29A1 **Pôrto Artur** Brazil
29B3 **Pôrto de Novembro** Brazil
29B1 **Pôrto dos Meinacos** Brazil
25F2 **Pôrto E Cunha** Brazil
29A2 **Pôrto Esperança** Brazil
40C2 **Portoferraio** Italy
23E4 **Port of Spain** Trinidad
37E2 **Portogruaro** Italy
29A2 **Porto Jofre** Brazil
28D1 **Porto Lucena** Brazil
37D2 **Portomaggiore** Italy
29B3 **Porto Mendez** Brazil
29A3 **Porto Murtinho** Brazil
71G4 **Porto Novo** Benin
25F2 **Pôrto Primavera, Represa** *Res* Brazil
18B1 **Port Orchard** USA
37E3 **Porto Recanati** Italy
18B2 **Port Orford** USA
70A1 **Porto Santo** *I* Medeira
29B3 **Porto São José** Brazil
27L7 **Pôrto Seguro** Brazil
40B2 **Porto Torres** Sardegna
29B4 **Porto União** Brazil
40B2 **Porto Vecchio** Corse
26F5 **Pôrto Velho** Brazil
78A3 **Port Pegasus** *B* NZ
75B3 **Port Phillip B** Aust
75A2 **Port Pirie** Aust
10P2 **Port Radium** Can
34B3 **Portree** Scot
18B1 **Port Renfrew** Can
23J2 **Port Royal** Jamaica
15C2 **Port Royal Sd** USA
34B4 **Portrush** N Ire
65B3 **Port Said** Egypt
15B3 **Port St Joe** USA
74D3 **Port St Johns** S Africa
7N4 **Port Saunders** Can
74E3 **Port Shepstone** S Africa
3B3 **Port Simpson** Can
23Q2 **Portsmouth** Dominica
35E6 **Portsmouth** Eng
14E1 **Portsmouth** New Hampshire, USA
12C3 **Portsmouth** Ohio, USA
13D3 **Portsmouth** Virginia, USA
75D2 **Port Stephens** *B* Aust
72D2 **Port Sudan** Sudan
17E3 **Port Sulphur** USA
32K5 **Porttipahdan Tekojärvi** *Res* Fin
39A2 **Portugal** Republic, Europe
14A1 **Portville** USA
12B2 **Port Washington** USA
55C5 **Port Weld** Malay
26E6 **Porvenir** Bol
25E3 **Posadas** Arg
39A2 **Posadas** Spain
37D1 **Poschiavo** Switz
63D2 **Posht-e Badam** Iran
57B3 **Poso** Indon
54A4 **Posŏng** S Korea
44M2 **Pos Polvy** Russian Fed
29C1 **Posse** Brazil
16B3 **Post** USA
43F1 **Postavy** Belorussia
74C2 **Postmasburg** S Africa
40C1 **Postojna** Slovenia, Yugos
53C3 **Pos'yet** Russian Fed
57B4 **Pota** Indon
74D2 **Potchetstroom** S Africa
17D2 **Poteau** USA
40D2 **Potenza** Italy
74D1 **Potgietersrus** S Africa
16C4 **Poth** USA
45G7 **Poti** Georgia
71J3 **Potiskum** Nig
18C1 **Potlatch** USA
74C3 **Potloer** *Mt* S Africa
18C1 **Pot Mt** USA
13D3 **Potomac** *R* USA
14A3 **Potomac South Branch** *R* USA
26E7 **Potosi** Bol
25C3 **Potrerillos** Chile
42C2 **Potsdam** Germany
5G5 **Potsdam** USA
16B1 **Potter** USA
14C2 **Pottstown** USA
14B2 **Pottsville** USA
14D2 **Poughkeepsie** USA
29C3 **Pouso Alegre** Brazil
78C1 **Poverty B** NZ
44E3 **Povonets** Russian Fed
45G5 **Povorino** Russian Fed
7L4 **Povungnituk** Can
11A2 **Powder** *R* USA
11A3 **Powder River** USA
18E2 **Powell** USA
76C2 **Powell Creek** Aust
19D3 **Powell,L** USA
3D4 **Powell River** Can
35D5 **Powys** County, Wales
29B2 **Poxoréo** Brazil
52D4 **Poyang Hu** *L* China
53B2 **Poyarkovo** Russian Fed
64C2 **Pozantı** Turk
22C1 **Poza Rica** Mexico
42D2 **Poznań** Pol
25E2 **Pozo Colorado** Par
40C2 **Pozzuoli** Italy
71F4 **Pra** *R* Ghana
55C3 **Prachin Buri** Thai
55B3 **Prachuap Khiri Khan** Thai
42D2 **Praděd** *Mt* Czech Republic
38C3 **Pradelles** France
29E2 **Prado** Brazil
Prague = Praha
42C2 **Praha** Czech Republic
70A4 **Praia** Cape Verde
29A1 **Praia Rica** Brazil
26F5 **Prainha** Brazil
16B3 **Prairie Dog Town Fork** *R* USA
12A2 **Prairie du Chien** USA
17D2 **Prairie Village** USA
55C3 **Prakhon Chai** Thai
29C2 **Prata** Brazil
29C2 **Prata** *R* Brazil
Prates = Dongsha Qundao
37D3 **Prato** Italy
37D3 **Pratomagno** *Mt* Italy
14C1 **Prattsville** USA
15B2 **Prattville** USA
38B1 **Prawle Pt** Eng
56E4 **Praya** Indon
37D1 **Predazzo** Italy
49L4 **Predivinsk** Russian Fed
49Q3 **Predporozhnyy** Russian Fed
43E2 **Pregolyu** *R* Russian Fed
55D3 **Prek Kak** Camb
12A1 **Prentice** USA
42C2 **Prenzlau** Germany
62E2 **Preparis I** Burma
55A2 **Preparis North Chan** Burma
55A3 **Preparis South Chan** Burma
42D3 **Přerov** Czech Republic
22C1 **Presa de les Adjuntas** Mexico
22B2 **Presa del Infiernillo** Mexico
28D2 **Presa de Salto Grande** Urug
22D2 **Presa Netzahualcóyotl** Mexico
19D4 **Prescott** Arizona, USA
17D3 **Prescott** Arkansas, USA
13D2 **Prescott** Can
11B3 **Presho** USA
25D3 **Presidencia Roque Sáenz Peña** Arg
29B3 **Presidente Epitácio** Brazil
79G2 **Presidente Frei** *Base* Ant
22C2 **Presidente Migúel Aleman** *L* Mexico
29B2 **Presidente Murtinho** Brazil
29B3 **Presidente Prudente** Brazil
29B3 **Presidente Venceslau** Brazil
16B4 **Presidio** USA
22A1 **Presidio** *R* Mexico
43E3 **Prešov** Slovakia
41E2 **Prespansko Jezero** *L* Macedonia, Yugos
13F1 **Presque Isle** USA
71F4 **Prestea** Ghana
35D5 **Preston** Eng
8B2 **Preston** Idaho, USA
11D3 **Preston** Minnesota, USA
17D2 **Preston** Missouri, USA
34C4 **Prestwick** Scot
27J8 **Prêto** Brazil
29C2 **Prêto** *R* Brazil
74D2 **Pretoria** S Africa
41E3 **Préveza** Greece
55D3 **Prey Veng** Camb
10E4 **Pribilof Is** USA
19D3 **Price** USA
3C3 **Price I** Can
15B2 **Prichard** USA
45E6 **Prichernomorskaya Nizmennost'** *Lowland* Ukraine
23M2 **Prickly Pt** Grenada
43F3 **Pridneprovskaya Vozvyshennost'** *Upland* Ukraine
43E1 **Priekule** Lithuania
74C2 **Prieska** S Africa
18C1 **Priest L** USA
18C1 **Priest River** USA
Prikaspiyskaya Nizmennost' = Caspian Depression
41E2 **Prilep** Macedonia, Yugos
45E5 **Priluki** Ukraine
28C2 **Primero** *R* Arg
32K6 **Primorsk** Russian Fed
45F6 **Primorsko-Akhtarsk** Russian Fed
3G3 **Primrose L** Can
3G3 **Prince Albert** Can
74C3 **Prince Albert** S Africa
6F2 **Prince Albert,C** Can
3G3 **Prince Albert Nat Pk** Can
6G2 **Prince Albert Pen** Can
6G2 **Prince Albert Sd** Can
7L3 **Prince Charles I** Can
79G10 **Prince Charles Mts** Ant
xxviiiC7 **Prince Edward** *I* Indian O
7M5 **Prince Edward I** Province, Can
3D3 **Prince George** Can
6H2 **Prince Gustaf Adolp Sea** Can
10E2 **Prince of Wales,C** USA
51H8 **Prince of Wales I** Aust
6H2 **Prince of Wales I** Can
3B2 **Prince of Wales I** USA
6G2 **Prince of Wales Str** Can
6G2 **Prince Patrick I** Can
7J2 **Prince Regent Inlet** *Str* Can
3B3 **Prince Rupert** Can
76D2 **Princess Charlotte B** Aust
3C3 **Princess Royal I** Can
23L1 **Princes Town** Trinidad
3D4 **Princeton** Can
12B2 **Princeton** Illinois, USA
12B3 **Princeton** Kentucky, USA
17D1 **Princeton** Missouri, USA
14C2 **Princeton** New Jersey, USA
12C3 **Princeton** W Virginia, USA
10J3 **Prince William Sd** USA
70C4 **Principe** *I* W Africa
18B2 **Prineville** USA
10J2 **Pringle,Mt** USA
7O3 **Prins Christian Sund** *Sd* Greenland
79F12 **Prinsesse Astrid Kyst** Region, Ant
79F12 **Prinsesse Ragnhild Kyst** Region, Ant
48C2 **Prins Karls Forland** *I* Barents S
21D3 **Prinzapolca** Nic
44E3 **Priozersk** Russian Fed
43F2 **Pripet** *R* Belorussia
Pripyat' = Pripet
41E2 **Priština** Serbia, Yugos
42C2 **Pritzwalk** Germany
44G5 **Privolzhskaya Vozvyshennost'** *Upland* Russian Fed
41E2 **Prizren** Serbia, Yugos
56D4 **Probolinggo** Indon
11D2 **Proctor** USA
62B2 **Proddatūr** India
21D2 **Progreso** Mexico
53B2 **Progress** Russian Fed
18B2 **Project City** USA
45G7 **Prokhladnyy** Russian Fed
48K4 **Prokop'yevsk** Russian Fed
45G6 **Proletarskaya** Russian Fed
49P2 **Proliv Dmitriya Lapteva** *Str* Russian Fed
48G2 **Proliv Karskiye Vorota** *Str* Russian Fed
49T2 **Proliv Longa** *Str* Russian Fed
49L2 **Proliv Vilkitskogo** *Str* Russian Fed
Prome = Pyè
29A2 **Promissão** Brazil
43G2 **Pronya** *R* Belorussia
3D2 **Prophet** *R* Can
27L6 **Propriá** Brazil
14C1 **Prospect** New York, USA
18B2 **Prospect** Oregon, USA
76D3 **Prosperine** Aust
42D3 **Prostějov** Czech Republic
7N2 **Prøven** Greenland
38D3 **Provence** Region, France
14E2 **Providence** USA
49U3 **Provideniya** Russian Fed
14E1 **Provincetown** USA
36B2 **Provins** France
19D2 **Provo** USA
3F3 **Provost** Can
29B4 **Prudentópolis** Brazil
10J1 **Prudhoe B** USA
10J1 **Prudhoe Bay** USA
7M2 **Prudhoe Land** *Region* Greenland
43E2 **Pruszkow** Pol
43F3 **Prut** *R* Rom/Moldova
45D6 **Prutul** *R* Rom
43E2 **Pruzhany** Belorussia
17C2 **Pryor** USA
43E3 **Przemyśl** Pol
41F3 **Psará** *I* Greece
44D4 **Pskov** Russian Fed
43F2 **Ptich** *R* Belorussia
41E2 **Ptolemaïs** Greece
54A3 **Puan** S Korea
26D5 **Pucallpa** Peru
52D4 **Pucheng** China
28A3 **Pucón** Chile
32K5 **Pudasjärvi** Fin
44F3 **Pudozh** Russian Fed
62B2 **Pudukkottai** India
39A1 **Puebai de Trives** Spain
22C2 **Puebla** Mexico
22C2 **Puebla** State, Mexico
39A1 **Puebla de Sanabria** Spain
16B2 **Pueblo** USA
28B3 **Puelches** Arg
28B3 **Puelén** Arg
22B2 **Puenta Ixbapa** Mexico
28B2 **Puente del Inca** Arg
26B5 **Puerta Aguja** Peru
26D7 **Puerta Coles** Peru
28B2 **Puerta de los Llanos** Arg
22A1 **Puerta de Mita** Mexico
27L5 **Puerta do Calcanhar** *Pt* Brazil
74E2 **Puerta do Oro** *Pt* S Africa
22C2 **Puerta Galera** Mexico
26D1 **Puerta Gallinas** Colombia
22C2 **Puerta Maldonado** *Pt* Mexico
26B2 **Puerta Mariato** Panama
25C7 **Puerta Médanosa** *Pt* Arg
22B2 **Puerta Mongrove** Mexico
22C2 **Puerta Roca Partida** Mexico
21E4 **Puerta San Blas** *Pt* Panama
22B2 **Puerta San Telmo** Mexico
29B3 **Puerto Adela** Brazil
25B7 **Puerto Aisén** Chile
22C2 **Puerto Angel** Mexico
21D4 **Puerto Armuelles** Panama
27G6 **Puerto Artur** Brazil
26C3 **Puerto Asis** Colombia
26E2 **Puerto Ayacucho** Ven
21D3 **Puerto Barrios** Guatemala
26D2 **Puerto Berrio** Colombia
26E1 **Puerto Cabello** Ven
21D3 **Puerto Cabezas** Nic
26E2 **Puerto Carreño** Ven
29A3 **Puerto Casado** Brazil
26B1 **Puerto Cavezas** Nic
29A3 **Puerto Cooper** Brazil
21D4 **Puerto Cortes** Costa Rica
21D3 **Puerto Cortés** Honduras
70A2 **Puerto del Rosario** Canary Is
27H8 **Puerto E Cunha** Brazil
22C2 **Puerto Escondido** Mexico
26D1 **Puerto Fijo** Ven
27J5 **Puerto Franco** Brazil
29A3 **Puerto Guarani** Brazil
26E6 **Puerto Heath** Bol
21D2 **Puerto Juarez** Mexico
26F1 **Puerto la Cruz** Ven
39B2 **Puertollano** Spain
23C4 **Puerto Lopez** Colombia
25D6 **Puerto Madryn** Arg
26E6 **Puerto Maldonado** Peru
22C2 **Puerto Marquéz** Mexico
25B6 **Puerto Montt** Chile
24C7 **Puerto Moritt** Chile
27G8 **Puerto Murtinho** Brazil
25B8 **Puerto Natales** Chile
21A1 **Puerto Peñasco** Mexico
29A3 **Puerto Pinasco** Brazil
25D6 **Puerto Pirámides** Arg
23C3 **Puerto Plata** Dom Rep
57E9 **Puerto Princesa** Phil
26C3 **Puerto Rico** Colombia
23D3 **Puerto Rico** *I* Caribbean
23D3 **Puerto Rico Trench** Caribbean
22B2 **Puerto San Juan de Lima** Mexico
27H4 **Puerto Santanga** Brazil
29A3 **Puerto Sastre** Brazil
25E1 **Puerto Suárez** Bol
22A1 **Puerto Vallarta** Mexico
25B6 **Puerto Varas** Chile
26F7 **Puerto Villarroel** Bol
45H5 **Pugachev** Russian Fed
60C3 **Pugal** India
39C1 **Puigcerdá** Spain
54A2 **Pujŏn** N Korea
54A2 **Pujŏn Res** N Korea
78B2 **Pukaki,L** NZ
4D4 **Pukaskwa Nat Park** Can
4A2 **Pukatawagan** Can
54A2 **Pukchin** N Korea
53B3 **Pukch'ŏng** N Korea
78B1 **Pukekobe** NZ
78B2 **Puketeraki Range** *Mts* NZ
44G3 **Puksoozero** Russian Fed
40C2 **Pula** Croatia, Yugos
13D2 **Pulaski** New York, USA
15B1 **Pulaski** Tennessee, USA
12C3 **Pulaski** Virginia, USA
51G7 **Pulau Kolepom** *I* Indon
57D2 **Pulau Pulau Asia** *Is* Indon
57D2 **Pulau Pulau Ayu** *Is* Indon
56A2 **Pulau Pulau Banyak** *Arch* Indon
56A3 **Pulau Pulau Batu** *Is* Indon
76A1 **Pulau Pulau Kangean** *Is* Indon
76B1 **Pulau Pulau Macan** *Is* Indon
57D3 **Pulau Pulau Pisang** *Is* Indon
56A3 **Pulautelo** Indon
43E2 **Pulawy** Pol
62C2 **Pulicat,L** India
60B1 **Pul-i-Khumri** Afghan
62B3 **Puliyangudi** India
36E3 **Pullendorf** Germany
18C1 **Pullman** USA
51G6 **Pulo Anna Merir** *I* Pacific I
57F7 **Pulog,Mt** Phil
32L5 **Pulozero** Russian Fed
43E2 **Pultusk** Pol
25C3 **Puna de Atacama** Arg
61C2 **Punakha** Bhutan
60C2 **Punch** Pak
74E1 **Punda Milia** S Africa
62A1 **Pune** India
22B2 **Punéper** Mexico
54A2 **Pungsan** N Korea
54A2 **Pungso** N Korea
72C4 **Punia** Zaïre
28A2 **Punitaqui** Chile
60C2 **Punjab** Province, Pak
60D2 **Punjab** State, India
26D7 **Puno** Peru
21A2 **Punta Abreojos** *Pt* Mexico
40D3 **Punta Alice** *Pt* Italy
28C3 **Punta Alta** Arg
25B8 **Punta Arenas** Chile
21A2 **Punta Baja** *Pt* Mexico
28C4 **Punta Bermeja** *Pt* Arg
28A2 **Punta Curaumilla** *Pt* Chile
73B5 **Punta da Marca** *Pt* Angola
73D6 **Punta de Barra Falsa** *Pt* Mozam
28E2 **Punta del Este** Urug
37C2 **Punta di Portofino** *Pt* Italy
21A2 **Punta Eugenia** *Pt* Mexico
28A3 **Punta Galera** Chile
21D3 **Punta Gorda** Belize
15E4 **Punta Gorda** USA
28A3 **Punta Lavapié** *Pt* Chile
28A2 **Punta Lengua de Vaca** *Pt* Chile
40C2 **Punta Licosa** *Pt* Italy
28D3 **Punta Norte** *Pt* Arg
28D3 **Punta Piedras** *Pt* Arg
28A1 **Punta Poroto** *Pt* Chile
28C4 **Punta Rasa** *Pt* Arg
26B1 **Puntarenas** Costa Rica
28C4 **Punta Rubia** *Pt* Arg
8B4 **Punta San Antonio** *Pt* Mexico
28D3 **Punta Sur** Arg
28A2 **Punta Topocalma** Chile
57B4 **Puntjak Ranakah** *Mt* Indon
14A2 **Punxsutawney** USA
57D3 **Puper** Indon
52C4 **Puqi** China
46J3 **Pur** *R* Russian Fed
17C2 **Purcell** USA
10G2 **Purcell Mt** USA
3E3 **Purcell Mts** Can
28A3 **Purén** Chile
16B2 **Purgatoire** *R* USA
61C3 **Puri** India

Pūrna Rawlins

62B1 **Pūrna** India
61C2 **Pūrnia** India
55C3 **Pursat** Camb
22B1 **Puruandro** Mexico
26F4 **Purus** *R* Brazil
17E3 **Purvis** USA
56C4 **Purwokerto** Indon
48J3 **Pur** *R* Russian Fed
56D4 **Purworejo** Indon
60D5 **Pusad** India
53B4 **Pusan** S Korea
44E4 **Pushkin** Russian Fed
44F3 **Pushlakhta** Russian Fed
43F1 **Pustoshka** Russian Fed
28A2 **Putaendo** Chile
61E2 **Putao** Burma
78C1 **Putaruru** NZ
52D4 **Putian** China
14E2 **Putnam** USA
14D1 **Putney** USA
62B3 **Puttalam** Sri Lanka
42C2 **Puttgarden** Germany
26C4 **Putumayo** *R* Ecuador
56D2 **Putussibau** Indon
32K6 **Puulavesl** *L* Fin
18B1 **Puyallup** USA
38C2 **Puy de Sancy** *Mt* France
28A4 **Puyehue** Chile
78A3 **Puysegur Pt** NZ
73C4 **Pweto** Zaïre
35C5 **Pwllheli** Wales
44F3 **Pyal'ma** Russian Fed
44E2 **Pyaozero, Ozero** *L* Russian Fed
55B2 **Pyapon** Burma
49K2 **Pyasina** *R* Russian Fed
45G7 **Pyatigorsk** Russian Fed
61E4 **Pyè** Burma
61E4 **Pyinmana** Burma
54A2 **Pyŏktong** N Korea
54A3 **Pyonggang** N Korea
54A3 **Pyŏnggok-dong** S Korea
54A3 **P'Yŏngsann** N Korea
54A3 **P'yongt'aek** S Korea
53B4 **P'yŏngyang** N Korea
75B3 **Pyramid Hill** Aust
5J2 **Pyramid Hills** Can
19C2 **Pyramid L** USA
78A2 **Pyramid,Mt** NZ
38B3 **Pyrénées** *Mts* France
43F1 **Pytalovo** Russian Fed
55B2 **Pyu** Burma

Q

65C2 **Qabatiya** Israel
67E3 **Qabr Hūd** Yemen
65D3 **Qā'el Hafīra** *Mud Flats* Jordan
65D3 **Qa'el Jinz** *Mud Flats* Jordan
7O3 **Qagssimiut** Greenland
50C3 **Qaidam Pendi** *Salt Flat* China
63E1 **Qaisar** Afghan
65D2 **Qa Khanna** *Salt Marsh* Jordan
63E2 **Qala Adras Kand** Afghan
72D2 **Qala'en Nahl** Sudan
63E2 **Qala Nau** Afghan
60B2 **Qalat** Afghan
65D1 **Qal'at al Hisn** Syria
65C1 **Qal'at al Marqab** *Hist Site* Syria
66D2 **Qal'at Bīshah** S Arabia
64E3 **Qal'at Sālih** Iraq
50C3 **Qamdo** China
69E3 **Qandala** Somalia
69B2 **Qara** Egypt
45H8 **Qareh Dāgh** *Mts* Iran
63B2 **Qaṛe Shīrīn** Iran
67E1 **Qaryat al Ulyā** S Arabia
65D3 **Qasr el Kharana** Jordan
63E3 **Qasr-e-Qand** Iran
69B2 **Qasr Farafra** Egypt
65D2 **Qaṭana** Syria
67F1 **Qatar** Emirate, Arabian Pen
65D3 **Qatrāna** Jordan
69B2 **Qattāra Depression** Egypt
63D2 **Qāyen** Iran
63C1 **Qazvīn** Iran
66B1 **Qena** Egypt
63B1 **Qeydār** Iran
63C3 **Qeys** *I* Iran
45H8 **Qezel Owzan** *R* Iran
65C3 **Qeziot** Israel
53A3 **Qian'an** China
53A2 **Qian Gorlos** China
52B5 **Qian Jiang** *R* China
52E1 **Qian Shan** *Upland* China
52E3 **Qidong** China
52B4 **Qijiang** China
63E3 **Qila Ladgasht** Pak
60B2 **Qila Saifullah** Pak
52A2 **Qilian** China
50C3 **Qilian Shan** China
52B3 **Qin'an** China
52E2 **Qingdao** China
53B2 **Qinggang** China
52A2 **Qinghai** Province, China
50C3 **Qinghai Hu** *L* China
52D3 **Qingjiang** Jiangsu, China
52D4 **Qingjiang** Jiangxi, China
52B3 **Qing Jiang** *R* China
52C2 **Qingshuihe** China
52B2 **Qingshui He** *R* China
52B2 **Qingtonxia** China
52B2 **Qingyang** China
53B3 **Qingyuan** Liaoning, China
52D4 **Qingyuan** Zhejiang, China
59G2 **Qing Zang** *Upland* China
52B5 **Qingzhou** China
52D2 **Qinhuangdao** China
52B3 **Qin Ling** *Mts* China
55E2 **Qionghai** China
52A3 **Qionglai Shan** *Upland* China
55D1 **Qiongzhou Haixia** *Str* China
53A2 **Qiqihar** China
65C2 **Qiryat Ata** Israel
65C3 **Qiryat Gat** Israel
65C2 **Qiryat Shemona** Israel
65C2 **Qiryat Yam** Israel
67F3 **Qishn** Yemen
65C2 **Qishon** *R* Israel
66C2 **Qishran** *I* S Arabia
49K5 **Qitai** China
53C2 **Qitaihe** China
53C2 **Qixing He** *R* China
52C4 **Qiyang** China
52B1 **Qog Qi** China
45J8 **Qolleh-ye-Damavand** *Mt* Iran
63C1 **Qolleh-ye Damavand** *Mt* Iran
63C2 **Qom** Iran
63C2 **Qomisheh** Iran
Qomolangma Feng = Everest,Mt
65D1 **Qornet es Saouda** *Mt* Leb
7N3 **Qôrnoq** Greenland
63B1 **Qorveh** Iran
63D3 **Qotābad** Iran
45H8 **Qotúr** *R* Iran
14D1 **Quabbin Res** USA
74C2 **Quaggablat** S Africa
14C2 **Quakertown** USA
55C3 **Quam Phu Quoc** *I* Viet
16C3 **Quanah** USA
55D2 **Quang Ngai** Viet
55D2 **Quang Tri** Viet
55D4 **Quan Long** Viet
52D5 **Quanzhou** Fujian, China
52C4 **Quanzhou** Guangxi, China
11B1 **Qu'Appelle** Can
6H4 **Qu' Appelle** *R* Can
28D2 **Quarai** *R* Urug
28D2 **Quaral** Brazil
67G2 **Quarayyāt** Oman
69D4 **Quardho** Somalia
71F3 **Quarkoye** Burkina
19D4 **Quartzsite** USA
3C3 **Quatsino Sd** Can
63D1 **Quchan** Iran
75C3 **Queanbeyan** Aust
5G4 **Québec** Can
7L4 **Quebec** Province, Can
29C2 **Quebra-Anzol** *R* Brazil
28D2 **Quebracho** Urug
25F3 **Quedas do Iguaçu** Brazil/Arg
14C3 **Queen Anne** USA
3C3 **Queen Bess,Mt** Can
3B3 **Queen Charlotte** Can
3B3 **Queen Charlotte Is** Can
3B3 **Queen Charlotte Sd** Can
3C3 **Queen Charlotte Str** Can
6H1 **Queen Elizabeth Is** Can
79G9 **Queen Mary Land** Region, Ant
6H3 **Queen Maud G** Can
79E **Queen Maud Mts** Ant
14D2 **Queens** *Borough* New York, USA
51F8 **Queens Ch** Aust
75B3 **Queenscliff** Aust
76D3 **Queensland** State, Aust
75E3 **Queenstown** Aust
78A3 **Queenstown** NZ
74D3 **Queenstown** S Africa
14B3 **Queenstown** USA
73B4 **Quela** Angola
73D5 **Quelimane** Mozam
16A3 **Quemado** USA
71G4 **Quémé** *R* Benin
28C3 **Quemuquemú** Arg
4C4 **Quentico Prov Park** Can
28D3 **Quequén** Arg
28D3 **Quequén** *R* Arg
22B1 **Querétaro** Mexico
22B1 **Queretaro** *State* Mexico
3D3 **Quesnel** Can
3D3 **Quesnel** *L* Can
60B2 **Quetta** Pak
21C3 **Quezaltenango** Guatemala
57F8 **Quezon City** Phil
73B5 **Quibala** Angola
73B4 **Quibaxe** Angola
26C2 **Quibdó** Colombia
38B2 **Quiberon** France
73B4 **Quicama Nat Pk** Angola
29A4 **Quiindy** Par
52A4 **Quijing** China
28A2 **Quilima** Chile
28C2 **Quilino** Arg
26D6 **Quillabamba** Peru
26E7 **Quillacollo** Bol
38C3 **Quillan** France
3H3 **Quill Lakes** Can
28A2 **Quillota** Chile
62B3 **Quilon** India
75B1 **Quilpie** Aust
28A2 **Quilpué** Chile
73B4 **Quimbele** Angola
28C1 **Quimili** Arg
38B2 **Quimper** France
38B2 **Quimperlé** France
19B3 **Quincy** California, USA
12A3 **Quincy** Illinois, USA
14E1 **Quincy** Massachusetts, USA
28B2 **Quines** Arg
10F4 **Quinhagak** USA
55D3 **Qui Nhon** Viet
39B2 **Quintanar de la Orden** Spain
28A2 **Quintero** Chile
28C2 **Quinto** *R* Arg
28A3 **Quirihue** Chile
73B5 **Quirima** Angola
75D2 **Quirindi** Aust
73E5 **Quissanga** Mozam
73D6 **Quissico** Mozam
26C4 **Quito** Ecuador
27L4 **Quixadá** Brazil
74D3 **Qumbu** S Africa
75A2 **Quorn** Aust
6G3 **Qurlurtuuq** Can
66B1 **Qus** Egypt
67F4 **Quṣayir** Oman
66B1 **Quseir** Egypt
7N3 **Qutdligssat** Greenland
Quthing = Moyeni
52B3 **Qu Xian** Sichuan, China
52D4 **Qu Xian** Zhejiang, China
55D2 **Quynh Luu** Viet
52C2 **Quzhou** China
61D2 **Qūzū** China

R

32J6 **Raahe** Fin
34B3 **Raasay** *I* Scot
34B3 **Raasay,Sound of** *Chan* Scot
67F4 **Raas Caseyr** *C* Somalia
40C2 **Rab** *I* Croatia, Yugos
56E4 **Raba** Indon
42D3 **Rába** *R* Hung
66B4 **Rabak** Sudan
71A2 **Rabat** Mor
76E1 **Rabaul** PNG
65C3 **Rabba** Jordan
3H2 **Rabbit Lake** Can
66C2 **Rabigh** S Arabia
37B2 **Racconigi** Italy
7N5 **Race,C** Can
14E1 **Race Pt** USA
65C2 **Rachaya** Leb
42C3 **Rachel** *Mt* Germany
55D3 **Rach Gia** Viet
12B2 **Racine** USA
66D4 **Radā'** Yemen
43F3 **Rădăuţi** Rom
12B3 **Radcliff** USA
12C3 **Radford** USA
60C4 **Radhanpur** India
23L1 **Radix,Pt** Trinidad
43E2 **Radom** Pol
43D2 **Radomsko** Pol
43F2 **Radomyshl'** Ukraine
37E1 **Radstadt** Austria
43E1 **Radviliškis** Lithuania
3H4 **Radville** Can
6G3 **Rae** Can
61B2 **Rāe Bareli** India
7K3 **Rae Isthmus** Can
6G3 **Rae L** Can
78C1 **Raetihi** NZ
28C2 **Rafaela** Arg
65C3 **Rafah** Egypt
72C3 **Rafai** CAR
64D3 **Rafhā Al Jumaymah** S Arabia
63D2 **Rafsanjān** Iran
72C3 **Raga** Sudan
23Q2 **Ragged Pt** Barbados
40C3 **Ragusa** Italy
57B3 **Raha** Indon
66C4 **Rahad** *R* Sudan
66D4 **Raheita** Eth
60C3 **Rahimyar Khan** Pak
63C2 **Rāhjerd** Iran
28D2 **Raíces** Arg
62B1 **Rāichur** India
61B3 **Raigarh** India
75B3 **Rainbow** Aust
15B2 **Rainbow City** USA
3E2 **Rainbow Lake** Can
18B1 **Rainier** USA
18B1 **Rainier,Mt** USA
11D2 **Rainy** *R* USA
4C4 **Rainy L** Can
10H3 **Rainy P** USA
11D2 **Rainy River** Can
61B3 **Raipur** India
62C1 **Rājahmundry** India
56D2 **Rajang** *R* Malay
60C3 **Rajanpur** Pak
62B3 **Rājapālaiyam** India
60C3 **Rājasthan** State, India
60D3 **Rājgarh** India
60D4 **Rājgarh** State, India
60C4 **Rājkot** India
61C3 **Rājmahāl Hills** India
61B3 **Raj Nāndgaon** India
60C4 **Rājpīpla** India
61C3 **Rajshahi** Bang
60D4 **Rajur** India
78B2 **Rakaia** *R* NZ
56C4 **Rakata** *I* Indon
59G3 **Raka Zangbo** *R* China
43E3 **Rakhov** Ukraine
63E3 **Rakhshan** *R* Pak
67F3 **Rakhyūt** Oman
74C1 **Rakops** Botswana
43F2 **Rakov** Belorussia
15D1 **Raleigh** USA
65C4 **Ram** Jordan
65C2 **Rama** Israel
65C3 **Ramallah** Israel
62B3 **Rāmanāthapuram** India
50H3 **Ramapo Deep** Pacific O
4E4 **Ramore** Can
65C2 **Ramat Gan** Israel
36D2 **Rambervillers** France
36A2 **Rambouillet** France
61C3 **Rāmgarh** Bihar, India
60C3 **Rāmgarh** Rajosthan, India
63B2 **Rāmhormoz** Iran
65C3 **Ramla** Israel
67G2 **Ramlat Al Wahibah** Region, Oman
67E3 **Ramlat as Sab'atayn** Region, Yemen
19C4 **Ramona** USA
60D3 **Rāmpur** India
60D4 **Rāmpura** India
61D4 **Ramree** *I* Burma
45J8 **Rāmsar** Iran
35C4 **Ramsey** Eng
14C2 **Ramsey** USA
35C6 **Ramsey I** Wales
35F6 **Ramsgate** Eng
65D2 **Ramtha** Jordan
76D1 **Ramu** *R* PNG
56E1 **Ranau** Malay
28A2 **Rancagua** Chile
3B1 **Rancheria** *R* Can
11A3 **Ranchester** USA
61C3 **Rānchi** India
61B3 **Rānchi Plat** India
74D2 **Randburg** S Africa
32F7 **Randers** Den
74D2 **Randfontein** S Africa
14A1 **Randolph** New York, USA
13E2 **Randolph** Vermont, USA
20D3 **Randsburg** USA
78B3 **Ranfurly** NZ
61D3 **Rangamati** Bang
16A1 **Rangely** USA
78B2 **Rangiora** NZ
78C1 **Rangitaiki** *R* NZ
78B2 **Rangitate** *R* NZ
78C1 **Rangitikei** *R* NZ
Rangoon = Yangon
61C2 **Rangpur** India
62B2 **Rānībennur** India
61C3 **Rānīganj** India
7J3 **Rankin Inlet** Can
75C2 **Rankins Springs** Aust
60B4 **Rann of Kachchh** *Flood Area* India
55B4 **Ranong** Thai
56A2 **Rantauparapat** Indon
57A3 **Rantepao** Indon
12B2 **Rantoul** USA
29B1 **Ranuro** *R* Brazil
53C2 **Raohe** China
36D2 **Raon-l'Etape** France
77H3 **Raoul** *I* NZ
37C2 **Rapallo** Italy
28A2 **Rapel** *R* Chile
7M3 **Raper,C** Can
11B3 **Rapid City** USA
12B1 **Rapid River** USA
13D3 **Rappahannock** *R* USA
57A3 **Rappang** Indon
37C1 **Rapperswil** Switz
14C2 **Raritan B** USA
66C2 **Ras Abū Dâra** *C* Egypt
66C2 **Ra's Abu Madd** *C* S Arabia
66C2 **Ras Abu Shagara** *C* Sudan
64D2 **Ra's al 'Ayn** Syria
67G2 **Ra's al Hadd** *C* Oman
67G1 **Ras al Kaimah** UAE
67E4 **Ra's al Kalb** *C* Yemen
67G1 **Ras-al-Kuh** *C* Iran
67G3 **Ra's al Madrakah** *C* Oman
66D3 **Ras Andadda** *C* Eritrea
67G3 **Ra's ash Sharbatāt** *C* Oman
66C3 **Ra's Asis** *C* Sudan
66D3 **Ra's at Tarfā** *C* S Arabia
67E1 **Ra's az Zawr** *C* S Arabia
66C2 **Râs Bânas** *C* Egypt
65B3 **Ras Burûn** *C* Egypt
66C4 **Ras Dashan** *Mt* Eth
67G3 **Ra's Duqm** Oman
63B2 **Ra's-e-Barkan** *Pt* Iran
63E3 **Ra's-e-Fasteh** *C* Iran
65A3 **Râs el Barr** *C* Egypt
64A3 **Râs el Kenâyis** *Pt* Egypt
65C4 **Ras el Nafas** *Mt* Egypt
65B4 **Râs El Sudr** *C* Egypt
65C4 **Ras en Naqb** *Upland* Jordan
67F3 **Ra's Fartak** *C* Yemen
66B1 **Râs Ghârib** Egypt
72D2 **Rashad** Sudan
66C2 **Ras Hadarba** *C* Egypt
65C3 **Rashādīya** Jordan
64B3 **Rashîd** Egypt
63B1 **Rasht** Iran
65C1 **Ra's ibn Hāni** *C* Syria
63E3 **Ra's Jaddi** *C* Pak
67G2 **Ra's Jibish** *C* Oman
63E3 **Rāsk** Iran
66C3 **Ra's Kasar** *C* Sudan
72E2 **Ras Khanzira** *C* Somalia
60B3 **Ras Koh** *Mt* Pak
65B4 **Râs Maʿarma** *C* Egypt
67F4 **Ra's Momi** *C* Socotra
66B1 **Râs Muhammad** *C* Egypt
70A2 **Ras Nouadhibou** *C* Maur
63E3 **Ra's Nuh** *C* Pak
63E3 **Ra's Ormara** *C* Pak
67F3 **Ra's Sharwayn** *C* Yemen
50J2 **Rasshua** *I* Russian Fed
67F4 **Ra's Shu'ab** *C* Socotra
71E1 **Rass Kaboudia** *Pt* Tunisia
45G5 **Rasskazovo** Russian Fed
67E1 **Ra's Tanāqib** *C* S Arabia
67F1 **Ra's Tannūrah** S Arabia
42B3 **Rastatt** Germany
66D3 **Ra's 'Tsa** *C* Yemen
Ras Uarc = Cabo Tres Foreas
65C4 **Ras Um Seisaban** *Mt* Jordan
69E3 **Ras Xaafuun** *C* Somalia
60C3 **Ratangarh** India
55B3 **Rat Buri** Thai
60D3 **Rath** India
42C2 **Ratherow** Germany
34B4 **Rathlin** *I* N Ire
10B6 **Rat I** USA
10B6 **Rat Is** USA
60C4 **Ratlām** India
62A1 **Ratnāgiri** India
62C3 **Ratnapura** Sri Lanka
43E2 **Ratno** Ukraine
16B2 **Raton** USA
37D1 **Rattenberg** Austria
32H6 **Rättvik** Sweden
3B2 **Ratz,Mt** Can
57C2 **Rau** *I* Indon
56F7 **Raub** Malay
28D3 **Rauch** Arg
78C1 **Raukumara Range** *Mts* NZ
29D3 **Raul Soares** Brazil
32J6 **Rauma** Fin
61B3 **Raurkela** India
63B2 **Ravānsar** Iran
63D2 **Rāvar** Iran
43E2 **Rava Russkaya** Ukraine
14D1 **Ravena** USA
37E2 **Ravenna** Italy
42B3 **Ravensburg** Germany
76D2 **Ravenshoe** Aust
35F4 **Ravenspurn** *Oilfield* N Sea
60C2 **Ravi** *R* Pak
60C2 **Rawalpindi** Pak
45G3 **Rawāndiz** Iraq
42D2 **Rawicz** Pol
76B4 **Rawlinna** Aust
8C2 **Rawlins** USA

Romang St James,C

57C4 **Romang** *I* Indon
45C6 **Romania** Republic, E Europe
15E4 **Romano,C** USA
38D2 **Romans sur Isère** France
10E3 **Romanzof,C** USA
10K2 **Romanzof Mts** USA
57F8 **Romblon** Phil
Rome = Roma
15B2 **Rome** Georgia, USA
14C1 **Rome** New York, USA
13D2 **Rome** USA
38C2 **Romilly-sur-Seine** France
71A2 **Rommani** Mor
13D3 **Romney** USA
45E5 **Romny** Ukraine
42B1 **Rømø** *I* Den
37B1 **Romont** Switz
38C2 **Romoratin** France
56G7 **Rompin** Malay
56G7 **Rompin** *R* Malay
37D2 **Ronco** Italy
39A2 **Ronda** Spain
26F6 **Rondônia** Brazil
26F6 **Rondônia** State, Brazil
29B2 **Rondonópolis** Brazil
52B4 **Rong'an** China
52B4 **Rongchang** China
52E2 **Rongcheng** China
52B4 **Rongjiang** China
52B4 **Rong Jiang** *R* China
55A1 **Rongklang Range** *Mts* Burma
32G7 **Rønne** Denmark
32H7 **Ronneby** Sweden
79F2 **Ronne Ice Shelf** Ant
36B1 **Ronse** Belg
36A1 **Ronthieu** Region, France
8C3 **Roof Butte** *Mt* USA
60D3 **Roorkee** India
36C1 **Roosendaal** Neth
19D2 **Roosevelt** USA
79E **Roosevelt I** Ant
3C2 **Roosevelt,Mt** Can
10O3 **Root** *R* Can
11D3 **Root** *R* USA
76C2 **Roper** *R* Aust
37A3 **Roquevaire** France
26F3 **Roraima** State, Brazil
26F2 **Roraime** *Mt* Ven
4B3 **Rorketon** Can
32G6 **Røros** Nor
37C1 **Rorschach** Switz
32G6 **Rørvik** Nor
43G3 **Ros'** *R* Ukraine
23Q2 **Rosalie** Dominica
20C3 **Rosamond** USA
20C3 **Rosamond L** USA
22A1 **Rosamorada** Mexico
28C2 **Rosario** Arg
27K4 **Rosário** Brazil
22A1 **Rosario** Mexico
29A3 **Rosario** Par
28D2 **Rosario** Urug
28D2 **Rosario del Tala** Arg
28E2 **Rosário do Sul** Brazil
29A1 **Rosário Oeste** Brazil
14C2 **Roscoe** USA
38B2 **Roscoff** France
33B3 **Roscommon** Irish Rep
35B5 **Roscrea** Irish Rep
23E3 **Roseau** Dominica
4B4 **Roseau** *R* Can/USA
75E3 **Rosebery** Aust
5K4 **Rose Blanche** Can
11A2 **Rosebud** USA
18B2 **Roseburg** USA
17C4 **Rosenberg** USA
42C3 **Rosenheim** Germany
3G3 **Rosetown** Can
20B1 **Roseville** USA
41E2 **Rosiorii de Verde** Rom
32G7 **Roskilde** Den
44E5 **Roslavl'** Russian Fed
44G4 **Roslyatino** Russian Fed
78B2 **Ross** NZ
10M3 **Ross** *R* Can
33B3 **Rossan** *Pt* Irish Rep
40D3 **Rossano** Italy
17E3 **Ross Barnet Res** USA
13D1 **Rosseau L** Can
77E2 **Rossel** *I* Solomon Is
79E **Ross Ice Shelf** Ant
18B1 **Ross L** USA
3E4 **Rossland** Can
35B5 **Rosslare** Irish Rep
78C2 **Ross,Mt** NZ
70A3 **Rosso** Maur
35D6 **Ross-on-Wye** Eng
45F5 **Rossosh** Russian Fed
6E3 **Ross River** Can
79F6 **Ross S** Ant
63C3 **Rostāq** Iran
3G3 **Rosthern** Can
42C2 **Rostock** Germany
44F4 **Rostov** Russian Fed
45F6 **Rostov-na-Donu** Russian Fed
15C2 **Roswell** Georgia, USA
16B3 **Roswell** New Mexico, USA
51H5 **Rota** Pacific O
36E1 **Rotenburg** Hessen, Germany
42B2 **Rotenburg** Niedersachsen, Germany
36E1 **Rothaar-Geb** *Region* Germany
79G3 **Rothera** *Base* Ant
35E5 **Rotherham** Eng
5H4 **Rothesay** Can
34C4 **Rothesay** Scot
57B5 **Roti** *I* Indon
75C2 **Roto** Aust
78B2 **Rotoiti,L** NZ
78B2 **Rotoroa,L** NZ
78C1 **Rotorua** NZ
78C1 **Rotorua,L** NZ
36E2 **Rottenburg** Germany
42A2 **Rotterdam** Neth
36E2 **Rottweil** Germany
77G2 **Rotuma** *I* Fiji
36B1 **Roubaix** France
38C2 **Rouen** France
35F5 **Rough** *Oilfield* N Sea
Roulers = Roeselare
73F6 **Round I** Mauritius
20D1 **Round Mountain** USA
75D2 **Round Mt** Aust
18E1 **Roundup** USA
34D2 **Rousay** *I* Scot
38C3 **Roussillon** Region, France
74D3 **Rouxville** S Africa
4F4 **Rouyn** Can
32K5 **Rovaniemi** Fin
37D2 **Rovereto** Italy
37D2 **Rovigo** Italy
40C1 **Rovinj** Croatia, Yugos
43F2 **Rovno** Ukraine
63B1 **Row'ān** Iran
75C1 **Rowena** Aust
7L3 **Rowley I** Can
76A2 **Rowley Shoals** Aust
57E8 **Roxas** Palawan, Phil
57F8 **Roxas** Panay, Phil
15D1 **Roxboro** USA
78A3 **Roxburgh** NZ
18E1 **Roy** USA
35B5 **Royal Canal** Irish Rep
35E5 **Royal Leamington Spa** Eng
12C2 **Royal Oak** USA
35F6 **Royal Tunbridge Wells** Eng
38B2 **Royan** France
36B2 **Roye** France
35E5 **Royston** Eng
43E3 **Rožňava** Slovakia
36B2 **Rozoy** France
45G5 **Rtishchevo** Russian Fed
37E2 **Rt Kamenjak** *C* Croatia, Yugos
73D4 **Ruaha Nat Pk** Tanz
78C1 **Ruahine Range** *Mts* NZ
78C1 **Ruapehu,Mt** NZ
67D3 **Rub al Khālī** *Desert* S Arabia
34B3 **Rubha Hunish** Scot
25F2 **Rubinéia** Brazil
29B3 **Rubinéia** Brazil
48K4 **Rubtsovsk** Russian Fed
10G3 **Ruby** USA
19C2 **Ruby Mts** USA
63D3 **Rudan** Iran
63E2 **Rudbar** Afghan
63B1 **Rūdbār** Iran
53D3 **Rudnaya Pristan'** Russian Fed
43G2 **Rudnya** Russian Fed
53C3 **Rudnyy** Russian Fed
41E2 **Rudoka Planina** *Mt* Macedonia, Yugos
48G1 **Rudol'fa, Ostrov** *I* Russian Fed
52E3 **Rudong** China
12C1 **Rudyard** USA
36A1 **Rue** France
66B4 **Rufa'a** Sudan
38C2 **Ruffec** France
73D4 **Rufiji** *R* Tanz
28C2 **Rufino** Arg
70A3 **Rufisque** Sen
73C5 **Rufunsa** Zambia
35E5 **Rugby** Eng
11B2 **Rugby** USA
32G8 **Rügen** *I* Germany
42B2 **Ruhr** *R* Germany
52D4 **Ruijin** China
41E2 **Rujen** *Mt* Macedonia, Bulg/Yugos
73D4 **Rukwa** *L* Tanz
34B3 **Rum** *I* Scot
41D1 **Ruma** Serbia, Yugos
67E1 **Rumāh** S Arabia
72C3 **Rumbek** Sudan
23C2 **Rum Cay** *I* Caribbean
13E2 **Rumford** USA
37A2 **Rumilly** France
76C2 **Rum Jungle** Aust
54D2 **Rumoi** Japan
73D5 **Rumphi** Malawi
78B2 **Runanga** NZ
78C1 **Runaway,C** NZ
73B5 **Rundu** Namibia
73D4 **Rungwa** Tanz
73D4 **Rungwa** *R* Tanz
73D4 **Rungwe** *Mt* Tanz
59G2 **Ruoqiang** China
50D2 **Ruo Shui** *R* China
56F7 **Rupat** *I* Indon
41F1 **Rupea** Rom
18D2 **Rupert** USA
7L4 **Rupert** *R* Can
36D1 **Rur** *R* Germany
26E6 **Rurrenabaque** Bol
73D5 **Rusape** Zim
41F2 **Ruse** Bulg
12A2 **Rushville** Illinois, USA
11B3 **Rushville** Nebraska, USA
75B3 **Rushworth** Aust
17C3 **Rusk** USA
15E4 **Ruskin** USA
3H2 **Russel L** Can
3H3 **Russell** Can
78B1 **Russell** NZ
16C2 **Russell** USA
4A2 **Russell L** Can
15B2 **Russellville** Alabama, USA
17D2 **Russellville** Arkansas, USA
12B3 **Russellville** Kentucky, USA
19B3 **Russian** *R* USA
44E4 **Russian Federation**
49L2 **Russkiy, Ostrov** *I* Russian Fed
64E1 **Rustavi** Georgia
74D2 **Rustenburg** S Africa
17D3 **Ruston** USA
72C4 **Rutana** Burundi
57B4 **Ruteng** Indon
74E1 **Rutenga** Zim
19C3 **Ruth** USA
36E1 **Rüthen** Germany
22C2 **Rutla** Mexico
13E2 **Rutland** USA
62E2 **Rutland** *I* Andaman Is
60D2 **Rutog** China
Ruvu = Pangani
73E5 **Ruvuma, R** Tanz/Mozam
72D3 **Ruwenzori Range** *Mts* Uganda/Zaïre
73D5 **Ruya** *R* Zim
43D3 **Ružomberok** Slovakia
72C4 **Rwanda** Republic, Africa
44F5 **Ryazan'** Russian Fed
44G5 **Ryazhsk** Russian Fed
32L5 **Rybachiy, Poluostrov** *Pen* Russian Fed
44F4 **Rybinsk** Russian Fed
44F4 **Rybinskoye Vodokhranilishche** *Res* Russian Fed
43F3 **Rybnitsa** Moldova
3E2 **Rycroft** Can
35E6 **Ryde** Eng
35F6 **Rye** Eng
18C2 **Rye Patch Res** USA
45E5 **Ryl'sk** Russian Fed
45H6 **Ryn Peski** *Desert* Kazakhstan
54A3 **Ryoju** S Korea
53D4 **Ryōtsu** Japan
43F3 **Ryskany** Moldova
50F4 **Ryūkyū Retto** *Arch* Japan
43E2 **Rzeszów** Pol
44E4 **Rzhev** Russian Fed

S

63C2 **Sa'ādatābād** Iran
66B2 **Saad el Aali** *Dam* Egypt
42C2 **Saale** *R* Germany
37B1 **Saanen** Switz
36D2 **Saar** *R* Germany
36D2 **Saarbrücken** Germany
36D2 **Saarburg** Germany
32J7 **Saaremaa** *I* Estonia
36D2 **Saarland** State, Germany
36D2 **Saarlouis** Germany
28C3 **Saavedra** Arg
65B3 **Saba'a** Egypt
41D2 **Šabac** Serbia, Yugos
39C1 **Sabadell** Spain
54C3 **Sabae** Japan
56E1 **Sabah** State, Malay
10A6 **Sabak,C** USA
57B3 **Sabal** Indon
23C4 **Sabanalarga** Colombia
56A1 **Sabang** Indon
57A2 **Sabang** Indon
62C1 **Sabari** *R* India
65C2 **Sabastiya** Israel
26E7 **Sabaya** Bol
64C3 **Sab'Bi'ār** Syria
66C3 **Sabderat** Eth
65D2 **Sabhā** Jordan
69A2 **Sabhā** Libya
73D6 **Sabi** *R* Zim
74E2 **Sabie** *R* S Africa
21B2 **Sabinas** Mexico
21B2 **Sabinas Hidalgo** Mexico
17C3 **Sabine** *R* USA
17D4 **Sabine L** USA
67F2 **Sabkhat Maţţi** *Salt Marsh* UAE
65B3 **Sabkhet El Bardawīl** *Lg* Egypt
57F8 **Sablayan** Phil
7M5 **Sable,C** Can
15E4 **Sable,C** USA
7N5 **Sable I** Can
63D1 **Sabzevār** Iran
18C1 **Sacajawea Peak** USA
14C1 **Sacandaga Res** USA
11D3 **Sac City** USA
9D1 **Sachigo** *R* Can
4C3 **Sachigo L** Can
54A3 **Sach'on** S Korea
42C2 **Sachsen** State, Germany
42C2 **Sachsen-Anhalt** State, Germany
6F2 **Sachs Harbour** Can
37E2 **Sacile** Italy
37B1 **Säckingen** Germany
5J4 **Sackville** Can
13E2 **Saco** Maine, USA
11A2 **Saco** Montana, USA
20B1 **Sacramento** USA
20B1 **Sacramento** *R* USA
19B2 **Sacramento** *V* USA
16A3 **Sacramento Mts** USA
66D3 **Sa'dah** Yemen
41E2 **Sadanski** Bulg
67G3 **Sadh** Oman
61E2 **Sadiya** India
39A2 **Sado** *R* Port
53D4 **Sado-shima** *I* Japan
60C3 **Sādri** India
Safad = Zefat
60A2 **Safed Koh** *Mts* Afghan
63E2 **Safer** Afghan
32G7 **Saffle** Sweden
19E4 **Safford** USA
64C3 **Safi** Jordan
71A2 **Safi** Mor
63E2 **Safidabeh** Iran
65D1 **Şāfītā** Syria
43G1 **Safonovo** Russian Fed
44H2 **Safonovo** Russian Fed
64E3 **Safwān** Iraq
61C2 **Saga** China
54B4 **Saga** Japan
55B1 **Sagaing** Burma
54C4 **Sagami-nada** *B* Japan
60D4 **Sāgar** India
10J2 **Sagavanirktok** *R* USA
14D2 **Sag Harbor** USA
12C2 **Saginaw** USA
12C2 **Saginaw B** USA
7M4 **Saglek B** Can
54A3 **Sagŏ-ri** S Korea
16A2 **Saguache** USA
23B2 **Sagua de Tánamo** Cuba
23B2 **Sagua la Grande** Cuba
7L5 **Saguenay** *R* Can
39B2 **Sagunto** Spain
65D3 **Sahāb** Jordan
39A1 **Sahagún** Spain
70C2 **Sahara** *Desert* N Africa
60D3 **Saharanpur** India
60C2 **Sahiwal** Pak
64D3 **Şahrā al Hijārah** *Desert Region* Iraq
66B1 **Sahra esh Sharqiya** *Desert Region* Egypt
22B1 **Sahuayo** Mexico
65D1 **Sahyun** *Hist Site* Syria
76D1 **Saibai I** Aust
71C2 **Saïda** Alg
65C2 **Saïda** Leb
63D3 **Sa'īdabad** Iran
39B2 **Saidia** Mor
61C2 **Saidpur** India
60C2 **Saidu** Pak
54B3 **Saigō** Japan
Saigon = Ho Chi Minh
61D3 **Saiha** India
50E2 **Saihan Tal** China
54B4 **Saijo** Japan
53C5 **Saiki** Japan
44D3 **Saimaa** *L* Fin
22B1 **Sain Alto** Mexico
63E3 **Saindak** Pak
34D4 **St Abb's Head** *Pt* Scot
5G4 **St Agapit** Can
5G4 **Ste Agathe-des-Monts** Can
5K4 **St Albans** Can
35E6 **St Albans** Eng
13E2 **St Albans** Vermont, USA
12C3 **St Albans** West Virginia, USA
35D6 **St Albans Head** *C* Eng
3F3 **St Albert** Can
36B1 **St Amand-les-Eaux** France
38C2 **St Amand-Mont Rond** France
37A1 **St-Amour** France
73E5 **St André** *C* Madag
36A2 **St-André-de-l'Eure** France
15B3 **St Andrew B** USA
34D3 **St Andrews** Scot
15C2 **St Andrew Sd** USA
11C2 **Ste Anne** Can
5G4 **Ste Anne de Beaupré** Can
5H4 **Ste-Anne-des-Monts** Can
23H1 **St Ann's Bay** Jamaica
7N4 **St Anthony** Can
18D2 **St Anthony** USA
75B3 **St Arnaud** Aust
5K3 **St Augustin** *R* Can
15C3 **St Augustine** USA
5K3 **St Augustin-Saguenay** Can
35C6 **St Austell** Eng
36D2 **St-Avold** France
35D4 **St Bees Head** *Pt* Eng
4B4 **St Boniface** Can
37B2 **St-Bonnet** France
35C6 **St Brides B** Wales
38B2 **St-Brieuc** France
36A3 **St-Calais** France
4F5 **St Catharines** Can
23M2 **St Catherine,Mt** Grenada
15C2 **St Catherines I** USA
35E6 **St Catherines Pt** Eng
38C2 **St Chamond** France
18D2 **St Charles** Idaho, USA
17D2 **St Charles** Missouri, USA
12C2 **St Clair** USA
12C2 **St Clair,L** USA/Can
12C2 **St Clair Shores** USA
38D2 **St Claud** France
11D2 **St Cloud** USA
37B1 **Ste Croix** Switz
23E3 **St Croix** *I* Caribbean
12A1 **St Croix** *R* USA
13F1 **St Croix** *R* USA/Can
12A1 **St Croix Falls** USA
35C6 **St Davids Head** *Pt* Wales
36B2 **St Denis** France
73F6 **St Denis** Réunion
36D2 **St-Dié** France
36C2 **St Dizier** France
10K3 **St Elias,Mt** USA
10L3 **St Elias Mts** Can
38B2 **Saintes** France
38C2 **St Étienne** France
37B2 **St Étienne-de-Tinée** France
13E1 **St-Félicien** Can
5K4 **St Fintan's** Can
36B2 **St-Florentin** France
16B2 **St Francis** USA
17D2 **St Francis** *R* USA
74C3 **St Francis B** S Africa
74C3 **St Francis,C** S Africa
37C1 **St Gallen** Switz
38C3 **St-Gaudens** France
75C1 **St George** Aust
15C2 **St George** South Carolina, USA
19D3 **St George** Utah, USA
10E4 **St George** *I* Alaska, USA
15C3 **St George I** Florida, USA
36E2 **St Georgen im Schwarzwald** Germany
18B2 **St George,Pt** USA
5H4 **St George** Can
13E1 **St-Georges** Can
23E4 **St George's** Grenada
5K4 **St George's B** Can
35B5 **St Georges Chan** Irish Rep/ Wales
77E1 **St Georges Chan** PNG
37A1 **St Germain-du-Bois** France
36A2 **St German-en-laye** France
37B2 **St-Gervais** France
37C1 **St Gotthard** *P* Switz
35C6 **St Govans Head** *Pt* Wales
20A1 **St Helena** USA
xxxH5 **St Helena** *I* Atlantic O
74B3 **St Helena B** S Africa
15C2 **St Helena Sd** USA
75E3 **St Helens** Aust
35D5 **St Helens** Eng
18B1 **St Helens** USA
18B1 **St Helens,Mt** USA
38B2 **St Helier** Jersey
37B1 **St Hippolyte** France
36C1 **St-Hubert** Belg
7L5 **St-Hyacinthe** Can
12C1 **St Ignace** USA
12B1 **St Ignace I** Can
35C6 **St Ives** Eng
11D3 **St James** Minnesota, USA
17D2 **St James** Missouri, USA
3B3 **St James,C** Can

San Jose Sawara

20B2 **San Jose** USA
8B4 **San José** *I* Mexico
26F7 **San José de Chiquitos** Bol
28D2 **San José de Feliciano** Arg
28B2 **San José de Jachal** Arg
28C2 **San José de la Dormida** Arg
28A3 **San José de la Mariquina** Chile
8C4 **San José del Cabo** Mexico
28D2 **San José de Mayo** Urug
22B1 **San José de Raices** Mexico
25G2 **San José do Rio Prêto** Brazil
21B2 **San Joseé del Cabo** Mexico
54A3 **Sanju** S Korea
28B2 **San Juan** Arg
23D3 **San Juan** Puerto Rico
28B2 **San Juan** State, Arg
23L1 **San Juan** Trinidad
20B3 **San Juan** USA
26E2 **San Juan** Ven
23B2 **San Juan** *Mt* Cuba
28B2 **San Juan** *R* Arg
20B3 **San Juan** *R* California, USA
22C2 **San Juan** *R* Mexico
21D3 **San Juan** *R* Nicaragua/Costa Rica
19D3 **San Juan** *R* Utah, USA
22C2 **San Juan Bautista** Mexico
25E3 **San Juan Bautista** Par
20B2 **San Juan Bautista** USA
21D3 **San Juan del Norte** Nic
23D4 **San Juan de los Cayos** Ven
22B1 **San Juan de loz Lagoz** Mexico
22B1 **San Juan del Rio** Mexico
21D3 **San Juan del Sur** Nicaragua
22C2 **San Juan Evangelista** Mexico
18B1 **San Juan Is** USA
16A2 **San Juan Mts** USA
22C2 **San Juan Tepozcolula** Mexico
25C7 **San Julián** Arg
28C2 **San Justo** Arg
44E4 **Sankt-Peterburg** Russian Fed
72C4 **Sankuru** *R* Zaïre
20A2 **San Leandro** USA
28E1 **San Leopoldo** Brazil
64C2 **Şanlıurfa** Turk
28C2 **San Lorenzo** Arg
26C3 **San Lorenzo** Colombia
24C3 **San Lorenzo** Ecuador
20B2 **San Lucas** USA
28B2 **San Luis** Arg
28B2 **San Luis** State, Arg
19D4 **San Luis** USA
22B1 **San Luis de la Paz** Mexico
28D1 **San Luis del Palma** Arg
20B3 **San Luis Obispo** USA
20B3 **San Luis Obispo B** USA
22B1 **San Luis Potosi** Mexico
22B1 **San Luis Potosi** State, Mexico
20B2 **San Luis Res** USA
40B3 **Sanluri** Sardegna
22D2 **San Magallanes** Mexico
26E2 **San Maigualida** *Mts* Ven
28D3 **San Manuel** Arg
28A2 **San Marcos** Chile
22C2 **San Marcos** Mexico
17C4 **San Marcos** USA
37E3 **San Marino** Republic, Europe
28B1 **San Martin** Catamarca, Arg
28B2 **San Martin** Mendoza, Arg
79G3 **San Martin** *Base* Ant
28A4 **San Martin de los Andes** Arg
37D2 **San Martino di Castroza** Italy
22C2 **San Martin Tuxmelucan** Mexico
20A2 **San Mateo** USA
27G7 **San Matias** Brazil
52C3 **Sanmenxia** China
21D3 **San Miguel** El Salvador
20B3 **San Miguel** USA
20B3 **San Miguel** *I* USA
22B1 **San Miguel del Allende** Mexico
28D3 **San Miguel del Monte** Arg
25C3 **San Miguel de Tucumán** Arg
52D4 **Sanming** China
8B3 **San Nicolas** *I* USA
28C2 **San Nicolás de los Arroyos** Arg
74D2 **Sannieshof** S Africa
70B4 **Sanniquellie** Lib
43E3 **Sanok** Pol
23B5 **San Onofore** Colombia
20D4 **San Onofre** USA
57F8 **San Pablo** Phil
20A1 **San Pablo B** USA
28D2 **San Pedro** Buenos Aires, Arg
70B4 **San Pédro** Ivory Coast
25D2 **San Pedro** Jujuy, Arg
25E2 **San Pedro** Par
19D4 **San Pedro** *R* USA
20C4 **San Pedro Chan** USA
8C4 **San Pedro de los Colonias** Mexico
21D3 **San Pedro Sula** Honduras
40B3 **San Pietro** *I* Medit S
21A1 **San Quintin** Mexico
28B2 **San Rafael** Arg
20A2 **San Rafael** USA
20C3 **San Rafael Mts** USA
37B3 **San Remo** Italy
16C3 **San Saba** *R* USA
28D2 **San Salvador** Arg
24B2 **San Salvador** El Salvador
22B1 **San Salvador** Mexico
23C2 **San Salvador** *I* Caribbean
25C2 **San Salvador de Jujuy** Arg
71G3 **Sansanné-Mango** Togo
39B1 **San Sebastian** Spain
37E3 **Sansepolcro** Italy
40D2 **San Severo** Italy
20B3 **San Simeon** USA
26E7 **Santa Ana** Bol
21C3 **Santa Ana** Guatemala
20D4 **Santa Ana** USA
20D4 **Santa Ana Mts** USA
16C3 **Santa Anna** USA
28A3 **Santa Bárbara** Chile
21B2 **Santa Barbara** Mexico
20C3 **Santa Barbara** USA
20C4 **Santa Barbara,I** USA
20B3 **Santa Barbara Chan** USA
20C3 **Santa Barbara Res** USA
20C4 **Santa Catalina** *I* USA
20C4 **Santa Catalina,G of** USA
25F3 **Santa Catarina** State, Brazil
23B2 **Santa Clara** Cuba
20B2 **Santa Clara** USA
20C3 **Santa Clara** *R* USA
25C8 **Santa Cruz** Arg
26F7 **Santa Cruz** Bol
28A2 **Santa Cruz** Chile
57F8 **Santa Cruz** Phil
25B7 **Santa Cruz** State, Arg
20A2 **Santa Cruz** USA
20C4 **Santa Cruz** *I* USA
77F2 **Santa Cruz** *Is* Solomon Is
19D4 **Santa Cruz** *R* USA
29E2 **Santa Cruz Cabrália** Brazil
20C3 **Santa Cruz Chan** USA
70A2 **Santa Cruz de la Palma** Canary Is
23B2 **Santa Cruz del Sur** Cuba
70A2 **Santa Cruz de Tenerife** Canary Is
73C5 **Santa Cruz do Cuando** Angola
29C3 **Santa Cruz do Rio Pardo** Brazil
28E1 **Santa Cruz do Sul** Brazil
20A2 **Santa Cruz Mts** USA
28D2 **Santa Elena** Arg
26F3 **Santa Elena** Ven
28C2 **Santa Fe** Arg
28C2 **Santa Fe** State, Arg
16A2 **Santa Fe** USA
29B2 **Santa Helena de Goiás** Brazil
52B3 **Santai** China
25B8 **Santa Inés** *I* Chile
28B3 **Santa Isabel** La Pampa, Arg
28C2 **Santa Isabel** Sante Fe, Arg
77E1 **Santa Isabel** *I* Solomon Is
28D2 **Santa Lucia** Urug
20B2 **Santa Lucia** USA
19B3 **Santa Lucia Range** *Mts* USA
70A4 **Santa Luzia** *I* Cape Verde
28C1 **Santa Margarita** Arg
20B3 **Santa Margarita** USA
8B4 **Santa Margarita** *I* Mexico
20D4 **Santa Margarita** *R* USA
37C2 **Santa Margherita** Italy
28E1 **Santa Maria** Brazil
23C4 **Santa Maria** Colombia
20B3 **Santa Maria** USA
70A1 **Santa Maria** *I* Açores
28E2 **Santa Maria** *R* Brazil
16A3 **Santa Maria** *R* Chihuahua, Mexico
22C1 **Santa Maria** *R* Queretaro, Mexico
29D1 **Santa Maria da Vitória** Brazil
22B1 **Santa Maria del Rio** Mexico
26D1 **Santa Marta** Colombia
20C3 **Santa Monica** USA
20C4 **Santa Monica B** USA
29D1 **Santana** Brazil
28D2 **Santana do Livramento** Brazil
26C3 **Santander** Colombia
39B1 **Santander** Spain
39C2 **Santañy** Spain
20C3 **Santa Paula** USA
29B3 **Santa Porto Helena** Brazil
27K4 **Santa Quitéria** Brazil
37E2 **Santarcangelo di Romagna** Italy
27H4 **Santarem** Brazil
39A2 **Santarém** Port
29B2 **Santa Rita do Araguaia** Brazil
28E1 **Santa Rosa** Brazil
20A1 **Santa Rosa** California, USA
21D3 **Santa Rosa** Honduras
28C3 **Santa Rosa** La Pampa, Arg
28B2 **Santa Rosa** Mendoza, Arg
16B3 **Santa Rosa** New Mexico, USA
28B2 **Santa Rosa** San Luis, Arg
20B3 **Santa Rosa** *I* USA
21A2 **Santa Rosalía** Mexico
18C2 **Santa Rosa Range** *Mts* USA
28C1 **Santa Sylvina** Arg
27L5 **Santa Talhada** Brazil
29D2 **Santa Teresa** Brazil
40B2 **Santa Teresa di Gallura** Sardegna
28E2 **Santa Vitoria do Palmar** Brazil
20B3 **Santa Ynez** *R* USA
20B3 **Santa Ynez Mots** USA
15D2 **Santee** *R* USA
37D2 **Santerno** *R* Italy
37C2 **Santhia** Italy
28A2 **Santiago** Chile
23C3 **Santiago** Dom Rep
22A1 **Santiago** Mexico
26B2 **Santiago** Panama
57F7 **Santiago** Phil
26C4 **Santiago** *R* Peru
39A1 **Santiago de Compostela** Spain
23B2 **Santiago de Cuba** Cuba
28C1 **Santiago del Estero** Arg
25D3 **Santiago del Estero** State, Arg
20D4 **Santiago Peak** *Mt* USA
27K7 **Santo** State, Brazil
77F2 **Santo** Vanuatu
29B3 **Santo Anastatácio** Brazil
28E1 **Santo Angelo** Brazil
70A4 **Santo Antão** *I* Cape Verde
29B3 **Santo Antonio da Platina** Brazil
29E1 **Santo Antônio de Jesus** Brazil
29A2 **Santo Antônio do Leverger** Brazil
22B1 **Santo Dominco** Mexico
23D3 **Santo Domingo** Dom Rep
29C3 **Santos** Brazil
29D3 **Santos Dumont** Brazil
19C4 **Santo Tomas** Mexico
28D1 **Santo Tomé** Arg
25B7 **San Valentin** *Mt* Chile
28A2 **San Vicente** Chile
22B1 **San Vicente** Mexico
37E2 **San Vito al Tagliamento** Italy
73B4 **Sanza Pomba** Angola
28D1 **São Borja** Brazil
29C3 **São Carlos** Brazil
29C1 **São Domingos** Brazil
27H5 **São Félix** Mato Grosso, Brazil
29D3 **São Fidélis** Brazil
29D2 **São Francisco** Brazil
27L5 **São Francisco** *R* Brazil
28D1 **São Francisco de Assis** Brazil
25G3 **São Francisco do Sul** Brazil
28E2 **São Gabriel** Brazil
29C2 **São Gotardo** Brazil
73D4 **Sao Hill** Tanz
29D3 **São João da Barra** Brazil
29C3 **São João da Boa Vista** Brazil
29C1 **São João d'Aliança** Brazil
29D2 **São João da Ponte** Brazil
29D3 **São João del Rei** Brazil
29D2 **São João do Paraíso** Brazil
29C3 **São Joaquim da Barra** Brazil
70A1 **São Jorge** *I* Açores
28E2 **São José do Norte** Brazil
29C3 **São José do Rio Prêto** Brazil
29C3 **São José dos Campos** Brazil
29C4 **São José dos Pinhais** Brazil
29A2 **São Lourenço** *R* Brazil
28E2 **São Lourenço do Sul** Brazil
27K4 **São Luis** Brazil
28E1 **Sao Luis Gonzaga** Brazil
29C2 **São Marcos** *R* Brazil
29D2 **São Maria do Suaçui** Brazil
29E2 **São Mateus** Brazil
29D2 **São Mateus** *R* Brazil
70A1 **São Miguel** *I* Açores
29B1 **São Miguel de Araguaia** Brazil
38C2 **Saône** *R* France
70A4 **São Nicolau** *I* Cape Verde
29D1 **São Onofre** *R* Brazil
29C3 **São Paulo** Brazil
29B3 **São Paulo** State, Brazil
28E1 **São Pedro do Sul** Brazil
24H3 **São Pedro e São Paulo** *Is* Brazil
27K5 **São Raimundo Nonato** Brazil
29C2 **São Romão** Brazil
29C3 **São Sebastia do Paraiso** Brazil
28E2 **São Sepé** Brazil
29B2 **São Simão** Goias, Brazil
25G1 **São Simão, Barragem de** *Res* Brazil
29C3 **São Simão** Sao Paulo, Brazil
70A4 **São Tiago** *I* Cape Verde
70C4 **São Tomé** *I* W Africa
70C4 **São Tomé and Principe** Republic, W Africa
70B2 **Saoura** *Watercourse* Alg
29A1 **Saouriuiná** *R* Brazil
29C3 **São Vicente** Brazil
70A4 **São Vincente** *I* Cape Verde
41F2 **Sápai** Greece
57C3 **Saparua** Indon
56E4 **Sape** Indon
71H4 **Sapele** Nig
53E3 **Sapporo** Japan
40D2 **Sapri** Italy
32G7 **Saprsborg** Nor
17C2 **Sapulpa** USA
63B1 **Saqqez** Iran
45H8 **Sarāb** Iran
41D2 **Sarajevo** Bosnia-Herzegovina, Yugos
63E1 **Sarakhs** Iran
45K5 **Saraktash** Russian Fed
49K4 **Sarala** Russian Fed
13E2 **Saranac L** USA
13E2 **Saranac Lake** USA
41E3 **Sarandë** Alb
28E1 **Sarandi** Brazil
28D2 **Sarandi del Yi** Urug
28D2 **Sarandi Grande** Urug
57G9 **Sarangani Is** Phil
44L3 **Saranpaul'** Russian Fed
44H5 **Saransk** Russian Fed
37C2 **Saranza** Italy
71H4 **Sara Peak** *Mt* Nig
44J4 **Sarapul** Russian Fed
29A3 **Sarasota** USA
41F1 **Sărat** Rom
43F3 **Sarata** Ukraine
11A3 **Saratoga** USA
14D1 **Saratoga Springs** USA
56D2 **Saratok** Malay
45H5 **Saratov** Russian Fed
45H5 **Saratovskoye Vodokhranilishche** *Res* Russian Fed
64A2 **Saraykoy** Turk
63E3 **Sarbāz** Iran
63D2 **Sarbīsheh** Iran
37D1 **Sarca** *R* Italy
69A2 **Sardalais** Libya
63B1 **Sar Dasht** Iran
40B2 **Sardegna** *I* Medit S
Sardinia = Sardegna
32H5 **Sarektjåkkå, Mt** Sweden
66C4 **Sarenga** Eth
60C2 **Sargodha** Pak
72B3 **Sarh** Chad
63C1 **Sārī** Iran
65C2 **Sarida** *R* Isreal
64D1 **Sarikamiş** Turk
76D3 **Sarina** Aust
37B1 **Sarine** *R* Switz
60B1 **Sar-i-Pul** Afghan
69B2 **Sarīr** Libya
69A2 **Sarir Tibesti** *Desert* Libya
53B4 **Sariwŏn** N Korea
38B2 **Sark** *I* UK
64C2 **Şarkişla** Turk
51G7 **Sarmi** Indon
25C7 **Sarmiento** Arg
32G6 **Särna** Sweden
37C1 **Sarnen** Switz
4E5 **Sarnia** Can
43F2 **Sarny** Ukraine
60B2 **Sarobi** Afghan
56B3 **Sarolangun** Indon
41E3 **Saronikós Kólpos** *G* Greece
37C2 **Saronno** Italy
41F2 **Saros Körfezi** *B* Turk
44M2 **Saroto** Russian Fed
7N2 **Sarqaq** Greenland
36D2 **Sarralbe** France
36D2 **Sarrebourg** France
36D2 **Sarreguemines** France
36D2 **Sarre-Union** France
39B1 **Sarrion** Spain
60B3 **Sartanahu** Pak
40B2 **Sartène** Corse
36A3 **Sarthe** Department, France
38B2 **Sarthe** *R* France
65D1 **Sārūt** Syria
63E3 **Sarvan** Iran
45J6 **Sarykamys** Kazakhstan
48H5 **Sarysu** *R* Kazakhstan
61B3 **Sasarām** India
53B5 **Sasebo** Japan
6H4 **Saskatchewan** Province, Can
6H4 **Saskatchewan** *R* Can
3G3 **Saskatoon** Can
49N2 **Saskylakh** Russian Fed
74D2 **Sasolburg** S Africa
44G5 **Sasovo** Russian Fed
70B4 **Sassandra** Ivory Coast
70B4 **Sassandra** *R* Ivory Coast
40B2 **Sassari** Sardegna
42C2 **Sassnitz** Germany
37D2 **Sassuolo** Italy
28C2 **Sastre** Arg
54A4 **Sasuna** Japan
62A1 **Sātāra** India
6G2 **Satellite B** Can
56E4 **Satengar** *Is* Indon
32H6 **Säter** Sweden
15C2 **Satilla** *R* USA
44K4 **Satka** Russian Fed
60D2 **Satluj** *R* India
61B3 **Satna** India
60C4 **Sātpura Range** *Mts* India
41E1 **Satu Mare** Rom
45C6 **Satu Mare** Rom
28D2 **Sauce** Arg
32F7 **Sauda** Nor
58C3 **Saudi Arabia** Kingdom, Arabian Pen
36D2 **Sauer** *R* Germany/Lux
36D1 **Sauerland** Region, Germany
32B1 **Sauðárkrókur** Iceland
12B2 **Saugatuck** USA
14D1 **Saugerties** USA
3C3 **Saugstad,Mt** Can
11D2 **Sauk Center** USA
12B2 **Sauk City** USA
4E4 **Sault Ste Marie** Can
12C1 **Sault Ste Marie** USA
51G7 **Saumlaki** Indon
38B2 **Saumur** France
73C4 **Saurimo** Angola
23M2 **Sauteurs** Grenada
41D2 **Sava** *R* Serbia, Yugos
77H2 **Savai'i** *I* Western Samoa
71G4 **Savalou** Benin
45H9 **Savan** *R* Iran
15C2 **Savannah** Georgia, USA
15B1 **Savannah** Tennessee, USA
15C2 **Savannah** *R* USA
55C2 **Savannakhet** Laos
23B3 **Savanna la Mar** Jamaica
4C3 **Savant L** Can
7J4 **Savant Lake** Can
55D2 **Savarane** Laos
71G4 **Savé** Benin
73D6 **Save** *R* Mozam
63C2 **Sāveh** Iran
36D2 **Saverne** France
37B2 **Savigliano** Italy
36B2 **Savigny** France
44G3 **Savinskiy** Russian Fed
37E3 **Savio** *R* Italy
38D2 **Savoie** *Region* France
37C2 **Savona** Italy
32K6 **Savonlinna** Fin
10D3 **Savoonga** USA
37E2 **Savudrija Rtič** *Pt* Croatia, Yugos
32K5 **Savukoski** Fin
57B4 **Savu S** Indon
55A1 **Saw** Burma
57C3 **Sawai** Indon
60D3 **Sawai Mādhopur** India
56B2 **Sawang** Indon
55C2 **Sawankhalok** Thai
54D3 **Sawara** Japan

Sawatch Mts Shasta,Mt

16A2 **Sawatch Mts** USA
5H3 **Sawbill** Can
10J2 **Sawtooth Mt** USA
18C2 **Sawtooth Range** *Mts* USA
76B2 **Sawu** *I* Indon
14A2 **Saxton** USA
71G3 **Say** Niger
60B1 **Sayghan** Afghan
67G3 **Sayh Hajmah** Oman
67F2 **Sayhūt** Yemen
45H6 **Saykhin** Kazakhstan
50D2 **Saynshand** Mongolia
16C2 **Sayre** Oklahoma, USA
14B2 **Sayre** Pennsylvania, USA
22C2 **Sayula** Mexico
22A1 **Sayulita** Mexico
45J7 **Say-Utes** Kazakhstan
14D2 **Sayville** USA
3C3 **Sayward** Can
42C3 **Sázava** *R* Czech Republic
39C2 **Sbisseb** *R* Alg
35D4 **Scafell Pike** *Mt* Eng
34E1 **Scalloway** Scot
34D2 **Scapa Flow** *Sd* Scot
13D2 **Scarborough** Can
35E4 **Scarborough** Eng
23E4 **Scarborough** Tobago
34B2 **Scarp** *I* Scot
40B1 **Schaffhausen** Switz
42C3 **Scharding** Austria
36D1 **Scharteberg** *Mt* Germany
7M4 **Schefferville** Can
36B1 **Schelde** *R* Belg
19D3 **Schell Creek Range** *Mts* USA
14D1 **Schenectady** USA
16C4 **Schertz** USA
36C1 **Schiedam** Neth
37D2 **Schio** Italy
36D1 **Schleiden** Germany
42B2 **Schleswig** Germany
42B2 **Schleswig Holstein** State, Germany
14C1 **Schoharie** USA
76D1 **Schouten Is** PNG
36E2 **Schramberg** Germany
7K5 **Schreiber** Can
19C3 **Schurz** USA
14C2 **Schuylkill** *R* USA
14B2 **Schuylkill Haven** USA
42B3 **Schwabische Alb** *Upland* Germany
74B2 **Schwarzrand** *R* Namibia
36E2 **Schwarzwald** *Mts* Germany
42B3 **Schwarzwald** *Upland* Germany
10G2 **Schwatka Mts** USA
37D1 **Schwaz** Austria
42C2 **Schweinfurt** Germany
74D2 **Schweizer Reneke** S Africa
42C2 **Schwerin** Germany
37C1 **Schwyz** Switz
40C3 **Sciacca** Italy
35B7 **Scilly Isles** *Is* UK
12C3 **Scioto** *R* USA
11A2 **Scobey** USA
75D2 **Scone** Aust
7Q2 **Scoresby Sd** Greenland
xxxF7 **Scotia Ridge** Atlantic O
xxxF7 **Scotia S** Atlantic O
34C3 **Scotland** Country, UK
79F7 **Scott** *Base* Ant
74E3 **Scottburgh** S Africa
3C3 **Scott,C** Can
16B2 **Scott City** USA
79G6 **Scott I** Ant
7L2 **Scott Inlet** *B* Can
3G2 **Scott L** Can
18B2 **Scott,Mt** USA
76B2 **Scott Reef** Timor S
11B3 **Scottsbluff** USA
15B2 **Scottsboro** USA
75E3 **Scottsdale** Aust
19D4 **Scottsdale** USA
14C2 **Scranton** USA
11C3 **Scribner** USA
37D1 **Scuol** Switz
Scutari = Shkodër
74C3 **Seacow** S Africa
6J4 **Seal** *R* Can
75B3 **Sea Lake** Aust
4B2 **Seal** Can
5K3 **Seal Bight** Can
45F6 **Sea of Azov** *S* Russian Fed
19D3 **Searchlight** USA
17D2 **Searcy** USA
20D3 **Searles** USA
20B2 **Seaside** California, USA
18B1 **Seaside** Oregon, USA
14C3 **Seaside Park** USA
18B1 **Seattle** USA
57B5 **Seba** Indon
13E2 **Sebago L** USA
56B2 **Sebanga** Indon
20A1 **Sebastopol** USA
58B4 **Sebderat** Eritrea
43F1 **Sebez** Russian Fed
13F1 **Seboomook L** USA
15E4 **Sebring** USA
37D2 **Secchia** *R* Italy
78A3 **Secretary I** NZ
17D2 **Sedalia** USA
36C2 **Sedan** France
10E5 **Sedanka** *I* USA
78B2 **Seddonville** NZ
65C3 **Sede Boqer** Israel
65C3 **Sederot** Israel
70A3 **Sédhiou** Sen
65C3 **Sedom** Israel
19D4 **Sedona** USA
74B2 **Seeheim** Namibia
79E **Seelig,Mt** Ant
36A2 **Sées** France
71B2 **Sefrou** Mor
78B2 **Sefton,Mt** NZ
55C5 **Segamat** Malay
44E3 **Segezha** Russian Fed
39B2 **Segorbe** Spain
70B3 **Ségou** Mali
Segovia = Coco
39B1 **Segovia** Spain
39C1 **Segre** *R* Spain
10D6 **Seguam** *I* USA
10D6 **Seguam Pass** USA
70B4 **Séguéla** Ivory Coast
70A2 **Seguia el Hamra** *Watercourse* Mor
17C4 **Seguin** USA
28C2 **Segundo** *R* Arg
56E2 **Seguntur** Indon
39B2 **Segura** *R* Spain
60B3 **Sehwan** Pak
16C2 **Seiling** USA
36D2 **Seille** *R* France
32J6 **Seinäjoki** Fin
11D2 **Seine** *R* Can
38C2 **Seine** *R* France
36B2 **Seine-et-Marne** Department, France
36A2 **Seine-Maritime** Department, France
72D4 **Sekenke** Tanz
72D2 **Sek'ot'a** Eth
18B1 **Selah** USA
51G7 **Selaru** *I* Indon
56E4 **Selat Alas** *Str* Indon
56C3 **Selat Bangka** *Str* Indon
56B3 **Selat Berhala** *B* Indon
51G7 **Selat Dampier** *Str* Indon
56C3 **Selat Gaspar** *Str* Indon
56E4 **Selat Lombok** *Str* Indon
56A3 **Selat Mentawi** *Str* Indon
56E4 **Selat Sape** *Str* Indon
57B4 **Selat Sumba** *Str* Indon
56C4 **Selat Sunda** *Str* Indon
57C4 **Selat Wetar** *Chan* Indon
57D3 **Selawati** *I* Indon
10F2 **Selawik** USA
10G2 **Selawik** *R* USA
10F2 **Selawik L** USA
35E5 **Selby** Eng
11B2 **Selby** USA
41F3 **Selçuk** Turk
10H4 **Seldovia** USA
74D1 **Selebi Pikwe** Botswana
53C1 **Selemdzha** *R* Russian Fed
53C1 **Selemdzhinsk** Russian Fed
49Q3 **Selennyakh** *R* Russian Fed
36D2 **Selestat** France
7Q3 **Selfoss** Iceland
11B2 **Selfridge** USA
72C1 **Selima Oasis** Sudan
43G1 **Selizharovo** Russian Fed
6J4 **Selkirk** Can
34D4 **Selkirk** Scot
3E3 **Selkirk Mts** Can
15B2 **Selma** Alabama, USA
20C2 **Selma** California, USA
15B1 **Selmer** USA
37A1 **Selongey** France
39B2 **Selouane** Mor
10M3 **Selous,Mt** Can
56C3 **Selta Karimata** *Str* Indon
28C1 **Selva** Arg
26D5 **Selvas** Region, Brazil
18C1 **Selway** USA
76D3 **Selwyn** Aust
3H1 **Selwyn L** Can
6E3 **Selwyn Mts** Can
56D4 **Semarang** Indon
44G4 **Semenov** Russian Fed
10A5 **Semichi Is** USA
10G4 **Semidi Is** USA
45F5 **Semiluki** Russian Fed
11A3 **Seminoe Res** USA
17C2 **Seminole** Oklahoma, USA
16B3 **Seminole** Texas, USA
15C2 **Seminole,L** USA
48K4 **Semipalatinsk** Kazakhstan
57F8 **Semirara Is** Phil
63C2 **Semirom** Iran
10B6 **Semisopochnoi** *I* USA
56D2 **Semitau** Indon
63C1 **Semnān** Iran
36C2 **Semois** *R* Belg
22C2 **Sempoala** Hist Site, Mexico
56E2 **Semporna** Malay
26E5 **Sena Madureira** Brazil
73C5 **Senanga** Zambia
17E3 **Senatobia** USA
53E4 **Sendai** Honshū, Japan
53C5 **Sendai** Kyūshū, Japan
60D4 **Sendwha** India
14B1 **Seneca Falls** USA
14B1 **Seneca L** USA
16A3 **Senecu** Mexico
70A3 **Senegal** Republic, Africa
70A3 **Sénégal** *R* Maur/Sen
74D2 **Senekal** S Africa
57B3 **Sengkang** Indon
27L6 **Senhor do Bonfim** Brazil
40C2 **Senigallia** Italy
40D2 **Senj** Croatia, Yugos
50F4 **Senkaku Gunto** *Is* Japan
53C3 **Senlin Shan** *Mt* China
36B2 **Senlis** France
72D2 **Sennar** Sudan
7L5 **Senneterre** Can
36D2 **Senones** France
36B2 **Sens** France
41E1 **Senta** Serbia, Yugos
72C4 **Sentery** Zaïre
3D3 **Sentinel Peak** *Mt* Can
60D4 **Seoni** India
Seoul = Soul
78B2 **Separation Pt** NZ
54A3 **Sep'o** N Korea
55D2 **Sepone** Laos
29A2 **Sepotuba** *R* Brazil
7M4 **Sept-Iles** Can
72B1 **Séquédine** Niger
20C2 **Sequoia Nat Pk** USA
65C1 **Serai** Syria
57C3 **Seram** *I* Indon
56C4 **Serang** Indon
56C2 **Serasan** *I* Indon
41D2 **Serbia** *Republic* Yugos
37D2 **Serchio** *R* Italy
45G5 **Serdobsk** Russian Fed
36B3 **Serein** *R* France
55C5 **Seremban** Malay
72D4 **Serengeti Nat Pk** Tanz
73D5 **Serenje** Zambia
43F3 **Seret** *R* Ukraine
44H4 **Sergach** Russian Fed
53C3 **Sergeyevka** Russian Fed
48H3 **Sergino** Russian Fed
27L6 **Sergipe** State, Brazil
44F4 **Sergiyev Posad** Georgia
56D2 **Seria** Brunei
56D2 **Serian** Malay
41E3 **Sérifos** *I* Greece
5H2 **Sérigny** *R* Can
37C2 **Serio** *R* Italy
69B2 **Serir Calanscio** *Desert* Libya
36C2 **Sermaize-les-Bains** France
7P3 **Sermilik** Greenland
44J5 **Sernovodsk** Russian Fed
44L4 **Serov** Russian Fed
74D1 **Serowe** Botswana
39A2 **Serpa** Port
44F5 **Serpukhov** Russian Fed
29A3 **Serra Amamba** Par
29B1 **Serra Azul** Brazil
29C3 **Serra da Canastra** *Mts* Brazil
39A1 **Serra da Estrela** *Mts* Port
29C3 **Serra da Mantiqueira** *Mts* Brazil
29B2 **Serra da Mombuca** Brazil
29B2 **Serra das Furnas** *Mts* Brazil
29C1 **Serra de Arrajas** *Mts* Brazil
29B4 **Serra de Fartura** *Mts* Brazil
29A3 **Serra de Maracaju** *Mts* Brazil
29A2 **Serra de São Jeronimo** Brazil
28D1 **Serra do Boquairao** *Mts* Brazil
29D2 **Serra do Cabral** *Mt* Brazil
27G5 **Serra do Cachimbo** *Mts* Brazil
29B2 **Serra do Caiapó** *Mts* Brazil
28E2 **Serra do Canguçu** *Mts* Brazil
29B3 **Serra do Cantu** *Mts* Brazil
29D3 **Serra do Caparaó** *Mts* Brazil
27K7 **Serra do Chifre** Brazil
29D2 **Serra do Espinhaço** *Mts* Brazil
28D1 **Serra do Espinilho** *Mts* Brazil
29C2 **Serra do Jibão** *Mts* Brazil
29C3 **Serra do Mar** *Mts* Brazil
29B3 **Serra do Mirante** *Mts* Brazil
27H3 **Serra do Navio** Brazil
29C3 **Serra do Paranapiacaba** *Mts* Brazil
29D1 **Serra do Ramalho** *Mts* Brazil
29B1 **Serra do Roncador** *Mts* Brazil
27G6 **Serra dos Caiabis** *Mts* Brazil
29B3 **Serra dos Dourados** *Mts* Brazil
29D1 **Serra do Sincora** *Mts* Brazil
26F6 **Serra dos Parecis** *Mts* Brazil
29C2 **Serra dos Pilões** *Mts* Brazil
29B2 **Serra do Taquaral** *Mts* Brazil
29B2 **Serra Dourada** *Mts* Brazil
29C1 **Serra Dourada** *Mts* Brazil
28E2 **Serra Encantadas** *Mts* Brazil
27G6 **Serra Formosa** *Mts* Brazil
29D2 **Serra Geral** *Mts* Bahia, Brazil
29B4 **Serra Geral** *Mts* Parona, Brazil
29C1 **Serra Geral de Goiás** *Mts* Brazil
29C2 **Serra Geral do Parana** *Mts* Brazil
41E2 **Sérrai** Greece
21D3 **Serrana Bank** *Is* Caribbean
39B1 **Serrana de Cuenca** *Mts* Spain
16B4 **Serranias del Burro** *Mts* Mexico
29B2 **Serranópolis** Brazil
26F3 **Serra Pacaraima** *Mts* Brazil/Ven
26F3 **Serra Parima** *Mts* Brazil
27H3 **Serra Tumucumaque** Brazil
36B2 **Serre** *R* France
37A2 **Serres** France
28B2 **Serrezuela** Arg
27L6 **Serrinha** Brazil
29D2 **Serro** Brazil
29B3 **Sertanópolis** Brazil
52A3 **Sêrtar** China
57D4 **Serua** *I* Indon
74D1 **Serule** Botswana
56A2 **Seruwai** Indon
56D3 **Seruyan** *R* Indon
53B1 **Seryshevo** Russian Fed
4D3 **Seseganaga L** Can
73B5 **Sesfontein** Namibia
73C5 **Sesheke** Zambia
37B2 **Sestriere** Italy
37C2 **Sestri Levante** Italy
53D3 **Setana** Japan
38C3 **Sète** France
29D2 **Sete Lagoas** Brazil
71D1 **Sétif** Alg
66C4 **Setit** *R* Sudan
54C3 **Seto** Japan
54B4 **Seto Naikai** *S* Japan
71A2 **Settat** Mor
35D4 **Settle** Eng
39A2 **Setúbal** Port
37A1 **Seurre** France
45H7 **Sevan, Ozero** *L* Armenia
45E7 **Sevastopol'** Ukraine
7K4 **Severn** *R* Can
35D5 **Severn** *R* Eng
44G3 **Severnaya Dvina** *R* Russian Fed
49L1 **Severnaya Zemlya** *I* Russian Fed
44L3 **Severnyy Sos'va** *R* Russian Fed
44K3 **Severnyy Ural** *Mts* Russian Fed
49M4 **Severo-Baykalskoye Nagorye** *Mts* Russian Fed
45F6 **Severo Donets** *R* Ukraine
44F3 **Severodvinsk** Russian Fed
48H3 **Severo Sos'va** *R* Russian Fed
44L3 **Severoural'sk** Russian Fed
19D3 **Sevier** *R* USA
19D3 **Sevier Desert** USA
19D3 **Sevier L** USA
39A2 **Sevilla** Spain
Seville = Sevilla
41F2 **Sevlievo** Bulg
70A4 **Sewa** *R* Sierra Leone
10J3 **Seward** Alaska, USA
17C1 **Seward** Nebraska, USA
10E2 **Seward Pen** USA
3E2 **Sexsmith** Can
68K8 **Seychelles,Is** Indian O
32C1 **Seyðisfjörðor** Iceland
32C1 **Seyðisfjörður** Iceland
64C2 **Seyhan** Turk
45F5 **Seym** *R* Russian Fed
49R3 **Seymchan** Russian Fed
75C3 **Seymour** Aust
14D2 **Seymour** Connecticut, USA
12B3 **Seymour** Indiana, USA
16C3 **Seymour** Texas, USA
37B2 **Seyne** France
37E2 **Sežana** Slovenia, Yugos
36B2 **Sézanne** France
71E2 **Sfax** Tunisia
41F1 **Sfînto Gheorghe** Rom
42A2 **'s-Gravenhage** Neth
52B3 **Shaanxi** Province, China
72C4 **Shabunda** Zaïre
59F2 **Shache** China
79G9 **Shackleton Ice Shelf** Ant
60B3 **Shadadkot** Pak
63C2 **Shādhām** *R* Iran
20C3 **Shafter** USA
35D6 **Shaftesbury** Eng
71G4 **Shagamu** Nig
4D2 **Shagamu** *R* Can
25J8 **Shag Rocks** *Is* South Georgia
63B2 **Shāhabād** Iran
56F7 **Shah Alam** Malay
65D2 **Shahbā** Syria
63D2 **Shahdap** Iran
61B3 **Shahdol** India
63B1 **Shāhīn Dezh** Iran
63D2 **Shāh Kūh** Iran
63E2 **Shahrak** Afghan
63D2 **Shahr-e Bābak** Iran
Shahresa = Qomisheh
63C2 **Shahr Kord** Iran
45J8 **Shahsavār** Iran
44L3 **Shaim** Russian Fed
62B1 **Shājābād** India
60D3 **Shājahānpur** India
60D4 **Shājāpur** India
53E2 **Shakhtersk** Russian Fed
45G6 **Shakhty** Russian Fed
44H4 **Shakhun'ya** Russian Fed
71G4 **Shaki** Nig
11D3 **Shakopee** USA
54D2 **Shakotan-misaki** *C* Japan
10F3 **Shaktoolik** USA
44K4 **Shamary** Russian Fed
72D3 **Shambe** Sudan
14B2 **Shamokin** USA
16B2 **Shamrock** USA
14C1 **Shandaken** USA
20B3 **Shandon** USA
52D2 **Shandong** Province, China
52C5 **Shangchuan Dao** *I* China
52C1 **Shangdu** China
52E3 **Shanghai** China
52C3 **Shangnan** China
73C5 **Shangombo** Zambia
52D4 **Shangra** China
52B5 **Shangsi** China
52C3 **Shang Xian** China
53B2 **Shangzhi** China
33B3 **Shannon** *R* Irish Rep
3H2 **Shannon L** Can
52D3 **Shanqiu** China
53B3 **Shansonggang** China
50G1 **Shantarskiye Ostrova** *I* Russian Fed
52D5 **Shantou** China
52C2 **Shanxi** Province, China
52D3 **Shan Xian** China
52C5 **Shaoguan** China
52E4 **Shaoxing** China
52C4 **Shaoyang** China
34D2 **Shapinsay** *I* Scot
65D2 **Shaqqā** Syria
67E3 **Shaqqat aj Kharitah** Region, S Arabia
67E1 **Shaqra'** S Arabia
67E4 **Shaqrā'** Yemen
67E3 **Sharawrah** S Arabia
52A1 **Sharhulsan** Mongolia
54D2 **Shari** Japan
63D1 **Sharifābād** Iran
67G1 **Sharjah** UAE
76A3 **Shark B** Aust
63D1 **Sharlauk** Turkmenistan
65C2 **Sharon,Plain of** Israel
14B3 **Sharpsburg** USA
44H4 **Sharya** Russian Fed
72D3 **Shashamenē** Eth
74D1 **Shashani** *R* Zim
74D1 **Shashe** *R* Botswana
52C3 **Shashi** China
18B2 **Shasta L** USA
18B2 **Shasta,Mt** USA

Shathah at Tahtā
Sirte,G of

65D1 Shathah at Tahtā Syria
64E3 Shatt al Gharrat R Iraq
65C3 Shaubak Jordan
3G4 Shaunavon Can
20C2 Shaver L USA
14C2 Shawangunk Mt USA
12B2 Shawano USA
17C2 Shawnee Oklahoma, USA
11A3 Shawnee Wyoming, USA
5G4 Shawinigan Can
52D4 Sha Xian China
76B3 Shay Gap Aust
65D2 Shaykh Miskīn Syria
66D4 Shaykh 'Uthmān Yemen
44F5 Shchekino Russian Fed
45F5 Shchigry Russian Fed
45E5 Shchors Ukraine
48J4 Shchuchinsk Kazakhstan
12B2 Sheboygan USA
72E3 Shebelë R Eth
72B3 Shebshi Mts Nig
53E2 Shebunino Russian Fed
5J4 Shediac Can
10K2 Sheenjek R USA
34B4 Sheep Haven Estuary Irish Rep
35F6 Sheerness Eng
5J5 Sheet Harbour Can
65C2 Shefar'am Israel
15B2 Sheffield Alabama, USA
35E5 Sheffield Eng
14A2 Sheffield Pennsylvania, USA
16B3 Sheffield Texas, USA
5K3 Shekalika Bay Can
60C2 Shekhupura Pak
3C2 Shelagyote Peak Mt Can
5H5 Shelburne Can
14D1 Shelburne Falls USA
12B2 Shelby Michigan, USA
18D1 Shelby Montana, USA
15C1 Shelby N Carolina, USA
12B3 Shelbyville Indiana, USA
15B1 Shelbyville Tennessee, USA
11C3 Sheldon USA
10M3 Sheldon,Mt Can
5J3 Sheldrake Can
10H4 Shelikof Str USA
3G3 Shellbrook Can
18D2 Shelley USA
75D2 Shellharbour Aust
78A3 Shelter Pt NZ
18B1 Shelton USA
64E1 Shemakha Azerbaijan
17C1 Shenandoah USA
13D3 Shenandoah R USA
14A3 Shenandoah Mt USA
13D3 Shenandoah Nat Pk USA
71H4 Shendam Nig
66B3 Shendi Sudan
44G3 Shenkursk Russian Fed
52C2 Shenmu China
52E1 Shenyang China
52C5 Shenzhen China
60D3 Sheopur India
43F2 Shepetovka Ukraine
14B3 Shepherdstown USA
75C3 Shepparton Aust
36A1 Sheppey,I of Eng
7K2 Sherard,C Can
35D6 Sherborne Eng
70A4 Sherbro I Sierra Leone
5G4 Sherbrooke Can
14C1 Sherburne USA
66B3 Shereik Sudan
60C3 Shergarh India
17D3 Sheridan Arkansas, USA
11A3 Sheridan Wyoming, USA
17C3 Sherman USA
3H2 Sherridon Can
42B2 s-Hertogenbosh Neth
10M4 Sheslay Can
3B2 Sheslay R Can
33C1 Shetland Is Scot
Shevchenko = Aktau
53C1 Shevli R Russian Fed
11C2 Sheyenne USA
11C2 Sheyenne R USA
63C3 Sheyk Sho'eyb I Iran
50J2 Shiashkotan I Russian Fed
60B1 Shibarghan Afghan
53D4 Shibata Japan
54D2 Shibetsu Japan
69C1 Shibin el Kom Egypt
65A3 Shibîn el Qanâtir Egypt
43D4 Shibogama L Can
54C3 Shibukawa Japan
14B2 Shickshinny USA
52C2 Shijiazhuang China
60B3 Shikarpur Pak
47H4 Shikoku,I Japan
54B4 Shikoku-sanchi Mts Japan
54D2 Shikotsu-ko L Japan
44G3 Shilega Russian Fed
61C2 Shiliguri India
50E1 Shilka Russian Fed
50E1 Shilka R Russian Fed
14C2 Shillington USA
61D2 Shillong India
44G5 Shilovo Russian Fed
54B4 Shimabara Japan
54C4 Shimada Japan
53B1 Shimanovsk Russian Fed
53D4 Shimizu Japan
60D2 Shimla India
54C4 Shimoda Japan
62B2 Shimoga India
53C5 Shimonoseki Japan
54C3 Shinano R Japan
67G2 Shināş Oman
63E2 Shindand Afghan
14A2 Shinglehouse USA
4D4 Shingleton USA
53D5 Shingū Japan
54D3 Shinjō Japan
53D4 Shinminato Japan
65D1 Shinshār Syria
72D4 Shinyanga Tanz
53E4 Shiogama Japan
54C4 Shiono-misaki C Japan
52A5 Shiping China
5J4 Shippegan Can
14B2 Shippensburg USA
16A2 Shiprock USA
67E3 Shiqāq al Ma'āṭīf Region, Yemen
52B3 Shiquan China
54D3 Shirakawa Japan
54C3 Shirane-san Mt Japan
54C3 Shirani-san Mt Japan
63C3 Shīraz Iran
65A3 Shirbîn Egypt
54D2 Shiriya-saki C Japan
63C2 Shīr Kūh Iran
54C3 Shirotori Japan
63D1 Shirvān Iran
10F5 Shishaldin V USA
10E2 Shishmaref USA
10E2 Shishmaref Inlet USA
52B2 Shitanjing China
12B3 Shively USA
60D3 Shivpuri India
65C3 Shivta Hist Site Israel
19D3 Shivwits Plat USA
73D5 Shiwa Ngandu Zambia
52C3 Shiyan China
52B2 Shizuishan China
54C3 Shizuoka Japan
41D2 Shkodër Alb
43G2 Shkov Belorussia
49L1 Shmidta, Ostrov I Russian Fed
75D2 Shoalhaven R Aust
54B4 Shobara Japan
62B2 Shoranūr India
62B1 Shorāpur India
19C3 Shoshone California, USA
18D2 Shoshone Idaho, USA
18E2 Shoshone R USA
18D2 Shoshone L USA
19C3 Shoshone Mts USA
18E2 Shoshoni USA
45E5 Shostka Ukraine
66C4 Showak Sudan
19D4 Show Low USA
17D3 Shreveport USA
35D5 Shrewsbury Eng
35D5 Shropshire County, Eng
53B2 Shuangcheng China
52E1 Shuanglia China
53C2 Shuangyashan China
45K6 Shubar-Kuduk Kazakhstan
5J4 Shubenacadie Can
10J2 Shublik Mts USA
44N2 Shuga Russian Fed
52D2 Shu He R China
52A4 Shuicheng China
60C3 Shujaabad Pak
60D4 Shujālpur India
53B3 Shulan China
50C2 Shule He China
10G5 Shumagin Is USA
41F2 Shumen Bulg
44H4 Shumerlya Russian Fed
52D4 Shuncheng China
10G2 Shungnak USA
52C2 Shuo Xian China
63D3 Shūr Gaz Iran
73C5 Shurugwi Zim
3E3 Shuswap L Can
44G4 Shuya Russian Fed
10H4 Shuyak I USA
61E3 Shwebo Burma
55B2 Shwegyin Burma
61E3 Shweli R Burma
63E3 Siahan Range Mts Pak
60A2 Siah Koh Mts Afghan
60C2 Sialkot Pak
Sian = Xi'an
57G9 Siarao, I Phil
57F9 Siaton Phil
57C2 Siau I Indon
43E1 Šiauliai Lithuania
44K5 Sibay Russian Fed
74E2 Sibayi L S Africa
40D2 Šibenik Croatia, Yugos
56A3 Siberut I Indon
60B3 Sibi Pak
53C3 Sibirtsevo Russian Fed
72B4 Sibiti Congo
72D4 Sibiti R Tanz
41E1 Sibiu Rom
11C3 Sibley USA
57A2 Siboa Indon
56A2 Sibolga Indon
61D2 Sibsāgār India
56D2 Sibu Malay
57F9 Sibuguay B Phil
72B3 Sibut CAR
56E1 Sibutu Pass Malay/Phil
57F8 Sibuyan I Phil
57F8 Sibuyan S Phil
52A3 Sichuan Province, China
40C3 Sicilia I Medit S
40C3 Sicilian Chan Italy/Tunisia
Sicily = Sicilia
26D6 Sicuari Peru
60C4 Siddhapur India
62B1 Siddipet India
61B3 Sidhi India
69B1 Sidi Barrani Egypt
71B1 Sidi bel Abbès Alg
71A2 Sidi Kacem Mor
34D3 Sidlaw Hills Scot
79F5 Sidley,Mt Ant
18B1 Sidney Can
11B2 Sidney Montana, USA
16B1 Sidney Nebraska, USA
14C1 Sidney New York, USA
12C2 Sidney Ohio, USA
15C2 Sidney Lanier,L USA
Sidon = Säida
29B3 Sidrolândia Brazil
43E2 Siedlce Pol
36D1 Sieg R Germany
36D1 Siegburg Germany
36D1 Siegen Germany
37A1 Sielle R France
55C3 Siem Reap Camb
40C2 Siena Italy
36C3 Siene R France
43D2 Sierpc Pol
22C2 Sierra Andrés Tuxtla Mexico
28B3 Sierra Auca Mahuida Mts Arg
16A3 Sierra Blanca USA
28B4 Sierra Blanca Mts Arg
28B4 Sierra Colorada Arg
39B1 Sierra de Albarracin Mts Spain
39B2 Sierra de Alcaraz Mts Spain
28B1 Sierra de Ancasti Mts Arg
28B2 Sierra de Cordoba Mts Arg
28B1 Sierra de Famantina Mts Arg
39A1 Sierra de Gredos Mts Spain
39A2 Sierra de Guadalupe Mts Spain
39B1 Sierra de Guadarrama Mts Spain
39B1 Sierra de Guara Mts Spain
39B1 Sierra de Gudar Mts Spain
22C2 Sierra de Juárez Mts Mexico
28C3 Sierra de la Ventana Mts Arg
39C1 Sierra del Codi Mts Spain
28D1 Sierra del Imán Mts Arg
28B2 Sierra del Morro Mt Arg
28B3 Sierra del Nevado Mts Arg
21B2 Sierra de los Alamitos Mts Mexico
39B2 Sierra de los Filabres Mts Spain
22B1 Sierra de los Huicholes Mts Mexico
22C2 Sierra de Miahuatlán Mts Mexico
22B1 Sierra de Morones Mts Mexico
39A2 Sierra de Ronda Mts Spain
28B2 Sierra de San Luis Mts Arg
39B2 Sierra de Segura Mts Spain
22C1 Sierra de Tamaulipas Mts Mexico
39B1 Sierra de Urbion Mts Spain
28B2 Sierra de Uspallata Mts Arg
28B1 Sierra de Valasco Mts Arg
28B2 Sierra de Valle Fértil Mts Arg
22B1 Sierra de Zacatécas Mts Mexico
22C2 Sierra de Zongolica Mts Mexico
28C2 Sierra Grande Mts Arg
70A4 Sierra Leone Republic, Africa
70A4 Sierra Leone,C Sierra Leone
57F7 Sierra Madre Mts Phil
22B2 Sierra Madre del Sur Mts Mexico
20B3 Sierra Madre Mts USA
21B2 Sierra Madre Occidental Mts Mexico
22B1 Sierra Madre Oriental Mts Mexico
28B2 Sierra Malanzan Mts Arg
8C4 Sierra Mojada Mexico
39A2 Sierra Morena Mts Spain
39B2 Sierra Nevada Mts Spain
19B3 Sierra Nevada Mts USA
26D1 Sierra Nevada de santa Marta Mts Colombia
28B2 Sierra Pié de Palo Mts Arg
19D4 Sierra Vista USA
37B1 Sierre Switz
29A3 Siete Puntas R Par
41E3 Sifnos I Greece
71B1 Sig Alg
44E2 Sig Russian Fed
56A3 Sigep Indon
43E3 Sighetu Marmaţiei Rom
41E1 Sighişoara Rom
56A1 Sigli Indon
32B1 Siglufjördur Iceland
36E2 Sigmaringen Germany
26A1 Siguatepeque Honduras
39B1 Sigüenza Spain
70B3 Siguiri Guinea
55C3 Sihanoukville Camb
60D4 Sihora India
64D2 Siirt Turk
50C3 Sikai Hu L China
3D2 Sikanni R Can
60D3 Sīkar India
60B2 Sikaram Mt Afghan
70B3 Sikasso Mali
57B4 Sikeli Indon
17E2 Sikeston USA
41F3 Sikinos I Greece
41E3 Sikionía Greece
61C2 Sikkim State, India
49O3 Siktyakh Russian Fed
39A1 Sil R Spain
37D1 Silandro Italy
22B1 Silao Mexico
57F8 Silay Phil
61D3 Silchar India
4C2 Silcox Can
70C2 Silet Alg
61B2 Silgarhi Nepal
64B2 Silifke Turk
65D1 Silinfah Syria
59G2 Siling Co L China
41F2 Silistra Bulg
44A3 Siljan L Sweden
32F7 Silkeborg Den
37E1 Sillian Austria
17D2 Siloam Springs USA
17D3 Silsbee USA
72B2 Siltou Well Chad
43E1 Šilute Lithuania
64D2 Silvan Turk
29C2 Silvania Brazil
60C4 Silvassa India
11D2 Silver Bay USA
19C3 Silver City Nevada, USA
16A3 Silver City New Mexico, USA
18B2 Silver Lake USA
20D2 Silver Peak Range Mts USA
14B3 Silver Spring USA
3C3 Silverthrone Mt Can
75B2 Silverton Aust
16A2 Silverton USA
37D1 Silvretta Mts Austria/Switz
56D2 Simanggang Malay
55C1 Simao China
63B2 Simareh R Iran
41F3 Simav Turk
41F3 Simav R Turk
44H5 Simbirsk Russian Fed
4F5 Simcoe,L Can
10G5 Simeohof I USA
56A2 Simeulue I Indon
45E7 Simferopol' Ukraine
41F3 Sími I Greece
61B2 Simikot Nepal
16B2 Simla USA
36D1 Simmern Germany
20C3 Simmler USA
74B3 Simonstown S Africa
3C3 Simoom Sound Can
38D2 Simplon Mt Switz
37C1 Simplon P Switz
6C2 Simpson,C USA
76C3 Simpson Desert Aust
10N2 Simpson L Can
3B2 Simpson Peak Mt Can
7K3 Simpson Pen Can
32G7 Simrishamn Sweden
50J2 Simushir I Russian Fed
56A2 Sinabang Indon
72E3 Sina Dhaqa Somalia
64B4 Sinai Pen Egypt
22A1 Sinaloa State, Mexico
37D3 Sinalunga Italy
26C2 Sincelejo Colombia
15C2 Sinclair,L USA
60D3 Sind R India
60B3 Sindh Region Pak
41F3 Sindirği Turk
61C3 Sindri India
53E2 Sinegorsk Russian Fed
39A2 Sines Port
72D2 Singa Sudan
55C5 Singapore Republic, S E Asia
55C5 Singapore,Str of S E Asia
56E4 Singaraja Indon
36E3 Singen Germany
72D4 Singida Tanz
61E2 Singkaling Hkamti Burma
56C2 Singkawang Indon
75D2 Singleton Aust
56B3 Singtep I Indon
55B1 Singu Burma
74E1 Singuédeze R Mozam
54A3 Sin'gye N Korea
54A2 Sinhŭng N Korea
40B2 Siniscola Sardgena
57B4 Sinjai Indon
64D2 Sinjár Iraq
60B2 Sinkai Hills Mts Afghan
66C3 Sinkat Sudan
59G1 Sinkiang Autonomous Region, China
36E1 Sinn R Germany
27H2 Sinnamary French Guiana
54A3 Sinnyong S Korea
64C1 Sinop Turk
54A2 Sinpa N Korea
54A2 Sinp'o N Korea
54A3 Sinp'yong N Korea
41E1 Sîntana Rom
56D2 Sintang Indon
17F4 Sinton USA
39A2 Sintra Port
26C2 Sinú R Colombia
53A3 Sinŭiju N Korea
43D3 Siofok Hung
37B1 Sion Switz
11C3 Sioux City USA
11C3 Sioux Falls USA
4C3 Sioux Lookout Can
57F9 Sipalay Phil
23L1 Siparia Trinidad
53A3 Siping China
4B3 Sipiwesk L Can
79F3 Siple Base Ant
79F5 Siple I Ant
57F8 Sipocot Phil
56A3 Sipora Indon
15B2 Sipsey R USA
22A1 Siqueros Mexico
57F9 Siquijor I Phil
62B2 Sira India
40D3 Siracusa Italy
61C3 Sirajganj Bang
3D3 Sir Alexander,Mt Can
71G3 Sirba R Burkina
67F2 Sīr Banī Yās I UAE
76C2 Sir Edward Pellew Group Is Aust
41F1 Siret R Rom
10N3 Sir James McBrien,Mt Can
62B2 Sir Kālahasti India
3D3 Sir Laurier,Mt Can
64D2 Şirnak Turk
60C4 Sirohi India
62C1 Sironcha India
60D4 Sironj India
41E3 Síros I Greece
20C3 Sirretta Peak,Mt USA
63C3 Sirri I Iran
60C3 Sirsa India
3E3 Sir Sandford,Mt Can
62A2 Sirsi India
69A1 Sirte Desert Libya
69A1 Sirte,G of Libya

Sisak Spjelkavik

40D1 **Sisak** Croatia, Yugos
55C2 **Sisaket** Thai
4A2 **Sisipuk L** Can
55C3 **Sisophon** Camb
20B3 **Sisquoc** USA
20C3 **Sisquoc** *R* USA
11C2 **Sisseton** USA
71F3 **Sissili** *R* Burkina
36B2 **Sissonne** France
63E2 **Sistan** Region, Iran/Afghan
38D3 **Sisteron** France
49L4 **Sistig Khem** Russian Fed
61B2 **Sītāpur** India
41F3 **Sitía** Greece
29C1 **Sitio d'Abadia** Brazil
6E4 **Sitka** USA
10H4 **Sitkalidak I** USA
10H4 **Sitkinak** *I* USA
55B2 **Sittang** *R* Burma
36C1 **Sittard** Neth
61D3 **Sittwe** Burma
56D4 **Situbondo** Indon
53B1 **Sivaki** Russian Fed
64C2 **Sivas** Turk
64C2 **Siverek** Turk
64B2 **Sivrihisar** Turk
69B2 **Siwa** Egypt
60D2 **Siwalik Range** *Mts* India
61B2 **Siwalik Range** *Mts* Nepal
44G3 **Siya** Russian Fed
52D3 **Siyang** China
42C1 **Sjaelland** *I* Den
32G7 **Skagen** Den
32F7 **Skagerrak** *Str* Nor/Den
18B1 **Skagit** *R* USA
18B1 **Skagit Mt** Can
6E4 **Skagway** USA
14B1 **Skaneateles** USA
14B1 **Skaneateles L** USA
32G7 **Skara** Sweden
43E2 **Skarzysko-Kamlenna** Pol
6F4 **Skeena** *R* Can
3C2 **Skeena Mts** Can
6D3 **Skeenjek** *R* USA
35F5 **Skegness** Eng
44B2 **Skellefte** *R* Sweden
32J6 **Skellefteå** Sweden
41E3 **Skíathos** *I* Greece
6E4 **Skidegate** Can
43E2 **Skiemiewice** Pol
32F7 **Skien** Nor
71D1 **Skikda** Alg
53C5 **Skikoku** *I* Japan
35E5 **Skipton** Eng
41E3 **Skíros** *I* Greece
32F7 **Skive** Den
42B1 **Skjern** Den
7O3 **Skjoldungen** Greenland
12B2 **Skokie** USA
41E3 **Skópelos** *I* Greece
41E2 **Skopje** Macedonia, Yugos
32G7 **Skövde** Sweden
49O4 **Skovorodino** Russian Fed
13F2 **Skowhegan** USA
74E1 **Skukuza** S Africa
6C3 **Skwentna** USA
42D2 **Skwierzyna** Pol
33B2 **Skye** *I* Scot
32G7 **Slagelse** Den
35B5 **Slaney** *R* Irish Rep
41E2 **Slatina** Rom
56D4 **Slaung** Indon
41D1 **Slav Brod** Yugos
6G3 **Slave** *R* Can
3F2 **Slave Lake** Can
43G2 **Slavgorod** Belorussia
48J4 **Slavgorod** Russian Fed
43F2 **Slavuta** Ukraine
45F6 **Slavyansk** Ukraine
34C3 **Sleat,Sound of** *Chan* Scot
4F2 **Sleeper Is** Can
10G3 **Sleetmute** USA
35B5 **Sleeve Bloom** *Mts* Irish Rep
17E3 **Slidell** USA
14C2 **Slide Mt** USA
33B3 **Sligo** Irish Rep
33B3 **Sligo** *B* Irish Rep
41F2 **Sliven** Bulg
19C3 **Sloan** USA
41F2 **Slobozia** Rom
3E4 **Slocan** Can
43F2 **Slonim** Belorussia
35E6 **Slough** Eng
20B2 **Slough** *R* USA
43D3 **Slovakia** *Republic* Europe
58C1 **Slovenia** *Republic* Europe
42C2 **Slubice** Pol
43F2 **Sluch'** *R* Ukraine
42D2 **Słupsk** Pol
43F2 **Slutsk** Belorussia
43F2 **Slutsk** *R* Belorussia
33A3 **Slyne Head** *Pt* Irish Rep
49M4 **Slyudyanka** Russian Fed
7M4 **Smallwood Res** Can
70A2 **Smara** Mor
41E2 **Smederevo** Serbia, Yugos
41E2 **Smederevska Palanka** Serbia, Yugos
45E6 **Smela** Ukraine
14A2 **Smethport** USA
53C2 **Smidovich** Russian Fed
53E2 **Smirnykh** Russian Fed
3F2 **Smith** Can
20C1 **Smith** USA
10O2 **Smith Arm** *B* Can
10H1 **Smith B** USA
3C3 **Smithers** Can
15D1 **Smithfield** N Carolina, USA
74D3 **Smithfield** S Africa
18D2 **Smithfield** Utah, USA
7L3 **Smith I** Can
3C2 **Smith River** Can
3C3 **Smith Sd** Can
4F5 **Smiths Falls** Can
75E3 **Smithton** Aust
3E2 **Smoky** *R* Can
16B2 **Smoky** *R* USA
75D2 **Smoky C** Aust
16C2 **Smoky Hills** USA
3F3 **Smoky Lake** Can
18D2 **Smoky Mts** USA
32F6 **Smøla** *I* Nor
44E5 **Smolensk** Russian Fed
41E2 **Smólikas** *Mt* Greece
41E2 **Smolyan** Bulg
3G3 **Smoothstone L** Can
43F2 **Smorgon'** Belorussia
14C3 **Smyrna** Delaware, USA
15C2 **Smyrna** Georgia, USA
35C4 **Snaefell** *Mt* Eng
32B2 **Snæfell** *Mt* Iceland
18C1 **Snake** USA
18D2 **Snake** *R* USA
8B2 **Snake River Canyon** USA
18D2 **Snake River Plain** USA
77F5 **Snares** *Is* NZ
42B2 **Sneek** Neth
20B2 **Snelling** USA
42D2 **Sněžka** *Mt* Pol/Czech Republic
32F6 **Snøhetta** *Mt* Nor
18B1 **Snohomish** USA
18B1 **Snoqualmie P** USA
55D3 **Snoul** Camb
3H1 **Snowbird L** Can
35C5 **Snowdon** *Mt* Wales
35C5 **Snowdonia Nat Pk** Wales
6G3 **Snowdrift** Can
19D4 **Snowflake** USA
6H4 **Snow Lake** Can
14B2 **Snow Shoe** USA
75A2 **Snowtown** Aust
18D2 **Snowville** USA
75C3 **Snowy Mts** Aust
16B3 **Snyder** USA
53B5 **Soan-kundo** *I* S Korea
54A3 **Sobaek Sanmaek** *Mts* S Korea
72D3 **Sobat** *R* Sudan
27K4 **Sobral** Brazil
43E2 **Sochaczew** Pol
45F7 **Sochi** Russian Fed
54A3 **Sŏch'on** S Korea
69A2 **Socna** Libya
16A3 **Socorro** USA
21A3 **Socorro** *I* Mexico
28A2 **Socos** Chile
67F4 **Socotra** *I* Yemen
20C3 **Soda L** USA
32K5 **Sodankylä** Fin
18D2 **Soda Springs** USA
32H6 **Soderhamn** Sweden
32H7 **Södertälje** Sweden
72C2 **Sodiri** Sudan
72D3 **Sodo** Eth
14B1 **Sodus Point** USA
57B4 **Soë** Indon
36E1 **Soest** Germany
Sofala = Beira
Sofia = Sofiya
41E2 **Sofiya** Bulg
53C1 **Sofiysk** Russian Fed
44E2 **Sofporog** Russian Fed
50H4 **Sofu Gan** *I* Japan
26D2 **Sogamoso** Colombia
53C1 **Sogda** Russian Fed
32F6 **Sognefjorden** *Inlet* Nor
54A4 **Sŏgwi-ri** S Korea
59H2 **Sog Xian** China
66B1 **Sohâg** Egypt
77E1 **Sohano** PNG
60D3 **Sohīpat** India
36B1 **Soignies** Belg
36B2 **Soissons** France
60C3 **Sojat** India
53A4 **Sŏjosŏn-man** *B* N Korea
54A3 **Sokcho** S Korea
64A2 **Söke** Turk
71G4 **Sokodé** Togo
44G4 **Sokol** Russian Fed
43E2 **Sokołka** Pol
70B3 **Sokolo** Mali
7Q3 **Søkongens Øy** *I* Greenland
71H3 **Sokoto** Nig
71H3 **Sokoto** State, Nig
71G3 **Sokoto** *R* Nig
78A3 **Solander I** NZ
57F7 **Solano** Phil
62B1 **Solapur** India
57B4 **Solar** *I* Indon
37D1 **Solbad Hall** Austria
37D1 **Sölden** Austria
10H3 **Soldotna** USA
23C4 **Soledad** Colombia
20B2 **Soledad** USA
28E1 **Soledade** Brazil
35E6 **Solent** *Sd* Eng
36B1 **Solesmes** France
43F2 **Soligorsk** Belorussia
44K4 **Solikamsk** Russian Fed
45J5 **Sol'Iletsk** Russian Fed
26D4 **Solimões** Peru
36D1 **Solingen** Germany
74B1 **Solitaire** Namibia
32H6 **Sollefteå** Sweden
37B3 **Solliès-Pont** France
36E1 **Solling** Region, Germany
53D1 **Solnenechnyy** Russian Fed
36A3 **Sologne** *R* France
56B3 **Solok** Indon
77E1 **Solomon Is** Pacific O
12A1 **Solon Springs** USA
37B1 **Solothurn** Switz
44F2 **Solovetskiye, Ostrova** *I* Russian Fed
53A1 **Solov'yevsk** Russian Fed
32F8 **Soltau** Germany
20B3 **Solvang** USA
14B1 **Solvay** USA
34D4 **Solway Firth** *Estuary* Scot/Eng
73C5 **Solwezi** Zambia
54D3 **Sōma** Japan
41F3 **Soma** Turk
58C5 **Somalia** Republic, E Africa
xxviiiD4 **Somali Basin** Indian O
41D1 **Sombor** Serbia, Yugos
62E3 **Sombrero Chan** Indian O
22B1 **Sombretete** Mexico
76D2 **Somerset** Aust
35D6 **Somerset** County, Eng
12C3 **Somerset** Kentucky, USA
14E2 **Somerset** Massachusetts, USA
13D2 **Somerset** Pennsylvania, USA
74D3 **Somerset East** S Africa
7J2 **Somerset I** Can
14D1 **Somerset Res** USA
14C3 **Somers Point** USA
14E1 **Somersworth** USA
14C2 **Somerville** USA
17C3 **Somerville Res** USA
41E1 **Somes** *R* Rom
36B2 **Somme** Department, France
36B2 **Somme** *R* France
36C2 **Sommesous** France
26A1 **Somoto** Nic
61B3 **Son** *R* India
53A4 **Sŏnch'ŏn** N Korea
74D3 **Sondags** *R* S Africa
32F8 **Sønderborg** Den
7N3 **Søndre Strømfjord** Greenland
7N2 **Søndre Upernavik** Greenland
37C1 **Sondrio** Italy
55D3 **Song Ba** *R* Viet
55D3 **Song Cau** Viet
54A3 **Sŏngch'on** N Korea
73D5 **Songea** Tanz
54A2 **Songgan** N Korea
53B2 **Songhua Jiang** *R* China
52E3 **Songjiang** China
54A3 **Songjŏng** S Korea
55C4 **Songkhla** Thai
53B4 **Songnim** N Korea
55C5 **Sông Pahang** *R* Malay
52A3 **Songpan** China
54A4 **Sŏngsan-ni** S Korea
53B3 **Sonhue Hu** *L* China
52C1 **Sonid Youqi** China
55C1 **Son La** Viet
60B3 **Sonmiani** Pak
60B3 **Sonmiani Bay** Pak
19D4 **Sonoita** Mexico
20A1 **Sonoma** USA
20B2 **Sonora** California, USA
19D4 **Sonora** State, Mexico
16B3 **Sonora** Texas, USA
21A2 **Sonora** *R* Mexico
8B3 **Sonoran Desert** USA
20C1 **Sonora P** USA
21D3 **Sonsonate** El Salvador
51G6 **Sonsorol** *I* Pacific O
9E2 **Soo Canals** USA/Can
3D4 **Sooke** Can
43D2 **Sopot** Pol
42D3 **Sopron** Hung
5K4 **Sop's Arm** Can
20B2 **Soquel** USA
40C2 **Sora** Italy
65C3 **Sored** *R* Israel
5G4 **Sorel** Can
75E3 **Sorell** Aust
37C2 **Soresina** Italy
64C2 **Sorgun** Turk
39B1 **Soria** Spain
32J5 **Sørkjosen** Nor
48C2 **Sørksop** *I* Barents S
45J6 **Sor Mertvyy Kultuk** *Plain* Kazakhstan
29C3 **Sorocaba** Brazil
44J5 **Sorochinsk** Russian Fed
51H6 **Soroi** *I* Pacific O
43F3 **Soroki** Moldova
54D2 **Soroma-ko** *L* Japan
51G7 **Sorong** Indon
57D3 **Sorong** Province, Indon
72D3 **Soroti** Uganda
32J4 **Sørøya** *I* Nor
40C2 **Sorrento** Italy
32K5 **Sorsatunturi** *Mt* Fin
32H5 **Sorsele** Sweden
57F8 **Sorsogon** Phil
44E3 **Sortavala** Russian Fed
53B4 **Sŏsan** S Korea
43D2 **Sosnowiec** Pol
37B3 **Sospel** France
44L4 **Sos'va** Russian Fed
71G3 **Sota** *R* Benin
22C1 **Soto la Manna** Mexico
72B3 **Souanké** Congo
70B4 **Soubré** Ivory Coast
14C2 **Souderton** USA
23P2 **Soufrière** St Lucia
23N2 **Soufrière** *V* St Vincent
38C3 **Souillac** France
71D1 **Souk Ahras** Alg
71A2 **Souk Larbat Gharb** Mor
53B4 **Soul** S Korea
39C2 **Soummam** *R* Alg
Sour = Tyr
74D2 **Sources,Mt aux** Lesotho
11B2 **Souris** Manitoba, Can
5J4 **Souris** Prince Edward I, Can
11B2 **Souris** *R* USA/Can
27L5 **Sousa** Brazil
71E1 **Sousse** Tunisia
73C7 **South Africa** Republic, Africa
14C2 **South Amboy** USA
4E5 **Southampton** Can
35E6 **Southampton** Eng
14D2 **Southampton** USA
7K3 **Southampton I** Can
62E2 **South Andaman** *I* Indian O
7M4 **South Aulatsivik I** Can
76C3 **South Australia** State, Aust
xxviiiH6 **South Australian Basin** Indian O
17E3 **Southaven** USA
16A3 **South Baldy** *Mt* USA
15E4 **South Bay** USA
12C1 **South Baymouth** Can
12B2 **South Bend** Indiana, USA
18B1 **South Bend** Washington, USA
13D3 **South Boston** USA
4E5 **South Branch** USA
14E1 **Southbridge** USA
South Cape = Ka Lae
9E3 **South Carolina** State, USA
51E5 **South China S** S E Asia
8C2 **South Dakota** State, USA
14D1 **South Deerfield** USA
35E6 **South Downs** Eng
75E3 **South East C** Aust
10E3 **Southeast C** USA
xxixO7 **South East Pacific Basin** Pacific O
78A2 **Southern Alps** *Mts* NZ
3H2 **Southend** Can
35F6 **Southend-on-Sea** Eng
77F5 **Southern Alps** *Mts* NZ
76A4 **Southern Cross** Aust
4B2 **Southern Indian L** Can
6J4 **Southern Indian L** Can
15D1 **Southern Pines** USA
23H2 **Southfield** Jamaica
xxixK6 **South Fiji Basin** Pacific O
35F6 **South Foreland** *Pt* Eng
16A2 **South Fork** USA
10H3 **South Fork** *R* Alaska, USA
20B1 **South Fork** *R* California, USA
20B1 **South Fork American** *R* USA
20C3 **South Fork Kern** *R* USA
24G9 **South Georgia** *I* S Atlantic O
35D6 **South Glamorgan** County, Wales
12B2 **South Haven** USA
6J3 **South Henik L** Can
13D3 **South Hill** USA
xxviiiJ3 **South Honshu Reige** Pacific O
78A2 **South I** NZ
14D2 **Southington** USA
4B2 **South Knife** *R* Can
53B4 **South Korea** Republic, S E Asia
19B3 **South Lake Tahoe** USA
xxviiiD6 **South Madagascar Ridge** Indian O
79G8 **South Magnetic Pole** Ant
15E4 **South Miami** USA
14B3 **South Mt** USA
6F3 **South Nahanni** *R* Can
23G1 **South Negril Pt** Jamaica
xxxF8 **South Orkney** *Is* Atlantic O
24B5 **South Pacific O**
16B1 **South Platte** *R* USA
79E **South Pole** Ant
12C1 **South Porcupine** Can
35D5 **Southport** Eng
23Q2 **South Pt** Barbados
14C2 **South River** USA
34D2 **South Ronaldsay** *I* Scot
xxxG7 **South Sandwich Trench** Atlantic O
20A2 **South San Francisco** USA
3G3 **South Saskatchewan** *R* Can
4B2 **South Seal** *R* Can
34E4 **South Shields** Eng
78B1 **South Taranaki Bight** *B* NZ
4F3 **South Twin I** Can
34B3 **South Uist** *I* Scot
South West Africa = Namibia
76D5 **South West C** Aust
10D3 **Southwest C** USA
xxviiiD6 **South West Indian Ridge** Indian O
xxixM6 **South West Pacific Basin** Pacific O
xxxD5 **South West Peru Ridge** Pacific O
35E5 **South Yorkshire** County, Eng
74D1 **Soutpansberg** *Mts* S Africa
43E1 **Sovetsk** Russian Fed
44H4 **Sovetsk** Russian Fed
53E2 **Sovetskaya Gavan'** Russian Fed
44L3 **Sovetskiy** Russian Fed
74D2 **Soweto** S Africa
54D1 **Sōya-misaki** *C* Japan
73B4 **Soyo Congo** Angola
43G2 **Sozh** *R* Belorussia
36C1 **Spa** Belg
39 **Spain** Kingdom, Europe
Spalato = Split
35E5 **Spalding** Eng
12C1 **Spanish** *R* Can
19D2 **Spanish Fork** USA
23B3 **Spanish Town** Jamaica
19C3 **Sparks** USA
12A2 **Sparta** USA
15C2 **Spartanburg** USA
41E3 **Spartí** Greece
53C3 **Spassk Dal'niy** Russian Fed
11B3 **Spearfish** USA
16B2 **Spearman** USA
23Q2 **Speightstown** Barbados
10J3 **Spenard** USA
11C3 **Spence** Iowa, USA
12B3 **Spencer** Indiana, USA
7J3 **Spencer Bay** Can
75A3 **Spencer,C** Aust
75A2 **Spencer G** Aust
7L3 **Spencer Is** *Is* Can
78B2 **Spenser Mts** NZ
34B4 **Sperrin** *Mts* N Ire
36E2 **Spessart** Region, Germany
34D3 **Spey** *R* Scot
42B3 **Speyer** Germany
23K1 **Speyside** Tobago
37B1 **Spiez** Switz
10K2 **Spike Mt** USA
37E1 **Spilimbergo** Italy
18C1 **Spirir Lake** USA
6G4 **Spirit River** Can
Spitsbergen = Svalbard
48C2 **Spitsbergen, I** Barents S
42C3 **Spittal** Austria
37E1 **Spittal an der Drau** Austria
32F6 **Spjelkavik** Nor

Split L Swale

4B2 **Split L** Can
40D2 **Split** Croatia, Yugos
37C1 **Splügen** Switz
18C1 **Spokane** USA
12A1 **Spooner** USA
18C2 **Spray** USA
42C2 **Spree** *R* Germany
74B2 **Springbok** S Africa
5K4 **Springdale** Can
17D2 **Springdale** USA
16B2 **Springer** USA
19E4 **Springerville** USA
16B2 **Springfield** Colorado, USA
12B3 **Springfield** Illinois, USA
14D1 **Springfield** Massachusetts, USA
11C3 **Springfield** Minnesota, USA
17D2 **Springfield** Missouri, USA
12C3 **Springfield** Ohio, USA
18B2 **Springfield** Oregon, USA
15B1 **Springfield** Tennessee, USA
13E2 **Springfield** Vermont, USA
74D3 **Springfontein** S Africa
5J4 **Springhill** Can
19C3 **Spring Mts** USA
74D2 **Springs** S Africa
14A1 **Springville** New York, USA
19D2 **Springville** Utah, USA
14B1 **Springwater** USA
18D2 **Spruce Mt** USA
35F5 **Spurn Head** *C* Eng
33D3 **Spurn Head** *Pt* Eng
18B1 **Spuzzum** Can
3D4 **Squamish** Can
49R3 **Sredhekolymsk** Russian Fed
49S4 **Sredinnyy Khrebet** *Mts* Russian Fed
44F5 **Sredne-Russkaya Vozvyshennost'** *Upland* Russian Fed
49M3 **Sredne Sibirskoye Ploskogorye** *Tableland* Russian Fed
44K4 **Sredniy Ural** *Mts* Russian Fed
55D3 **Srepok** *R* Camb
50E1 **Sretensk** Russian Fed
55C3 **Sre Umbell** Camb
62C1 **Srīkākulam** India
59G5 **Sri Lanka** Republic, S Asia
60C2 **Srīnagar** Pak
62A1 **Srīvardhan** India
42D2 **Sroda Wielkopolski** Pol
34C2 **Stack Skerry** *I* Scot
42B2 **Stade** Germany
34B3 **Staffa** *I* Scot
35D5 **Stafford** County, Eng
35D5 **Stafford** Eng
14D2 **Stafford Springs** USA
Stalingrad = Volgograd
3D2 **Stalin,Mt** Can
74B3 **Stallberg** *Mt* S Africa
7J1 **Stallworthy,C** Can
43E2 **Stalowa Wola** Pol
14D2 **Stamford** Connecticut, USA
14C1 **Stamford** New York, USA
16C3 **Stamford** Texas, USA
74B1 **Stampriet** Namibia
74D2 **Standerton** S Africa
12C2 **Standish** USA
18D1 **Stanford** USA
74E2 **Stanger** S Africa
20B2 **Stanislaus** *R* USA
41E2 **Stanke Dimitrov** Bulg
75E3 **Stanley** Aust
25E8 **Stanley** Falkland Is
18D2 **Stanley** Idaho, USA
11B2 **Stanley** N Dakota, USA
62B2 **Stanley Res** India
Stanleyville = Kisangani
21D3 **Stann Creek** Belize
50F1 **Stanovoy Khrebet** *Mts* Russian Fed
37C1 **Stans** Switz
75D1 **Stanthorpe** Aust
34B3 **Stanton Banks** *Sand-bank* Scot
16B1 **Stapleton** USA
43E2 **Starachowice** Pol
41E2 **Stara Planiná** *Mts* Bulg
44E4 **Staraya Russa** Russian Fed
41F2 **Stara Zagora** Bulg
42D2 **Stargard Szczecinski** Pol
17E3 **Starkville** USA
42C3 **Starnberg** Germany
43D2 **Starogard Gdanski** Pol
43F3 **Starokonstantinov** Ukraine
35D6 **Start Pt** Eng
45F5 **Staryy Oskol** Russian Fed
14B2 **State College** USA
14C2 **Staten I** USA
15C2 **Statesboro** USA
15C1 **Statesville** USA
13D3 **Staunton** USA
32F7 **Stavanger** Nor
36C1 **Stavelot** Belg
45G6 **Stavropol'** Russian Fed
75B3 **Stawell** Aust
42D2 **Stawno** Pol
18B2 **Stayton** USA
16A1 **Steamboat Springs** USA
10F3 **Stebbins** USA
10K3 **Steele,Mt** Can
14B2 **Steelton** USA
3E2 **Steen** *R* Can
3E2 **Steen River** Can
18C2 **Steens Mt** USA
7N2 **Steenstrups Gletscher** *Gl* Greenland
6H2 **Stefansson I** Can
74E2 **Stegi** Swaziland
37D1 **Steinach** Austria
4B4 **Steinbach** Can
44A3 **Steinkjer** Nor
74B2 **Steinkopf** S Africa
3D3 **Stein Mt** Can
74C2 **Stella** S Africa
5J4 **Stellarton** Can
74B3 **Stellenbosch** S Africa
22C2 **Stemaco** Mexico
36C2 **Stenay** France
42C2 **Stendal** Germany
45H8 **Stepanakert** Azerbaijan
11C2 **Stephen** USA
78B2 **Stephens,C** NZ
75B2 **Stephens Creek** Aust
12B1 **Stephenson** USA
10M4 **Stephens Pass** USA
7N5 **Stephenville** Can
16C3 **Stephenville** USA
10F4 **Stepovak B** USA
74D3 **Sterkstroom** S Africa
16B1 **Sterling** Colorado, USA
12B2 **Sterling** Illinois, USA
16C2 **Sterling** Kansas, USA
11B2 **Sterling** N Dakota, USA
16B3 **Sterling City** USA
12C2 **Sterling Heights** USA
44K5 **Sterlitamak** Russian Fed
3F3 **Stettler** Can
12C2 **Steubenville** USA
4B3 **Stevenson L** Can
12B2 **Stevens Point** USA
6D3 **Stevens Village** USA
3B2 **Stewart** Can
19C3 **Stewart** USA
10L3 **Stewart** *R* Can
10L3 **Stewart Crossing** Can
78A3 **Stewart I** NZ
77F1 **Stewart Is** Solomon Is
6E3 **Stewart River** Can
14B3 **Stewartstown** USA
11D3 **Stewartville** USA
74D2 **Steyn** S Africa
74D3 **Steynsburg** S Africa
42C3 **Steyr** Austria
74C3 **Steytlerville** S Africa
37D3 **Stia** Italy
10L4 **Stika** USA
3B2 **Stikine** *R* Can
10M4 **Stikine Ranges** *Mts* Can
11D2 **Stillwater** Minnesota, USA
17C2 **Stillwater** Oklahoma, USA
19C3 **Stillwater Range** *Mts* USA
4E4 **Stimson** Can
16B2 **Stinett** USA
75A2 **Stirling** Aust
34D3 **Stirling** Scot
36E3 **Stockach** Germany
14D1 **Stockbridge** USA
42D3 **Stockerau** Austria
32H7 **Stockholm** Sweden
35D5 **Stockport** Eng
20B2 **Stockton** California, USA
35E4 **Stockton** Eng
16C2 **Stockton** Kansas, USA
17D2 **Stockton L** USA
35D5 **Stoke-on-Trent** Eng
4E4 **Stokes Bay** Can
32A2 **Stokkseyri** Iceland
32G5 **Stokmarknes** Nor
49P2 **Stolbovoy, Ostrov** *I* Russian Fed
32K8 **Stolbtsy** Belorussia
43F2 **Stolin** Belorussia
14C3 **Stone Harbor** USA
34D3 **Stonehaven** Scot
17C3 **Stonewall** USA
10H3 **Stony** *R* USA
5K3 **Stony I** Can
3J2 **Stony L** Can
4E3 **Stooping** *R* Can
32H5 **Storavan** *L* Sweden
32G6 **Støren** Nor
75E3 **Storm B** Aust
11C3 **Storm Lake** USA
34B2 **Stornoway** Scot
43F3 **Storozhinets** Ukraine
14D2 **Storrs** USA
32G6 **Storsjön** *L* Sweden
32H5 **Storuman** Sweden
11A3 **Story** USA
3H4 **Stoughton** Can
14E1 **Stoughton** USA
36A1 **Stour** *R* Eng
35F5 **Stowmarket** Eng
53C1 **Stoyba** Russian Fed
34B4 **Strabane** N Ire
75E3 **Strahan** Aust
42C2 **Stralsund** Germany
74B3 **Strand** S Africa
32F6 **Stranda** Nor
32H7 **Strängnäs** Sweden
34C4 **Stranraer** Scot
38D2 **Strasbourg** France
13D3 **Strasburg** USA
20C2 **Stratford** California, USA
4E5 **Stratford** Can
14D2 **Stratford** Connecticut, USA
78B1 **Stratford** NZ
16B2 **Stratford** Texas, USA
35E5 **Stratford-on-Avon** Eng
75A3 **Strathalbyn** Aust
34C4 **Strathclyde** Region, Scot
3F3 **Strathmore** Can
13E1 **Stratton** USA
12B2 **Streator** USA
37C2 **Stresa** Italy
40D3 **Stretto de Messina** *Str* Italy/Sicily
40D3 **Stroboli** *I* Italy
28C4 **Stroeder** Arg
34D2 **Stromness** Scot
32D3 **Strømø** Faroes
17C1 **Stromsburg** USA
32H6 **Stromsund** Sweden
32G6 **Ströms Vattudal** *L* Sweden
34D2 **Stronsay** *I* Scot
35D6 **Stroud** Eng
14C2 **Stroudsburg** USA
41E2 **Struma** *R* Bulg
35C5 **Strumble Head** *Pt* Wales
41E2 **Strumica** Macedonia, Yugos
43E3 **Stryy** Ukraine
43E3 **Stryy** *R* Ukraine
75B1 **Strzelecki Creek** *R* Aust
15E4 **Stuart** Florida, USA
11C3 **Stuart** Nebraska, USA
3D3 **Stuart** *R* Can
10F3 **Stuart I** USA
3D3 **Stuart L** Can
37D1 **Stubaier Alpen** *Mts* Austria
32H8 **Stubice** Pol
55D3 **Stung Sen** Camb
55D3 **Stung Treng** Camb
4C2 **Stupart** *R* Can
40B2 **Stura** *R* Italy
79G7 **Sturge I** Ant
12B2 **Sturgeon Bay** USA
4F4 **Sturgeon Falls** Can
4C4 **Sturgeon L** Can
12B3 **Sturgis** Kentucky, USA
12B2 **Sturgis** Michigan, USA
11B3 **Sturgis** S Dakota, USA
76B2 **Sturt Creek** *R* Aust
75B1 **Sturt Desert** Aust
74D3 **Stuttemeim** S Africa
17D3 **Stuttgart** USA
42B3 **Stuttgart** Germany
32A1 **Stykkishólmur** Iceland
43F2 **Styr'** *R* Ukraine
49M4 **Styudyanka** Russian Fed
29D2 **Suaçuí Grande** *R* Brazil
66C3 **Suakin** Sudan
54A3 **Suan** N Korea
52E5 **Su-ao** Taiwan
28C2 **Suardi** Arg
56C2 **Subi** *I* Indon
41D1 **Subotica** Serbia, Yugos
45D6 **Suceava** Rom
22C2 **Suchixtepec** Mexico
26E7 **Sucre** Bol
29B2 **Sucuriú** R, Brazil
72C2 **Sudan** Republic, Africa
4E4 **Sudbury** Can
35F5 **Sudbury** Eng
72C3 **Sudd** *Swamp* Sudan
27G2 **Suddie** Guyana
65B4 **Sudr** Egypt
72C3 **Sue** *R* Sudan
10M4 **Suemez I** USA
64B4 **Suez** Egypt
64B3 **Suez Canal** Egypt
64B4 **Suez,G of** Egypt
14C2 **Suffern** USA
35F5 **Suffolk** County, Eng
13D3 **Suffolk** USA
13E2 **Sugarloaf Mt** USA
75D2 **Sugarloaf Pt** Aust
3H3 **Suggi L** Can
49R3 **Sugoy** *R* Russian Fed
67G2 **Suhār** Oman
50D1 **Sühbaatar** Mongolia
60B3 **Sui** Pak
53C2 **Suibin** China
52C2 **Suide** China
53C3 **Suifenhe** China
53B2 **Suihua** China
53B2 **Suileng** China
52B3 **Suining** China
36C2 **Suippes** France
33B3 **Suir** *R* Irish Rep
52C3 **Sui Xian** China
52E1 **Suizhong** China
60C3 **Sujāngarth** India
56C4 **Sukabumi** Indon
56D3 **Sukadana** Borneo, Indon
56C4 **Sukadana** Sumatra, Indon
53E4 **Sukagawa** Japan
56D3 **Sukaraya** Indon
44F5 **Sukhinichi** Russian Fed
44G4 **Sukhona** *R* Russian Fed
45G7 **Sukhumi** Georgia
7N3 **Sukkertoppen** Greenland
7N3 **Sukkertoppen Isflade** *Gl* Greenland
32L6 **Sukkozero** Russian Fed
60B3 **Sukkur** Pak
62C1 **Sukma** India
53D2 **Sukpay** *R* Russian Fed
73B6 **Sukses** Namibia
54B4 **Sukumo** Japan
3D2 **Sukunka** *R* Can
45F5 **Sula** *R* Russian Fed
60B3 **Sulaiman Range** *Mts* Pak
34B2 **Sula Sgeir** *I* Scot
57B3 **Sulawesi** *I* Indon
57B3 **Sulawesi Sulatan** Prov, Indon
57B3 **Sulawesi Tengah** Prov, Indon
57B3 **Sulawesi Tenggara** Prov, Indon
57B3 **Sulawesi Utara** Prov, Indon
71H4 **Suleja** Nig
34C2 **Sule Skerry** *I* Scot
41F1 **Sulina** Rom
32H5 **Sulitjelma** Nor
26B4 **Sullana** Peru
17D2 **Sullivan** USA
3C3 **Sullivan Bay** Can
3F3 **Sullivan L** Can
36B3 **Sully-sur-Loire** France
40C2 **Sulmona** Italy
17D3 **Sulphur** Louisiana, USA
17C3 **Sulphur** Oklahoma, USA
17C3 **Sulphur Springs** USA
4E4 **Sultan** Can
45E8 **Sultan Dağlari** *Mts* Turk
61B2 **Sultānpur** India
57F9 **Sulu Arch** Phil
51E6 **Sulu S** Philip
36E2 **Sulz** Germany
25D3 **Sumampa** Arg
56A2 **Sumatera** *I* Indon
57B4 **Sumba** *I* Indon
56E4 **Sumbawa** *I* Indon
56E4 **Sumbawa Besar** Indon
73D4 **Sumbawanga** Tanz
34E2 **Sumburgh Head** *Pt* Scot
56D4 **Sumenep** Indon
45H7 **Sumgait** Azerbaijan
73B5 **Sumbe** Angola
50H3 **Sumisu** *I* Japan
3E4 **Summerland** Can
5J4 **Summerside** Can
3B2 **Summer Str** USA
6F4 **Summit Lake** Can
19C3 **Summits Mt** USA
78B2 **Sumner,L** NZ
54B4 **Sumoto** Japan
15C2 **Sumter** USA
45E5 **Sumy** Ukraine
18D1 **Sun** *R* USA
54D2 **Sunagawa** Japan
54A3 **Sunan** N Korea
14B2 **Sunbury** USA
28C2 **Sunchales** Arg
28C1 **Suncho Corral** Arg
53B4 **Sunch'ŏn** N Korea
53B5 **Sunch'ŏn** S Korea
11B3 **Sundance** USA
61B3 **Sundargarh** India
61C3 **Sunderbans** *Swamp* India
34E4 **Sunderland** Eng
3F3 **Sundre** Can
13D1 **Sundridge** Can
32H6 **Sundsvaall** Sweden
56E3 **Sungaianyar** Indon
56B3 **Sungaisalak** Indon
56F6 **Sungai Siput** Malay
56F6 **Sungei Petani** Malay
57A4 **Sungguminasa** Indon
18C1 **Sunnyside** USA
19B3 **Sunnyvale** USA
12B2 **Sun Prairie** USA
49N3 **Suntar** Russian Fed
63E3 **Suntsar** Pak
18D2 **Sun Valley** USA
53B2 **Sunwu** China
71F4 **Sunyani** Ghana
44E3 **Suojarvi** Russian Fed
54B4 **Suō-nada** *B* Japan
32K6 **Suonejoki** Fin
61C2 **Supaul** India
19D4 **Superior** Arizona, USA
17C1 **Superior** Nebraska, USA
12A1 **Superior** Wisconsin, USA
12B1 **Superior,L** USA/Can
55C3 **Suphan Buri** Thai
64D2 **Süphan Dağ** Turk
51G7 **Supiori** *I* Indon
57C2 **Supu** Indon
66D3 **Sūq 'Abs** Yemen
64E3 **Suq ash Suyukh** Iraq
65D1 **Suqaylibīyah** Syria
52D3 **Suqian** China
Suqutra = Socotra
67G2 **Sūr** Oman
44H5 **Sura** *R* Russian Fed
56D4 **Surabaya** Indon
54C4 **Suraga-wan** *B* Japan
56D4 **Surakarta** Indon
65D1 **Sūrān** Syria
75C1 **Surat** Aust
60C4 **Sūrat** India
60C3 **Sūratgarh** India
55B4 **Surat Thani** Thai
60C4 **Surendranagar** India
14C3 **Surf City** USA
48J3 **Surgut** Russian Fed
62B1 **Suriāpet** India
38D2 **Sürich** Switz
57G9 **Surigao** Phil
55C3 **Surin** Thai
27G3 **Surinam** Republic, S America
20B2 **Sur,Pt** USA
35E6 **Surrey** County, Eng
37C1 **Sursee** Switz
69A1 **Surt** Libya
32A2 **Surtsey** *I* Iceland
56B3 **Surulangan** Indon
37B2 **Susa** Italy
54B4 **Susa** Japan
54B4 **Susaki** Japan
19B2 **Susanville** USA
37D1 **Süsch** Switz
10J3 **Susitna** *R* USA
14C2 **Susquehanna** USA
14B3 **Susquehanna** *R* USA
14C2 **Sussex** USA
35E6 **Sussex West** Eng
3C2 **Sustut Peak** *Mt* Can
74C3 **Sutherland** S Africa
16B1 **Sutherland** USA
60C2 **Sutlej** *R* Pak
19B3 **Sutter Creek** USA
12C3 **Sutton** USA
4E3 **Sutton** *R* Can
54D2 **Suttsu** Japan
10G4 **Sutwik I** USA
77G2 **Suva** Fiji
53D4 **Suwa** Japan
43E2 **Suwałki** Pol
15C3 **Suwannee** *R* USA
65C2 **Suweilih** Jordan
53B4 **Suwŏn** S Korea
52D3 **Su Xian** China
54C3 **Suzaka** Japan
52E3 **Suzhou** China
53D4 **Suzu** Japan
54C4 **Suzuka** Japan
54C3 **Suzu-misaki** *C* Japan
48C2 **Svalbard** *Is* Barents S
43E3 **Svalyava** Ukraine
7N2 **Svartenhuk Halvø** *Region* Greenland
32G5 **Svartisen** *Mt* Nor
55D3 **Svay Rieng** Camb
32G6 **Sveg** Sweden
32G7 **Svendborg** Den
7J1 **Sverdrup Chan** Can
6H2 **Sverdrup Is** Can
53D2 **Svetlaya** Russian Fed
43E2 **Svetlogorsk** Russian Fed
32K6 **Svetogorsk** Russian Fed
41E2 **Svetozarevo** Serbia, Yugos
41F2 **Svilengrad** Bulg
43F2 **Svir'** Belrussia
44E3 **Svir'** *R* Russian Fed
42D3 **Švitavy** Czech Republic
53B1 **Svobodnyy** Russian Fed
32G5 **Svolvaer** Nor
77E3 **Swain Reefs** Aust
77H2 **Swains** *I* American Samoa
15C2 **Swainsboro** USA
74B1 **Swakop** *R* Namibia
74A1 **Swakopmund** Namibia
35E4 **Swale** *R* Eng

Swallow Reef
Taurage

56D1 Swallow Reef I S E Asia
62B2 Swāmihalli India
21D3 Swan I Honduras
35E6 Swanage Eng
75B3 Swan Hill Aust
3E3 Swan Hills Can
3E3 Swan Hills Mts Can
23A3 Swan I Caribbean
4A3 Swan L Can
6H4 Swan River Can
35D6 Swansea Wales
35D6 Swansea B Wales
74C3 Swartberge Mts S Africa
74D2 Swartruggens S Africa
4E4 Swastika Can
Swatow = Shantou
74E2 Swaziland Kingdom, S Africa
32G7 Sweden Kingdom, N Europe
71F4 Swedru Ghana
18B2 Sweet Home USA
16B3 Sweetwater USA
11A3 Sweetwater R USA
74C3 Swellendam S Africa
42D2 Świdnica Pol
42D2 Świdwin Pol
42D2 Świebodzin Pol
43D2 Świecie Pol
3G3 Swift Current Can
11A1 Swift Current Creek R Can
3B1 Swift River Can
35E6 Swindon Eng
42C2 Świnoujście Pol
38D2 Switzerland Federal Republic, Europe
35B5 Swords Irish Rep
32D3 Syderø Faroes
75D2 Sydney Aust
7M5 Sydney Can
11D1 Sydney L Can
5J4 Sydney Mines Can
44J3 Syktyvkar Russian Fed
15B2 Sylacauga USA
32G6 Sylarna Mt Sweden
61D3 Sylhet Bang
42B1 Sylt I Germany
12C2 Sylvania USA
3D2 Sylvia,Mt Can
22B1 Symon Mexico
79G11 Syowa Base Ant
Syracuse = Siracusa
16B2 Syracuse Kansas, USA
14B1 Syracuse New York, USA
13D2 Syracuse USA
48H5 Syr Darya R Kazakhstan
64C2 Syria Republic, S W Asia
44L4 Sysert' Russian Fed
44H5 Syzran' Russian Fed
42C2 Szczecin Pol
42D2 Szczecinek Pol
43E2 Szczytno Pol
43E3 Szeged Hung
43D3 Székesfehérvár Hung
43D3 Szekszard Hung
43D3 Szolnok Hung
42D3 Szombathely Hung
42D2 Szprotawa Pol

T

74D3 Tabankulu S Africa
76E1 Tabar Is PNG
63D2 Tabas Iran
22B1 Tabasco Mexico
22D2 Tabasco State, Mexico
26E4 Tabatinga Brazil
70B2 Tabelbala Alg
55C3 Tabeng Camb
3F4 Taber Can
57F8 Tablas I Phil
74B3 Table Mt S Africa
10K2 Table Mt USA
17D2 Table Rock Res USA
56C3 Taboali Indon
42C3 Tábor Czech Republic
72D4 Tabora Tanz
44L4 Tabory Russian Fed
70B4 Tabou Ivory Coast
71D1 Taboursouk Tunisia
63B1 Tabrīz Iran
64C4 Tabūk S Arabia
22B2 Tacámbaro Mexico
59G1 Tacheng China
57G8 Tacloban Phil
26D7 Tacna Peru
19D4 Tacna USA
8A2 Tacoma USA
14D1 Taconic Range USA
28E2 Tacuan R Urug
28D2 Tacuarembó Urug
29A3 Tacuati Par
72E2 Tadjoura Djibouti
66D4 Tadjoura,G of Djibouti
4B2 Tadoule L Can
5H4 Tadoussac Can
62B2 Tādpatri India
53B4 Taebaek Sanmaek Mts S Korea
54A3 Taech'on S Korea
54A3 Taedong R N Korea
54A3 Taegang-got Pen N Korea
53B4 Taegu S Korea
53B5 Taehŭksan I S Korea
54A2 Taehung N Korea
53B4 Taejŏn S Korea
56G7 Taesek Dampar L Malay
39B1 Tafalla Spain
70C2 Tafasaset Watercourse Alg
35D6 Taff R Wales
65C3 Tafila Jordan
20C3 Taft USA
45F6 Taganrog Russian Fed
70A3 Tagant Region, Maur
61E3 Tagaung Burma
57F9 Tagbilaran Phil
3B2 Tagish L Can
37E1 Tagliamento R Italy
70B2 Taguenout Hagguerete Well Maur
77E2 Tagula I Solomon Is
57G9 Tagum Phil
Tagus = Tejo
70C2 Tahat, Mt Alg
xxixM5 Tahiti I Pacific O
63E3 Tahlab R Iran
17C2 Tahlequah USA
19B3 Tahoe City USA
19B3 Tahoe,L USA
16B3 Tahoka USA
70C3 Tahoua Niger
66B1 Tahta Egypt
57C2 Tahulandang I Indon
57C2 Tahuna Indon
52D2 Tai'an China
52B3 Taibai Shan Mt China
52D1 Taibus Qi China
52E5 T'ai-chung Taiwan
78B3 Taieri R NZ
52C2 Taihang Shan China
78C1 Taihape NZ
52E3 Tai Hu L China
54D2 Taiki Japan
53A2 Tailai China
56A3 Taileleo Indon
75A3 Tailem Bend Aust
34C3 Tain Scot
52E5 T'ai-nan Taiwan
29D2 Taiobeiras Brazil
52E5 T'ai pei Taiwan
55C5 Taiping Malay
54D3 Taira Japan
56B3 Tais Indon
54B3 Taisha Japan
25B7 Taitao,Pen de Chile
52E5 T'ai-tung Taiwan
32K5 Taivelkoski Fin
50F4 Taiwan Republic, China
Taiwan Haixia = Formosa Str
65C3 Taiyiba Jordan
52C2 Taiyuan China
52D3 Taizhou China
66D4 Ta 'izz Yemen
59E2 Tajikistan
39B1 Tajo R Spain
55B2 Tak Thai
53D4 Takada Japan
54B4 Takahashi Japan
78B2 Takaka NZ
53C5 Takamatsu Japan
53D4 Takaoka Japan
78B1 Takapuna NZ
53D4 Takasaki Japan
54C3 Takayama Japan
66C4 Takazie R Eth
53D4 Takefu Japan
56A2 Takengon Indon
55C3 Takeo Camb
54B4 Takeo Japan
Take-shima = Tok-do
63B1 Takestān Iran
54B4 Taketa Japan
54D2 Takikawa Japan
54D2 Takinoue Japan
6G3 Takiyvak L Can
72D2 Takkaze R Eth
3C2 Takla L Can
3C2 Takla Landing Can
10F3 Takslesluk L USA
3B2 Taku R Can
10M3 Taku Arm R Can
3B2 Taku Gl USA
71J4 Takum Nig
22B1 Tala Mexico
43D3 Talabanya Hung
57C3 Talaga Indon
60C2 Talagang Pak
28A2 Talagante Chile
62B3 Talaimannar Sri Lanka
70C3 Talak Desert, Region, Niger
56B3 Talangbetutu Indon
26B4 Talara Peru
76E1 Talasea PNG
65B3 Talata Egypt
39A1 Talavera de la Reina Spain
28A3 Talca Chile
28A3 Talcahuano Chile
61C3 Tālcher India
53A1 Talden Russian Fed
59F1 Taldy Kurgan Kazakhstan
57B3 Taliabu Indon
60B1 Taligan Afghan
72D3 Tali Post Sudan
56E4 Taliwang Indon
10H3 Talkeetna USA
10J3 Talkeetna Mts USA
65A3 Talkha Egypt
15B2 Talladega USA
64D2 Tall 'Afar Iraq
15C2 Tallahassee USA
37B2 Tallard France
65D1 Tall Bīsah Syria
44C4 Tallinn Estonia
64C3 Tall Kalakh Syria
17D3 Tallulah USA
50B1 Tal'menka Russian Fed
45E6 Tal'noye Ukraine
43E2 Talpaki Russian Fed
25B3 Taltal Chile
75C1 Talwood Aust
11D3 Tama USA
56E2 Tamabo Range Mts Malay
71F4 Tamale Ghana
70C2 Tamanrasset Alg
70C2 Tamanrasset Watercourse Alg
14C2 Tamaqua USA
Tamatave = Toamasina
22A1 Tamazula Durango, Mexico
22B2 Tamazula Jalisco, Mexico
22C2 Tamazulapán Mexico
22C1 Tamazunchale Mexico
70A3 Tambacounda Sen
28D2 Tambores Urug
45G5 Tambov Russian Fed
39A1 Tambre R Spain
57B3 Tambu Indon
72C3 Tambura Sudan
70A3 Tamchaket Maur
39A1 Tamega R Port
22C1 Tamiahua Mexico
62B2 Tamil Nādu State, India
55D2 Tam Ky Viet
15C3 Tampa USA
15E4 Tampa B USA
32J6 Tampere Fin
22C1 Tampico Mexico
56G7 Tampin Malay
50E2 Tamsagbulag Mongolia
37E1 Tamsweg Austria
61D3 Tamu Burma
22C1 Tamuis Mexico
75D2 Tamworth Aust
35E5 Tamworth Eng
44D1 Tana Nor
72D2 Tana L Eth
72E4 Tana R Kenya
32K5 Tana R Nor/Fin
54C4 Tanabe Japan
32K4 Tanafjord Inlet Nor
10C6 Tanaga I USA
56E3 Tanahgrogot Indon
57B4 Tanahjampea I Indon
51G7 Tanahmerah Indon
57A4 Tanakeke I Indon
10H2 Tanana USA
10J3 Tanana R USA
Tananarive = Antananarivo
10C6 Tananga Pass USA
37C2 Tanaro R Italy
53B3 Tanch'ŏn N Korea
28D3 Tandil Arg
56C2 Tandjong Datu Pt Indon
51G7 Tandjung d'Urville C Indon
56A1 Tandjung Jambuair C Indon
56E3 Tandjung Layar C Indon
56C3 Tandjung Lumut C Indon
56E2 Tandjung Mangkalihet C Indon
56D3 Tandjung Sambar C Indon
56D2 Tandjung Sirik C Malay
51G7 Tandjung Vals C Indon
60B3 Tando Adam Pak
60B3 Tando Muhammad Khan Pak
75B2 Tandou L Aust
62B1 Tāndūr India
78C1 Taneatua NZ
53C5 Tanega-shima I Japan
55B2 Tanen Range Mts Burma/Thai
70B2 Tanezrouft Desert Region Alg
63D3 Tang Iran
72D4 Tanga Tanz
77E1 Tanga Is PNG
72C4 Tanganyika,L Tanz/Zaïre
71A1 Tanger Mor
59H2 Tanggula Shan Mts China
Tangier = Tanger
54A3 Tangjin S Korea
56B2 Tangjungpinang Indon
56G7 Tangkak Malay
59G2 Tangra Yumco L China
52D2 Tangshan China
57F9 Tangub Phil
50D1 Tanguy Russian Fed
53B2 Tangwang He R China
53B2 Tangyuan China
Tanintharyi = Tenasserim
57F9 Tanjay Phil
56D4 Tanjong Bugel C Indon
56C4 Tanjong Cangkuang C Indon
56F7 Tanjong Malim Malay
56D3 Tanjong Puting C Indon
56D3 Tanjong Selatan C Indon
56E3 Tanjung Indon
56A2 Tanjungbalai Indon
57C3 Tanjungbaliha Indon
56B3 Tanjung Jabung Pt Indon
57A4 Tanjung Karossa Indon
57A2 Tanjung Manimbaya Pt Indon
56C3 Tanjungpandan Indon
56C4 Tanjung Priok Indon
56E2 Tanjungredeb Indon
76A1 Tanjung Selatan Pt Indon
56E2 Tanjungselor Indon
57B2 Tanjung Torawitan C Indon
76C1 Tanjung Vals Pt Indon
60C2 Tank Pak
77F2 Tanna I Vanuatu
50C1 Tannu Ola Mts Russian Fed
71F4 Tano R Ghana
70C3 Tanout Niger
22C1 Tanquián Mexico
52E4 Tan-shui Taiwan
61B2 Tansing Nepal
69C1 Tanta Egypt
70A2 Tan-Tan Mor
6B3 Tanunak USA
54A3 Tanyang S Korea
72D4 Tanzania Republic, Africa
53A2 Tao'an China
53A2 Tao'er He R China
52A3 Tao He R China
73E6 Taola168naro Madag
52B2 Taole China
16A2 Taos USA
71B2 Taounate Mor
71B2 Taourirt Mor
44D4 Tapa Estonia
21C3 Tapachula Mexico
56F6 Tapah Malay
27G4 Tapajós R Brazil
56A2 Tapaktuan Indon
28C3 Tapalquén Arg
56B3 Tapan Indon
22D2 Tapanatepec Mexico
78A3 Tapanui NZ
26E5 Tapauá R Brazil
28E2 Tapes Brazil
60D4 Tapi R India
61C2 Taplejung Nepal
71G3 Tapoa R Burkina
13D3 Tappahannock USA
78B2 Tapuaeniku Mt NZ
29C3 Tapuaritinga Brazil
57F9 Tapul Group Is Phil
26F4 Tapurucuara Brazil
29B2 Taquari R Brazil
75D1 Tara Aust
48J4 Tara Russian Fed
48J4 Tara R Russian Fed
41D2 Tara R Bosnia-Herzegovina/Montenegro, Yugos
71J4 Taraba R Nig
71J4 Taraba State Nig
26F7 Tarabuco Bol
Tarābulus = Tripoli
39B1 Taracón Spain
78C1 Taradale NZ
56E2 Tarakan Indon
57B4 Taramana Indon
34B3 Taransay I Scot
40D2 Taranto Italy
26C5 Tarapoto Peru
38C2 Tarare France
78C2 Tararua Range Mts NZ
44H2 Tarasovo Russian Fed
70C2 Tarat Alg
78C1 Tarawera NZ
39B1 Tarazona Spain
34D3 Tarbat Ness Pen Scot
60C2 Tarbela Res Pak
34C4 Tarbert Strathclyde, Scot
34B3 Tarbert Western Isles, Scot
38B3 Tarbes France
15D1 Tarboro USA
76C4 Tarcoola Aust
75C2 Tarcoon Aust
48H4 Tarda Russian Fed
53D2 Tardoki Yani, Gora Mt Russian Fed
75D2 Taree Aust
70A2 Tarfaya Mor
18D2 Targhee P USA
69A1 Tarhūnah Libya
67F2 Tarīf UAE
26F8 Tarija Bol
62B2 Tarikere India
67E3 Tarīm Yemen
72D4 Tarime Tanz
59G1 Tarim He R China
59G2 Tarim Pendi Basin China
60B2 Tarin Kut Afghan
74D3 Tarkastad S Africa
17C1 Tarkio USA
44J3 Tarko Sale Russian Fed
71F4 Tarkwa Ghana
57F7 Tarlac Phil
26C6 Tarma Peru
38C3 Tarn R France
43E2 Tarnobrzeg Pol
43E3 Tarnów Pol
37C2 Taro R Italy
76D3 Taroom Aust
70B1 Taroudannt Morocco
39C1 Tarragona Spain
75E3 Tarraleah Aust
39C1 Tarrasa Spain
14D2 Tarrytown USA
64B2 Tarsus Turk
34E2 Tartan Oilfield N Sea
37D2 Tartaro R Italy
44D4 Tartu Estonia
64C3 Tartūs Syria
29D2 Tarumirim Brazil
56A2 Tarutung Indon
37E1 Tarvisio Italy
13D1 Taschereau Can
58D1 Tashauz Turkmenistan
61D2 Tashigang Bhutan
59E1 Tashkent Uzbekistan
63E1 Tashkepri Turkmenistan
48K4 Tashtagol Russian Fed
49K4 Tashtyp Russian Fed
56C4 Tasikmalaya Indon
65C2 Tasīl Syria
5H2 Tasiujaq Can
7N2 Tasiussaq Greenland
72B2 Tasker Well Niger
78B2 Tasman B NZ
76D5 Tasmania I Aust
78B2 Tasman Mts NZ
75E3 Tasman Pen Aust
77E4 Tasman S NZ Aust
64C1 Taşova Turk
70C2 Tassili du Hoggar Desert, Region, Alg
70C2 Tassili N'jjer Desert, Region, Alg
70B2 Tata Mor
71E2 Tataouine Tunisia
48J4 Tatarsk Russian Fed
53E2 Tatarskiy Proliv Str Russian Fed
44H4 Tatarstan Respublika, Russian Fed
54C3 Tateyama Japan
3E1 Tathlina L Can
66D3 Tathlith S Arabia
10J3 Tatitlek USA
3D3 Tatla Lake Can
7J4 Tatnam, Cape Can
43D3 Tatry Mts Pol/Slovakia
54B4 Tatsuno Japan
60B4 Tatta Pak
29C3 Tatuí Brazil
16B3 Tatum USA
64D2 Tatvan Turk
77H2 Ta'u I American Samoa
27K5 Tauá Brazil
29C3 Taubaté Brazil
36E1 Taufstein Mt Germany
78C1 Taumarunui NZ
74C2 Taung S Africa
55B2 Taungdwingyi Burma
55B1 Taung-gyi Burma
55A2 Taungup Burma
60C2 Taunsa Pak
35D6 Taunton Eng
14E2 Taunton USA
36E1 Taunus Region, Germany
78C1 Taupo NZ
78C1 Taupo,L NZ
43E1 Taurage Lithuania

Tauranga Tione

78C1 **Tauranga** NZ
78C1 **Tauranga Harbour** *B* NZ
78B1 **Tauroa Pt** NZ
7J3 **Tavani** Can
48H4 **Tavda** *R* Russian Fed
77H2 **Taveuni** *I* Fiji
39A2 **Tavira** Port
35C6 **Tavistock** Eng
55B3 **Tavoy** Burma
55B3 **Tavoy Pt** Burma
64A2 **Tavsanli** Turk
78B2 **Tawa** NZ
17C3 **Tawakoni,L** USA
12C2 **Tawas City** USA
56E2 **Tawau** Malay
72C2 **Taweisha** Sudan
57F9 **Tawitawi** *I* Phil
57F9 **Tawitawi Group** *Is* Phil
22C2 **Taxco** Mexico
22C2 **Taxcoco** Mexico
34D3 **Tay** *R* Scot
56D3 **Tayan** Indon
72E3 **Tayeeglow** Somalia
10F2 **Taylor** Alaska, USA
3D2 **Taylor** Can
12C2 **Taylor** Michigan, USA
17C3 **Taylor** Texas, USA
16A2 **Taylor,Mt** USA
12B3 **Taylorville** USA
66C1 **Taymā'** S Arabia
49L3 **Taymura** *R* Russian Fed
49M2 **Taymyr, Ozero** *L* Russian Fed
49L2 **Taymyr, Poluostrov** *Pen* Russian Fed
55D3 **Tay Ninh** Viet
22A1 **Tayoltita** Mexico
49L4 **Tayshet** Russian Fed
50C2 **Tayshir** Mongolia
34D3 **Tayside** Region, Scot
57E8 **Taytay** Phil
63E2 **Tayyebāt** Iran
71B2 **Taza** Mor
54D3 **Tazawako** Japan
54D3 **Tazawa-ko** *L* Japan
3G2 **Tazin L** Can
69B2 **Tazirbu** Libya
10J3 **Tazlina L** USA
48J3 **Tazovskiy** Russian Fed
45G7 **Tbilisi** Georgia
71G4 **Tchaourou** Benin
72B4 **Tchibanga** Gabon
72B1 **Tchigai,Plat du** Niger
70C3 **Tchin Tabaradene** Niger
72B3 **Tcholliré** Cam
43D2 **Tczew** Pol
22A1 **Teacapán** Mexico
78A3 **Te Anau** NZ
78A3 **Te Anua,L** NZ
78C1 **Te Aroha** NZ
78C1 **Te Awamutu** NZ
71D1 **Tébessa** Alg
56A2 **Tebingtinggi** Indon
22B2 **Teboman** Mexico
22B2 **Tecailtlān** Mexico
19C4 **Tecate** Mexico
22B1 **Tecclotlán** Mexico
44L4 **Techa** *R* Russian Fed
22B2 **Tećpan** Mexico
22A1 **Tecuala** Mexico
41F1 **Tecuci** Rom
17C1 **Tecumseh** USA
58E2 **Tedzhen** Turkmenistan
48H6 **Tedzhen** *R* Turkmenistan
35E4 **Tees** *R* Eng
26F4 **Tefé** Brazil
56C4 **Tegal** Indon
56C4 **Tegineneng** Indon
21D3 **Tegucigalpa** Honduras
20C3 **Tehachapi** USA
20C3 **Tehachapi Mts** USA
19C3 **Tehachapi P** USA
6J3 **Tehek L** Can
57C3 **Tehoru** Indon
63C1 **Tehrān** Iran
22C2 **Tehuacán** Mexico
22C2 **Tehuantepec** Mexico
22C2 **Tehuitzingo** Mexico
35C5 **Teifi** *R* Wales
39A2 **Tejo** *R* Port
20C3 **Tejon P** USA
22B2 **Tejupilco** Mexico
11C3 **Tekamah** USA
78B2 **Tekapo,L** NZ
59F1 **Tekeli** Kazakhstan
64A1 **Tekirdağ** Turk
41F2 **Tekir Dağlari** *Mts* Turk
61D3 **Teknaf** Bang
57B3 **Teku** Indon
78C1 **Te Kuiti** NZ
21D3 **Tela** Honduras
45H7 **Telavi** Georgia
65C2 **Tel Aviv Yafo** Israel
3B2 **Telegraph Creek** Can
28B3 **Telén** Arg
19C3 **Telescope Peak** *Mt* USA
27G5 **Teles Pires** *R* Brazil
37D1 **Telfs** Austria
49K4 **Teli** Russian Fed
45F9 **Telkalakh** Syria
65C3 **Tell el Meise** *Mt* Jordan
10E2 **Teller** USA
62B2 **Tellicherry** India
55C5 **Telok Anson** Malay
57C2 **Tēlok Buli** *B* Indon
56E2 **Tēlok Darvel** Malay
57B2 **Tēlok Dondo** *B* Indon
51G7 **Tēlok Flamingo** *B* Indon
57C2 **Tēlok Kau** *B* Indon
56D3 **Tēlok Kumai** *B* Indon
56E1 **Tēlok Labuk** *B* Malay
56C4 **Tēlok Pelabuanratu** *B* Indon
56E4 **Tēlok Saleh** *B* Indon
56D3 **Tēlok Sampit** *B* Indon
56C3 **Tēlok Sukadona** *B* Indon
22C2 **Teloloapán** Mexico
43E1 **Telšiai** Lithuania
56D3 **Telukbatang** Indon
51G7 **Teluk Berau** *B* Indon
56C4 **Telukbetung** Indon
57B3 **Teluk Bone** *B* Indon
51G7 **Teluk Cendrawasih** *B* Indon
56A2 **Telukdalam** Indon
57A3 **Teluk Mandar** *B* Indon
57B3 **Teluk Tolo** *B* Indon
57B3 **Teluk Tomini** *B* Indon
57C2 **Tēluk Weda** *B* Indon
71F4 **Tema** Ghana
4E4 **Temagami,L** Can
22C2 **Temascal** Mexico
56B3 **Tembesi** *R* Indon
56B3 **Tembilahan** Indon
23E5 **Temblador** Ven
20B3 **Temblor Range** *Mts* USA
55C5 **Temerloh** Malay
48G5 **Temir** Kazakhstan
48J4 **Temirtau** Kazakhstan
13F1 **Témiscouata,L** Can
4F4 **Témiscaming** Can
75C2 **Temora** Aust
19D4 **Tempe** USA
17C3 **Temple** USA
35B5 **Templemore** Irish Rep
20B3 **Templeton** USA
22C1 **Tempoal** Mexico
28A3 **Temuco** Chile
78B2 **Temuka** NZ
26C4 **Tena** Ecuador
62C1 **Tenāli** India
22C2 **Tenancingo** Mexico
55B3 **Tenasserim** Burma
35C6 **Tenby** Wales
25D2 **Tenco** *R* Par
66D4 **Tendaho** Eth
37B2 **Tende** France
37B2 **Tende** *P* Italy
62E3 **Ten Degree Chan** Indian O
71B2 **Tendrara** Mor
72B2 **Ténéré** *Desert Region* Niger
70A2 **Tenerife** *I* Canary Is
71C1 **Ténès** Alg
16A2 **Tenessee P** USA
55B1 **Teng** *R* Burma
48H4 **Tengiz, Ozero** *L* Kazakhstan
56E3 **Tenggarong** Indon
52A2 **Tengger Shamo** *Desert* China
62B3 **Tenkāsi** India
73C5 **Tenke** Zaïre
71F3 **Tenkodogo** Burkina
37E3 **Tenna** *R* Italy
76C2 **Tennant Creek** Aust
9E3 **Tennessee** State, USA
17E2 **Tennessee** *R* USA
28A2 **Teno** Chile
56E1 **Tenom** Malay
21C3 **Tenosique** Mexico
71A2 **Tensift** *R* Mor
57B3 **Tentena** Indon
75D1 **Tenterfield** Aust
15E4 **Ten Thousand Is** USA
22B1 **Teocaltiche** Mexico
29D2 **Teófilo Otôni** Brazil
22C2 **Teotihiucan** Hist Site, Mexico
22C2 **Teotitlan** Mexico
57C4 **Tepa** Indon
22B1 **Tepatitlan** Mexico
21B2 **Tepehuanes** Mexico
22C2 **Tepeji** Mexico
22B1 **Tepic** Mexico
42C2 **Teplice** Czech Republic
78C1 **Te Puke** NZ
22B1 **Tequila** Mexico
22C2 **Tequistepec** Mexico
39C1 **Ter** *R* Spain
70C3 **Téra** Niger
54C3 **Teradomari** Japan
40C2 **Teramo** Italy
70A1 **Terceira** *I* Açores
43F3 **Terebovlya** Ukraine
29B2 **Terenoz** Brazil
27K5 **Teresina** Brazil
29D3 **Teresópolis** Brazil
62E3 **Teressa** *I* Indian O
56G7 **Teriang** Malay
64C1 **Terme** Turk
58E2 **Termez** Uzbekistan
40C2 **Termoli** Italy
57C2 **Ternate** Indon
53D3 **Terney** Russian Fed
40C2 **Terni** Italy
43F3 **Ternopol** Ukraine
20C3 **Terra Bella** USA
3C3 **Terrace** Can
12B1 **Terrace Bay** Can
40C2 **Terracina** Italy
73C6 **Terrafirma** S Africa
79G8 **Terre Adélie** Region, Ant
17D4 **Terre Bonne B** USA
12B3 **Terre Haute** USA
17C3 **Terrell** USA
5L4 **Terrenceville** Can
11A2 **Terry** USA
42B2 **Terschelling** *I* Neth
39B1 **Teruel** Spain
6C2 **Teshekpuk** USA
71G4 **Teshi** *R* Nig
54D2 **Teshikaga** Japan
53E3 **Teshio** *R* Japan
54D2 **Teshio dake** *Mt* Japan
50C2 **Tesiyn Gol** *Mts* Mongolia
10M3 **Teslin** Can
10M4 **Teslin** *R* Can
10M3 **Teslin L** Can
49L5 **Teslyn Gol** *R* Mongolia
70C2 **Tessalit** Mali
70C3 **Tessaoua** Niger
71A2 **Tessaout** *R* Mor
66C3 **Tessenei** Eth
73D5 **Tete** Mozam
22B2 **Tetela** Mexico
43F2 **Teterev** *R* Ukraine
18D1 **Teton** *R* USA
18D2 **Teton Range** *Mts* USA
71A1 **Tetouan** Mor
44H5 **Tetyushi** Russian Fed
26F8 **Teuco** *R* Arg
22B1 **Teúl de Gonzalez Ortega** Mexico
57C4 **Teun** *I* Indon
54D2 **Teuri-tō** *I* Japan
40C2 **Tevere** *R* Italy
34D4 **Teviot** *R* Scot
48J4 **Tevriz** Russian Fed
78A3 **Te Waewae B** NZ
56D3 **Tewah** Indon
75D1 **Tewantin** Aust
52A3 **Têwo** China
17D3 **Texarkana** USA
17D3 **Texarkana,L** USA
75D1 **Texas** Aust
8C3 **Texas** State, USA
17D4 **Texas City** USA
42A2 **Texel** *I* Neth
16B2 **Texhoma** USA
17C3 **Texoma,L** USA
74D2 **Teyateyaneng** Lesotho
60A2 **Teyuarah** Afghan
22C2 **Teziutlán** Mexico
29B2 **Tezouro** Brazil
61D2 **Tezpur** India
55C1 **Tha** Laos
74D2 **Thabana Ntlenyana** *Mt* Lesotho
74D2 **Thaba Putsoa** *Mt* Lesotho
74D1 **Thabazimbi** S Africa
55B3 **Thagyettaw** Burma
55D1 **Thai Binh** Viet
55C2 **Thailand** Kingdom, S E Asia
55C3 **Thailand,G of** Thai
55D1 **Thai Nguyen** Viet
55D2 **Thakhek** Laos
60C2 **Thal** Pak
Thalassery = Tellicherry
55C4 **Thale Luang** *L* Thai
75C1 **Thallon** Aust
67F3 **Thamarit** Oman
78C1 **Thames** NZ
35F6 **Thames** *R* Eng
67E3 **Thamūd** Yemen
62A1 **Thāne** India
55D2 **Thanh Hoah** Viet
62B2 **Thanjavur** India
Thanlwin = Salween
36D3 **Thann** France
60C3 **Thar Desert** India
75B1 **Thargomindah** Aust
61E4 **Tharrawaddy** Burma
41E2 **Thásos** *I* Greece
55B2 **Thaton** Burma
55A2 **Thayetmyo** Burma
61E3 **Thazi** Burma
11B3 **Thedford** USA
67F1 **The Gulf** S W Asia
3G1 **Thekulthili L** Can
6H3 **Thelon** *R* Can
36A1 **The Naze** Eng
76E3 **Theodore** Aust
19D4 **Theodore Roosevelt L** USA
41E2 **Thermaïkós Kólpos** *G* Greece
18E2 **Thermopolis** USA
6F2 **Thesiger B** Can
4E4 **Thessalon** Can
41E2 **Thessaloníki** Greece
35F5 **Thetford** Eng
5G4 **Thetford Mines** Can
74D2 **Theunissen** S Africa
17D4 **Thibodaux** USA
6J4 **Thicket Portage** Can
11C2 **Thief River Falls** USA
18B2 **Thielsen,Mt** USA
38C2 **Thiers** France
70A3 **Thiès** Sen
72D4 **Thika** Kenya
61C2 **Thimphu** Bhutan
38D2 **Thionville** France
41F3 **Thíra** *I* Greece
35E4 **Thirsk** Eng
Thiruvananthapuram = Trivandrum
32F7 **Thisted** Den
41E3 **Thívai** Greece
38C2 **Thiviers** France
3G1 **Thoa** *R* Can
20C2 **Thomas A Eddison,L** USA
15C2 **Thomaston** Georgia, USA
13F2 **Thomaston** Maine, USA
35B5 **Thomastown** Irish Rep
15B2 **Thomasville** Alabama, USA
15C2 **Thomasville** Georgia, USA
15D1 **Thomasville** N Carolina, USA
7J2 **Thom Bay** Can
6J4 **Thompson** Can
17D1 **Thompson** USA
18C1 **Thompson Falls** USA
6G3 **Thompson Landing** Can
3D3 **Thompson** *R* Can
14D2 **Thompsonville** USA
15C2 **Thomson** USA
76D3 **Thomson** *R* Aust
55C3 **Thon Buri** Thai
55B2 **Thongwa** Burma
37B1 **Thonon-les-Bains** France
16A2 **Thoreau** USA
34D4 **Thornhill** Scot
38B2 **Thouars** France
13D2 **Thousand Is** Can/USA
18D1 **Three Forks** USA
3F3 **Three Hills** Can
77G4 **Three Kings Is** NZ
12B1 **Three Lakes** USA
55B2 **Three Pagodas P** Thai
20C2 **Three Rivers** California, USA
12B2 **Three Rivers** Michigan, USA
17F4 **Three Rivers** Texas, USA
18B2 **Three Sisters** *Mt* USA
7M2 **Thule** Greenland
37B1 **Thun** Switz
4D4 **Thunder Bay** Can
10F2 **Thunder Mt** USA
37B1 **Thuner See** *L* Switz
55B4 **Thung Song** Thai
37C1 **Thur** *R* Switz
42C2 **Thüringen** State, Germany
42C2 **Thüringen Wald** *Upland* Germany
35B5 **Thurles** Irish Rep
51H8 **Thursday I** Aust
34D2 **Thurso** Scot
79F4 **Thurston I** Ant
37C1 **Thusis** Switz
75B1 **Thylungra** Aust
52B5 **Tiandong** China
52B5 **Tian'e** China
52D2 **Tianjin** China
52B5 **Tianlin** China
53B3 **Tianqiaoling** China
52B3 **Tianshui** China
52A2 **Tianzhu** China
71C1 **Tiaret** Alg
29B3 **Tibagi** *R* Brazil
71J4 **Tibati** Cam
65C2 **Tiberias** Israel
65C2 **Tiberias,L** Israel
Tiber,R = Tevere,R
18D1 **Tiber Res** USA
72B1 **Tibesti** *Mountain Region* Chad
59G2 **Tibet** Autonomous Region, China
75B1 **Tibooburra** Aust
61B2 **Tibrikot** Nepal
21A2 **Tiburón** *I* Mexico
70B3 **Tichitt** Maur
70A2 **Tichla** Mor
37C2 **Ticino** *R* Italy/Switz
13E2 **Ticonderoga** USA
21D2 **Ticul** Mexico
70A3 **Tidjikja** Maur
37C1 **Tiefencastel** Switz
36C1 **Tiel** Neth
53B2 **Tieli** China
53A3 **Tieling** China
36B1 **Tielt** Belg
36C1 **Tienen** Belg
36E3 **Tiengen** Germany
48J5 **Tien Shan** *Mts* China/ Kirgizia
52D2 **Tientsin** China
32H6 **Tierp** Sweden
28A1 **Tierra Amarilla** Chile
16A2 **Tierra Amarilla** USA
22C2 **Tierra Blanca** Mexico
22C2 **Tierra Colorada** Mexico
25C8 **Tierra del Fuego** Territory, Arg
24C9 **Tierra del Fuego** *I* Chile/ Arg
29C3 **Tietê** Brazil
29B3 **Tiete** *R* Brazil
12C2 **Tiffin** USA
15C2 **Tifton** USA
57C3 **Tifu** Indon
10F5 **Tigalda** *I* USA
49R4 **Tigil** Russian Fed
71J4 **Tignere** Cam
5J4 **Tignish** Can
26C4 **Tigre** *R* Peru
26F2 **Tigre** *R* Ven
64E3 **Tigris** *R* Iraq
22C1 **Tihuatlán** Mexico
19C4 **Tijuana** Mexico
60D4 **Tikamgarh** India
44E4 **Tikhin** Russian Fed
45G6 **Tikhoretsk** Russian Fed
77F2 **Tikopia** *I* Solomon Is
64D3 **Tikrīt** Iraq
49O2 **Tiksi** Russian Fed
57B2 **Tilamuta** Indon
36C1 **Tilburg** Neth
35F6 **Tilbury** Eng
25C2 **Tilcara** Arg
75B1 **Tilcha** Aust
55A1 **Tilin** Burma
70C3 **Tillabéri** Niger
18B1 **Tillamook** USA
62E3 **Tillanchong** *I* Indian O
70C3 **Tillia** Niger
41F3 **Tílos** *I* Greece
75B2 **Tilpa** Aust
26C3 **Tiluá** Colombia
44H2 **Timanskiy Kryazh** *Mts* Russian Fed
78B2 **Timaru** NZ
45F6 **Timashevsk** Russian Fed
41E3 **Timbákion** Greece
17D4 **Timbalier B** USA
70B3 **Timbédra** Maur
Timbuktu = Tombouctou
70B3 **Timétrine Monts,** *Mts* Mali
70C3 **Timia** Niger
70C2 **Timimoun** Alg
41E1 **Timiş** *R* Rom
41E1 **Timişoara** Rom
4E4 **Timmins** Can
76B1 **Timor** *I* Indon
76B2 **Timor S** Aust/Indon
28C3 **Timote** Arg
65B3 **Timsâh,L** Egypt
15B1 **Tims Ford L** USA
57G9 **Tinaca Pt** Phil
23D5 **Tinaco** Ven
62B2 **Tindivanam** India
70B2 **Tindouf** Alg
37B2 **Tinée** *R* France
20C2 **Tinemaha Res** USA
70B2 **Tinfouchy** Alg
70C2 **Tin Fouye** Alg
10F2 **Tingmerkpuk Mt** USA
7O3 **Tingmiarmiut** Greenland
26C5 **Tingo Maria** Peru
70B3 **Tingrela** Ivory Coast
61C2 **Tingri** China
51H5 **Tinian** Pacific O
28B1 **Tinogasta** Arg
41F3 **Tinos** *I* Greece
61E2 **Tinsukia** India
35C6 **Tintagel Head** *Pt* Eng
70C2 **Tin Tarabine** *Watercourse* Alg
75B3 **Tintinara** Aust
70C2 **Tin Zaouaten** Alg
11B2 **Tioga** USA
14B2 **Tioga** *R* USA
20C2 **Tioga P** USA
55C5 **Tioman** *I* Malay
4E4 **Tionaga** Can
37D1 **Tione** Italy

Tsogt Ovoo Üsküdar

52B1 **Tsogt Ovoo** Mongolia
74D3 **Tsomo** S Africa
50D2 **Tsomog** Mongolia
54C4 **Tsu** Japan
54C3 **Tsubata** Japan
53E4 **Tsuchira** Japan
53E3 **Tsugaru-kaikyō** *Str* Japan
73B5 **Tsumeb** Namibia
73B6 **Tsumis** Namibia
54C3 **Tsunugi** Japan
53D4 **Tsuruga** Japan
53D4 **Tsuruoka** Japan
54C3 **Tsushima** Japan
53B5 **Tsushima** *I* Japan
Tsushima-Kaikyō = Korea Str
53C4 **Tsuyama** Japan
39A1 **Tua** *R* Port
56A2 **Tuangku** *I* Indon
45F7 **Tuapse** Russian Fed
78A3 **Tuatapere** NZ
19D3 **Tuba City** USA
25G3 **Tubarão** Brazil
65C2 **Tubas** Israel
57E9 **Tubbataha Reefs** *Is* Phil
42B3 **Tübingen** Germany
69B1 **Tubruq** Libya
14C3 **Tuckerton** USA
19D4 **Tucson** USA
25C3 **Tucumán** State, Arg
16B2 **Tucumcari** USA
28B2 **Tucunuco** Arg
26F2 **Tucupita** Ven
39B1 **Tudela** Spain
10N2 **Tudenet L** Can
64C3 **Tudmur** Syria
28C2 **Tuerto** Arg
74E2 **Tugela** *R* S Africa
75D2 **Tuggerah** *L* Aust
10H4 **Tugidak** *I* USA
57F7 **Tuguegarao** Phil
49P4 **Tugur** Russian Fed
53D1 **Tugur** *R* Russian Fed
52D2 **Tuhai He** *R* China
71F3 **Tui** *R* Burkina
10M2 **Tuktoyaktuk** Can
43E1 **Tukums** Latvia
73D4 **Tukuyu** Tanz
60B1 **Tukzar** Afghan
22C1 **Tula** Mexico
44F5 **Tula** Russian Fed
22C1 **Tulancingo** Mexico
56B3 **Tulangbawang** *R* Indon
20C2 **Tulare** USA
20C2 **Tulare Lake Bed** USA
16A3 **Tularosa** USA
26C3 **Tulcán** Colombia
45D7 **Tulcea** Rom
43F3 **Tul'chin** Ukraine
20C2 **Tule** *R* USA
73C6 **Tuli** Zim
74D1 **Tuli** *R* Zim
16B3 **Tulia** USA
10E5 **Tulik V** USA
65C2 **Tulkarm** Israel
15B1 **Tullahoma** USA
35B5 **Tullarnore** Irish Rep
38C2 **Tulle** France
37A2 **Tullins** France
17D3 **Tullos** USA
35B5 **Tullow** Irish Rep
14B1 **Tully** USA
17C2 **Tulsa** USA
64C3 **Tulūl ash Shāmīyah** *Desert Region* Syria/ S Arabia
49M4 **Tulun** Russian Fed
56D4 **Tulungagung** Indon
26C3 **Tumaco** Colombia
49R3 **Tumany** Russian Fed
75C3 **Tumbarumba** Aust
26B4 **Tumbes** Ecuador
75A2 **Tumby Bay** Aust
53B3 **Tumen** China
62B2 **Tumkūr** India
63E3 **Tump** Pak
55C4 **Tumpat** Malay
60D4 **Tumsar** India
71F3 **Tumu** Ghana
75C3 **Tumut** Aust
75C3 **Tumut** *R* Aust
23L1 **Tunapuna** Trinidad
64C2 **Tunceli** Turk
73D4 **Tunduma** Zambia
73D5 **Tunduru** Tanz
41F2 **Tundzha** *R* Bulg
62B1 **Tungabhadra** *R* India
50E4 **Tung-Chiang** Taiwan
32B2 **Tungnafellsjökull** *Mts* Iceland
10N3 **Tungsten** Can
62C1 **Tuni** India
71E1 **Tunis** Tunisia
68E4 **Tunisia** Republic, N Africa
26D2 **Tunja** Colombia
14C2 **Tunkhannock** USA
10F3 **Tuntutuliak** USA
5H2 **Tunulik** *R* Can
10F3 **Tununak** USA
5J2 **Tunungayualok I** Can
28B2 **Tunuyán** Arg
28B2 **Tunuyán** *R* Arg
20C2 **Tuolumne Meadows** USA
29B3 **Tupã** Brazil
29C2 **Tupaciguara** Brazil
28E1 **Tupancireta** Brazil
17E3 **Tupelo** USA
43G1 **Tupik** Russian Fed
26E8 **Tupiza** Bol
20C3 **Tupman** USA
13E2 **Tupper Lake** USA
28B2 **Tupungato** Arg
25C4 **Tupungato** *Mt* Arg
61D2 **Tura** India
49M3 **Tura** Russian Fed
44L4 **Tura** *R* Russian Fed
66D2 **Turabah** S Arabia
63D1 **Turān** Iran
49L4 **Turan** Russian Fed
64C3 **Turayf** S Arabia
63E3 **Turbat** Pak
26C2 **Turbo** Colombia
41E1 **Turda** Rom
48K5 **Turfan Depression** China
48H5 **Turgay** Kazakhstan
49L5 **Turgen Uul** *Mt* Mongolia
4F3 **Turgeon** *R* Can
64A2 **Turgutlu** Turk
64C1 **Turhal** Turk
32K7 **Türi** Estonia
39B2 **Turia** *R* Spain
Turin = Torino
44L4 **Turinsk** Russian Fed
53C2 **Turiy Rog** Russian Fed
72D3 **Turkana,L** Kenya/Eth
58E1 **Turkestan** Region, C Asia
59E1 **Turkestan** Kazakhstan
64C2 **Turkey** Republic, W Asia
48G5 **Turkmenistan**
63C1 **Turkmenskiy Zaliv** *B* Turkmenistan
23C2 **Turks Is** Caribbean
32J6 **Turku** Fin
72D3 **Turkwel** *R* Kenya
20B2 **Turlock** USA
20B2 **Turlock L** USA
3C2 **Turnagain** *R* Can
78C2 **Turnagain,C** NZ
21D3 **Turneffe I** Belize
14D1 **Turners Falls** USA
36C1 **Turnhout** Belg
3G2 **Turnor L** Can
41E2 **Turnu Măgurele** Rom
41E2 **Turnu-Severin** Rom
49K5 **Turpan** China
23B2 **Turquino** *Mt* Cuba
58E1 **Turtkul'** Uzbekistan
17C2 **Turtle Creek Res** USA
3G3 **Turtle L** Can
49K3 **Turukhansk** Russian Fed
50D1 **Turuntayevo** Russian Fed
29B2 **Turvo** *R* Goias, Brazil
29C3 **Turvo** *R* São Paulo, Brazil
43E2 **Tur'ya** *R* Ukraine
17E3 **Tuscaloosa** USA
Tuscany = Toscana
14B2 **Tuscarora Mt** USA
12B3 **Tuscola** Illinois, USA
16C3 **Tuscola** Texas, USA
15B2 **Tuscumbia** USA
63D2 **Tusharík** Iran
14A2 **Tussey Mt** USA
Tutera = Tudela
62B3 **Tuticorin** India
41F2 **Tutrakan** Bulg
42B3 **Tuttlingen** Germany
77H2 **Tutuila** *I* American Samoa
22C2 **Tututepec** Mexico
50D2 **Tuul Gol** *R* Mongolia
77G1 **Tuvalu** *Is* Pacific O
49L4 **Tuvinskaya** Respublika, Russian Fed
65C4 **Tuwayilel Haj** *Mt* Jordan
66C2 **Tuwwal** S Arabia
22B2 **Tuxpan** Jalisco, Mexico
22A1 **Tuxpan** Nayarit, Mexico
22C1 **Tuxpan** Veracruz, Mexico
22C2 **Tuxtepec** Mexico
21C3 **Tuxtla Gutiérrez** Mexico
39A1 **Túy** Spain
3B2 **Tuya** *R* Can
55D3 **Tuy Hoa** Viet
64B2 **Tuz Gölü** *Salt L* Turk
64D3 **Tuz Khurmātū** Iraq
41D2 **Tuzla** Bosnia-Herzegovina, Yugos
34D4 **Tweed** *R* Scot/Eng
75D1 **Tweed Heads** Aust
34D4 **Tweedsmuir Hills** Scot
19C4 **Twentynine Palms** USA
7N5 **Twillingate** Can
18D1 **Twin Bridges** USA
16B3 **Twin Buttes Res** USA
18D2 **Twin Falls** USA
78B2 **Twins,The** *Mt* NZ
4B4 **Twin Valley** USA
20B3 **Twitchell Res** USA
12A1 **Two Harbors** USA
18D1 **Two Medicine** *R* USA
12B2 **Two Rivers** USA
49O4 **Tygda** Russian Fed
17C3 **Tyler** USA
53E1 **Tymovskoye** Russian Fed
50F1 **Tynda** Russian Fed
34E4 **Tyne** *R* Eng
34E4 **Tyne and Wear** Metropolitan County, Eng
34E4 **Tynemouth** Eng
32G6 **Tynset** Nor
10H4 **Tyonek** USA
65C2 **Tyr** Leb
Tyre = Tyr
53C1 **Tyrma** Russian Fed
53C1 **Tyrma** *R* Russian Fed
34B4 **Tyrone** County, N Ire
16A3 **Tyrone** New Mexico, USA
14A2 **Tyrone** Pennsylvania, USA
4B3 **Tyrrel** Can
75B3 **Tyrrell,L** Aust
40C2 **Tyrrhenian S** Italy
45J7 **Tyuleni, Ostrova** *Is* Kazakhstan
48H4 **Tyumen'** Russian Fed
49O3 **Tyung** *R* Russian Fed
35C5 **Tywyn** Wales
41E3 **Tzoumérka** *Mt* Greece
74E1 **Tzaneen** S Africa

U

29D3 **Ubá** Brazil
29D2 **Ubaí** Brazil
29E1 **Ubaitaba** Brazil
72B3 **Ubangi** *R* CAR
37B2 **Ubaye** *R* France
54B4 **Ube** Japan
39B2 **Ubeda** Spain
7N2 **Ubekendt Ejland** *I* Greenland
29C2 **Uberaba** Brazil
29C2 **Uberlândia** Brazil
55D2 **Ubon Ratchathani** Thai
43F2 **Ubort** *R* Belorussia
72C4 **Ubundi** Zaïre
26D5 **Ucayali** *R* Peru
60C3 **Uch** Pak
53E3 **Uchiura-wan** *B* Japan
49P4 **Uchar** *R* Russian Fed
18A1 **Ucluelet** Can
49L4 **Uda** *R* Russian Fed
60C4 **Udaipur** India
61C2 **Udaipur Garhi** Nepal
28D3 **Udaquoila** Arg
32G7 **Uddevalla** Sweden
32H5 **Uddjaur** *L* Sweden
62B1 **Udgir** India
60D2 **Udhampur** India
37E1 **Udine** Italy
44J4 **Udmurtskaya** Respublika, Russian Fed
55C2 **Udon Thani** Thai
49P4 **Udskaya Guba** *B* Russian Fed
53C1 **Udskoye** Russian Fed
62A2 **Udupi** India
53D1 **Udyl', Ozero** *L* Russian Fed
49N2 **Udzha** Russian Fed
54C3 **Ueda** Japan
72C3 **Uele** *R* Zaïre
49U3 **Uelen** Russian Fed
42C2 **Uelzen** Germany
72C3 **Uere** *R* Zaïre
44K5 **Ufa** Russian Fed
44K4 **Ufa** *R* Russian Fed
73B6 **Ugab** *R* Namibia
72D4 **Ugalla** *R* Tanz
10H4 **Ugak B** USA
72D3 **Uganda** Republic, Africa
10G4 **Ugashik B** USA
10G4 **Ugashik L** USA
37B2 **Ugine** France
66D1 **'Uglat as Suqūr** S Arabia
53E2 **Uglegorsk** Russian Fed
44F4 **Uglich** Russian Fed
53C3 **Uglovoye** Russian Fed
44F5 **Ugra** *R* Russian Fed
34B3 **Uig** Scot
73B4 **Uige** Angola
54A3 **Ŭijŏngbu** S Korea
45J6 **Uil** Kazakhstan
18D2 **Uinta Mts** USA
54A3 **Ŭiryŏng** S Korea
54A3 **Uisŏng** S Korea
74D3 **Uitenhage** S Africa
5J2 **Uivak,C** Can
43E3 **Ujfehértó** Hung
54C4 **Uji** Japan
72C4 **Ujiji** Tanz
25C2 **Ujina** Chile
60D4 **Ujjain** India
57B4 **Ujung** Indon
76A1 **Ujung Pandang** Indon
72D4 **Ukerewe** *I* Tanz
61D2 **Ukhrul** India
44J3 **Ukhta** Russian Fed
19B3 **Ukiah** California, USA
18C1 **Ukiah** Oregon, USA
8A3 **Ukiah** USA
43E1 **Ukmerge** Lithuania
45D6 **Ukraine**
54A4 **Uku-jima** *I* Japan
50D2 **Ulaanbaatar** Mongolia
50C2 **Ulaangom** Mongolia
52C1 **Ulaan Uul** Mongolia
59G1 **Ulangar Hu** *L* China
52B1 **Ulansuhai Nur** *L* China
50D1 **Ulan Ude** Russian Fed
50C3 **Ulan Ul Hu** *L* China
28B2 **Ulapes** Arg
49Q3 **Ul'beya** *R* Russian Fed
53B4 **Ulchin** S Korea
41D2 **Ulcinj** Montenegro, Yugos
50E2 **Uldz** Mongolia
50C2 **Uliastay** Mongolia
43F1 **Ulla** Lithuania
75D3 **Ulladulla** Aust
34C3 **Ullapool** Scot
32H5 **Ullsfjorden** *Inlet* Nor
35D4 **Ullswater** *L* Eng
53C4 **Ullung-do** *I* S Korea
42C3 **Ulm** Germany
53C2 **Ul'ma** *R* Russian Fed
75A1 **Uloowaranie,L** Aust
53B4 **Ulsan** S Korea
35B4 **Ulster** Region, N Ire
57C2 **Ulu** Indon
48K5 **Ulungur He** *R* China
48K5 **Ulungur Hu** *L* China
34B3 **Ulva** *I* Scot
35D4 **Ulverston** Eng
75E3 **Ulverstone** Aust
49Q4 **Ulya** *R* Russian Fed
43G3 **Ulyanovka** Ukraine
16B2 **Ulysses** USA
45E6 **Uman** Ukraine
7N2 **Umanak** Greenland
61B3 **Umaria** India
60B3 **Umarkot** Pak
75A1 **Umaroona,L** Aust
18C1 **Umatilla** USA
44E2 **Umba** Russian Fed
72D4 **Umba** *R* Tanz
37E3 **Umbertide** Italy
76D1 **Umboi I** PNG
32H6 **Ume** *R* Sweden
32J6 **Umea** Sweden
74E2 **Umfolozi,R** S Africa
10H2 **Umiat** USA
74E3 **Umkomaas** *R* S Africa
67G1 **Umm al Qaiwain** UAE
67G2 **Umm as Samīm** *Salt Marsh* Oman
72C2 **Umm Bell** Sudan
66B3 **Umm Inderaba** Sudan
72C2 **Umm Keddada** Sudan
66C1 **Umm Lajj** S Arabia
72D2 **Umm Ruwaba** Sudan
67G2 **Umm Sa'id** Qatar
66B4 **Umm Saiyala** Sudan
73C5 **Umnaiti** *R* Zim
10E5 **Umnak I** USA
18B2 **Umpqua** *R* USA
60D4 **Umred** India
74D3 **Umtata** S Africa
29B3 **Umuarama** Brazil
74D3 **Umzimkulu** S Africa
74E3 **Umzimkulu** *R* S Africa
74D3 **Umzimvubu** *R* S Africa
74D1 **Umzingwane** *R* Zim
29E2 **Una** Brazil
40D1 **Una** *R* Bosnia-Herzegovina/Croatia, Yugos
14C1 **Unadilla** USA
14C1 **Unadilla** *R* USA
29C2 **Unai** Brazil
10F3 **Unalakleet** USA
10E5 **Unalaska** *I* USA
66D1 **Unayzah** S Arabia
14D2 **Uncasville** USA
16A2 **Uncompahgre Plat** USA
74D2 **Underberg** S Africa
11B2 **Underwood** USA
44E5 **Unecha** Russian Fed
65C3 **Uneisa** Jordan
10G4 **Unga** *I* USA
7M4 **Ungava B** Can
25F3 **União de Vitória** Brazil
10F5 **Unimak Bight** USA
10F5 **Unimak I** USA
10E5 **Unimak Pass** USA
28B3 **Unión** Arg
17D2 **Union** Missouri, USA
15C2 **Union** S Carolina, USA
13D2 **Union City** Pennsylvania, USA
15B1 **Union City** Tennessee, USA
74C3 **Uniondale** S Africa
15B2 **Union Springs** USA
13D3 **Uniontown** USA
67F2 **United Arab Emirates** Arabian Pen
30E3 **United Kingdom** Kingdom, W Europe
2H4 **United States of America**
7K1 **United States Range** *Mts* Can
3G3 **Unity** Can
18C2 **Unity** USA
16A3 **University Park** USA
36D1 **Unna** Germany
61B2 **Unnão** India
54A2 **Unsan** N Korea
34E1 **Unst** *I* Scot
57B3 **Unuana** *I* Indon
3B2 **Unuk** *R* USA
64C1 **Ünye** Turk
44G4 **Unzha** *R* Russian Fed
26F2 **Upata** Ven
73C4 **Upemba Nat Pk** Zaïre
7N2 **Upernavik** Greenland
74C2 **Upington** S Africa
20D3 **Upland** USA
77H2 **Upolu** *I* Western Samoa
3E3 **Upper Arrow L** Can
78C2 **Upper Hutt** NZ
18B2 **Upper Klamath L** USA
18B2 **Upper L** USA
35B4 **Upper Laugh Erne** *L* N Ire
23L1 **Upper Manzanilla** Trinidad
11D2 **Upper Red L** USA
14B3 **Upperville** USA
Upper Volta = Burkina
32H7 **Uppsala** Sweden
11D2 **Upsala** Can
11B3 **Upton** USA
52B1 **Urad Qianqi** China
67E1 **Urairah** S Arabia
54D2 **Urakawa** Japan
45J5 **Ural** *R* Kazakhstan
75D2 **Uralla** Aust
45J5 **Ural'sk** Kazakhstan
48G4 **Uralskiy Khrebet** *Mts* Russian Fed
29D1 **Urandi** Brazil
6H4 **Uranium City** Can
51G8 **Urapunga** Aust
16A2 **Uravan** USA
54C3 **Urawa** Japan
44L3 **Uray** Russian Fed
12B2 **Urbana** Illinois, USA
12C2 **Urbana** Ohio, USA
37E3 **Urbino** Italy
35D4 **Ure** *R* Eng
44H4 **Uren'** Russian Fed
48J3 **Urengoy** Russian Fed
53C1 **Urgal** Russian Fed
58E1 **Urgench** Uzbekistan
60B2 **Urgun** Afghan
53B1 **Urkan** *R* Russian Fed
41F3 **Urla** Turk
53C2 **Urmi** *R* Russian Fed
71H4 **Uromi** Nig
41E2 **Uroševac** Serbia, Yugos
27J6 **Uruaçu** Brazil
29C1 **Uruaçu** Brazil
22B2 **Uruapan** Mexico
29C2 **Urucuia** *R* Brazil
28E1 **Uruguai** *R* Brazil
28D1 **Uruguaiana** Brazil
25E4 **Uruguay** Republic, S America
25E4 **Uruguay** *R* Urug
63B1 **Urumīyeh** Iran
59G1 **Ürümqi** China
50J2 **Urup** *I* Russian Fed
49Q5 **Urup, Ostrov** *I* Russian Fed
67E3 **'Urūq al Awārik** Region, S Arabia
53A1 **Urusha** Russian Fed
60B2 **Uruzgan** Afghan
54D2 **Uryū-ko** *L* Japan
45G5 **Uryupinsk** Russian Fed
44J4 **Urzhum** Russian Fed
41F2 **Urziceni** Rom
59G1 **Usa** China
54B4 **Usa** Japan
44L2 **Usa** *R* Russian Fed
64A2 **Uşak** Turk
74B1 **Usakos** Namibia
48J1 **Ushakova, Ostrov** *I* Russian Fed
72D4 **Ushashi** Tanz
48J5 **Ush Tobe** Kazakhstan
25C8 **Ushuaia** Arg
49O4 **Ushumun** Russian Fed
35D6 **Usk** *R* Wales
64A1 **Üsküdar** Turk

Villa Neuva Warmbad

22B1 **Villa Neuva** Mexico
39A1 **Villa Nova de Gaia** Port
39A2 **Villanueva de la Serena** Spain
39C1 **Villanueva-y-Geltrú** Spain
28C1 **Villa Ojo de Agua** Arg
28B3 **Villa Regina** Arg
39B2 **Villarreal** Spain
28A3 **Villarrica** Chile
25E3 **Villarrica** Par
39B2 **Villarrobledo** Spain
28D2 **Villa San José** Arg
28C1 **Villa San Martin** Arg
28C2 **Villa Valeria** Arg
26D3 **Villavicencio** Colombia
38C2 **Villefranche** France
7L5 **Ville-Marie** Can
39B2 **Villena** Spain
36B2 **Villeneuve-St-Georges** France
38C3 **Villeneuve-sur-Lot** France
36B2 **Villeneuve-sur-Yonne** France
17D3 **Ville Platte** USA
36B2 **Villers-Cotterêts** France
38C2 **Villeurbanne** France
74D2 **Villiers** S Africa
36E2 **Villingen-Schwenningen** Germany
62B2 **Villupuram** India
43F2 **Vilnius** Lithuania
49N3 **Vilyuy** *R* Russian Fed
49O3 **Vilyuysk** Russian Fed
36A2 **Vimoutiers** France
71J4 **Vina** *R* Cam
28A2 **Viña del Mar** Chile
39C1 **Vinaroz** Spain
12B3 **Vincennes** USA
28B1 **Vinchina** Arg
32H5 **Vindel** *R* Sweden
60D4 **Vindhya Range** *Mts* India
14C3 **Vineland** USA
14E2 **Vineyard Haven** USA
55D2 **Vinh** Viet
55D3 **Vinh Cam Ranh** *B* Viet
55D4 **Vinh Loi** Viet
55D3 **Vinh Long** Viet
17C2 **Vinita** USA
41D1 **Vinkovci** Croatia, Yugos
43F3 **Vinnitsa** Ukraine
79F3 **Vinson Massif** *Upland* Ant
11D3 **Vinton** USA
74B2 **Vioolsdrift** S Africa
37D1 **Vipiteno** Italy
57C4 **Viqueque** Indon
57F8 **Virac** Phil
62B2 **Virddhāchalam** India
11B2 **Virden** Can
73B5 **Virei** Angola
29D2 **Virgem da Lapa** Brazil
19D3 **Virgin** *R* USA
74D2 **Virginia** S Africa
9F3 **Virginia** State, USA
11D2 **Virginia** USA
13D3 **Virginia Beach** USA
19C3 **Virginia City** USA
23E3 **Virgin Is** Caribbean
12A2 **Viroqua** USA
40D1 **Virovitica** Croatia, Yugos
36C2 **Virton** Belg
62B3 **Virudunagar** India
40D2 **Vis** *I* Croatia, Yugos
20C2 **Visalia** USA
57F8 **Visayan S** Phil
32H7 **Visby** Sweden
6H2 **Viscount Melville Sd** Can
41D2 **Višegrad** Bosnia-Herzegovina, Yugos
39A1 **Viseu** Port
62C1 **Vishākhapatnam** India
44K3 **Vishera** *R* Russian Fed
37B1 **Visp** Switz
38C1 **Vissingen** Neth
19C4 **Vista** USA
Vistula = Wisla
42C3 **Vitavia, R** Czech Republic
62A1 **Vite** India
43G1 **Vitebsk** Belorussia
40C2 **Viterbo** Italy
39A1 **Vitigudino** Spain
77G2 **Viti Levu** *I* Fiji
49N4 **Vitim** *R* Russian Fed
39B1 **Vitora** Spain
27L8 **Vitória** Brazil
27K6 **Vitória da Conquista** Brazil
38B2 **Vitré** France
36C2 **Vitry-le-Francois** France
32J5 **Vittangi** Sweden
36C2 **Vittel** France
40C3 **Vittoria** Italy
37E2 **Vittorio Veneto** Italy
50J2 **Vityaz Depth** Pacific O
Viveiro = Vivero
39A1 **Vivero** Spain
49L3 **Vivi** *R* Russian Fed
28D3 **Vivorata** Arg
49M4 **Vizhne-Angarsk** Russian Fed
62C1 **Vizianagaram** India
37A2 **Vizille** France
44J3 **Vizinga** Russian Fed
41E1 **Vládeasa** *Mt* Rom
44G4 **Vladimir** Russian Fed
43E2 **Vladimir Volynskiy** Ukraine
53C3 **Vladivostok** Russian Fed
42A2 **Vlieland** *I* Neth
36B1 **Vlissingen** Neth
41D2 **Vlorë** Alb
42C3 **Vöcklabruck** Austria
37E2 **Vodnjan** Croatia, Yugos
55D3 **Voeune Sai** Camb
71J4 **Vogel Peak** *Mt* Nig
36E1 **Vogelsberg** Region, Germany
37C2 **Voghera** Italy
73F5 **Vohémar = Vohimarina** Madag
73E5 **Vohibinany** Madag
73F5 **Vohimarina** Madag
72D4 **Voi** Kenya
70B4 **Voinjama** Lib
38D2 **Voiron** France
41D1 **Vojvodina** *Aut Republic* Serbia, Yugos
11A2 **Volborg** USA
23A5 **Volcán Baru** *Mt* Panama
22C2 **Volcán Citlaltepetl** *Mt* Mexico
26E8 **Volcán Lullaillaco** *Mt* Chile
28A3 **Volcáno Copahue** *Mt* Chile
28A3 **Volcáno Dumuyo** *Mt* Arg
Volcano Is = Kazan Retto
28A3 **Volcáno Lanin** *Mt* Arg
26E8 **Volcán Ollagüe** *Mt* Chile
28A3 **Volcáno Llaima** *Mt* Chile
28B2 **Volcáno Malpo** *Mt* Arg
28A3 **Volcáno Peteroa** *Mt* Chile
28B3 **Volcáno Tromen** *V* Arg
28A3 **Volcáno Villarrica** *Mt* Chile
22B2 **Volcán Paracutin** *Mt* Mexico
26C3 **Volcán Puraće** *Mt* Colombia
28A2 **Volcán Tinquiririca** *Mt* Chile/Arg
44K4 **Volchansk** Russian Fed
45H6 **Volga** *R* Russian Fed
45G6 **Volgodonsk** Russian Fed
45G6 **Volgograd** Russian Fed
45H5 **Volgogradskoye Vodokhranilishche** *Res* Russian Fed
44E4 **Volkhov** Russian Fed
44E4 **Volkhov** *R* Russian Fed
43E2 **Volkovysk** Belorussia
74D2 **Volksrust** S Africa
49L2 **Volochanka** Russian Fed
44G4 **Vologda** Russian Fed
38B2 **Volognes** France
41E3 **Vólos** Greece
45H5 **Vol'sk** Russian Fed
20B2 **Volta** USA
71G4 **Volta** *R* Ghana
71F3 **Volta Blanche** *R* Burkina
71F4 **Volta,L** Ghana
71F3 **Volta Noire** *R* Burkina
29D3 **Volta Redonda** Brazil
71F3 **Volta Rouge** *R* Burkina
37D3 **Volterra** Italy
37C2 **Voltri** Italy
45G6 **Volzhskiy** Russian Fed
10H3 **Von Frank Mt** USA
44F3 **Vonguda** Russian Fed
7R3 **Vopnafjörður** Iceland
37C1 **Voralberg** Province, Austria
37C1 **Vorder Rhein** *R* Switz
42C1 **Vordingborg** Den
45C8 **Voriái** *I* Greece
44L2 **Vorkuta** Russian Fed
32G6 **Vorma** *R* Nor
45F5 **Voronezh** Russian Fed
32M5 **Voron'ya** *R* Russian Fed
45F6 **Voroshilovgrad** Ukraine
32K7 **Võru** Estonia
36D2 **Vosges** Department, France
38D2 **Vosges** *Mts* France
32F6 **Voss** Nor
53E2 **Vostchnyy** Russian Fed
53E1 **Vostochnyy** Russian Fed
49L4 **Vostochnyy Sayan** *Mts* Russian Fed
79F9 **Vostok** *Base* Ant
44J4 **Votkinsk** Russian Fed
36C2 **Vouziers** France
36A2 **Voves** France
11D2 **Voyageurs Nat Pk** USA
44K3 **Voy Vozh** Russian Fed
45E6 **Voznesensk** Ukraine
63E1 **Vozvyshennost' Karabil'** *Desert Region* Turkmenistan
49T2 **Vrangelya, Ostrov** *I* Russian Fed
41E2 **Vranje** Serbia, Yugos
41E2 **Vratsa** Bulg
41D1 **Vrbas** Serbia, Yugos
40D2 **Vrbas** *R* Serbia, Yugos
40C1 **Vrbovsko** Bosnia-Herzegovina, Yugos
74D2 **Vrede** S Africa
74B3 **Vredendal** S Africa
27G2 **Vreed en Hoop** Guyana
37F2 **Vrhnika** Slovenia, Yugos
41E1 **Vršac** Serbia, Yugos
40D2 **Vrtoče** Bosnia-Herzegovina, Yugos
74C2 **Vryburg** S Africa
74E2 **Vryheid** S Africa
10E5 **Vsevidof,Mt** USA
41D1 **Vukovar** Croatia, Yugos
44K3 **Vuktyl'** Russian Fed
3F3 **Vulcan** Can
35G5 **Vulcan** *Oilfield* N Sea
40C3 **Vulcano** *I* Italy
55D3 **Vung Tau** Viet
32J5 **Vuollerim** Sweden
44E3 **Vyartsilya** Russian Fed
44J4 **Vyatka** *R* Russian Fed
53C2 **Vyazemskiy** Russian Fed
44E4 **Vyaz'ma** Russian Fed
44G4 **Vyazniki** Russian Fed
44D3 **Vyborg** Russian Fed
44F3 **Vygozero, Ozero** *L* Russian Fed
44J3 **Vym** *R* Russian Fed
35D5 **Vyrnwy** *R* Wales
44E4 **Vyshniy Volochek** Russian Fed
42D3 **Vyškov** Czech Republic
53D1 **Vysokogornyy** Russian Fed
44F3 **Vytegra** Russian Fed

W

71F3 **Wa** Ghana
36C1 **Waal** *R* Neth
3F2 **Wabasca** Can
6G4 **Wabasca** *R* Can
3F2 **Wabasca L** Can
12B2 **Wabash** USA
12B3 **Wabash** *R* USA
12C1 **Wabatongushi L** Can
6J4 **Wabowden** Can
7M4 **Wabush** Can
15C3 **Waccasassa B** USA
14E1 **Wachusett Res** USA
17C3 **Waco** USA
5H3 **Wacouno** *R* Can
60B3 **Wad** Pak
69A2 **Waddān** Libya
6F4 **Waddington,Mt** Can
3H3 **Wadena** Can
11C2 **Wadena** USA
65D3 **Wadi Abu 'Amūd** *V* Jordan
65B4 **Wadi Abu Tarfa** *V* Egypt
66D2 **Wadi ad Dawāsin** *Watercourse* S Arabia
67E3 **Wadi Adhanah** *Watercourse* Yemen
67F3 **Wadi al Amilhayt** *Watercourse* Oman
64E4 **Wadi al Bātin** *Watercourse* Iraq
64D3 **Wadi al Ghudāf** *Watercourse* Iraq
65D2 **Wadi al Harīr** *V* Syria
67F3 **Wadi al Masilāh** *Watercourse* Yemen
64D3 **Wadi al Mirah** *Watercourse* S Arabia/Iraq
64D3 **Wadi al Ubayyid** *Watercourse* Iraq
67F3 **Wadi Aman** *Watercourse* Yemen
65C3 **Wadi 'Araba** *V* Israel
64D3 **Wadi Ar'ar** *Watercourse* S Arabia
67E2 **Wadi as Hsabā'** *Watercourse* S Arabia
64C3 **Wadi as Sirhān** *V* Jordan/ S Arabia
45G8 **Wadi ath Thamhar** *R* Iraq
65D2 **Wadi az Zaydi** *V* Syria
66D2 **Wadi Bishah** *Watercourse* S Arabia
65D3 **Wadi edh Dhab'i** *V* Jordan
65C4 **Wadi el'Aqaba** *V* Egypt
65B3 **Wadi el 'Arish** *V* Egypt
65B3 **Wadi el Brûk** *V* Egypt
65A3 **Wadi el Gafa** *V* Egypt
65D3 **Wadi el Ghadaf** *V* Jordan
65C3 **Wadi el Hasa** *V* Jordan
65B3 **Wadi el Higayib** *V* Egypt
65D3 **Wadi el Janab** *V* Jordan
65C3 **Wadi el Jeib** *V* Israel/ Jordan
65D4 **Wadi el Khush Shah** *V* Jordan
72C2 **Wadi el Milk** *Watercourse* Sudan
64A3 **Wadi el Natrun** *Watercourse* Egypt
65B4 **Wadi el Saheira** *V* Egypt
65B4 **Wadi el Sîq** Egypt
65C3 **Wadi es Sir** Jordan
65C3 **Wadi Fidan** *V* Jordan
66D3 **Wadi Habawnāh** *Watercourse* S Arabia
66B2 **Wadi Haifa** Sudan
65C3 **Wadi Hareidin** *V* Egypt
65B3 **Wadi Hasana** *V* Egypt
64D3 **Wadi Hawrān** *R* Iraq
72C2 **Wadi Howa** *Watercourse* Sudan
72C2 **Wadi Ibra** *Watercourse* Sudan
67E3 **Wadi Jawf** *Watercourse* Yemen
65D2 **Wadi Luhfi** *Watercourse* Jordan
67E3 **Wadi Makhay** *Watercourse* Yemen
66D3 **Wadi Mawr** *Watercourse* Yemen
67F3 **Wadi Mugshin** *Watercourse* Oman
65C3 **Wadi Mujib** *V* Jordan
65C3 **Wādi Mūsa** Jordan
66B1 **Wadi Ouena** *Watercourse* Egypt
65D4 **Wadi Qa'ash Shubyk** *V* Jordan
67F3 **Wadi Qināb** *Watercourse* Yemen
65C3 **Wadi Qîtaiya** *V* Egypt
66D2 **Wadi Ranyah** *Watercourse* S Arabia
65D4 **Wadi Ratiyah** *V* Jordan
65D4 **Wadi Ruweila** *V* Jordan
66B2 **Wadi Sha'it** *Watercourse* Egypt
67F3 **Wadi Shihan** *Watercourse* Oman
66D2 **Wadi Tathlith** *Watercourse* S Arabia
66D2 **Wadi Turabah** *Watercourse* S Arabia
65C3 **Wadi Ugeiqa** *V* Jordan
72D2 **Wad Medani** Sudan
54A3 **Waegwan** S Korea
64E4 **Wafra** Kuwait
36C1 **Wageningen** Neth
7K3 **Wager B** Can
7J3 **Wager Bay** Can
75C3 **Wagga Wagga** Aust
76A4 **Wagin** Aust
11C3 **Wagner** USA
57C3 **Waha** Indon
20E5 **Wahaiwa** Hawaiian Is
17C1 **Wahoo** USA
11C2 **Wahpeton** USA
62A1 **Wai** India
20E5 **Waialua** Hawaiian Is
78B2 **Waiau** NZ
78A3 **Waiau** *R* NZ
78B2 **Waiau** *R* NZ
57C3 **Waigama** Indon
51G6 **Waigeo** *I* Indon
78C1 **Waihi** NZ
57A4 **Waikabubak** Indon
78C1 **Waikaremoana,L** NZ
78C1 **Waikato** *R* NZ
57A4 **Waikelo** Indon
75A2 **Waikerie** Aust
78B3 **Waikouaiti** NZ
20E5 **Wailuku** Hawaiian Is
78B2 **Waimakariri** *R* NZ
78B2 **Waimate** NZ
20E5 **Waimea** Hawaiian Is
76B1 **Waingapu** Indon
3F3 **Wainwright** Can
10F1 **Wainwright** USA
78B2 **Waipara** NZ
78C2 **Waipukurau** NZ
78C2 **Wairarapa,L** NZ
78B2 **Wairau** *R* NZ
78C1 **Wairoa** NZ
78C1 **Wairoa** *R* NZ
78B2 **Waitaki** *R* NZ
78B1 **Waitara** NZ
78C1 **Waitomo** NZ
78B1 **Waiuku** NZ
54C3 **Wajima** Japan
72E3 **Wajir** Kenya
54C3 **Wakasa-wan** *B* Japan
78A3 **Wakatipu,L** NZ
3G3 **Wakaw** Can
53D5 **Wakayama** Japan
16C2 **Wa Keeney** USA
35E5 **Wakefield** Eng
23H1 **Wakefield** Jamaica
12B1 **Wakefield** Michigan, USA
14E2 **Wakefield** Rhode Island, USA
55B2 **Wakema** Burma
53E2 **Wakkanai** Japan
75B3 **Wakool** *R* Aust
57D3 **Wakre** Indon
5H2 **Wakuach L** Can
42D2 **Walbrzych** Pol
75D2 **Walcha** Aust
42D2 **Walcz** Pol
36D1 **Waldbröl** Germany
14C2 **Walden** USA
36E3 **Waldshut** Germany
35D5 **Wales** Country, UK
10E2 **Wales** USA
7K3 **Wales I** Can
71F3 **Walewale** Ghana
75C2 **Walgett** Aust
79F4 **Walgreen Coast** Region, Ant
72C4 **Walikale** Zaïre
11D2 **Walker** USA
20C1 **Walker L** USA
20C3 **Walker Pass** USA
12C2 **Walkerton** Can
11B3 **Wall** USA
18C1 **Wallace** USA
75A2 **Wallaroo** Aust
75C3 **Walla Walla** Aust
18C1 **Walla Walla** USA
36E2 **Walldürn** Germany
14D2 **Wallingford** USA
xxixK5 **Wallis and Futuna** *Is* Pacific O
18C1 **Wallowa** USA
18C1 **Wallowa Mts** *Mts* USA
75C1 **Wallumbilla** Aust
17D2 **Walnut Ridge** USA
78C1 **Walouru** NZ
14D1 **Walpole** USA
35E5 **Walsall** Eng
16B2 **Walsenburg** USA
15C2 **Walterboro** USA
15B2 **Walter F George Res** USA
16C3 **Walters** USA
14E1 **Waltham** USA
14C1 **Walton** USA
68F9 **Walvis Bay** Namibia
74A1 **Walvis Bay** S Africa
xxxJ6 **Walvis Ridge** Atlantic O
71H4 **Wamba** Nig
72B4 **Wamba** *R* Zaïre
17C2 **Wamego** USA
57C3 **Wamsasi** Indon
18E2 **Wamsutter** USA
60B2 **Wana** Pak
75B1 **Wanaaring** Aust
78A2 **Wanaka** NZ
78A2 **Wanaka,L** NZ
4E4 **Wanapitei L** Can
53C2 **Wanda Shan** *Upland* China
54A4 **Wando** S Korea
75C1 **Wandoan** Aust
75B3 **Wanganella** Aust
78B2 **Wanganui** NZ
78C1 **Wanganui** *R* NZ
75C3 **Wangaratta** Aust
57B4 **Wangiwangi** *I* Indon
53B2 **Wangkui** China
71F4 **Wango Fitini** Ivory Coast
53B3 **Wangqing** China
68G9 **Wankie** Zim
72E3 **Wanle Weyne** Somalia
55E2 **Wanning** China
62B1 **Wanparti** India
52B3 **Wanxian** China
52B3 **Wanyuan** China
3H3 **Wapawekka L** Can
3D3 **Wapiti** *R* Can
17D2 **Wappapello,L** USA
14D2 **Wappingers Falls** USA
11D3 **Wapsipinicon** *R* USA
71J3 **Wara Nat Pk** Cam
62B1 **Warangal** India
75E3 **Waratah** Aust
75C3 **Waratah B** Aust
36E1 **Warburg** Germany
75C3 **Warburton** Aust
75A1 **Warburton** *R* Aust
75C1 **Ward** *R* Aust
74D2 **Warden** S Africa
72E3 **Warder** Eth
60D4 **Wardha** India
78A3 **Ward,Mt** NZ
3C2 **Ware** Can
14D1 **Ware** USA
14E2 **Wareham** USA
36D1 **Warendorf** Germany
75D1 **Warialda** Aust
55D2 **Warin Chamrap** Thai
74B2 **Warmbad** Namibia

Warmbad

Wind Cave Nat Pk

73C6 **Warmbad** S Africa
14C2 **Warminster** USA
19C3 **Warm Springs** USA
42C2 **Warnemünde** Germany
18B2 **Warner Mts** USA
15C2 **Warner Robins** USA
75B3 **Warracknabeal** Aust
75A1 **Warrandirinna,L** Aust
76D3 **Warrego** *R* Aust
17D3 **Warren** Arkansas, USA
75C2 **Warren** Aust
11C2 **Warren** Minnesota, USA
12C2 **Warren** Ohio, USA
4E5 **Warren** Michigan, USA
13D2 **Warren** Pennsylvania, USA
14E2 **Warren** Rhode Island, USA
35B4 **Warrenpoint** N Ire
17D2 **Warrensburg** USA
74C2 **Warrenton** S Africa
13D3 **Warrenton** USA
71H4 **Warri** Nig
75A1 **Warrina** Aust
35D5 **Warrington** Eng
15B2 **Warrington** USA
75B3 **Warrnambool** Aust
11C2 **Warroad** USA
Warsaw = Warszawa
14A1 **Warsaw** USA
72E3 **Warshiikh** Somalia
43E2 **Warszawa** Pol
43D2 **Warta** *R* Pol
75D1 **Warwick** Aust
35E5 **Warwick** County, Eng
35E5 **Warwick** Eng
14C2 **Warwick** New York, USA
14E2 **Warwick** Rhode Island, USA
19D3 **Wasatch Range** *Mts* USA
74E2 **Wasbank** S Africa
20C3 **Wasco** USA
11D3 **Waseca** USA
3G2 **Wasekamio L** Can
63E3 **Washap** Pak
12A1 **Washburn** USA
6H2 **Washburn L** Can
18D2 **Washburn,Mt** USA
60D4 **Wāshīm** India
9F3 **Washington** District of Columbia, USA
15C2 **Washington** Georgia, USA
12B3 **Washington** Indiana, USA
11D3 **Washington** Iowa, USA
17D2 **Washington** Missouri, USA
15D1 **Washington** N Carolina, USA
14C2 **Washington** New Jersey, USA
12C2 **Washington** Pennsylvania, USA
8A2 **Washington** State, USA
19D3 **Washington** Utah, USA
12C3 **Washington Court House** USA
7M1 **Washington Land** *Region* Can
13E2 **Washington,Mt** USA
16C2 **Washita** *R* USA
35F5 **Wash,The** Eng
60A3 **Washuk** Pak
10J3 **Wasilla** USA
7L4 **Waskaganish** Can
23A4 **Waspán** Nic
20C1 **Wassuk Range** *Mts* USA
36C2 **Wassy** France
4F4 **Waswanipi L** *L* Can
57B3 **Watampone** Indon
57A3 **Watansoppeng** Indon
74D3 **Waterberge** *Mts* S Africa
14D2 **Waterbury** USA
3G2 **Waterbury L** Can
35B5 **Waterford** County, Irish Rep
33B3 **Waterford** Irish Rep
35B5 **Waterford Harbour** Irish Rep
36C1 **Waterloo** Belg
4E5 **Waterloo** Can
11D3 **Waterloo** USA
12B1 **Watersmeet** USA
18D1 **Waterton-Glacier International Peace Park** USA
13D2 **Watertown** New York, USA
11C3 **Watertown** S Dakota, USA
12B2 **Watertown** Wisconsin, USA
74E2 **Waterval-Boven** S Africa
13F2 **Waterville** Maine, USA
14C1 **Waterville** New York, USA
14D1 **Watervliet** USA
6G4 **Waterways** Can
35E6 **Watford** Eng
11B2 **Watford City** USA
14B1 **Watkins Glen** USA
16C2 **Watonga** USA
8C1 **Watrous** Can
16B2 **Watrous** USA
72C3 **Watsa** Zaïre
10N3 **Watson Lake** Can
20B2 **Watsonville** USA
3E2 **Watt,Mt** Can
57B3 **Watukancoa** Indon
51H7 **Wau** PNG
72C3 **Wau** Sudan
75D2 **Wauchope** Aust
15E4 **Wauchula** USA
12B2 **Waukegan** USA
12B2 **Waukesha** USA
12B2 **Waupaca** USA
12B2 **Waupun** USA
17C3 **Waurika** USA
12B2 **Wausau** USA
12B2 **Wauwatosa** USA
76C2 **Wave Hill** Aust
35F5 **Waverey** *R* Eng
11D3 **Waverly** Iowa, USA
14B1 **Waverly** New York, USA
12C3 **Waverly** Ohio, USA
36C1 **Wavre** Belg
7K5 **Wawa** Can
71G4 **Wawa** Nig
69A2 **Wāw Al Kabīr** Libya
69A2 **Wāw an Nāmūs** *Well* Libya
20C2 **Wawona** USA
17C3 **Waxahachie** USA
57C2 **Wayabula** Indon
15C2 **Waycross** USA
11C3 **Wayne** USA
15C2 **Waynesboro** Georgia, USA
17E3 **Waynesboro** Mississippi, USA
14B3 **Waynesboro** Pennsylvania, USA
13D3 **Waynesboro** Virginia, USA
17D2 **Waynesville** Missouri, USA
15C1 **Waynesville** N Carolina, USA
60B2 **Wazi Khwa** Afghan
35F6 **Weald,The** *Upland* Eng
34D4 **Wear** *R* Eng
16C2 **Weatherford** Oklahoma, USA
17C3 **Weatherford** Texas, USA
18B2 **Weaverville** USA
12C1 **Webbwood** Can
14B1 **Webster** New York, USA
11C2 **Webster** S Dakota, USA
14E1 **Webster** USA
11D3 **Webster City** USA
12A3 **Webster Groves** USA
57C2 **Weda** Indon
25D8 **Weddell I** Falkland Is
79G2 **Weddell S** Ant
3D3 **Wedge Mt** Can
5H5 **Wedgeport** Can
18B2 **Weed** USA
14A2 **Weedville** USA
74E2 **Weenen** S Africa
75C2 **Wee Waa** Aust
52D1 **Weichang** China
42C3 **Weiden** Germany
52D2 **Weifang** China
52E2 **Weihai** China
52C3 **Wei He** *R* Henan, China
52C2 **Wei He** *R* Shaanxi, China
75C1 **Weilmoringle** Aust
36E2 **Weinheim** Germany
52A4 **Weining** China
76D2 **Weipa** Aust
12C2 **Weirton** USA
18C2 **Weiser** USA
52D3 **Weishan Hu** *L* China
42C2 **Weissenfels** Germany
15B2 **Weiss L** USA
3G2 **Weitzel L** Can
4B3 **Wekusko** Can
12C3 **Welch** USA
72E2 **Weldiya** Eth
20C3 **Weldon** USA
74D2 **Welkom** S Africa
13D2 **Welland** Can
35E5 **Welland** *R* Eng
76C2 **Wellesley Is** Aust
10L3 **Wellesley L** Can
14E2 **Wellfleet** USA
35E5 **Wellingborough** Eng
75C2 **Wellington** Aust
16B1 **Wellington** Colorado, USA
17C2 **Wellington** Kansas, USA
20C1 **Wellington** Nevada, USA
78B2 **Wellington** NZ
74B3 **Wellington** S Africa
16B3 **Wellington** Texas, USA
7J2 **Wellington Chan** Can
3D3 **Wells** Can
35D6 **Wells** Eng
18D2 **Wells** Nevada, USA
14C1 **Wells** New York, USA
14B2 **Wellsboro** USA
78B1 **Wellsford** NZ
76B3 **Wells,L** Aust
4A2 **Wells L** Can
14B1 **Wellsville** USA
42C3 **Wels** Austria
35D5 **Welshpool** Wales
3E2 **Wembley** Can
7L4 **Wemindji** Can
18B1 **Wenatchee** USA
18C1 **Wenatchee** *R* USA
71F4 **Wenchi** Ghana
52E2 **Wenden** China
18D2 **Wendover** USA
52E4 **Wenling** China
52A5 **Wenshan** China
76D4 **Wenthaggi** Aust
75B2 **Wentworth** Aust
3F2 **Wentzel L** Can
52A3 **Wen Xian** China
52E4 **Wenzhou** China
52C4 **Wenzhu** China
74D2 **Wepener** S Africa
74C2 **Werda** Botswana
10L2 **Wernecke Mts** Can
42C2 **Werra** *R* Germany
75D2 **Werris Creek** Aust
36D1 **Wesel** Germany
42B2 **Weser** *R* Germany
16B2 **Weskan** USA
17F4 **Weslaco** USA
7N5 **Wesleyville** Can
76C2 **Wessel Is** Aust
36E1 **Wesser** *R* Germany
36E1 **Wesserbergland** Region, Germany
11C3 **Wessington Springs** USA
12B2 **West Allis** USA
xxviiiF5 **West Australian Basin** Indian O
xxviiiF6 **West Australian Ridge** Indian O
17E3 **West B** USA
61C3 **West Bengal** State, India
14C1 **West Branch Delaware** *R* USA
14A2 **West Branch Susquehanna** *R* USA
35E5 **West Bromwich** Eng
13E2 **Westbrook** USA
12A2 **Westby** USA
14C3 **West Chester** USA
20D3 **Westend** USA
36D1 **Westerburg** Germany
42B2 **Westerland** Germany
14E2 **Westerly** USA
76B3 **Western Australia** State, Aust
62A1 **Western Ghats** *Mts* India
34B3 **Western Isles** Scot
70A2 **Western Sahara** Region, Mor
77H2 **Western Samoa** *Is* Pacific O
36B1 **Westerschelde** *Estuary* Neth
36D1 **Westerwald** Region, Germany
38D1 **Westfalen** Region, Germany
25D8 **West Falkland** *I* Falkland Is
14D1 **Westfield** Massachusetts, USA
13D2 **Westfield** New York, USA
14B2 **Westfield** Pennsylvania, USA
12B3 **West Frankfort** USA
75C1 **Westgate** Aust
35D6 **West Glamorgan** County, Wales
13F1 **West Grand L** USA
xxxE4 **West Indies** *Is* Caribbean S
12C3 **West Liberty** USA
3F3 **Westlock** Can
12C2 **West Lorne** Can
35B5 **Westmeath** County, Irish Rep
17D2 **West Memphis** USA
35E5 **West Midlands** County, Eng
35E6 **Westminster** Eng
14B3 **Westminster** Maryland, USA
15C2 **Westminster** S Carolina, USA
74D1 **West Nicholson** Zim
56E1 **Weston** Malay
12C3 **Weston** USA
35D6 **Weston-super-Mare** Eng
15E4 **West Palm Beach** USA
17D2 **West Plains** USA
20B1 **West Point** California, USA
17E3 **West Point** Mississippi, USA
11C3 **West Point** Nebraska, USA
14D2 **West Point** New York, USA
10K3 **West Point** *Mt* USA
78B2 **Westport** NZ
4A3 **Westray** Can
33C2 **Westray** *I* Scot
3D3 **West Road** *R* Can
35F5 **West Side** *Oilfield* N Sea
9E3 **West Virginia** State, USA
20C1 **West Walker** USA
75C2 **West Wyalong** Aust
18D2 **West Yellowstone** USA
35E5 **West Yorkshire** County, Eng
57C4 **Wetar** *I* Indon
3F3 **Wetaskiwin** Can
72D4 **Wete** Tanz
36E1 **Wetter** *R* Germany
36E1 **Wetzlar** Germany
Wevok = Cape Lisburne
76D1 **Wewak** PNG
17C2 **Wewoka** USA
35B5 **Wexford** County, Irish Rep
35B5 **Wexford** Irish Rep
6H5 **Weyburn** Can
35D6 **Weymouth** Eng
14E1 **Weymouth** USA
78C1 **Whakatane** NZ
78C1 **Whakatane** *R* NZ
34E1 **Whalsay** *I* Scot
78B1 **Whangarei** NZ
35E5 **Wharfe** *R* Eng
17C4 **Wharton** USA
11A3 **Wheatland** USA
14B3 **Wheaton** Maryland, USA
11C2 **Wheaton** Minnesota, USA
3G2 **Wheeler** *R* Can
19D3 **Wheeler Peak** *Mt* Nevada, USA
16A2 **Wheeler Peak** *Mt* New Mexico, USA
20C3 **Wheeler Ridge** USA
5H2 **Wheeler** *R* Can
12C2 **Wheeling** USA
3D3 **Whistler** Can
35E4 **Whitby** Eng
4F5 **Whitby** Can
17D2 **White** *R* Arkansas, USA
10K3 **White** *R* Can
16A1 **White** *R* Colorado, USA
12B3 **White** *R* Indiana, USA
11B3 **White** *R* S Dakota, USA
7N4 **White B** Can
11B2 **White Butte** *Mt* USA
75B2 **White Cliffs** Aust
33C2 **White Coomb** *Mt* Scot
3E3 **Whitecourt** Can
18D1 **Whitefish** USA
4D4 **Whitefish B** Can/USA
12B1 **Whitefish Pt** USA
7M4 **Whitegull L** Can
13E2 **Whitehall** New York, USA
14C2 **Whitehall** Pennsylvania, USA
12A2 **Whitehall** Wisconsin, USA
35D4 **Whitehaven** Eng
10L3 **Whitehorse** Can
78C1 **White I** NZ
17D4 **White L** USA
75E3 **Whitemark** Aust
19C3 **White Mountain Peak** *Mt* USA
20C2 **White Mountain Peak** *Mt* USA
20C2 **White Mountain Peak** *Mt* USA
10J2 **White Mts** Alaska, USA
20C2 **White Mts** California, USA
13E2 **White Mts** New Hampshire, USA
72D2 **White Nile** *R* Sudan
4C4 **White Otter L** Can
14D2 **White Plains** USA
7K5 **White River** Can
11B3 **White River** USA
13E2 **White River Junction** USA
White S = Beloye More
3C3 **Whitesail L** Can
18B1 **White Salmon** USA
3H3 **Whitesand** *R* Can
4B3 **Whiteshell Prov Park** Can
18D1 **White Sulphur Springs** USA
15D2 **Whiteville** USA
71F4 **White Volta** *R* Ghana
12B2 **Whitewater** USA
3H3 **Whitewood** Can
34C4 **Whithorn** Scot
15C2 **Whitmire** USA
4F4 **Whitney** Can
20C2 **Whitney,Mt** USA
10J3 **Whittier** Alaska, USA
20C4 **Whittier** California, USA
6H3 **Wholdaia L** Can
75A2 **Whyalla** Aust
12C2 **Wiarton** Can
71F4 **Wiawso** Ghana
11B2 **Wibaux** USA
17C2 **Wichita** USA
16C3 **Wichita** *R* USA
16C3 **Wichita Falls** USA
16C3 **Wichita Mts** USA
34D2 **Wick** Scot
19D4 **Wickenburg** USA
35B5 **Wicklow** County, Irish Rep
35B5 **Wicklow** Irish Rep
35B5 **Wicklow** *Mts* Irish Rep
75C1 **Widgeegoara** *R* Aust
36D1 **Wied** *R* Germany
43D2 **Wielun** Pol
42D3 **Wien** Austria
42D3 **Wiener Neustadt** Austria
43E2 **Wieprz** *R* Pol
36E1 **Wiesbaden** Germany
36D3 **Wiese** *R* Germany
35D5 **Wigan** Eng
17E3 **Wiggins** USA
34C4 **Wigtown** Scot
34C4 **Wigtown B** Scot
37C1 **Wil** Switz
18C1 **Wilbur** USA
75B2 **Wilcannia** Aust
19C3 **Wildcat Peak** *Mt* USA
37B1 **Wildhorn** *Mt* Switz
3F4 **Wild Horse** Can
37D1 **Wildspitze** *Mt* Austria
15C3 **Wildwood** Florida, USA
14C3 **Wildwood** New Jersey, USA
16B2 **Wiley** USA
74D2 **Wilge** *R* S Africa
76D1 **Wilhelm,Mt** PNG
42B2 **Wilhelmshaven** Germany
14C2 **Wilkes-Barre** USA
79F8 **Wilkes Land** Ant
3G3 **Wilkie** Can
18B2 **Willamette** *R* USA
75B2 **Willandra** *R* Aust
18B1 **Willapa B** USA
19E4 **Willcox** USA
23D4 **Willemstad** Curaçao
3G2 **William** *R* Can
75A1 **William Creek** Aust
75B3 **William,Mt** Aust
19D3 **Williams** Arizona, USA
19B3 **Williams** California, USA
13D3 **Williamsburg** USA
3D3 **Williams Lake** Can
12C3 **Williamson** USA
14B2 **Williamsport** USA
15D1 **Williamston** USA
14D1 **Williamstown** Massachusetts, USA
12C3 **Williamstown** W Virginia, USA
14D2 **Willimantic** USA
14C2 **Willingboro** USA
3E3 **Willingdon,Mt** Can
76E2 **Willis Group** *Is* Aust
15C3 **Williston** Florida, USA
11B2 **Williston** N Dakota, USA
74C3 **Williston** S Africa
3D2 **Williston L** Can
11C2 **Willmar** USA
75A3 **Willoughby,C** Aust
3D3 **Willow** *R* Can
11A2 **Willow Bunch** Can
74C3 **Willowmore** S Africa
18B2 **Willow Ranch** USA
19B3 **Willows** USA
17D2 **Willow Springs** USA
75A2 **Wilmington** Aust
14C3 **Wilmington** Delaware, USA
15D2 **Wilmington** N Carolina, USA
14D1 **Wilmington** Vermont, USA
16C2 **Wilson** Kansas, USA
15D1 **Wilson** N Carolina, USA
14A1 **Wilson** New York, USA
9F3 **Wilson** USA
16C2 **Wilson** *L* USA
75B1 **Wilson** *R* Aust
7K3 **Wilson,C** Can
20C3 **Wilson,Mt** California, USA
16A2 **Wilson,Mt** Colorado, USA
18B1 **Wilson,Mt** Oregon, USA
75C3 **Wilsons Promontory** *Pen* Aust
35E6 **Wiltshire** County, Eng
36C2 **Wiltz** Lux
76B3 **Wiluna** Aust
12B2 **Winamac** USA
74D2 **Winburg** S Africa
14D1 **Winchendon** USA
13D1 **Winchester** Can
35E6 **Winchester** Eng
12C3 **Winchester** Kentucky, USA
14D1 **Winchester** New Hampshire, USA
13D3 **Winchester** Virginia, USA
18E2 **Wind** *R* USA
14A2 **Windber** USA
11B3 **Wind Cave Nat Pk** USA

Windermere
Yirol

35D4 **Windermere** Eng
74B1 **Windhoek** Namibia
11C3 **Windom** USA
76D3 **Windorah** Aust
18E2 **Wind River Range** *Mts* USA
75D2 **Windsor** Aust
14D2 **Windsor** Connecticut, USA
35E6 **Windsor** Eng
5K4 **Windsor** Newfoundland, Can
15D1 **Windsor** N Carolina, USA
7M5 **Windsor** Nova Scotia, Can
4E5 **Windsor** Ontario, Can
5G4 **Windsor** Quebec, Can
15C2 **Windsor Forest** USA
14D2 **Windsor Locks** USA
23E4 **Windward Is** Caribbean
23C3 **Windward Pass** Caribbean
3F2 **Winefred L** Can
15B2 **Winfield** Alabama, USA
17C2 **Winfield** Kansas, USA
75D2 **Wingham** Aust
4E5 **Wingham** Can
28C3 **Winifreda** Arg
4D2 **Winisk** Can
7K4 **Winisk** *R* Can
7K4 **Winisk L** Can
55B2 **Winkana** Burma
18B1 **Winlock** USA
71F4 **Winneba** Ghana
11D3 **Winnebago** USA
12B2 **Winnebago,L** USA
18C2 **Winnemucca** USA
11C3 **Winner** USA
17D3 **Winnfield** USA
11D2 **Winnibigoshish L** USA
6J4 **Winnipeg** Can
6J4 **Winnipeg,L** Can
4B3 **Winnipeg** *R* Can
6J4 **Winnipegosis** Can
4A3 **Winnipegosis,L** Can
13E2 **Winnipesaukee,L** USA
11D3 **Winona** Minnesota, USA
17E3 **Winona** Mississippi, USA
13E2 **Winooski** USA
19D4 **Winslow** USA
14D2 **Winsted** USA
15C1 **Winston-Salem** USA
36E1 **Winterberg** Germany
15C3 **Winter Garden** USA
15C3 **Winter Park** USA
20B1 **Winters** USA
36D1 **Winterswijk** Neth
37C1 **Winterthur** Switz
11D3 **Winthrop** USA
76D3 **Winton** Aust
78A3 **Winton** NZ
35F5 **Wisbech** Eng
9E2 **Wisconsin** State, USA
12A2 **Wisconsin** *R* USA
12B2 **Wisconsin Dells** USA
7K5 **Wisconsin Rapids** USA
10H2 **Wiseman** USA
43D2 **Wisla** *R* Pol
42C2 **Wismar** Germany
36D2 **Wissembourg** France
27G2 **Witagron** Suriname
74D2 **Witbank** S Africa
8D3 **Witchita Falls** USA
35E5 **Witham** *R* Eng
35F5 **Withernsea** Eng
35E6 **Witney** Eng
36D1 **Witten** Germany
42C2 **Wittenberg** Germany
76A3 **Wittenoom** Aust
36D1 **Wittlich** Germany
74B1 **Witvlei** Namibia
43D2 **Wladyslawowo** Pol
43D2 **Włocławek** Pol
43E2 **Włodawa** Pol
75C3 **Wodonga** Aust
37C1 **Wohlen** Switz
51G7 **Wokam** Indon
35E6 **Woking** Eng
14B1 **Wolcott** USA
51H6 **Woleai** *I* Pacific O
12B1 **Wolf** *R* USA
36E2 **Wolfach** Germany
18B2 **Wolf Creek** USA
16A2 **Wolf Creek P** USA
3B1 **Wolf L** Can
12A1 **Wolf Point** USA
42C3 **Wolfsberg** Austria
42C2 **Wolfsburg** Germany
3H2 **Wollaston L** Can
3H2 **Wollaston Lake** Can
6G3 **Wollaston Pen** Can
75D2 **Wollongong** Aust
74D2 **Wolmaransstad** S Africa
42D2 **Wolow** Pol
57B4 **Wolowaru** Indon
75B3 **Wolseley** Aust
35D5 **Wolverhampton** Eng
14B2 **Womelsdorf** USA
75D1 **Wondai** Aust
53B4 **Wŏnju** S Korea
75B2 **Wonominta** *R* Aust
3D2 **Wonowon** Can
53B4 **Wŏnsan** N Korea
75C3 **Wonthaggi** Aust
75A2 **Woocalla** Aust
14C3 **Woodbine** USA
13D3 **Woodbridge** USA
3F2 **Wood Buffalo Nat Pk** Can
75D1 **Woodburn** Aust
18B1 **Woodburn** USA
14C3 **Woodbury** USA
10K2 **Woodchopper** USA
20C1 **Woodfords** USA
3H2 **Wood L** Can
20C2 **Woodlake** USA
19B3 **Woodland** California, USA
20B1 **Woodland** USA
18B1 **Woodland** Washington, USA
77E1 **Woodlark** *I* PNG
76C4 **Woodmera** Aust
76C3 **Woodroffe,Mt** Aust
5H3 **Woods L** Can
12B2 **Woodstock** Illinois, USA
13F1 **Woodstock** New Brunswick, Can
4E5 **Woodstock** Ontario, Can
14A3 **Woodstock** Virginia, USA
14C3 **Woodstown** USA
78C2 **Woodville** NZ
17D3 **Woodville** USA
16C2 **Woodward** USA
75A2 **Woomera** Aust
13E2 **Woonsocket** USA
12C2 **Wooster** USA
35D5 **Worcester** Eng
74B3 **Worcester** S Africa
14E1 **Worcester** USA
37E1 **Wörgl** Austria
35D4 **Workington** Eng
18E2 **Worland** USA
36E2 **Worms** Germany
35C6 **Worms Head** *Pt* Wales
35E6 **Worthing** Eng
11C3 **Worthington** USA
12C2 **Worthington** USA
11B3 **Wounded Knee** USA
57B3 **Wowoni** *I* Indon
10M4 **Wrangell** USA
10A5 **Wrangell,C** USA
10M4 **Wrangell I** USA
10K3 **Wrangell Mts** USA
33B2 **Wrath,C** Scot
16B1 **Wray** USA
35D5 **Wrexham** Wales
19D4 **Wrightson** USA
15C2 **Wrightsville** USA
20D3 **Wrightwood** USA
6F3 **Wrigley** Can
42D2 **Wrocław** Pol
43D2 **Września** Pol
53B3 **Wuchang** China
55E1 **Wuchuan** China
52E2 **Wuda** China
67E3 **Wuday'ah** S Arabia
71H3 **Wudil** Nig
52C2 **Wuding He** *R* China
52A3 **Wudu** China
52C4 **Wugang** China
52B2 **Wuhai** China
52C3 **Wuhan** China
52D3 **Wuhu** China
52D5 **Wuhua** China
60D2 **Wūjang** China
52B1 **Wujia He** *R* China
52B4 **Wu Jiang** *R* China
71H4 **Wukari** Nig
57D4 **Wuliaru** *I* Indon
52B4 **Wuling Shan** *Mts* China
71J4 **Wum** Cam
52A4 **Wumeng Shan** *Upland* China
4D3 **Wunnummin L** Can
61E3 **Wuntho** Burma
36D1 **Wuppertal** Germany
52B2 **Wuqi** China
52D2 **Wuqing** China
42B3 **Würzburg** Germany
42C2 **Wurzen** Germany
53C2 **Wusuli Jiang** *R* China
52C2 **Wutai Shan** *Mt* China
51H7 **Wuvulu** *I* Pacific O
52A2 **Wuwei** China
52E3 **Wuxi** China
52E3 **Wuxing** China
52C2 **Wuyang** China
53B2 **Wuyiling** China
52D4 **Wuyi Shan** *Mts* China
52B1 **Wuyuan** China
53B2 **Wuyur He** *R* China
55D2 **Wuzhi Shan** *Mts* China
52B2 **Wuzhong** China
52C5 **Wuzhou** China
12C2 **Wyandotte** USA
75C1 **Wyandra** Aust
35D6 **Wye** *R* Eng
35D6 **Wylye** *R* Eng
35F5 **Wymondham** Eng
76B2 **Wyndham** Aust
17D2 **Wynne** USA
6G2 **Wynniatt B** Can
75E3 **Wynyard** Aust
3H3 **Wynyard** Can
8B2 **Wyoming** State, USA
12B2 **Wyoming** USA
18D2 **Wyoming Peak** *Mt* USA
18D2 **Wyoming Range** *Mts* USA
75D2 **Wyong** Aust
12C3 **Wytheville** USA

X

60D1 **Xaidulla** China
52D1 **Xai Moron He** *R* China
74E2 **Xai Xai** Mozam
22C2 **Xaltinguis** Mexico
73B5 **Xangongo** Angola
36D1 **Xanten** Germany
41E2 **Xánthi** Greece
74C1 **Xau,L** Botswana
12C3 **Xenia** USA
50C4 **Xiaguan** China
52A2 **Xiahe** China
52D5 **Xiamen** China
52B3 **Xi'an** China
52B4 **Xianfeng** China
52C3 **Xiangfan** China
52C4 **Xiang Jiang** *R* China
52C4 **Xiangtan** Province, China
52C4 **Xianning** China
52B3 **Xianyang** China
53A2 **Xiao'ergou** China
52C4 **Xiao Shui** *R* China
52D4 **Xiapu** China
52A4 **Xichang** China
22C1 **Xicoténcatl** Mexico
22C1 **Xicotepec** Mexico
55C2 **Xieng Khouang** Laos
52B4 **Xifeng** China
61C2 **Xigazê** China
52A1 **Xi He** *R* China
52B2 **Xiji** China
52C5 **Xi Jiang** *R* China
52E1 **Xiliao He** *R* China
52B5 **Xilin** China
22C1 **Xilitla** Mexico
52D4 **Xinfeng** China
52C1 **Xinghe** China
53C2 **Xingkai Hu** *L* China/Russian Fed
52D5 **Xingning** China
52B4 **Xingren** China
52C2 **Xingtai** China
27H4 **Xingu** *R* Brazil
50C2 **Xingxingxia** China
52A4 **Xingyi** China
53B3 **Xinhan** China
52A2 **Xining** China
52E2 **Xinjin** Liaoning, China
52A3 **Xinjin** Sichuan, China
53A3 **Xinkai He** *R* China
52D2 **Xinwen** China
52C2 **Xin Xian** China
52C2 **Xinxiang** China
52C3 **Xinyang** China
52C5 **Xinyi** Guangdong, China
52D3 **Xinyi** Jiangsu, China
52D1 **Xi Ujimqin Qi** China
53A3 **Xiuyan** China
22C2 **Xochimilco** Mexico
52D3 **Xuancheng** China
52B3 **Xuanhan** China
52D1 **Xuanhua** China
52A4 **Xuanwei** China
52C3 **Xuchang** China
72E3 **Xuddur** Somalia
52A2 **Xunhua** China
52C5 **Xun Jiang** *R* China
53B2 **Xunke** China
52D5 **Xunwu** China
52C4 **Xupu** China
55E1 **Xuwen** China
52B4 **Xuyong** China
52D3 **Xuzhou** China

Y

52A4 **Ya'an** China
75B3 **Yaapeet** Aust
72B3 **Yabassi** Cam
53E2 **Yablochnyy** Russian Fed
50D1 **Yablonovyy Khrebet** *Mts* Russian Fed
65D2 **Yabrūd** Syria
18B2 **Yachats** USA
26F8 **Yacuiba** Bol
62B1 **Yādgīr** India
69A1 **Yafran** Libya
54D2 **Yagishiri-tō** *I* Japan
43G2 **Yagotin** Ukraine
28D2 **Yaguari** *R* Urug
28E2 **Yaguaron** *R* Urug
22B1 **Yahualica** Mexico
72C3 **Yahuma** Zaïre
54C3 **Yaita** Japan
54C4 **Yaizu** Japan
52A4 **Yajiang** China
18B1 **Yakima** USA
18B1 **Yakima** *R* USA
71F3 **Yako** Burkina
72C3 **Yakoma** Zaïre
53C5 **Yakujima-kaikyō** *Str* Japan
53E3 **Yakumo** Japan
53C5 **Yaku-shima** *I* Japan
10L4 **Yakutat** USA
10L4 **Yakutat B** USA
49O3 **Yakutsk** Russian Fed
49N3 **Yakutskaya** Respublika, Russian Fed
55C4 **Yala** Thai
22C2 **Yalalag** Mexico
18B1 **Yale** Can
72C3 **Yalinga** CAR
75C3 **Yallourn** Aust
50C3 **Yalong** *R* China
52A4 **Yalong Jiang** *R* China
41F2 **Yalova** Turk
45E7 **Yalta** Ukraine
53A2 **Yalu He** *R* China
53B3 **Yalu Jiang** *R* China
54D3 **Yamada** Japan
53D4 **Yamagata** Japan
53C5 **Yamaguchi** Japan
48J2 **Yamal, Poluostrov** *Pen* Russian Fed
50E1 **Yamarovka** Russian Fed
75D1 **Yamba** New S Wales, Aust
75B2 **Yamba** S Australia, Aust
72C3 **Yambio** Sudan
41F2 **Yambol** Bulg
57D4 **Yamdena** *I* Indon
61E3 **Yamethin** Burma
Yam Kinneret = Tiberias,L
75B1 **Yamma Yamma,L** Aust
16A1 **Yampa** *R* USA
49R4 **Yamsk** Russian Fed
60D3 **Yamuna** *R* India
61D2 **Yamzho Yumco** *L* China
49P3 **Yana** *R* Russian Fed
75B3 **Yanac** Aust
54B4 **Yanagawa** Japan
62C1 **Yanam** India
52B2 **Yan'an** China
66C2 **Yanbu'al Bahr** S Arabia
75B2 **Yancannia** Aust
52E3 **Yancheng** China
52B2 **Yanchi** China
75B1 **Yandama** *R* Aust
72C3 **Yangambi** Zaïre
50B2 **Yanggi** China
54A3 **Yanggu** S Korea
52C1 **Yang He** *R* China
52C5 **Yangjiang** China
55B2 **Yangon** Burma
52C2 **Yangquan** China
54A3 **Yangsan** S Korea
52C5 **Yangshan** China
52C3 **Yangtze Gorges** China
52E3 **Yangtze,Mouths of the** China
54A3 **Yangyang** S Korea
52D3 **Yangzhou** China
52B4 **Yanhe** China
53B3 **Yanji** China
75C3 **Yanko** Aust
49P2 **Yankskiy Zaliv** *B* Russian Fed
11C3 **Yankton** USA
59G1 **Yanqqi** China
52D1 **Yan Shan** *Hills* China
75B1 **Yantabulla** Aust
52E2 **Yantai** China
52D2 **Yanzhou** China
72B3 **Yaoundé** Cam
51G7 **Yapen** *I* Indon
28D1 **Yapeyú** Arg
51G6 **Yap Is** Pacific O
21B2 **Yaqui** *R* Mexico
44H4 **Yaransk** Russian Fed
44H3 **Yarenga** Russian Fed
44H3 **Yarensk** Russian Fed
26D3 **Yari** *R* Colombia
53D4 **Yariga-dake** *Mt* Japan
59F2 **Yarkant He** *R* China
61D2 **Yarlung Zangbo Jiang** *R* China
66D4 **Yarmin** Yemen
7M5 **Yarmouth** Can
65C2 **Yarmūk** *R* Syria/Jordan
44F4 **Yaroslavl'** Russian Fed
65C2 **Yarqon,R** Israel
75C3 **Yarram** Aust
75D1 **Yarraman** Aust
75C3 **Yarrawonga** Aust
44N2 **Yar Sale** Russian Fed
44E4 **Yartsevo** Russian Fed
49L3 **Yartsevo** Russian Fed
26C2 **Yarumal** Colombia
77G2 **Yasawa Group** *Is* Fiji
71H3 **Yashi** Nig
71G4 **Yashikera** Nig
45G6 **Yashkul'** Russian Fed
60C1 **Yasin** Pak
43E3 **Yasinya** Ukraine
53B1 **Yasnyy** Russian Fed
75C2 **Yass** Aust
75C2 **Yass** *R* Aust
54B3 **Yasugi** Japan
17C2 **Yates Center** USA
6J3 **Yathkyed L** Can
72C3 **Yatolema** Zaïre
53C5 **Yatsushiro** Japan
65C3 **Yatta** Israel
26D4 **Yavari** Peru
60D4 **Yavatmāl** India
53C5 **Yawatahama** Japan
55D2 **Ya Xian** China
63C2 **Yazd** Iran
63C2 **Yazd-e Khvāst** Iran
17D3 **Yazoo** *R* USA
17D3 **Yazoo City** USA
55B2 **Ye** Burma
43F3 **Yedintsy** Moldova
75A2 **Yeelanna** Aust
44F5 **Yefremov** Russian Fed
45G6 **Yegorlyk** *R* Russian Fed
72D3 **Yei** Sudan
71F4 **Yeji** Ghana
44L4 **Yekaterinburg** Russian Fed
53B1 **Yekaterinoslavka** Russian Fed
45F5 **Yelets** Russian Fed
33C1 **Yell** *I* Scot
62C1 **Yellandu** India
Yellow = Huang He
6G4 **Yellowhead P** Can
6G3 **Yellowknife** Can
75C2 **Yellow Mt** Aust
50F3 **Yellow Sea** China/Korea
8C2 **Yellowstone** *R* USA
18D2 **Yellowstone L** USA
18D2 **Yellowstone Nat Pk** USA
43G2 **Yel'nya** Russian Fed
43F2 **Yel'sk** Belorussia
7K1 **Yelverton B** Can
71G3 **Yelwa** Nig
58C4 **Yemen** Republic, Arabian Pen
55C1 **Yen Bai** Viet
71F4 **Yendi** Ghana
55B1 **Yengan** Burma
48K3 **Yenisey** *R* Russian Fed
49L4 **Yeniseysk** Russian Fed
49L3 **Yeniseyskiy Kryazh** *Ridge* Russian Fed
48J2 **Yeniseyskiy Zaliv** *B* Russian Fed
10H3 **Yentna** *R* USA
35D6 **Yeo** *R* Eng
75C2 **Yeoval** Aust
35D6 **Yeovil** Eng
49M3 **Yerbogachen** Russian Fed
45G7 **Yerevan** Armenia
19C3 **Yerington** USA
44J2 **Yermitsa** Russian Fed
19C4 **Yermo** USA
49O4 **Yerofey-Pavlovich** Russian Fed
65C3 **Yeroham** Israel
49S3 **Yeropol** Russian Fed
45H5 **Yershov** Russian Fed
Yerushalayim = Jerusalem
64C1 **Yeşil** *R* Turk
49M3 **Yessey** Russian Fed
65C2 **Yesud Hama'ala** Israel
75D1 **Yetman** Aust
70B2 **Yetti** Maur
61E3 **Yeu** Burma
45H7 **Yevlakh** Azerbaijan
45E6 **Yevpatoriya** Ukraine
52E2 **Ye Xian** China
45F6 **Yeysk** Russian Fed
28D2 **Yi** *R* Urug
65C1 **Yialousa** Cyprus
53B2 **Yi'an** China
41E2 **Yiannitsá** Greece
52A4 **Yibin** China
52C3 **Yichang** China
53B2 **Yichun** China
52B2 **Yijun** China
64C2 **Yıldızeli** Turk
53A1 **Yilehuli Shan** *Upland* China
52A5 **Yiliang** China
52B2 **Yinchuan** China
52D3 **Ying He** *R* China
52E1 **Yingkou** China
52D3 **Yingshan** Hubei, China
52B3 **Yingshan** Sichuan, China
52D4 **Yingtan** China
59G1 **Yining** China
52B1 **Yin Shan** *Upland* China
72D3 **Yirga' Alem** Eth
72D3 **Yirol** Sudan

ASIA

48-49
50-51
53
54
54
65
64
63
58-59
52
66-67
60
61
55
57
62
56
57

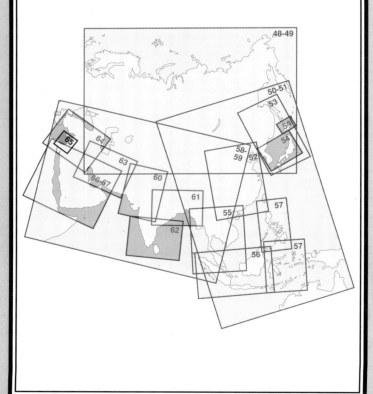

AFRICA

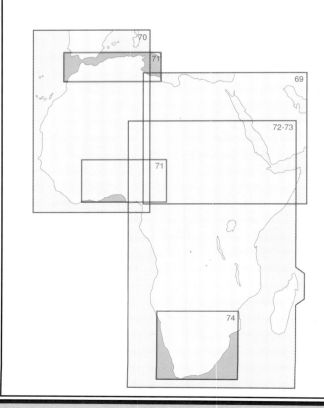

70
71
69
72-73
71
74